American Politicians Confront the Court

Politicians have long questioned, or have even been openly hostile to, the legitimacy of judicial authority, but that authority seems to have become more secure over time. What explains the recurrence of hostilities and yet the security of judicial power? Addressing this question anew, Stephen M. Engel points to the gradual acceptance of dissenting views of the Constitution, that is, the legitimacy and loyalty of stable opposition. Politicians' changing perception of the threat posed by opposition influenced how manipulations of judicial authority took shape. As politicians' views toward opposition changed over time, their approach toward the judiciary – where opposition could become entrenched – changed as well. Once opposition was no longer seen as a fundamental threat to the Constitution's survival and multiple constitutional interpretations were considered legitimate, judicial power could be construed less as the seat of an illegitimate opposition and more as an instrument to achieve political ends. Politicians were more likely to harness it to serve their aims than to openly undermine its legitimacy. In short, conflicts between the elected branches and the judiciary have not subsided. They have changed form. They have shifted from measures that undermine judicial legitimacy to measures that harness judicial power for political ends. Engel's book brings our understanding of these manipulations into line with other developments, such as the establishment of political parties, the acceptance of loyal opposition, the development of different modes of constitutional interpretation, and the emergence of rights-based pluralism.

Stephen M. Engel is an assistant professor of politics at Bates College and an Affiliated Scholar of the American Bar Foundation. He holds a doctorate in political science from Yale University, an interdisciplinary master of arts in Social Thought from New York University, and a bachelor of arts from the multidisciplinary College of Social Studies at Wesleyan University. His research is at the intersection of political development, constitutional law and theory, and sexuality politics. He is the author of *The Unfinished Revolution: Social Movement Theory and the Gay and Lesbian Movement*, also published by Cambridge University Press. His research has appeared in *Studies in American Political Development*, *Journal of the Philosophy of Education*, and the *Advertising and Society Review*.

T0371375

"Stephen Engel's elegant and deeply empirical account traces the history of political attacks on America's independent judiciary, showing how these attacks have evolved and provoked changes in both law and politics. His narrative deftly weaves constitutional development into political development, showing how we have gotten to today's political and politicized federal courts. This book is essential reading for those interested in the American courts. It also poses an unanswerable challenge to anyone who believes that America's national development can be understood without an account of the courts' place in it."

– Julie Novkov, SUNY Albany

American Politicians Confront the Court

Opposition Politics and Changing Responses to Judicial Power

STEPHEN M. ENGEL

Bates College and American Bar Foundation

CAMBRIDGE
UNIVERSITY PRESS

CAMBRIDGE
UNIVERSITY PRESS

University Printing House, Cambridge CB2 8BS, United Kingdom

One Liberty Plaza, 20th Floor, New York, NY 10006, USA

477 Williamstown Road, Port Melbourne, VIC 3207, Australia

314-321, 3rd Floor, Plot 3, Splendor Forum, Jasola District Centre, New Delhi - 110025, India

103 Penang Road, #05-06/07, Visioncrest Commercial, Singapore 238467

Cambridge University Press is part of the University of Cambridge.

It furthers the University's mission by disseminating knowledge in the pursuit of education, learning and research at the highest international levels of excellence.

www.cambridge.org
Information on this title: www.cambridge.org/9780521153980

First published 2011

A catalogue record for this publication is available from the British Library

Library of Congress Cataloging in Publication data
Engel, Stephen M.
   American politicians confront the court : opposition politics and changing responses
   to judicial power / Stephen M. Engel.
      p.   cm.
   ISBN 978-0-521-19295-8 (hardback) – ISBN 978-0-521-15398-0 (pbk.)
      1. Political questions and judicial power – United States.   2. United States – Politics
   and government.   I. Title.
   KF5130.E45   2011
   342.73´044–dc22   2010054310

ISBN 978-0-521-19295-8 Hardback
ISBN 978-0-521-15398-0 Paperback

Contents

Acknowledgments   *page* vii

Introduction: Had Americans "Stopped Understanding
about the Three Branches"?   1

PART I   POLITICAL DEVELOPMENT AND ELECTED-BRANCH
RELATIONS WITH THE JUDICIARY

1. Beyond the Countermajoritarian Difficulty   19
2. A Developmental Theory of Politicians' Confrontations
    with Judicial Authority   43

PART II   HOSTILITY TO JUDICIAL AUTHORITY AND THE
POLITICAL IDIOM OF CIVIC REPUBLICANISM

3. In Support of Unified Governance: Undermining the Court
    in an Anti-Party Age   71
4. Party against Partisanship: Single-Party Constitutionalism
    and the Quest for Regime Unity   131
5. "As Party Exigencies Require": Republicanism, Loyal
    Opposition, and the Emerging Legitimacy of Multiple
    Constitutional Visions   170

PART III   HARNESSING JUDICIAL POWER AND THE
POLITICAL IDIOM OF LIBERAL PLURALISM

6. Clashing Progressive Solutions to the Political Problem
    of Judicial Power   225
7. A Polity Fully Developed for Harnessing (I): Living
    Constitutionalism and the Politicization of Judicial
    Appointment   285

8. A Polity Fully Developed for Harnessing (II): A Conservative
   Insurgency Innovates and a Self-Styled Majoritarian
   Court Responds   337

Conclusion: On the Return of Opposition Illegitimacy
and the Prospects for New Development   372

Index   385

Acknowledgments

For all the solitude that often comes with writing a book, the research involved can also be collaborative and involve family, friends, students, and colleagues. During the years spent on this project, I have had the privilege of knowing and working with faculty, colleagues, and students who offered much-needed encouragement through some of the darker doldrums that periodically stymied my research and writing, and for whom I am immensely grateful.

This project began as a dissertation prospectus at Yale University in the fall of 2005 under the guidance of Stephen Skowronek, who has remained foremost among my mentors. Steve introduced me to the subfield of American political development (APD), offering me access to APD's leading scholars and newest voices when he took me on as an editorial assistant for the journal *Studies in American Political Development*. His insights, questions, and commentary throughout the writing of the dissertation and the development of this book are appreciated beyond measure.

My deepest gratitude extends also to Bruce Ackerman and Greg Huber. Bruce introduced me to constitutional law and pushed me to consider how processes of legal interpretation and development extend far beyond judges' chambers. His revisionist scholarship stands as an inspirational model of creativity and rigor. Greg has been a constant in my intellectual development, proving himself to be a truly excellent mentor and, more important, a friend, throughout my graduate school years and beyond.

The research undertaken to complete this book required not only the commitment of skilled and empathetic mentors and a borderline sense of self-destructive self-obsession on the part of the writer, but money! Travel to various archives for data could not have been completed without generous financial support. The National Science Foundation provided a Dissertation Improvement Grant in Law and Social Science (SES-0719031) in 2007–8 and a grant extension in 2008–9. Columbia University's School of International and Public Affairs graciously offered an appointment as a visiting research scholar during the summer of 2010 so that I might make final revisions to the manuscript while living near family and friends in and around New York

City. Yale University provided a doctoral dissertation-writing grant in 2008 and 2009 as well as a John W. Enders grant in the summer of 2006 to begin my research at the Maryland Historical Society. Thanks also to Alan Gerber's Center for the Study of American Politics at Yale for funding my research at the Massachusetts Historical Society in 2006.

The American Bar Foundation (ABF) in Chicago deserves special mention. The Foundation offered me a pre-doctoral fellowship in 2007–8, which not only provided funding and office space but, much more importantly, also gave me access to a rich and vibrant interdisciplinary intellectual community just when frustrations with my project and home discipline were beginning to mount. My year at the ABF stands as a highlight of my time in graduate school; it reaffirmed my commitment to seeking out research areas and questions that transcend disciplinary domains. My particular thanks to Robert Nelson, Laura Beth Nielsen, Bonnie Honig, Terry Haliday, and Traci Burch at the ABF.

Numerous scholars offered helpful commentary on earlier iterations of many of these chapters. Thanks to Richard Adelstein, Julia Azari, Dan Carpenter, Elizabeth Clemens, Stephen Daniels, Giulio Gallarotti, Daniel Galvin, Scott James, David Mayhew, Cecilia Miller, and Don Moon for their assessments of early drafts of my work on Jefferson, Van Buren, and Lincoln. Thanks to Justin Crowe, Don Greene, Jacob Hacker, Bradley Hayes, Thomas Keck, Kevin McMahon, Shep Melnick, Bruce Peabody, Sarah Staszak, Steven Teles, and McGee Young for their helpful commentary on earlier versions of my theory chapters. Thanks also to my colleagues in the Department of Political Science at Marquette University for encouraging the successful completion of this project and to colleagues at Marquette Law School, particularly Chad Oldfather, who offered me access to their faculty research seminar to present parts of this study. Thanks also to John Baughman and my new colleagues at Bates College for helping to make my transition to a new position, while in the midst of editing this book, so easy. Finally, a special thanks to Mark Graber, Paul Frymer, Robert Lieberman, and Ken Kersch, who have offered invaluable critiques and professional advice and who have encouraged me to push and test my ideas at conferences, further introducing me to the growing community of scholars interested in questions at the intersection of law, politics, and history.

My research required a fair bit of rooting around in archives and going bleary-eyed in front of microfilm readers. It could only have been accomplished with the help of numerous archivists across the country. Thanks to staffs at the New York Public Library, Connecticut Historical Society, Massachusetts Historical Society, Maryland Historical Society, Franklin D. Roosevelt Presidential Library, Richard M. Nixon Presidential Library, the Bancroft Library at University of California-Berkeley, the Library of Congress, and the National Archives and Records Administration. Thanks to Bert Brandenberg and Bill Saunders at Justice at Stake and the Family Research

Council, respectively, who graciously provided sundry materials and invited me to interview them about their campaigns involving judicial authority.

Over the past five years – at Yale, the Bar Foundation, and Marquette – I have had the good fortune to build a community of friends and colleagues who have made my work a joy. These intensely smart, caring, and wonderfully witty, sarcastic, and oft-times just goofy men and women made the periodic frustrations of this research and writing not merely bearable but an eminently conquerable challenge. My most heartfelt thanks to Abbey Steele, Alex Kirshner, Shatema Threadcraft, Stephen Kaplan, Robert Person, Nicole Kazee, Dominika Koter, Amelia Hoover, Steve Shewfelt, Christine Kim, Justin Zaremby, Sandy Henderson, Joseph Lampert, Ana Arjona, Turkular Isiksel, Ryan Sheely, Jud Mathews, Meredith Levine, Matt Hall, Tiffany Davenport, Laia Balcells, and Beth Lauer. Thanks to friends who provided much-needed respites in New York; Boston; Chicago; Milwaukee; Washington, DC; and Berkeley, as well as beds to crash on when research funding was nearing its limits: Carter Clements, Jenna and Ethan Dabbs, Becca Gerner, Kevin Staszowski, Andrew Grossman, John Gage, Maya Seiden, Sean Maloney, Kara Cruoglio, Blair Hanzlik, Prana Topper, Rob Finn, Dave Gomez, Peter Friedman, Dena Rosenberg, Amin Ghaziani, Ellen Berrey, Gabrielle Ferales, Christopher McGuinness, Michael Phillips, Matt Bianco, Patrick Hunt, Luke Schluesener, Max Polonsky, Scott Grabarski, and Brian Falb, who, each in their own way, helped me to see this project through. Thanks to my undergraduate students at Marquette and Yale for continuously reminding me of the reasons I decided to become a professor in the first place. A few students deserve special mention for invaluable research, administrative, and editorial assistance. Thanks to Nick Franchot, Yale '07, for his assistance combing through years of *Congressional Record* indices; thanks also to Marquette graduate students – Patricia Rodda, Joseph Struble, Lauren Reeves, Meaghan Moen, and Nathan Conroy – for their editorial comments and criticism on earlier drafts.

At Cambridge University Press, I am grateful to my editor Lew Bateman for his unflagging belief in my project. Anne Lovering Rounds has been extremely supportive throughout the editing process. Thanks also to my copy editor Patterson Lamb and to Soniya Ashok for her skilled production management. Earlier versions of portions of Chapters 3 and 4 appeared in *Studies in American Political Development* 23 (October 2009): 189–217 under the title "Before the Countermajoritarian Difficulty: Regime Unity, Loyal Opposition, and Hostilities toward Judicial Authority in Early America." Thank you to Cambridge University Press for granting permission to reprint those portions.

The phrase "thank you" hardly captures my gratitude to my parents and brothers who I am sure wondered on too many occasions when I would finish this book. My father spent hundreds of hours discussing my ideas, reading chapters, offering critiques – always with a self-deprecating caveat of "what do I know, I'm an eye doctor" – and calling me when spotting a news article that was relevant to my research. My mother spent hundreds of hours getting me to think about and do things *other* than work on this book, making sure that I remained a whole person, getting enough exercise and nagging me to eat right. My brothers, Jarrett and David, my sister-in-law, Jennifer, and my two nieces, Emma Hayes and Charlotte, each had a hand in helping me complete this project. I dedicate this book to my family, on whose shoulders I have always stood and without whom I would not have accomplished what I have.

Stephen M. Engel
Milwaukee, WI
January 31, 2011

Introduction

Had Americans "Stopped Understanding about the Three Branches"?

On 3 March 2009, former Justice Sandra Day O'Connor, as a guest on *The Daily Show with Jon Stewart*, voiced concerns about a perceived rising tide of anti-judicial hostilities:

> What I became aware of increasingly in those last years [since my retirement] was all the criticism of judges across America. We heard a lot from Congress and in state legislatures, we heard a lot about activist judges, didn't we – secular godless humanists trying to tell us all what to do – I mean that was what we were hearing. And I just didn't see it that way. And, I thought perhaps a lot of Americans had stopped understanding about the three branches of government.

That O'Connor, a Reagan appointee, would warn against this antagonism is notable. For, while hostilities toward judges and courts have, over time, known no particular partisan color, during the 1990s and early 2000s such anger was voiced primarily by a conservative insurgency that made inroads to power with Ronald Reagan in 1980.[1] Around that time, Republican national platforms began to give vent to anti-judge tirades. Republican members of Congress have since followed with court-curbing bills, and a conservative legal movement has developed, making its judicial preferences widely known.[2]

---

[1] Accusations of judicial activism are not limited to one side of the political spectrum. While conservatives criticized the Court as "imperial" following *Roe*, liberals have assailed the Court for its *Lochner*-era jurisprudence and accuse the Rehnquist and Roberts Courts of conservative judicial activism. See Laura Kalman, *The Strange Career of Legal Liberalism* (New Haven: Yale University Press, 1996) and Thomas Keck, *The Most Activist Supreme Court in History: The Road to Judicial Conservatism* (Chicago: University of Chicago Press, 2004). Although one scholar has noted, "Everyone seems opposed to judicial activism, yet no one agrees what it means," judicial activism usually connotes the act of reaching beyond the question involved in the case to rule according to personal substantive views. See Viet Dinh, "Threats to Judicial Independence, Real or Imagined," *Georgetown Law Journal* 95 (2007), 938–9.

[2] Party platforms are discussed in subsequent chapters. For a summary of court-curbing legislation, see Citizens for Independent Courts, *Uncertain Justice: Politics and America's Courts*

By 1996, some congressional Republicans contemplated impeaching federal judges.[3] These threats escalated when some called for impeaching Reagan-appointed Justice Anthony Kennedy.[4] In 2005 and 2006, the conservative interest group, the Family Research Council, sponsored "Justice Sunday" telecasts dedicated to showing "how activist judges ... threaten our nation's future" and suggesting that Christian values were increasingly in conflict with judicial rulings.[5] Former Representative Tom DeLay (R-TX) summed up the complaint: "moral values that have defined the progress of human civilization for millennia are cast aside in favor of those espoused by a handful of unelected, lifetime-appointed judges."[6]

These telecasts followed Congress's manipulation of judicial process in the battle over Terri Schiavo's life. Schiavo, a woman in a vegetative state, presented the Republican majority with the opportunity to champion its "culture of life" against the Court-sponsored presumption of choice.[7] Schiavo's husband

(New York: Century Foundation Press, 2000), 131–47. Examples of recent legislation include the Judicial Transparency and Ethics Enhancement Bill of 2006, which created an Inspector General of the Judicial Branch, a congressional officer charged with financial oversight of the judiciary. This bill followed jurisdiction-stripping legislation passed in the 108th session of the House, "Safeguarding Our Religious Liberties Act," preventing federal courts from hearing cases involving the Ten Commandments, Pledge of Allegiance, and marriage. Another bill, the "Life-Protecting Judicial Limitation Act of 2003," had similar aims with respect to hearing abortion cases. The Constitution Restoration Act restricted federal jurisdiction on multiple fronts, including in matters relating to belief in God, excluded foreign legal principles from having relevant bearing on constitutional interpretation, and provided for removal of federal judges ignoring jurisdictional limitations imposed by the act. On the rise of a conservative legal movement and its objections to George W. Bush's nomination in 2005 of Harriet Meiers to the Supreme Court, see Steve Teles, *The Rise of the Conservative Legal Movement: The Battle for Control of the Law* (Princeton: Princeton University Press, 2008), 1.

3 Dinh, 934–5. See Alison Mitchell, "Clinton Pressing Judge to Relent," *New York Times*, 22 March 1996; Ian Fisher, "Gingrich Asks Judge's Ouster for Ruling Out Drug Evidence," *New York Times*, 7 March 1996, B4; Laurie Kellman, "Republicans Rally 'Round Judge-impeachment Idea; Constitution Would Be Violated, Foes Say," *Washington Times*, 13 March 1996, A1; Linda Greenhouse, "Judges as Political Issues: Clinton Move in New York Case Imperils Judicial Independence, Bar Leaders Say," *New York Times*, 23 March 1996, A4.

4 In 2005, some Republicans threatened to bring impeachment charges against Justice Anthony Kennedy, since his positions in some decisions including decriminalization of consensual homosexual sex placed him at odds with the more conservative wing of that party. See Jason DeParle, "In Battle to Pick Next Justice, Right Says Avoid a Kennedy: Conservatives See Him as a Turncoat on the Bench," *New York Times*, 27 June 2005, A1.

5 http://www.sourcewatch.org/index.php?title=Justice_Sunday. The full-page ad in the *New York Times* depicts a young man looking quizzically at a gavel and at a Bible, thereby suggesting that, increasingly, citizens are confronted with supporting either allegedly activist judicial rulings or Christian values.

6 Thomas Edsall, "Conservatives Rally for Justices; Leaders Ask for Nominees Who Will End Abortion and Gay Rights," *Washington Post*, 14 August 2005, A02.

7 The presumption of choice extends beyond abortion jurisprudence. In *Cruzon v. Director, Missouri Department of Health* 497 U.S. 261 (1990), the Supreme Court declared a right to refuse medical treatment under the due process clause. Five justices agreed that it covered the refusal of food and water to the point of death.

sought removal of her feeding tube while her parents sued to keep it in place. When the state court refused to grant the restraining order, Congress transferred jurisdiction to the federal district court.[8] Republicans appeared to serve notice that judicial opinions contrary to the policy aims of their majority were not to be countenanced.[9]

And yet, even as the antagonism against courts and judges has accelerated since the 1990s, scholars argue that judicial power has remained intact: the heightened level of anti-court agitation in recent years appears mostly to have fallen flat. Few pieces of legislation curbing judicial power have passed, and those that have belie their sponsors' aggressive rhetoric by only nibbling at the edges of jurisdiction.[10] Moreover, the Supreme Court, for all of its more recent controversial rulings – on federalism, abortion, voting rights, gay rights, eminent domain, and campaign finance – is said to maintain a level of public esteem higher than the elected branches.[11] The ambiguity surrounding these hostilities extends to the "Justice Sunday" speakers themselves. Anyone listening carefully would have heard them couple their assaults on the legitimacy of

[8] The legislation transferring jurisdiction from the state to the federal court was "An Act for the Relief of the Parents of Theresa Marie Schiavo," PL- 109-3, 119 Stat. 15. Abby Goodnough and Carl Hulse, "Despite Congress, Woman's Feeding Tube Is Removed," *New York Times*, 19 March 2005, A1; and "Terri Schiavo Has Died," 31 March 2005, http://www.cnn.com/2005/ LAW/03/31/schiavo/index.html. While the action could be considered bi-partisan, the vote indicates a heavy tilt toward Republican support: 156 Republicans and 47 Democrats favored the jurisdictional transfer while 53 Democrats and 5 Republicans voted against it. Charles Hulse and David Kirkpatrick, "Congress Passes and Bush Signs Legislation on Schiavo Case," *New York Times*, 21 March 2005, A1.

[9] On Republican hostilities toward the judiciary, particularly from evangelical interest groups, see Mark C. Miller, *The View of the Courts from the Hill* (Charlottesville: University of Virginia Press, 2009), 105-33.

[10] In 1996, Congress passed the Antiterrorism and Effective Death Penalty Act, which limited federal courts' jurisdiction to consider habeas corpus challenges in state courts. PL-104-132, 110 Stat. 1214 (1996). That year Congress also passed the Illegal Immigration Reform and Immigrant Responsibility Act, which prevented federal court review of an Immigration and Naturalization Service final order to deport a person convicted of a crime. PL-104-208, 110 Stat. 3009 (1996). In 2006, Congress passed the Military Commissions Act (MCA) (PL-109-366, 120 Stat. 2600 [Oct. 17, 2006]) in response to *Hamdan v. Rumsfeld* (2004), which ruled that military commissions trying detainees at Guantanamo Bay violated the Uniform Code of Military Justice and the Geneva Convention. William Glaberson, "In Shift, Justices Agree to Review Detainee's Case," *New York Times*, 30 June 2007, A1.

[11] On public approval of the Court, see Gregory Caldeira, "Neither the Purse nor the Sword: The Dynamics of Public Confidence in the United States Supreme Court," *American Political Science Review* 80 (1986), 1209-26; Roger Handberg, "Public Opinion and the United States Supreme Court, 1935-1981," *International Social Science Review* 59 (1984), 3-13; Richard Lehne and John Reynolds, "The Impact of Judicial Activism on Public Opinion," *American Journal of Political Science* 22 (1978), 896-904; Joseph Tanenhaus and Walter Murphy, "Patterns of Public Support for the Supreme Court: A Panel Study," *Journal of Politics* 43 (1981), 24-39; Barbara Perry, *The Priestly Tribe: The Supreme Court's Image in the American Mind* (Westport, CT: Praeger, 1999), 5; and H. W. Perry, Jr., and L. A. Powe, Jr., "The Political Battle for the Constitution," *Constitutional Commentary* 21 (2004), 641-96.

independent judicial authority with a plea to advance conservative policy aims on the bench by confirming John Roberts and Samuel Alito.[12] If these conservatives voiced hostility to judicial power in principle, it would appear that they were not wholly committed to restraining its practical exercise.

I. Courts, Parties, and the Politics of Opposition

The central question of this book is how can the recurrence of anti-judicial hostilities over American history be squared with repeated scholarly and journalistic assessments that judicial power has grown, is secure, and is even supreme. Inter-branch relations are not always or even frequently hostile. Madisonian claims of ambition countering ambition not withstanding, much scholarship has shed light on how inter-branch relations are, if not always cordial, at least politically strategic and often cooperative such that the judicial authority is empowered to serve the needs of the elected branches.[13] But, even as we might differentiate between hostile actions meant to curb judicial power and actions to enhance that power, we should also attend to how manifestation of hostilities have changed over time, and what that change may tell us about American political and constitutional development more generally. At stake are not only questions of whether, how, and why judicial power has been and continues to be politically constructed, but also how instances of antagonism toward judges and courts have changed over time in ways that serve partisan objectives and, ironically, may maintain judicial power to further partisan ends.

Contrary to more common claims that these attacks have never succeeded or that they never succeeded after a certain time, I show that courts have never been insulated from attack.[14] Rather, what has changed over time is the nature of antagonism. This book traces and explains this shift; the

---

[12] Justice Sunday II on 14 August 2005 was, in part, a rally to support the appointment of Roberts; Justice Sunday III on 8 January 2006 was, in part, a rally to support the appointment of Alito.

[13] For James Madison's claim, "Ambition must be made to counteract ambition," see *Federalist 51*. Recent scholarship on how judicial power is constructed to serve the interests of the majority party controlling Congress, the presidency, or both includes Howard Gillman, "How Political Parties Can Use the Courts to Advance Their Agendas: Federal Courts in the United States, 1875–1891," *American Political Science Review* 96 (September 2002), 511–24; Keith Whittington, *Political Foundations of Judicial Supremacy* (Princeton: Princeton University Press, 2007); and Justin Crowe, "Cooperation over Conflict: Congress and the Court in American Political Development," presented at the 2010 New England Political Science Association Annual Meeting, Newport, Rhode Island, 23 April 2010.

[14] Charles Black remarked, "the strongest claim of judicial review's historically attested legitimacy would point to the fact that it has been under attack continuously since its beginning, but that the attacks have always failed." Black, *The People and the Court* (New York: MacMillan, 1960), 183. On the assumption that Congress has not successfully curbed judicial power since Reconstruction, see Lee Epstein and Thomas Walker, *Constitutional Law for a Changing America*, 4th ed. (Washington, DC: Congressional Quarterly Press, 2000).

explanation takes the legitimacy of holding differing views of the Constitution's meaning as its central point.

Today, holding differing views about the meaning of the Constitution or modalities of interpretation used to uncover that meaning is more common than it was at the moment of Founding or through much of the nineteenth century.[15] Our constitutional culture has developed over two centuries to allow for such disagreement to occur without threatening the stability of the republic.[16] However, such a pluralistic constitutional culture has not always characterized American experience. Furthermore, holding differing views about the Constitution's meaning is a manifestation of a broader perspective toward political opposition. And, for much of this country's first century, the legitimacy and loyalty of such stable, formed, and permanent opposition was not fully granted by elected officials.[17]

By legitimate opposition, I mean that those in power accept a stable out-group as natural, unavoidable, and manageable. As discussed in later chapters, although early recognition of this idea is evident in James Madison's *Federalist 10* and in writings by Martin Van Buren, the Founding generation tended to associate stable and permanent opposition with civil unrest and constitutional instability. Consequently, they sought mechanisms to minimize if not squash it altogether; diluting this threat by enlarging the size of the republic, as Madison advocated in *Federalist 10*, was one such mechanism.

---

[15] Philip Bobbit, *Constitutional Fate: Theory of Constitutionalism* (New York: Oxford University Press, 1982), 3–8. See also Sotirios Barber and James E. Fleming, *Constitutional Interpretation: The Basic Questions* (New York: Oxford University Press, 2007), 64–188.

[16] I adopt Reva Siegel's definition of "constitutional culture" as "the understandings of role and practices of argument that guide interactions among citizens and officials in matters of the Constitution's meaning." (3) Siegel argues that the Civil War was a turning point in how disagreements about constitutional meaning would be vocalized; after the war, "those who disagree about the Constitution's meaning must advance their views without resort to violent coercion." (30) I seek to uncover the processes that made this turn from coercion and toward persuasion possible. Siegel, "Constitutional Culture, Social Movement Conflict and Constitutional Change: The Case of the De Facto ERA," *California Law Review* 94 (2006), 1323–419.

[17] While one of my aims is to demonstrate this shift from the illegitimacy of opposition to the idea that stable opposition could be loyal, I do not argue against a reversal. Rhetoric and behavior during the 2009–10 debate on health insurance reform included manifestations of the illegitimacy of opposition such as political violence (e.g., racial and homophobic epithets and vandalism against congressional members' offices) to pursuing legal arguments similar to nullification. These events led economist Paul Krugman to note how some within the Republican Party do not accept the legitimacy of opposition: "For today's G.O.P. is ... a party in which paranoid fantasies about the other side – Obama is a socialist, Democrats have totalitarian ambitions – are mainstream. And, as a result, it's a party that fundamentally doesn't accept anyone else's right to govern." Krugman, "Going to Extreme," *New York Times*, 26 March 2010, A27. Paranoia and conspiracy are – as evaluated in Chapters 2 and 5 – indicators of the illegitimacy of opposition. On recent political violence, see Phillip Rucker, "Lawmakers Concerned as Health-Care Overhaul Foes Resort to Violence," *Washington Post*, 25 March 2010, A1. On the resurgence of nullification, see E. J. Dionne, "The New Nullifiers," *Washington Post*, 25 March 2010, A21.

Loyal opposition refers to those in power not only viewing out-group mobilization as a natural effect of democratic politics – that is, as legitimate – but also understanding that its potential to gain power through electoral procedures does *not* destabilize or threaten the Constitution. I suggest that we do not see this idea take strong root until Abraham Lincoln's presidency and not bloom fully until after Reconstruction.

Former Vice President Al Gore's 2000 concession speech helps make the concepts of legitimate and loyal opposition less abstract:

> Almost a century and a half ago, Senator Stephen Douglas told Abraham Lincoln, who had just defeated him for the presidency, "Partisan feeling must yield to patriotism. I'm with you, Mr. President, and God bless you." Well, in that same spirit, I say to President-elect Bush that what remains of partisan rancor must now be put aside, and may God bless his stewardship of this country. Neither he nor I anticipated this long and difficult road. Certainly neither of us wanted it to happen. Yet it came, and now it has ended, resolved, as it must be resolved, through the honored institutions of our democracy.[18]

Gore's comments summarize the political norm of loyal opposition as the stabilizing element of democratic elections and transitions of power.

Peaceful rotations in office, as occurred between John Adams and Thomas Jefferson after the contested election of 1800 and as followed the 2000 election, are necessary but not sufficient indicators that opposition is considered legitimate. A more complete assessment hinges on how new leadership treats those who have lost power. Jefferson's aim, discussed in Chapter 3, to *absorb* the opposition and *minimize* its voice, suggests the illegitimacy of opposition. By contrast, Abraham Lincoln's exhortations to southern Democrats, reviewed in Chapter 5, to try again in the next election rather than secede – to remain loyal by using their voice rather than exiting the Union – indicate that he considered his political opposition not only legitimate but also loyal.[19]

Assumptions that stable opposition is illegitimate or disloyal carry a particular stance toward constitutional interpretation. They allow for an interpretation to be framed as anti-constitutional, that is, as undermining the republic. Therefore, as ideas about opposition shift over time, parallel shifts likely took place in constitutional culture, namely, granting the legitimacy of differing takes on the Constitution's meaning. Examining change in hostilities toward judicial authority points to the need to probe not only the relationship between the limits of nineteenth-century constitutional culture and the republic's collapse into Civil War but also the relationship between courts and the primary institution of organized opposition in American politics, namely, political parties.[20]

---

[18] Albert Gore, Jr., "2000 Presidential Concession Speech," delivered 13 December 2000.
[19] Albert Hirschman, *Exit, Voice, and Loyalty*, new ed. (Cambridge: Harvard University Press, 2006).
[20] I respond to Gillman's (2002) call to assess how the simultaneous development of courts and parties affected one another:

> We might encourage students of party politics or delegation of powers to focus more attention on the ways in which executives and legislators use judges as extensions of

The relationship between courts and parties, and its periodic renegotiation, lies at the heart of political and constitutional development. To link this changing perspective on opposition politics to the politics of manipulating judicial authority, I suggest that politicians' gradual recognition of legitimacy and loyalty of opposition altered their perceptions of courts and parties in tandem, ultimately influencing their outlooks on the value of judicial power and how that power could be manipulated.

Courts and parties have always had an uneasy relationship in American politics. Historians have recorded the Jeffersonians' drive toward judicial impeachments, the Civil War Republicans' zeal for jurisdiction stripping, and Franklin D. Roosevelt's ill-fated Court-packing initiative. These episodes seem to illustrate a recurrent pattern of insurgent parties newly ensconced in power confronting entrenched judges of the old regime in cataclysmic showdowns. And they have figured in empirical and normative theorizing primarily through the idea of "countermajoritarian difficulty."[21] The concept summarizes the power of unelected judges to overrule laws passed by the elected branches. This paradigm of inter-branch dynamics renders judicial power an unchanging dilemma for American democracy, which inevitably follows from the structure of the federal branches. As such, it obscures important differences among successive instances. Rather than seek out and explain what is new in each episode, scholars, operating from this model, have viewed these confrontations as enduring emblems of American governance.[22]

I recast this history by focusing on courts and parties' *changing relationship to one another*, primarily by focusing on the process through which ideas

conventional political or policy agendas. Conversely, students of law and courts might be encouraged to locate the scope and direction of judicial decision making into a broader analysis of party systems and partisan control of those institutions that are responsible for the jurisdiction and the staffing of courts. (522)

Ronald Kahn and Ken Kersch called for inquiry into the "relationship between law and politics by refusing to isolate questions involving legal doctrines and judicial decisions and the special qualities of courts as decision-making units from the consideration of developments elsewhere in the political system – be they in ideologies, elite and popular political thought, social movements, or in formal institutions, such as Congress, the presidency, state and federal bureaucracies, and state and federal court decisions." Kahn and Kersch, eds., *The Supreme Court and American Political Development* (Lawrence: University Press of Kansas, 2006), 13. Perry and Powe (2004) note the stultifying scholarly disconnect between these two institutions: "Focusing on political parties is not something legal academics tend to do.... When it comes to constitutional analysis, they fall off the radar screen." (643)

[21] Alexander Bickel coined the phrase "countermajoritrarian difficulty" in his *The Least Dangerous Branch* (New Haven: Yale University Press, 1986), 16. Erwin Chemerinsky refers to the concept as the "dominant paradigm of constitutional law and scholarship" in his "The Supreme Court, 1988 Term – Forward: The Vanishing Constitution," 103 *Harvard Law Review* 43 (1989), 61. Barry Friedman calls it an "academic obsession" in his "The Birth of an Academic Obsession: The History of the Countermajoritarian Difficulty, Part Five," 112 *Yale Law Journal* (2002), 153.
[22] Keith Whittington sees the problem as enduringly cyclic. He has formulated a model of presidential conflict with the federal courts that corresponds to Skowronek's typology of presidential authority; see Whittington (2007).

about opposition changed. In particular, I highlight specific entrepreneurial actions that enabled this relationship to be continuously reevaluated and
redefined. While scholars have studied dynamics underlying episodes of presidential and/or congressional manipulation of judicial power, and they have
examined how parties have changed over time, they have yet to consider fully
how court development and party development link together.[23] Each institution is treated as a separate problem.[24] Or, if they are connected, it is more
often than not to bear out Mr. Dooley's aphorism that the Court follows the
election returns via the mechanism of presidential nomination and senatorial
confirmation. Little attention is paid to whether and how any of the participating institutions or aims of actors within them change over time, how those
actors respond to or promote new ideas or aims, or how the development of
wholly new agents affects this process.[25]

Connection between judicial and party development is evident in my central claim: anti-judicial animus reflects politicians' changing ideas about the
threat posed by formed, stable, and permanent opposition. This animus is
motivated by more than just an alleged structural abnormality of an unelected
branch in a democracy. We limit our understanding of this hostility and how
it has manifested differently over time when we see it only as a static characteristic of American democracy. We ought to think about these inter-branch
tensions as changing over time and illustrating shifting imperatives to tame,
contain, harness, or otherwise manipulate judicial power. By shining light
on change and development rather than recurrence, I show how inter-branch
confrontation has turned on the legitimacy and loyalty of opposition, not just
on the structural legitimacy of judicial review. Furthermore, this explanation comes into view only when the kind of cross-institutional analysis – as

[23] On presidential-court clashes, see Whittington (2007). On Congress-court relations, see
Miller (2009) and Charles Geyh, *When Courts and Congress Collide* (Ann Arbor: University
of Michigan Press, 2007). On party development in the electorate and as an organization,
see Scott James, *Presidents, Parties, and the State* (New York: Cambridge University Press,
2000); Earl Black and Merle Black, *Rise of Southern Republicans* (Cambridge: Belknap Press
of Harvard, 2002); and Daniel Galvin, *Presidential Party Building: Dwight D. Eisenhower
to George W. Bush* (Princeton: Princeton University Press, 2009). On party systems, see John
Aldrich, *Why Parties?* (Chicago: University of Chicago Press, 1995). On judicial development, see Felix Frankfurter and James Landes, *The Business of the Supreme Court* (New
Brunswick, NJ: Transaction, 2007 [1928]); and Justin Crowe, "The Forging of Judicial
Autonomy: Political Entrepreneurship and the Reforms of William Howard Taft," *Journal of
Politics* 69 (February 2007), 73–87.
[24] Two exceptions are works by Stephen Skowronek and Bruce Ackerman. For Skowronek,
courts and parties were the foremost political institutions of the nineteenth-century American
state. Ackerman sees entrenched courts and insurgent parties as a recurring dynamic. See
Skowronek, *Building a New American State* (New York: Cambridge University Press,
1981); Ackerman, *We the People: Foundations* (Cambridge, MA: Belknap Press of Harvard
University, 1991); and Ackerman, "The Living Constitution," *Harvard Law Review* 120
(2007), 1737–812.
[25] Mr. Dooley is the fictional creation of the author and humorist, Finley Peter Dunne (1867–
1936), who commented that the Supreme Court follows the election returns.

opposed to studying each institution's development in isolation – that this book attempts is undertaken.

The matter of the opposition's right to rule was not resolved at a single moment, and I tie its gradual resolution to politicians' eventual recognition of the strategic value of judicial power in partisan combat. Along this line of development, I uncover a shift in emphasis: hostilities toward the federal judiciary come to be less about broadly undermining judicial authority and more about targeted harnessing of judicial power for new political purposes. As politicians' perceptions toward opposition changed, their approach toward the judiciary – where opposition could become entrenched due to lifetime appointment – changed in tandem. Therefore, where existing scholarship points to a structural dilemma of eternal recurrence, I point to a developmental transformation. By focusing on development, I highlight entrepreneurial innovation undertaken by particular leaders in defining and redefining the central ideas characterizing American democratic politics and constitutional culture. In short, I am less interested in the repetition of these instances than in what emerges through them.

Put more concretely, politicians from the Founding era through the mid-nineteenth century were suspicious of political party and thus of stable opposition because they were long-committed to the notion of one proper constitutional interpretation that was fixed by the popular act of ratification and subsequently discoverable through textual analysis, an interpretive methodology known as textual originalism.[26] Propelled by fears of civil unrest, they insisted on a certain regime unity among governing branches behind one interpretation, and they attacked displays of judicial independence with blunt instruments. Amid the secession crisis of 1860 and 1861 and especially in the wake of the Civil War, politicians – armed with a fuller recognition of the inability to construct one perpetually dominant party, the inevitability of periodic rotation in power, and the need to grant the loyalty of opposition lest civil strife recur – were compelled to concede the legitimacy of multiple equally plausible interpretations of the Constitution. In this new ideational context, they would shift their strategies toward the judiciary, attempting tactics that would not undermine judicial authority but harness it for future policy gains. Their attacks would become more targeted and instrumental, aiming to enlist the Court's legitimacy to secure particular political priorities.

[26] On early American commitments to textual originalism, or the practice of seeking the Framers' intentions through textual analysis, as the only legitimate interpretive methodology, see Howard Gillman, "The Collapse of Constitutional Originalism and the Rise of the Notion of the 'Living Constitution' in the Course of American State-Building," *Studies in American Political Development* 11 (1997), 191–247. Although disagreements on the meaning of the Constitution obviously existed during the republic's first century, "none of the disputants fundamentally rejected the [interpretive] methods of their adversaries." Johnathan O'Neill, *Originalism in American Law and Politics: A Constitutional History* (Baltimore: Johns Hopkins University Press, 2005), 17. See also Kent Greenfield, "Original Penumbras: Constitutional Interpretation in the First Year of Congress," *Connecticut Law Review* 26 (1993), 79–144.

While this book offers a thorough tracing of the gradual change from viewing opposition as illegitimate and disloyal to legitimate and loyal, it should *not* be assumed that the developmental path is unidirectional. More recent qualities of American politics – heightened party polarization in Congress and the electorate; Tea Party anti-government sentiment; accusations that President Obama is a socialist, not born in the United States or, in the words of Newt Gringich, "outside our comprehension" – all open the possibility that a rhetoric of the illegitimacy of one's political opposition is thriving.[27] In the Conclusion, I raise the possibility that contemporary originalism actually fosters this outcome, as it has become a closed system of absolutes. Nevertheless, I am skeptical as to whether the illegitimacy of opposition would ever again rise to heights seen prior to the Civil War and Reconstruction for reasons discussed in Chapter 8 and the Conclusion. In short, while this book critically responds to cyclic notions of American political development by, instead, marking an arc of development toward political and constitutional pluralism, this is not simply a story of a *steady* arc. Although we are on an arc from regime unity and the illegitimacy of opposition toward granting opposition loyalty and the consequent imperative to harness judicial power, this progress is not steady. Multiple steps in that direction are interrupted by periodic and striking steps back; the Roberts Court may represent a retrenchment. And yet, it may be a retrenchment that can only go so far.

Finally, my intention is not only to examine politicians' behavior toward judicial power, for the judiciary is not merely acted upon. A second question is how judges adapted to this changing ideational environment in which multiple differing constitutional interpretations could vie for legitimacy. This context of equally plausible meanings compelled a rationale for why *judicial* renderings should be given more weight. Consequently, from the 1870s onward, legal scholars and judges engaged in a systematic enterprise of constructing jurisprudential history into a clear pattern of judicial supremacy. This process involved a deliberate re-imagining of *Marbury v. Madison* (1803). Scholars found within that ruling an allegedly strong articulation of judicial supremacy from the republic's earliest days.[28] This move in American constitutional development would have profound effects on the dynamics of inter-branch relations and the politically strategic value of deference to judicial authority.

---

[27] For accusations that Obama was not born in the United States, see Eric Etheridge, "Birther Boom," *Opinionator Online Commentary of the New York Times*, 22 July 2009, http://opinionator.blogs.nytimes.com/2009/07/22/birther-boom/?scp=4&sq=obama%20not%20born%20in%20the%20united%20states&st=cse. For Gingrich's comments that Obama is "so outside our comprehension," see Robert Costa, "Gingrich: Obama's 'Kenyan, Anti-Colonial' Worldview," *National Review Online*, 11 September 2010, http://www.nationalreview.com/corner/246302/gingrich-obama-s-kenyan-anti-colonial-worldview-robert-costa.

[28] Robert Clinton, "Precedent as Mythology: A Reinterpretation of *Marbury v. Madison*," *American Journal of Jurisprudence* 35 (1990), 55.

II. Moving Forward

Connections among ideas about opposition, party development, and constitutional culture are not immediately apparent; the burden of this book is to make them clear. My challenge is compounded by two factors. First, we must be aware of multiple interlocking dynamics, which are not wholly discrete and separable. The first, a shift in how manipulations of judicial power occur, is explained by the second, a larger pattern of ideational change and party development over time. The third dynamic – the Court's reaction to all of this by declaring its own supremacy – is a necessary component to understand why harnessing judicial authority, as opposed to attacking the legitimacy of that authority, has become the dominant political dynamic. Second, we must recognize that few actors involved in episodes of judicial manipulation were aware of the ideational drift of their efforts. Fewer still anticipated how future politicians might utilize the precedents they set to propel the observable movement from undercutting judicial legitimacy to harnessing judicial power.[29] But this is all to say that important aspects of politics can be revealed only by carefully tracing institutional and ideational interaction and development over time.

The payoffs for building theory once we engage in this multifaceted cross-institutional and ideational analysis should be evident on a variety of fronts. For students of American political development, I elaborate on themes of recurrence and emergence, on the interplay and interactive effects of contemporaneous institutional development, and on the role entrepreneurial politicians play in redefining ideas. For students of courts and of parties, I examine instances of conflict that have too long been viewed as structural, static, and functionalist rather than dynamic, political, and historically embedded. Ultimately, I demonstrate that successive iterations of seemingly engrained syndromes can produce new politics.

Part I of this book lays out the theoretical context in which relations between courts and parties have been understood and re-conceptualizes them around the problem of legitimate and loyal political opposition. In Chapter 1, I assess existing accounts, many of which deal with anti-judiciary hostility by attempting to resolve tensions between democracy and judicial review. The static conception of these hostilities as recurrently emanating from structural constitutional design does not consider tactical variation evident in manipulations of judicial power over time. I reconsider these actions by constructing and analyzing a dataset of proposed legislation involving the judiciary.

In Chapter 2, I articulate an alternative theory that draws on patterns in these data and focuses attention on institutional and ideational development

---

[29] On altering the original meaning of ideas and using them for unanticipated ends, see Gordon Wood's account of Federalist redefinition of sovereignty in *The Creation of the American Republic, 1776–1787*, 2nd ed. (Chapel Hill: University of North Carolina Press, 1998); and Stephen Skowronek, "The Reassociation of Ideas and Purposes: Racism, Liberalism, and the American Political Tradition," *American Political Science Review* 100 (2006), 385–401.

over time. This theory closely attends to how politicians' views toward stable opposition, their understandings of legitimate methods of constitutional
interpretation, and their manipulations of judicial authority may be connected
and grounded in a set of common assumptions, which have changed over two
hundred years. The chapter discusses the role of ideational entrepreneurs, how
and why they were able to articulate new ways of understanding the threats
posed by political opposition, and why those new ideas became entrenched as
assumptions guiding strategic behavior. By framing their found circumstances
as indicators of constitutional crisis, certain entrepreneurs including presidents,
members of Congress, and judges, could transform formerly considered illegitimate ideas about institutional relations and norms of political behavior into the
very solutions to the crisis.[30] Whether such ideational transformations would
hold depended on a variety of factors including whether the entrepreneur was
recognized and respected as speaking from authority and whether the opponents of this transformation expressly acquiesced to the new action or, at least,
tacitly did so by their participation in new institutional configurations.[31] This
developmental theory linking constrained ideational innovation, institutional
development, rationality, and strategic inter-branch actions leads to a set of
expectations about political behavior, detailed in this chapter.

The remaining chapters are case studies of inter-branch relations and ideational and institutional innovation and development over time. Part II, which
includes Chapters 3, 4, and 5, examines how politicians viewed opposition,
parties, and judicial authority prior to and during the Civil War. Part III,

---

[30] Ideational transformations compelled by crisis and serving strategic interests abound. For
example, early civil rights movement commitments to a "color-blind" society blocked gains
to be had from affirmative action. The crisis of urban riots in the 1960s provided opportu-
nity to re-frame the policy not as antithetical to the color-blind ideal but as a "crisis management" solution and a step toward realizing that ideal. See John Skretny, *The Ironies of
Affirmative Action: Politics, Culture, and Justice in America* (Chicago: University of Chicago
Press, 1996).
   On the role of exogenous crisis as an instigator of institutional and ideational innovation, see
William Sewell's "A Theory of Structure: Duality, Agency, and Transformation," *American
Journal of Sociology* 98 (1992), 1–29. Importantly, the crisis/opportunity need not be created
by an exogenous force. Institutional and ideational change can have endogenous inducements
created, for example, by the unanticipated consequences of layering new policy or institutional innovations upon pre-existing ones. See Elisabeth Clemens and James Cook, "Politics
and Institutionalism: Explaining Durability and Change," *Annual Review of Sociology* 25
(1999), 441–66; and Stephen Skowronek and Karen Orren, *The Search for American Political
Development* (New York: Cambridge University Press, 2004). For my purposes, the important
action to take note of is how actors are able to frame particular circumstances as crisis and use
that framing as justification for ideational and institutional innovation.
[31] On the relationship between recognized authority and legitimacy, see Max Weber, "Politics
as a Vocation," in *From Max Weber: Essays in Sociology*, H. H. Gerth and C. Wright Mills,
eds. (New York: Routledge, 2001 [1948]); and Martin Spencer, "Weber on Legitimate Norms
and Authority," *British Journal of Sociology* 21 (June 1979), 123–34. On the role of acquiescence and legitimacy, see Stanley Elkins and Eric McKitrick, *The Age of Federalism: The
Early American Republic*, 1788–1800 (New York: Oxford University Press, 1993), 32.

which includes Chapters 6, 7, and 8, examines how opposition, parties, and judicial authority have come to be understood after Reconstruction. Each of these chapters discusses both presidential-judicial relations and congressional-judicial relations. Since presidents nominate Supreme Court justices who tend to share their ideological perspective, but Congress defines jurisdiction per the Constitution's third article, studying both allows for a fuller perspective on the changing dynamics of inter-branch relations.[32]

Each case study relies on qualitative materials: letters, speeches, manuscripts, executive branch memoranda, and congressional debates. My aim in each is threefold. First, I illustrate how politicians viewed the threat posed by opposition and the purpose of political parties. Second, I evaluate the actions these politicians took toward the judiciary and show that how they articulated the crisis confronted and the threat posed by opposition helps to explain their relations with the federal judiciary. Third, I connect these cases across time by arguing that the resolution of each episode was taken up by later generations in ways unanticipated, in part, because views about opposition continued to change in response to both new strategic interests and crisis. In short, these case studies trace shifts in strategic behavior toward judicial authority and detail more general processes of deliberate institutional recalibration that occur when inter-branch relations become unmoored as a consequence of ideational change.[33]

Chapter 3 examines the Federalist/Jeffersonian period with attention to hostilities culminating in the 1805 impeachment of Justice Samuel Chase. The impeachment's consequence, namely the transformation of what judicial independence means – from independence from executive and/or legislative corruption to a more robust sense of absolute political neutrality – re-structured the relationship between courts and newly emergent political alignments. By setting the judiciary apart not only from partisanship but from politics altogether, this Jeffersonian construction had a perhaps unanticipated effect. It allowed subsequent attackers to frame their initiatives as efforts to re-establish the judiciary's neutrality rather than as campaigns seeking partisan policy outcomes.

---

[32] Lee Epstein and Jeffrey Segal, *Advise and Consent: The Politics of Judicial Appointment* (New York: Oxford University Press, 2005), 130–5; and Charles Cameron et al., "Senate Voting on Supreme Court Nominees: A Neoinstitutional Model," *American Political Science Review* 84 (1990), 530–1. As legal scholar, Charles Fairman, once noted, "the historian of the Court should keep his watch in the halls of Congress." Fairman, *Reconstruction and Reunion*, Part One (New York: Macmillan, 1971), 118.

[33] A full account of why anti-court attacks occur must investigate when they do *not* occur and explain their absence; otherwise, the researcher has selected on the dependent variable. If my question were under what circumstances do anti-court attacks occur, then investigating only cases of anti-judicial hostility would be inappropriate. Since the question underlying this book is not why do anti-judicial hostilities manifest themselves, but whether, how, and why they vary over time, narrowing the focus to identifiable instances of hostility is appropriate. See John Gerring, *Case Study Research: Principles and Practices* (New York: Cambridge University Press, 2006).

Chapter 4 examines the institutionalization of party permanence in the Jacksonian era. This permanence was primarily one-sided as shown by Martin Van Buren's ideas, which were foundational to the establishment of and justification for political parties. Van Buren understood opposition as natural and unavoidable, but he stopped short of endorsing party competition and rotation in office as the normal state of national political affairs. He advocated maintaining a single permanent party – his "Democracy" – that could defend the Constitution's meaning and principles against inevitable threats posed by a persistent minority faction. As such, party and constitutional interpretation were tied together in a way that maintained the disloyalty of opposition and its threat to constitutional stability, even if its legitimacy were nonetheless conceded. This formulation sets up a discernible disposition toward the judiciary, particularly as to whether judicial rulings would be observed and how appointments would occur. The chapter reconciles Van Buren's seemingly incongruent and opportunistic support for President Andrew Jackson's attacks on the Court, his support for the expansion of judicial power in the Judiciary Act of 1837, and his condemnation of Chief Justice Roger Taney for his *Dred Scott v. Sanford* (1857) ruling.[34]

Chapter 5 considers Lincoln's views on political party and constitutional meaning as well as congressional Republican manipulations of judicial power during the Civil War and Reconstruction. Some Republicans clung to Van Buren's notion of a single constitutional party designed to contain a conspiratorial opposition and ensure national stability, but Lincoln offered a different idea. While insisting on a baseline of constitutional agreement – grounded in procedural legitimacy so as to undermine the anarchic logic of secession – Lincoln acknowledged that there were numerous questions on which the Constitution did not speak clearly and on which the people could legitimately and loyally disagree. While still reliant on Van Buren's construction of political party as the vehicle of constitutional interpretation, Lincoln laid the groundwork for claiming the plausibility of *multiple* different constitutional interpretations. For, if multiple parties could loyally exist and parties were the institutionalized vehicles of constitutional interpretation, then so too could multiple constitutional interpretations. As each political party rose to power through legitimate electoral means, its leaders would be free to enact its particular constitutional vision; judicial authority was a tool to do so. Judicial power was thus a tool of electoral democracy.

Lincoln's position sets the foundation for Progressive-era development of the idea of living constitutionalism and the legal realist school, which are explored in Chapter 6. This chapter calls attention to the successful passage of court-curbing legislation during the 1910s and 1930s. At the same time, it grapples with that legislation's comparative narrowness and conceptual ambiguities. Pointing to other aspects of the fractured Progressive movement, in particular its budding recognition of interest-group competition, the

---

[34] *Dred Scott v. Sanford*, 60 U.S. 393 (1857).

contingency of constitutional interpretation, and scholarly efforts to construct judicial supremacy, it links the changing mode of anti-judicial hostilities to a more fully articulated imperative to harness judicial power for political use. The chapter concludes by examining evidence of the Court's recognition of pluralism's ascendance even as it articulated its own supremacy in certain circumstances. The justices re-conceptualized the Court as an overseer of the democratic political process and, under certain circumstances, an advocate for particular groups.[35] In doing so, it laid out the conditions under which judicial authority might be most likely harnessed for political ends.

Chapters 7 and 8 detail inter-branch dynamics in a polity fully developed for harnessing judicial power for political ends. They examine these relations when each branch is calibrated to the assumptions of interest-based pluralism and thus where multiple constitutional interpretive claims are not only plausible but also de-coupled from parties as their primary articulators. These chapters identify and discuss various tactics to harness judicial power in the wake of the Court's reorientation. Chapter 7 focuses on jurisdiction stripping, judicial appointment, and use of the filibuster from the 1950s through the present. Chapter 8 examines the development of contemporary originalism as a jurisprudential philosophy as well as a political strategy. It also discusses more recent innovations, such as utilizing presidential signing statements to solicit judicial interpretation in line with partisan aims.

Given the multiplicity of constitutional meanings that follows from a pluralist political culture as well as from a constitutional culture that recognizes the legitimacy and loyalty of opposition, it has become all the more imperative for the Court to justify why its interpretation should be determinative. As reviewed in Chapter 8, the Court has recently striven to justify its authority on majoritarian grounds. Justices have emphasized the democratic credentials of their holdings, stressing how they follow majoritarian trends, however defined, evident in the broader polity. Some scholars have praised the Court's interaction with democratic processes.[36] Yet, while this strategy may blunt the countermajoritarian accusation, it is disturbing for anyone concerned with minority rights and the sanctity of democratic processes. It is far from clear that democracy leads to just outcomes.[37] And why should the

---

[35] The culminating decision in this regard was *United States v. Carolene Products Co.*, 304 U.S. 144 (1938).

[36] On "democratic constitutionalism," see Robert Post and Reva Siegel, "*Roe* Rage: Democratic Constitutionalism and Backlash," *Harvard Civil-Rights Civil Liberties Law Review* 42 (2007), 373–434.

[37] Jeremy Waldron has argued against strong judicial review as long as certain conditions of good working democratic institutions and a cultural commitment to individual rights are met. Yet, it is far from clear that these conditions have been historically met in the United States, or under conditions of descriptive representation, can even be said to exist now. Waldron, "The Core Case against Judicial Review," *Yale Law Journal* 115 (2006),1346–407. On how democracy and justice are often considered at odds, see Ian Shapiro, *Democratic Justice* (New Haven: Yale University Press, 1999).

Court identify democratic trends as a part of its judicial decision making? Doing so seems fundamentally at odds with its claims of political neutrality.[38] By having it both ways – in touting its neutrality while grounding rulings in majoritarian processes – the Court exacerbates the imperative to compel it to hold a party line.

   In their attempts to redirect the stigma of countermajoritarian tendencies onto polarized parties, some justices have only rationalized their increasing power within the political system. As examined in the Conclusion, our more recent polarized politics may indicate a turn away from ideas about loyal opposition and the plausibility of multiple constitutional meanings that have marked our development. And the seeming triumph of originalism, such that "we are all originalists now," may foster a sense of singular meaning undercutting a sense of loyal opposition.[39] Taken together, judicial empowerment and originalism's ascension may unwittingly set the stage not just of only one legitimate constitutional interpretation but ultimately position the Court as the only legitimate articulator of that interpretation. As such, we the people may lose our constitutional voice and civic responsibility in the process.

---

[38] David Savage, "Roberts Sees Role as Judicial 'Umpire.'" *Los Angeles Times*, 13 September 2005, A1. Senator John Cornyn's reaction to the empathy standard was emblematic of Republican reliance on the concept of a judge as a neutral umpire: "The problem is you've got to call balls and strikes as a judge and the ethnicity focus – the focus on sex and on race and saying that there may be different outcomes depending who the judge is – is antithetical to the whole idea of the rule of law objective and neutral justice. And that's the reason why this deserves some questions." Cornyn quoted in Janie Lorber, "The Sunday Word: Confirmations and Torture Investigations," The Caucus: The Politics and Government Blog of the *Times*, 12 July 2009. http://thecaucus.blogs.nytimes.com/2009/07/12/the-sunday-word-confirmations-and-torture-investigations/?scp=37&sq=republican%20reaction%20to%20empathy%20standard%20for%20judges&st =cse.

[39] James Fleming, "The Balkanization of Originalism," *Maryland Law Review* 67 (2007), 10.

PART I

POLITICAL DEVELOPMENT
AND ELECTED-BRANCH RELATIONS
WITH THE JUDICIARY

I

Beyond the Countermajoritarian Difficulty

Politicians have challenged the judiciary's legitimate independent authority throughout American history. Yet scholars contend that the judiciary, and particularly the Supreme Court, has become more powerful and secure over time. Nothing in twentieth-century American politics matches how Jeffersonians reined in the judiciary in the early 1800s or what congressional Republicans achieved in the 1860s. Franklin Delano Roosevelt's (FDR's) court-packing plan collapsed and the impeachment and jurisdiction-curbing threats lobbed against the Warren Court went nowhere. Recent attacks notwithstanding, the Court is unfazed; it and has "intensified its political activity" since the mid-twentieth century, and it shows "few signs of reversing course."[1] Some scholars assert not only that the judiciary reigns supreme in matters of constitutional interpretation but that such supremacy has been deliberately sought and constructed by elected politicians.[2]

It appears that attacks focused on the Court's democratic deficit have become less potent over time even as the polity as a whole has become more democratic. One way to reconcile this paradox is to suggest that judicial aggrandizement has not come at the expense of the elected branches. Political attacks on the federal courts that do not result in undermining judicial power could be a win-win for all sides. Or, a strong judiciary might serve some advantage despite its countermajoritarian potential, and thus that potential needs to be grudgingly accommodated.[3] Even if either of these accounts were

[1] William Lasser, *The Limits of Judicial Power: The Supreme Court in American Politics* (Chapel Hill: University of North Carolina Press, 1988), 2, 6.
[2] Keith Whittington, *Political Foundations of Judicial Supremacy* (Princeton: Princeton University Press, 2007); and Justin Crowe, "Cooperation over Conflict: Congress and the Court in American Political Development," presented at the New England Political Science Association Annual Meeting, Newport, Rhode Island, 23 April 2010.
[3] Consider Richard Bensel's argument that because centralized state development was opposed during Reconstruction by a newly powerful Northern financial class, an opportunity for judicial empowerment developed as the judiciary could be utilized as the vehicle of federal interests absent a formed bureaucracy. See Bensel, *Yankee Leviathan* (New York: Cambridge University

so, we would still be left with the question of why it took so long – the first
century of the republic's existence – for elected politicians to figure out that
they could have it both ways, that they could couple electorally beneficial
rhetorical attacks on the judiciary with the accountability deflection provided
by a strong judiciary.

This chapter begins the process of accounting for that development. It
starts by examining responses to the countermajoritarian difficulty, which has
been called "the dominant paradigm of constitutional law and scholarship."[4]
While each rejoinder motivates the theory presented here, none provides an
adequate account of a history in which hostilities recur while courts appear
increasingly invulnerable. This chapter then takes a closer look at what counts
as an attack on judicial independence. Most accounts of these hostilities have
grouped together an array of tactics without attention to how the tactics differ from one another. While all of them infringe on judicial independence, all
infringements are not the same. Broadly speaking, two types of moves can be
distinguished: some undermine judicial legitimacy while others channel judicial power toward partisan ends. With this distinction in mind, the chapter's
third part examines proposed federal legislation concerning the judiciary since
1789. Categorizing these proposals over time reveals a shift in emphasis from
undermining the courts' legitimacy to harnessing judicial power. This pattern
sets the stage for building an explanatory theory in Chapter 2.

I. The Countermajoritarian Difficulty and Four Responses

Judicial review is the power of courts to consider the constitutionality of
legislation and to affirm or overturn it. When judges appointed for life wield
this power, control over the Constitution seems transferred beyond the reach
of the people it affects. Legal scholar, Alexander Bickel, viewed attacks on the
Warren Court, which characterized the judicial politics of his day, as driven
by the structural deviance of unelected judges in an otherwise democratic

Press, 1990). This account dovetails with Howard Gillman's analysis of Republican-led judi-
cial empowerment in the 1870s and 1890s to serve partisan interests. See Gillman, "How
Political Parties Can Use the Courts to Advance Their Agendas: Federal Courts in the United
States, 1875–1891," *American Political Science Review* 96 (September 2002), 511–24.

   Given the development of federal state apparatus from the early twentieth century onward,
courts could have easily proven redundant to newly created bureaucratic commissions.
Therefore, courts could have, in fact, been less necessary under circumstances of bureaucratic
expansion and *more* susceptible to having their powers stripped. In the nineteenth-century
state of "courts and parties," courts would seem most crucial to national stability and federal governmental power, and yet, ironically, these were the years when their powers were
most severely threatened. The phrase, a state of "courts and parties," was coined by Stephen
Skowronek to characterize the nineteenth-century American state. See Skowronek, *Building
a New American State* (New York: Cambridge University Press, 1982). Thanks to Stephen
Skowronek and Shep Melnick for their insights on this point.

[4] Erwin Chemerinsky, "The Supreme Court, 1988 Term – Forward: The Vanishing
   Constitution," *Harvard Law Review* 103 (1989), 61.

polity.[5] But he was hardly the first to do so. Judicial review's legitimacy preoccupied Americans from the Founding through the Progressive era.[6]

Bickel sought to curb anti-court hostilities by appealing to judges to exercise their "passive virtues" or their capacity to decide not to decide. If neutrality and the rule of law were to be maintained, judicial review must be undertaken "rigorously on principle, else it undermines the justification of [the Court's] power."[7] Bickel contended that judges should exercise restraint in their controversial prerogative precisely because he assumed the principles of legal realism to be true, namely, that judges did not discover law but created it to fill in the gaps of the Constitution and thus always already imposed their values.[8] And yet, if "the secret of [the Court's] ability to maintain itself in the tension between principle and expediency" lies in inaction, then judicial supremacy would be retained mostly as a theoretical possibility, never fully actualized.[9] In practice, the Court is cowered into avoiding cases lest it suffer the angry hordes.

Like Bickel's solution, many other responses to the countermajoritarian problem seek to regulate judicial behavior. They rationalize review as essential for protecting minority rights, prescribe boundaries on its exercise, or even advocate popular review. They assume that hostilities toward judges are motivated by the countermajoritarian difficulty, and that this difficulty requires resolution or accommodation.[10] But the Court is not anomalous among governing institutions in its countermajoritarian impulse. The Electoral College, presidential veto, filibuster, and Senate's non-proportional representation scheme are all countermajoritarian.[11] Thus, something other than claims of

---

[5] Alexander Bickel, *The Least Dangerous Branch* (New Haven: Yale University Press, 1986), 239, 18.

[6] Charles Beard, "The Supreme Court – Usurper or Grantee?" *Political Science Quarterly* 27 (March 1912),1–35.

[7] Bickel, 69. See pages 111–98 for a fuller discussion of what Bickel means by "passive virtue."

[8] Jonathan O'Neill, *Originalism in American Law and Politics: A Constitutional History* (Baltimore: Johns Hopkins University Press, 2007), 43–66.

[9] Bickel, 69.

[10] On the judiciary as protecting minority rights, see John Hart Ely, *Democracy and Distrust* (Cambridge: Harvard University Press, 1980); and William N. Eskridge, Jr., "Pluralism and Distrust: How Courts Can Support Democracy by Lowering the Stakes of Politics," *Yale Law Journal* 114 (2005), 1279–328. On boundary conditions for judicial review, see Ian Shapiro, *Democratic Justice* (New Haven: Yale University Press, 1999); Jeremy Waldron, "The Core Case against Judicial Review," *Yale Law Journal* 115 (2006), 1346–406; and, Ronald Dworkin, *Freedom's Law: The Moral Reading of the American Constitution* (New York: Oxford University Press, 1996). On popular review, see Larry Kramer, *The People Themselves* (New York: Oxford University Press, 2004); and Mark Tushnet, *Taking the Constitution Away from the Court* (Princeton: Princeton University Press, 2000) and "Is Judicial Review Good for the Left?" *Dissent* (Winter 1998), 65.

[11] On how various American political institutions are not democratic, see Sanford Levinson, *Our Undemocratic Constitution* (New York: Oxford University Press, 2006) and Robert Dahl, *How Democratic Is Our Constitution?* 2nd ed. (New Haven: Yale University Press, 2001).

countermajoritarianism motivates persistent attacks on the Court and the ferocity of the antebellum and Reconstruction-era hostilities in particular.

Some research suggests that the problem is not what legal scholars have traditionally thought it to be. Three theories in particular point beyond countermajoritarianism as the core difficulty and beyond the normative preoccupation of legitimizing judicial review. They show, alternatively, that even if countermajoritarian problems arise, they do not persist for long due to electoral realignment; that judicial power, even in its countermajoritarian form, serves politicians' interests; and that the potential to raise popular ire by highlighting the Court's countermajoritarian potential has declined over time.

I.a. *Dahl's Response: Countermajoritarianism Is Short-Lived*

In a seminal essay, written a few years before Bickel's study, political scientist, Robert Dahl, conceded judicial review's undemocratic implications. He nonetheless claimed that its countermajoritarian threat fails to materialize for a significant length of time: "even without examining actual cases, it would appear on political grounds, somewhat unrealistic to suppose that a Court whose members are recruited in the fashion of Supreme Court justices would long hold to norms of Right or Justice substantially at odds with the rest of the political elite."[12] The Court, lacking power to implement its rulings without the support of the other branches, represents little threat to democracy.[13] As justices are appointed by the president with senatorial advice and consent, they are, according to Dahl, part of a unified regime. Rather than counter popular will, judicial review more often reflects and reinforces it.[14] The countermajoritarian difficulty does not materialize for long because judges are either pressured to "switch-in-time" or they are replaced via retirement with others who endorse the new order.[15]

Scholars have advanced Dahl's insights by developing a regime theory, which elaborates how judges advance the appointing party's objectives, particularly in cases of unified government.[16] Even as some scholars have pointed out that

---

[12] Robert Dahl, "Decision Making in a Democracy: The Supreme Court as a National Policy-Maker," *Journal of Public Law* 6 (1957), reprinted in the *Emory Law Journal* 50 (2001), 578.

[13] In *Federalist 78*, Hamilton characterizes the Court as the "least dangerous branch" since it lacks the executive's power of the sword and the legislature's power of the purse.

[14] Dahl posits, "The fact is, then, that the policy views dominant on the Court are never for long out of line with the policy views dominant among the lawmaking majorities of the United States." (570).

[15] On "switches," see Bruce Ackerman, *We the People: Transformations* (Cambridge, MA: Belknap Press of Harvard University, 1998), 333–50; and Ackerman, *The Failure of the Founding Fathers* (Cambridge, MA: Belknap Press of Harvard University, 2005), 188–98; see also William Leuchtenberg, *The Supreme Court Reborn: The Constitutional Revolution in the Age of Roosevelt* (New York: Oxford University Press, 1995), 213–36. On partisan entrenchment, see Jack Balkin and Sanford Levinson, "Understanding the Constitutional Revolution," *Virginia Law Review* 87 (October 2001), 1045–109.

[16] See Gillman, 2002; Keith Whittington, "Interpose Your Friendly Hand: Political Supports and the Exercise of Judicial Review by the United States Supreme Court," *American Political*

because justices spend increasingly lengthy terms on the bench and that therefore periods of judicial recalcitrance may be prolonged, "these arguments are not fundamentally different from others in the Dahlian tradition: it simply takes longer for the legal markets to clear (that is, to align with the 'dominant political alliance')."[17] Yet, these scholarly illustrations of Mr. Dooley's maxim are problematic on multiple fronts.

First, Dahl's empirics are problematic. As he penned his essay before many contentious Warren Court rulings, his data exclude a period of heightened popular hostility toward the Court.[18] And his coding includes only constitutional questions, leaving out instances when the Court weighed in on statutory construction.[19] Furthermore, his findings do not consider intensity of attacks, how they vary, or whether, even if briefly, they undermine judicial authority. But most important from a political development perspective, the tithing of judicial rulings to electoral outcomes, primarily through the mechanism of judicial appointment, ignores the institutional thickening characterizing American political development beginning in the early twentieth century and exploding since 1960s, that is, that multiple interests have increasing institutional resources and bases from which to stake claims on constitutional meaning. Therefore, partisan entrenchment on the judiciary is not a simple outcome of winning an election. Other institutions – a professionalized and politicized bar and interest groups and social movement actors – play a role in appointment, thereby dulling connections between party victory and judicial rulings.[20]

As such, Dahl's underlying assumptions can be challenged. His statement that "presidents are not famous for appointing justices hostile to their own views on public policy nor could they expect to secure confirmation of a man whose stance on key questions was flagrantly at odds with that of the dominant majority in the Senate" may predate Eisenhower's widely known disillusionment with Warren.[21] His claim that judges fall in line with the partisan leanings of the presidents who appoint them does not comport with either the failure of Nixon's four appointments to shift the direction taken by the

Science Review 99 (November 2005), 583–95; and J. Mitchell Pickerill and Cornell Clayton, "The Rehnquist Court and the Political Dynamics of Federalism," *Perspectives on Politics* 2 (2004), 233–48.

[17] Steven Teles, *The Rise of the Conservative Legal Movement: The Battle for Control of the Law* (Princeton: Princeton University Press, 2008), 11.

[18] Jonathan Casper, "The Supreme Court and National Policy Making," *American Political Science Review* 70 (1976), 52.

[19] Ibid., 60.

[20] Teles, 11. On institutional thickening generally, see Stephen Skowronek, *The Politics Presidents Make* (Cambridge: Harvard University Press, 1997). On the explosion and professionalization of interest groups since the 1960s, see Theda Skocpol, *Diminished Democracy: From Membership to Management in American Civic Life* (Norman: University of Oklahoma Press, 2003).

[21] Dahl, 569–70. Eisenhower is said to have called his nomination of Warren to be "the biggest damn-fool mistake I ever made." See David Nichols, *A Matter of Justice* (New York: Simon & Schuster, 2007), 296.

Warren Court or more recent episodes of Republican anti-judicial hostility. Republican presidents have dominated the federal judicial appointment process since 1968. Dahl contends, "the policy views dominant on the Court are never for long out of line with the policy views dominant among the lawmaking majorities of the United States." And yet, a mostly Republican-appointed Supreme Court has upheld (limited) abortion access, expanded gay rights, and maintained affirmative action in ways very much out of synch with Republican policy objectives evidenced in national party platforms since at least 1980.[22]

Finally, Dahl's prediction that the countermajoritarian difficulty will subside once the Court aligns through pressure or replacement rests on the idea that the Constitution is what the people, or at least their representatives, say it is at a given time. In other words, Dahl assumes the legitimacy of multiple possible interpretations, and thus the right of opposition to rule, to be an underlying tenet of American politics throughout. But the idea that if one side to a conflict gains the reins of power legitimately, it can implement its particular constitutional vision until such time as it loses its electoral grip has not always held currency. Indeed, that idea was slow in dawning.

I.b. *Strategic Interest: Politicians Want Strong Judiciaries*
A second model dismisses the countermajoritarian threat not because the Court eventually falls in line with the aims of the governing regime but because strong judicial power, even if periodically countermajoritarian, serves politicians' interests. Some of this work builds and tests its claims with game-theoretic models, which, while compelling, sometimes do not sufficiently address if and how actors' behaviors are contingent on circumstances, what those institutional and ideational circumstances might be, and how and why those circumstances change over time.[23] The general claim that follows is put sharply by constitutional scholars Neal Devins and Louis Fisher: "When lawmakers find it convenient to seek cover in a Court ruling ... Congress's willingness to both interpret the Constitution and challenge the Court gives way to political expediency.... Like Congress, the White House sometimes finds it easier to hide behind a Court decision than to take the heat for independently interpreting the Constitution."[24] Politicians can and will use courts to pursue policy goals or to deflect accountability.

---

[22] Ibid. Recent years have witnessed continued support for the underlying principles of *Roe v. Wade*, 410 U.S. 113 (1973) even as the Court has put some restrictions on access to abortion. See, for example, *Planned Parenthood v. Casey*, 505 U.S. 833 (1992). Note also the Court's overturning of the criminalization of consensual homosexual sex in its decision in *Lawrence and Garner v. Texas*, 539 U.S. 558 (2003) and its upholding of affirmative action in university admissions in *Grutter v. Bollinger*, 539 U.S. 306 (2003).

[23] See Jeffrey Segal, "Separation-of-Powers Games in the Positive Theory of Congress and Courts," *American Political Science Review* 91 (March 1997), 28–44; and McNollgast, "Politics and the Courts: A Positive Theory of Judicial Doctrine and the Rule of Law," *Southern California Law Review* (1994–95), 1631–84; Tom S. Clark, "The separation of Powers, Court Curbing, and Judicial Legitimacy," *American Journal of Political Science* 53(October 2009), 971–89.

[24] Neal Devins and Louis Fisher, *The Democratic Constitution* (New York: Oxford University Press, 2004), 11.

Keith Whittington, Mark Graber, Howard Gillman, George Lovell, and Ran Hirschl explore how the judiciary holds strategic political value. In line with Dahl's thesis, Whittington contends that judges may be aligned ideologically with the elected branches. Judicial review may promote congressional and/ or presidential policy; as such, we should expect more cooperation than conflict between the elected branches and the judiciary.[25] For Graber, the legislature can avoid inflaming internal party cleavages on divisive issues by passing controversial issues to the Court for resolution. The legislature avoids accountability, and popular antipathy is deflected toward the judiciary.[26] Similarly, Lovell examines judicial invalidation of Progressive and labor legislative gains in the 1910s and 1920s to argue that ambiguous legislative statutes "could create the appearance of democratic responsiveness while allowing much of the blame for difficult policy choices to fall on less accountable judges."[27] Gillman assesses the expansion of federal judicial power in late nineteenth-century America through jurisdictional transfer from state to federal courts and the establishment of new administrative courts; he interprets this expansion as a "partisan or programmatic entrenchment that we frequently associate with legislative delegations to executive or quasi-executive agencies."[28] And Ran Hirschl argues that politicians benefit from increased "judicial intervention in the political sphere."[29] Furthermore, a strong judiciary may promote investor security thereby spurring economic development.[30] It may stabilize the rule of law.[31] In all these ways, strong and secure judicial power may serve politicians' interests.

When the Madisonian assumption of conflict among the branches is dropped – and many of the scholars who focus on the politically strategic value of judicial power take this view – it brings into clearer relief how judicial review promotes ends sought by a governing coalition. These scholars have catalogued tactics and motives to harness that power. Their insights figure prominently in this book. But there is a shortcoming in these accounts: they deal with half of the problem. If independent judicial power is politically valuable, then, as John Ferejohn asks, why "leave the door open for political meddling in the future by allowing the political branches to influence the

---

[25] Whittington, 2005.
[26] Mark Graber, "The Nonmajoritarian Difficulty: Legislative Deference to the Judiciary," *Studies in American Political Development* 7 (Spring 1993), 35–73.
[27] George Lovell, *Legislative Deferrals: Statutory Ambiguity, Judicial Power, and American Democracy* (New York: Cambridge University Press, 2003), 3.
[28] Gillman, 2002, 512.
[29] Ran Hirschl, *Toward Juristocracy: The Origins and Consequences of the New Constitutionalism* (Cambridge, MA: Harvard University Press, 2004), 39.
[30] Mancur Olsen, "Dictatorship, Democracy, and Development," *American Political Science Review* 87 (September 1993), 567–76; Barry Weingast, "The Political Foundations of Democracy and the Rule of Law," *American Political Science Review* 91 (June 1997), 245–63.
[31] Jon Elster and Rune Stagstad, eds., *Constitutionalism and Democracy* (New York: Cambridge University Press, 1988); Alec Stone Sweet, "Judicialization and the Construction of Governance," *Comparative Political Studies* 32 (1989), 147–84.

judiciary as a whole?"[32] Or, if politicians recognize that judicial power may serve their interests, then they can recognize that it may periodically operate against those interests, so why not curb courts and secure interests whenever possible? More pointedly, models focusing on the underlying political strategy of judicial supremacy tend not to account adequately for the expansive and successful court-curbing tactics of the nineteenth century or more recently passed jurisdiction stripping.

One possible answer, further explored in the next section, is that acceptance of strong independent judicial power constitutes a cultural norm. Yet, Ferejohn dismisses the development of a norm: "in a profoundly pluralist society it can hardly be hoped that acceptance of legal norms will always be sufficient to restrain groups from interfering; particularly when a value they hold very dear is at stake in a judicial proceeding."[33] Instead, he turns to problems of collective action to explain the failure to curb judicial power.[34] Judicial power is secure when the federal government is divided or when party discipline is weak, that is, circumstances characterizing much of twentieth-century American politics: "courts have more freedom of action when the political branches are too fragmented to make decisions directly."[35] If mustering votes to stop the Court is difficult, the judiciary will be more powerful.

By specifying a generalizeable political dynamic, Ferejohn's account does explain why attacks on judicial independence persist and why FDR's court-packing proposal and Nixon's jurisdiction-stripping proposal failed. Yet, his focus on collective action problems leads to an unsatisfying truism: Congress constrains the judiciary when Congress is hostile toward it and can overcome transaction costs. And, problematically, he does not assess the opposite possibility, namely, that anti-judicial legislation may aggregate different interests and serve as a common carrier. Such legislation might, in fact, function to overcome the collective action problems he relies upon as his explanatory mechanism.

In other words, interest-based theories need to account for strategies that aim to use the judiciary *and* for those that seek to undermine it. At present, none of these accounts explain the persistence of anti-judicial rhetoric. Nor do they grapple with the radical character of action taken in the early republic.[36] A theory is necessary that can explain when interests in strong judicial power

---

[32] John Ferejohn, "Independent Judges, Dependent Judiciary: Explaining Judicial Independence," *Southern California Law Review* 72 (1999), 376.

[33] Ibid., 370-1.

[34] Ibid., 372–82. Similarly, Tom Ginsburg suggests that anti-Court initiatives fail because governing systems are often characterized by "political diffusion" which "hinders authorities from overruling or counterattacking the courts." Ginsburg, *Judicial Review in New Democracies* (New York: Cambridge University Press, 2003), 261.

[35] John Ferejohn, "Judicializing Politics, Politicizing Law," *Law and Contemporary Problems* 65 (September 2002), 59.

[36] More generally, these interest-based models do not explain the persistence of anti-Court rhetoric or assess its strategic and possible electoral value. Most importantly, they do not consider how politicians' preferences for judicial power change over time and why. This critique is not to suggest that these accounts do not consider the effects of structural

are observable as well as the circumstances under which these interests would be overcome and judicial legitimacy undermined.

I.c. *A Norm of Deference: An Account of Gradual Change over Time*
Neither Dahl's theory nor the strategic-interest models examine change over time to account for why the countermajoritarian potential may not be as dangerous as normative legal scholars suggest. A third theory does. It posits the development of a pervasive norm of deference to judicial authority or acceptance of the Court as the ultimate interpreter of the Constitution.[37] Such judicial supremacy suggests that when the Supreme Court rules, "whether legitimately or not, as to that issue *the democratic process is at an end*."[38] As Whittington puts it, "judges, lawyers, politicians, and the general public today accept the principle of judicial supremacy – indeed they assume it as a matter of course."[39] And, Susan Burgess has contended, "scholars of both the political right and left support the ultimate interpreter reading as simply given," even though "judicial supremacy rests on tenuous grounds logically and historically."[40]

influences on rationality or the possibility of actors "updating" information after repeated interactions. Even when such interaction is built into these models, their underlying parameters constituting actors' rationality are generally held constant. By contrast, a longer time horizon afforded by a more historical study may demonstrate that *rationality itself should not be held constant*, and that rationality is, in fact, contextually contingent. See Ira Katznelson and Barry Weingast, "Intersections between Historical and Rational Choice Institutionalism," in *Preferences and Situations: Points of Intersection between Historical and Rational Choice Institutionalism*, Katznelson and Weingast, eds. (New York: Russell Sage Foundation, 2005), 11.

[37] Prominent work in this vein includes Barry Friedman's five-part series "The Countermajoritarian Difficulty." See "The History of Countermajoritarian Difficulty, Part One: The Road to Judicial Supremacy," *New York University Law Review* 73 (May 1998), 333–433. "The History of the Countermajoritarian Difficulty, Part II: Reconstruction's Political Court," *Georgetown Law Review* 91 (November 2002), 1–66; "The History of the Countermajoritarian Difficulty, Part III: The Lesson of Lochner," *New York University Law Review* 76 (November 2001), 1383–455; "The History of the Countermajoritarian Difficulty, Part Four: Law's Politics," *University of Pennsylvanian Law Review* 148 (April 2000), 971–1064; "The Birth of an Academic Obsession: The History of the Countermajoritarian Difficulty, Part Five," *Yale Law Journal* 112 (November 2002), 153–259. See also Charles Gardner Geyh's *When Congress and the Court Collide* (Ann Arbor: University of Michigan Press, 2006).

[38] Robert Bork, *The Tempting of America* (New York: Free Press, 1993), 199. Emphasis added.

[39] Keith Whittington, "Extrajudicial Constitutional Interpretation: Three Objections and Responses," *North Carolina Law Review* (2002), 776–7. On the assumption that judicial supremacy is a norm, see Louis Fisher, *Constitutional Dialogues* (Princeton: Princeton University Press, 1988); and Kevin Yingling, "Justifying the Judiciary: A Majoritarian Response to the Countermajoritarian Problem," *Journal of Law & Politics* 15 (1999), 81, 84, 106. On scholarly assumption that the public endorses judicial supremacy, see Steven Calabresi, "A Political Question," in *Bush v. Gore: The Question of Legitimacy*, Bruce Ackerman, ed. (New Haven: Yale University Press, 2002), 129–44; and Sanford Levinson, "Bush v. Gore and the French Revolution: A Tentative List of Some Early Lessons," *Law and Contemporary Problems* 65 (Summer 2002), 7–39.

[40] Susan Burgess, "Beyond Instrumental Politics: The New Institutionalism, Legal Rhetoric, and Judicial Supremacy," *Polity* 25 (Spring 1993), 454. While normative judicial supremacy is

Accounts of normative judicial supremacy claim that nineteenth-century court-curbing occurred before this norm was entrenched. The cultural shift was anchored in late nineteenth-century legal institutional development, particularly the establishment of bar associations and professionalized education. It was strengthened by reforms undertaken in the 1920s by Chief Justice Taft, which gave the Supreme Court control of its docket. Contemporaneously, judges and scholars began to characterize John Marshall's ruling in *Marbury v. Madison* (1803), particularly his claim that "it is emphatically the province and duty of the judicial department to say what the law is" as the doctrinal basis for judicial supremacy.[41]

The fates of FDR's court-packing proposal, the campaign to impeach Earl Warren, and the Nixon-era jurisdiction stripping lend some credibility to this thesis. As legal historian, Charles Geyh, notes when postulating this norm, "whereas threats to diminish and control judges are commonplace, making good on those threats is not."[42] Geyh argues that politicians have accepted the judiciary over time, despite its anti-democratic roots, and defer to its authority.[43] The value of this claim lies in its direct engagement with a fundamental change in inter-branch relations and in its recognition that accounting for that change is essential for any understanding of what is occurring today. What I put at issue is the precise nature of the normative change that took place. I do not seek to discredit norm development as an explanation for change over time; my own explanation elaborated in Chapter 2 relies on a normative shift. I do question the evidence gathered to prove the development of this particular norm of deference to judicial authority.

First, the normative judicial supremacy thesis tends to deal with the vehemence of recent anti-court rhetoric by dismissing it as the clamoring of an impotent minority. It assumes attacks on judicial authority are insignificant if advocated actions are not followed through, for example, if judges are not impeached or jurisdiction-stripping legislation does not pass. In measuring success in this way, it does not examine the strategic purposes rhetoric serves. Rhetoric may have electoral value as symbolic position-taking. And, if anti-court rhetoric garners votes, it is not clear that actual weakening of judicial

---

assumed across a range of literature, existing data fail to confirm public endorsement of it. See Brian Feldman, "Evaluating Public Endorsement of the Weak and Strong Forms of Judicial Supremacy," *Virginia Law Review* 89 (September 2003), 979–1036.

[41] *Marbury v. Madison*, 5 U.S. (1 Cranch) 137 (1803); Devins and Fisher, 9–19. See also Justin Crowe, "The Forging of Judicial Autonomy: Political Entrepreneurship and the Reforms of William Howard Taft," *Journal of Politics* 69 (February 2007), 73–87. The Supreme Court did not cite the case to support judicial review until 1887. Robert Clinton, "Precedent as Mythology: A Reinterpretation of *Marbury v. Madison*," *American Journal of Jurisprudence* 35 (1990), 55. The Court cited *Marbury* in *Mugler v. Kansas* 123 U.S. 623 (1887), but as Clinton points out, "The *Mugler* reference is an obvious misreading of *Marbury*. The Court there uses *Marbury* in support of the developing idea of substantive due process, in a passage which is *obiter dicta*." (56)

[42] Geyh, 5.

[43] Ibid., 11, 18–21, 253–82.

authority must follow, especially if the issue of judicial power does not hold public attention. Furthermore, evidence of recurrent position-taking against judicial authority would call into question a judicial supremacy norm at the popular level. In short, failure to pass court-curbing legislation cannot be considered a failed attack without a clearer understanding of politicians' multiple and simultaneous goals.

Second, and more fundamentally, a judicial supremacy norm cannot explain why politicians persist in drafting bills that undercut judicial authority and making speeches that emphasize the Court's undemocratic character. If normative judicial supremacy does in fact promote deference to judicial authority throughout the broader electorate, these actions would be irrational from an electoral incentive perspective.[44]

More specifically, Geyh points to three manifestations of this norm. First, the Senate's acquittal of Justice Samuel Chase in 1805, despite the House's impeachment, is an alleged initial encounter with the norm.[45] Second, Geyh details "a preference for conserving the structure of the Judiciary Act of 1789, which was viewed as an implementation of the constitutional framers' vision for an independent judiciary" in nineteenth-century congressional debate concerning alterations to federal judicial structure.[46] Third, Geyh sees the norm in "the gradual establishment of an independent, self-governing judicial branch, beginning in 1891 and continuing throughout the twentieth century."[47] On the basis of these indicators, Geyh argues that the norm strengthened over time thereby explaining the decline of judicial impeachments and why jurisdiction-stripping campaigns increasingly seem to fall flat.

However, each of these manifestations can be explained without postulating a norm of deference to judicial authority. Declining rates of impeachment are not evidence of a burgeoning norm of deference to the Court. The rarity of impeachment does not necessarily mean norms prohibit its use; it could just as likely indicate that judges have learned to avoid provoking it. For Ferejohn, its rarity "may be due as much to judges' reluctance to make politically controversial decisions as to any display of congressional virtue."[48] They may engage their "passive virtues," and, as detailed in the Introduction, calls for judicial impeachment still pepper recent Republican national platforms. Furthermore, while some tactics may decline, new ones have emerged such as legislation requiring supermajorities on the Court to overrule statute, creating judge or judicial decision recall, and filibustering senatorial consideration of judicial nominees. How these tactics vary in their impact needs to be more thoroughly assessed, but none suggest a norm of deference to the judiciary. Therefore,

---

[44] David Mayhew, *Congress: The Electoral Connection* (New Haven: Yale University Press, 1974), 49–77.
[45] Geyh, 55.
[46] Ibid., 57.
[47] Ibid., 101.
[48] Ferejohn, 1999, 358.

I question whether this norm can credibly be said to have developed at either the level of political elites or the wider electorate.

Consider the difficulties in amending the Judiciary Act of 1789 in the 1820s, 1830s, and 1860s. Failure to restructure the judiciary illustrates difficulties with altering the status quo as institutions acquire vested interests over time.[49] And, as to Geyh's third claim, while reforms were taken to strengthen judicial independence in the late nineteenth century, including the 1891 Evarts Act, a senatorial Republican majority encouraged these reforms because it could control, to a large extent, judicial appointments; the legislation was an opportunity to entrench party interests within the judiciary. Doing so held the promise of removing those interests from congressional contestation, an especially important objective since Republicans were aware of a recent rise in divided government and their tenuous hold on majority status.[50]

Finally, the idea of normative judicial supremacy promotes questionable assessments of relevant history. For example, while Progressive Era anti-judicial rhetoric has been called a "muted fury," legislation, which restricted the federal judiciary from issuing injunctions against labor, enjoined the enforcement of utility rates as set by state commissions, and limited diversity jurisdiction, did pass during the 1910s and 1930s.[51] Furthermore, when the Supreme Court declared the National Recovery Administration unconstitutional leading to FDR's Judicial Reorganization Bill, it was not at all apparent that the Court would evade the packing scheme.[52] It was similarly not clear that jurisdiction-stripping attempts were doomed to fail in the 1950s, 1960s, or 1970s.[53] As the chapters to follow detail, multiple pieces of jurisdiction-stripping legislation in the 1950s and in the 1970s did pass in the House of Representatives and were quite close to passage in the Senate.[54] The 2005 Detainee Treatment Act and the 2006 Military Commissions Act did strip the judiciary of habeas corpus jurisdiction.[55] The proposal of such legislation and its periodic passage undercut claims that normative deference to judicial authority has prevailed since

---

[49] On various reasons for entrenchment of legislation, see Paul Pierson, *Dismantling the Welfare State? Reagan, Thatcher, and the Politics of Retrenchment* (New York: Cambridge University Press, 1994), 27–50.

[50] Gillman, 2002. For a broader discussion of legislators empowering unelected judges to entrench their partisan interests, see Hirschl, 2004. On divided government in the 1870s through the 1890s, see Morris Fiorina, "An Era of Divided Government," *Political Science Quarterly* 107 (Autumn 1992), 387–410.

[51] William Ross, *A Muted Fury* (Princeton: Princeton University Press, 1994).

[52] Leuchtenberg, 132–62.

[53] On presidential delays on school desegregation, see Dean Kotlowski, "With All Deliberate Delay: Kennedy, Johnson, and School Desegregation," *Journal of Policy History*, 17 (April 2005), 155–92.

[54] Walter Murphy, *Congress and the Court* (Chicago: University of Chicago Press, 1962); Lucas Powe, Jr., *The Warren Court and American Politics* (Cambridge: Belknap Press of Harvard University, 2000), 60–2, 99–102, 127–42; Gary Orfield, "Congress, the President, and Anti-Busing Legislation, 1966–1974," *Journal of Law and Education* 4 (January 1975), 108.

[55] The United States Military Commissions Act of 2006, Pub. L. No. 109–366 (2006); and Detainee Treatment Act of 2005, Pub. L. No. 109–148 (2005).

the late nineteenth century and that collective action problems account for their failure.

The alarm bells currently rung by judges confronting heightened rhetorical hostility also cut against the deference thesis. As one interest group organized to defend judicial authority observed:

> interest groups and political partisans have been trying to weaken the author-
> ity and legitimacy of our courts by painting them as the enemy of main-
> stream values. They respond to controversial decisions – or any decision they
> don't like – by calling judges "activists" and even "tyrants," and by seeking
> to intimidate the judiciary and weaken Americans' access to justice. This
> drumbeat has gone unanswered for too long.[56]

In short, a norm of deference to judicial authority would lead to problematic assessments of relevant history. It cannot explain why jurisdiction-stripping actions were taken in the 1910s, 1930s, and 2006, when that norm should have prevented them. And it would discount worry about more recent hostili-ties toward judges as so much hysterics.

The claim that anti-judiciary attacks have subsided due to the develop-ment of a norm of deference to judicial authority is suspect. However, this theory usefully grapples with the categorical difference between attacks on judicial independence in the early 1800s and the 1860s on the one side and all those that followed on the other. This is precisely where regime models and strategic interest-based models come up short. I advance the insights of these different strands of scholarship with an alternative synthesis, one that brings the development of norms to bear on politicians' preferences, interests, and strategies.

II. Manipulating the Court: Undermining Judicial Legitimacy or Harnessing Judicial Power

As a first step toward re-conceptualizing the politics of hostility toward the judiciary, we might consider what an attack on judicial power actually is. Relevant literature offers an undifferentiated list of hostile congressional moves: (1) judicial impeachment, (2) tampering with bench size, (3) congres-sional override procedures, (4) altering jurisdictional boundaries, (5) altering appointment via term limits, recall, or re-confirmation, (6) lowering the Court's operational budget, (7) refusing to raise judges' salaries, (8) requiring supermajorities, (9) adding courts to allow appeal to a more "representative" body such as a proposed "Court of the Union," and (10) offering constitu-tional amendments overturning decisions.[57]

---

[56] Roger Warren and Bert Brandenburg, *Speak to American Values: A Handbook for Winning the Debate for Fair and Impartial Courts* (Washington, DC: Justice at Stake, 2006), i.

[57] This list is based on Stuart Nagel, "Court-Curbing Periods in American History," *Vanderbilt Law Review* 18 (1964–65), 925–44; and Gerald Rosenberg, "Judicial Independence and the Reality of Political Power," *Review of Politics* 54 (1992), 369–98.

This list is problematic on several counts. For example, constitutional amendments overturning decisions are neither necessary nor sufficient to constitute an attack on the judiciary.[58] They may reflect disagreement with a particular ruling, not an assault on the Court's institutional legitimacy.[59] And this point can be generalized. The current definition assumes that all these tactics entertain the same goal. Attending more closely to tactical objectives opens the possibility that they do not all seek the same ends.

A similar definitional problem mars accounts of presidential relations with the federal judiciary, which have been viewed as either judicial supremacist or departmentalist.[60] While judicial supremacy considers the Court's opinion to be synonymous with constitutional meaning, and thus that the president and all other government actors are bound to enforce it, departmentalism, by contrast, refers to the idea that while the Court may make persuasive rulings, its interpretation does not bind the other branches, leaving Congress, the president, or even states free to follow their own interpretations.[61] This doctrine has enjoyed recurring prominence among certain presidents, and as Keith Whittington has argued, presidential assertions of authority to interpret the Constitution correspond to Stephen Skowronek's characterization of particular presidents who come to office unencumbered by the commitments of a previous regime. These presidents, including Jefferson, Jackson, Lincoln, FDR, and Reagan, have more freedom and legitimacy to assert not only their policy claims but also their own constitutional claims.[62] Yet, while FDR's actions remind us of Jefferson's, they were not an exact replay. FDR sought to pack the Court; Jefferson sought to impeach judges and eliminate courts. Jefferson wanted to push the judiciary aside; FDR wanted to pull it to his side. Simply

---

[58] See the Eleventh Amendment (1798), which overturned *Chisholm v. Georgia*, 2 U.S. 419 (1793) and clarified jurisdictional boundaries of suits between states and private citizens; the Thirteenth, Fourteenth, and Fifteenth Amendments, which negated *Dred Scott v. Sanford*, 60 U.S. 393 (1857); the Sixteenth Amendment (1913), which established the income tax overruling *Pollock v. Farmers' Loan and Trust Company*, 157 U.S. 429 (1895); and the Twenty-Sixth Amendment (1971) setting the voting age at eighteen negating *Oregon v. Mitchell*, 400 U.S. 112 (1970).
  Similarly, statutory reversals of judicial rulings are not necessarily attempts to discipline the Court but to clarify existing statute in an ongoing inter-branch colloquy. Judges may clarify legislation that was either intentionally or unintentionally vague, asking legislators to respond. See Jeb Barnes, *Overruled?* (Stanford: Stanford University Press, 2004); and Shep Melnick, *Between the Lines* (Washington, DC: Brookings Institution, 1994).
[59] This is the distinction between diffuse and specific support. Specific support refers to popular agreement with a ruling; diffuse support is support for the institution even if a ruling provokes disagreement. See Jeffrey Mondak and S. I. Smithey, "The Dynamics of Public Support for the Supreme Court," *Journal of Politics* 59 (1997), 1114–42; and Gregory Caldeira and James Gibson, "The Etiology of Public Support for the Supreme Court," *American Journal of Political Science* 36 (1992), 635–64.
[60] Susan Burgess, *Contest for Constitutional Authority: The Abortion and War Powers Debates* (Lawrence: University Press of Kansas, 1992); and Whittington, 2007.
[61] Whittington, 2007, xi; Murphy, 411–2.
[62] Whittington, 2007; and Stephen Skowronek, *The Politics Presidents Make* (Cambridge: Belknap Press of Harvard University, 1997).

considering FDR's actions to be a static recurrence of Jeffersonian themes misses nuanced differences between them that point to the potential for a developmental shift, which deserves explanation.

Scholars have tended to view both the congressional actions listed earlier and presidential departmentalism as uniformly hostile because all infringe on judicial independence. Yet, this position assumes that the judiciary was intended to operate totally independent of the other branches. The Constitution denies this possibility: jurisdictional boundaries and structure are congressional prerogatives.[63] Stripping jurisdiction is a case in point. Manipulations of jurisdictional boundaries affect the types of cases that can be brought and the parties that may seek redress. Congress can alter jurisdiction according to the Constitution's Exceptions Clause in Article III, Section Two: "In all Cases affecting Ambassadors, other public Ministers and Consuls, and those in which a State shall be Party, the supreme Court shall have original Jurisdiction. In all the other Cases before mentioned, the Supreme Court shall have appellate Jurisdiction, both as to Law and Fact, with such Exceptions, and under such Regulations as the Congress shall make." Generally, this clause is understood to mean that the Constitution empowers Congress to remove jurisdiction from the Supreme Court or lower federal courts, and historically, Congress has done so or proposed bills to do so.[64]

Acknowledging the extent of congressional prerogative raises the question of whether the actions that politicians advocate undermine judicial legitimacy or do something more limited, something that actually relies on judicial legitimacy and seeks to channel the exercise of judicial power toward particular political ends. Viewing attacks on judicial independence as at least these two distinguishable strategies allows for assessments of variation in how these strategies were employed over time. Table 1.1 reclassifies the actions as one of these two strategies while Figure 1.1 suggests how these actions may be arrayed along a spectrum from attempts to actively undermine judicial legitimacy to more passive measures to do so and to measures that harness judicial power. By attending to this variation, we can consider additional tactics that do not fall within the traditional array of hostile actions, such as filibustering judicial nominations, ignoring a ruling, or a presidential signing statement

---

[63] See Article III, Section 1, and Article I, Section 8, of the U.S. Constitution.

[64] Martin Redish, "Congressional Power to Regulate Supreme Court Appellate Jurisdiction under the Exceptions Clause: An Internal and External Examination," *Villanova Law Review* 27 (1980), 900–28. Steven Calabresi and Gary Lawson argue that the Constitution allows for the transfer of jurisdiction between appellate and original, not removal of jurisdiction. However, politicians have behaved as if the Exception Clause grants removal power, and judges have responded in kind. For example, as discussed in Chapter 8, Justice Antonin Scalia dissented in *Hamdan v. Rumsfeld*, 548 U.S. 557 (2006), arguing that the Detainees Treatment Act removed jurisdiction on the question before the Court so the Court could not rule. This argument follows the precedent of *Ex parte McCardle*, 74 U.S. 506 (1868) discussed in Chapter 5. See Calabresi and Lawson, "The Unitary Executive, Jurisdiction Stripping, and the Hamdan Opinions: A Textualist Response to Justice Scalia," *Columbia Law Review* 107 (2007), 1002–47.

TABLE 1.1. *Tactical Measures Constituting an Attack on the Judiciary*

Traditional Definition	Parsing the Traditional Definition
Battery of Tactics	*Undermining Judicial Legitimacy*
Judicial impeachment	Politically motivated judicial impeachment
Tampering with bench size	Altering the Court's decision rules
Congressional override procedures	Congressional override procedures
Manipulating jurisdiction (stripping or transfer)	Lowering Court's operational budget
	Refusal to raise judges' salaries
Altering appointment/removal procedures	Eliminating courts or judges
	Ignoring the Court's decisions*
Lowering the Court's operational budget	Decision and judicial recall
Refusal to raise judge's salaries	
Altering the Court's decision rules	*Harnessing Judicial Power*
Eliminating/adding courts or judges	Tampering with bench size
Constitutional amendments overturning decisions	Manipulating jurisdiction (stripping or transfer)
	Altering appointment or removal procedures
	Adding courts or judges
	Filibustering judicial appointments*
	Presidential signing statements*

* Ignoring the Court – as was done by Jackson in the Cherokee decision or by massive Southern resistance to *Brown v. Board of Education* – filibustering judicial appointments, and signing statements were not included in Nagel or Rosenberg's definitions, but each is discussed in this book.

prompting judges to a particular interpretation of statute. Thus, my conceptual move increases the actions meriting interrogation and allows for some needed distinctions.

A strategy of undermining judicial legitimacy might lead to politically motivated judicial impeachment – a broad construction of impeachment whereby judges are impeached if congressional majorities disagree with rulings – or establishing procedures for congressional overruling authority or forcing the Court to take on restrictive decision rules like supermajorities.[65] A strategy of harnessing judicial power for political ends might lead to manipulating jurisdictions, establishing administrative courts to diminish the judiciary's influence in certain policy domains, altering bench size, or filibustering judicial appointments. This latter group of actions does not necessarily de-legitimize the judiciary, but it alters and directs the judiciary toward new political purposes.

Divisions between undermining judicial legitimacy and harnessing judicial power are not clear-cut, and I have arranged these tactics as a spectrum in

[65] This broad construction of impeachment was mostly discredited after Samuel Chase's 1805 trial; Gerald Ford failed to revive it against Justice William Douglas in the early 1970s. Politically motivated impeachments are discussed in Chapters 3 and 7.

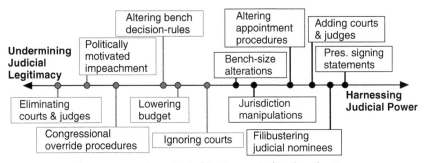

FIGURE 1.1. A spectrum of tactics infringing on judicial authority.

Figure 1.1 to highlight this. For example, increasing bench size may appear to place the Court at the mercy of the elected branches thereby undermining its legitimacy, but it also relies on the Court's authority to make rulings considered legitimate. Indeed, FDR's Court-packing plan was not supported by many Progressives who had wanted to weaken the judiciary for decades, precisely because it *relied too much* on judicial legitimacy. As one scholar observed, "the remedy proposed for that situation was, in effect, a change in the Court's size and personnel, not in its role."[66]

Similarly, jurisdiction-stripping measures can blur the line between harnessing power and undermining legitimacy. Indeed, carried to their logical extreme, Congress could remove nearly all federal jurisdiction and incapacitate the judiciary.[67] And yet, a primary aim of these bills may be to reverse or head off a court ruling; a secondary objective may be to lodge final appellate decision with a court friendlier to the legislators' political perspective. Legislators seek a policy outcome, and in the latter case at least, they rely on the courts, in part, to maintain that outcome. Jurisdiction-stripping measures are often offered in tandem with legislation that limits federal funding or restricts other departments from acting in the same policy area. That coupling suggests that multiple tactics are employed to achieve a single policy

---

[66] Stephen Strickland, "Congress, the Supreme Court and Public Policy: Activism, Restraint and Interplay," *American University Law Review* 18 (March 1968), 273–4.

[67] Former Representative Charles Mathias (D-MD) commented on the slippery slope of jurisdiction-curbing that leads toward undermining judicial authority. When discussing this congressional authority, he noted:

It is obvious that these provisions mean something. They give Congress some authority to regulate the jurisdiction of both the Supreme Court and the lower federal courts. But it is equally obvious that they do not provide the Congress with the power to deprive our federal system of the jurisdiction to decide certain types of constitutional issues.... Once Congress starts down this road, there is no area of human endeavor that could not be reached by a simple act of Congress altering the jurisdiction of federal courts to control the outcome of cases. Tomorrow, our most basic constitutional protections could be at stake.

Charles Mathias, Jr., "The Federal Courts under Siege," *Annals of the American Academy of Political and Social Science* 462 (July 1982), 29.

objective. For example, in response to the Supreme Court's busing rulings in the 1970s, separate bills curbed federal jurisdiction, cut funding to the Department of Health, Education, and Welfare to enforce busing, and prohibited the Department of Justice from initiating or supporting litigation that might promote busing. As such, jurisdiction-stripping was only one of many tactics to achieve the policy aim of ending busing.

Given porous boundaries between the strategies, assessing what is going on in a particular episode of inter-branch hostility will demand closer readings of political context and actors' understandings, which will be accomplished in the subsequent case-study chapters. At this point, it is sufficient to stipulate a strategic difference. Some tactics *attack* the judiciary's legitimacy, harping on its democratic deficit and particularly referencing the specter of countermajoritarianism. Others *exploit* the judiciary's legitimacy and seek to redirect its power toward partisan objectives. The harnessing strategy indicates a tacit recognition of the Court's legitimacy as a policy-making body; the countermajoritarian strategy does not.

III. Mapping Legislation: Patterns Over Time

Subtleties aside, quantification does reveal a general historical pattern in the kinds of attacks leveled at the judiciary over time. A crude first cut will not substitute for a closer look within each episode, but it does motivate such an investigation. To assess whether any pattern to harnessing or undermining strategies exists, I built a dataset of proposed congressional legislation on judicial power between 1789 and 1982.[68] I searched indexes of the *Annals of Congress, Register of Debates, Congressional Globe,* and *Congressional Record* using key words: "amendment," "court," "constitution," "impeachment," "judges," "judiciary," "justice," and "supreme court."[69] The set was culled based on the following rules:

1. Impeachments unrelated to the judiciary and constitutional amendments reversing a decision were excluded.[70]

---

[68] Stuart Nagel constructed a dataset – extended by Gerald Rosenberg – of proposed legislation impinging on judicial independence since 1800. See Nagel, 1965, 925 and Rosenberg, 1992, 379. Rosenberg told me that his data were no longer available, so I constructed a new dataset. I stopped my dataset at 1982 so I could cross-check my results with Rosenberg's. My counts differ from the Nagel-Rosenberg data for four reasons: (1) I include amendments to alter federal judicial structure, (2) I count legislation other than jurisdiction-stripping, (3) I include the early 1970s because President Nixon advocated stripping federal jurisdiction on integrative busing legislation, and (4) I keep sessions of Congress intact to assess how anti-judiciary legislation may decline within a session.

[69] I conducted a second sweep of the national party platforms between 1840 and 2004 for anti-judicial rhetoric to corroborate these periods, and such rhetoric is evident in the 1996, 2000, and 2004 Republican platforms.

[70] Resolutions for a pro-life amendment were not included in the dataset. However, bills curbing jurisdiction such that lower federal courts could no longer rule on matters of abortion were included.

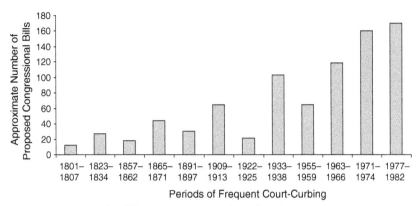

FIGURE I.2. Periods of frequent Court-curbing legislation.

2. Duplicate entries under distinct index headings were excluded.
3. Actions against personnel aside from judges, for example, marshals or district attorneys, were excluded.
4. Bills and resolutions for building courthouses or dividing states into new districts were eliminated, but the creation of circuits was included.
5. Index entries in which the bill's directionality could not be determined were excluded.

Figure I.2 depicts the absolute total number of proposed legislation for these periods.

Since the volume of all proposed legislation has grown over time, the pattern of increasing court-curbing proposals reveals very little information. Therefore, I disaggregated the proposed congressional legislation involving the judiciary by tactic and normalized it across time as percentages of total judiciary legislation. This information is included in an appendix to this chapter. When these percentages are re-aggregated as either the strategy of undermining judicial legitimacy or of harnessing judicial power, the two distinct strategies can be mapped over time. Figure I.3 depicts these two strategies as mirror images as I have simply divided the tactics traditionally considered anti-court attacks into one of the two strategies. While harnessing tactics are more prevalent in the twentieth century, no trend is immediately apparent in the nineteenth century. Yet, some of the noise in this data, which may obscure a clearer pattern, can be dealt with easily.

First, before 1891, altering the size of the Supreme Court bench was a structural artifact of the admission of new states since Supreme Court Justices also served as circuit judges. As such, bench increases cannot be credibly categorized as pure political harnessing.[71] After 1891, bench packing is more clearly

---

[71] The federal judiciary, as designed by the 1789 Judiciary Act, had district courts, circuit courts, and a Supreme Court. Supreme Court justices manned the circuits with a district judge. As traveling was difficult, this structure was amended in 1794 so that a circuit panel included one

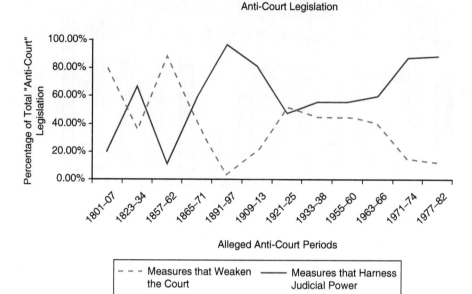

FIGURE 1.3. Proposed legislation concerning judicial power.

a tactic attempting to harness judicial power to a particular political end. Second, we should distinguish between whether hostile measures come proposed as normal legislation or as constitutional amendments. My expectation is not that legislators will propose less court-weakening measures over time, but that proposals will allow for position-taking credit without damaging a plausible longer term interest in a strong judiciary. Amendments can function as symbolic politics: by advocating them, politicians exploit short-term electorally strategic rhetoric while not taking additional, potentially costly action to weaken courts that may be strategically beneficial in the long term.

When alterations of Supreme Court bench size and all constitutional amendments are separated out from normal legislation, a clearer pattern emerges. Figure 1.4 confirms and deepens the finding that politicians focus more on harnessing judicial power after the 1870s than before.

Normal legislation undermining judicial legitimacy is a higher proportion of all proposed legislation infringing on judicial independence compared with normal legislation harnessing judicial power until about the late 1860s. The pattern then reverses, and harnessing legislation is a greater proportion of total proposed legislation. Second, constitutional amendments taken together – those that harness the judiciary and those that undermine it – are a

justice and one district judge. So, the number of justices was tied to the number of circuits. To accommodate the addition of new states, new circuits were created, and new justices added in Judiciary Acts of 1807, 1837, and 1862. In 1891, justices were relieved from circuit-riding responsibilities.

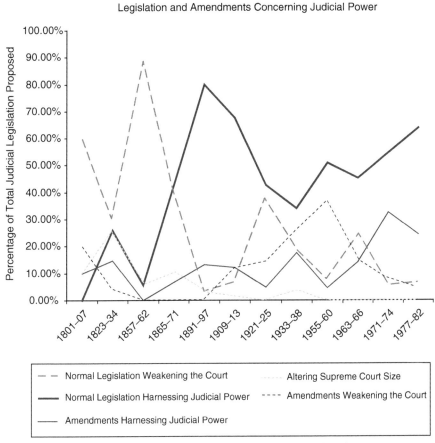

Legislation and Amendments Concerning Judicial Power

FIGURE I.4. Disaggregating normal legislation concerning judicial power.

higher proportion of total judiciary legislation in the twentieth century than earlier. This pattern may indicate that attacks on judicial independence are becoming increasingly symbolic. Third, both normal and higher legislation that undermines judicial authority are less evident from the mid-twentieth century onward, which indicates that legislators are focusing more on harnessing tactics.

This preliminary exercise leaves two matters to be explained. One is the apparent shift in elite tactics around 1870; the other is the persistence of anti-Court rhetoric geared toward the wider electorate that focuses on the countermajoritarian difficulty.

IV. Conclusion

Discussion of the federal judiciary in American politics traditionally starts from the premise that it is a deviant institution because it is structurally countermajoritarian. This chapter points to the limits of that framing. It leads to a normative preoccupation with the legitimate role of the judge in a democracy, and it conceptualizes attacks on judicial independence as reactions against the Court's structural democratic deficit. It has fixated on recommendations for how judges should decide, advocating either avoiding contentious issues or narrowing the breadth of rulings so as not to quell democratic deliberation.

Several scholars have recently delimited the actual problem posed by countermajoritarianism and pointed to strategic tactics in inter-branch relations. Yet much of this newer scholarship has assumed some of what needs to be explained. By classifying all tactics that encroach on judicial independence as hostile attacks and failing to consider differences among them, studies of inter-branch hostility miss or misconstrue important changes in inter-branch relations over time.

I have shown here that all attacks are not the same. While my initial distinction between attacks that undermine judicial legitimacy and attacks that harness judicial power is crude, it is nevertheless truer to the constitutionally enshrined idea that none of the branches, including the judiciary, is fully independent. Mapping these tactics over time gives reason to suspect that a systemic shift in inter-branch relations did indeed occur in the latter part of the nineteenth century. Chapter 2 offers a theory to explain this shift.

Appendix: Proposed Congressional Legislation Involving the Judiciary Disaggregated by Type

In the table shown here, legislation that would weaken judicial power is displayed in **bold**; legislation that I argue harnesses judicial power, but which has traditionally also been considered an attack on the Court in the relevant scholarship, is *italicized*. The percentages refer to how much a certain tactic was a percentage of all legislation proposed that targeted judicial power in that particular set of years, and thus allows for some comparison across time given the increase in legislation proposed over time.

	1801–07	1823–34	1857–62	1865–71	1891–97	1909–13	1921–25	1933–38	1955–60	1963–66	1971–74	1977–82
ALTER FEDERAL JUDICIAL SYSTEM												
Restrict the Meeting Time of the Supreme Court per Year	1 (10%)											
Alter Supreme Court Size (both raise and lower)		7 (25.93%)	1 (5.56%)	5 (11.11%)	1 (3.33%)	1 (1.54%)		4 (3.88%)				
Congressional Constitutional Overrides				1 (2.22%)	1 (3.33%)			3 (2.91%)	1 (1.54%)	30 (25.21%)	7 (4.38%)	2 (1.18%)
Reorganize / Eliminate Lower Courts	2 (20%)	6 (22.22%)	13 (72.2%)	14 (31.11%)				2 (1.94%)		1 (0.63%)	1 (0.63%)	3 (1.76%)
Supreme Court Decision Rules (Usually Requiring Supermajorities)							5 (23.81%)	16 (15.53%)	4 (6.15%)		1 (.63%)	1 (.59%)
JURISDICTION STRIPPING LEGISLATION (REMOVING FEDERAL JURISDICTION)												
Lower Federal Courts	4 (14.8%)			12 (26.67%)	15 (50.0%)	18 (27.69%)	4 (19.05%)	16 (15.53%)	13 (20.0%)	10 (8.40%)	24 (15.0%)	58 (34.12%)
Supreme Court Only	3 (11.11%)			4 (8.89%)	3 (10.0%)			2 (1.94%)	6 (9.23%)	12 (10.08%)	10 (6.25%)	2 (1.18%)
JUDGE-BASED LEGISLATION												
Election of Judges						1 (1.54%)					1 (0.63%)	3 (1.76%)
Age Restrictions/ Forced Retirement				2 (4.44%)	2 (6.67%)	1 (1.54%)		3 (2.91%)		10 (8.40%)	11 (6.88%)	12 (7.06%)
Oaths/Restricting Judge Behavior				1 (2.22%)		25 (38.46%)	5 (23.81%)	3 (2.91%)	3 (4.62%)		10 (6.25%)	19 (11.18%)
Qualifications								1 (.97%)	10 (15.38%)	11 (9.24%)	4 (2.50%)	
Require Reconfirmation											2 (1.25%)	
Restrict Judicial Ruling												
Salary Alterations				3 (6.67%)	4 (13.33%)		3 (14.29%)			1 (0.84%)		5 (2.94%)
Term of Office/Tenure											2 (1.25%)	2 (1.18%)

(continued)

	1801–07	1823–34	1857–62	1865–71	1891–97	1909–13	1921–25	1933–38	1955–60	1963–66	1971–74	1977–82
INVESTIGATIONS												
Judicial Rulings								4 (3.88%)			4 (2.50%)	3 (1.76%)
Judicial Behavior		2 (7.41%)	1 (5.56%)					6 (5.83%)	1 (1.54%)		3 (1.88%)	9 (5.29%)
Impeachment Resolutions & Trials	3 (30%)		3 (16.67%)			3 (4.62%)						1 (.59%)
CONSTITUTIONAL AMENDMENTS												
Eliminate Federal Courts	2 (20%)	1 (3.70%)										
Add Federal Courts				1 (2.22%)						1 (.84%)	1 (0.63%)	3 (1.76%)
Alter Supreme Court Size				2 (4.44%)			1 (4.76%)	6 (5.83%)	2 (3.08%)	1 (.84%)	2 (1.25%)	1 (0.59%)
Congressional Override							1 (4.76%)	8 (7.77%)	1 (1.54%)	5 (4.20%)	8 (5.00%)	5 (2.94%)
Supreme Court Decision Rule (Usually Requiring Supermajorities)								9 (8.74%)		3 (2.52%)	2 (1.25%)	
Jurisdiction Stripping (Removing Federal Jurisdiction)						5 (7.69%)	1 (4.76%)	5 (4.85%)	18 (27.69%)	9 (7.56%)	1 (.63%)	2 (1.18%)
Election of Judges						3 (4.62%)	1 (4.76%)	3 (2.91%)	5 (7.69%)	1 (.84%)	1 (.63%)	3 (1.76%)
Forced Retirement/Age Limit						2 (3.08%)		3 (2.91%)		3 (2.52%)	11 (6.88%)	4 (2.36%)
Prevent from Holding Public Office					1 (3.33%)							
Qualifications										1 (0.84%)	9 (5.63%)	1 (0.84%)
Requiring Reconfirmation										1 (0.84%)	11 (6.88%)	6 (3.53%)
Tenure/Term of Office	1 (10%)	4 (14.8%)			3 (10.0%)	6 (9.23%)		9 (8.74%)	1 (1.54%)	10 (8.40%)	18 (11.25%)	26 (15.29%)
Total	10	27	18	45	30	65	21	103	65	119	160	170

2

A Developmental Theory of Politicians' Confrontations with Judicial Authority

This chapter lays out a theory of elected branch-judiciary relations, which anchors individual interests and strategies in perceptions, ideas, and norms. It offers an explanation of the observed shift, detailed in Chapter 1, in emphasis of attacks on judicial authority, that is, a move from undermining judicial legitimacy to harnessing judicial power, which, in its general outlines, pivots the years of Civil War and Reconstruction.

Strategic-interest models offer one possible explanation for the harnessing strategy: deference to judicial authority may serve political purposes. Yet, many of these theories tend to take preferences as given – even if they are institutionally constrained – and hold the underlying parameters of rationality constant; the ideas and norms constituting the boundaries of rationality and structuring the range of legitimate political choices are not themselves closely scrutinized.[1] In short, they "relegate ideas, however they are conceived, to the sidelines in explanatory accounts of political processes."[2] As such, ideas are often viewed as derivative of or epiphenomenal to interests rather than constituting them.

However, entrenched ideas, like norms and institutions, limit and motivate political action. Entrenched ideas constrain how challenges to a political regime can take shape: "challengers to a dominant regime do not operate in an empty playing field, but are forced to challenge inherited norms and institutions, or to adapt their insurgency to the regime they seek to dislodge."[3] Political agents are situated in an inherited regime of ideas and institutions

---

[1] Such accounts of contextualized rationality are associated with historical institutionalism, which moves beyond the radical individualism of rational choice to see choice as embedded within institutions, defined as negative constraints or positive enabling rules and orders. See Elisabeth Clemens and James Cook, "Politics and Institutionalism: Explaining Durability and Change," *Annual Review of Sociology* 25 (1999), 441–46.

[2] Robert Lieberman, "Ideas, Institutions, and Political Order: Explaining Political Change," *American Political Science Review* 96 (December 2002), 699.

[3] Steven Teles, *The Rise of the Conservative Legal Movement: The Battle for Control of the Law* (Princeton: Princeton University Press, 2008), 6.

that set the boundaries and delimit the range of legitimate preferences.[4] Such ideational and institutional regimes endure when those invested in their continuity can make their precepts seem natural.[5] Often, entrepreneurial challengers exploit a sense of crisis – a disruption of normalcy – to displace and replace underlying ideas and foundational assumptions. Often, we observe this struggle between new and existing ideas through rhetoric.[6]

If ideas and assumptions set the range of legitimate preferences and interests, then changing ideational contexts alters those limits: "actors' understanding of their own interests is apt to evolve as the ideological setting of politics changes."[7] Rationality is thickly situated in an ideational context (as well as an institutional context) that changes over time.[8] The challenge is to illustrate the deliberate processes of how and why new ideas are created, voiced, accepted as legitimate, and underlie changes to institutional relationships and politically strategic behaviors. In this process, crisis and political entrepreneurship take center stage.

To the extent that changing norms and ideas have figured into explanations of inter-branch relations, scholars have relied primarily on the normative acceptance of judicial supremacy. The theory presented in this chapter takes different ground. It relates politicians' strategies on judicial authority to their perceptions of danger posed by differing interpretations of the Constitution, which are implicated more generally by ideas about loyalty of opposition and the legitimacy of party competition. Norms did develop over time, they did alter perceptions, and those changes did alter inter-branch relations systemically. But the change entailed recognition that no one group held a monopoly

---

[4] No political behavior or institutional development begins on a blank slate, but instead is mediated and limited by what exists already. See Stephen Skowronek, *Building a New American State* (New York: Cambridge University Press, 1982), 285 (noting, "Whether a given state changes or fails to change, the form and timing of the change, and the governing potential in the change – all of these turn on a struggle for political power and institutional position, a struggle defined and mediated by the organization of the preestablished state").

[5] Antonio Gramsci describes stable ideational regimes as hegemony, or the circumstance by which control is maintained through consent rather than coercion. Other scholars have referred to this circumstance by which a set of ideas is taken for granted as the natural or normal state of affairs and thereby constituting the assumptions that structure rational decision-making as the "third face of power." See Antonio Gramsci, *Selections from the Prison Notebooks*, trans. Quentin Hoare and Geoffrey Nowell Smith (London: Lawrence and Wishart, 1971), 182; John Gaventa, *Power and Powerlessness: Quiescense and Rebellion in an Appalachian Valley* (Urbana: University of Illinois Press, 1980), 13–19.

[6] Celeste Condit, *Decoding Abortion Rhetoric* (Urbana: University of Illinois Press, 1990), 3.

[7] Lieberman, 698. On ideas as constitutive of social reality, see James Tully, ed., *Meaning and Context: Quentin Skinner and His Critics* (Princeton: Princeton University Press, 1988).

[8] Ira Katznelson, "Situated Rationality: A Preface to J. David Greenstone's Reading of V. O. Key's The Responsible Electorate" in *The Liberal Tradition in American Politics: Reassessing the Legacy of American Liberalism*, David Ericson and Louisa Bertch Green, eds. (New York: Routledge, 1999). The idea of contextualized rationality as "thick rationality" comes from Victor Nee, "Sources of the New Institutionalism," *The New Institutionalism in Sociology*, Mary Brinton and Victor Nee, eds. (New York: Russell Sage, 1988), 10–11.

on legitimate claims to rule. At issue is not acceptance of judicial supremacy but the gradual acceptance of dissenting views of the Constitution. Once politicians granted that no single interpretation of the Constitution would hold absolute authority and that different interpretations could contend – indeed, must contend – as a matter of course, their strategic repertoire expanded. They were free to challenge the finality and independence of judicial power *and* to try to use that power as best they could. Simultaneously, judges were compelled to find new ground on which to build the claim that their particular interpretations should carry more weight than other leaders' alternatives. Without proper specification of the normative foundations of this historical shift, important aspects of inter-branch relations as well as various justifications of judicial authority made today would scarcely make sense.

This perspective on opposition politics tracks a cultural shift long familiar to historians of American political culture, which is the movement from the idiom of civic republicanism, with its emphasis on consensualism, substantive common good, and conflation of stable opposition with conspiratorial threat and civic instability, to the idiom of liberal pluralism. An idiom is a set of shared assumptions that structure the legitimate set of an actor's preferences and actions. Liberal pluralism holds that conflict, disagreement, and competition are not only unavoidable but also signs of a healthy body politic; it tends to be procedurally agnostic toward the outcome.[9] Evidence detailed in subsequent chapters reveals how these two idioms bounded politicians' assumptions and choices as they contemplated the problem of judicial power and how politicians moved those boundaries over time.

To sum up, underlying norms and ideas about opposition legitimacy and loyalty constrain or enable legitimate actions. If other actions are to be pursued, political entrepreneurs must strive to reconfigure the ideational context. This book is concerned with the processes politicians undertake to re-shape these contexts, how actors in other institutional settings recalibrate their own legitimate purposes in these new contexts, and how these new contexts shaped manipulations of judicial power.

---

[9] Neither idiom has fully displaced the other, but most observers agree that the balance between them has changed, such that pluralism describes the dynamics of contemporary politics. Historians and political scientists have argued about which idiom defines the American political tradition. Louis Hartz argued that American politics is liberal, while Berard Bailyn and J. G. A. Pocock highlighted the nation's republican underpinnings and Rogers Smith saw liberalism as one of multiple traditions. In this book, I reference David Ericson's notion of republicanism and pluralism as variants of American liberalism while highlighting the distinctive traditions that undergirded American law and policy during the nation's first century relative to its second. See Ericson, *The Shaping of American Liberalism* (Chicago: University of Chicago Press, 1993); Hartz, *The Liberal Tradition in America* (New York: Harcourt Brace, 1955); Bailyn, *The Ideological Origins of the American Revolution* (Cambridge, MA: Belknap Press of Harvard University, 1967); Pocock, *The Machiavellian Moment: Florentine Political Thought and the Atlantic Republican Tradition* (Princeton: Princeton University Press, 1975); Smith, "Beyond Tocqueville, Myrdal, and Hartz: The Multiple Traditions in America," *American Political Science Review* 87 (September 1993), 549–66.

The first part of this chapter explains the rationality of politicians' hostile rhetoric toward courts and judges by examining popular presumptions of judicial neutrality, popular ambivalence about judicial power, the judiciary's low levels of long-term salience, and politicians' goals of election and policy implementation. It accounts for the persistence of this rhetoric across time. Part II examines the idioms that have characterized American political culture – civic republicanism and liberal pluralism – and notes how they have gradually shifted over time. It relates the legitimization of opposition to the gradual rise of pluralism as the predominant idiom and links party development and attacks on judicial independence through changing perspectives on opposition that follow from pluralism. It then lays out a set of observable expectations for political behavior under changing assumptions. Part III discusses how judges re-cast their role in this pluralist environment. Not only did elected politicians alter their relations with the judiciary, but judges reset their relationship to the polity at large. Part IV concludes.

I. The Presumption of Judicial Neutrality and Persistence of Anti-Judicial Hostilities

Anti-judicial rhetoric persists over time because the general public is ambivalent toward judicial power and is not fully cognizant of court rulings or of how courts operate. Politicians exploit this circumstance of low knowledge by taking two seemingly contradictory actions.[10] They attack judicial legitimacy aggressively in their rhetoric and simultaneously seek to maintain that power through their legislative actions, as it may prove useful toward implementing particular political ends. The rhetoric serves valuable electoral position-taking purposes while maintaining that judicial power serves policy goals. Crucially, this disjuncture between aggressive rhetoric and minimalist court-curbing is perpetuated by a presumption of judicial neutrality that took root early in the republic's history.[11] So long as this presumption holds sway, politicians cannot ask directly for policy outcomes from judges; instead, they are driven to advocate structural reforms or to mask their political intentions through the frame of maintaining judicial neutrality, for example, by calling for judicial appointments who will interpret the Constitution "faithfully" rather than "legislate from the bench."

Anchoring the popular politics surrounding the judiciary in the presumption of neutrality puts us on firmer empirical ground than would a presumption of judicial supremacy. A common assumption underlies much legal and judicial politics scholarship that the public respects the federal judiciary, particularly the Supreme Court, and therefore endorses it as the privileged interpreter of

---

[10] Low knowledge of the federal judiciary is rational. Since judges are not elected and they deal with complex issues, paying attention may not be an efficient use of time. See Gregory Huber and Sanford Gordon, "Accountability and Coercion: Is Justice Blind When It Runs for Office?" *American Journal of Political Science* 48 (April 2004), 247–8.

[11] See Chapter 3.

constitutional meaning. However, there is little direct empirical data supporting a judicial supremacy norm in contemporary American politics. The norm is not isolated in polling data, and it does not follow from available evidence of popular respect for or confidence in the Court.[12] Neither "specific" support for a ruling nor "diffuse" support for the institution indicates anything about an endorsement of judicial supremacy.[13] The flawed assumption underlying contentions that this norm exists is that when "people favor judicial constitutional interpretations, people like judicial supremacy; when people dislike judicial constitutional interpretations, people disfavor judicial supremacy."[14] But, agreement with outcome does not imply agreement with process, and viewing courts as legitimate does not necessarily lead to an endorsement of judicial supremacy.[15] To be sure, Supreme Court justices have articulated their institution's supremacy in constitutional interpretation at least since *Cooper v. Aaron* (1958). In that case, they held that *Marbury v. Madison* "declared the basic principle that the federal judiciary is supreme in the exposition of the law of the Constitution, and that principle has ever since been respected by this Court and the Country as a permanent and indispensable feature of our constitutional system."[16] But, declarations of this sort are not proof of popular endorsement of judicial supremacy. Scholars may assume the idea, and judges may rely on it, but the proposition of public acceptance proves shaky nonetheless.

Robert Dahl was closer to the mark when, rather than stipulate public endorsement of judicial supremacy, he noted that Americans harbored competing sentiments: "the Court is highly unusual, not least because Americans are not quite willing to accept the fact that it *is* a political institution and not quite capable of denying it; so that frequently we take both positions at once."[17] Citizens may be uncomfortable with the judiciary's undemocratic implications, but they may also value its checking function. To the extent that the public is ambivalent, opportunities are made available for politicians to sway popular perceptions of judicial power.

Confidence levels garnered from public opinion polling do indicate that the judiciary is considered legitimate.[18] Evidence suggests that this legitimacy is

---

[12] Brian Feldman, "Evaluating Public Endorsement of the Weak and Strong Forms of Judicial Supremacy," *Virginia Law Review* 89 (September 2003), 1010.

[13] David Easton, "A Re-Assessment of the Concept of Political Support," *British Journal of Political Science* 5 (October 1975), 435–57.

[14] Feldman, 1011.

[15] Ibid., 1016.

[16] *Cooper v. Aaron*, 358 U.S. 1 (1958). The traditional account characterizes Marshall as articulating judicial supremacy in his ruling in *Marbury v. Madison*, 5 U.S. 137 (1803). More recent scholarship contends that Marshall was only articulating the equality of the branches and the judicial responsibility to review. See Larry Kramer, *The People Themselves: Popular Constitutionalism and Judicial Review* (New York: Oxford University Press, 2004).

[17] Robert Dahl "Decision-Making in a Democracy: The Supreme Court as a National Policy-Maker," *Journal of Public Law* (1957), 279.

[18] Gregory Caldeira, "Neither the Purse nor the Sword: The Dynamics of Public Confidence in the United States Supreme Court," *American Political Science Review* 80 (1986), 1209–26;

grounded in a sense of judges as neutral arbiters. Political scientists Gregory Caldeira and James Gibson have posited that public support for the Supreme Court draws on its perceived role in protecting liberty: "the mass public does not seem to condition its basic loyalty to the Court as an institution upon the satisfaction of demands for particular policies or ideological positions."[19] The public distinguishes between judges' partisan inclinations and the Supreme Court as a disembodied corporate entity, which should remain neutral.[20] Legal scholar, Eric Posner, takes note of this separation:

> Americans believe that the court has a valuable institutional role, but they resent the fact that these nine people exercise so much power over them. The more that these individuals have distinct personalities, flaw, quirks, recognizable ambitions, and so forth – the more they seem like ordinary human beings rather than disembodied spirits – the more difficult it is to acknowledge their exalted status in a democracy where authority is supposed to flow from the people.[21]

As Posner indicates, identifying the Court's most important political asset points to its most serious political vulnerability. Public respect for the Court is contingent on that institution's self-presentation as more than just one set of judges as partisan decision makers beating out another set of partisan decision makers. Judicial review functions because the public perceives judges to be "fair and unbiased, neutral in their application of the law.... They are believed to be able to do this because they are insulated from politics and are not elected officials" and thus "the general perception of Supreme Court justices held by the American public (a perception often buttressed by the

Gregory Caldeira, "Public Opinion and the Supreme Court: FDR's Court-Packing Plan," *American Political Science Review* 81 (1987), 1139–54; Roger Handberg, "Public Opinion and the United States Supreme Court, 1935–1981," *International Social Science Review* 59 (1984), 3–13; Richard Lehne and John Reynolds, "The Impact of Judicial Activism on Public Opinion," *American Journal of Political Science* 22 (1978), 896–904; Joseph Tanenhaus and Walter Murphy, "Patterns of Public Support for the Supreme Court: A Panel Study," *Journal of Politics* 43 (1981), 24–39.

[19] Gregory Caldeira and James Gibson, "The Etiology of Public Support for the Supreme Court," *American Journal of Political Science* 36 (1992), 658.
[20] A recent poll found marked disparity between favorability ratings for individual justices and ratings for the Court: 41 percent of "likely voter" respondents rated the Court as excellent or good, but the best-known justice, Clarence Thomas, an originalist, had a favorability rating of 38 percent (the highest among his brethren). The ratings do not correspond with the judges' interpretive methods; self-proclaimed originalists like Samuel Alito and Antonin Scalia had favorability ratings of 26 and 27 percent, respectively, while Ruth Bader Ginsberg, who is not an originalist, is rated at 36 percent. The survey was conducted by Rasmussen on May 14 and May 15, 2008, of 800 likely voters. See "Thomas Most Familiar Supreme Court Justice to Voters," Rasmussen Reports, 21 May 2008. http://www.rasmussenreports.com/public_content/politics/mood_of_america/thomas_most_familiar_supreme_court_justice_to_voters.
[21] Eric Posner, "Reply to Diane, Kenji, and Dahlia," at Slate.com's legal blog, "Convictions." Posted on May 22, 2008, at 6:25 P.M. http://www.slate.com/blogs/blogs/convictions/default.aspx. Posner attributes the original hypothesis of his claim to an earlier posting by Slate's legal correspondent, Dahlia Lithwick.

justices themselves) is that they are neutral interpreters of our laws and our Constitution."[22] If perceptions of fairness and neutrality are compromised, the judiciary is vulnerable to a crisis of legitimacy.

Next to the public's presumption of judicial neutrality, the most important factor conditioning the politics of anti-judicial hostilities is the public's minimal knowledge of judicial rulings and operations. As Lee Epstein and Jeffrey Segal have assessed, "most Americans lack even a passing familiarity with courts and judges."[23] This lack of awareness deepens the institution's vulnerability to misrepresentation by political entrepreneurs. Acknowledging first that judicial rulings may be out of line with how the public understands the judiciary's role and second that the Court's decision-making processes are not publicly salient, Caldeira and Gibson venture that politicians' framing of rulings may be more relevant to the Court's legitimacy than the legal matters dealt with or the ruling itself.[24] Entrepreneurial politicians may manipulate public understandings by framing decisions as politically motivated and violating the keystone standard of judicial neutrality. Thus, it is hardly surprising that the courts become "pawns in the culture wars," and hostile rhetoric focuses on rulings involving stark and uncompromising sociocultural questions, such as *Roe v. Wade* (1973) on abortion, *Parents Involved in Community Schools v. Seattle School District No. 1* (2007) on integrative busing, or *Lawrence v. Texas* (2003) on consensual homosexual sex, which are more readily comprehensible because they involve "primordial loyalties."[25] These issues do not easily submit to calm deliberation; one scholar has suggested, "pro-choice and pro-life people see themselves engaged in a death struggle for America's soul, as do pro-gay and traditional-family-values people."[26]

---

[22] Eliot Slotnick and Jennifer Segal, *Television News and the Supreme Court: All the News That's Fit to Air?* (New York: Cambridge University Press, 1998), 4.

[23] Lee Epstein and Jeffrey Segal, *Advice and Consent: The Politics of Judicial Appointment* (New York: Oxford University Press, 2005), 56. The salience of the Supreme Court ebbs and flows; nominations trigger public attention as the contentious evaluations of Robert Bork and Clarence Thomas have shown. However, public attention to the lower federal judiciary is even lower than to the Supreme Court (ibid.). See also Barbara Perry, *The Priestly Tribe: The Supreme Court's Image in the American Mind* (Westport, CT: Praeger, 1999), 123. These assessments, however, stand in some contrast to Barry Friedman's claim: "The public takes interest in Supreme Court decisions and appears widely to accept the role of the judiciary in resolving constitutional disputes." Friedman, "Dialogue and Judicial Review," *Michigan Law Review* 91 (1993), 624. Friedman suggests a broad interest where Epstein and Siegal suggest a shallow and sporadic one.

[24] Caldeira and Gibson, 659.

[25] On language of "the courts as pawns in the culture wars," see Mark C. Miller, *The View of the Courts from the Hill* (Charlottesville: University of Virginia Press, 2009), 105. On primordial loyalties, see Clifford Geertz, "The Integrative Revolution: Primordial Sentiments and Civil Politics in the New States," in *The Interpretations of Cultures* (New York: Basic Books, 1973), 255, 259. *Roe v. Wade*. 410 U.S. 113 (1973); *Parents Involved in Community Schools v. Seattle School District No. 1*, 551 U.S. 701 (2007); *Lawrence and Garner v. Texas*, 539 U.S. 558 (2003).

[26] William N. Eskridge, Jr. "Pluralism and Distrust: How Courts Can Support Democracy by Lowering the Stakes of Politics," *Yale Law Journal* 114 (2005), 1295.

Elected politicians' support for the judiciary, in sharp contrast to the broader public's support, is said to be attuned to case outcomes: "for opinion leaders, the Court has not become less salient and has not become less politicized" and "the commitments to the Court among the opinion leaders go together with their views of proper policy."[27] This difference points to the potential for strategic elite behavior, especially in light of politicians' multiple simultaneous aims. They seek to (1) be re-elected; (2) pass legislation;[28] (3) maintain or enlarge power within one's own institution;[29] (4) maintain their institution's standing in the public eye;[30] and (5) preserve or increase institutional capacity of their branch relative to other branches.[31] Rhetoric on the judiciary's undemocratic usurpation of power may serve these interests in different ways.

Politicians' anti-judicial rhetoric has value as electoral position-taking; as historian Lee Benson argued, rhetoric may not represent fervently sincere objectives, but "no one can deny" that it reflects politicians' "convictions on what the voters want to hear."[32] Anti-court rhetoric is evident in the campaigns of 1800, 1832, 1860, 1896, 1912, 1924, 1936, 1980, 1984, 1996, and 2004, which has led to the supposition that "every serious debate over judicial review in this country has occurred during a time that encompasses one of these campaigns."[33] Anecdotal evidence suggests that the rhetoric of "judicial activism" was raised during the last month of the 2008 presidential campaign to shore up support of the Republican base.[34] At the very least, the pattern suggests that anti-judicial hostilities can be exploited as a voter mobilization tool.

---

[27] Caldeira and Gibson, 660.

[28] David Mayhew, *Congress: The Electoral Connection* (New Haven: Yale University Press, 1974); R. Doug Arnold, *Logic of Congressional Action* (New Haven: Yale University Press, 1992).

[29] Mayhew, 1974; Eric Schickler, *Disjointed Pluralism* (Princeton: Princeton University Press, 2001).

[30] Schickler, 2001; members of Congress have a collective incentive to maintain or improve the stature of Congress. Legislators do not want to damage their institution's power relative to another branch nor diminish its standing in public opinion. This incentive may operate among Supreme Court justices, although since justices are not elected, their desire to maintain standing is not expected to be particularly strong. Rather, justices may be concerned with the legal integrity of their rulings and thus may be more responsive to the legal professional elite than the mass public.

[31] Schickler, 2001; Keith Kreihbel, *Information and Legislative Organization* (Ann Arbor: University of Michigan Press, 1991). Members of Congress are cautious in advocating institutional reform and innovation of other branches because to do so threatens their own branch. If Congress threatens the Court, the Court can similarly retaliate and invalidate legislation.

[32] Lee Benson, *Merchants, Farmers, and Railroads* (Cambridge: Harvard University Press, 1955), 138.

[33] Donald Stephenson, Jr., *Campaigns and the Court* (New York: Columbia University Press, 1999), 234.

[34] See Patrick Healy, "Seeking to Shift Attention to Judicial Nominees," *New York Times*, 6 October 2008, A15.

If anti-judicial rhetoric mobilizes voters, then it is not at all clear that the rhetoric must represent a sincere policy aim for the politician. Indeed, much journalistic coverage suggests that rhetoric mobilizes voters, leading one scholar to note that "the courts have thus become a highly salient issue for both parties, although more so for the Republicans."[35] A 2008 poll found that, although seven of nine Supreme Court justices and the vast majority of lower level federal judges had been, at that time, nominated by Republican presidents, 30 percent of Republicans still rated judicial appointments as their "top voting issue."[36] The finding suggests that "activists on the right have found in recent years that their supporters are the ones for whom changing the federal judiciary has become a movement."[37] A Republican operative characterized the battle over judicial appointments as a "unifying issue in many ways for Republicans" and analogized it to "becom[ing] like anti-communism was during the Cold War."[38]

And yet, politicians who may seek to garner support by voicing hostility toward judges find some room to maneuver once elected. Because the Court is not publicly salient in the long term or even well understood by most voters, politicians can make a series of moves. First, they may be able to frame the Court as hostile to their interests even if its rulings suggest otherwise. In recent years, Republican politicians have done so: "The courts have delivered the kinds of policy many conservatives want, while simultaneously providing them with a succinct and passionate rationale to persuade the public to vote

---

[35] Miller, 130. Some studies indicate judicial activism is inversely related to voter turnout. See Philip Klinkner, "Dwarfing the Political Capacity of the People? The Relationship between Judicial Activism and Voter Turnout, 1840–1988," *Polity* 25 (Summer 1993),633–46. But accounts of diminished turnout causally linked to judicial activism ignore efforts of entrepreneurs to mobilize the electorate against the Court, *making the Court's behavior itself a voting issue*, and thus utilizing the Court's alleged countermajoritarian behavior to broaden electoral support. See, for example, pro-life mobilization after *Roe* assessed by Kristin Luker in her *Abortion and the Politics of Motherhood* (Berkeley: University of California Press, 1984), 137–57. Further, hostility toward the judiciary may galvanize the electorate on the broader issues on which a case centers, for example, racial equality, feminism, and homosexuality. Journalistic accounts of G. W. Bush's 2004 victory cite anti-same-sex marriage ballot measures as a tactic to mobilize the Republican evangelical base. See Gary Segura, "A Symposium on the Politics of Same-Sex Marriage – An Introduction and Commentary," *PS: Political Science & Politics* 38 (2005), 189–93. Some analysis disputes this finding. See D. Sunshine Hillygus and Todd Shields, "Moral Issues and Voter Decision Making in the 2004 Presidential Election," *PS: Political Science & Politics* 38 (2005), 201–9. However, perception matters: "If Republican strategists and anti-gay activists believe that these ballot measures helped them at the ballot box, more are certain to follow" (Segura, 189).

[36] The poll was conducted by Rasmussen on 19 and 20 May 2008 of 800 likely voters. "For Republicans, Judicial Appointments Matter More than Iraq," Rasmussen Reports," 21 May 2008, http://rasmussenreports.com/public_content/politics/election_20082/2008_presidential_election/for_republicans_judicial_appointments_matter_more_than_iraq.

[37] Robert Barnes and John Cohen, "Fewer See Balance in Court's Decisions," *Washington Post*, 29 July 2007, A03, http://www.washingtonpost.com/wp-dyn/content/article/2007/07/28/AR2007072800645.html.

[38] Gregory Mueller, quoted in ibid.

Republican."[39] Second, to the extent that undermining judicial legitimacy carries costs, that is, politicians lose another tool by which to achieve and entrench their interests, the public's general lack of knowledge about and attention to the Court provides politicians with the capacity to not necessarily act on the implications of their rhetoric. Thus, whether or not politicians intend to effect change, they can make use of a ruling to build a base of support and reap the electoral benefits of position-staking against the "elitist" and "activist" judiciary. To the extent that they have strategic interests in perpetuating judicial power, their public attacks may come with relatively low cost. And, if this rhetoric gains support and the prospects of following through on court-curbing brighten, then politicians alert to the strategic uses of a strong judiciary may have room to pull back.

This is not to say that politicians are unconstrained. They want particular policy outcomes – they may want the judiciary to act as an extension of their party or ideological beliefs more broadly – but at the same time, given the public presumption of judicial neutrality and independence already detailed, politicians cannot openly demand that courts reach their favored outcomes.[40] Their only legitimate claim against the judiciary is that its rulings are inappropriately partisan and, as such, confound legitimate interpretive techniques. It is little wonder that much of conservative antagonism toward the judiciary that began in the 1970s and 1980s has come in the guise of originalist criticism.

Originalism is an interpretive technique that regards the Constitution as an act of sovereign lawmaking with fixed meaning; subsequent interpretation must "be bound by the meaning the document had for those who gave it legal authority."[41] Thus, originalist interpretation has often been used by its exponents to characterize judges as umpires, neutrally calling "balls and strikes" to contrast it with the allegedly politically motivated judicial activism that has been ascribed to non-originalist interpretive methodology.[42] However, originalism is more than that; it is the interpretive manifestation of movement conservatism, which took root in the late 1970s.[43] According to legal scholar, Reva Seigel, originalism served conservative political purposes while stipulating that its interpretive mode was fundamentally apolitical: "Originalism ... is not merely a jurisprudence. It is a discourse employed in politics to mount an attack on courts. ... [O]riginalism [is] a language employed

---

[39] Andrew Taylor, *Elephant's Edge: The Republicans as a Ruling Party* (Westport, CT: Praeger, 2005), 96.

[40] On the public's perception of the judiciary as a neutral arbiter, see Tom R. Tyler and Kenneth Rasinski, "Procedural Justice, Institutional Legitimacy, and the Acceptance of Unpopular U.S. Supreme Court Decisions: A Reply to Gibson," *Law & Society Review* 25 (1991), 621–30.

[41] Johnathan O'Neill, *Originalism in American Law and Politics: A Constitutional History* (Baltimore: Johns Hopkins University Press, 2005), 2.

[42] Jack Shafer, "How the Court Imitates the World Series: John Roberts' Winning Baseball Analogy," *Slate.com.* 13 September 2005.

[43] Robert Post and Reva Siegel, "Originalism as a Political Practice: The Right's Living Constitutionalism," *Fordham Law Review* 75 (2006), 545–74.

to pursue constitutional change in *politics and through adjudication*."[44] In other words, the claim that adherence to text or founders' intent – depending on the originalism practiced – is the only legitimate interpretive framework serves a politically charged movement with particular policy aims.

In short, to define antagonism toward a ruling in the language of policy difference is to concede that the judiciary is and can be political.[45] To seek policy responsiveness openly from judges is to concede that they can and even should behave precisely in the politicized way that politicians often argue is illegitimate. The upshot is that even if politicians care more about case outcomes than the judiciary's structural legitimacy – even when they want to harness judicial power instrumentally to policy ends – they tend to be driven in their public rhetoric to more hyperbolic assaults on the courts as structurally undemocratic and illegitimate.

Consider the endorsement of judicial review in the Republican national party platform of 2000:

> The rule of law ... has been under assault, not only by criminals from the ground up, but also from the top down.... Many judges disregard the safety, values, and freedom of law-abiding citizens.... [T]hey make up laws, invent new rights, free vicious criminals, and pamper felons in prison. They have arbitrarily overturned state laws enacted by citizen referenda, utterly disregarding the right of the people and the democratic process. The sound principle of judicial review has turned into an intolerable presumption of judicial supremacy. A Republican Congress, working with a Republican president, will restore the separation of powers and reestablish a government of law. There are different ways to achieve that goal – setting terms for federal judges, for example, or using Article III of the Constitution to limit their appellate jurisdiction – but the most important factor is the appointing power of the presidency.[46]

This plank does not advocate overt change in policy but recommends working through constitutional measures of defining jurisdiction and appointment to

---

[44] Emphasis in original. Reva Siegel, "Constitutional Culture, Social Movement Conflict, and Constitutional Change: The Case of the de facto ERA," *California Law Review* 94 (2006), 25. See Chapter 8 for further discussion of the political strategy inherent in the development of originalist interpretation.

[45] For example, organizations such as the Family Research Council (FRC) that have driven contemporary mobilization on judges as a political issue defines its purpose as preventing judicial activism or "upending the will of the people on important social issues" arguing that "judges have an obligation to interpret the law as it is written and not to impose their own policy preferences." Groups such as Justice at Stake (JAS), who defend state and federal judges against accusations of activism, aim "to educate the public and work for reforms to keep politics and special interests out of the courtroom – so judges can do their job protecting the Constitution, individual rights and the rule of law." Both organizations utilize the same terms to defend their actions: judicial independence, rule of law, policy preferences, and special interests. Yet the motivations of each – as FRC is evangelical and conservative, though officially non-partisan, while JAS is more liberal, though officially non-partisan – are distinct despite similar terminology. See http://www.frc.org/the-courts and http://faircourts.org/contentViewer.asp?breadcrumb=8,284.

[46] 2000 Republican National Party Platform.

re-establish the "sound principle" of judicial review. Even appointment, a tactic that harnesses judicial power rather than undermines judicial legitimacy, is not framed as serving partisan policy ends but as a means to maintain a de-politicized judiciary.

To sum up, manipulations of judicial power may appear increasingly *shallow* over time relative to the rhetoric behind them; yet, this shallowness does not necessarily indicate normative deference to judicial authority. Empirical evidence of acceptance of judicial supremacy is thin, but, as we shall see, there is evidence that politicians strive to harness the judiciary and become increasingly frustrated when the judiciary refuses to operate as an ideological tool of their parties and/or ideological movements. Politicians cloak themselves in the mantle of democratic values, of countering an unelected cadre of culturally elitist judges or, in Sandra Day O'Connor's terms, "secular godless humanists." All the while they maintain judicial authority to achieve preferred policies.[47] Rhetoric aimed at undermining judicial legitimacy followed by actions that actually *harness* judicial power allow politicians to have it both ways, to stand four square for democracy and to use the courts' insulation from democratic control for their own ends. By not structurally weakening the judiciary, politicians can (1) protect a mechanism to promote their own longer term policy interests and ideological agendas; (2) maintain the basis for mobilizing rhetoric useful in their short-term electoral ambitions; and (3) avoid undermining their own basis of support (especially if court-curbing legislation exacerbates the cleavages among intra-party factions). And because of the judiciary's low public salience, elites may find this hypocrisy comes at low cost. This is all quite cold calculation for politicians who have come to understand that judicial power can be harnessed to a variety of different constitutional meanings. It remains to uncover how the legitimacy of these multiple renderings developed.

II. Opposition Legitimacy and Loyalty as Manifestations of Political Idiom

The assumption that alternative constitutional meanings are credible does not hold across American political history. To investigate how it developed over time, this book focuses on how shifts in ideational context have re-oriented the preferences and rationales of politicians' relations with the judiciary. As a rule, politicians do not seek to act in ways considered illegitimate. When their interests lead them in that direction, the entrepreneurs among them will strive to re-shape the existing ideational framework via extensive public rhetorical argument to bring norms into alignment with their interests. Often

---

[47] While politicians are often understood as likely to discount longer term aims given uncertainty about the future and lack of credible commitment from peers to maintain institutional rules, Sarah Binder posits "still, such long-term forecasting might in fact be quite prevalent amongst senators when thinking about institutions of advice and consent" such as the judiciary. Binder, "Where Do Institutions Come From? Exploring the Origins of the Senate Blue Slip," *Studies in American Political Development* 21 (Spring 2007), 4.

this process entails framing a crisis as having occurred and as demanding new approaches. These new approaches often appropriate accepted concepts and subtly transform their meaning. Importantly, the entrepreneurial leader does not promote new ideas unconstrained; these ideas must resonate with what people already hold to be legitimate. Sociologist Aldon Morris highlighted this process when civil rights leaders, like Martin Luther King, Jr., utilized Christian theology to support their activism:

> For the first half of the twentieth century most black churches taught that the meek would inherit the earth ... and that a good Christian was more concerned with perfecting his or her spiritual life rather than with material wellbeing.... King carried a new message [that "a religion true to its nature must also be concerned about man's social conditions"].... A refocusing of the cultural content of the church was required to operationalize King's view of religion. This "militant" view of religion has always existed in the black church.... However, refocusing black religion was made easier for King and his counterparts because they were activating a religious view latent in the church rather than creating it in a vacuum.[48]

Leaders in the Southern Christian Leadership Conference did not create new Christian tenets out of whole cloth but shifted emphasis to focus on a particular aspect of a commonly understood tradition. This process of ideational transformation is not unique to the civil rights movement or to Christian theology. The example demonstrates generalizable processes of entrepreneurial actors framing ideas to legitimate their political action as well as illustrating the constraints under which they act.[49]

In the chapters that follow I examine how politicians manipulated ideas in ways that would gradually re-shape relations between the elected branches and the judiciary, particularly how manipulations of judicial power would be made. Two broad ideational transformations are central to the changing perception of judicial power: first is the shift from understanding opposition outside the bounds of parliamentary debate as wholly illegitimate to acknowledging opposition as unavoidable and finally to accepting it as non-threatening; and, second is the transition from being hostile to all political parties to accepting a party as an organizational form and finally to promoting multiple

---

[48] Aldon Morris, *Origins of the Civil Rights Movement* (New York: Free Press, 1984), 96–8. The passage defining the "new message" is taken from Martin Luther King, Jr., *Stride toward Freedom* (New York: Harper & Row, 1958), 36, quoted in Morris, 97.

[49] For example, Gordon Wood illustrates how Federalists re-conceptualized sovereignty to bolster their idea of a government further removed from the people than the Articles of Confederation. See Wood, *The Creation of the American Republic, 1776–1787* (Chapel Hill: University of North Carolina Press, 1998), 519–64. For additional studies in the transformation of meaning in similar ways, see J. David Greenstone, "Political Culture and American Political Development: Liberty, Union, and Liberal Bipolarity," *Studies in American Political Development* 1 (Spring 1986), 1–49, and Stephen Skowronek, "The Reassociation of Ideas and Purposes: Racism, Liberalism, and the American Tradition," *American Political Science Review* 100 (August 2006), 385–401.

party competition. Both of these changes are manifestations of a broader, gradual, and halting shift in the idiom of political contestation from civic republicanism to liberal pluralism.[50]

To some extent, elements of civic republican and the liberal pluralist traditions have been evident in American political culture since the Founding. However, over time, the balance between these traditions shifted. Historians have long recognized that the Civil War and Reconstruction marked a turning point in the balance between these idioms: "republicanism had survived vigorously through Andrew Jackson's presidency, only to fade into a 'translucent' half-life" and the Civil War "consummated the consensus shift from republicanism to pluralism."[51] Scholars have also noted that the Civil War represented a turning point in American constitutional culture, that is, that after the war, argument about the meaning of the Constitution needed to occur through persuasion rather than violent coercion.[52] This temporal congruence suggests underlying connections between political and constitutional culture worthy of exploration. And if historians and legal scholars have taken note of this transition and cultural shift, it remains to draw out their implications for changing patterns in inter-branch relations.

Civic republicanism has been dubbed the "ideological substratum" and "the foundation of the partisan ideologies" prior to the Civil War.[53] It "constituted the antebellum period's deeper political conscience" such that "the common frame of reference itself stoked the fires of controversy."[54] It differs from pluralism to the extent that it values public welfare above private interest, holds that a discernible singular public good exists, strives for consensualism, shuns disunity, and views the state as not promoting legislation favorable to a particular class. By contrast, in its broadest brushstrokes, pluralism defines politics as competitive and interest-based rather than consensual. It emphasizes individual freedoms and tends to reject a singular notion of public good; it attends more to process than substantive ends.[55]

---

[50] Following David Ericson, I suggest that antebellum civic republicanism was supplanted by modern liberal pluralism, both of which drew upon a liberal foundation emphasizing liberty rather than substantive justice. See Ericson, 1993, 1–9. However, importantly, I make a crucial distinction between the pluralism that developed in the wake of Reconstruction and which Lincoln endorsed in his first inaugural and the more modern "interest-based" pluralism defining much mid-twentieth century political science.

[51] Daniel Rodgers, "Republicanism: The Career of a Concept," *Journal of American History* 79 (June 1992), 30. Micahel Pfau, *The Political Style of Conspiracy* (East Lansing: Michigan State University Press, 2005), 147. Ericson, 9.

[52] Seigel, 2006, 30.

[53] Pfau, 160. See also Pocock, 506–52.

[54] Pfau, 160; Ericson, 4.

[55] On a definable good as a cornerstone of republicanism, see Ericson, 11. On republican and pluralist strands of American political culture and definitions of each idiom, see Smith, 1993; Michael Sandel, *Democracy's Discontent: America in Search of a Public Philosophy* (Cambridge: Belknap Press of Harvard University, 1998), 5–6, and Ian Shapiro, *The State of Democratic Theory* (Princeton: Princeton University Press, 2003), 21–33.

Early American republicanism rejected the abstract individual constrained by civil society; instead, the individual was understood as constituted by society. Law and regulation did not limit but enabled liberty. Rights were derived from government rather than existing prior to it.[56] As legal theorist, John Hart Ely, points out, the liberal first line of the Declaration of Independence that certain truths are "self-evident," which suggests fundamental values exist prior to law and governance, came with a republican tag line. The second clause of that sentence – "that to secure these rights governments are constituted among men" – indicates a belief that government secures rights to the degree that they are recognized and maintained.[57] Hannah Arendt distinguishes the American Revolution from its French counterpart on similar grounds. For her, the American Revolution "proclaims no more than the necessity of civilized government for all mankind" whereas the French Revolution makes the critical move associated with a priori rights: "the French revolution ... proclaims the existence of rights independent of and outside the body public."[58]

Because government constituted rights, politicians grounded in the civic republican tradition were preoccupied with its possible collapse. And because republican thinkers conceptualized a singular notion of the good as identifiable and achievable, alternative views were not only not credible but also potentially harmful to civic stability and signals of collapse. Hence, this idiom "stressed the existence of internal conspiracies designed to overthrow republican government and eradicate liberty."[59] Inherent in republican theories were assumptions about the danger of opposition, the susceptibility of governance to internal conspiracy, and the rejection of party as the form of conspiracy, giving rhetoric a seemingly "paranoid style."[60] Richard Hofstadter contends that this style is engrained and recurrent in American political history. Other historians see it as limited to the Framers' allegedly unique preoccupation with consensual and elite-led governance.[61] I find this style to be a manifestation of republican precepts that gradually lost currency over the course of the antebellum era, and while re-emerging in particular periods, most notably the Progressive era, never regained their dominance.

In short, so long as civic republicanism was the dominant idiom of national politics, only one conception of constitutional government could be considered

---

[56] William Novak, *The People's Welfare* (Chapel Hill: University of North Carolina Press, 1996), 45.

[57] John Hart Ely, *Democracy and Distrust: A Theory of Judicial Review* (Cambridge: Harvard University Press, 1980), 88–101.

[58] Hannah Arendt, *On Revolution* (New York: Penguin Classics, 1990), 149.

[59] William Giennapp, *The Origins of the Republican Party, 1852–1856* (New York: Oxford University Press, 1987), 4.

[60] On the "paranoid style," see Richard Hofstadter, *The Paranoid Style of American Politics and Other Essays* (Cambridge, MA: Harvard University Press, 1964).

[61] Bailyn and Wood, by contrast, view the conspiratorial tone as a manifestation of early American republicanism. Michael Pfau illustrates civic republican tropes – especially themes of internal conspiracy – coursing through Republican "slave power" rhetoric of the 1850s.

legitimate. So long as civic republicanism was the dominant idiom of American political culture, the contemporaneous constitutional culture would condone violence as a legitimate means of argument about constitutional meaning precisely because, given republican assumptions about permanent disagreement necessarily leading to civil strife, the stakes were so high. Thus, early American constitutional disputes are characterized by recurrent episodes of mob violence.[62] The opposition's position could not be permitted. Carrying this idea into the realm of judicial behavior, if judges offered a vision that challenged the commitments underlying the presidential administration and/or the ruling party in Congress, they would be seen to represent not simply an alternative vision of the good but a fundamental threat to civic stability. In other words, when opposition – defined as a minority coalition that does not hold power – is not granted legitimacy so that it is considered anti-constitutional, a civic republican concern for stable governance demands that it be kept weak if not eradicated altogether.[63]

Accordingly, when republican precepts hold sway, ironically politicians will engage freely in constitutional interpretation of their own, but they will not grant the legitimacy of any interpretation except their own. The judiciary has no special authority to say what the Constitution means and that the president, Congress, and even the people themselves have the responsibility to defend the Constitution even when that means acting against the judiciary. In other words, such multiple interpretive locality is demanded by the perception that judges might threaten the Constitution and civic stability.

Furthermore, within the parameters of the republican idiom, politicians will pursue tactics that broadly undermine the judiciary's legitimacy, such as congressional overrides of constitutional rulings or imposing supermajority decision-rules on the bench, or even secession. This is because an opposition-controlled judiciary would, by definition, threaten national survival and must be weakened.

By contrast, to the extent that liberal pluralism is the dominant political cultural idiom, a range of conceptions of constitutional meaning is credible. In this context, party actors recognize the legitimacy of their competitors to rule and to implement their constitutional vision. Politicians may expect that judges serve as instruments for the implementation of these particular visions, and political parties will therefore seek to harness judicial authority for their own ends. Put differently, once opposition is viewed as natural, unavoidable, *and* loyal so that its rule does not threaten civic instability, then each political party can lay claim to the constitutionality of its policy aims. While interpretive disputes need no longer devolve into high-stakes violent action, stable

---

[62] Kramer, 2004, 24–39.

[63] This perspective follows from the republican fear of factionalism, aim for governing consensus – what one scholar has called "the authoritative ideology of the new American Republic" – and consequent sense of conspiratorial threat to government stability. See Howard Gillman, *The Constitution Besieged: The Rise and Demise of Lochner Era Police Powers Jurisprudence* (Durham, NC: Duke University Press, 1993), 62.

governance necessarily requires some way to arbitrate equally viable constitutional claims. Thus, not only does this context create the need to justify some definitive interpreter, but also politicians, constrained to support judicial neutrality but intent on exploiting judicial power for partisan policy aims, will adjust their tactics to harness that interpreting agent.[64]

Four expectations about political relations with the judiciary follow when pluralism is the dominant ideational framework. First, politicians' rhetoric emphasizing democratic illegitimacy and countermajoritarianism may continue, but it will be paired with difficult-to-pass constitutional amendments or similar vehicles that maximize position-taking. Alternatively, politicians will promote statutory measures to curb judicial power, such as jurisdiction-stripping, but this legislation will actually achieve little beyond what judges' decisions have already stipulated. As such, these actions are primarily symbolic.

Second, attacks on judicial legitimacy may not subside, but politicians will limit the judiciary's power by narrowly manipulating jurisdiction either by stripping it or transferring it between state and federal courts.

Third, politicians will intentionally draft statutes in ambiguous language to invite judicial interpretation. Doing so avoids accountability, allows credit-claiming on passing legislation, and maintains the judiciary as an "undemocratic foil" if judges overrule the statute.

Last, since politicians want to maintain their respective institutions' power, that is, engage in institutional preservation, court-curbing legislation may fail if pursuing it threatens these power bases, meaning the political party or politicians' respective branch. As such, politicians' retreat from this legislation should not be interpreted as deference to judicial authority.[65] It may

[64] The logic draws on Adam Przeworski's theory of why opposition does not revolt in democracy. See Przeworski, *Democracy and the Market* (New York: Cambridge University Press, 1991). In this application, the cost to politicians of weakening the Supreme Court is too high. The model depends on longer time horizons, which may be applicable to institutions illustrating dynamics of advise and consent. William Lasser, for example, assumed longer time horizons when he argued that presidents like Lincoln and FDR "remained essentially friendly to the idea of a strong federal judiciary" because they expected "the Court [to] become their ally in the long run." As such, "they set out not to destroy the Court but only to capture it." While this book aims to prove that Lasser's assessment of Lincoln and FDR is correct, it also seeks to unearth the assumption on which Lasser's articulation of harnessing relies, namely, that judicial moves are not viewed as destabilizing to the Constitution or the republic's longevity. Tactics associated with harnessing only follow when the stakes are lowered by reason of a loyal opposition. Lasser, *The Limits of Judicial Power: The Supreme Court in American Politics* (Chapel Hill: University of North Carolina Press, 1988), 258.

[65] This expectation assumes (1) parties are legitimate, otherwise why protect their power; (2) that they shift between minority and majority status; and (3) that intra-party factionalism can occur, otherwise no concern with court-curbing's potential to destabilize party unity would follow. Such factionalism is evident from the 1880s through the 1970s as Democrats split among northern liberals and southern racial conservatives and as Republicans split between western Progressives and eastern economic conservatives. See James MacGregor Burns, *The Deadlock of Democracy: Four-Party Politics in America* (Englewood Cliffs, NJ: Prentice-Hall, 1963), 93–203. For analysis of roll call votes that captured twentieth-century fluctuation of congressional party polarization, see Keith Poole, "The Decline and

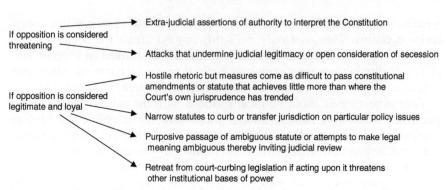

FIGURE 2.1. Propositions Linking Opposition and Relations with the Judiciary.

instead reflect interests in maintaining those particular institutional bases of power and have little to do with deference to or support for judges or courts.[66] Figure 2.1 summarizes these expectations.

In short, acceptance of opposition as legitimate and loyal could develop only after assumptions inherent in civic republicanism were abandoned and party's purposes re-cast. As parties and opposition were considered legitimate, politicians' perceptions of the judiciary's value and their justifications of manipulations of judicial power could likewise change.[67]

> Rise of Party Polarization in Congress during the 20th Century," working paper accessible at www.voteview.com. Such factionalism does not mean that collective action problems cannot be overcome. Intra-party factions may foster cross-party majority coalitions; however, party leaders may engage in parliamentary techniques to avoid court-curbing measures, not out of any deference toward judicial authority but motivated by the desire to avoid party division. See examples in Chapter 7.
>
> [66] A variant of this expectation of institutional preservation is that politicians secure judicial power even as they attack it because of a longer term perspective that they may utilize it downstream. Consider advice once offered to John Quincy Adams: "Always love your friend as though one day he might become your enemy; and always hate your enemy as though one day he might become your friend." Walter Murphy, *Congress and the Court* (Chicago: University of Chicago Press, 1962), 261. A difficulty with testing this idea is that the behavior is functionally indistinguishable from expectations of judicial supremacy. Also, it is unlikely – though not impossible – that politicians would announce this strategy as doing so undermines judicial neutrality. FDR did so during his March 1937 fireside chat discussing his judicial reform proposal, which took a different frame than his speech to Congress on the same topic a month earlier. See Chapter 6.
>
> [67] It should generally be expected that the narrow scope, symbolic politics, purposive ambiguity, or institutional preservation hypotheses are less evident prior to the Civil War. Essentially, the antebellum cases constitute a least-likely case of the post-Reconstruction expectations. Yet a clear division between these two periods cannot be fully expected since ideational change is gradual. Therefore, the transition is likely to occur over the course of the case studies, rather than a clear breakpoint that divides them. In particular, the case study on the Lincolnian Republicans would likely illustrate this transition as Republican leaders – Lincoln and Seward, foremost among them – represented different positions on the opposition's loyalty and legitimacy. See generally John Gerring, *Case Study Research: Principles and Practices* (New York: Cambridge University Press, 2006).

It should be emphasized that I do not claim that the dominant political idiom is completely hegemonic or static. Nor does one ever *entirely* replace the other over time. Elements of civic republicanism and liberal pluralism underlay the political ideas motivating the Founding. And the meaning of each changed over time. For example, republicanism adapted from its eighteenth-century English origins to Jacksonian democracy, which emphasized majority rule and universal white manhood suffrage. Consequently, its tenet of vigilance against conspiracy relied less on English virtue and more on the American vote.[68] And if the process of the legitimization of opposition is a reflection of the slow degradation of republicanism and the rise of pluralism, then the entire span of the antebellum era should reveal movement from the first set of expectations toward the second set of expectations, not simply a dramatic or immediate shift from the first set to the second. Instead, a gradual shift in emphasis toward the four propositions that assume opposition legitimacy and loyalty should be evident. This pattern is confirmed in the data sweeps detailed in Chapter 1. Figure 1.3 showed that legislation seeking to harness judicial power outpaced legislation that undermined judicial legitimacy from the 1870s onward.

More generally, the interactive pattern of ideational change is simply this: when confronting the exigencies of their times and particularly when confronting perceived constitutional crises, political entrepreneurs manipulated the precepts of republicanism and, through a deliberate process of adaptation, elimination, and addition, gradually developed the cluster of ideas that we have come to identify as liberal pluralism. Thus, instead of viewing these idioms as competing and discrete multiple traditions, we can understand the one as developing from the other.[69] For example, while some historians have argued that James Madison was republican and others see his *Federalist 10* as the foundation of pluralism, we might be on firmer footing to suggest that Madison was neither republican nor a precocious pluralist, as if those idioms were fully formed, opposed, and available for articulation. Rather, Madison, and other thinkers discussed in this book, including Van Buren and Lincoln, "remained republican as they became liberal."[70] As such, one of the broader aims of this book is to trace the markers of this transformation until it is apparent that actors in all three federal branches tended to endorse assumptions associated with pluralism. As will be shown, this transformation did not occur all of a piece, and indeed, the Supreme Court was the last mover.

[68] Pfau, 43, 160–1.
[69] This model of ideational change is best captured by Andreas Kalyvas and Ira Katznelson's examination of how political thinkers adapted the core tenets of classic republicanism to the exigencies of their political experience and how through that process of adaptation in which new tenets (such as popular sovereignty and individual right) were grafted onto existing ones (such as public good) and others (such as civic religion) were abandoned, liberalism developed. See Kalyvas and Katznelson, *Liberal Beginnings: Making a Republic for the Moderns* (New York: Cambridge University Press, 2008).
[70] Ibid., 90.

Furthermore, by conceptualizing these idioms as developing gradually over time, we can recognize the gradual endorsement of the component parts of each idiom. Put differently, what we now understand as contemporary pluralism is different from earlier versions of pluralism that Lincoln advocated. Contemporary definitions of pluralism capture the notion, popularized by Dahl and other political scientists of the mid-twentieth century, that politics is a competitive group-based system in which individuals operate through various institutionalized associations, including but not limited to political parties, to achieve various ends.[71] Later variants of this school of thought began to recognize systemic power differentials among the various competing groups, but the core principle of pluralism is that popular political participation occurs through a range of institutional outlets, including interest groups, political parties, social movements, labor unions, religious organizations, and non-profit legal entities.[72] By contrast, Lincoln's pluralism – expanded upon in Chapter 5 – recognized only political parties as vehicles of constitutional interpretation and as the only legitimate vehicles of popular interests; and it did not recognize that systemic power differentials might exist among these competing interests.[73] This limited pluralistic understanding of parties dictated a particular stance toward the judiciary, which only makes sense within the confines of a particular stage of ideational development about the legitimacy of opposition and the parameters of constitutional culture.

Once pluralism is conceptualized as incorporating elements of and evolving from republicanism – rather than seen as wholly distinct from republicanism – then the republican specter of government instability and conspiracy could very much remain a potent if sometimes latent theme even when the pluralist idiom is dominant. Thus, rhetoric that judicial action threatened national survival, which is evident in the 1930s in the context of an economic crisis, in the 1950s in the context of an alleged communist threat, in the 1990s in the

[71] Dahl defines pluralism as "organizational pluralism," meaning "the existence of a plurality of relatively autonomous (independent) organizations (subsystems) within the domain of a state." (5) Political parties are only one type of organization that holds power in a pluralist democracy: "Of organizations, partial societies, associations, groups, and subsystems there is no end, and in various times and places diverse associations have claimed a measure of independence from the state and other associations." (27) See Robert Dahl, *Dilemmas of Pluralist Democracy: Autonomy vs. Control* (New Haven: Yale University Press, 1982). See also Theodore Lowi's summary of pluralism in his *The End of Liberalism*, 2nd ed. (New York: W.W. Norton, 1979), 31–41.

[72] For critiques of pluralism, see E. E. Schatttschneider, *The Semi-Sovereign People* (New York: Holt, Rinehart and Winston, 1960); Peter Bachrach and Morton Baratz, *Power and Poverty: Theory and Practice* (New York: Oxford University Press, 1970); Gaventa, 1980, 5–20.

[73] If Lincoln had recognized power differentials, he potentially would have lent legitimacy to the secessionist claim that slave states had become an insular congressional minority due to national demographic shifts. See Mark Graber, *Dred Scott and the Problem of Constitutional Evil* (New York: Cambridge University Press, 2006), 126–7, and Eric Foner, *Free Soil, Free Labor, Free Men: The Ideology of the Republican Party before the Civil War* (New York: Oxford University Press, 1970), 234–7.

context of alleged moral decline, and more recently in the context of terrorist threats and the passage of health insurance reform, is far less surprising.[74]

But while the recurrence of rhetoric suggesting a position of illegitimate opposition must be noted, we should attend to *who* articulates these ideas and who the audience is. Normative acceptance of the opposition's right to rule and dissenting views of the Constitution's meaning may be more apparent among political elites than among the voting public. Former Republican presidential nominee John McCain's explicit statements that his opponent, Barack Obama, was a good man from whom Republicans had nothing to fear and Obama's statements that McCain was similarly honorable, are telling in this regard. They indicate that a norm of loyal opposition held among political elites even as it seemed increasingly strained in the later months of the 2008 elections season.[75] McCain reiterated this sentiment in the days following the shootings at a constituent event in Tuscon, Arizona, hosted by Congresswoman Gabrielle Giffords. Amid media commentary that the seemingly heightened level of polarized rhetoric contributed to a context in which civil debate was increasingly difficult to foster, McCain maintained that opposing viewpoints did not threaten national stability:

> We should respect the sincerity of the convictions that enliven our debates but also the mutual purpose that we and all preceding generations of Americans serve: a better country; stronger, more prosperous and just than the one we inherited. We Americans have different opinions on how best to serve that noble purpose. We need not pretend otherwise or be timid in our advocacy of the means we believe will achieve it. But we should be mindful as we argue about our differences that so much more unites than divides us.... I disagree with many of the president's policies, but I believe he is a patriot sincerely intent on using his time in office to advance our country's cause. I reject accusations that his policies and beliefs make him unworthy to lead America or are opposed to its founding ideals. And I reject accusations that Americans who vigorously oppose his policies are less intelligent, compassionate or just than those who support them.[76]

While presidents and other politicians may tend to recognize a general norm of loyal and legitimate political opposition, the broader public may not subscribe as strongly or as regularly to this norm. And politicians may strategically rely on its absence to mobilize a base and gain election. Recognizing this possibility does not conflict with the larger historical pattern, namely, that

[74] On the 1930s, see FDR's March 1937 fireside chat and Senate speeches and constituent letters discussed in Chapter 6. On anti-communism fears and judicial power, see Chapter 7. On the judiciary as weakening congressional responses to the War on Terror, see John McCain's reaction to the 2008 *Boumediene* decision (discussed in Chapter 8). Linda Greenhouse, "Over Guantanamo, Justices Come under Election-Year Spotlight," *New York Times*, 14 June 2008, A10.

[75] Elisabeth Bumiller, "McCain Draws Line on Attacks as Crowds Cry 'Fight Back,'" *New York Times*, 10 October 2008, A12.

[76] John McCain, "After the Shootings, Obama Reminds the Nation of the Golden Rule," *Washington Post*, 16 January 2011, B7.

attacks undermining judicial legitimacy do and will probably always persist, but clearly their emphasis since Reconstruction is on tactics that are more targeted and seek to harness periodically oppositional judicial authority toward particular political ends.

III. Multiple Constitutional Visions and the Rise of a Majoritarian Court

My aim in this book is not merely to move the time line as to when the legitimacy and loyalty of opposition came to be understood as a precept of functional American democratic politics. Nor is it just to trace the concomitant rise of judicial harnessing by the elected branches. The displacement of republicanism by pluralist ideas and norms, the corresponding claims of multiple equally-valid constitutional interpretations and interpretive methods, and the stabilization of constitutional culture in which violent coercion was replaced by trust and persuasion, influenced elected politicians' relations with the judiciary as well as the judiciary's own understanding of its particular governmental purpose. The shift in ideational context restructured the repertoire of strategic actions available for politicians to pursue just as it unmoored the pre-existing rationale justifying judicial authority. In outlining a developmental theory of manipulations of judicial authority, I have addressed how politicians adjusted to and promoted liberal pluralism. It remains to be understood how the judiciary re-anchored itself in this shifting context.

While I argue in later chapters that the modern competitive political party took recognizable shape during Reconstruction and that pluralism henceforth increasingly operated as an organizing principle of American politics, important changes continued to take place, especially with regard to the espousal of multiple credible constitutional visions. Throughout the late nineteenth and early twentieth centuries, new organizational forms competed with political parties, each espousing their own claims of what policies followed from their respective views on constitutional meaning. Additionally, legal scholars and judges increasingly abandoned the interpretive methodology of "textual originalism," which dominated much of the first century of American constitutional interpretation, creating a range of new methods and consequent interpretive possibilities.

This institutional and interpretive pluralism continued to develop over the course of the twentieth century. Governance and participation became increasingly diffuse and professionalized as policy-making and constitutional claims fell within the domain of new bureaucratic agencies, interest groups, social movements, think tanks, and charitable foundations. In short, actors who might have stakes in controlling constitutional meaning had proliferating institutional bases from which to speak, and political parties, which, as we shall see, had been understood throughout the nineteenth century as articulators of constitutional vision, were, if not wholly displaced, reshaped to include previously unincorporated interests.[77] In recognizing this context

[77] Teles, 7–8.

of institutional thickening and ideational transformation, the Court was the last mover. When it did recognize this new pluralist world, it needed to justify its own interpretive authority against these multiplying interests.[78] For, in an environment in which multiple constitutional interpretations were plausible and each garnered entrenched and mobilized interests, the judiciary's critical move – which was bolstered by deliberate actions taken in legal scholarship and the legal profession more generally – was to assert that its rendering of constitutional meaning, regardless of whether it corresponded to that of the party which held Congress, the presidency or both (that is, its independent interpretation), was final.

This possibility of a fully independent judicial interpretation developed only during the late nineteenth and early twentieth centuries as judges and legal scholars re-imagined the judiciary's purpose. It is evident in the reforms that justices on the Supreme Court undertook in the 1890s and 1920s to manage the Court's own docket. It is evident in Progressive legal scholars' construction of judicial supremacy as a concept to justify why judicial constitutional interpretation should carry more weight than plausible alternatives. And it is evident in how justices began to re-frame the Court's orientation toward democratic politics in their rulings. In particular, the justices slowly discarded republican ideas of the Court as a neutral arbiter among competing classes, interests, or factions.[79] Instead, they re-cast the Court as an actor engaged in pluralist politics, one that would side with groups shut out from participating in democratic contestation, that is, insular and discrete minorities, and simultaneously declare the supremacy of its ruling. This re-imagining of the Court's self-presentation is reflected in its seemingly contradictory economic substantive due process jurisprudence of the late nineteenth and early twentieth centuries, is epitomized by its 1938 ruling in *United States v. Carolene Products*, and has continued with the development of the doctrine of suspect classes, each receiving a particular threshold of scrutiny.[80] In short, by proclaiming that the Court would function to oversee political processes as well as periodically intervene in those processes to assure that all had equal access, the Justices redefined its purpose to fit within liberal pluralist premises.

---

[78] The concept of "institutional thickening" is used in new institutionalist scholarship to describe the development of new institutions, agencies, and litigants with entrenched interests, which tends to make policy innovation more difficult over time. See Clemens and Cook, 457. Here, I use the concept not only to connote that process but to help justify the imperative for the Court to assert its interpretive authority against these multiplying interests, which each had a stake in whichever interpretation was rendered.

[79] See Chapter 6. On procedural reforms, see Felix Frankfurter and James Landis, *The Business of the Supreme Court: A Study in the Federal Judicial System* (New Brunswick: Transaction, 2007), 187–298. On Progressive constructions of *Marbury*, see Davison Douglas, "The Rhetorical Uses of *Marbury v. Madison*: The Emergence of a Great Case," *Wake Forest Law Review* 38 (2003), 375–413.

[80] See the fourth footnote in *United States v. Carolene Products Co.*, 304 U.S. 144 (1938). While *Carolene's* famous footnote set the definition of insular and discrete minorities, earlier jurisprudence of the late nineteenth and early twentieth centuries set women apart as a special class necessitating government protections. See Chapter 6.

Thus, while the Supreme Court is often understood as capitulating to the elected branches after some period of pressure in the mid-1930s, it is a mistake to understand the Court's moves as merely caving to the threat of Court-packing.[81] Rather, the Court was an active agent in its own transformation. Its jurisprudential move was the completion of a long period of alignment by all three branches to the assumptions of pluralism, an alignment that still constitutes the constitutional politics of our era. Put differently, while the Court's ruling in *West Coast Hotel v. Parish* (1937) was no doubt an important step toward judicial validation of New Deal policies, what is at stake for my argument is not whether the Court made an abrupt turn in response to political pressure, but in identifying which is the more crucial turning point: the Court's assent to New Deal policies signaled in *West Coast Hotel* or its conceptualization of a fundamentally new role for itself that accepted the underlying precepts of pluralism signaled in *Carolene Products*. The former had substantial policy implications for the development of the American welfare state, but the latter had substantial implications for the institutional role played by the Court and thus for inter-branch relations and its own institutional capacity, legitimacy, and authority.

Just as we cannot fully grasp politicians' behavior through the lens of a norm of deference to judicial authority, we miss important aspects of judicial development by viewing judicial politics simply as a game of inter-branch brinksmanship. Through *Carolene*, the Court became a political branch in its own right, entrenched in the assumptions and values of liberal pluralism. That the Court maintains itself in this guise is not a reflection of deference to judicial supremacy by other actors. It is an indicator of the extent to which the old conceit that there is but one proper understanding of the Constitution has been displaced. In short, through *Carolene*, the Court re-calibrated itself to the increasingly dominant ideational context emergent since Reconstruction.

As already suggested, the one place where that old conceit endures is in the public's presumption of judicial neutrality. The persistence of that standard in the public mind makes judicial politics today especially volatile and the search for a standard of judicial legitimacy so enduring. As the Supreme Court has relinquished the civic republican notion of state neutrality and engaged the pluralist implication that the Court can be a proactive agent in its own right, it has, in effect, opened itself to intensified political action on two fronts. On one side, it has laid bare incentives for prospective litigants to enlist it as an ally. Once the Court made clear that it would actively agitate for its own vision, keeping judicial power in harness became all the more imperative

---

[81] While the Court supported minimum wage legislation in *West Coast Hotel Co. v. Parish* (1937), that is, the so-called "switch-in-time" that saved nine, I argue a more important shift was the Court's re-conceptualization of its own purpose within democracy, which came in *Carolene*. My emphasis on *Carolene* follows from recent revisionism suggesting that the *West Coast Hotel* decision was not a dramatic switch but a more gradual process. See Barry Cushman, "Rethinking the New Deal Court," *Virginia Law Review* 80 (1994), 201–61. For more general coverage of this debate see "AHR Forum: The Debate over the Constitutional Revolution of 1937," *American Historical Review* 110 (October 2005), 1046–1115.

for other actors. Its capture by various interest groups (via appointment, for example) became an overriding goal. On the other side, in its willingness to abandon the presumption of neutrality for more effective political advocacy, the Court remains subject to intense and sustained rhetorical assaults from elected officials. The cause of re-establishing judicial neutrality and the institutional legitimacy of judicial authority lives on not only in public campaigns against "activist judges" – campaigns that exploit the widening gap between the reality of pluralist politics and the lingering allure of republican precepts – but also in the Court's own jurisprudence.

IV. Conclusion

This book's primary claim is that politicians' manipulations of the judiciary depend on an ideational context that is not constant across American history. Shifts between tactics that undermine judicial legitimacy and those that exploit that legitimacy in order to harness judicial power correlate with ideational developments related to the legitimacy of opposition. Hostilities toward courts and hostilities toward parties reflect a set of common underlying assumptions about the legitimacy or illegitimacy of opposition and not simply the structural problem presented by unelected judges. By viewing the development of manipulations of judicial power in this way, we can integrate these actions into the broader idiomatic and constitutional cultural shifts long recognized by political and legal historians. For the illegitimacy of opposition is one of the core characteristics of the predominant political idiom of the antebellum era: civic republicanism. Thus, as republican fears of conspiratorial threats to the Constitution and national stability gave way to pluralist acceptance of the opposition's right to rule, the legitimacy of multiple constitutional visions followed, and hostilities toward the judiciary become more targeted. To state this idea in more general terms, the rationality of a tactic toward judicial power is contingent upon or situated within an ideational context changing over time. As that context changes, so does the meaning and expression of rationality itself.

Since the public has demonstrated ambivalence toward judicial power, politicians have a strategic electoral interest in de-legitimizing the judiciary by harping on its unelected status. They also have a policy-driven interest to maintain or at least not damage that power in the longer term. And since courts lack long-term public salience, politicians have room to maneuver between their rhetoric and its implications. Therefore, the scope of anti-judicial hostilities during the modern interest-based pluralist era is a rhetorical politics exploited for electoral gain. If this claim is accurate, then political behavior after Reconstruction should fit expectations that court-curbing legislation be targeted, narrow, and/or purposively ambiguous, and tend to come as vehicles showcasing their symbolic nature, for example, constitutional amendment. Their failure to secure passage should be explainable by referencing politicians' attempts to maintain institutional bases of power as opposed to positing a norm of deference to judicial authority.

To be sure, pluralism's ascension with its new assumptions regarding the legitimacy and loyalty of opposition was not a change to which politicians merely reacted. Political entrepreneurs themselves redefined ideas that would subsequently alter relations between the elected branches and the judiciary. By seizing upon crises as opportunities to alter the meaning of existing political practices and concepts, often to antithetical effect, they legitimized their confrontations with or utilizations of judicial power. There were limits to the legitimate actions they could take; nevertheless, entrepreneurial leaders pushed the boundaries of the politics in which they were situated, working within clear constraints to create new ideational circumstances for those who would follow.[82] Subsequent chapters investigate how politicians' behavior toward the judiciary reflects this shift in rational preferences and how its range is bounded by the dominant political idiom, but also how politicians' actions drive that idiomatic shift itself.

In summary, once we consider the right of the opposition to rule and its consequent implication that multiple constitutional interpretations be considered plausible, conflicts with the judiciary no longer need to be seen as a structural matter that recurs ad infinitum. They are phenomena for which changing tactics over time should be expected since the idea of multiple credible and valid constitutional interpretations did not exist throughout American history. My developmental theory predicts that efforts to control judicial power will continue, not necessarily decline, over time, but, more important, that their *mode* will change; actions like jurisdiction-stripping, filibustering judicial nominations, and advocating appointment of those who hold to particular interpretive philosophies will become more prominent as they do not undermine the legitimacy of the judiciary per se but have the potential to achieve policy aims through judicial rulings.

In its broadest implication, the theory suggests that when assessing the politicization of courts, we should not restrict our analysis to the alleged partisan leanings of judges as they might be measured on a uni-dimensional left to right scale and to those of the presidents who appointed them. Nor should we be solely preoccupied with an allegedly measurable level of "activism" demonstrated by a particular Court. Rather, we must examine how politicians make use of the Court in their rhetoric and their strategizing, and we must explain how and why these actions have changed over time. Ultimately, if rhetorical patterns and tactical legislation suggestive of anti-judicial hostility persist, then scholarly recommendations for judicial restraint – as has been the norm in constitutional studies – to avoid offending democratic sensibilities may be for naught. Even the most restrained Court will find itself unable to avoid being used as a political tool and as a mobilizing issue.

---

[82] As Karl Marx recognized, "Men make their own history, but they do not make it just as they please; they do not make it under circumstances chosen by themselves, but under circumstances directly found, given, and transmitted from the past." Marx, "The Eighteenth Brumaire of Louis Bonaparte," (1852) in *The Marx-Engels Reader*, Robert C. Tucker, ed. (New York: W.W. Norton, 1978), 595.

PART II

HOSTILITY TO JUDICIAL AUTHORITY AND THE POLITICAL IDIOM OF CIVIC REPUBLICANISM

3

In Support of Unified Governance

Undermining the Court in an Anti-Party Age

The Jeffersonian assault on judicial authority was grounded in civic republican ideas that did not grant the validity of dissenting views on constitutional meaning and thus did not acknowledge the legitimacy of opposition. Additional telltale characteristics of the republican idiom were made manifest during these years including rhetoric of a substantive and identifiable common good and conflation of political opposition with anti-constitutional conspiracy.[1] Notwithstanding images of separate institutional powers checked and balanced against one another, the Founding generation expected the federal judiciary to be part of a unified governing regime, which served an identified common good and which was guided by a Constitution of fixed and discoverable meaning.[2] If anything, Jeffersonians (or Republicans as they came to identify themselves) were more insistent on this point than Federalists. They could not conceive of a legitimate federal government in which the different branches would act on competing principles since they considered those principles to be "immutably fixed" by a written Constitution approved by the people themselves.[3] As such, many Jeffersonians considered the practice of

---

[1] Jefferson and Madison wrote "oblique references" to hide their meaning, and during the politically tense 1790s "letters written to close personal confidants, responding to their inquiries about strategy and philosophy are, not so curiously, missing.... Madison likely asked the recipients of these letters to destroy them." Gaps in the documentary record are uncharacteristic for a prodigious record-keeper such as Madison. See David Siemers, *Ratifying the Republic: Antifederalists and Federalists in Constitutional Time* (Stanford: Stanford University Press, 2002), 106.

[2] For a generation that held no idea that parties would exist and that a circumstance of divided government was therefore possible, the concept of a unified federal governing regime is more plausible than we might consider once two parties are entrenched.

[3] On the Framers' assumption of branch unity, see G. Edward White, "Recovering Coterminous Power Theory: The Lost Dimension of Marshall Sovereignty Cases," in *Origins of the Federal Judiciary: Essays on the Judiciary Act of 1789*, Maeva Marcus, ed. (New York: Oxford University Press, 1992), 66–105. On their ideas about a Constitution as fixed and immutable, see Siemers, 58–61; Leonard Levy, *Original Intent and the Framers' Constitution* (New York: Macmillan, 1988), 143; and Phillip Hamburger, "The Constitution's Accommodation of Social Change," *Michigan Law Review* 88 (1989), 241.

constitutional interpretation to be illegitimate and to signal a move away from the Framers' limited intentions for national power; as one member of Congress put it during early debates on establishing a national bank, "We have already gone much too far in explaining the constitution; and if we continue on the same plan, there is a danger that we shall at length persuade ourselves, that every power which is not expressly refused is given to us."[4]

By the same token, however, Jeffersonian experience of Federalist rule pushed another concern to the fore: that federal branches working in concert might be animated by the *wrong* principles and operate together to swallow up the authority of the separate states. For Jeffersonians, the problem of institutional reconstruction in 1801 was to re-establish *unity* in the national government and to do so on the basis of what they considered to be the *proper* constitutional principles.

The judiciary that Jeffersonians inherited in 1801 posed a double threat. First, it was animated by Federalist principles that had proven a danger to the sovereignty of the several states and were considered to contradict the intentions of the Framers. Second, it could continue as an entrenched minority opposed to the elected national governing regime. In attempting to eradicate these threats, Jeffersonians unleashed the most radical and thoroughgoing assault on the federal judiciary in American history. As is well known, this assault imploded in a program of judicial impeachments. My concern in reviewing this history is to mark the outcome of the Jeffersonian quest for unity as a new settlement, one which moved beyond the Framers' assumptions of unified governance and of each branch, including the judiciary, as representative of popular sovereignty. That settlement would serve as an essential building block for modern practices of harnessing judicial power. But it would still maintain that the Constitution had a discoverable fixed meaning and that contention would position opposition to that meaning as an anti-constitutional threat.

The history of Jeffersonian hostilities toward the judiciary has been told as the opening salvo in what would become an American tradition of hostility to judicial review. I re-frame this history to highlight the assumptions it reveals about the illegitimacy of opposition and to draw out implications of these assumptions for politicians' relations with the judiciary. In Part I, I show that Federalists and many Anti-Federalists accepted the legitimacy of judicial review precisely because it was grounded in notions of *written* constitutionalism and popular sovereignty. These ideas set interpretation as a process of discovery that would *not* grant equally valid alternatives but which constructed constitutions to be "fixed codes," deviation from which represented "a grave political ill."[5] Thus, judicial review and its implication of *structural* countermajoritarianism cannot be taken as the sole motivator of anti-judicial animus

---

[4] Thomas Tudor Tucker, quoted in Charlene Bangs Bickford, et al., eds., *The Documentary History of the First Federal Congress, 1789–1791*, 14 vols. (Baltimore, MD: Johns Hopkins University Press, 1972–), Vol. 10, 481.

[5] Siemers, 58.

in this period. Part II locates the hostility toward the judiciary within the larger antipathy toward formed, stable, and permanent opposition. It details the Framers' conception of party politics as a harbinger of civil instability, which was an assumption drawn from eighteenth-century English political thought. It attends to Madison's later cutting-edge defense of parties, written in the 1790s, but highlights both the extent to which Madison conceptualized his defense of party as guarding against an anti-constitutional minority faction and how his ideas went beyond and were abandoned in favor of the Jeffersonian anti-party party. Part III assesses Jeffersonian attacks on the judiciary in this light, where opposition by Federalist judges was viewed as tantamount to anti-constitutional threat. Part IV focuses on judicial impeachment as a tool to remove that opposition and, in particular, on the impeachment of Justice Samuel Chase. While the Senate acquitted Chase, his impeachment not only dichotomized law and politics but also yielded a fuller conception of separated federal powers. In effect, the acquittal was a compromise. No longer viewing the judiciary as representative of the popular sovereignty but seemingly anathema to it, politicians were compelled from that point onward to hold the judiciary as a branch apart. Judges were henceforth promoted as neutral arbiters of constitutional meaning divorced from politics, and particularly from representation altogether, a framing that would profoundly affect later debates about judicial reform.

I. Judges as Representatives of Popular Sovereignty

The traditional account of the development of judicial power and, indeed, judicial supremacy begins by detailing how, given a colonial history of judges tied to corrupt executives, the principle of judicial review was highly contentious in the new republic.[6] It highlights that the Articles of Confederation did not contemplate a national judicial body.[7] It emphasizes that judicial review was not much discussed in any direct way at the constitutional convention.[8] It showcases how, during the late 1770s and 1780s, through their constitutions, various states tended to eliminate executive control over judicial appointment and lodged it with the legislature to tie the judiciary closer to the people. And it points out that through the early 1780s, juries were the basis of democratic legal construction whereas judges were criticized as lackeys of executive corruption. In short, judges were not regarded as democratic bulwarks against tyranny in colonial America. Yet by the early 1800s, the judge's image appeared curiously and rapidly rehabilitated.[9] To account for this transformation, legal

---

[6] Richard Ellis, *The Jeffersonian Crisis: Courts and Politics in the Young Republic* (New York: Oxford University Press, 1971), 139–229.

[7] Ibid., 3–10.

[8] Shannon Stimson, *The American Revolution in the Law: Anglo-American Jurisprudence before John Marshall* (Princeton: Princeton University Press, 1990), 48–56.

[9] Jack Rakove, "The Origins of Judicial Review: A Plea for New Contexts," *Stanford Law Review* 49 (May 1997), 1062.

scholars have looked to the judges themselves and, in particular, to an alleged early articulation of judicial supremacy. This explanation has focused on Chief Justice John Marshall's *Marbury v. Madison* (1803) ruling as the definitive expression of judicial muscle.[10]

Yet this account fails to recognize that judicial review was justified during the Constitution's ratification debates, was articulated and accepted by some Anti-Federalists, and was promoted through judicial rulings of the 1790s, albeit the conception of review power did *not* entail judicial supremacy. If Federalists and Anti-Federalists accepted judicial review, then the Jeffersonian assault on the judiciary cannot flow from a notion of that branch's structural countermajoritarian illegitimacy. The attack's underlying logic must be grounded in another concern.

The critical move was not Marshall's but the Framers'. By shifting the location of sovereignty from the legislature to the people themselves, they placed federal judges on equal representational footing with Congress and the president. Each branch, in its own way, would represent the people and preserve constitutional principles.[11] It was in this original frame – where judges were conceptualized as representatives of the people and servants of the popular sovereignty equal to the other branches and not necessarily as neutral arbitrators held apart from politics – that judicial review initially claimed legitimacy. It was a fundamentally democratic principle that did not entail or require any assertion of judicial supremacy.

If the structural separation of powers implied judicial independence, it may be initially unclear how the judiciary's dual functions of representation and independence were to work together. Harmony of these two principles requires an assumption – which the Founding generation embraced – that constitutional meaning amounted to uncovering the Framers' intentions as ratified by the people.[12] That the American Constitution was written, as opposed to its English predecessor, was not only the consummate expression of Enlightened principles of Lockean social contracting but also served to convey real and limited constitutional meaning, which had been "fixed" by the public and sovereign act of formal popular ratification.[13] During the years of the Founding through much of the nineteenth century, these assumptions

---

[10] Robert McKeever, *The United States Supreme Court: A Political and Legal Analysis* (New York: Manchester University Press, 1997), 47, 48. Many constitutional law casebooks begin with *Marbury v. Madison*. See, for example, William Lockhart et al., *Constitutional Law: Cases, Comments, and Questions*, 8th ed. (St. Paul: West Publishing, 1996).

[11] On judges as preserving constitutional principles, see Bruce Ackerman, *We the People: Foundations* (Cambridge, MA: Belknap Press of Harvard University, 1991).

[12] The assumption implies the limited impact of judicial interpretation. Interpretation would not alter constitutional meaning; it would uncover it. See Hamburger, 280–1. On discovery and original intent, see Howard Gillman, "The Collapse of Constitutional Originalism and the Rise of the Notion of the 'Living Constitution' in the Course of American State-Building," *Studies in American Political Development* 11 (Fall 1992), 191–203.

[13] Johnathan O'Neill, *Originalism in American Law and Politics: A Constitutional History* (Baltimore: Johns Hopkins University Press, 2005), 2–4.

about fixed constitutional meaning stemming from the very written nature of the Constitution itself, assumptions commonly associated with the contemporary jurisprudential philosophy now known as textual "originalism," were predominant among legal scholars and political thinkers: "In this period the originalist approach directly implied by a written constitution was most often simply assumed as a principle of the regime.... Interpreters typically expressed the originalist idea confidently and axiomatically.... Accordingly, there was little drive to offer a detailed theoretical defense of originalism."[14] Given this underlying assumption of only one legitimate interpretive modality, any constitutional reading that seemed to move beyond the plain text was often considered derisively to be "interpretation" or "construction."[15] As one constitutional scholar has noted, for many of the Founding generation, "the very purpose of having a written constitution would be circumvented by the process of interpretation."[16]

By the assumptions of this interpretive viewpoint, the legitimacy of multiple interpretations could not be granted. If the Constitution had a singular, fixed, and discoverable meaning ratified by the people, then judicial interpretation contradicting that meaning would be anti-constitutional. In so ruling, judges would abandon their responsibility to represent and preserve the expression of popular sovereignty that the Constitution entailed. These ideas linking interpretation to popular sovereignty, in conjunction with republican fears about opposition, would animate inter-branch conflict, ultimately motivating Federalist and Jeffersonians alike to squash what each considered to be a threatening anti-constitutional opposition.

I.a. *Accepting Judicial Review, Presuming Unity, and Fearing Consolidation*

One indicator of the Framers' acceptance of judicial review is how they discussed the judiciary's role at the constitutional convention. That role was raised mostly in conjunction with proposals for a congressional or national veto over state law and a Council for Revision armed with a limited veto over congressional legislation. These proposals fell not only to concerns about feasibility – how could Congress review state legislation and attend to federal business? – but to claims of redundancy. The judiciary would suffice to take on both the vertical and horizontal responsibilities.[17] Thus, judicial review was assumed by many of the Framers in the organizational roles of the proposed government.[18]

---

[14] Ibid., 5. O'Neill cautions against "ahistorically equating" what he calls nineteenth-century "traditional textual originalism" with "contemporary originalism." (13)

[15] Early American interpretation relied on William Blackstone's *Commentaries*, which counseled focusing on the text's "plain meaning" to discover legislative intent.

[16] Siemers, 67.

[17] Rackove, 1046–7; Larry Kramer, *The People Themselves: Popular Constitutionalism and Judicial Review* (New York: Oxford University Press, 2004), 59–60.

[18] On acceptance of judicial review as part of the institutional structure of the new republic, see P. Allan Dionisopoulos and Paul Peterson, "Rediscovering the American Origins of Judicial

James Iredell, a future Supreme Court Justice, offered an early working out of these assumptions of vertical and horizontal review and the parameters of judicial authority. He conceded that "the judicial power is not to presume to question the power of an act of Assembly," but he also considered resort to the people "either by humble petition" or "universal resistance" to be inefficient.[19] Such popular resistance would be difficult to mobilize, and it would offer no safety against majority tyranny. In place of such populist review, Iredell defended judicial review. This power to validate or nullify law was "not a usurped or discretionary power, but one inevitably resulting from the constitution of their office, they being judges *for the benefit of the whole people*, not *mere servants of the Assembly*."[20] Judicial review's representative justification depended on the Framers' relocation of sovereignty from the legislature to the people.[21] In this framework, elected representatives might pass legislation in conflict with the Constitution, and it fell to the judiciary, in their similar capacity as popular servants, to correct those errors.[22]

Iredell's argument should be familiar as it is essentially the same as Hamilton's rationale offered in his *Federalist 78*. In that essay, Hamilton specified the logic of horizontal judicial review:

> There is no position which depends on clearer principles, than that every act of a delegated authority, contrary to the tenor of the commission under which it is exercised is void. No legislative act therefore contrary to the constitution can be valid. To deny this principle would be to affirm that the deputy is greater than his principal; that the servant is above his master; that the representatives of the people are superior to the people themselves.[23]

This conception of judicial review does not imply supremacy. It does claim that the Constitution, as fundamental or higher law, takes precedence over statute – as statute is passed by the legislature while the Constitution was ratified by the people themselves – and makes no one branch supreme. It maintains judges as equal participants in a representative democracy, doing their part to safeguard the Constitution from an internal aristocratic minority threat that might lead to civil war. If judges voided an act of Congress, they would only be giving preference to "the intention of the people [over] the intention of their agents" not assuming their own supremacy.[24] They would be performing their

---

Review: A Rebuttal to the Views Stated by Currie and Other Scholars," *John Marshall Law Review* 18 (1984), 49–76.

[19] An Elector, "To the Public," in Griffith McRee, *Life and Correspondence of James Iredell* (1857), Vol. 2, 145, 148, quoted in Kramer, 61.

[20] Ibid.

[21] On Federalist relocation of sovereignty from the legislature to the people, see Gordon Wood, *The Creation of the American Republic, 1776–1787*, 2nd ed. (Chapel Hill: University of North Carolina Press, 1998), 373–83, 519–36.

[22] For a fuller examination of this interpretation, see Gerald Leonard, "Iredell Reclaimed: Farewell to Snowiss's History of Judicial Review," *Chicago-Kent Law Review* 80 (2006), 867–82.

[23] Alexander Hamilton, "Federalist 78," in *The Federalist*, Jacob Cooke, ed. (Middletown, CT: Wesleyan University Press, 1961), 524.

[24] Ibid.

function as representatives of the popular sovereignty. Hamilton did not posit courts to be the *only* branch that passes on a law's constitutionality. He contended that it held a responsibility to do so lest it become party to an unconstitutional act: "Nor does this conclusion by any means suppose a superiority of the judicial to the legislative power. It only supposes that the power of the people is superior to both."[25] Taking the Constitution to be an artifact of popular sovereignty and judges as representatives of the people are cornerstones of judicial review's original legitimacy.

Hamilton's *Federalist* essays on the judiciary responded to Anti-Federalist Brutus, who criticized the judiciary's lack of popular accountability.[26] Yet in his critique, Brutus did *not* question the legitimacy of independent judicial review itself:

> If the legislature pass laws, which, in the judgment of the court, they are not authorised to do by the constitution, the court will take notice of them; for it will not be denied that the constitution is the highest or supreme law. And the courts ... cannot, therefore, execute a law, which, in their judgment, opposed the constitution, unless we can suppose they can make a superior law give way to an inferior.[27]

While many of the Anti-Federalists criticized the proposed Constitution as confusingly locating sovereignty in both the state and national governments, the quoted passage indicates that Brutus, like Iredell and Hamilton, recognized the people as sovereign, not the particular state or national governments, and that judges must remain as faithful to that sovereignty as legislators would. Brutus even agreed that the judiciary *cannot* be elected because "their business requires that they should possess a degree of law knowledge, which is acquired only by a regular education" and because "in an independent situation" these judges "may maintain in their firmness and steadiness their decisions."[28] If Brutus conceded all this, what was the basis of his concern with the newly proposed federal judiciary?

In other words, if Brutus stipulated that "the proper province of judicial power, in any government, is, as I conceive, to declare what is the law of the land," then his concern was not with an unelected judiciary as potentially countermajoritarian, but that federal judicial and federal legislative power were mutually reinforcing.[29] His preoccupation was not with *judicial* power per se, but with *federal* judicial power as a threat to state sovereignty. He

[25] Ibid.
[26] Brutus's identity is unclear. Scholars generally agree Brutus was New York Supreme Court judge Robert Yates, a delegate to the Constitutional Convention who left it because he thought the participants exceeded their authority. Publius responded to this question of authority in *Federalist 40*.
[27] Herbert Storing, ed. *The Complete Anti-Federalist* (Chicago: University of Chicago Press, 1981), 2, 9, 148, quoted in Shlomo Slonim, "Federalist No. 78 and Brutus' Neglected Thesis on Judicial Supremacy," *Constitutional Commentary* 23 (2006), 10.
[28] Brutus XVI, 10 April 1788, http://www.constitution.org/afp/brutus16.htm.
[29] Brutus XIII, 21 February 1788, http://www.constitution.org/afp/brutus13.htm.

feared "what arises from the undue extension of legislative power ... [and] that judicial power would be commensurate with the legislative."[30] He contended that federal judicial authority would develop in tandem with congressional authority and that each branch would support the others to expand their respective powers at the expense of the states:

> the general legislature might pass one law after another, extending the general and abridging the state jurisdictions, and to sanction their proceedings would have a course of decisions of the judicial to whom the constitution has committed the power of explaining the constitution. If the states remonstrated, the constitutional mode of deciding upon the validity of the law, in with the supreme court, and neither people, nor state legislatures, nor the general legislature can remove them or reverse their decrees.[31]

For Brutus, the Framers constructed a system of reinforcing federal power aggrandizement against the sovereignty of the state governments. He assumed that the Supreme Court would be biased toward federal power and would extend the limits of federal power to its own and to Congress's advantage.

The primary cause for Brutus's concern was the balance of federal power against states' rights, not how to guard a democratic Congress from an unelected judiciary.[32] Brutus entertained little to no notion of federal judicial power as a horizontal check on congressional power or vice versa. While he agreed abstractly with Madison's separation-of-powers design, he maintained "But *still* each of these bodies should be accountable for their conduct."[33] That phrasing suggests that the branches would *not* in and of themselves hold one another accountable, that ambition of one federal branch would not counter ambition of another. Formal separation was not enough; the branches would nevertheless find ways to concentrate power against the states. Brutus sought to curb federal power as a whole, not simply the powers of judges, precisely because he accepted what Hamilton called a "political axiom" in his *Federalist 80*, namely, that "the judicial power of a government is coextensive with its legislative power."[34] In short, Hamilton and Brutus assumed that not only was judicial review acceptable but that the branches would form a unified governing regime.[35] For Brutus, this possibility presented a grave danger. For Hamilton, who strove to build and consolidate a strong national government, it proved a great opportunity.[36]

---

[30] Ibid.

[31] Brutus XV, 20 March 1788, http://www.constitution.org/afp/brutus15.htm.

[32] Saul Cornell, *The Other Founders: Anti-Federalism and the Dissenting Tradition in America, 1788–1828* (Chapel Hill: University of North Carolina Press, 1999), 26–34.

[33] Brutus XVI. Emphasis added.

[34] Alexander Hamilton, *Federalist 80*. http://avalon.law.yale.edu/18th_century/fed80.asp.

[35] For a fuller detailing of this assumption and how it underlay many decisions of the Marshall Court, see White, 1992.

[36] On Hamilton's designs for a strong national government, in sharp contrast with anti-Federalist fears and Madison's ideas, see Siemers, 78–89.

This fear of consolidation against the states motivated Anti-Federalist objections to Article III and later attempts to clarify and restrict its meaning through the Judiciary Act of 1789. Since members of the Constitutional Convention spent less time debating the terms of Article III, and since many of the members of that convention went on to serve in the first Congress, scholars have tended to assume that debate on the Judiciary Act of 1789 stands in as the working out of the Framers' intent not achieved at the Convention.[37] However, more recent scholarship has argued that this Act is better understood as a political compromise between states' rights advocates and supporters of a powerful national government. As such, the Judiciary Act's provisions are motivated by similar concerns underlying the Bill of Rights.[38]

Debate on the Judiciary Act of 1789 centered on the structure of the new federal judiciary. As such, there was little discussion about how judges should behave. This is unsurprising for at least two reasons. First, in the early republic, juries were, in many regards, more important than judges; they were considered a democratic bulwark against a judge who might be tied to a corrupt executive or legislature. Juries held final say on questions of law and fact: "Judges were not empowered to make authoritarian common-law decisions."[39] Rather, "the eighteenth-century judge 'found' the law," which meant that in the common-law tradition, it was the number and repetition of judges and juries that "found" the law to have similar meaning that conferred its legitimacy.[40] Second, the proposed hierarchical structure and distinction among judges at the federal level had no equivalent in the respective states or in England; therefore, it needed to be wholly worked out.[41] Much of the debate and many of the Judiciary Act's provisions dealt with demarcating the jurisdictions of the lower federal courts versus that of state judiciaries since state courts already existed. The various sections were geared to alleviate concerns that an extensive federal courts system would swamp state authority and individual rights. For example, by setting a high financial threshold for an amount in controversy, federal courts would be accessible for only certain cases, ensuring that wealthy litigants would not abuse the system against the

---

[37] Charles Warren, "New Light on the History of the Federal Judiciary Act of 1789," *Harvard Law Review* 37 (1923), 431–65; W. R. Casto, "The First Congress's Understanding of Its Authority over the Federal Courts' Jurisdiction," *Boston College Law Review* 26 (1985), 1101–42.

[38] Maeva Marcus and Natalie Wexler, "The Judiciary Act of 1789: Political Compromise or Constitutional Interpretation?" *Origins of the Federal Judiciary: Essays on the Judiciary Act of 1789*, Maeva Marcus, ed. (New York: Oxford University Press, 1992); Wilfred Ritz, *Rewriting the History of the Judiciary Act of 1789: Exposing Myths, Challenging Premises, and Using New Evidence*, Wythe Holt and L. H. LaRue, eds. (Norman: University of Oklahoma Press, 1990).

[39] Ritz, 10.

[40] Ibid., 28.

[41] State courts were horizontal: trials were conducted by any of a pool of judges; trials could be re-done in their entirety on questions of law and fact; and there was little to no hierarchy among judges. See Ritz, 6, 10, 27–52.

poor. Also, access to the Supreme Court was limited through procedures such as application for a writ of error.[42] Such restrictions assured an ongoing role for state judiciaries, suggesting that they were meant, in part, to quell concerns about federal power overtaking state autonomy.

In short, much of the Judiciary Act of 1789 indicates a continued concern with the balance of federal and state power. This focus on the vertical balance of power stands in marked contrast with later congressional concerns about judges' behavior and how best to insulate it from the corrupting influences of the partisan elected branches of the national government. These concerns would dominate the next extensive debate on judicial structure undertaken in 1826.[43]

I.b. *Judges' Early Steps to Secure Judicial Review*
As the essays of both Hamilton and Brutus reveal, Chief Justice Marshall tilled little new ground in articulating the democratic logic of judicial review in his *Marbury* ruling.[44] And the legitimacy of such review was strengthened by judicial rulings made throughout the 1790s.[45] For example, Justice William Patterson elaborated upon horizontal judicial review in *Vanhorne's Lessee v. Dorrance* (1795):

> What is a Constitution? It is a form of government, delineated by the mighty hand of the people, in which certain first principles of fundamental laws are established.... What are Legislatures? Creatures of the Constitution; they owe their existence to the Constitution ... there can be no doubt, that every act of the Legislature, repugnant to the Constitution, is absolutely void.[46]

---

[42] See Sections 9, 11, 12, 21, 22, and 25 of the 1789 Act.

[43] See Section II of Chapter 4.

[44] For a summary of evidence on acceptance of judicial review prior to *Marbury*, see Michael Klarman, "How Great Were the 'Great' Marshall Court Decisions?" *Virginia Law Review* 87 (2001), 1113–17. On the related claim that Marshall was interpreting the Constitution in line with judicial precedent and was therefore not acting politically toward the Jefferson administration, see Christopher Wolfe, "A Theory of U.S. Constitutional History," *Journal of Politics* 43 (May 1981), 292–316. *Marbury* and *Dred Scott* are often cited as the only times before the Civil War when the Court reviewed and repudiated congressional statutes. This skews the degree to which such review was understood as a legitimate exercise. Judicial review is as much a process of validation as it is of possible negation. As Charles Black notes, "The prime and most necessary function the Court has been that of *validation*, not that of invalidation." Black, *The People and the Court* (New York: Macmillan, 1960), 52.

[45] Maeva Marcus, "Judicial Review in the Early Republic," in *Launching the 'Extended Republic': The Federalist Era*, Ronald Hoffman and Peter Albert, eds. (Charlottesville: University of Virginia Press, 1996). On the foundation laid for the *Marbury* ruling during the 1790s, see R. Kent Newmyer, "Thomas Jefferson and the Rise of the Supreme Court," *Journal of Supreme Court History* 31 (July 2006), 126–40; Mark Graber, "Establishing Judicial Review: Schooner Peggy and the Early Marshall Court," *Political Research Quarterly* 51 (March 1998), 221–39; and, Robert Frankel, Jr., "Before *Marbury*: Hylton v. United States and the Origins of Judicial Review," *Journal of Supreme Court History* 28 (April 2003), 1–13.

[46] *Vanhorne's Lessee v. Dorrance*, 2 U.S. 304 (1795), 308.

The idea that the people hold ultimate power and that the three branches collectively act in their stead is readily evident in this passage. The branches are not only united in their representative function but also in their responsibility to protect the Constitution from corrupt politicians who might attempt to undermine it.

That judicial review was accepted among governing elites in the 1790s is further evidenced by rulings and machinations involved in the *Hayburn Case* (1792), *United States v. Yale Todd* (1794), *Hylton v. United States* (1796), and *Cooper v. Telfair* (1800).[47] *Hayburn* was decided in the circuit court for the district of Pennsylvania with Justices James Wilson and John Blair sitting in their dual capacity as circuit judges. The case involved the constitutionality of the Invalid Pensions Act, which charged federal judges (serving as commissioners and not as judges) to determine whether a petitioner was entitled to government compensation if his injury resulted from fighting for the Revolutionary cause. The Secretary of War then reviewed the judges' assessments. William Hayburn filed a claim for a pension, but the circuit court refused to hear the case. No records exist of the judges' reasoning; however, Representative Elias Boudinot reported the judges' statements in the House of Representatives:

> it appeared that the Court thought the examination of invalids a very extraordinary duty to be imposed on the Judges; and looked on the law which imposes that duty as an unconstitutional one, inasmuch as it directs the Secretary of War to state the mistakes of the Judges to Congress for their revision; they could not, therefore, accede to a regulation tending to render the Judiciary subject to Legislative and Executive powers, which from a regard for liberty and the Constitution, ought to be kept carefully distinct; it being a primary principle of the utmost importance, that no decision of the Judiciary Department should, under any pretext, be brought in revision before either the Legislative or Executive Departments of the Government, neither of which have, in any instance, a revisionary authority over the judicial proceedings of the courts of justice.[48]

In essence, the Pensions Act set the executive branch above the judiciary. During discussion of this incident, it was conceded that the circuit court for the district of New York had already heard petitioners' claims, but they had done so in their capacity as commissioners not as judges, thereby circumventing the separation-of-powers issue raised by Wilson and Blair.[49] As this case was "the first instance in which a court of justice had declared a law of Congress to be unconstitutional,"[50] the judges wrote to President Washington

---

[47] Marcus, 36–40; Kramer, 95–6. *Hayburn Case*, 2 Dallas 409 (1792); *United States v. Yale Todd*, 488 U.S. 361 (1794); *Hylton v. United States*, 3 U.S. 171 (1796); *Cooper v. Telfair*, 4 U.S. 14 (1800).

[48] *Annals of Congress*, 2nd Congress, 1st Session, 556.

[49] Ibid., 557.

[50] Ibid. On federal judges holding multiple judicial positions simultaneously, see Mark Tushnet, "Dual Office Holding and the Constitution: A View from Hayburn's Case," in *Origins of the Federal Judiciary*, Maeva Marcus, ed. (New York: Oxford University Press, 1992).

that their actions were "far from being pleasant" and that horizontal review "excited feelings in us, which we hope never to experience again."[51] Attorney General Randolph informed Washington that Wilson's and Blair's refusal to hear the case was tantamount to overtly striking down a congressional act.[52]

If governing elites already accepted judicial review, why would Wilson and Blair agonize over it?[53] The focus on judicial review misses the point. These justices did not want to express *open* opposition to Congress's objective. They considered such displays to be anathema to the norms of civic republicanism as they exposed disunity in the government. Antipathy toward opposition will be further discussed in Part II of this chapter. Suffice it to say that the Supreme Court's reaction to the attorney general's application for a writ of mandamus ordering the Pennsylvania circuit to hear Hayburn's case supports my interpretation. The Court postponed ruling on this application, thereby signaling not only that the justices harbored doubts about the Invalid Pensions Act's constitutionality, but also buying time for "Congress to correct the Invalid Pension Act before the Supreme Court embarrassed the legislature by declaring the act unconstitutional."[54] Congress did so in 1793 and mooted the need for a Court opinion. Furthermore, as Larry Kramer notes, the judiciary faced little rebuke in its potential exercise of review: "no one was heard shrieking about a usurpation of power, and there were no calls for anyone's impeachment, at least none that were taken seriously."[55]

Judicial statements in *United States v. Yale Todd* further confirm acceptance of judicial review. By ordering Todd to reapply for his pension under the 1793 law, the Court essentially declared the 1792 Act invalid. However, it offered no rationale for its decision, perhaps highlighting that it did not want to draw attention to its actions, not because its actions were illegitimate from the standpoint of exercising review of congressional action but because review would highlight open opposition within the governing regime. An opinion in this case would only draw attention to an ongoing inter-branch dispute, opening the way to possible factional conflict that Federalist ideology sought to avoid at all cost.

This cautious exercise of review exhibited in *Hayburn* and *Yale Todd*, which indicated a desire to minimize disagreement among the branches, is further evident in *Hylton v. United States* where the constitutionality of the Carriage Tax Act was at stake. Hamilton, who wanted the Act preserved as part of his national economic plan, brought the case, and ultimately the Court ruled the

[51] *Hayburn Case*, 2 U.S. (2 *Dallas*) 409, 412.
[52] Edmund Randolph to Washington, 5 April 1792, George Washington Papers, Library of Congress, cited in Marcus, 39.
[53] Justices Jay, Cushing, and Iredell supported Wilson's and Blair's reading of the law even if they heard petitioners' claims in New York and North Carolina. They wrote of their support in a letter to Washington dated 10 April 1792. *Hayburn Case*, 2 U.S. (2 *Dallas*) 409, 410, 412–14.
[54] Marcus, 40.
[55] Kramer, 96.

Act constitutional.[56] The machinations necessary to bring it before the Supreme Court suggested that all parties to the case understood that the Court could review a congressional act's constitutionality well before Marshall clearly stipulated the idea in *Marbury*.[57] And finally, the connection of review to popular sovereignty is made explicit by Justice Samuel Chase in his ruling in *Cooper v. Telfair*: "It is, indeed, a general opinion, it is expressly admitted by all this bar, and some of the Judges have, individually, in the Circuits, decided, that the Supreme Court can declare an act of congress to be unconstitutional, and, therefore, invalid; but there is no adjudication of the Supreme Court itself upon the point."[58] While Chase pointed out that in no existing ruling had the Court struck down congressional acts, the ability to do so was readily understood.[59] Justice Iredell affirms Chase's view in *Calder v. Bull* (1798): "If any act of Congress, or of the Legislature of a State, violates those constitutional provisions, it is unquestionably void; though I admit, that as the authority to declare it void is of a delicate and awful nature, the Court will never resort to that authority, but in a clear and urgent case."[60] Iredell specifies the logic of both vertical and horizontal review to be supported by federal supremacy and the separation of powers, respectively.

These examples of judges' own specifications of authority to review legislative acts should not be considered to be merely self-serving. As the 1790s debate on the extent of the president's removal authority demonstrated, members of Congress also understood and accepted the legitimacy of judicial review. In that debate Representative William Smith of South Carolina argued that reinstatement of an executive officer was a judicial matter rectified by a writ of mandamus, not a congressional prerogative to limit executive authority. Senate participation in dismissing an executive branch officer would distort the principle that "it is the duty of the Legislature to make laws; your judges are to expound them."[61] In this instance, then, judges held legitimate authority to review presidential actions.

Madison countered that Smith's assertion implied judicial supremacy. How, Madison asked, is it that "any one department draws from the Constitution greater powers than another? ... I do not see that any one of these independent departments has more right than another to declare their sentiments on that point."[62] The question suggests that all three branches have the right and

---

[56] Marcus, 41–4; Kramer, 103.

[57] These machinations involved inflating the disputed sum such that it met the monetary threshold for the Court to hear it. See 3 *United States Reports* (3 *Dallas*) 171 (1796). That the Court found the act constitutional indicates that it exercised review well before Marshall took a seat on the Supreme bench.

[58] 4 *United States Reports* (4 *Dallas*) 19 (1800).

[59] *Hayburn* avoided striking down a law by signaling to Congress the need to re-write existing law and *Hylton* exercised review only to affirm the law passed by Congress.

[60] *Calder v. Bull*, 3 U.S. 386 (1798), 399.

[61] William Loughton Smith, *Annals of Congress*, First Congress, First Session, 470 quoted in Marcus, 30.

[62] James Madison, *Annals of Congress*, First Congress, First Session, 500 quoted in Marcus, 32.

responsibility of constitutional interpretation, which would be more fully developed in Madison's Virginia Resolution.[63] Elbridge Gerry responded by defending judicial review: it is a judicial responsibility to "declare a law a nullity."[64] If Congress could do the same, then the separation of powers had no meaning. As such, Gerry rejected the idea of congressional interpretation of the Constitution. He later noted, "I am decidedly against putting any construction whatever on the constitution."[65] By asserting that the Court held the power of review, Gerry, Iredell, and Hamilton were not rejecting popular sovereignty in favor of judicial supremacy; they were relying on it to motivate and legitimize that judicial power as serving a representative function.

I.c. *Judicial Review as Discovering the Act of Popular Sovereignty*
In the traditional telling of the rise of judicial authority, reviewed at the beginning of this section, Marshall's elitist Federalist assertion of judicial supremacy is pitted against Jefferson's democratic populism.[66] And Jefferson's animus toward the Court is captured by his oft-quoted claim, "the judiciary of the United States is the subtle corps of sappers and miners constantly working under ground to undermine the foundations of our confederated fabric."[67] Criticizing constitutional interpretation as "the eccentric impulses of whimsical, capricious designing men," Jefferson sought to transform it into "a mere machine" requiring little special education.[68] Doing so would allegedly guard against discretionary abuse of law.[69]

And yet, Jefferson supported the structural design of the federal judiciary, that is, life-termed judges who are appointed by the president with the consent of the Senate. By drafting provisions in the Virginia constitution for judicial appointment and creating life tenure for judges under conditions of good behavior, Jefferson, like Anti-Federalist Brutus, seemingly conceded the structural legitimacy of the federal system of judicial review. In a letter to Madison, which discussed the proposed Bill of Rights, Jefferson even noted the benefit of independent judicial authority:

> In the arguments in favor of a declaration of rights, you omit one which has great weight with me, the legal check which it puts into the hands of the

---

[63] See Part II of this chapter.

[64] Elbridge Gerry, *Annals of Congress*, First Congress, First Session, 504 quoted in Marcus, 33.

[65] Elbridge Gerry quoted in Bickford, 1972–, Vol. 11, 1021.

[66] See, for example, James Simon, *What Kind of Nation: Thomas Jefferson, John Marshall, and the Epic Struggle to Create a United States* (New York: Simon & Schuster, 2003).

[67] Jefferson, letter to Thomas Ritchie, 25 December 1820, in *The Writings of Thomas Jefferson*, ed. Paul L. Ford, Vol. 10, 17071.

[68] Thomas Jefferson to Edmund Pendleton (26 August 1776) in *The Papers of Thomas Jefferson*, Vol. 1, Julian P. Boyd, ed. (1950), quoted in Gordon Wood, "The Origins of Judicial Review Revisited, or How the Marshall Court Made More Out of Less," *Washington and Lee Law Review* 56 (1999), 790.

[69] Charles Cook, *The American Codification Movement: A Study of Antebellum Legal Reform* (New York: Greenwood Press, 1981). See also Karen Orren, *Belated Feudalism: Labor, Law, and Liberal Development in the United States* (New York: Cambridge University Press, 1991), 62–7.

judiciary. This is a body, which if rendered independent, and kept strictly to their own department merits great confidence for their learning and integrity. In fact what degree of confidence would be too much for a body composed of such men as Wythe, Blair, and Pendleton?[70]

Thus, Jefferson was not hostile to courts or judicial review to the extent that judges were unelected and thereby embodied a democratic deficit. To understand the reason and the timing of Jefferson's anti-judicial animus, it is necessary to understand how he – as well as others in the Founding generation – linked interpretation, popular sovereignty, and legitimacy.

That connection underlies the logic of Jefferson's qualifying statement, which followed his oft-quoted "sappers and miners" criticism: "A judiciary independent of a king or executive alone, is a good thing; but independence of the will of the nation is a solecism, at least in a republican government."[71] Here, Jefferson revealed two assumptions about the expected role of judges in the new republic. First, judicial independence meant independence from corrupt politicians, not from politics altogether. If judges were representatives of the people charged with protecting the higher law of the Constitution, it does not follow that they would necessarily be cast as separate and distinct, as neutral apolitical statesmen "making" the law, which is a more modern conception of the judge and the judiciary.[72] Conflating political neutrality with judicial independence to create the concept of judicial neutrality would come, I argue, only in the wake of the Chase impeachment.

Second, since independence from the people is nonsensical in a democratic republic, judicial interpretation should accord with the popular will since the Constitution is, by definition, an act of popular sovereignty. If judges ruled otherwise, they would represent the aims of an aristocratic minority to the detriment of principles as ratified by the people themselves.[73] Jefferson complained that through interpretation the Marshall Court betrayed its responsibility to preserve the Constitution as an act of popular sovereignty: "The constitution ... is a mere thing of wax in the hands of the judiciary, which they may twist and shape in to any form they please."[74] The criticism implies not that the judiciary was necessarily anti-democratic, only that certain judges

---

[70] Jefferson to Madison, 15 March 1789, in *Papers of Thomas Jefferson*, J. Boyd, ed. (Princeton: Princeton University Press, 1958), Vol. 14, 659.

[71] Jefferson to Ritchie, 25 December 1820, in *Writings*, 1707I.

[72] Matthew Frank locates this idea of judicial authority as neutral in Tocqueville's interpretation of the Framers' actions. If it is a predominant theme by the 1830s, as congressional debate discussed in Chapter 4 indicates, it is not a predominant theme during the 1780s or 1790s. See Frank, "Statesmanship and the Judiciary," *The Review of Politics* 51 (Autumn 1989), 510–32. See Alexis de Tocqueville, *Democracy in America*, Harvey Mansfield and Delba Winthrop, eds. (Chicago: University of Chicago Press, 2000 [1835, 1840]), 93–9, 130–42, 251–63.

[73] See Richard Hofstadter, *The Idea of a Party System: The Rise of Legitimate Opposition in the United States, 1780–1840* (Berkeley: University of California Press, 1969), 127. See also Lance Banning, *The Jeffersonian Persuasion: Evolution of a Party Ideology* (Ithaca: Cornell University Press, 1980), 129, 135–40, 208–70.

[74] Jefferson to Roane quoted in Gillman, 212.

abused their power via the tool of interpretation. In other words, the Marshall Court abandoned the Constitution's proper principles and discoverable singular meaning and turned it into something it was not. Interpretive authority was used to undermine rather than maintain the Constitution. Those circumstances, as we shall see later in this chapter, were made evident, according to Jefferson, by the passage and litigation of the 1798 Sedition Act.[75]

Of course, Jefferson's anti-judicial animus is grounded in a particular interpretive perspective that we now associate with originalism. However, the Federalist perspective was not anti-originalist or anti-textualist; Federalists did not base their ideas about constitutional meaning on a wholly distinct interpretive method such as the legal realism school that would only develop a century later. Given their common assumptions about the fixed meaning conferred by the sovereign act of ratification, Federalists and Anti-Federalists adopted the same interpretive modality such that "if the debate between narrow and broad readings introduced a measure of flexibility into early constitutional interpretation, it was a flexibility firmly anchored in the premises of originalism."[76] In other words, their shared interpretive mode de-legitimized the possibility of two or more distinct interpretive outcomes. As such, the one faction was compelled, by its very assumptions about how constitutional meaning was rendered, to view the other faction as anti-constitutional. In short, anti-judicial animus for which Jefferson would become known follows from a particular grounding of judicial authority in popular sovereignty and an assumption that alternative constructions amounted to an anti-constitutional and conspiratorial threat.

If many members of the Founding generation – Hamiltonian Federalists and Anti-Federalists alike – agreed that the Court could legitimately review congressional legislation, why did Marshall's ruling in *Marbury* – which did just that – agitate Jeffersonians with whom Anti-Federalists had come to identity? The traditional focus on the structural illegitimacy of judicial review, that is, of its undemocratic countermajoritarian potential, points in the wrong direction. Jeffersonians were angered that the outcome of judicial review implied the Justices' refusal to recognize that the people had repudiated Federalism in the election of 1800. That outcome did illustrate the judiciary's independence from the elected branches, but was that the Framers' notion of judicial independence, much less Jefferson's own?

Federalists and Anti-Federalists agreed that judges should be independent of corrupt executives and legislators. But for Jefferson, if his election were taken to be an expression of popular sovereignty on par with constitutional ratification, Federalist judges, through rulings subsequent to that election, revealed independence from the people themselves.[77] That was intolerable because it

[75] Ellis, 26.
[76] Morton Horowitz, "Foreword: The Constitution of Change: Legal Fundamentality without Fundamentalism," *Harvard Law Review* 107 (1993), 51.
[77] Jefferson, of course, was fond of referring to his election as the Revolution of 1800, thereby granting it more importance than a regular election.

suggested that agents of government would actively contradict the expressed popular sovereignty. As such, the Marshall Court's review demonstrated that the governing regime was not unified in its representative function. It was splintered by the open opposition of a recalcitrant judiciary. Stable opposition was now entrenched in government and threatened instability. From the Jeffersonian perspective, Marshall had not acted illegitimately because he reviewed the Judiciary Act of 1789 and found its Section 13 unconstitutional; he acted illegitimately because he represented an aristocratic minority faction out to repudiate the people's expressed choice and undermine the Constitution itself.

II. An Age of Party Illegitimacy

Traditional accounts of American political parties, which divide party competition into six systems punctuated by critical elections, tend to organize conflict around policy differences within a constitutional consensus. Each system has two parties: Federalists battled Jeffersonian Republicans, Democrats battled Whigs, Republicans battled Democrats, and so on.[78] This paradigm skims over the possibility that politicians conceptualized parties in their own time in ways that may not accord or wholly resonate with contemporary functionalist definitions of party purposes.[79] Therefore, it does not consider how assumptions about opposition, conflict, and competition have changed over time. It problematically explains party practices as the necessary intentions of their designers such that contemporary parities are colored with a sense of inevitability. As one historian notes, "this view misconstrues the two-party system as having been consensual, relatively stable, and undramatic in its evolution and as having remained relatively unchanged since its inception."[80] This account glosses over the intensity of conflict during the antebellum era, or it is acknowledged merely as a difference of degree relative to post-Reconstruction politics rather than of kind.[81] By examining the aims and objectives of these politicians in their own time, what becomes apparent is a deep mistrust bordering on the conspiratorial among politicians who *"failed to recognize*

[78] Walter Dean Burnham, *Critical Elections and the Mainsprings of American Politics* (New York: W.W. Norton, 1971). A cogent rebuttal of the first party system thesis is offered by R. Formisano, "Federalists and Republicans: Parties, Yes – System, No" in Paul Kleppner et al., eds. *The Evolution of American Electoral Systems* (Westport, CT: Greenwood Press, 1981). On consensus underlying American politics, see Louis Hartz, *The Liberal Tradition in America* (New York: Harcourt, Brace, & World, 1955), and Richard Hofstadter, *The American Political Tradition and the Men Who Made It* (New York: Vintage, 1989 [1948]).
[79] For critiques of functionalism, see Paul Pierson, *Politics in Time: History, Institutions, and Social Analysis* (Princeton: Princeton University Press, 2004), 46–8, 104–22.
[80] James Sharp, *American Politics in the Early Republic* (New Haven: Yale University Press, 1993), 7.
[81] See John Hoadley, *Origins of American Political Parties, 1789–1803* (Lexington: University Press of Kentucky, 1986); Joseph Charles, *The Origins of the American Party System* (Williamsburg, VA: Institute of Early American History and Culture, 1956); William Chambers, *Political Parties in a New Nation* (New York: Oxford University Press, 1963).

that they *shared* a consensus," a consensus, I argue, grounded in civic republicanism. But the terms or underlying assumptions of that consensus – about
the illegitimacy of formed and stable opposition and about the strict textualist
bounds of constitutional interpretation – drove politicians in both factions to
view one another as threatening civil strife. The ideational boundaries of these
politicians' worldviews, in short, raised the stakes of political contestation to
constitutional heights.

II.a. *Not Just Anti-Partisan, but Anti-Party*

Between 1789 and potentially as late as the Monroe presidency, the organizational form of political parties was almost entirely illegitimate: "If anyone
publicly defended 'party' or 'party spirit' as inherent goods before 1815, it was
a rare event."[82] Indeed, James Madison provided a rare defense, which is discussed below; yet even his defense was distinct from contemporary notions of
the purpose of parties, and its core ideas were abandoned by Jeffersonians and
remained to be taken up by Marin Van Buren in the 1820s.[83] The Founders'
education did not support the implications of open, stable, and popular-based
institutions' opposition that seemingly followed from the First Amendment's
guarantees of speech and association: "they were far from clear as to how
opposition should make itself felt, for they valued social harmony, and they
had not arrived at the view that opposition, manifested in organized political
parties, could sustain freedom without fatally shattering social harmony."[84] In
one *Federalist* essay, Madison cautioned against appealing to the public too
often as it might foster instability:

> frequent appeals ... deprive the government of that veneration which time
> bestows on every thing, and without which perhaps the wisest and freest
> governments would not possess the requisite stability.... The danger of dis-
> turbing the public tranquility by interesting too strongly the public passions,
> is a still more serious objection against a frequent reference of constitutional
> questions to the decision of the whole society.[85]

For Madison, civic stability was "essential to national character and to the
advantages annexed to it, as well as to that repose and confidence in the minds
of the people, which are among the chief blessings of civil society."[86] One historian has captured this generation's antipathy to party-based opposition and

---

[82] Ronald Formisano, *The Transformation of Political Culture: Massachusetts Parties, 1790s–1840s* (New York: Oxford University Press, 1983), 88–9 (noting that the Federalist-Jeffersonian Republican divide was not a fully developed two-party system because participants held little to no expectation of rotation in office). See also Formisano, "Deferential-Participant Politics: The Early Republic's Political Culture, 1789–1840," *American Political Science Review* 68 (1973), 473–87, and Formisano (1981), 33–76.

[83] See Chapter 4.

[84] Hofstadter, 1967, 9.

[85] James Madison, *Federalist 49*, http://www.constitution.org/fed/federa49.htm.

[86] James Madison, *Federalist 37*, http://www.constitution.org/fed/federa37.htm.

how it was rooted in a claim of fixed and discoverable constitutional meaning: "To the Federalist it was obvious that Republican opposition was malicious mischief.... Since both parties could not be correct, one must be the foe
of order. Protestations of the loyalty of an opposition party were insincere."[87]

Thus, while battles between Federalists and Jeffersonians seem similar
to contemporary two-party competition, Federalist rhetoric is qualitatively
distinct and is grounded in different assumptions regarding constitutional
interpretation and the legitimacy of opposition.[88] My point is not that no
legitimate dissenting tradition existed in the early republic. The Constitution
was born amid active dissent, and after its ratification, Anti-Federalists were
elected to Congress and participated in the amendment process producing
the Bill of Rights.[89] But if dissent in parliamentary debate was accepted, open
and permanent opposition was perceived as a stepping-stone to civil unrest.
Once the people voted, their role in deliberation was at an end until the
next election.[90]

[87] Marshall Smelser, "The Federalist Period as an Age of Passion," *American Quarterly* 10
(Winter 1958), 395. For a discussion on the constitutional interpretive claims of the Federalists
and the Jeffersonians, see Keith Whittington, "Give 'The People' What They Want?" *Chicago-
Kent Law Review* 81 (2006), 911–22.

[88] Gordon Wood, "Launching the 'Extended Republic': The Federalist Era," in *Launching
the 'Extended Republic': The Federalist Era*, Ronald Hoffman and Peter Albert, eds.
(Charlottesville: University Press of Virginia, 1996), 2. For example, the Jefferson-Adams contest was driven by an animosity that brewed throughout the 1790s. Adams condemned Jefferson
as "poisoned with Ambition" and referred to his supporters as "Demons" (John Adams to
Abigail Adams, 26 November 1793, 13 March 1796, Adams Family Papers, Massachusetts
Historical Society, Boston, 1954–59, microfilm edition, quoted in John Ferling, *Adams vs.
Jefferson: The Tumultuous Election of 1800* [New York: Oxford University Press, 2004],
82). Hamilton wrote his "Letter from Alexander Hamilton, concerning the Public Conduct
and Character of John Adams," to accomplish two purposes. First, he sought to defend himself against Adams's public insults toward him. Adams called Hamilton "a Bastard," a "man
devoid of every moral principle," and an "insolent coxcomb who rarely dined in good company" and who could be found "getting silly and vaporing about his administration like a
young girl about her brilliants and trinkets." Second, Hamilton sought to undermine Adams
in the 1800 election and position his High Federalist ally, Charles Cotesworth Pinckney,
for victory. For Adams's insults, see James McHenrey to Oliver Wolcott, Jr., 9 November
1800, in George Gibbs, *Memoirs of the Administrations of Washington and Adams*
(New York: 1846), Vol. 2, 455; see also Adams to Rush, 25 January 1806, in John A. Schutz
and Douglass Adair, *The Spur of Fame: Dialogues of John Adams and Benjamin Rush, 1805–
1813* (San Marino: Huntington Library, 1966), 48, and Adams to Jefferson, 12 July 1813,
*The Adams-Jefferson Letters: The Complete Correspondence between Thomas Jefferson
and Abigail and John Adams*, Lestor Cappon, ed. (Chapel Hill: University of North Carolina
Press, 1988), 354. See generally Jo Ann Freeman, *Affairs of Honor: National Politics in the
New Republic* (New Haven: Yale University Press, 2004), 105–9 and 116–20.

[89] Eleven of the first sixty-five representatives and three of the first twenty-six senators were
Anti-Federalists.

[90] For a synopsis of Federalist theories of representation and how they cut against modern ideas
of democracy, see James Martin, "When Repression Is Democratic and Constitutional: The
Federalist Theory of Representation and the Sedition Act of 1798," *University of Chicago
Law Review* 66 (Winter 1999), 117–82.

This anti-opposition principle is clearly at play in the Anti-Federalist response to the ratification of the Constitution. Anti-Federalists offered vociferous objections to the document drawn up in Philadelphia, but when it became clear that majorities in at least eleven states voted to ratify the Constitution and reconstruct the national government accordingly, many Anti-Federalists acquiesced, recognizing that the people had spoken and that continued opposition was not only inappropriate but potentially de-stabilizing.[91] As Pennsylvanian Anti-Federalist, James Hanna noted, "the worst that we can expect from a bad form of government is anarchy and confusion ... and by an opposition in the present situation of affairs, we are sure of it." Furthermore, according to Hanna, refusal to acquiesce amounted to "a crime of very detrimental consequence to our country."[92] In short, by continuing to oppose the newly ratified Constitution, Anti-Federalists would only assure that civil strife would ensue. No continued opposition would be legitimate. And other Anti-Federalists echo this idea. John Quincy Adams, an Anti-Federalist early in his political career, conceded, "In our Government, opposition to the acts of a majority of the people is rebellion to all intents and purposes."[93] Even the firebrand Virginian Anti-Federalist, Patrick Henry, chose civil stability over maintaining his political conviction by declaring his intent to "submit as a quiet citizen" were the Constitution ratified.[94] Indeed, by mid-1788, George Washington recognized how such spirited dissent transformed into the much-needed acquiescence to provide the Constitution with a sense of legitimacy: "I am induced to believe the [Anti-Federalist] minorities have acquiesced not only with a good grace, but also with a serious design to give the government a fair chance to discover its operation by being carried into effect."[95] Indeed, many Anti-Federalists confirmed their allegiance by taking oaths of fidelity to the Constitution. Nevertheless, some Federalists were skeptical of this rapid transition among Anti-Federalists and continued to view them as anti-constitutional. As Virginian Federalist James Gordon wrote to James Madison, "there appears to be to be little or no opposition from the Anties ... but I rather think their conduct is intended to lull the friends of the new government into a state of security and then in the fall to make a violent attack."[96]

---

[91] As David Siemers *Federalists* argues, Anti-Federalists supported the Constitution primarily because they feared that their continued opposition would foster civil war and that the process of ratification had adhered to legitimate republican principles. The decision had been made; ongoing opposition served no purpose: "either one agreed to abide by it or one was a rebel – there was no middle ground." (30)

[92] Jack Hanna to John Vandegrift, Nathan Vansant, and Jacob Vandegrift (15 August 1788) in Merrill Jensen and John P. Kaminski, eds., *The Documentary History of the Ratification of the Constitution* (Madison: Madison State Historical Society of Wisconsin, 1976–), Vol. 1, 250 and 262, quoted in Siemers, 26.

[93] John Quincy Adams, diary entry of 7 February 1788, quoted in Siemers, 30.

[94] Henry quoted in Siemers, 32.

[95] Jensen and Kaminski, eds., Vol. 1, 55–6, quoted in Siemers, 32.

[96] Gordon to Madison, 31 August 1778, Jensen and Kaminski, eds., Vol. 2, 258, quoted in Siemers, 33.

Such fears suggest not only the fragility of the new government but also the extent to which permanent and stable oppositional viewpoints were considered to be harbingers of civil unrest.

Lest this antipathy toward opposition be interpreted as solely confined to questions of establishing the parameters of the governing structure such that opposition within the system could be construed as legitimate or loyal, attention should be paid to the politics of the 1790s.[97] Conflating opposition with anti-constitutional conspiracy continued well into that decade's controversy over the Democratic-Republican clubs. Having lost the battle to scuttle the first national bank, some members of Congress sought direct public support giving rise to these organizations. Yet their very existence contradicted Federalist theories of representation. They were an illegitimate response to the outcome of parliamentary debate. Precisely because they showcased dissent *outside* the legislature, New York Federalist, Rufus King, denounced them as contrary to the Constitution: "It was never expected that the executive should sit with folded Arms, and that the Government should be carried on by Town Meetings, and those irregular measures, which disorganize the Society, destroy the salutary influence of regular Government, and render the Magistracy a mere pageant."[98] While these clubs defined their purpose as educational, Federalists saw them as akin to the revolutionary committees of correspondence with the potential for upheaval that that analogy implied.[99]

While scholars have used congressional voting and the organization of extra-legislative opposition as evidence of party formation, these patterns do not indicate any acceptance of opposition as legitimate.[100] *The forming of party-like groups implies nothing about whether the one party would concede the other party's legitimacy.* The party-like behavior of these factions needs to be understood as distinct from modern parties.[101] Normative assumptions

---

[97] Saul Cornell argues that once the Constitution was ratified, Anti-Federalists played the role of a loyal opposition, forgoing a second convention movement and working within the established system to seek amendments to the Constitution. I do not quarrel with that assessment; I only point out that throughout the 1790s each faction held to the notion that the Constitution had a singular discoverable meaning, and that this contention led each to describe the other not as loyal to the Constitution but as seeking to destroy it. See Cornell, 136–94.

[98] Rufus King to Alexander Hamilton, 3 August 1793, quoted in Freeman, 92–3.

[99] For Jeffersonian assessment of these societies, see Cornell, 196–9. For Federalist perception, see Freeman, 91–9. See also Ferling, 60–1, 63–4, and Bernard Fay, "Early Party Machinery in the United States: Pennsylvania in the Election of 1796," *Pennsylvania Magazine of History and Biography* 66 (1936), 375–90.

[100] John Hoadley analyzes congressional roll call votes to reveal two-bloc voting behavior in the fourth Congress (1795–97). See Hoadley, "The Emergence of Political Parties in Congress," *American Political Science Review* 74 (September 1980), 575–779. Sean Theriat sees a pattern of partisan blocs incorporating electoral considerations into their voting patterns, thereby suggesting fuller party development than previously recognized. See Theriat, "Party Politics during the Louisiana Purchase," *Social Science History* 30 (Summer 2006), 293–323.

[101] Using these patterns as a basis, scholars have argued that economic-based parties existed since the establishment of the Constitution, that partisanship cemented around the Jay

underlying civic republicanism – unity in governance, fear of faction, worry of civil instability – structured responses to opposition. Politicians conceptualized party competition as a constitutional threat. Therefore, we should not read contemporary systemic party divisions and managed partisanship back in time to see our reflection in the Federalist-Jeffersonian conflicts. While they acted in partisan fashion, few on either side conceded that they did so as that would mean admitting the perpetuity of factional politics.[102]

Viewing opposition as illegitimate underscores the rationality of seemingly radical actions taken with respect to judicial power. If permanent opposition is anathema to republican assumptions, then silencing a recalcitrant judiciary would be a rational course of action. If party is taken to endanger constitutional principles, then shoring up the branch structurally separate from potentially party-driven electoral politics is a rational action. In short, the civic republican assumptions animating Federalists and Jeffersonians triggered a set of rational actions that had less to do with maintaining policy preferences and everything to with their fears of civil war and the collapse of the Constitution.

II.b. *An Inherited Political Tradition Fearful of Open, Stable, and Permanent Opposition*

Federalist and Jeffersonian positions toward opposition assumed that parties were dangerous and, if needed, *temporary* organizations. This conception of party came from English political thought, which itself was not a uniform tradition.[103] Its diversity explains, in part, differences between Hamilton's and Madison's discussion of stable faction, articulated in *Federalist 9* and *Federalist 10* essays, respectively. Hamilton's recommendation to *suppress* faction drew on Bolingbroke's writings while Madison's hope to *manage* faction drew on those by David Hume.[104]

Treaty, or that parties were defined by their relationship to the Adams administration. Charles Beard, *Economic Origins of Jeffersonian Democracy* (New York: Macmillan, 1915); Rudolph Bell, *Party and Faction in American Politics: The House of Representatives, 1789–1801* (Westport, CT: Greenwood Press, 1973); Noble Cunningham, Jr., *The Jeffersonian Republicans: The Formation of Party Organization, 1789–1801* (Chapel Hill: University of North Carolina Press, 1957); Jerald Combs, *The Jay Treaty: Political Battleground of the Founding Fathers* (Berkeley: University of California Press, 1970).

[102] One notable exception was Madison, who in a series of essays from 1792 considered whether explicit partisanship could serve the common good by forcing Federalists out of office. See Section B of Part II.

[103] See Stanley Elkins and Eric McKitrick, *The Age of Federalism: The Early American Republic, 1788–1800* (New York: Oxford University Press, 1993). On the influence of English political thought on the Founders, see Bernard Bailyn, *The Origins of American Politics* (New York: Vintage, 1970),14–23, and Ralph Ketcham, *Presidents above Party: The First American Presidency, 1789–1829* (Chapel Hill: University of North Carolina Press, 1984), 51–55.

[104] Douglass Adair, "'That Politics May Be Reduced to a Science': David Hume, James Madison, and the Tenth Federalist," in *Fame and the Founding Fathers*, Trevor Colbourn, ed. (New York: W. W. Norton, 1974). For a rebuttal arguing that Madison was responding to

Bolingbroke characterized the English civil war as a conflict between a "court" party of the King's allies and a "country" party of the people. He wrote that the latter is "improperly called party. It is the nation speaking and acting in the discourse and conduct of particular men."[105] As such, the country party is always defined as the popular majority. Perhaps even more important, the country party was compelled to rise *temporarily* to eradicate corruption, re-establish good government, and then fade away. If the country party was a party at all, it was as a "party that is to end all parties."[106] This characterization would infuse Jeffersonian rhetoric with Federalists as the aristocratic "court" and Jeffersonians as "country."[107] Such anti-partyism also permeated Hamilton's *Federalist 9*. For him, government was "a barrier against domestic faction and insurrection."[108] Washington, identified with Federalists by his second term, made the destructive effect of party a central theme of his farewell address.[109] Monroe similarly characterized the lack of opposition during his presidency as the mark of progress and American exceptionalism.[110]

Where Bolingbroke defined "court" and "country" divisions as temporary abnormalities that would re-establish the equilibrium of civic tranquility and governing unity, Hume, while acknowledging that "they oft threaten the total dissolution of the government," saw these divisions as the "real causes of its permanence and vigour."[111] Faction was the unavoidable outcome of

Virginian politics, see Edward Morgan, "Safety in Numbers: Madison, Hume and the Tenth *Federalist*," *Huntington Library Quarterly* 49 (1986), 95–112. For a response to Morgan and extension of Adair, see Mark Spencer, "Hume and Madison on Faction," *William and Mary Quarterly* 59 (October 2002), 869–96.

[105] Henry St. John Viscount Bolingbroke, *A Dissertation upon Parties* (1733–1734), Letter IV, Vol. 2, 48, in *The Works of Lord Bolingbroke*, Carey and Hart, eds. 4 vols., 1841.

[106] Giovanni Sartori, *Parties and Party Systems: A Framework for Analysis* (New York: Cambridge University Press, 1976), Vol. 1, 7.

[107] Elkins and McKitrick, 13–29; Hofstadter, 1967, 122–8.

[108] Hamilton, "Federalist 9" in *The Federalist*, Jacob E. Cooke, ed. (Middletown, CT: Wesleyan University Press, 1961), 50.

[109] Washington's Farewell Address is one of the more potent indictments of partisan behavior and the conflation of opposition to government with opposition to the republic. It also identifies government as the instantiation of national unity driven to discover and promote the common good; http://www.yale.edu/lawweb/avalon/washing.htm.

[110] In his 1817 inaugural, Monroe noted that "discord does not belong to our system" and that Americans "constitute one great family with a common interest" to have created a government that "has approached perfection; that in respect to it we have no essential improvement to make." In his 1821 inaugural, following an election in which he ran unopposed, Monroe noted how American democracy had overcome the divisions that tore apart historical antecedents. Monroe's association of order, harmony, and republican tranquility with political perfection carries the imprint of Bolingbroke's ideas. See James Monroe, First Inaugural Address, 4 March 1817, http://odur.let.rug.nl/~usa/P/jm5/speeches/monroe1.htm, and James Monroe, Second Inaugural Address, 5 March 1821, http://odur.let.rug.nl/~usa/P/jm5/speeches/monroe2.htm.

[111] David Hume, *History of England from the Invasion of Julius Caesar to the Revolution in 1688*, Foreword by William Todd, 6 vols. (Indianapolis: Liberty Fund, 1983), Vol. 6, 123, and Vol. 4, 290.

democratic government.[112] If partisan divisions were natural, republican governance should manage them without being subsumed and ultimately destroyed by them. Madison saw "the latent causes of faction" to be "sown in the nature of man."[113] Just as Hume had written "to abolish all distinctions of party may not be practicable," Madison contended that to destroy faction would be to destroy liberty.[114]

Consequently, the primary solution Madison offered to the problem of factionalism was to enlarge the republic. In *Federalist 10*, Madison maintains the republican principle that the state must remain disinterested among factions, that "the government [be] *neutral* with respect to the conflicts that arose between and among market competitors."[115] Enlarging the republic would ensure that the agents operating within the federal government would not abandon the republican responsibilities toward common good and neutral good governance to serve the interests of a particular faction. In other words, a representative system in a large territorial expanse would "refine and enlarge" elected leaders' perspectives, thereby nurturing statesmen "whose wisdom may best discern the true interest of their country, and whose patriotism and love of justice will be least likely to sacrifice it to temporary or partial considerations."[116] The structure of representative government would induce politicians to rise above factional politics. *Federalist 10* is not an inchoate celebration of interest-based pluralist politics, but a republican blueprint of how to diminish harmful factionalism.[117] The essay advocated structural means to *minimize* the deleterious effects of factional politics – an essentially republican goal – not to celebrate them.[118]

By the early 1790s, as David Siemers observes, Madison began to abandon his ideas laid out in *Federalist 10*. The years spent representing Virginia in the House of Representatives during the First Congress convinced him that the large size of the republic had not sufficed to guard against the capture of the government by a minority interest unconcerned with the common good.[119] While he continued, in true republican form, to maintain that a

---

[112] Sartori, 7–10, 31.

[113] James Madison, "Federalist No. 10" in *The Federalist*, Jacob E. Cooke, ed. (Middletown, CT: Wesleyan University Press, 1961), 58.

[114] Hume quoted in Spencer, 2002.

[115] Howard Gillman, *The Constitution Besieged* (Durham, NC: Duke University Press, 1993), 29.

[116] James Madison. *Federalist 10*, http://www.constitution.org/fed/federa10.htm.

[117] For characterization of Madison as a pluralist, see Edward Erler, "The Problem of the Public Good in The Federalist," *Polity* 13 (1981), 649–67, and James Conniff, "On the Obsolescence of the General Will: Rousseau, Madison, and the Evolution of Republican Political Thought," *Western Political Quarterly* 28 (1975), 49–51. For a discussion of *Federalist 10* as entrenched in the republican tradition, see Garry Wills, *Explaining America: The Federalist* (New York: Penguin Books, 1981); see also Gillman, 1993, 32.

[118] Andreas Kalyvas and Ira Katznelson, *Liberal Beginnings: Making a Republic for the Moderns* (New York: Cambridge University Press, 2008), 88, 96–105.

[119] Siemers, 108–21.

common good was identifiable and reachable, his sociological theory had not yielded the proper circumstances for its attainment. Madison turned his efforts in the early 1790s to what Siemers calls "cultivating a connective majority," or the idea of motivating the people themselves to right the constitutional ship.[120] In January 1792, Madison penned the first essay of a series, which was published anonymously in the *National Gazette*. The first essay, "Parties," defined the solution to the instability that followed from partisanship to be, ironically, the establishment of political parties such that one party could check the other.[121]

While this essay holds a recognizable kernel of the contemporary two-party system where parties check each other and alternately gain power after winning the favor of a popular majority, Madison's ideas are more similar to Bolingbroke's notion of the favored perpetual majority "country party" battling to cleanse the government of the self-interested aristocratic and minority "court party" in at least two ways. First, Madison's Republicans were, like the "country party," by definition, the protectors of constitutional principles, and therefore the opposition was inherently anti-constitutional. In another essay in that series, "The Union, Who Are Its Real Friends," Madison describes the Federalists as anti-constitutional and as engaged in "arbitrary [constitutional] interpretations and insidious precedents" in their collective effort to "pervert the limited government of the Union."[122] In his most famous essay in the series, "A Candid State of Parties," Madison defines the Federalists as a clearly anti-constitutional opposition. The Federalists, whom he now calls "Anti-republicans," advocated a government "carried only by the pageantry of rank, the influence of money and emoluments, and the terror of military force."[123] By contrast, Madison defined his own Republicans as the only true republicans who believed "that mankind are capable of governing themselves, and ... are naturally offended by every public measure that does not appeal to the understanding and to the general interest of the country."[124] In short, Madison did not advocate a bi-partisan system in which each party had a legitimate and valid but also distinct interpretation of the Constitution; rather, he set one as the true supporters of the Constitution and the other as an insidious and dangerous faction.

Second, drawing on the concept of the necessarily majority "country party," Madison wrote of the Republicans that their "superiority of numbers is so great that no temperate observer of human affairs will be surprised if the issue in the present stance shall be reversed, and the government be administered in the spirit and form approved by the great body of the people."[125] Not only had

---

[120] Ibid., 114.
[121] William Hutchinson et al., *The Papers of James Madison* (Chicago and Charlottesville: University of Chicago Press and University of Virginia Press, 1962–), Vol. 14, 197.
[122] Ibid., Vol. 14, 274–5.
[123] Ibid., Vol. 14, 371.
[124] Ibid.
[125] Ibid., Vol. 14, 372.

the Federalists steered the government in the direction of anti-constitutional policies, but Madison's new Republicans would embrace partisanship to correct the misdirection.

For Madison, such partisanship was not really fostering civil strife as it was serving the common good precisely because it represented the interest of the popular majority. And indeed, once Republicans were in power, plurality of opinion was to be *avoided*. This idea is expressed in another essay in this series, "Consolidation." Here, Madison describes how the partisan action he advocated could eventually subside, that is, party could be temporary once the proper advocates of the Constitution had gained power. In a reversal from his ideas espoused in *Federalist 10*, Madison sees the consolidation of public opinion, not the proliferation of many opposing views, as the source of republican stability: "the greater the concord and confidence throughout the great body of the people, the more readily must they sympathize with each other, the more seasonably can they interpose a common manifestation of their sentiments, the more certainly they will take the alarm at usurpation or oppression, and the more effectually will they consolidate their defense of the public liberty."[126]

In other words, as David Siemers has cogently argued, the theory of territorial enlargement, espoused in *Federalist 10*, failed to insulate the government from the evils of faction. For Madison, no longer did expanding the multiplicity of opinions protect the government from falling under the control of a minority faction preoccupied more with personal gain than with common good. Thus, Madison's advocacy for party was for an institution very different from our contemporary conception. Madison's Republicans were meant to restore constitutional government. The party, by definition, represented the Constitution and thus the principles ratified by the majority of the people. The party could potentially be a temporary if periodically recurrent institution.

As discussed below, Madison's new ideas and his abandonment of theories for managing faction outlined in *Federalist 10* undergirded, to an extent, the anti-party sentiments espoused by Jefferson and his supporters. Indeed, Jefferson advocated such consolidation in his 1800 inaugural speech and hoped his election marked an end to the partisan developments and civil instability preceding his election. Therefore, to the limited extent that Madison's writings do set the foundation for two-party competition – and that foundation is shallow – they were ultimately abandoned by Jefferson and Monroe in favor of the civil tranquility that anti-partyism allegedly provided and supposedly was evident in the "era of good feeling."

II.c. *Sedition and the Kentucky Resolution: Hostility to Court-Centered Interpretation*

Passage of and reaction to the 1798 Sedition Act offers an additional glimpse into how this generation of politicians viewed opposition.[127] The Act had two

---

[126] Ibid., Vol. 14, 138–9.
[127] Riding high in public support following the XYZ Affair and quasi-war with France, Adams secured a variety of policy aims, including some he never asked for, such as the Alien and

parts, and the second part dealing with prosecution for libel has received far more scholarly attention. The first part banned organized and assembled opposition to any passed legislative measure. Federalist Robert Goodloe Harper commented on this aspect of the law, noting that it "has never been complained of, nor has any objection been made to its constitutionality. The objections are confined to the second section."[128] The comment underscores the boundaries of legitimate opposition during this period. It is telling that objection to a law banning open opposition by assembled groups was not considered to be particularly loud.

The Sedition Act's second section criminalized any utterance or publication about Congress or the president considered false or malicious. Highlighting its bias, the act did not criminalize actions that made the vice president, Thomas Jefferson, their target. Fisher Ames praised the law's effect to demarcate the line between whom he considered the friends and the enemies of the Constitution. He belittled Jeffersonian criticism of the law as hypocritical: "The implacable foes of the Constitution – foes before it was made, while it was making, and since, – became full of tender fears lest it should be violated by the alien and sedition law."[129] Ames viewed anti-Federalism and Jeffersonianism of a piece, as illegitimate opposition aiming to unmake the constitutional order.[130]

The Sedition Act, while seemingly an assault on First Amendment speech rights, is consistent with Federalist theories on representation and civic republican fears of civil instability. Antagonism toward the law did *not* stem from its curbing of speech. Rather, Jeffersonians challenged the law because it represented an aggrandizement of national power at the expense of state sovereignty; many Jeffersonians harbored the same fears of federal consolidation against the states to which Brutus had given voice.[131] Jefferson himself was not

Sedition Acts of 1798. As Elkins and McKitrick note, "there is no evidence that a campaign against sedition was one of Adams's primary concerns." (590)

[128] Robert Goodloe Harper, "Letter to His Constituents," 10 February 1798, in Noble E. Cunningham, Jr., ed., *Circular Letters of Congressmen to Their Constituents, 1789–1829* (Chapel Hill: University of North Carolina Press, 1978), 146–7.

[129] Fisher Ames to Christopher Gore, 18 December 1798, in W. B. Allen, ed., *Works of Fisher Ames*, 2 vols. (Indianapolis: Liberty Classics, 1983), Vol. 2, 1302–3.

[130] Jeffersonians did not remain silent. In particular, James Callender, a pamphleteer, attacked Adams for this Act. Callender's pamphlet, *The Prospect before Us*, insinuated that Adams stole the presidency in 1796 and that Hamilton's financial plans would bring the new nation once again under British domination. Callender did not hedge on his objective; his pamphlet begins, "The design of this book is to exhibit the multiplied corruptions of the Federal Government, and more especially of the President, Mr. Adams." (1) He characterized Federalist members of Congress as "Aristocrats." He dismissed the XYZ affair as a Federalist conspiracy: "By sending these ambassadors to Paris, Mr. Adams and his British faction designed to do nothing but mischief. This is, and it always has been, the universal opinion of the republican party." (141). James Callender, *The Prospect before Us* (Richmond: M. Jones, S. Pheasants, and J Lyon, 1800). As discussed in Part IV, Callender was tried and imprisoned for sedition in a trial presided over by Samuel Chase, and Chase's conduct provided the basis of several articles of impeachment.

[131] As Mark Graber has argued, opposition to federal law and judicial support for such law stemmed less from fears about countermajoritarianism than from fears of federal

opposed to state-level sedition laws, testifying to his own entrenchment in a system that refused to concede the legitimacy of organized opposition.[132]

To oppose the Sedition Act, Jefferson and Madison anonymously penned the Kentucky and Virginia Resolutions, respectively, and had them introduced through third parties. Both argued that the act was an unconstitutional federal infringement upon state sovereignty. They articulated a theory of constitutional review of federal law by state legislatures thereby enabling states to reject laws. Their logic seemingly reversed that of Madison's national veto, which had been proposed at the Philadelphia convention, and the Constitution's supremacy clause.

While Madison's theory limited state-level review to be an expression of opinion with only educational impact, Jefferson's resolution was more radical. It hinted toward nullification.[133] Jefferson argued that the Constitution was a compact joined by several states in order to constitute "a general government for special purposes – delegated to that government certain definite powers, reserving, each State to itself, the residuary mass of right to their own self-government; and that whensoever the general government assumes undelegated powers, its acts are unauthoritative, void, and of no force." More importantly, Jefferson claimed that this general government "was not made the exclusive or final judge of the extent of the powers delegated to itself; since that would have made its discretion, and not the Constitution, the measure of its powers; but that, as in all other cases of compact among powers having no common judge, each party has an equal right to judge for itself, as well of infractions as of the mode and measure of redress."[134] His characterization of the relationship between state governments and the federal government is emblematic of assumptions of regime unity and that the federal branches would allegedly

consolidation of power against the states. See Graber, "James Buchanan as Savior? Judicial Power, Political Fragmentation, and the Failed 1831 Repeal of Section 25," *Oregon Law Review* 88 (2009), 95–155. Jefferson shared such concerns: "After twenty years' confirmation of the federated system by the voice of the nation, declared through the medium of elections, the judiciary on every occasion [is] still driving us into consolidation." Jefferson to Spencer Roane, 6 September 1819, in *The Writings of Jefferson*, Albert Ellery Bergh, Richard Holland Johnson, and Andrew A. Lipscomb, eds. (Washington, DC: Thomas Jefferson Memorial Association of the United States, 1900), Vol. 15, 212.

[132] Martin, 124–7. On Jefferson's support for sedition law, see Leonard Levy, *Jefferson and Civil Liberties: The Darker Side* (Cambridge, MA: Harvard University Press, 1963), 46–8.

[133] Cornell, 238–45.

[134] http://www.constitution.org/cons/kent1798.htm. Virginia and Kentucky were not the only states to challenge federal supremacy, although at the time of their resolutions no other state signed on. Yet most states, even as they might illustrate "a steady stream of intermittent but fierce resistance" to judicial authority, took a more passive route to undermining judicial legitimacy, which was to ignore rulings. Leslie Goldstein, *Constituting Federal Sovereignty: The European Union in Comparative Context* (Baltimore: Johns Hopkins University Press, 2001), 31. Local noncompliance was enabled by the judiciary's lack of formal enforcement mechanisms and by the underdeveloped national infrastructure. The route of noncompliance remained open to states and "the Court acquiesced in the party's disobedience." Ruth Wedgwood, "Cousin Humphrey," *Constitutional Commentary* 14 (1997), 266.

work in tandem to absorb the power of the states. To maintain their own sovereignty, according to this logic, the states had to assert their own power as an arbitrator of constitutional meaning since federal officials would act in a corrupt fashion to concentrate power and thereby undermine the Constitution.

The Kentucky Resolution highlighted the legitimacy of multiple *interpreters* of the Constitution, but it did not concede the legitimacy of multiple *interpretations*. Again, the meaning was fixed, singular, discoverable, and transparent; there could only be one. Alternatives, such as that which would have supported the Sedition Act, were contrary to constitutional principle. In the Resolution, Jefferson advocated state authority to interpret the Constitution; the document was more focused on vertical relationships in federalism than the horizontal separation of powers. Jefferson spoke to the horizontal relationship in a later letter to Abigail Adams in which he summarized his constitutional interpretive authority relative to the other federal branches: "You seem to think it devolved on the judges to decide on the validity of the sedition law. But nothing in the Constitution has given them a right to decide for the Executive, more than the Executive to decide for them. Both magistrates are equally independent in the sphere of action assigned to them."[135] He thereby extended his theory of interpretive authority to include all public officers in both the state and federal governments.

That Federalists responded to open dissent with measures to squash it altogether and that Jeffersonians would articulate arguments to ignore judicial rulings testify to the Founding generation's grounding in a political theory of republican unity and stability. Thus, Jefferson's logic is similar to Hamilton's to the extent that each relies on the people as sovereign and government officials as only representative of that sovereignty. In essence, Jefferson's logic remains that of the Framers' notion of popular sovereignty, but taken to the extreme of disrupting federalism's vertical hierarchy in order to secure constitutional principles from what Jefferson viewed as a dangerous minority aristocratic faction. In short, the irony is that if opposition's legitimacy and loyalty are not granted, what rationally follows is a constitutional theory that promotes either the interpretive chaos of Jeffersonian departmentalism or an assault on the judiciary so radical that it may exceed its own constitutional bounds. Jeffersonians would proceed on the latter path.

---

[135] Andrew A. Lipscomb, ed., *Writings of Thomas Jefferson* (Washington, DC: Thomas Jefferson Memorial Association, 1903), Vol. 11, 50–1. The Kentucky Resolution stipulated that state governments could nullify federal law if they considered such law unconstitutional: "this commonwealth [Kentucky] considers the federal union, upon the terms and for the purposes specified in the late compact, as conducive to the liberty and happiness of the several states ... the several states who formed that instrument, being sovereign and independent, have the unquestionable right to judge of its infraction; and that a nullification, by those sovereignties, of all unauthorized acts done under colour of that instrument, is the rightful remedy." Jefferson's letter to Abigail Adams suggests a similar sentiment. Both indicate that presidential interpretive authority is implied in the text of the Constitution and did not specify this power as deriving from outside it. For the text of the Resolution, see http://www.yale.edu/lawweb/avalon/kenres.htm.

II.d. 1800: A Peaceful Transition but No Acceptance
of Opposition Legitimacy or Loyalty

While the 1800 election marked a peaceful transfer of power after a highly contentious election, it did not herald the emergence of any notion of legitimate or loyal opposition. In fact, the eventual outcome was preceded by at least a year of rumors and threats of violence and insurrection.[136] Virginia threatened secession if Jefferson were not selected once the choice was thrown to the House of Representatives. Some of Jefferson's supporters indicated that if Jefferson were not the victor, they would call a new constitutional convention. The governor of Pennsylvania informed Jefferson that he could muster 20,000 militia troops to take the newly constructed White House if Adams refused to vacate.[137] Jefferson absolved himself of responsibility for any actions by his supporters, telling Adams that there might be violence if Federalists attempted to hold the presidency.[138] Adams wrote, "civil war was expected."[139]

Having themselves once been the opposition, Jeffersonians did not translate that experience into a more cordial perspective toward the ousted Federalists. Jefferson, like Madison, continued to view Federalism as a dangerous aristocratic minority.[140] The Jeffersonian view on Federalism's illegitimacy was evident in two ways. First, more extreme Jeffersonians like John Randolph, William Branch Giles, and James Monroe called for the removal of Federalists from political appointments altogether. Randolph, for example, interpreted the 1800 election outcome as a first step toward the restoration of the republic: "we think that the great work is only begun: and that without substantial reform, we have little reason to congratulate ourselves on the mere change of men."[141] Second, more moderate Jeffersonians like Madison, Pierce Butler, Alexander Dallas, and Albert Gallatin sought to absorb Federalists, essentially consolidating public opinion – as Madison had described in his series of essays on parties – by cutting the extremes of both factions from political power. Each strategy – to remove Federalists or to absorb them "inducing the mass of the Federal citizens to make a common cause with [Jeffersonians]" – exemplifies the Founding generation's underdeveloped sense of legitimate or loyal opposition organized as a party.[142]

---

[136] By 1799, Jeffersonians in Richmond, Virginia, so feared Federalist power that they stockpiled arms and organized militia to prepare for armed resistance against the Adams administration. See Jane Elsmere, *Justice Samuel Chase* (Muncie, IN: Janevar, 1980), 117.

[137] Ferling, 188.

[138] Sharp, 267–71.

[139] John Adams to James Lloyed, 6 February 1815 in *Works of John Adams, Second President of the United States: With a Life of the Author*, Charles Frances Adams, ed. (Boston: Little Brown, 1850–56), Vol. 10, 115.

[140] Peter Onuf, *Jefferson's Empire: The Language of American Nationhood* (Charlottesville: University of Virginia Press, 2001), 85–88.

[141] John Randolph to Joseph Hooper Nicholson, 26 July 1801, Nicholson Papers, Library of Congress.

[142] Albert Gallatin to Thomas Jefferson, 10 August 1801, in Henry Adams, ed. *The Writings of Albert Gallatin* (Philadelphia, 1879), Vol. 1, 33.

While Jefferson's peace-making statement in his inaugural – "We have called by different names brethren of the same principle. We are all republicans; we are all federalists" – may suggest reconciliation, it should not be construed to imply the legitimacy of Federalism or party competition.[143] Jefferson's private statements regarding the suppression of party-based opposition were more apt: "Nothing shall be spared on my part to obliterate the traces of party and *consolidate* the nation if it can be done without abandonment of principle."[144] Thus, the inaugural's theme did less to concede the legitimacy of the Federalist perspective and more to explore whether and how to bring Federalists into the Republican fold. Such reconciliation and consolidation still aimed to do away with party rancor altogether, or in Hofstadter's terms, Jefferson contended that the two groups could be "not so much reconciled as merged, and merged under his own standards."[145]

Some Federalists like Robert Goodloe Harper hoped Jefferson's ascendance was temporary and took comfort in the tone of Jefferson's inaugural: "The speech which he delivered previous to taking the oath was well calculated to inspire these sentiments [of respect], and to afford the hope of such an administration, as may conduce to his own glory and the public good. Before the evening all was quiet, as if no change had taken place."[146] Yet in this same letter, Harper acknowledged the need for vigilance and characterized opposition against Jefferson as necessary to save the republic, essentially viewing the Jeffersonians as misguided. He spoke of his fellow Federalists as saviors of the public good:

> Should they [Federalists] be compelled ultimately to oppose the administration, by its adopting systems and principles essentially hostile to the public good, they will commence their opposition with reluctance, support it with energy, and conduct it with candour, dignity, and effect: that they will not sully the fair reputation which they have obtained, nor dishonour the noble principles on which they have acted, by resorting to those factions and profligate arts which have been employed against themselves ... that relying on their known and acknowledged superiority in talents, services, knowledge, and character, they will always spurn the little arts of which inferior men sometimes obtain success.[147]

[143] Thomas Jefferson, "First Inaugural Address," Washington, DC, 4 March 1801. Accessed at http://www.yale.edu/lawweb/avalon/presiden/inaug/jefinau1.htm.

[144] Jefferson, quoted in Noble E. Cunningham, *Jeffersonian Republicans in Power: Party Operations, 1801–09* (Chapel Hill: University of North Carolina Press, 1963), 8. Emphasis added.

[145] Hofstadter, 1967, 154.

[146] Robert Goodloe Harper, "A Letter Containing a short view of the political principles and the system of the Federalists, and of the situation in which they found and left government" (Washington, DC, 5 March 1801) in *Selected Works of Robert Goodloe Harper* (Baltimore: O. H. Neilson, Market Street, 1814), 324. Massachusetts Historical Society. Call Number E187.

[147] Ibid., 324–5.

The ideas of civic tranquility, fear of faction, and illegitimacy of opposition are evident. Harper denigrates the Jeffersonians as "inferior men" and characterizes Federalist opposition as patriotic, virtuous, and necessarily temporary to effect a restoration of constitutional principles. By 1803, rather than concede Jefferson's legitimacy, the more ardent Federalists considered seceding from the Union and forming a "Northern confederacy."[148] Consideration of exit is, by definition, the clearest expression that the opposition is not granted governing authority.[149] John Quincy Adams wrote that the secessionist impulse was grounded in a fundamental mistrust of the Jeffersonian majority:

> But the acquisition of Louisiana, although the immediate occasion of this project of disunion, was not its only, nor even its most operative, cause. The election of Mr. Jefferson to the presidency was.... [I]t was the victory of professed democracy over Federalism.... The party overthrown was the whole Federal party, – the disciples of Washington, the framers and supporters of the Constitution of the United States.[150]

The telling sentence – "The party overthrown was ... the framers and supporters of the Constitution of the United States" – implies that Jeffersonians opposed the Constitution. The stakes of politics, given the illegitimacy of opposition, were correspondingly high. Without achieving what Jefferson called his "most important object ... to consolidate the nation once more into a single mass, in sentiment & in object," politicians envisioned a future where "parties will continue always equally to divide the nation; every Federalist will become a conspirator; every Republican will be a tyrant; and each general election will involve the hazard of a civil war."[151]

How does this perspective toward opposition connect to the underlying logic of hostility toward judicial power? In his study of this period, Larry Kramer dismisses what he considers a semantic debate among historians and political scientists about whether the Federalists or Jeffersonians were parties, because, in his estimation, they became so in spite of themselves:

---

[148] Samuel Chase wrote to Gouverneur Morris that secession and establishment of a new government was the only option: "There is but one event (which will probably never happen) in which I will interfere with politics. I mean the establishment of a new government. I believe nothing can save the present one from dissolution. Some events, as war with France, may delay it for a few years. The seeds are sown and they ripen daily." Chase to Morris, 6 March 1803, Samuel Chase Correspondence, Maryland Historical Society.

[149] On the relationship between right to exit and right to voice dissent, see Albert Hirschman, *Exit, Voice, and Loyalty*, 2nd ed. (Cambridge: Harvard University Press, 2006). On the connection of this dynamic to loyal opposition, see Ian Shapiro, *The State of Democratic Theory* (Princeton: Princeton University Press, 2006), 90–1.

[150] John Quincy Adams, "Reply to the Appeal of the Massachusetts Federalists," in *Documents relating to New England Federalism, 1800–1815*, Henry Adams, ed. (Boston: B. Franklin, 1877), 149.

[151] Thomas Jefferson to David Denniston and James Cheetham, 6 June 1801, Jefferson Papers, Library of Congress. Alexander J. Dallas to Albert Gallatin, 14 June 1801, Gallatin Papers, New York Historical Society.

> It is when we focus on these concrete manifestations of party politics that
> we see the irrelevance of the endless debate among historians and political
> scientists about whether these first parties really were "parties" or really
> were a "party system." ... However much they hated what they were doing,
> they did it. However much they longed to undo it, they failed. It may have
> taken until the 1840s or 1850s for modern attitudes about parties to develop.
> But the crucial practices of party politics – the use of stable institutionalized
> means to recruit candidates, organize campaigns, and arrange the govern-
> ment within to implement policy – were all in place by 1800. And it is those
> practices, however grudgingly followed, that mattered.[152]

Yet distinguishing among parties, party systems, and partisanship and more
fully considering the attitudes taken toward political party and stable and permanent opposition are *critical* to understanding the ferocity of the Jeffersonian
assault on the Court. As the quoted passage indicates, Kramer does not address
the conceptual shift in perception of opposition that had not yet occurred
because he views the attack on the Court to be about the structural legitimacy of judicial review. This view is too narrow. Rather, attacking the Court
is a symptom of a more general dynamic of attack on opposition. The legitimacy of courts and the legitimacy of parties were inextricably connected
through this disposition toward open opposition as disloyal and illegitimate.
To skim over the development of changing perspectives toward opposition is
to lose sight of larger ideational developments in which anti-Court attacks
were embedded.

By ignoring views toward opposition, accounts of this era's judicial politics –
beginning with the repeal of the Judiciary Act of 1801, gaining steam with
Marbury, and culminating in Chase's impeachment – have tended to focus on
the legitimacy of judicial review and alleged articulations of judicial supremacy.[153] But Jeffersonians were not attacking judicial review; they were attacking what they considered a repudiated opposition. They were attacking the
very idea that the federal branches of government could be divided against
themselves and that constitutional interpretations might vary. They sought to
construct and maintain that very same image of unity that underlay the reti-
cence of judges to contradict Congress and their plea to Washington to fore-
stall such displays of disunity. By giving a fuller accounting of this perspective
on opposition, these hostilities can now be understood not as attacks on the
structural legitimacy of judicial review and the alleged democratic deficit of
the judiciary, but as expression of broader concerns regarding an opposition's
right to rule.

---

[152] Kramer, 167.
[153] See William Rehnquist, *Grand Inquests: The Historic Impeachments of Justice Samuel Chase
and President Andrew Johnson* (New York: Harper Perennial, 1999); Robert McCloskey, *The
American Supreme Court*, 2nd ed., revised by S. Levinson (Chicago: University of Chicago
Press, 1994); Robert Clinton, *Marbury v. Madison and Judicial Review* (Lawrence: University
Press of Kansas, 1989).

III. The Jeffersonian Assault on the Judiciary

As this chapter has thus far demonstrated, Federalists understood judicial review as constitutionally provided and many Anti-Federalists and Jeffersonians agreed. An independent judiciary was part of the conservative drive against legislative excesses exhibited by the states under the Articles of Confederation.[154] Removed from popular selection and extending deep into localities, this judiciary would promote supremacy of federal law, quell internal dissent, especially in the absence of a standing military, and secure fundamental liberties, namely, a regime of contracts and property rights.[155] But, Jefferson interpreted his election in 1800 as connoting a fundamental shift in politics, as a "revolution."[156] Federalists did not, and that disagreement forced the issue of what the appropriate parameters of judicial authority should be in a democratic republic.

As reviewed earlier, the Framers – and Jefferson – viewed judges as representatives of popular sovereignty. As such, together with the elected branches, judges served as part of a unified regime that would steer the Constitution clear of civil strife. Under these assumptions, judges, Supreme Court Justice Samuel Chase foremost among them, took it as their role to speak out against Jefferson and his supporters. They saw his leadership as supported by a dangerous party-like apparatus and thus as inimical to the Constitution itself. But such judicial public speech would amount to a repudiation of the victors of 1800 and thus for Jeffersonians would not only betray the democratic impulses motivating the revolution and the Constitution but also showcase the open opposition considered so de-stabilizing to regime unity. Judicial interpretation – such as Chase's repeated rulings upholding the Sedition Act – represented only infidelity in the face of constitutional principles that Jefferson held as reaffirmed by his election in 1800.

Jeffersonians responded with various measures that would either bring in line or silence what they saw as an aristocratic factional minority threat entrenched in the judiciary. The impeachment of Samuel Chase in 1805 represented the last stage in a series of hostilities between the Supreme Court and the elected branches triggered by the passage of the Judiciary Act of 1801. These included the repeal of that act in 1802 (the Repeal Act), limitations

---

[154] Many of the Framers considered the 1780s to exemplify the worst tendencies of legislative government; state governments undermined contracts by supporting wage earners, debtors, and small farmers through issuing debt relief, price controls, and paper currency. Such actions betrayed basic republican ideas against class legislation and maintaining a neutral state. Cathy Matson and Peter Onuf, *A Union of Interests: Political and Economic Thought in Revolutionary America* (Lawrence: University Press of Kansas, 1990); Isaac Kramnick, "The 'Great National Discussion': The Discourse of Politics in 1787," *William and Mary Quarterly* 45 (September 1988): 3–32.

[155] Wood, 1996, 12–13; Gillman, 1993, 22–33.

[156] Thomas Jefferson to Spencer Roane, 6 September 1819, in *The Writings of Thomas Jefferson*, Vol. 12, 136.

placed on the Court's convening calendar by the Judiciary Act of 1802, a publicity campaign and debate on a memorial to Congress drafted by thirteen ousted federal appellate judges, the Supreme Court rulings in *Marbury v. Madison* and *Stuart v. Laird* in 1803, and the impeachment of federal Judge Pickering in 1804.

III.a. *Framing the Reform of 1801: Civil Stability versus Party Threat*

The Judiciary Act of 1801 is often characterized as nothing more than a measure of partisan entrenchment akin to Franklin Roosevelt's 1937 Court-packing scheme. The outgoing Federalist politicians drafted its provisions to harness judicial power to maintain their policy interests.[157] If that assessment is accurate, then the radical nature of the Jeffersonian response – repealing the act (an action which could be considered unconstitutional to the extent that judges who had *not* violated standards of good behavior lost their positions) and embarking on a strategy of systematic impeachments – only serves to highlight how illegitimate such harnessing was taken to be in a context when opposition within regime was viewed as so threatening. Additionally, the Federalist view toward the illegitimacy of the Jeffersonian faction and the threat of civil strife it portended suggests that this measure was understood by political actors at the time as qualitatively different from contemporary notions of partisan entrenchment to secure policy aims.[158] If Federalists took refuge in the judiciary, they did so, in their terms, to secure the Constitution from the party-based actions of an illegitimate opposition, from a faction that had already threatened violence while the House of Representatives attempted to resolve the election.

The federal judiciary, as established by the Judiciary Act of 1789, was a vertical system of district courts at its base; circuit courts of appeal, which were presided over by one district judge and two Supreme Court justices, in the middle; and the Supreme Court at its apex. The six Supreme Court justices rode a particular circuit and met in the national capital twice per year. Circuit-riding was onerous: one judge refused Washington's nomination because he could not "resolve to spend six Months in the Year ... on Roads at Taverns chiefly and often in Situations where the most moderate Desires are disappointed."[159] The justices pushed to end circuit-riding in the early 1790s, and a compromise measure was ratified so that only one Supreme Court justice and one district judge would compose a respective circuit court.[160] The Judiciary Act of 1801 put an end to circuit-riding responsibilities, allowing

[157] See Bernard Schwartz, *A History of the Supreme Court* (New York: Oxford University Press, 1994), 30.

[158] Examples are examined in later chapters.

[159] Thomas Johnson to George Washington, 16 January 1793, quoted in Maeva Marcus, ed., *The Documentary History of the Supreme Court of the United States, 1789–1800* (New York: Columbia University Press, 1985), Vol. 1, 344.

[160] Kathryn Turner, "Federalist Policy and the Judiciary Act of 1801," *William and Mary Quarterly* 22 (January 1965), 3–32.

the justices to sit permanently in the nation's capital. The law also established sixteen federal judgeships; if the justices were not riding circuit, judges were needed to fill gaps left by their absence.

Much of the 1801 Act had been considered as early as 1790. Characterizing its reforms as partisan measures by a lame duck president and Congress is therefore somewhat inaccurate. And the necessary addition of circuit judges once circuit-riding was eliminated fit with the Federalist view of the judiciary as a republican schoolmaster that would minimize opposition and promote national unity.[161] In 1799, Hamilton proposed a larger judiciary (along with a larger army) to curb "a rising tide of rebellion in Virginia and Kentucky."[162] These two institutions would "surround the Constitution with more ramparts and ... disconcert the schemes of its enemies."[163] Federalist Theodore Sedgwick contended that an expanded judiciary could be a weapon against Jeffersonian threat: "We ought to spread out the judicial so as to render the justice of the nation acceptable to the people, to aid the national economy, to overawe the licentious, and to punish the guilty."[164] The Federalist newspaper, *Columbian Centinnel*, made this link explicit:

> If free government can ever be maintained without a standing army it can only be effected by a firm, independent, and extensive Judiciary ... it has been the constant endeavor of the Federalists, to extend the protecting power of the judiciary to every part of the union, and to every case provided in the Constitution. Unhappily a mistaken timidity, and a disposition too prevalent, during the first years of the existence of our government, to conciliate the opposition, induced the First Congress not to invest the Federal Judiciary with the powers which the constitution authorized them to bestow. The error has been deeply felt and sincerely lamented.[165]

In other words, the Judiciary Act of 1801 not only fulfilled a long-observed and lamented logistical failing of the 1789 Act. Its advocates also conceptualized it in republican terms of preventing civil unrest.

Almost immediately after President Adams signed the 1801 Judiciary Act on 13 February, Jefferson's supporters discussed its repeal.[166] Jeffersonians and Federalists characterized the 1801 Act and the 1802 Repeal Act, respectively, as wholly illegitimate. Each law was characterized in the same terms: as destroying judicial independence, as motivated by the dangerous spirit of

---

[161] According to Richard Ellis, "there is substantial if indirect evidence to indicate that federal judges were expected not only to bring home the authority of the national government to the people, but also, by means of their charges to grand juries to inculcate in their listeners an understanding for the intricacies of self-government and a respect for the judiciary." (12)

[162] Turner, 9.

[163] Alexander Hamilton to Jonathan Dayton, 1799, in Henry Cabot Lodge, ed., *The Works of Alexander Hamilton* (New York, 1904), Vol. 10, 336.

[164] Theodore Sedgewick to Rufus King, 15 November 1799, in Charles King, ed., *The Life and Correspondence of Rufus King* (New York, 1894–1900), Vol. 3, 146–7.

[165] *Columbian Centinel* (Boston), 14 January 1801.

[166] Turner, 15–21.

party, and as fundamentally threatening to the principles of the Constitution and national stability. Some Jeffersonians saw the enlarged judiciary as the seat of illegitimate opposition and called for its complete abolition and re-building. Senator William Giles wrote to Jefferson once the election had been resolved:

> What concerns us most is the situation of the Judiciary as now organized. It is constantly asserted that the Revolution is incomplete, as long as that strong fortress is in possession of the enemy; and it is surely a most singular circumstance that the public sentiment should have forced itself into the Legislative and Executive Department, and that the Judiciary should not only not acknowledge its influence, but should pride itself in resisting its will, under the misapplied idea of "independence." ... No remedy is competent to redress the evil system, but an absolute repeal of the whole Judiciary and terminating the present offices and creating a new system.[167]

In this letter, Giles characterized Federalist judges as "the enemy" further illustrating that opposition was not legitimate. He also considered Federalism to have been wholly repudiated by the recent election. As such, he stipulated that the judiciary must give way to the demands of the elected branches thereby testifying to a united regime theory of government. Finally, he wanted the judiciary to be re-constructed not eliminated. This concession is a crucial admission that the structure of an unelected judiciary was not the object of Giles's ire. Put more generally, the legitimacy of judicial review and the legitimacy of opposition are tightly intertwined, and when disaggregated, the illegitimacy of opposition remains as the motivating impetus for Jeffersonian animus, not the illegitimacy of structurally unelected judges.

The Federalist *Gazette of the United States* defended the judiciary against Jeffersonian actions: "It was, clearly, the design of the framers of the constitution, and of the respective state conventions which ratified it, that such should be the stability of our judiciary, that it should never be affected by the changes and revolutions to which, from the nature of the government, the other departments would be subject."[168] In this reading, the proposed repeal would not reform the judiciary. It would mold it to the partisan whims of a party-driven faction to the detriment of the Constitution.

For Jeffersonians, the repeal would accomplish the opposite. It would remove the influence of party from the judiciary. The Federalists, as Madison had written in his 1792 essays, were a corrupt aristocratic minority. By expanding the judiciary for members of its own faction, Federalists had ignored the people's voice. In re-structuring the judiciary, they had denied its representative function. The Repeal Act would be part of a larger process by Jeffersonians to re-set the judiciary as representative of the popular sovereignty and righting the constitutional ship. The Philadelphia *Aurora*

---

[167] William Branch Giles to Thomas Jefferson, 1 June 1801, Jefferson Papers, Library of Congress, quoted in Ellis, *The Jeffersonian Crisis*, 20–1.
[168] Philadelphia *Gazette of the United States*, 9 November 1801.

emphasized re-establishing "the moderate principles which subsisted in the administration of Washington," before factional divisions had created such potential for civil conflict: "It has been proved that the Judiciary system, as it then stood, was equal to all the purposes of distributive justice, and yet some who pretend to be republicans are not satisfied to the return of the old system, but must have more than enough.... How many years will it take to eradicate the seeds of discord sown in the days of John Adams?"[169] Each side saw the other's action as motivated by partisan spirit. Both framed their objectives in republican language and logic and as avoiding civil war.

On 6 January 1802, John Breckenridge, who had introduced Jefferson's Kentucky Resolution, now introduced a bill repealing the 1801 Judiciary Act.[170] The Repeal Act eliminated sixteen judgeships even though the standard of good behavior had not been violated; it set the judicial system back to the 1789 design.[171] The Federalist press treated the move as ominous; one editorial declared after the bill's passage that "the Constitution is no more."[172] Another declared the "JUDICIARY LOST!"[173] Representative Roger Griswold of Connecticut echoed the sentiment: "The fate of the Judiciary I consider settled – the independence of the Department is to be prostrated, and this invasion of the Constitution is probably to be followed by other invasions which will mark the Constitution the leaves of an Old Almanac."[174]

As evidence for their claim of Jeffersonian intent to wreck the Constitution, Federalist senators insisted that the elimination of judgeships violated the parameters of Article III since such judgeships were understood as a property right. Senator John Ross of Pennsylvania made this point directly: "Whatever its title may be, the bill itself is nothing less than an act of the Legislature removing from office *all* the judges of *all* the circuit courts of the United States. It is a declaration that those officers hold their offices at your will and pleasure.... This is a direct and palpable violation of the Constitution."[175] Ross further argued that if the bill passed, the Supreme Court would declare it unconstitutional, thereby verifying that Federalists fully understood the logic of judicial review *before* Marshall articulated it in *Marbury*:

> There is no analogy in this respect between our national Government and that of Great Britain. There an act of Parliament can change the constitution. Here the written Constitution, established by the people, restrains the

---

[169] Philadelphia *Aurora*, 4 February 1802.

[170] *Journal of the Senate*, 6 January 1802, 166.

[171] The constitutionality of eliminating the sixteen federal judgeships was never fully arbitrated. As detailed later, the case of *Stuart v. Laird* addressed whether Supreme Court justices could ride circuit, but the ruling avoided the question of whether the newly established circuit judgeships could be eliminated.

[172] Washington *Federalist*, 3 March 1801, quoted in Ellis, 57.

[173] Philadelphia *Gazette of the United States*, 23 January 1802.

[174] Roger Griswold to Fanny Griswold, 26 February 1802, Griswold Family Papers, Box 3, Manuscripts and Archives, Yale University.

[175] *Annals of Congress*, Senate, 7th Congress, 1st Session, 3 February 1802, 163.

> Legislature to the exercise of delegated power, our Judiciary, sworn to sup-
> port the Constitution, must declare that the great *irrepealable statute* made
> by the people shall restrain and control the unauthorized acts of agents who
> have exceeded the limits of a special authority.[176]

Ross's statement also suggests the extent to which the Founding generation understood judicial authority to rest on the basis of representing the original act of public sovereignty. Ultimately, the Supreme Court would address the constitutionality of the Repeal Act in *Stuart v. Laird*. However, its ruling would not accord with Federalist expectations.[177]

III.b. *The Justices' Failed Strike Plan and Their Concession*

Shortly after the Repeal Act passed, Justice Chase wrote to Chief Justice Marshall to argue that the Act was unconstitutional and the Court should declare as much. He suggested the proper action would be to advise Jefferson against the law as their predecessors had Washington in the *Hayburn* case:

> I think it would be proper to lay the result [the Repeal Act] before the
> President; as our predecessors did in a familiar Case.... It is a great doubt
> with me whether the Circuit Court, established by the Law, can be abol-
> ished; but I have no doubt, that the Circuit Judges cannot directly or indi-
> rectly, be deprived of their offices, or commissions, or salaries, during their
> lives, unless only on impeachment for, and conviction of high Crimes &
> Misdemeanors.... I admit that Congress may, in their discretion, increase
> the number of judges in any of the Courts established; they may also lessen
> the number of Judges in such Courts on the death of any of them; they may
> diminish or enlarge or contract the extent of the Districts or the Circuits; and
> they may require additional Judicial Duties, of any of the Judges, agreeably
> to the provision of the Constitution; But still the Judges and their offices must
> remain independent of the Legislature.... The Judicial power is most feeble
> indeed; and if the Legislative and Executive united to impair or to destroy its
> Constitutional rights, they must be irresistible, unless the great body of the
> people take the alarm and give their aid.[178]

That Chase would advise consultation with Jefferson *before* the president signed the law again reflects a continued republican wariness of open conflict within a governing regime. And even Chase, the staunchest of Federalists, acknowledged the constitutionality of congressional prerogatives to manipulate judicial power.

Chase sought a meeting with his fellow justices, but it would not occur because Congress passed the Judiciary Act of 1802. This Act reduced the Court's convening calendar from twice per year to once in February.[179] The

---

[176] Ibid., 164.
[177] See discussion of *Stuart v. Laird* in Part III.c of this chapter.
[178] Samuel Chase to John Marshall, 24 April 1802, Baltimore, MD, Samuel Chase Correspondence, Maryland Historical Society, Call Number 1234, Item ID: 000000003265.
[179] Ellis, 59–60. The Court would not convene until February 1803, over a year since it met in December 1801.

legislation prevented the justices from sitting together in a timely fashion to react to the Repeal Act. The passage of the 1802 Judiciary Act is itself evidence that Jeffersonians understood that the Court could overrule the Repeal Act. It thereby indicates, if obliquely, their own understanding of the legitimate possibility of judicial review. Indeed, once the Repeal Act was passed, members of Congress waited to see what the Court would do. Federalist Representative Griswold summed up the reason for patience: "The only hope in correcting [this] usurpation remains with the Judges themselves, who may perhaps still pronounce the Act to be void.... My own opinion is, that the Legislature will give way because there is not nerve enough to persevere, & because many of those who have voted in the present bill, still admit that the Courts may pronounce on the Constitutionality of the Laws."[180] Griswold believed the Jeffersonians conceded the legitimacy of judicial review; yet he underestimated their desire to eliminate opposition and did not predict the 1802 Judiciary Act.

The strategic purpose of the 1802 Judiciary Act did not escape Chase. He saw it as an attempt to squash Federalism, which he refers to as "the friends of the Constitution," implying that Jeffersonians were the enemies. He wrote to Justice William Patterson:

> The object of postponing the meeting of the Judges of the Supreme Court until February is obvious.... I believe a day of severe trial is fast approaching for the friends of the Constitution and we I fear must be the principal actors, and maybe sufferers therein.... [I]f the *office* of circuit Judge is *full*, and it is so if not taken away by the Law act, we are to made instruments to destroy the independence of the Judiciary.[181]

Chase identified the question: was the Repeal Act constitutional if it removed the newly appointed circuit judges without impeaching them? If the justices agreed to resume riding circuit, they would essentially answer that question in a way that Chase warned would all but confirm legislative supremacy.

The justices considered going on strike. Marshall wrote to Justice Patterson: "the constitution requires distinct appointments & commissions for the Judges of the inferior courts from those of the supreme court."[182] In other words, the 1801 Act corrected an error of the 1789 Act; the Repeal Act only re-established the mistake. Marshall also acknowledged, "the consequences of refusing to carry the law into effect may be very serious," which suggests that he understood that Jeffersonians viewed his Court's rulings as problematic in the wake of the recent election.[183] Justice Chase, by contrast, was less tentative:

---

[180] Roger Griswold to Oliver Wollcott, 5 March 1802, Oliver Wolcott Papers, Box 11, Folder 10, Connecticut Historical Society.

[181] Samuel Chase to William Patterson, 6 April 1802, Maryland Historical Society, Samuel Chase Correspondence.

[182] Marshall, quoted in Bruce Ackerman, *The Failure of the Founding Fathers* (Cambridge, MA: Belknap Press of Harvard University, 2005), 165.

[183] Ibid. Ellis posits that Marshall was always against the strike. He cites a letter from Marshall to Patterson dated 3 May 1802 in which Marshall agrees with Justice Washington's

> I think (as at present advised) that a judge of the Supreme Court cannot accept and act under a Commission as Judge of a Circuit Court.... It appears to me, that Congress cannot, by Law, give the Judges of the Supreme Court original jurisdiction of the same Cases of which it expressly gives them appellate Jurisdiction.... I acted as a Circuit Judge, because my predecessors had done so before me.... But I now see that my holding the Circuit Courts will certainly do an injury to the Rights of other judges.[184]

Chase suggested that when they had served as circuit judges in the 1790s they had acted incorrectly. His logic mirrors the argument offered in *Hayburn* by Justices Wilson and Blair, namely, the justices had not been commissioned by the Constitution to act in this capacity. However, the issue in *Hayburn* was distinct in the sense that the justices were being asked to act in a non-judicial function. The Repeal Act (and the 1789 Judiciary Act), by contrast, required justices to take on additional *judicial* functions and in Jefferson's own words, simply to "restore our judiciary to what it was while justice & not federalism was its object."[185]

While the justices contemplated a strike, thirteen of the sixteen circuit judges, now stripped of their judgeships, drafted a memorial to Congress to seek redress. Their effort failed.[186] Meanwhile, Federalist lawyers brought a series of test cases to assess the Repeal Act's constitutionality. One was *Stuart v. Laird*. A week before that case reached the Court, the justices considered William Marbury's famous application for a writ of mandamus to receive his post as a justice of the peace. Marshall ruled that Marbury should receive the commission, but that the Court was powerless to issue a writ because the section of the 1789 Judiciary Act granting jurisdiction to do so was unconstitutional. The statutory law was in conflict with the higher law. If the Court compelled Madison to act, then it would be enforcing an improper law, acting as the servant of the legislature rather than of the people, and thereby calling its own legitimacy into question. If Marshall ruled that the Court had no power to compel the writ in order to avoid direct confrontation with the Jefferson administration, he nonetheless assumed a broad power to determine the constitutionality of another branch's actions. By issuing a ruling that could

---

objection: "Mr. Washington also states it as his opinion that the question respecting the constitutional right of the Judges of the supreme court to sit as circuit Judges ought to be considered as settled & should not again be movd [*sic*]. I have no doubt myself but that policy dictates this decision to us all." Ackerman sees Marshall as keeping open the possibility of striking. He stresses that Marshall reports on Chase's support of the strike and ends by suggesting that "if we determine certainly to proceed to do circuit duty it will I presume be entirely unnecessary to meet in August. If we incline to the contrary opinion, or are undecided we ought to meet & communicate verbally our difficulties to each other."

[184] Samuel Chase to John Marshall, 24 April 1802, Baltimore, MD, Samuel Chase Correspondence, Maryland Historical Society, Call Number 1234.

[185] Thomas Jefferson to M. Volney, 20 April 1802, Jefferson Papers, Library of Congress.

[186] For discussion of these "judges-without-judgeships" activities, see Jed Glickstein, "After Midnight: The Circuit Judges and the Repeal of the Judiciary Act of 1801," unpublished manuscript of Yale University undergraduate thesis on file with the author.

potentially undercut the claims of the Jeffersonian-majority Congress or the president's aims, the ruling served to showcase the breakdown of national regime unity.

In *Stuart*, the defendant's lawyer denied the legitimacy of the circuit courts as re-established by the Repeal Act. He argued that if a case were carried over from the previous term, then it could only be heard by an 1801 Act circuit court, not the 1802 Repeal Act court. Marshall, now serving in his re-instituted role as circuit judge, found for the plaintiff, compelling appeal to the Supreme Court.[187] Given *Marbury*, the prospects for the defendant in *Stuart v. Laird* appeared positive. If, in the earlier case, the Supreme Court reviewed the Judiciary Act of 1789 and found its provisions unconstitutional, then that Act's circuit-riding provision, which had been re-established by the Repeal, conferred an institutional capacity similarly unconstitutional. Justice Chase had already laid out the unconstitutionality in his private correspondence with Marshall. In the justices' dual role as circuit court judges, they held a jurisdiction that the Constitution did not contemplate; they were acting as original court judges and not appellate court judges. The 1801 Act had remedied that error by establishing specific circuit-court judgeships. The Repeal Act only served to recommit the original error.

Again, the logic of this claim had already been much discussed in Marshall and Chase's letters and underlay their reasons for considering a strike. Yet Marshall, by his very act of sitting as circuit judge to preside over *Stuart*, indicated that the Federalist case was already lost. By returning to their circuits, the justices conceded to the Jeffersonians with their feet if not yet with their words. When ruling for the Supreme Court in *Stuart*, Justice Patterson disregarded *Marbury* and offered the prudential argument that circuit-riding had always existed and could not now be disturbed. He did not engage the constitutional merits of the argument that the justices did not have distinct commissions as circuit court judges. He merely asserted, "it is sufficient to observe, that practice and acquiescence under it for a period of several years, commencing with the organization of the judicial system affords an irresistible answer, and has indeed fixed the construction."[188] As Patterson contended to Marshall on their earlier correspondence, there was no reason to disturb that system. The words in his letters and his ruling were nearly identical.[189] Patterson's ruling, days after *Marbury*, may have been an attempt to avoid further clashes with the Jefferson administration.[190]

---

[187] Ellis, 63; Ackerman, 188–94; Elsmere, 146–8.

[188] *Stuart v. Laird*, 5 U.S. 299, 308–9.

[189] Patterson killed the strike plan with a prudential claim: "the practical exposition is too old and strong & obstinate to be shaken or controlled. The question is at rest." In his holding in *Stuart*, Patterson wrote of circuit-riding: "This practical exposition is too strong and obstinate to be shaken or controlled, and ought not now be disturbed." Patterson's letter is cited by Ackerman, 170.

[190] Dean Alfange, Jr., "Marbury v. Madison and Original Understandings of Judicial Review: In Defense of Traditional Wisdom," *Supreme Court Review* (1993), 349–72.

The actions taken by both factions around the Judiciary Act of 1801 reveal the extent to which party and opposition were viewed as illegitimate. While the structural improvements that the legislation provided had been sought for nearly a decade, the manner in which it was passed only served to highlight, for Jeffersonians, that Federalists were intent on denying the people's will. The legislation seemed to epitomize that Federalists were an aristocratic faction sowing the seeds of open dissent and thereby upsetting the twin expectations of regime unity and the judiciary as equally representative of popular sovereignty. By contrast, Federalists viewed their actions not as harnessing judicial power for their own policy interests, which a Jeffersonian congressional majority might block, but as protecting the Constitution from the dangers of party-driven factionalism. They were saving the republic from a group of men who had already revealed a penchant for violence and civil strife. Ultimately, even as Jefferson had initially expressed an interest in his inaugural of bringing Federalists within the Jeffersonian fold, and even as the Supreme Court justices had signaled in *Stuart*, and to a lesser extent in *Marbury*, a willingness to be conciliatory with the new administration, Jefferson's supporters turned from absorbing Federalism to silencing it. Justice Patterson's gambit had failed. Calls for judicial impeachments reached new heights.

IV. Impeaching Justice Samuel Chase and Neutrality as a Second-Best Solution

Even before decisions in *Marbury* and *Stuart* were handed down, Jeffersonians struck upon a means to secure a unified Jeffersonian federal government: impeachment. Impeachment had already been successfully tested as a way to expel state judges.[191] Despite lamenting at the time of Chase's impeachment, "This business of removing Judges by impeachment is a bungling way," Jefferson gave his assent to the House of Representatives to begin impeachment proceedings against U.S. District Judge John Pickering of New Hampshire.[192]

---

[191] In 1803, Pennsylvanian judge Alexander Addison's impeachment and conviction triggered impeachment proceedings against other state judges including Thomas Passmore, Edward Shippen, Thomas Smith, and Jasper Yeates. Elsmere, 150–2. Because Pennsylvania, with a lower house dominated by Jeffersonians and an upper house with a significant Federalist minority, mirrored the federal Congress, the Pennsylvania judicial impeachments were considered important test cases for the viability of federal judicial impeachment. See Richard Neumann, Jr., "The Revival of Impeachment as a Partisan Political Weapon" (2006), Hofstra University Legal Studies Research Paper No. 06–22, available at SSRN: http://ssrn.com/abstract=923834.

[192] Entry of 5 January 1804, *Plumer Memorandum*, 101, quoted in Ellis, 72. The precise role Jefferson played as an advocate of impeachments is unclear, perhaps because he may have been subject to the charge himself if the Blount trial (see later) had been successful. Jefferson biographer, Dumas Malone, wrote that "Political enemies of Jefferson in his lifetime and numerous later writers contended that he planned a 'campaign' against the judiciary from the very start, but as a cautious politician, he put this into effect only step by step lest he jeopardize the popularity of his party." Malone rejects this claim and instead argues that

Jefferson's negative attitude toward impeachment only suggested that it was not his preferred means to root out opposition and unify the branches. Martin Van Buren's commentary on Jefferson's attitude is instructive. Van Buren noted that Jefferson "spoke of the power of Impeachment with great severity not only as a mockery in itself, but as having exercise in preventing a resort to a more thorough remedy, which he thought was only to be found in a change in the tenure of the judicial office."[193] Jefferson was lukewarm toward impeachment not because he opposed removing judges, but because it was a less effective means of ensuring removal of an opposition entrenched in government. It was a bumbling way to establish regime unity.

IV.a. *Impeachment as Removal of Illegitimate Opposition*

Impeachment refers to the procedure by which the Congress tries a federal official for "Treason, Bribery, or other high Crimes or Misdemeanors" before the full Senate acting as a court.[194] The range of offenses is not clearly specified by the Constitution.[195] This ambiguity created the possibility that impeachments could be used as a tool either to remove officials who abused the public trust by engaging in corruption or to remove officials who simply offended political sensibilities of the congressional majority.[196] Indeed, in England, an impeachable offense was given the latter wider meaning.[197]

At the Constitutional Convention, the boundaries of who could be impeached and for what reasons were debated.[198] The Convention settled on the language of "high Crimes and Misdemeanors."[199] While that phrase secured a compromise, it did not clarify the meaning. It left open the possibility of impeachment for acts of corruption but also impeachment for demonstrated opposition to majority interests.

he never advocated anything akin to what Randolph and Giles proposed as the total reconstruction of the judiciary. See Malone, *Jefferson and His Time: Jefferson the President, First Term*, 6 vols. (Charlottesville: University of Virginia Press, 1970), Vol. 4, 115–6.

[193] Martin Van Buren, *The Autobiography of Martin Van Buren*, John C. Fitzpatrick, ed. (New York: Augustus M. Kelley 1967 [1920]), 184.

[194] See Article II, Section 4, of the U.S. Constitution.

[195] Raoul Berger, *Impeachment: The Constitutional Problems* (Cambridge: Harvard University Press, 1974), 2–53; Peter Charles Hoffner and N. E. H. Hull, *Impeachment in America: 1635–1805* (New Haven: Yale University Press, 1984), 6–59.

[196] For discussion of these two tracks of impeachment, see Neumann 2006.

[197] Hoffner and Hull, 6–59. On English impeachable offenses, see Michael J. Gerhardt, "The Lessons of Impeachment History," *George Washington Law Review* 67 (March 1999), 605.

[198] George Mason objected to restricting impeachment to treason and bribery and wanted "maladministration" included in the list of offenses. Madison notes that Mason argued, "Why is the provision restrained to Treason & bribery only? Treason as defined in the Constitution will not reach many great and dangerous offenses.... Attempts to subvert the Constitution may not be Treason as above defined." Mason's stipulation that the Constitution is vulnerable to subversion beyond treason highlights the republican wariness of conspiracy. James Madison, *Notes of Debates in the Federal Convention of 1787* (New York: W.W. Norton, 1987 [1840]), 605.

[199] Ibid.

Hamilton acknowledged this latter possibility in *Federalist 65* by contending that the boundaries of an impeachable offense could not be fixed in ways similar to how other criminal acts were defined. When describing the impeachment proceeding, Hamilton wrote, "this can never be tied down by such strict rules, either in the delineation of the offense by the prosecutors, or in the construction of it by the Judges, as in common cases serve to limit the discretion of courts in favor of personal security."[200] Hamilton indicated that impeachments "are of a nature which may with peculiar property be denominated POLITICAL, as they relate chiefly to the injuries done immediately to the society itself."[201] This claim accords with George Mason's attempt to widen the range of offenses beyond indictable crimes to the more elastic concept of using a civil office to harm the republic. In an era, when opposition is not considered fully legitimate or loyal, this definition was wide indeed. Hamilton accepted the notion that impeachments would have a partisan character, that they would pit factions against one another and would be used to secure power:

> The prosecution of them, for this reason, will seldom fail to agitate the passions of the whole community, and to divide it into parties, more or less friendly or inimical, to the accused. In many cases, it will connect itself with the pre-existing factions, and will inlist [*sic*] all their animosities, partialities, influence and interest on one side, or on the other, and in such cases there will always be the greatest danger, that the decision will be regulated more by the comparative strength of parties than by the real demonstration of innocence or guilt.[202]

To lessen the possibility that an impeachment ruling and conviction might be "dangerous to the public tranquility," Hamilton explains that the Framers lodged prosecution authority with the Senate, which in his terms would be "sufficiently dignified" and "sufficiently independent."[203]

The first federal impeachment charges were raised against Senator William Blount of Tennessee, who was nominally a Federalist, but whose voting pattern in Congress illustrated an early alliance with Jeffersonians.[204] Blount was expelled from the Senate when evidence surfaced four months after he took his seat in 1797 that he was involved in a scheme to seize control of the territory of Louisiana from Spain and profit off the sale of his lands west of the Mississippi.[205] The House simultaneously began impeachment proceedings against him, but the trial was not conducted until December 1798.[206] While

[200] Alexander Hamilton, "Federalist 65," in *The Federalist*, Jacob E. Cooke, ed. (Middletown, CT: Wesleyan University Press, 1961), 441.
[201] Ibid., 439.
[202] Ibid., 439–40.
[203] Ibid., 441.
[204] Buckner Melton, Jr., *The First Impeachment: The Constitutional Framers and the Case of Senator William Blount* (Macon, GA: Mercer University Press, 1998), 76–7.
[205] Ibid., 116–25.
[206] Ibid., 190–231.

the case ultimately settled that senators could not be subject to impeachment, the incident suggests more than a new government fumbling its way toward making its Constitution operational. The trial reveals how Federalists laid the groundwork to utilize impeachment as a weapon to remove opposition in conjunction with the premises of the Sedition Act, which had been passed five months earlier.

By the time of the trial, Blount had already been expelled from the Senate; accordingly, his lawyers fought the charges of impeachment on the grounds that he was not a civil officer and thus not subject to impeachment. Put differently, given his prior expulsion, the impeachment was essentially redundant. Representative James Bayard, who conducted the impeachment trial, responded that the relevant constitutional clause only structured the effect of impeachment, that is, removal, not who was subject to the charge itself.[207] Bayard made the bold claim that "all persons, without the supposed limitation, are liable to impeachment."[208] Bayard's broad construction would permit wielding impeachment as a tool to prevent citizens from holding political office. Bayard defended this interpretation by arguing that influential individuals may foment civil unrest to seize office, perhaps even the presidency, and that preventing such an individual from ever holding office through the charge and conviction of impeachment, would secure civic tranquility against this possibility.[209] As one historian notes of Bayard's hypothetical, "Obviously Bayard employed this scenario to play upon the same Federalist fears that had produced the Alien and Sedition Acts ... the best weapon against the evildoer would be a vote of perpetual disqualification from public office, imposed via impeachment."[210] In an era when opposition was considered de-stabilizing and foreshadowing civil unrest, a broad impeachment authority would theoretically promote civil peace by keeping opposition permanently out of government.[211] Once Federalists lost power to the Jeffersonians, the Jeffersonians seized upon this broad definition of impeachment to remove the Federalist opposition. Their first target was federal district judge, John Pickering.[212]

---

[207] *Annals of Congress*, Senate, 5th Congress, 3rd Session, 2250–1.

[208] Ibid., 2251.

[209] Ibid., 2253–4.

[210] Melton, 211.

[211] Impeachment and conviction of Blount may have paved the way to impeach Vice President Jefferson, who was not protected by the terms of the Sedition Act. See Irving Brant, *Impeachment: Trials and Errors* (New York: Alfred A. Knopf, 1972), 44. Jefferson's liability to the charge may have led him to support the narrow charge against Chase. Representative Randolph disregarded the idea and sought trial under all eight articles of impeachment.

[212] Of the thirty lower federal judges in place after the passage of the 1801 Act, three were removed for political reasons and fifteen were removed by the Repeal Act, reducing the number of Federalist judges from thirty to twelve. This was accomplished "even though the President lacked the removal power in every instance." Carl Prince, "The Passing of the Aristocracy: Jefferson's Removal of the Federalists, 1801–1805," *Journal of American History* 57 (December 1970), 568.

The Pickering impeachment was the first successful impeachment of a federal judge, and the trial laid some precedent for using impeachment as a political weapon against judges. Jefferson's secretary of treasury, Albert Gallatin, requested that the U.S. district attorney for New Hampshire, John Samuel Sherburne, gather depositions regarding district Judge Pickering's increasingly erratic behavior on the bench.[213] These depositions were forwarded by Jefferson to the House of Representatives with a note indicating that the House was "to whom the constitution has confided a power of instituting proceedings of redress, if they shall be of opinion that the case calls for them," that is, a not-so-subtle reference to judicial impeachment.[214] John Quincy Adams, who as senator served as one of the judges at the Pickering trial, characterized Federalist belief regarding Jefferson's involvement: "At the same session of Congress which sanctioned the Louisiana purchase, a system of impeachment disclosed itself against the remaining judges of the courts of the United States, which was believed by the Federalists to be not only countenanced but stimulated by Mr. Jefferson. It was not then discountenanced by him." Thus, Quincy Adams viewed the Pickering impeachment as "merely an entering wedge" against the judiciary.[215] Federalist Timothy Pickering viewed impeachment as part of a larger Jeffersonian project to destroy the Constitution:

> The violation of the Constitution, though not commenced, yet most remarkable in overthrowing the judiciary, is becoming habitual. The judges of the Supreme Court are all Federalists. They stand in the way of the ruling power.... The judges, therefore, are, if possible, to be removed.... The men of stern, inflexible virtue, who dare expose and resist the public corruption, will be the first victims; and the best portion of the community, already humbled, will be trodden underfoot.[216]

That Timothy Pickering gave full vent to the illegitimacy of Jefferson's administration is evidenced by his discussion of a Federalist plan to secede from the Union:

> Although the end of all our Revolutionary labors and expectations is disappointment, and our fond hopes of republican happiness are vanity, and the real patriots of '76 are overwhelmed by the modern pretenders to that character, I will not yet despair: I will rather anticipate a new confederacy, exempt from the corrupt and corrupting influence and oppression of the aristocratic Democrats of the South. There will be – and our children at farthest will see

213 Lynn Turner, "The Impeachment of John Pickering," *American Historical Review* 54 (April 1949), 490–1.

214 *Documents Relative to John Pickering*, printed by order of the House of Representatives (Washington, 1803), 3. These documents include the depositions gathered against Pickering and Jefferson's letter to the House of Representatives dated 3 February 1804, quoted in ibid., 491.

215 John Quincy Adams, "Reply to the Appeal of the Massachusetts Federalists," in *Documents relating to New England Federalism, 1800–1815*, 160, 161.

216 Timothy Pickering to Theodore Lyman, Washington, DC, 11 February 1804, in *Documents relating to New England Federalism, 1800–1815*, 344.

it – a separation.... The British Provinces, even with the assent of Britain, will become members of the Northern confederacy. A continued tyranny of the present ruling sect will precipitate that event.[217]

In this letter, Jefferson is deemed a tyrant, the Federalist vision is lost, the Constitution is overrun, and the solution is secession. Northern secession was a common theme in Federalists' correspondence.[218]

Pickering's impeachment was complicated to the extent that his Federalist supporters attempted to show that the judge was insane and therefore not subject to impeachment. However, the House investigatory committee viewed Pickering's misbehavior as the consequence of drunkenness, not insanity, and the House voted to impeach by 45 to 8.[219] No method of judicial removal existed beyond either resignation or impeachment.[220] Thus, while the House managers interpreted the impeachment parameters narrowly to the extent that they attempted to deny evidence of insanity and attempted to show that Pickering was guilty of a crime, this strategy's effect paralleled the Federalist impeachment of Blount: "by confusing insanity with criminal misbehavior they also wiped out the line between good administration and politics and made any word or deed which a political majority might think objectionable the excuse for impeachment and removal from office."[221] Jefferson seemed to endorse this construction of impeachment. When Senator Plumer of New Hampshire inquired as to whether Jefferson thought insanity was cause for Pickering's impeachment, Jefferson replied, "If the facts of his denying an appeal & of his intoxication, as stated in the impeachment are proven, that will be sufficient cause of removal without further enquiry."[222]

Federalists were now forced to offer a narrow interpretation of impeachment for only indictable offenses; Senator Plumer wrote that impeachment

[217] Timothy Pickering to Richard Peters, Washington, DC, 24 December 1803, in *Documents relating to New England Federalism, 1800–1815*, 338.

[218] Northern secession after Jefferson's election is discussed in the following letters: Tapping Reeve to Uriah Tracy, 7 February 1804, Washington, DC; Cabot to Pickering, 14 February 1804; Theodore Lyman to Pickering, 29 February 1804, Boston; Pickering to Rufus King, Washington DC, 4 March 1804; Roger Griswold to Oliver Wolcott, 11 March 1804, Washington, DC; Stephen Higginson to Pickering, 17 March 1804. While Federalists discussed reasons for seceding, there was far from universal agreement on whether secession should be undertaken. Higginson's letter is instructive: "on the question of separation ... we all agree there can be no doubt of its being desirable; but of the expediency of attempting it, or discussing it now at this moment, we all very much doubt. It is dangerous to continue under the Virginia system: but how to extricate ourselves at present we see not" (361). See Adams, *Documents relating to New England Federalism, 1800–1815*, 331–66.

[219] *Annals of Congress*, 7th Congress, 2nd Session, 642.

[220] A method for removal without impeachment had been prescribed by the Judiciary Act of 1801. By that Act, one of the new class of circuit judges could take over district Judge Pickering's court. However, when this Act was negated in 1802, so was this solution. See Albert J. Beveridge, *The Life of John Marshall* (Boston: Houghton Mifflin, 1916), Vol. 3, 165.

[221] Turner, 1949, 493.

[222] Everett Somerville Brown, ed., *William Plumer's Memorandum of Proceedings in the United States Senate, 1803–1807* (New York: Macmillan, 1923), 100.

demands "to allege & prove crimes and misdemeanors in the accused."[223] To that end, Federalists proposed to limit the language of the offense and thereby bypass a conviction. Senator White proposed that the senators vote on whether Pickering was guilty of "high crimes and misdemeanors," but the Senate accepted the language offered by Jeffersonian Senator Anderson, who recommended that Pickering be voted either guilty or not guilty "as charged" thereby leaving the broader construction intact.[224] The Jeffersonians' tactic was widely understood; Quincy Adams fumed, "This form, by blending all the law and facts together under the shelter of general terms, put at ease a few of the weak brethren who scrupled on the law, and a few who doubted of the facts."[225] On 12 March 1804, the Senate convicted Pickering on four counts by a vote of 19 Republicans against 7 Federalists.[226] Eight senators refused to vote.[227] Plumer wrote despairingly of the trial just before the final Senate vote, suggesting secession as the appropriate response:

> Tomorrow, no doubt, an insane man will be convicted of high crimes & misdeamers [*sic*]; & probably the next day John Samuel Sherburne will be announced as his successor – for it is not yet necessary to enquire whether the Candidate is honest, or attached to the constitution. There is nothing here to induce me to tarry much longer, either as it respects myself or my country. I fondly hope I shall live to see the righteous separated from the wicked by a geographical line. True policy demands it.[228]

Secession seemed a likely response when one views opposition as not "attached to the constitution."

IV.b. *Samuel Chase on Sedition and the Illegitimacy of Opposition*
Judge Pickering's impeachment created a broad notion of the procedure. Capitalizing on this possibility, Representative John Randolph moved to impeach Justice Samuel Chase, who was widely known to contend that the ascension of Jeffersonians sounded the death knell of the Constitution. Chase had been a target since at least 1800 when the Baltimore newspaper, *The American*, characterized him as "subtle-sharp-scheming-subtle-sly-simpering-smiling-slippery Sam of speculative memory."[229]

Chase's appointment to the Supreme Court in 1796 is, in part, a consequence of the onerous responsibilities of circuit-riding that made the position unappealing. Washington had struggled to find anyone else. The Senate confirmed Chase unanimously, but some Federalists expressed reservations.

---

[223] William Plumer, "Autobiography," 130, quoted in Turner, 1949, 494.

[224] Turner, 1949, 504.

[225] John Quincy Adams diary 27, 1 January 1803–4 August 1809, 75 [electronic edition]. *The Diaries of John Quincy Adams: A Digital Collection.* Boston, MA: Massachusetts Historical Society, 2005, http://www.masshist.org/jqadiaries.

[226] *Journal of the Senate of the United States of America*, Vol. 3, 12 March 1804, 506–7.

[227] Ellis, 72–5.

[228] William Plumer to Jeremiah Smith, 11 March 1804, quoted in Turner, 1949, 503–4.

[229] *The American*, 6 November 1800, quoted in Elsmere, 136.

Secretary of the Treasury Oliver Wolcott wrote of his "unworthy opinion" of Chase. Perhaps alluding to Chase's entanglement in a flour speculation scheme during the Revolution, Justice Iredell was "not impressed with a very favorable opinion of [Chase's] moral character, whatever his professional abilities might be." Echoing this sentiment, Senator Plumer thought Chase's appointment could undermine "the respectability and dignity of the Judiciary.[230]

While Chase was the most vocal justice in the 1790s to elaborate judicial review, it was his vigorous enforcement of the Sedition Act that raised Jeffersonian ire.[231] That enforcement was evident in three cases over which Chase presided in his role as circuit judge in 1800: the trial of Thomas Cooper, *United States v. John Fries*, and *United States v. Callender*.[232] His behavior

---

[230] Iredell, Wolcott, and Plumer are quoted in Charles Warren, *The Supreme Court in United States History* (Boston: Little Brown, 1928), Vol. 1, 143. See also Elsmere, 57.

[231] On Chase's views on judicial review, see John J. Dolan, "The Constitutional Opinions of Mr. Justice Samuel Chase," Juris Doctoral Dissertation, Georgetown Law School (1938), 148–150, Maryland Historical Society. Chase's support for the Sedition Act is unsurprising. In a 1784 letter to the *Baltimore Daily Intelligencer* while commenting on a grand jury charge, Chase signed his name as "An Enemy to the Unrestrained Liberty of the Press." See Samuel Chase, "Essay on Liberty of the Press," *Baltimore Daily Intelligencer* 1794, Vertical File, Maryland Historical Society. Two years later Chase commented on the Republican newspaper of Philadelphia, *The Aurora*, to his former student and secretary of war, James McHenry: "I think the printer ought to be indicted for a false and base libel on our government. A free press is the support of liberty and Republican govt. but a licentious press is the base of freedom, and the peril of society, and will do more to destroy real liberty than any other instrument in the hands of knaves and fools." Samuel Chase to James McHenry, 4 December 1796, McHenry Papers, Library of Congress, also lodged with Samuel Chase Correspondence, Maryland Historical Society.

[232] Thomas Cooper published essays critical of President Adams in the *Sunbury and Northumberland Gazette*, was charged with seditious libel, and was brought to trial before Justice Chase and district judge Richard Peters in Philadelphia. The trial gained notoriety when Cooper made the request to call members of Congress as witnesses, but Chase refused. Chase advised the jury that Cooper admitted to drafting these editorials, and a guilty verdict was returned. See Elsmere, 92–8. Chase endorsed the sedition law, stating at trial his intent to "restrain, as far as I can, all such licentious attacks on the government of the country." Chase, quoted in Francis Wharton, *State Trials of the United States during the Administrations of Washington and Adams* (Philadelphia, 1849), 678, quoted in Elsmere, 97.

John Fries was arrested for leading a riot against tax collectors gathering monies to support a war with France. Testifying to the fear of opposition, Federalists saw in this "Fries Rebellion" larger signs of civil instability. Oliver Wolcott noted that the rebellion could "be nursed into something formidable." Oliver Wolcott to Frederick Wolcott, quoted in Elsmere, 101. On 12 March, President Adams authorized Secretary of War McHenry to use troops to disperse the uprising and arrest the insurgents. Fries was convicted of treason at the district level and appealed to the circuit court manned by Chase and Judge Peters. Fries's lawyers subsequently withdrew from the case contending that, in light of Chase's actions, their ability to represent Fries was compromised. Fries was found guilty and sentenced to hang, but President Adams pardoned him. Chase was lambasted in the Republican press. Editor of the Philadelphia *Aurora*, William Duane, wrote of Chase, "no lawyer of the present day can boast of more original and surprising ideas ... and whether the question be of treason ... of sedition law; or flour contracts, his abilities still shine with superior lustre" (22 and 27 May 1800). The Richmond *Examiner* declared Chase "totally unfit to be intrusted [*sic*] with power over the lives or liberties of the *free Citizens* of America" (6 June 1800). See Elsmere, 98–113.

during each would serve as the basis for eight articles of impeachment. Over the course of these trials, Chase would not only elaborate on the Court's responsibility to review acts of Congress but would also demonstrate his unwillingness to concede the legitimacy of the Jeffersonians.

Chase's behavior in *United States v. Callender* sealed his reputation as a despised Federalist. Callender, a fiery critic of the Adams administration, had been targeted for possible arrest by Adams's Secretary of State, Timothy Pickering, who instructed the U.S. district attorney in Richmond to scour Callender's newspaper, *The Examiner*, for evidence of libel.[233] Callender's defense sought to prove his innocence by claiming that the Sedition Act was unconstitutional, laying open the issue of determining the constitutionality of a congressional act.[234] Callender's lawyers attempted to steer around Chase – who was likely to validate the Act – by offering a theory of jury nullification. Chase rejected that logic by reaffirming judicial review: "the judicial power of the United States is the only proper and competent authority to decide whether any statute made by Congress (or any of the State Legislatures) is contrary to, or in violation of, the Federal Constitution."[235] Callender's lawyers withdrew in protest, and Callender was found guilty on 3 June 1800.[236] Jeffersonian vitriol against Chase reached new heights. He was accused of wearing a "party colored robe," and Jeffersonians created a toast: "Curse of thy father, scum of all that's base. Thy sight is odious and thy name is Chase."[237] Jeffersonian newspaper editor James Wilson, whom Chase failed to convince a grand jury in Delaware to indict on sedition charges, wrote "We hope the day is not far off, when Judge Chase will be impeached for this and other arbitrary acts of his."[238]

Chase's clearest articulation against Jefferson came in a charge to a Baltimore grand jury on 2 May 1803. These charges were common practice in this era as judges took it as part of their task to educate the public, hence the characterization of the judiciary as the republican schoolmaster. In this charge, Chase framed the Repeal Act as undermining liberty of property:

> Where law is *uncertain, partial,* or *arbitrary*; where justice is not *impartially* administered to *all*; where property is insecure, and the person is liable to insult and violence without redress by *law*; the people are *not free*; whatever may be that form of government. To *this* situation I greatly fear we are fast approaching!

---

[233] Elsmere, 116. Timothy Pickering to Thomas Nelson, 12 August 1799. Timothy Pickering Papers, Massachusetts Historical Society.

[234] If Chase had found the Sedition Act unconstitutional, it is plausible that his impeachment might not have occurred.

[235] Chase's charge is contained in Francis Wharton, *State Trials,* 712–17, and is quoted in Dolan, 152.

[236] Ellis, 78; Elsmere, 120–2.

[237] Richmond *Examiner,* 29 July 1800; Philadelphia *Aurora,* 8 August 1800.

[238] *Mirror of the Times and General Advertiser,* 3 July 1800, quoted in the *Trial of Judge Chase* (Washington?: 1804?), 81, Massachusetts Historical Society.

You know, gentleman, that our state, and national institutions were framed to secure to every member of society, *equal liberty* and *equal rights*; but the late abolition of the offices of the sixteen circuit court judges ... take[s] away all security for property and personal liberty ... our republican constitution will sink into a *mobocracy*, the worst of all possible governments.[239]

Jeffersonian criticism of this grand jury charge was published in the *Baltimore American*, the *National Intelligencer*, and the *Philadelphia Aurora*.[240] Federalists countered by publishing the full charge in various papers or by mocking these arguments.[241] Jefferson, having been made aware of the charge, wrote to Representative Joseph Nicholson, who had brought impeachment charges against Pickering, asking if action might not be taken against Chase:

> You must have heard of the extraordinary charge of Chace [*sic*] to the Grand Jury at Baltimore. Ought this seditious and official attack on the principles of our Constitution, and on the proceedings of a State, to go unpunished? And to whom so pointedly as yourself will the public look for the necessary measure? I ask these questions for your consideration, for myself it is better that I should not interfere.[242]

The letter reveals not only Jefferson's prodding to begin impeachment proceedings against Chase but also that he was not averse to invoking the language and implications of sedition when it served his purposes. That he characterized Chase's charge as seditious speaks to Jefferson's unease with political opposition.

IV.c. *The Chase Impeachment: Toward Judicial Independence as Political Neutrality*

For Jeffersonians, judicial power per se was not the problem. A judiciary out of line with the popular will and the newly elected federal regime was. It only served to demonstrate that a threatening opposition was entrenched in government. If Jefferson's election did not secure a unified governing regime,

---

[239] A judgeship was considered property. Washington *Federalist*, 5 September 1803; see also *Impeachment of Judge Chase* (Appendix), Massachusetts Historical Society.

[240] See Elsmere, 163–5; see also *Impeachment of Judge Chase*, 115–7, which quotes from the *National Intelligencer*, 20 May 1803, Massachusetts Historical Society.

[241] See Elsmere, 164–5. In particular, see Chase's response to the Republican press published in the *Anti-Democrat* and republished in the *National Intelligencer* 5 August 1803. Chase writes, "It is with great reluctance I comply with your request to send you a copy of the part of my charge to the grand jury of this district (in May last) which has been misunderstood by some editors, and shamefully misrepresented by others. I have uniformly declined the publication of any charge I have delivered. In some instances judicial opinions have been imputed to me that I never gave; and in other instances they have been grossly and willfully misrepresented (particularly in the case of Fries for treason) and I believe for base political purposes." *Impeachment of Judge Chase*, 117, Massachusetts Historical Society.

[242] Thomas Jefferson to Joseph Nicholson, 13 May 1803, Thomas Jefferson Papers, Library of Congress.

judicial impeachments might. Like the Pickering trial, at issue in Chase's trial was not only whether Chase was guilty of impeachable offenses but also what counted as an impeachable offense.

Pickering's conviction suggested a broad interpretation. Senator Plumer recognized this: "the process of impeachment is to be considered in effect as a *mode of removal*, and not as a charge and conviction of high crimes and misdemeanors."[243] Senator Giles put the relationship of impeachment and opposition in stark terms: "removal by impeachment was nothing more than a declaration by Congress to this effect: you hold *dangerous* opinions and if you are suffered to carry them into effect, you will work the destruction of the Union."[244] Furthermore, Giles targeted the actions of the Court in its *Marbury* ruling to pave the way toward an impeachment of the chief justice:

> If the Judges of the Supreme Court should dare, AS THEY HAD DONE, to declare an act of Congress unconstitutional, or to send a mandamus to the Secretary of STATE, AS THEY HAD DONE, it was the undoubted right of the House of Representatives to impeach them, and of the Senate to remove them, for giving opinions, however honest or sincere they may have been in entertaining them. Impeachment was not a criminal prosecution, it was no prosecution at all.[245]

This phrasing – "destruction of the Union" and "dangerous opinions" – indicates that Giles was unwilling to grant Federalists legitimacy whereas the phrase "nothing more" suggests that impeachment was a simple constitutional means to control the Court akin to altering jurisdiction.

Timothy Pickering characterized Randolph's view of impeachment: "the provision in the Constitution that the judges shall hold their offices *during good behavior* was intended to guard them against the *executive* alone, and not by means to control the power of Congress, on whose representation against the judges the President could remove them."[246] Impeachments were an appropriate means to remove judges who had demonstrated an unwillingness to uphold the expressed popular will. Judicial independence was necessary to the extent that it would guard against corrupt executives appointing judges as lackeys. But the concept could not be used as a rationale to defy the people's will. For Randolph and Giles, judicial independence could not be a shield to protect the views of a repudiated and aristocratic minority. That construction would only serve to create a stable opposition within government and promote instability. In short, Randolph and Giles saw impeachment as a tool to remove

---

[243] William Plumer to Theodore Lyman, 17 March 1804, Plumer Papers, Library of Congress.
[244] William Branch Giles, quoted in Dice Robins Anderson, *William Branch Giles: A Study in the Politics of Virginia and the Nation from 1790 to 1830* (Gloucester, MA: Peter Smith, 1965), 96. Emphasis added.
[245] Ibid.
[246] Timothy Pickering to Theodore Lyman, 11 February 1804, in Henry Cabot Lodge, *Life and Letters of George Cabot* (Boston, 1877), 444.

judges who demonstrated themselves opposed to the popular will and thereby ignoring their expected role as representatives.[247]

On 5 January 1804, Randolph introduced a resolution to begin an inquiry into Samuel Chase's conduct in the various sedition cases reviewed above.[248] Federalists pounced on the resolution as a Jeffersonian attempt to establish legislative supremacy and threaten judicial independence. The resolution would "make judges the flexible tools of this House."[249] Further,

> It will establish a precedent that any member may procure an investigating committee to inquire into the conduct of any executive or judicial officer merely upon his opinion, unsupported by facts that such an inquiry is necessary. Suppose parties to be nearly equally divided; a member has only to propose an inquiry into the conduct of any officer to whom he may feel inimical, and thereby throw a cloud upon his character, and render him the object of suspicion.... [T]his precedent will furnish the instrument of vengeance of one party against another.[250]

Again, apparent in this protest are the ill effects of party and a lack of clarity on the meaning of judicial independence given the assumption of the judiciary as representative of popular sovereignty. Were judges to be independent of politicians, party, or the people themselves? Would that independence help them to protect the Constitution or endanger its principles? Regardless of Federalist protest, a committee was formed with Randolph as its chair. On 6 March, Randolph presented the committee's findings, and on 12 March, the day the Senate convicted Judge Pickering, the House resolved to impeach Chase.[251]

Federalists and Jeffersonians alike viewed this impeachment as the first step toward impeaching other justices, most notably Chief Justice Marshall. Jefferson is rumored to have commented "Now we have caught the *whale*, let us have an eye to the *boat*."[252] Timothy Pickering viewed the impeachment less as an assault on the judiciary and more on Federalism: "New judges, of characters and tempers suited to the object, will be the selected ministers of vengeance."[253] The Federalist *Connecticut Courant* commented on the widening definition of impeachment:

---

[247] As Randolph led the House managers and Giles chaired the committee establishing guidelines for the trial, their views are particularly important.

[248] *Annals of Congress*, House of Representatives, 8th Congress, 1st Session, 805–20.

[249] *Annals of Congress*, 8 Congress, First Session, 825.

[250] Ibid., 826.

[251] Elsmere, 175.

[252] New York *Evening Post*, 9 March 1805. While this statement was attributed to Jefferson, there is no clear evidence that he said it. Richard Ellis argues that no evidence links Jefferson to the Chase impeachment; after Jefferson's hyperbolic response to Chase's grand jury charge in Baltimore, Jefferson remained quiet on impeachment proceedings. Ellis, "The Impeachment of Samuel Chase," *American Political Trials*, Michal Belknap, ed. (Westport, CT: Greenwood Press, 1981), 57–78.

[253] Timothy Pickering to George Cabot, 29 January 1804. Henry Adams, ed., *Documents Relating to New England Federalism, 1800–1815* (New York: B. Franklin, 1965 [1877]), 340.

> The fancied independence of the United States Judiciary vanishes before the omnipotence of Congress.... Now that their majority amounts to two-thirds, some of the Judges of the Supreme Court are threatened with impeachment, without even a specific charge against them. The others will understand the lesson – if they wish to keep their places, they must act so as to please those who hold them in their power, and who can make a high crime or misdemeanor out of an error of judgment, or a difference from them in opinion.[254]

Noting that judicial independence was intertwined with the legitimacy of partisanship, James Bayard declined to represent Chase at trial. He contended that if he did so, Chase would only be seen as a Federalist rather than as a judge: "The spirit & pride of the Party would be enlisted on the side of the prosecution. The Individual would be forgotten and in & out of doors the sole consideration would be which Party was to triumph."[255] Robert Goodloe Harper, who did represent Chase, also recognized how the illegitimacy of opposition animated the impeachment: "I am convinced that the leaders of this prosecution have in this matter an ulterior motive to accomplish ... this prosecution & the time of its commencement ... is designed to destroy the independence of the Judiciary, to cast an odium on the Federal party." [256]

Randolph, an increasingly polarizing figure, led the House team prosecuting Chase on eight articles of impeachment.[257] His strategy was to overwhelm

---

[254] *Connecticut Courant*, 1 February 1804.

[255] James Bayard to Robert Goodloe Harper, 30 January 1804, Etting Collection, Historical Society of Pennsylvania.

[256] Samuel Chase, Jr., to Eliza Chase Dugan Coale, date unspecified, 1824, Chase Papers, Maryland Historical Society.

[257] A record of the trial's proceedings can be found in *Annals of Congress*, Senate, 8th Congress, 2nd Session, 83–676, "Trial of Judge Chase." The sectional division over the Yazoo scandal has often been cited as the reason for Chase's eventual acquittal. See Ellis, "The Impeachment of Samuel Chase," 65–6; Ellis, *Jeffersonian Crisis*, 87–9, 93; Ackerman, 212. The Yazoo issue was debated in the House only a week before the impeachment trial, and during it Randolph attacked his fellow Jeffersonians likening them to Federalists:
   What is the spirit against which we now struggle and which we have vainly endeavored to stifle? A monster generated by fraud, nursed in corruption, that in grim silence awaits its prey! *It is the spirit of federalism*.... When I behold a certain party supporting and clinging to such a measure, almost to a man, I see only men faithful to their own principles.... But when I see, associated with them, in firm compact, others who once rallied under the standard of opposite principles, I am filled with apprehension and concern. Of what consequence is it that a man smiles in your face, holds out his hand, and declares himself the advocate of those political principles to which you are also attached, when you see him acting with your adversaries upon other principles, which the voice of the nation has put down, *never to rise again in this section of the globe*. (Randolph, quoted in Henry Adams, *John Randolph: A New Edition with Primary Documents and Introduction by Robert McColley* [Armonk, NY: M. E. Sharpe, 1996], 92). Emphasis added.
   Randolph's speech suggests the illegitimacy with which he views Federalism; however, attacking fellow Jeffersonians was a step too far. Following this speech, quiet dislike of Randolph turned to open animosity, and from this point onward, according to one Federalist observer, the Republicans "seem broken and divided, and do not act with their usual concert" (quoted in Ellis, "Impeachment of Samuel Chase," 68).

Chase's defense: one article might stick.[258] Article One dealt with Chase's conduct at the Fries trial. Articles Two, Three, Four, Five, and Six dealt with Chase's conduct during the Callender trial. Article Seven accused Chase of refusing to discharge a grand jury at New Castle, Delaware, until it filed an indictment under the Sedition Act. Article Eight characterized Chase's Baltimore grand jury charge as a political tirade.[259] Tellingly, no article referenced Chase's elaborations of judicial review in cases from the 1790s as problematic.

Randolph's and Giles's broadly political construction of impeachment cut against Chase's legalistic defense. Chase testified: "I shall contend, that all acts admitted to have been done by me, were *legal*; I deny, in every instance, the *improper* intentions ... in which their supposed criminality altogether exists."[260] For Chase, impeachment was a legal procedure, and the attempt to transform it into a political weapon wielded by the legislative majority endangered the separation of powers. He contended that his offenses were not indictable crimes and thus, he could not be found guilty.[261] Chase pointed to the prosecution's failure to impeach the district judges with whom he sat on the circuit bench as evidence that he was being tried for his political beliefs.[262] His legalistic interpretation of impeachment is evident in his response to the eighth impeachment article: "Admitting these opinions to have been incorrect and unfounded, this respondent denies that there was any law which forbid him to express them, in a charge to a grand jury.... The very essence of despotism consists, in punishing acts which, at the time when they were done, were forbidden by no law."[263] While a majority of the

---

[258] Henry Adams notes, "Conscious that he [Randolph] would meet with strong opposition in the Senate, he determined to make his attack overwhelming by proving criminality, even though in doing it he gave up for the time his theory that impeachment need imply no criminal offense; and therefore, placing the real cause of impeachment last in the order of his articles, he threw into the foreground a long series of charges, which concerned only questions of law." (97).

[259] Samuel H. Smith and Thomas Lloyd, *The Trial of Samuel Chase An Associate Justice of the Supreme Court of the United States, Impeached by the House of Representatives, for High Crimes and Misdemeanors before the Senate of the United States*, 2 vols. (Washington City: Printed for Samuel H. Smith, 1805), Massachusetts Historical Society.

[260] Smith and Lloyd, Vol. 1, 14.

[261] See *Columbian eloquence being the speeches of the most celebrated American orations, as delivered in the late interesting trial of the Hon. Samuel Chase, before the Senate of the United States*, 3 vols. (Baltimore, MD: Printed for S. Butler and S. Cole, 1806), 110–12, Massachusetts Historical Society, microfilm.

[262] Randolph responded to Chase's claim that he could not be guilty if his fellow circuit judges were not also impeached with incredulity: "But we shall be told that in all those acts with which the respondent stands charged, that he was associated with other judges, who concurred in opinion with him, and were therefore, equally guilty with the respondent.... This court will take all the acts together, and will observe that in all of them the respondent appeared to be the sole actor. With talents so conspicuous, and a disposition so irritable ... the acts for which he is impeached, were committed with men perhaps of timid minds, and with talents very far inferior to those of the respondent that they were overawed by him," *Columbian Eloquence*, 43–4.

[263] Smith and Lloyd, Vol. 1, 95–6.

Senate disagreed with Chase's assessment, the necessary two-thirds threshold to convict was not reached.

The prosecution and defense spoke past one another. Chase claimed he could not be convicted because he had not committed a misdemeanor or a crime, and thus, the impeachment was politically motivated. Randolph agreed; the impeachment *was* politically motivated. It aimed to remove opposition from government after an election if the sitting judges refused to recognize the expressed will of the people and thereby abandoned their representative function. It aimed to establish regime unity. Randolph did not engage Chase on legal merits. He accused Chase of abusing his judicial role by defaming the Jeffersonian administration: "He has no right in his judicial capacity, to pervert the bench of justice into the theatre of his political declamations."[264] Chase could be convicted because he no longer represented the will of the people.

A compromise was reached by the terms of the charge laid before the Senate. Senator James Bayard, who had previously advocated a broad interpretation of impeachment for Senator Blount, now sought to impose limits. Chase's charge was worded, "Is Samuel Chase, guilty or not guilty of a high crime or misdemeanor, as charged in the ... article of impeachment."[265] The Chase wording framed the issue at stake to be whether the justice's behavior had risen to the level of a high crime or misdemeanor, not simply whether his actions were against the political majority. The wording of Pickering's charge had not highlighted that distinction. Thus, Chase could be guilty of an offense, but that offense might not be deemed as rising to the level of an impeachable high crime or misdemeanor. Senators could thereby hold Chase's actions to be inappropriate but still vote to acquit.[266]

Chase escaped conviction even as a majority voted to convict on numerous charges.[267] Voting patterns on some of the impeachment articles reveal that while Chase may have been acquitted, the Federalist vision of the judiciary, that

---

[264] *Columbian Eloquence*, 43.

[265] Smith and Lloyd, Vol. 2, 484.

[266] This phrasing prevailed in a vote of seventeen to sixteen with one abstention. Given that at the highest count, Federalists held only ten seats in the Senate, at least seven Jeffersonians were searching for some way to avoid a conviction. Elsmere, 296–7.

[267] Part of the explanation for Chase's acquittal is that by 1805 the furor over the Federalist judiciary had cooled. While Jeffersonians had not taken the *Stuart* ruling as a signal of judicial acquiescence, the Court had not antagonized the administration or the congressional majority since. See Ackerman, 2005, 219–22. Even so, the most ardent Jeffersonians pursued other measures to de-legitimize the judiciary. Randolph introduced a constitutional amendment to allow for the removal of judges without impeachment. Another impeachment House manager introduced an amendment to allow States to recall senators (see Beveridge, Vol. 3, 221). Senator Johnson of Kentucky offered an amendment that would turn the Senate into a court of final resort if the Supreme Court declared a state law unconstitutional. Another amendment required a supermajority of the Court to declare a law unconstitutional. Jefferson, having come to regard impeachment as a "farce," promoted an amendment offering federal judges six-year terms with re-appointment conditional on the consent of both congressional chambers. See John Reinhardt, "The Impeachment Proceedings against Judge James Hawkins Peck," *University of Kansas City Law Review* 12 (1944), 108–9.

is, as serving an educative function and as representative of popular sovereignty as the elected branches, had given way to a newer notion that judges should be removed from politics altogether. This construction was a seemingly unforeseen compromise that served to cool tensions. It may explain why senators who voted for conviction nevertheless expressed relief at the acquittal.[268]

The vote on the eighth article of impeachment is telling in this regard. That article dealt with Chase's grand jury charge in Baltimore, which criticized the Jefferson administration and which framed the Repeal Act as an unconstitutional negation of a property right. It received the most votes, falling only four votes shy of the two-thirds threshold. The vote on Article Eight suggests an emerging consensus that judges should not be directly involved in politics. The article did not condemn Chase's views per se but found fault with his airing of those views in the context of his judicial capacity: "The Republicans did not denounce Chase's politics as illegitimate, but rather insisted that his office precluded his acting on those political views."[269] As such, judicial independence was no longer constructed simply as independence from executive or legislative authority but as removal from politics altogether. The meaning of judicial independence was now conflated with an emerging notion of political neutrality. Although judges had a long history of advising juries through grand jury charges such as that which Chase offered in Baltimore, the impeachment suggested that new parameters were to be placed on the content of that speech. The lesson of the impeachment was that the judiciary should be a sphere apart; it should be de-politicized.

Imposing this vision of judicial neutrality was a second-best solution. If judges could not be reliably considered or compelled to be part of a unified representative regime, and if their behavior exposed an entrenched opposition potentially threatening to civic stability, then they must be quarantined from politics. If they functioned as an aristocratic minority, ensconced in their lifetime tenure and untouchable in the wake of the impeachment's failure, they must be neutralized. Hence, Jefferson's lament:

> Having found, from experience, that impeachment is an impracticable thing, a mere scare-crow, [judges] consider themselves secure for life; they sculk [sic] from responsibility to public opinion, the only remaining hold on them.... An opinion is huddled up in a conclave, perhaps by a majority of one, delivered as if unanimous, and with the silent acquiescence of lazy or timid associates, by a crafty chief judge, who sophisticates the law to his mind, by the turn of his own reasoning.[270]

The passage suggests that Jefferson did not recognize the impeachment's consequence. The impeachment, according to one House manager, Representative Caesar A. Rodney, was intended "to teach a lesson of instruction to future

[268] Elsmere, 298–9.
[269] Keith Whittington, *Constitutional Construction* (Cambridge: Harvard University Press, 1999), 50.
[270] Jefferson to Thomas Ritchie, 25 December 1820, in *Writings* (1859), 1892.

judges, that when intoxicated by the spirit of party, they may recollect the scale of power may one day turn, and preserve the scales of justice equal."[271] And federal judges took it as a warning that they should be removed from politics. It had, in effect, broached a compromise that re-shaped the role of judge in a democratic republic. As that compromise shook out, judges were held apart from the electoral branches in hopes of rendering them less threatening to elected-branch unity.

V. Conclusion

The Founding generation occupied a transitional period, one in which the rights of minorities and of open political opposition seemed to flow from the Declaration of Independence and the Constitution, but the shape that such opposition would take as a stable party cut against the civic republican tenets of their political educations. Both Federalists and Jeffersonians held civic republican assumptions about the unity and concentration of power that led each faction to take for granted a symbiotic and reinforcing relationship among the federal branches rather than view them as checks on one another. Both assumed judges to represent the Constitution as an act of popular sovereignty and that, as such, judicial rulings would merely uncover the singular and fixed constitutional principles. Under these assumptions, the parameters of legitimate interpretation corresponded to and reinforced assumptions about the threat posed by a stable opposition. Interpretations that favored the positions maintained by the opposition were necessarily anti-constitutional and endangered the stability of the republic.

Even as Federalists and Jeffersonians agreed that judges must be kept independent from corrupt politicians, by demonstrating independence from Jefferson's administration, the justices of the Supreme Court revealed to Jeffersonians a refusal to acknowledge popular will. In their eyes, these justices abdicated their representative responsibility. Instead, they protected an aristocratic minority that, within the ideational parameters of republicanism, sought to undermine the Constitution. As Federalists operated equally under these assumptions, they construed Jeffersonians as party-driven and politically corrupt. As such, an assertion of independent judicial will was *necessary* to protect the Constitution. When attention is paid to these civic republican assumptions about unity within the government, opposition as a harbinger of civil war, constitutional meaning as fixed and discoverable, and judges as representative of popular sovereignty, then Jeffersonian attacks on the judiciary reveal themselves not only to be more about the illegitimacy of opposition than the structural legitimacy of judicial review, but also to be rationally strategic actions given the parameters of these assumptions.

That Jeffersonians continued to be hostile toward the Court even after it conceded the constitutionality of the Repeal Act reveals the depth of this

[271] Smith and Lloyd, Vol. 2, 363–4.

fear of entrenched opposition and desire for constitutional stability. It did not matter that the Court had acquiesced in *Stuart v. Laird* and that the Jeffersonians won the partisan policy game because what was considered at stake was not policy but the very security of the Constitution against an aristocratic opposition. Jeffersonians turned to impeachment to remove that opposition from government and to secure civic tranquility under a unified Jeffersonian regime.

When impeachment failed, Jefferson lamented that an aristocratic minority would henceforth be able to use "interpretation" to twist the Constitution from its original principles as ratified by the people, that is, that interpretation could be used to undermine the singular, fixed, and discoverable meaning of the Constitution. That sentiment is captured in Jefferson's letters to Roane and Ritchie cited earlier in this chapter. Yet, Jefferson did not recognize that the Chase trial had begun to alter views about whether judges could or should be considered representative of popular sovereignty. As such, in the face of the Jeffersonians' inability to achieve unification of all federal branches, the meaning of judicial independence was transformed. It came to signify not merely independence from the influence of corrupt executives or legislators, but independence from politics altogether. In short, the concepts of judicial independence and political neutrality were conflated. If judges could no longer be relied upon to serve a representative function, their role had to be re-constructed. The judiciary was relegated to its own unique sphere, one that had no representative function. Judges were to take on a countenance of detachment and neutrality.[272] This construction was a second-best outcome to achieving an elusive regime unity. Instead of seeking this seemingly improbable unity among the three branches, politicians were now directed to clamor for politically neutral judges. But, as the next chapter argues, the dream of unity did not die. Alternative means to achieve it were sought even as they would now compete with this newer framing of judicial independence as political neutrality.

[272] Justice Frankfurter captured this neutral ideal in his dissent in *Baker v. Carr* (1962): "The Court's authority – possessed of neither the purse nor the sword – ultimately rests on sustained public confidence in its moral sanction. Such feeling must be nourished by the Court's complete detachment, in fact and in appearance, from political entanglements and by abstention from injecting itself into the clash of political forces in political settlements," 369 U.S. 186. The Supreme Court remains a symbolic "font of impartiality and legitimacy, of near-infallibility amidst the chaos of conflicting notions of legality." See Harry P. Stumpf, "The Political Efficacy of Judicial Symbolism," *Western Political Quarterly* 19 (June 1966), 294, for this characterization of the Supreme Court.

4

Party against Partisanship

Single-Party Constitutionalism and the Quest for Regime Unity

The Chase impeachment set an ideal of judicial independence as political neutrality, but it hardly resolved the underlying antagonism with the judiciary. By showing that the federal judiciary could not easily be brought into alignment with the other branches, the impeachment began to unravel the idea of regime unity among political leaders; however, it did not diminish their hope that it could be achieved. As this chapter details, the Framers' presumptions of such unity and corresponding fears about federal consolidation against states' rights continued to color politicians' actions well into the next generation. But ideas about opposition also continued to evolve, and with them came a new attitude toward the judiciary. This chapter examines that evolution during the Jacksonian era (1828–60), which witnessed changes in how politicians viewed parties, the opposition's right to rule, and the advantages and threats posed by judicial power. More specifically, it draws out connections among these dynamics.

The Jacksonian era lacked the explosive anti-judicial hostilities of the early Jeffersonian years. This was a relative calm, at best, but the contrast with what came before is indicative of a newly emergent state of affairs. These years mark an intermediate stage between Jeffersonian attempts to undermine judicial authority when it could not be brought to heel and later Lincolnian attempts to manipulate judicial power to implement a particular political party's constitutional vision. In the main, as debate over judicial reforms in the 1820s and 1830s reveal, politicians did not seek to dislodge the judiciary; instead, they debated the best means to maintain it as a branch apart, that is, as neutral, walled-off, and de-politicized. In this way, the new baseline established by the fallout from the Chase impeachment is evident.

The great innovations of the period came in the realm of party building, and as national political organizations were knit together throughout the country, they changed the operations of American government as a whole. Many of these changes, including the relationship between courts and parties, were subtle and incremental. Martin Van Buren, the intellectual champion of the *permanent* party organization, never countenanced the idea of harnessing judicial power for particular partisan purposes. Rather, as will be detailed, he contended that the judiciary needed only to be brought in line with what he would characterize as a perpetual constitutional majority. As such, his intellectual indebtedness to Madison, particularly to the latter's essays from 1792, is highly evident. The ideal of a unified federal regime to protect the Constitution remained fundamental. Van Buren merely stipulated that the Jeffersonian Republicans had failed to achieve that ideal because they had not maintained sufficient discipline. And that lack of discipline stemmed from what Van Buren contended was a mistaken propensity to view party as a temporary tool to cleanse corruption rather than as a permanent organization to maintain the Constitution's principles. His invention, the permanent political party, would achieve what Jeffersonians had not.

The period covered in this chapter opened with President Jackson ignoring an adverse Supreme Court opinion, but closed with the last Jacksonian, President Buchanan, turning to the Court to solve the critical question looming since the Founding, that is, the status of slavery and, more generally, states' rights.[1] The Democratic presidential candidate in 1860, Stephen Douglas, argued that the Court could not be ignored, thereby turning Jackson's position on its head and ironically enabling Republican Abraham Lincoln to claim the Jacksonian tradition as his own.[2] Between these bookends, Democratic politicians seem remarkably inconsistent in their dealings with the federal judiciary. Jackson passively undermined the Marshall Court's legitimacy when it condemned the removal of the Cherokee from Georgia by ignoring the Court's ruling in *Worcester v. Georgia* (1832). He later supported federal judicial authority against South Carolinian assertions for nullification. Yet he actively repudiated the Court's decision in *McCulloch v. Maryland* (1819) when vetoing the re-charter of the national bank.[3]

Additional seemingly contradictory yet opportunistic actions toward the judiciary are evident. For example, Martin Van Buren, as senator from New York, fought against a long-sought judicial reform bill, only to advocate its passage when he served as vice-president, ultimately appointing additional Supreme Court justices by its provisions during his presidency. And when James Buchanan pleaded for the Court to resolve the slavery question and

---

[1] Stephen Skowronek's model of presidents in "political time" sets Jackson as a transformative president whose era closed with the "disjunctive" politics of James Buchanan. Skowronek, *The Politics Presidents Make: Leadership from George Washington to Bill Clinton* (Cambridge: Belknap Press of Harvard University, 1997), 129–96.

[2] See Chapter 5 for a discussion of how Lincoln claimed the mantle of Jackson and made early moves to structure the Republican Party as the replacement of the Democrats as the lone constitutional party.

[3] *Worcester v. Georgia*, 31 U.S. 515 (1832); *McCulloch v. Maryland*, 17 U.S. 316 (1819); see Robert Remini, *Andrew Jackson and the Bank War* (New York: W.W. Norton, 1967); William Freehling, *Prelude to Civil War: The Nullification Controversy in South Carolina, 1816–1836* (New York: Oxford University Press, 1992); and, Richard Ellis, *The Union at Risk: Jacksonian Democracy, States' Rights, and the Nullification Crisis* (New York: Oxford University Press, 1989).

praised it for doing so, Van Buren criticized Buchanan and Chief Justice Taney as traitors to the Constitution.[4] Consistent principles underlying Jackson's or Van Buren's course seem difficult to identify.

Calculations of immediate advantage play some role in explaining these inconsistencies. But this chapter makes sense of these inconsistent moves by placing them in the context of evolving ideas about party politics and the threat that opposition was understood to pose to civil stability. Much can be gained by more closely calibrating the advance on these assumptions.

As detailed in the previous chapter, scholars generally agree that Federalists and Jeffersonians held an underdeveloped sense of legitimate opposition, but the date demarcating the legitimacy of two-party competition and loyal opposition has increasingly been disputed.[5] The received wisdom, which finds modern notions of party and opposition formed no later than 1840, has been challenged, and the history of party development is now being refined in ways that prove helpful in untangling the twisted course of political relations with the judiciary during these years. By taking note of the persistence of anti-party rhetoric by Jacksonian Democrats and, even more so, by Whigs, scholars have pushed the date of modern stable competitive party norms further out.[6] They have pointed to a conception of parties in this period that was different from what came before and distinct from the modern definition of parties as federated groups organized to win elections and advocate policy. Historian Gerald Leonard contends that Jacksonians conceptualized party as the organizational embodiment and protector of the Constitution. And, since the idea that constitutional meaning was fixed, singular, and discoverable still held sway, the legitimacy of party apparatus was predicated upon the existence of only *one* party meant to protect that *one* meaning. Thus, Jacksonians created "a body called 'the democracy' and [held] that the Constitution made the democracy sovereign. Party [was] ... the institutional device by which the democracy might

---

[4] On using the Court to avoid accountability on slavery, see Mark Graber, "The Nonmajoritarian Difficulty: Legislative Deference to the Judiciary," *Studies in American Political Development* 7 (1993), 35–72. On Van Buren's assessment of Taney and Buchanan, see Martin Van Buren, *An Inquiry into the Origin and Course of Political Parties in the United States* (New York: Augustus M. Kelly, 1967), 356–76, as well as the third section of this chapter.

[5] On the traditional history of the evolution of parties, see Richard Hofstadter, *The Idea of a Party System* (Berkeley: University of California Press, 1969); Giovani Sartori, *Parties and Party System* (New York: Cambridge University Press, 1976); Michael Wallace, "Changing Concepts of Party in the United States: New York, 1815–1828," *American Historical Review* 74 (December 1968), 453–91; Ronald Formisano, "Federalists and Republicans: Parties, Yes – System, No," in *The Evolution of American Electoral Systems*, Paul Kleppner et al., eds. (Westport, CT: Greenwood Press, 1981); and James Sharp, *American Politics in the Early Republic* (New Haven: Yale University Press, 1993).

[6] For revisionism on fears of opposition during the second party system, see Gerald Leonard, *The Invention of Party Politics: Federalism, Popular Sovereignty, and Constitutional Development in Jacksonian Illinois* (Chapel Hill: University of North Carolina Press, 2002); Mark Voss-Hubbard, *Beyond Party: Cultures of Antipartisanship in Northern Politics before the Civil War* (Baltimore: Johns Hopkins University Press, 2002); and, Adam I. P. Smith, *No Party Now: Politics in the Civil War North* (New York: Oxford University Press, 2006).

exercise its sovereignty in practice."⁷ Even as they embraced the permanence of party, Jacksonians still "rejected party division *within* the democracy; and so they reaffirmed a kind of antipartyism.... It is this idea – party as the embodiment of the undivided democracy – that has been largely missing from the historiography of party."⁸

This chapter builds on Leonard's observation by arguing that early Jacksonian anti-party sentiment illustrates lingering discomfort with party competition and deeper concerns about a stable opposition's loyalty to the Constitution. It extends this revisionist scholarship to bring this intermediate stage in the development of politicians' ideas about party and opposition to bear on confrontations with judicial power. This chapter pays close attention to Van Buren's explanation of Jackson's relations with the Supreme Court. While Jackson's position on opposition is similar to that of the Founders, Van Buren's explanation suggests a different perspective on opposition and thus on whether and how to manipulate an oppositional Court. Van Buren's perspective is particularly important given his status as the founder of the Democratic Party. The chapter then examines congressional consideration of measures to re-structure the federal judiciary and Van Buren's interpretation of the *Dred Scott* decision. While no single logic underlying all of these actions can be wholly identified, a fuller understanding of views toward opposition on loyalty suggests that they were more than purely instrumental. The principles involved build a bridge to more modern ideas and practices.

I. Unease with Opposition and Jacksonian Views of Judicial Authority

Just as Jefferson's hostilities toward the Court are summarized by his "sappers and miners" statement, Jackson's hostility toward the judiciary is often summarized by the legend of his baiting Chief Justice Marshall: "John Marshall has made his decision, now let him enforce it."⁹ Jackson's comment, which is of dubious historical accuracy, followed *Worcester v. Georgia.*¹⁰ Jackson's

---

⁷ Leonard, 5.

⁸ Ibid. Emphasis mine.

⁹ The statement is attributed to Jackson, but it is unclear whether he said it. Horace Greeley reported it and claimed Representative George Briggs as his source. Remini claims that Jackson never made the statement. If he did, it is possible, as detailed later in this chapter, he meant that the decision left nothing to enforce. Robert Remini, *Andrew Jackson and the Course of American Freedom, 1822–1832* (New York: Harper & Row, 1981), Vol. 2, 276–7.

¹⁰ The case involved Samuel Worcester, who led missionaries in the Cherokee Nation and who opposed a state law requiring all whites living in tribal areas to take a loyalty oath. Worcester refused and was arrested. State court ruled the missionaries were federal employees (Worcester was the federal postmaster to the Cherokee Nation) and were thus exempted from the loyalty oath. The governor convinced the postmaster general to dismiss Worcester, forcing him to take the oath. Worcester refused, was arrested, and was convicted. Worcester applied for a writ of error, leading to a Supreme Court ruling. The Marshall Court overturned the conviction, but the ruling focused on supporting Cherokee independence against the recently passed Removal Act. Gerald Magliocca, *Andrew Jackson and the Constitution: The Rise and Fall of Generational Regimes* (Lawrence: University Press of Kansas, 2007), 22–5, 34–47.

veto of the reauthorization of the Second National Bank, which repudiated the ruling in *McCulloch*, reinforces an alleged pattern: the parallel sentiments and actions seemingly undermining Supreme Court rulings mark Jefferson and Jackson as kindred spirits in their antipathy toward federal judicial power. While Jackson's hostilities were more passive-aggressive – he tended to ignore the Court rather than attempt to dismantle it – they, in conjunction with congressional efforts in the late 1820s to undo federal supremacy by repealing Section 25 of the 1789 Judiciary Act, create a sense that Jackson and his supporters were "vigorous critics of the federal judiciary."[11]

This standard characterization also comports with the portrayal of Jackson's election as a trigger of realignment; anti-judicial sentiment is said to fit and affirm the realignment model.[12] In general terms, undermining judges of the old regime is part of a larger dynamic of political change heralded by the critical election of 1828, change that included expanded suffrage and acceptance of political parties. Yet, as detailed later, Jackson's position on the judiciary is never so clear-cut, and much important variation and need for explanation is lost if we ignore differences between Jefferson's and Jackson's stances toward judicial power and see only the cyclical recurrence of departmentalist presidencies. Jackson did call the authority of the Court into question, but he did not go as far as Jefferson. As will be shown, Jackson did not support the nullification doctrine toward which Jefferson hinted in his Kentucky Resolution. More important, Van Buren justified Jackson's seemingly opportunistic relationship with the judiciary not only through the structural constitutional logic of the presidency as a co-equal branch – as Jefferson had in his letter to Abigail Adams discussed in Chapter 3 – but also through the *extraconstitutional* authority granted to the president by virtue of his leadership of a permanent national political party.

Furthermore, Jackson never supported the effort to repeal Section 25 of the 1789 Judiciary Act, which establishes federal supremacy over state law, and Jackson sustained the legitimacy of judicial review against South Carolina's nullification doctrine.[13] All of these actions indicate that the standard

Jackson is rumored to have belittled the *Worcester* ruling as "stillborn." Chris Tomlins interprets Jackson's response as a "dismissal of the Court's significance." Tomlins, ed., *The United States Supreme Court* (New York: Houghton Mifflin, 2005), xi. However, Jackson's attorney general, Benjamin Butler, noted that the Militia Act of 1795 authorized the federal marshal to enforce the ruling. Only if the marshal encountered resistance could Jackson call up state militia to suppress insurrection. Thus, Jackson's comment may reflect the reality that the president had little way to enforce the ruling.

[11] Richard Longaker, "Andrew Jackson and the Judiciary," *Political Science Quarterly* 71 (September 1956), 341.
[12] Walter Dean Burnham, "Critical Realignment: Dead or Alive?" *The End of Realignment? Interpreting American Electoral* (Madison: University of Wisconsin Press, 1991), 124.
[13] Section 25 of the Judiciary Act of 1789 authorized the Supreme Court to review state court rulings that either upheld state laws against federal prosecution, declared federal laws unconstitutional, or rejected rights claims grounded in the federal Constitution. 1 U.S. Stat. 73, 85–6 (1789). Repealing that provision would severely undermine the federal government's ability

characterization of Jackson as maintaining a Jeffersonian anti-judicial tradition goes too far. Attention to underlying changes in perspectives on opposition and party politics helps to explain why traditional characterizations of departmentalist similarities between Jefferson and Jackson miss the mark.

I.a. *Consistency in Jackson's Relations with the Court: The Threat of Opposition*

Jackson was no foe of judicial review. No evidence exists of Jackson supporting anti-judicial legislation, which included measures to limit judicial tenure and to require bench unanimity on constitutional questions.[14] Nor did he support the repeal of Section 25 of the 1789 Judiciary Act.[15] Jackson wrote to his nephew criticizing this legislation, "the constitution is worth nothing and a mere buble [*sic*] except guaranteed to them by an independent and virtuous judiciary."[16] In short, Jackson grasped the importance of independent judicial power as a bulwark against anti-constitutional forces.

This comprehension is also evident in Jackson's response to the nullification crisis. South Carolinian protest against the tariffs of 1828 and 1832 was based on the idea that states could reject federal law, thereby reviving elements of Jefferson's Kentucky Resolution as well as rehashing an argument against Section 25. In a message to Congress, the president rejected nullification; he argued that state governments had no authority to counter federal law except by seeking redress through federal courts. The alternative was tantamount to expressing a desire for disunion. He took particular note of South Carolina's failure to use available legal channels; that state "has not only not appealed in her own name to those tribunals under the Constitution and the laws of the United States but has endeavored to frustrate their proper action on her citizens by drawing cognizance of cases under the revenue laws to her tribunals."[17] By referring South Carolina's grievance to the judiciary, Jackson again indicated a clear understanding of and support for a federal judicial role in reviewing state legislation. Therefore, Jackson's position toward judicial power cannot be credibly characterized as simply Jeffersonian redux. Still, the puzzle remains: if the judiciary was the proper branch in this case, why would Jackson ignore *McCulloch v. Maryland* and articulate in his veto of the

to assert the supremacy of the federal Constitution over the individual states. If the Supreme Court had no appellate jurisdiction to review state rulings, the Constitution's Supremacy Clause would have been a dead letter. See Maeva Marcus and Natalie Wexler, "The Judiciary Act of 1789: Political Compromise or Constitutional Interpretation?" *Origins of the Federal Judiciary: Essays on the Judiciary Act of 1789*, Maeva Marcus, ed. (New York: Oxford University Press, 1992).

[14] Ibid, 361. See *Register of Debates*, 24 February 1832, 1855–6, http://memory.loc.gov/cgi-bin/ampage?collId=llrd&fileName=012/llrd012.db&recNum=219.

[15] See discussion of Section 25 in Part II.

[16] Andrew Jackson to Andrew Jackson Donelson, 5 July 1822, in John Spencer Bassett et. al., eds. *The Correspondence of Andrew Jackson* (Washington, DC: Carnegie Institute, 1926–1935), Vol. 3, 167.

[17] "Special Message to Congress," 16 January 1833, quoted in Longaker, 360.

national bank re-charter bill a constitutional theory weakening the legitimacy of judicial precedent? Why would Jackson refer South Carolina to the Court in 1833, implying that that outcome would be legitimate, but hold that when Maryland went before the Court in 1819, that outcome was not so?

Opportunistic flip-flopping is one answer. Perhaps Jackson sought to hold together his fragile coalition or aggrandize presidential power, and doing so required supporting judicial authority in some circumstances and denying it others.[18] This explanation, while plausible, is de-contextualized. It ignores evidence of Jackson's skepticism of opposition. Jackson shared the Founding generation's aspirations toward civic tranquility defined by its "demand for internal unity, social solidarity, and virtue." This gave it "utopian dimensions."[19] He was not an early supporter of Van Buren's idea of a permanent political party; instead, he maintained the idea that party was a harbinger of civil instability.[20] His depiction of nullifications' supporters bears out this underdeveloped sense of legitimate opposition. He renounced them in the republican terms of conspiratorial demagogues, as "unprincipled men who would rather rule in hell, than subordinate in heaven."[21] Their "wickedness, madness, and folly ... has not its paralel [*sic*] in the history of the world."[22] Jackson characterized the leader of the nullification movement, John Calhoun, as motivated by "unholy ambition."[23] These words demonstrate all the characteristics of what legal scholar Robert Burt has called the Framers' search for "political unanimity" which "was not simply rhetorical" and which "meant much more than grudging or temporary acquiescence by the losers."[24] Jackson held to the Framers' "belief that all social conflict was polarized dispute."[25] The republic's early politics operated under ideas linking stable opposition to instability, and Jackson's views revealed these assumptions.[26]

Nullification undermined federal supremacy as stipulated in the Constitution's supremacy clause. The doctrine did curtail federal judicial power, but it also limited the federal government's ability to maintain a

[18] Longaker argues that Jackson refused to support the Cherokee decision because doing so would encourage other states to support nullification. Skowronek (1997) views Jackson as going "out of his way to emphasize gradualism and mutual accommodation" to hold together support (136).

[19] Richard Lattner, "The Nullification Crisis and Republican Subversion," *Journal of Southern History* 43 (February 1977), 28.

[20] Gerald Leonard, "Party as a 'Political Safeguard of Federalism': Martin Van Buren and the Constitutional Theory of Party Politics," *Rutgers Law Review* 54 (Fall 2001), 248.

[21] Andrew Jackson to John Coffee, 17 July 1832, *Correspondence of Andrew Jackson*, Vol. 4, 462–3.

[22] Andrew Jackson to Joel Poinsett, 9 December 1832, ibid., 498.

[23] Andrew Jackson to John Coffee, 13 May 1831, ibid., 177.

[24] Robert Burt, *The Constitution in Conflict* (Cambridge: Belknap Press of Harvard University, 1992), 45.

[25] Ibid.

[26] Robert Shallhope, "Toward a Republican Synthesis: The Emergence of an Understanding of Republicanism in American Historiography," *William and Mary Quarterly* 29 (January 1972), 49–80.

semblance of legal uniformity among the states. More pointedly, the nullification doctrine (as well as efforts to repeal the 1789 Judiciary Act's Section 25) *laid bare the idea that political opposition was intent on undermining the Constitution*; both measures would set federal-state relations back to circumstances under the failed Articles of Confederation. Thus, Jackson's seemingly contradictory positions toward judicial power are coherent when it is recognized that they are each motivated by a singular republican aim to protect the Constitution from an anti-constitutional opposition. On the Bank question, the Court claimed an unconstitutional level of federal power at the expense of the states. On the nullification issue, South Carolina claimed a degree of state power that threatened national unity. On the Cherokee removal, the Court denied state authority to regulate the liberties and status of its residents.[27]

Whereas Jackson's defense is a limited Jeffersonianism to the extent that Jackson stopped short of endorsing nullification, Martin Van Buren's explanation of Jackson's position toward judicial power is conceptually distinct from the constitutional claims made by both Jefferson and Jackson. This difference stems from Van Buren's particular position toward opposition politics and the purpose of political parties. As the next section explains, rather than ground presidential authority to interpret the Constitution within the framework of separation of powers, as Jefferson and Jackson had done, Van Buren went outside of the Madisonian architecture. He positioned Jackson's authority as not only drawing on his executive position, but on his popular authority, that is, his position as party leader. Van Buren's explicit focus on the party as the basis for interpretive authority indicates a new development in ideas about the purpose of parties, on views toward stable opposition as it gains shape through parties, and on judicial power as it may represent an entrenched opposition.

I.b. *Van Buren's Democratic Party as Permanent Constitutional Majority*

If Jackson's perspective on opposition hearkens back to that held by many of the Founders, Van Buren's ideas present a clearer epistemological break. Van Buren is a particularly important figure in the development of party politics

---

[27] According to Jackson, implementing the Court's ruling, would compel him to deny state sovereignty: "like other citizens or people resident within the limits of the States, they [the Cherokee] are subject to their jurisdiction and control. To maintain a contrary doctrine and to require the Executive to enforce it ... would be to place in his hands a power to make war upon the rights of the States and the liberties of the country – a power which should be placed in the hands of no individual." "Special Message to Congress," 22 February 1831, http://www.presidency.ucsb.edu/ws/index.php?pid=66803&st=andrew+jackson&st1. See Joseph Burke, "The Cherokee Cases: A Study in Law, Politics, and Morality," *Stanford Law Review* 21 (February 1969), 500–31. Jackson's logic captures the antebellum idea that state citizenship was prior to national citizenship, which Justice Curtiss elaborated in his opinion in *Dred Scott v. Sanford* (1857). See Herman Belz, *A New Birth of Freedom: The Republican Party and Freedman's Rights, 1861 to 1866* (New York: Fordham University Press, 2000), 26.

in the United States, and his writings shed light on connections among changing ideas about the threat posed by opposition, the purpose of party, and
the logic of confronting, ignoring, or otherwise manipulating the judiciary.
He was recognized in his own time and by subsequent generations of historians as the founder of the Democratic Party. He has been called one of "the
organizers/managers of American political life ... who earned their way by
their ability to conceptualize, establish, and run the machinery of politics and
governing ... [and who] took the lead among his contemporaries in remolding
the political order."[28] By the 1840s, however, Van Buren, especially after his
1848 third-party bid for the presidency, was an outlier. His ideas, reflecting
some republican assumptions about the conspiratorial dangers of opposition,
underlay his idiosyncratic perspective on the *Dred Scott* case evaluated later
in this chapter.

Traditionally, Van Buren is considered the founder of modern American
competitive party politics. James Ceaser, for example, described Van Buren
as the "one individual [who] can be accorded the distinction of establishing
permanent party competition in the United States ... [and who] viewed party
competition as a new 'institution' in the constitutional system that could help
eliminate personal factionalism, manage electoral conflict, and prevent presidential elections from being decided by the House under the widely distrusted
auxiliary plan."[29] This depiction ascribes to Van Buren an intention to create two parties battling over policy within an agreed constitutional context.[30]
Richard Hofstadter advanced this thesis when he characterized Democrats
as "less fixed in their view of issues, considerably less ideological" than their
predecessors.[31] Van Buren allegedly had a sensibility that moved past the
Founders' "paranoid" politics of high constitutional stakes.[32]

Van Buren did aim to maintain a party, which he referred to as the
"Democracy." He disparaged President Monroe for undermining the unity
that marked the administrations of Jefferson and Madison. By abandoning
factional divisions, Monroe did "openly all that a man ... could be expected
to do to promote the amalgamation of parties and the overthrow of that
exclusive and towering supremacy which the republican party had for many
years maintained in our national councils."[33] Van Buren blamed the collapse of Jeffersonian dominance on Monroe's decisions to bring Federalists

[28] Joel Silbey, *Martin Van Buren and the Emergence of American Popular Politics* (Lanham, MD: Rowman and Littlefield, 2002), xii–xiii.
[29] James Ceaser, *Presidential Selection: Theory and Development* (Princeton: Princeton University Press, 1979), 123.
[30] Examples of traditional scholarship include Richard McCormick, *The Second American Party System: Party Formation in the Jacksonian Era* (Chapel Hill: University of North Carolina Press, 1966); Joel Silbey, *The American Political Nation, 1838–1893* (Stanford, CA: Stanford University Press, 1994); and Clinton Rossiter, *Parties and Politics in America* (Ithaca: Cornell University Press, 1960).
[31] Hofstadter, *Party System*, 213.
[32] Ibid., 224–5.
[33] Van Buren, *Autobiography of Martin Van Buren*, 303, quoted in Leonard, 2001, 260.

into his cabinet and to support aristocratic Hamiltonian fiscal policies.[34]
Nevertheless, Van Buren considered opposition to be less threatening than
many of the Founders had. For example, in an 1839 speech, he stated, "The
constitution of man, and the nature of public questions ... render a diversity of
views ... almost a moral necessity; and the conflict which such a division of
sentiment invites, when it is divested of personal malignity, is by no means a
public evil."[35] Opposition was a natural state of affairs. Still, acknowledging
the naturalness or persistent character of opposition is not the same as a clear
intent to establish a permanent competitive two-party system, an intent usually ascribed to Van Buren.

Van Buren's wariness toward stable opposition capable of periodically winning power is evident in his telling of history. For Van Buren, history was a
static narrative of a permanent majority defending the Constitution against
an aristocratic minority seeking to undermine it.[36] This dichotomy structured
the Revolution, the ratification debate, and the 1790s.[37] Whereas some politicians attributed the Federalist-Jeffersonian divide "to causes which had either
become obsolete or had been compromised by mutual concession – such as the
early difficulties growing out of our relations with Great Britain and France,
the expediency of a navy, or similar questions," Van Buren contended that it
centered on support for the Constitution. Federalists and Whigs, which Van
Buren referred to as Hamiltonian, aimed "to absorb ... all power from its
legitimate sources, and to condense it in a single head"; Jeffersonians and
Democrats were "laboring as assiduously to resist the encroachments, and
limit the extent of executive authority."[38]

---

[34] Van Buren was aghast that "one of the most dangerous principles ever advocated by Alexander
Hamilton," which is "so much to be deprecated," should be uttered by "one of the first mem-
bers of the old republican party." Van Buren, *Autobiography of Martin Van Buren*, John C.
Fitzpatrick, ed. (New York: Augustus M. Kelley, 1969), 302–5. On Van Buren's interpreta-
tion of the 1824 election, the resulting "corrupt bargain," and the motivation to re-invent the
Jeffersonian party, see Robert Remini, *Martin Van Buren and the Making of the Democratic
Party* (New York: Columbia University Press, 1959), 12–92.

[35] Speech at Schenectady, NY, as quoted in the *Albany Argus*, 5 August 1839.

[36] Martin Van Buren, "Thoughts on the Approaching Election in New York," Papers of Martin
Van Buren, Library of Congress, 33. See also Leonard, 2001, 235–6.

[37] Van Buren, 1867, 7.

[38] Van Buren, "Substance of Mr. Van Buren's Observations in the Senate of the United States
on Mr. Foot's Amendment to the Rules of the Senate," Papers of Martin Van Buren, Library
of Congress, Series 2, Box 7, Microfilm 7, page 8. Van Buren characterizes the main division
at the constitutional convention to be on federal consolidated power versus dispersed state
power. Madison wrote to Van Buren that his characterization was mistaken:

> You will not, I am sure, take it amiss, if I here point to an error in fact in your "obser-
> vations on Mr. Foot's amendment." ... The threatening contest in the Convention of
> 1787 did not, as you supposed, turn on the degree of power to be granted to the Federal
> Government, but on the rule by which the States were to be represented and vote in
> the Government: the smaller states insisting on the rule of equality in all subjects, the
> larger on the rule of proportion to inhabitants: and the compromise which ensued was
> that which established an equality in the Senate, and an inequality in the House of

Although Federalists won popular assent to the Constitution, Anti-Federalism, according to Van Buren, had always been the majority sentiment, and Federalism gained support only through misdirection. The Federalists' name misrepresented their actual position: a "signal perversion of the true relations between party names and party objects" had developed.[39] The "true *federalists*" were but "a single misnomer ... immediately after called *anti-federalists*" to the extent that the federalists were, according to Van Buren, actually nationalists who sought consolidation and an end to states' rights.[40] As such, Federalism was disloyal to constitutional principles; in Van Buren's words, its "influential and leading men forgot that the administration did not, in point of fact, represent the political opinions in respect to the proper uses and spirit of governments in general of a majority of the people."[41] This perversion was made manifest in the promotion of Hamilton's fiscal policy through undemocratic mechanisms, particularly by turning to the Court such as in the *Hylton* case.[42] Van Buren held that Federalist constitutional claims had "been adjudged erroneous and unjust by the judges in the last resort – *the people themselves.*"[43]

Even as Van Buren conceded the inevitability of opposition, rule by the aristocratic minority faction of Hamiltonians, regardless of its changing name, epitomized constitutional collapse.[44] When he made this claim, Van Buren's civic republican assumptions were at their most transparent. He criticized the "old Federal party and its successors for their persevering efforts to destroy the balances of the Constitution."[45] Hamiltonian policy positions represented

---

Representatives. The contests and compromises turning on the grants of power, tho [*sic*] very important in some instances, were knots of a less Gordian character.

Madison to Van Buren, 13 May 1828, Martin Van Buren Papers, Library of Congress, Series 2, Box 7, Microfilm reel 7. See also Van Buren, 1867, 5–8.

[39] Van Buren, 1867, 36.
[40] Van Buren, "Substance," 9.
[41] Van Buren, 1867, 63.
[42] Ibid., 261. That Hamilton chose to work through the judiciary rather than through the electoral process or through an Article V amendment indicated for Van Buren that Hamiltonian positions were the minority. Hamiltonians advocated "government of more energy than was provided for by the Constitution presented by the Convention. This they had a right to desire and to work for through amendments in the way appointed by the Constitution, but in this way they knew they could not obtain what they wanted, and they therefore yielded their ready aid to the measures he proposed by which the Constitution was to be made to mean anything" (Van Buren, 1867, 262).
[43] Van Buren, "Substance," 10.
[44] Van Buren was an intellectual descendant of Madison, even as Madison was an outlier among the Founders. In contrast to Hamilton's *Federalist 9*, which advocated outright suppression of opposition, Madison understood opposition as an inevitable externality of democratic politics, and both sought institutional mechanisms to quell civic unrest. For Madison, the *structure* of government would propel politicians to rise above incentives toward factional politics. As such, *Federalist 10* is not an inchoate celebration of difference and interest-based politics, as has been suggested by some pluralists, but a blueprint of how to lessen factionalism.
[45] Van Buren, 1867, 353.

the interests of a permanent aristocratic minority always defined as anti-Constitutional. Hamilton "designedly gave it [the Constitution] construction, in cases where he deemed that course necessary to the public interest, *in opposition to what he knew to have been the intentions of the Convention.*"[46] The economic policy disputes of the 1790s were illustrative:

> If the Constitution had been upheld in good faith on both sides partisan contests must of necessity have been limited to local or temporary measures and to popular excitements and opposing organizations as shifting and short-lived.... But Hamilton took special care that such halcyon days should not even dawn on the country. He had a riveted conviction ... that the Constitution must *prove a signal failure,* unless it could be made to bear measures *little dreamed of by those who made and had adopted it.*[47]

Political conflict could not be based on policy conflicts within an agreed constitutional framework because Hamilton had turned against that framework almost immediately after it had been ratified. Partisan debate could not be on "evanescent measures" in which adherence might shift among multiple fluid factions in ways Madison foretold in *Federalist 10.* That vision was the "halcyon" dream precluded by entrenched opposition, a dream that even Madison began to abandon in the 1790s. American politics remained fundamentally constitutional and, thus, permanently, high stakes.

Therefore, while opposition was unavoidable for Van Buren, stipulating that fact does not necessarily, much less inevitably, lead to a claim that Van Buren conceptualized a stable system of party rotation. While opposition could not be eliminated, it nevertheless remained anti-constitutional in nature. It was a constant harbinger of instability and civil war. Van Buren's remedy to this problem was different from that of Madison and Jefferson. Van Buren did not entertain Jefferson's inclination "to consolidate the nation once more into a single mass, in sentiment & in object" and thereby eradicate divisions.[48] And while Van Buren agreed with Madison that opposition could be managed, their management solutions were different. According to Van Buren, Madison's solution of separating powers, detailed in *Federalist 51,* failed to guard against aristocratic corruption. Nowhere was this made clearer than in the election debacle of 1824 in which the people were, in Van Buren's eyes, denied their presidential choice.

Van Buren took that election to demonstrate how the Madisonian system failed to guard against the corruption of the aristocratic or "courtly" minority faction. In the months preceding that election, the congressional caucus presidential nominating system collapsed. Four candidates ran: John Quincy Adams, Andrew Jackson, Henry Clay, and the man nominated by the caucus, William Crawford. Despite winning the plurality of popular votes, Andrew

---

[46] Ibid., 137. Emphasis added.
[47] Ibid., 271. Emphasis added.
[48] Thomas Jefferson to David Denniston and James Cheetham, 6 June 1801, Jefferson Papers, Library of Congress.

Jackson lost the presidency to John Quincy Adams through a "corrupt bargain" in which Henry Clay allegedly persuaded representatives to vote for Adams in exchange for the position of secretary of state, a position then understood as a stepping stone to the presidency. Van Buren considered Quincy Adams to be part of the aristocratic minority inclined to manipulate the Constitution to consolidate power in the national government. That he succeeded to the presidency through seemingly "corrupt" machinations only further proved for Van Buren that Adams's faction was anti-democratic and anti-constitutional. Such seeming corruption of democratic processes inclined Van Buren to contend that Madison's institutional design could not guarantee outcomes in line with the common good. If Madison had himself abandoned the *Federalist 10* notion of the enlarged republic making the government safe against aristocratic control, Van Buren now abandoned the idea that the separation of powers, as detailed in *Federalist 51*, held the key to good outcomes.[49]

The 1824 election provided Van Buren the opportunity to re-conceptualize the source of and solution to corruption; he seized upon the contested election as the very reason a new take on the meaning of party was necessary. A permanent party was now *needed* to secure the Constitution.[50] As historian Gerald Leonard has argued, "politicians could not just state the obvious: that organization of party was an effective way to advance an agenda. Everyone knew that; yet, party remained out of bounds as ultimately inconsistent with popular sovereignty and confederated government."[51] Party's earlier connotation as promoting civil instability had to be abandoned and its meaning transformed given new realities, that is, the persistence of an aristocratic corrupt minority. For Van Buren, the "country" majority, the "Democracy," would continue to battle the "courtly" minority, but no longer was it stipulated that the country party would or should fade away as Bollingbroke and, to a lesser extent, Madison had suggested.

Van Buren's "Democracy" was not just an organizational replacement of the caucus system. He characterized it as the institutional embodiment of the Constitution's principles. His writings reveal a clear lack of symmetry between his Democracy and what he called the Hamiltonian faction of Federalists, National Republicans, and/or Whigs. Thus, the Democracy and the Hamiltonian faction were not two parties espousing different but equally valid interpretations of the Constitution. Their interpretations could not be equally legitimate if one were nothing more than the substantive personal agendas of a permanent aristocratic minority. Hamiltonians' periodic

---

[49] For Van Buren's assessment of the 1824 election and how House selection gave power to the anti-democratic and aristocratic Quincy Adams, see Martin Van Buren, "Thoughts on the Approaching Election in New York," Papers of Martin Van Buren, Library of Congress, 34–9.

[50] According to Gerald Leonard, one of Van Buren's "central purposes and justifications" as leader of the Democratic Party in 1836, was "the effective amendment of the Constitution to prevent elections by the House of Representatives." See Leonard, 2001, 223, 247–9.

[51] Leonard, 2002, 232.

electoral victory was, at best, aberrant. They gained power only through the Democracy's lack of organization, Van Buren's explanation for the electoral crisis of 1824, or by the beguilement of the voting public, his explanation for his own loss in 1840.[52]

According to Van Buren, the Federalists, National Republicans, and Whigs were "constructed principally of a network of special interests" and "the policy of their leaders has been from the beginning to discountenance and explode all usages or plans designed to secure party unity, so essential to their opponents and substantially unnecessary to themselves."[53] Federalist policies "rested upon substantial principles," a phrase that Van Buren used derisively to indicate certain pre-determined ends regardless of the procedures used to achieve them.[54] The Democracy, by contrast, lacked "substantive" policy aims, seeking only to promote the constitutional proceduralism of states' rights and popular sovereignty through the mechanism of majority rule. Since the Democracy did not espouse substantive ends, Van Buren maintained that it could not resort to the Hamiltonians' demagogic persuasive impulses.

Van Buren's contention that there could be only one legitimate party is further evidenced by how he defined his opposition. And this one-sided notion is fully embedded in the language of civic republican anti-partyism.[55] For Van Buren, Hamiltonianism was nothing more than a factious vehicle for the pursuit of personal glory and substantive policy outcomes at the expense of fair democratic procedures. It was not parallel in any sense to Van Buren's new invention. Since Van Buren's Democracy supported the Constitution's commitments rather than substantive policy objectives, it needed institutional mechanisms – the caucus, the platform, and so on – to ensure that personality was subservient to party principles; the platform, not the candidate, would matter.[56] In short, Van Buren's Democracy was "an antiparty party of last resort," an organization constructed to defend the Constitution from the machinations of an aristocratic minority intent on consolidating power in the federal government.[57] It was a constitutional party, similar to the idea Madison formulated in 1792, in that it was a party animated by its hostility toward partisanship and meant to guard the Constitution from

---

[52] Silbey, 2002, 153–7; and, Van Buren, 1867, 349.
[53] Van Buren, 1867, 226.
[54] Ibid., 5.
[55] Similarly, Whigs retained the Founders' anti-party animus, and their rhetoric drew on anti-party tropes. In the 1836 election, they ran multiple candidates as if to personify their aversion to the group loyalty of Van Buren's party. In 1840, they avoided writing a platform of principles and instead campaigned through pomp and pageantry bewildering Democrats who sought to debate stated principles. See Michael Holt, *The Rise and Fall of the American Whig Party: Jacksonian Politics and the Onset of the Civil War* (New York: Oxford University Press, 1999), 30–2, 104, 270–3, 345–7; Harry Watson, *Liberty and Power: The Politics of Jacksonian America* (New York: Hill and Wang, 2006), 201–5, 212–27.
[56] Joel Silbey, *The Partisan Imperative: The Dynamics of American Politics before the Civil War* (New York: Oxford University Press, 1985), 62.
[57] Leonard, 2001, 250.

"interpretation" or "construction". Unlike Madison's idea, Van Buren's party would not fade away precisely because the aristocratic faction could likewise never be eliminated.

In summary, by defining opposition in static terms and by linking the majority with constitutionalism, Van Buren reworked the Founders' fear of the stable and permanent party into the very solution needed. Party was no longer the cause of civil strife and constitutional collapse but the means to civic stability. Party served this end because it was, for Van Buren, the institutional embodiment of the Constitution's procedural commitments. It espoused the principle of states' rights, which Van Buren set against the consolidationist aims of the aristocratic minority.

Therefore, Van Buren's tolerance for political opposition should not be conflated with an intention to establish a two-party system that concedes *loyal* opposition. His notion of the purpose of party and his idea of opposition as natural and unavoidable does move beyond most of the Founding generation. His perspective on the legitimacy of opposition represents an intermediary point between the Founders' hostility and the modern acceptance of loyal opposition. Yet his language justifying his institutional innovation reveals the extent to which he remained steeped in traditionally civil republican fears of opposition and concerns about civic instability. Republican concepts of "court" and "country" and the potential threat of opposition underlay Jefferson, Jackson, and Van Buren's readings of politics.[58] Van Buren's party theory is a product of a partisan environment in which "all parties were obsessed with a sense of history and their historical obligation to protect the republican experiment in self-government ... and it was their duty to be ever vigilant that the achievements of the Revolutionary fathers were not squandered by their sons."[59]

I.c. *Van Buren's Party-based Justification of Jackson's Relations with the Judiciary*

If politicians feared opposition as a harbinger of civil strife and maintained that it could be suppressed if not eliminated, and if opposition were entrenched in the judiciary, then one would expect that they would pursue tactics that broadly undermine judicial authority. Hence, the more extreme Jeffersonians sought a broad construction of impeachment for Federalist judges even after the Supreme Court seemingly acquiesced to Jeffersonian demands. If, however, opposition were considered a permanent character of the political landscape yet also understood as excludable through specific institutional mechanisms that promote unity – as Van Buren stipulated – then more passive measures, such as simply ignoring judicial rulings made by that opposition, might be a preferred approach until that opposition could be replaced. The opposition would be

---

[58] Major Wilson, "The 'Country' versus the 'Court': A Republican Consensus and Party Debate during the Bank War," *Journal of the Early Republic* 15 (Winter 1995), 619–47.

[59] Michael Holt, *Political Crisis of the 1850s* (New York: Oxford University Press, 1978), 261.

troubling, but attempting to eradicate or actively suppress it was political folly. Instead, responsible politics required isolating and/or ignoring it.

Because Van Buren's Democracy, by his definition, was synonymous with the Constitution and always represented the majority, then judges whose rulings supported Hamiltonian or opposition principles undermined constitutional commitments. However, if the judiciary were brought into alignment with the properly elected Democracy through the nomination process, then judicial interpretation would maintain the Constitution as much as the constitutional party itself. Unified regime leadership would be achieved. In effect, Van Buren set his single constitutional party above the federal branches as a defender of the Constitution, which made strategic sense if realities on the ground demonstrated the branches to be susceptible to political corruption. For Van Buren, by selecting Quincy Adams as president, the House of Representatives had shown itself to be as susceptible as the Court.

With this understanding of how Van Buren linked his party, the Constitution, and civic stability, his justification of Jackson's veto of the re-charter of the second national bank can now be read as neither purely opportunistic nor as motivated by an assertion of executive supremacy. It flows from Van Buren's conception of Jackson's unique role as leader of the permanent constitutional majority, as leader of the Democracy. The veto struck down legislation and was therefore primarily a conflict with Congress. However, when Jackson vetoed the Bank bill, he did not restrain himself to policy-based objections enunciated in Madison's earlier veto of a re-charter.[60] Jackson made a constitutional claim. He viewed the Bank question not as a matter of fiscal policy but of constitutional meaning, thereby questioning the bounds of legitimate judicial authority. Van Buren contended that the constitutional claim was justified, as he saw the Bank as a tool of the aristocratic Hamiltonian faction. As an institutional form, the Bank violated Democratic Party principles and, what were synonymous, the Constitution's own principles.[61]

Jackson countered the determinacy of judicial interpretation: "The opinion of the judges has no more authority over Congress than the opinion of Congress have over the judges, and on that point the President is independent of both."[62] This assertion follows from Jackson's claim that "each public officer who takes an oath to support the Constitution swears that he

---

[60] Madison vetoed the bill authorizing the Bank on 30 January 1815. He limited his objections to policy claims conceding that a constitutional objection was "precluded in my judgment by repeated recognitions under varied circumstances of the validity of such an institution in acts of the legislative, executive, and judicial branches of the Government, accompanied by indications, in different modes, of a concurrence of the general will of the nation." Therefore, Jackson's Bank Veto is less interesting because it contained policy objections and more so because he articulated a constitutional claim that Madison saw as null. For Madison's veto, see James D. Richardson, ed., *A Compilation of the Messages and Papers of the Presidents, 1789–1897*, 10 vols. (Washington, DC: Government Printing Office, 1899), Vol. 1, 555.

[61] Leonard, 2002, 250–1.

[62] President Jackson's Veto Message Regarding the Bank of the United States, 10 July 1832, http://www.yale.edu/lawweb/avalon/presiden/veto/ajveto01.htm.

will support it as he understands it, and not as it is understood by others."[63] Jackson wrote, "it is maintained by the advocates of the bank that its constitutionality in all its features ought to be considered as settled by precedent and by the decision of the Supreme Court. To this I cannot assent."[64] Jackson's distinction between legislative and judicial precedent suggests a more robust understanding of each branch as engaged in constitutional interpretation. However, it also suggests that judicial power per se was not the direct or only target of the veto.

Rather, the direct target was the old Anti-Federalist fear of consolidation of power in the hands of the federal government and a particular manifestation of that consolidation as Hamiltonian fiscal policy. That policy, in Jackson's view, not only threatened the balance of federal and state power but also was advocated by an aristocratic minority. The president, as representative of the Democracy, was obligated to oppose it. The logic paralleled that offered by Marshall in *Marbury v. Madison* and Jackson's own logic underlying his reaction to *Worcester v. Georgia*. Just as the Court must not abet what it considered an unconstitutional act thereby forcing it to commit a necessarily unconstitutional act, the president must not either.

We need to distinguish between Jackson's logic and Van Buren's characterization of the veto. Jackson's language is Jeffersonian, and Senator Daniel Webster attacked it on the grounds that laying responsibility for constitutional interpretation in so many hands would create chaos: "If the opinions of the President be maintained, there is an end of all law and all judicial authority."[65] In his rebuttal, Webster devoted three pages to judicial authority to interpret the Constitution and seventeen pages on legislative precedent.[66] His speech reveals that Congress too made a constitutional claim. The Bank had been sustained by Congress, the Court, and former presidents:

> It is true that each branch of the legislature has an undoubted right, in the exercise of its functions, to consider the constitutionality of a law proposed to be passed. This is naturally a part of its duty, and neither branch can be compelled to pass any law, or do any other act, which it deems to be beyond the reach of its constitutional power. The President has the same right when a bill is presented for his approval for he is doubtless bound to consider, in all cases, whether such bill be compatible with the Constitution, and whether he can approve it consistently with his oath of office.[67]

Quoting Webster in his treatise, *An Inquiry into the Origin and Course of Political Parties in the United States*, Van Buren took the senator to be conceding

---

[63] Ibid.

[64] Ibid.

[65] Daniel Webster, quoted in Merrill Peterson, *The Great Triumvirate: Webster, Clay, and Calhoun* (New York: Oxford University Press, 1987).

[66] Magliocca, note 42, 145–6.

[67] Daniel Webster, "In the Senate of the United States on the President's Veto of the Bank Bill, July 11, 1832," in *Speeches and Forensic Arguments* (Boston: Perkins & Marvin, 1839), Vol. 2, 112.

that interpretation was not only the judiciary's province.[68] For Van Buren, Webster agreed that Jackson could and did interpret the Constitution: "That in all this [Jackson] was perfectly right, it will be seen even Mr. Webster ... did not venture to controvert."[69]

According to Van Buren, Jackson's interpretive authority did not negate judicial review; it guarded against judicial supremacy. The courts would interpret law, but Jackson could not allow a ruling to have ultimate authority when determining "the true meaning of a doubtful clause of the Constitution."[70] That power resided with the popular majority, which he defined as always synonymous with the Democracy. As such, Van Buren quoted Senator White's defense of the veto: "Each of the departments is the agent of the people ... and where there is disagreement as to the extent of these powers, the people themselves, through the ballot-boxes, must settle it."[71] Van Buren praised this statement, which calls to mind the Framers' notion of representative quality of all three branches (as discussed in Chapter 3), as "the true view of the Constitution" and the perspective of "the founders of the Democratic party."[72]

For Van Buren, Webster's response conflated Jackson's veto with Jeffersonian departmentalism. However, Van Buren distinguished these two claims to constitutional interpretive authority. This distinction is evident in his critique of the veto as substantively correct, but intemperate and exaggerated. He noted that although it was "open to my inspection," he had "little direct agency in its construction."[73] This caveat is important as Van Buren narrowed Jackson's Jeffersonian assertion that "each public officer" must interpret the Constitution as "he understands it." Opponents, like Webster, latched onto that phrase to undermine its legitimacy. Van Buren *agreed*. Still, he contended that the emphasis on Jackson's phrase amounted to "gross perversions of his message."[74] Such Jeffersonian sentiments were, according to Van Buren, merely "unguarded words."[75]

---

[68] Although Van Buren excerpts only the above portion of Webster's speech in his *Inquiry* (317), Webster's next sentence makes clear the boundaries of presidential interpretive right and responsibility: "But when a law has been passed by Congress, and approved by the President, it is now no longer in the power, either of the same President, or his successors, to say whether the law is Constitutional or not.... After a law has passed through all the requisite forms; after it has received the requisite legislative sanction and the executive approval, the question of its Constitutionality then becomes a judicial question, and a judicial question alone" (Ibid.).

[69] Van Buren, 1867, 316.

[70] This quote is taken from Remini, 1984, 339. Remini indicates that Francis Blair wrote the quoted statements in an editorial from the *Washington Globe* dated 27 July 1832, but posits "they clearly carry Jackson's imprimatur. The two men discussed them at the time the Bank Veto was written" (577).

[71] Van Buren, 1867, 330.

[72] Ibid.

[73] Ibid., 315.

[74] Ibid., 329.

[75] Ibid., 316.

While Van Buren defended the veto by noting of the three federal branches that "they each have the right, and it is the duty of each to judge for themselves in respect to the authority and requirements of the Constitution, without being controlled or interfered with by their co-departments," he repudiated Jeffersonian departmentalist implications that would undermine *federal* supremacy.[76] If "each public officer" could interpret the Constitution, that meant that state legislators, state courts, and state governors were set on equal interpretive footing to authorize or construct constitutional meaning. For Van Buren, the Constitution's supremacy clause denied this possibility, and therein lay the constitutional interpretive distinction between Van Buren and Jefferson. The Jeffersonian claim in the Kentucky Resolution, which seemed reiterated in Jackson's "unguarded words," was "too preposterous for credulity itself to swallow."[77] Judicial review was appropriate to maintain *federal* supremacy over the states.

Presidential authority and federal supremacy were connected through Van Buren's notion of party as the permanent static majority. Like Jefferson, Van Buren grounded Jackson's authority to interpret the Constitution in the unique nature of the executive oath of office: "To single out one department from the rest by placing its incumbent under a special oath ... and then to make it his duty to obey the directions of another in that very function, absolutely and unconditionally, would ... be going quite as far in that direction as the character of any people for justice and wisdom could bear."[78] However, he went *further.* He also grounded that authority in the unique position of the president as "the only officer, except the Vice-President, who is chosen by the whole people of the United States," and, by extension, as the Democracy's leader, because that party is always the majority.[79]

Not only did the vertical hierarchy of federalism follow from the Constitution, but the president's position as party leader and therefore representative of the whole Democracy set his constitutional interpretive authority above that of the state officers. The horizontal separation of powers was an altogether different matter. To deny the legitimacy of extra-judicial interpretation would, for Van Buren, render the executive branch and the legislative officers as "ministerial officers only" such that they are "bound, at every important step, to look to the judiciary for guidance, and if they omit to adopt its decisions ... they do so at their peril."[80] By this logic, as leader of the Democracy and as personification of those principles, Jackson was obligated to act against the *McCulloch* ruling but *not* to claim that the president simply could interpret the Constitution as he saw fit.

---

[76] Ibid., 336.
[77] Ibid., 317.
[78] Ibid., 351.
[79] Ibid., 335.
[80] Ibid., 342.

According to Jackson's opponents, the President's refusal to support the Court's decisions in *Worcester* and *McCulloch* confirmed his demeaning of judicial power.[81] Nevertheless, Van Buren turned that argument on its head, viewing the opposition as an aristocratic faction forsaking the Constitution in a desperate attempt to secure its policy objectives through the only means available, judicial supremacy. For Van Buren, recourse to judicial supremacy followed from Hamiltonianism. Only by avoiding the elected branches could the Constitution be twisted in favor of minority aims precisely because elections, held under proper circumstances, would always render a victory for the Democratic majority. Van Buren defined judicial supremacy as "so clearly anti-republican in its character and tendencies" that it had to be "long kept on foot under a system so truly republican as ours." Its rationale drew on the aristocratic distrust of democracy, which "proceeded the most tenacious of our party divisions" and which was fundamentally "an inextinguishable distrust, on the part of numerous and powerful classes, of the capacities and dispositions of the great body of their fellow-citizens."[82] Aristocratic recourse to judicial supremacy stemmed from the dichotomous nature of politics. Minority opposition, although natural, posed a fundamental threat to the Constitution's integrity. Not only did it advocate substantive measures that the people did not support, but it also aimed to achieve those measures through mechanisms and means that were fundamentally undemocratic.

In summary, for Van Buren, as for Jefferson, presidential constitutional interpretation would secure the republic against an opposition if it were entrenched in another branch, but the Jeffersonian and Van Buren logics are distinct. Van Buren advocated a permanent party whereas Jefferson did not. Party would be an instrument to protect the Constitution. Van Buren's party-based authority to interpret the Constitution is grounded in discomfort with opposition if the underlying assumption is that only one constitutional party should and would exist. Multiple valid interpretations of the Constitution are not contemplated.

Van Buren's assessment of Jackson's relations with the judiciary constitutes a civic republican partyism. Jackson could not, in Jeffersonian fashion, simply disagree with the Court on his own executive authority. He nevertheless had the right and responsibility to disagree when judicial rulings were antithetical to constitutional commitments, which Van Buren defined as synonymous with his Democracy's commitments. Jackson's authority to interpret the Constitution was channeled through his position as party leader, that is, as leader of the perpetual majority. He was charged with protecting the Constitution to combat an opposition always defined as anti-constitutional. Jackson's seemingly opportunistic positions toward judicial power were therefore unified, in Van Buren's eyes, by an underlying civic republican motivation to stamp out this threat and to maintain the Constitution against the

[81] Peterson, 236–52.
[82] Van Buren, 1867, 352.

encroachments of an aristocratic minority. Van Buren institutionalized the majority as a constitutional party.

The connection between party and anti-judicial hostilities during the Jacksonian era becomes explicit when we investigate how politicians understood the purpose of their parties in their *own* time. As long as the Democratic Party was considered synonymous with the majority, and the distinction between majority and minority was based on the former supporting the Constitution and the latter undermining it, judicial rulings could be framed as fundamentally anti-constitutional and a threat to civic stability. By focusing on Van Buren's underdeveloped sense of the opposition's right to rule, on his advocacy of a new institutional solution to manage that opposition, and on his inherited presumption of federal branch unity, I have identified a justification of Jackson's position toward the judiciary that is neither wholly hostile to judicial authority nor a purely opportunistic attempt to empower the executive. Furthermore, the purpose of party and the permanence of majority would need to be re-conceptualized if a different relationship with the judiciary were to be forged.[83]

II. The Anti-Partyist Debate to Maintain Judicial Neutrality

Confrontation with the judiciary was not limited to presidential actions. Congress repeatedly took up the question of whether and how to reshape a judiciary that was manifestly inadequate for an expanding nation. The Judiciary Act of 1837 increased the Supreme Court from seven justices to nine; in so doing, it followed the precedent of the 1807 Act, which expanded the Court from six justices to seven. The 1837 Act also extended the circuit court system to newly admitted states.[84] The familiar form of this expansion has led scholars to pay little attention to the Act or the nearly twenty years of debate, particularly an exhaustive debate in 1826, that preceded its passage.[85] By doing the least possible to disturb the system, the 1837 Act allegedly represented deference to the 1789 Act.[86] Traditionally, the 1837 Act is interpreted

---

[83] That re-working is undertaken by Lincoln. See Chapter 5.
[84] In 1807, to accommodate the new states of Ohio, Kentucky, and Tennessee, Congress created a seventh circuit and thus a seventh Supreme Court justice to man that circuit. By 1826, Alabama, Indiana, Illinois, Louisiana, Missouri, and Mississippi joined (Maine became part of New England circuit). These states had federal district courts, but had no recourse to appeal to a circuit court.
[85] Remini devotes no discussion to the 1837 Act in his study of Jackson, *Andrew Jackson and the Course of American Democracy*. David Cole devotes one paragraph to it. See Cole, *The Presidency of Andrew Jackson* (Lawrence: University Press of Kansas, 1993), 242. Felix Frankfurter and James Landis discuss the Act only to the extent that it continued the existing connection between the Supreme Court and the circuits. See Frankfurter and Landis, *The Business of the Supreme Court: A Study in the Federal Judicial System* (New York: Transaction, 2006 [1927]).
[86] Charles Geyh, *When Courts and Congress Collide* (Ann Arbor: University of Michigan Press, 2006), 52–65.

as providing Jackson the opportunity to pack the Court with his fellow partisans; it thereby serves to foreshadow Radical Republican actions thirty years
later as well as FDR's failure to do the same one hundred years later.[87] It is
partisan appointment, pure and simple.

However, this interpretation fails to take note of political context. First,
like the tendency to view President Adam's so-called midnight appointments
as purely partisan, this interpretation ignores that the judiciary's inadequate
and inefficient structure was a constant source of congressional concern since
its very inception. It downplays the reality that congressional debate on judicial reform had taken place each year since 1815, that Presidents Madison,
Monroe, Quincy Adams, and Jackson each called for reform, and that expansion of the Supreme bench was not the only reform considered.[88] The main
alternative – downsizing the Supreme Court and relieving justices of circuit-
riding responsibilities, which had been exactly what the 1801 Judiciary Act
had done before it was repealed – was taken up in three weeks of nearly unin-
terrupted House debate on judicial reform in January of 1826.[89] And it was
taken seriously enough that the Senate Judiciary Committee admitted in 1829
its inability to agree on whether to endorse simple expansion of the Supreme
bench or a complete overhaul ending circuit-riding. Such indecision is evidence
against a clear norm of deference to the 1789 plan.[90]

Second, the traditional interpretation does not allow for the conceptual distinction between "partisan appointment" and what might be termed "party
appointment." The former phrase represents the idea that judicial appointments are given to fellow partisans in hopes of securing judicial rulings that
comport with substantive policy aims. The latter phrase, by contrast, captures the idea that during the antebellum era, when the opposition's right to
rule was not fully granted, judicial appointment operated at the higher stakes
of securing the Constitution against an anti-constitutional threat. It was
not about securing a particular constitutional vision with substantive policy
implications and thereby viewing appointment as a spoil of electoral victory.

---

[87] Maggliocca, 65.
[88] Cole, 242; an 1819 bill, which the Senate passed, re-created the 1801 Act by downsizing the
Supreme Court and relieving the justices of circuit-riding. *Register of Debates*, House of
Representatives, 12 January 1826, 19th Congress, First Session, 954; *Annals of Congress*, 9
December 1817, Senate, 15th Congress, First Session, 419.
[89] Geyh dismisses this alternative as failing because it could not "distinguish the adverse precedent set by 1801"(61).
[90] On 16 December 1828, Senator White of the Senate Judiciary Committee indicated that the
committee considered three reform plans: (1) increase the number of Supreme Court justices
to accommodate new circuits incorporating new stages, (2) divorce the justices from circuit-
riding and lower the number of justices, and (3) locate the Court in Washington, DC, and
appoint more circuit judges. See *Register of Debates*, 16 December 1828, Senate, 2–3. On
Tuesday, 29 January 1829, this committee reported that while all members "agreed that there
was an inequality [in the current system] that should be removed; ... when the committee
came to inquire what was the remedy, they found it impossible to report any specific plan."
See *Register of Debates*, 29 January 1829, Senate, 49.

Party appointment, in the context of Van Buren's single constitutional party, still assumed the ideal of secure governance to be unity among the federal branches. Party appointment, therefore, was about securing the Constitution against civil collapse.

Ultimately, the outcomes of the judicial reform debates can be explained without referencing normative deference to judicial authority or competitive partisan advantage. The debate on judicial structure reveals (1) an intense desire to maintain the judiciary as politically neutral, (2) argument about the best means to do so, and (3) the continued framing of the opposition's alternative proposal in the civic republican language of conspiratorial politics. The 1826 discussion about structure dropped much of 1789's preoccupation with maintaining state court power and distinguishing the roles of the federal courts. Debate about how to structure the judiciary now took on a completely different valance. The 1826 debate focused on how best to keep federal judges walled off from the elected branches. The preoccupation was how best to maintain judicial neutrality. As the spirit of party remained much maligned at the time of these debates, harnessing judicial power for partisan ends was illegitimate. Rather, both sides debated from the same premise: not how to best achieve their substantive policy objectives, but how to insulate the judiciary from substantive political involvement.

II.a. *Judicial Reform: The Jeffersonian Construction of Political Neutrality as the New Paradigm*

During the 1826 debate on judicial structure, members of Congress considered a total re-design of the system including eliminating circuit-riding and establishing a permanent staff of circuit court judges versus simply adding three Supreme Court justices to cover the unmanned circuits. Discussion of both proposals dealt with how best to provide efficiency, uniformity, and equality of access to all citizens, and, more important, how the Court remain beyond the throes of politics. Any particular deference to judicial authority per se is difficult to discern.

Representative Daniel Webster introduced the House Judiciary Committee's proposal on 4 January 1826, which called for ten circuits. Maintaining circuit-riding responsibilities, the bill authorized the appointment of three additional Supreme Court justices (from seven to ten) so that all circuit courts could be staffed. Webster noted that "from the commencement, the System has not been uniform" and that the proposal would relieve the overburdened seventh circuit, provide federal judicial infrastructure to Western states, and ensure representation of new states on the bench.[91] Because the possibility of removing circuit-riding and downsizing the Supreme Court to five justices

---

[91] *Register of Debates*, 4 January 1826, House of Representatives, 19th Congress, First Session, 872–80. Webster notes that the Supreme Court justice who occupies the seventh circuit is so overburdened that he has become physically ill: "it might well be supposed that the Judge there had fallen a martyr to the heavy burden imposed upon him: for he is said to be upon his death bed" (1040).

was considered the primary alternative, Webster also commented on that plan. He conceded that it too would achieve desired systemic uniformity, but he fretted over potential consequences of isolating the justices from the people by keeping them in the national capital: "an intercourse as the Judges of the Supreme Court are enabled to have with the Profession, and with the People, in their respective Circuits, is itself an object of no inconsiderable importance. It naturally inspires respect and confidence, and it communicates and reciprocates information through all the branches of the Judicial Department."[92]

Webster recycled the Federalist ideas, reviewed in Chapter 3, that circuit-riding would bring the Supreme Court closer to the people, that the federal judiciary would unify the various states, and that interaction would mollify hostility toward the unelected branch. He further contended that the alternative proposal to end circuit-riding would inspire anti-judicial hostilities: "if the number of the Court were reduced, and its members wholly withdrawn from the Circuits it might become an object of unpleasant jealousy, and great distrust."[93]

Advocates of the proposal to end circuit-riding responded by inverting the corruption argument. They argued that judges were equally corruptible by their contact with the people as they would be if they were insulated from them. Representative Mercer saw judicial corruption as the necessary *result* of circuit-riding: "You are to send a Judge from this Court into a distant circuit, popularity hunting. You send him to imbibe the taint of popular prejudice, and then bring him back to inoculate the Court."[94] Judges who would have otherwise been neutral statesmen would be corrupted by their contact with popular prejudices.

The proposal to expand the Supreme Court to man new circuits was also criticized for undermining judicial neutrality by fostering "judicial representation." Bench expansion, some members of Congress alleged, would lead to appointments from particular regions; doing so would incorporate local prejudices into the interpretation of federal law at the expense of judicial neutrality.

---

[92] Ibid., 877–8.
[93] *Register of Debates*, 4 January 1826, House of Representatives, 19th Congress, First Session, 880. This logic was again stipulated in the 1830 debate about judicial structure. In that later debate, Representative Polk reiterated this claim by linking circuit-riding to maintaining public confidence in the Court: "By withdrawing the judges of this court from the view of the people, and constituting them a corporation of dignitaries at the seat of Government, ... with no direct responsibility to the people, and only liable to punishment for gross crimes and misdemeanors, there is danger that public confidence in their integrity may be weakened – that they may become odious, and their decisions cease to be regarded with that respect and submission which it is desirable they should be" (*Register of Debates*, 20 January 1830, 550). Polk's speech illustrated how judges, promoted as neutral statesmen, had gained "public confidence." If they were confined to the nation's capital, they would be vulnerable to the factious divisions that defined legislative politics. Exposure to the people and time away from the capital would prevent this.
[94] Ibid., 6 January 1826, 906.

In Representative Burges's estimation, an expanded Supreme bench would foster judicial representation even though "no such provision is found in the Constitution" to support this aim.[95] Further, if the bill did not specify that the justices were to be appointed from particular regions of the country – which it did not – then advocates of such representation must, according to Burges, be motivated by party to the detriment of judicial neutrality:

> Although they have not committed themselves to the restraint of definition, yet, if their representation be not of talent, if it be not of statistics, then, sir, it must be a representation of the political parties.... It must comprehend all the great doctrine of electioneering: the whole learning of public address, either from the press or the stump; and the entire array of interests, sections, families, patronage, proper to be brought into service, to push a man, either into office, or out of it. Can any man, not lost to reason, desire a plan for carrying this kind of representation into the Supreme Judicial Court of our country? The naked possibility that such an event may ever happen, fills the mind with horror.... From whatever point of view ... you look at this political representation, in our august tribunal of national justice, you see it at war with the Constitution.[96]

The anti-partyist tenor of this statement is clear. Representative Mercer opposed bench expansion on similar grounds: "should it [the Supreme Court] not therefore be elevated far, far above party feeling, and sectional prejudice?"[97] The House bill, it was maintained, would merely pack the Court with political rather than judicial characters. When advocating the alternative proposal to end circuit-riding and countering the objection that doing so was likewise partisan, Burges turned his own argument on its head by suggesting that such partisanship had long since passed: "Those unhappy days are past and we are indeed now all 'brothers of the same principle.'"[98] As such, no partisan motivations could be assigned to the alternative plan, even if structurally it was nearly identical to the 1801 Judiciary Act.

In support of the Bench expansion, Representative Wickliffe agreed with Burges's characterization of the political atmosphere; the days of faction had ended, and that was precisely why Burges's fears about judicial representation were nonsensical. For Wickliffe, no significant opposition existed, party spirit had retreated, and representation on the bench could therefore not reify divisive factions if none existed:

> But the gentlemen from Virginia says, new parties have arisen in the country, and new doctrines are afloat; and they are now introduced into this House; and if this bill passes, they are to be introduced upon the bench of the Supreme Court. What parties does the gentleman allude to? And what are the new doctrines at which he is so much alarmed? He has not furnished

[95] Ibid., 23 January 1826, 1087.
[96] Ibid., 1088.
[97] Ibid., 11 January 1826, 942.
[98] Ibid., 1094.

the Committee with that evidence which will authorize them to arrive at the conclusions he desires.[99]

This claim about the end of party was paired with rhetoric that defined judicial independence as political neutrality and that defended judges as neutral statesmen. Advocates of the House bill argued that judicial representation would not exacerbate partisan, factional, or sectional sentiment, but support the neutrality ideal. For example, Wickliffe stated, "I do not mean, nor did the gentleman alluded to [Clay of Kentucky] mean, that all the passions and party feelings and factious notions of all or part of this Union should be represented upon the Supreme Bench."[100] The justices "will never be seduced from that high and firm Republican stand which they have taken, by motives so base: nor will they become the blind and foolish opposers of an administration, for the mere honor of being in the opposition."[101] This rhetoric drew directly on the Jeffersonian re-construction of the Court brought forth by the Chase impeachment. Similarly, against the claim that three new Justices would bring "injustice, prejudice, and party feeling" to the bench and thereby corrupt sitting judges and that circuit-riding would expose the Justices to "political contagion," Representative Livingston asserted:

> Sir, the operation would be vain! Those respectable men have been vaccinated by honor, integrity, and truth; they need not fear the infection – even if it corrupt others, they are safe.... I cannot reconcile to it the fear, that, under any circumstances, they can become converts to the heresies, in law and morals, which are apprehended. The effect, sir, must be the reverse: if any political partisan should be selected to fill that high station, he will, himself, be converted to the truth by the reason, firmness, and learning, of his associates. The air of that tribunal is too pure for any reptile who might creep to the seat in order to poison it with his venom. And if there be any man in this assembly – I will not do it the injustice to believe there is one – who supports this bill under a belief that it is to be made the vehicle for carrying political opinions to the bench, that man grossly deceives himself.[102]

Not only is the spirit of party maligned in this passage, but also judges are perceived and promoted as immune to such spirit.

Besides this concern with maintaining judicial neutrality against corruption, representatives hostile to the elimination of circuit-riding recycled civic republican ideas of the judiciary as national unifier, invoked fears of civil unrest, and utilized rhetoric of faction and "courtly" corruption. For example, Representative Williams advocated the House committee bill because the judiciary's unifying effect would quell unrest: "By rejecting [the bill], discontent and uneasiness will prevail throughout the whole Western country – whereas,

---

[99] *Register of Debates*, 11 January 1826, House of Representatives, 19th Congress, First Session, 948.
[100] Ibid., 951.
[101] Ibid., 953.
[102] Ibid., 17 January 1826, 1013.

if we pass it, the People will be rendered tranquil to a very considerable extent. Let the spirit of nation, through the Judiciary, move upon those elements, so agitated and convulsed."[103] Representative Dorsey similarly contended that in the absence of reform, residents in newer states would rebel: "If, in the administration of justice, they seem themselves in a position inferior to that in which the rest of the People of the United States are placed, it will abate their attachment to the Union."[104] If this bill failed, he predicted "discontent and uneasiness will prevail in the whole Western country."[105] In parallel phrasing, Representative Ingersoll foretold of "alienat[ing] their attachments to this Union."[106]

Similarly, Representative Wright defended bench expansion, characterizing the judiciary as having a unifying and salutary effect on the large nation:

> If such beneficial results have followed the sending of your Judges into the fourteen Atlantic States, why will you still exclude the Western States from participation in these results? ... Why have you afforded your aid to quiet the alarms, and remove the jealousies of the People in the Atlantic States, and refuse to dissipate the fears and disquietudes, said to be so prevalent in the West?[107]

Wright's speech focused on how the bill achieved uniformity, thereby eliminating grievances of unequal access. Only in the last sentence did he mention the 1789 Act. And even here, he did not raise the Act as precedent but only to counter arguments by Representatives Pearce and Powell, who advocated an end to judicial appointment entirely. Pearce and Powell's extreme alternative again suggests that the debate included quite radical proposals and was not animated by deference to the 1789 design.[108]

Representative Livingston invoked the republican concern with maintaining civic tranquility. Echoing Webster, he argued that ending circuit-riding would lead to judicial corruption: "I fear no evil from the Judges mixing with the People. I fear much more from confining them to the performance of duties within the District of Columbia. If the [alternative] system ... [is] perserved [*sic*] in for half a century, the principles of this Government, at the end of that time will, in my opinion, be very little more like that which prevailed in 1798, than the present Government of England is like that which existed in the reign of William the Conqueror."[109] In other words, Livingston framed the potential consequences of re-designing the whole system as undermining the Constitution entirely, just as the Jeffersonians had framed the Sedition Act and the Adams administration more generally.

---

[103] Ibid., 12 January 1826, 968–69, 970.
[104] Ibid., 963.
[105] Ibid., 968.
[106] Ibid., 17 January 1826, 1015.
[107] Ibid., 19 January 1826, 1048.
[108] Ibid., 1051.
[109] Ibid., 17 January 1826, 1006.

In short, advocates of both proposals started from the premise that judges were or should be neutral and completely shielded from politics. The simple proposal for adding justices and maintaining circuit-riding was criticized for exposing judges to popular prejudices and fostering judicial representation that would bring sectional prejudices onto the bench. The total re-design, which would have ended circuit-riding, was criticized for entrenching the judges in the "courtly" and corrosive atmosphere of the national capital, likewise undermining judicial independence, conceptualized as absolute political neutrality. Far from showing any deference to the 1789 Act, the 1826 debate and its briefer recurrences throughout the 1830s demonstrate an obsession with judicial neutrality, but no agreement on how to maintain that ideal. Each alternative was viewed as leading to a politicized judiciary and thus undermining the Jeffersonian legacy of the Chase impeachment.

Frankfurter and Landis contend that the 1826 bill succumbed to congressional indifference.[110] The extensive debate raises doubts about this assessment. Alternatively, Geyh argues that the 1826 debate collapsed under the weight of "conflicting notions of judicial independence and accountability."[111] While a burgeoning sense that the Court should be insulated from party and politics is apparent in these debates, Geyh offers no assessment of the language of faction that underlies this motivation. No connection is drawn to the way in which party is disparagingly framed and how anti-partyism reflects ongoing fears of opposition inherited from the Framers' generation. Without focusing on the fear of opposition, the eventual passage of the 1837 Act is misread as deference to the 1789 Act.

The ultimate death of the 1826 bill illustrates congressional efforts to keep the Quincy Adams administration weak, tainted as an illegitimate minority by the election crisis of 1824. The Senate appended an amendment calling for a new arrangement of states in each circuit and restricted the president's selection of a justice from a pool of residents within a particular circuit. In other words, the Senate explicitly wrote into the bill the very prospect of judicial representation that had caused so much ire in the House. The House called for a conference with the Senate, which the latter refused. Van Buren, then senator for New York, introduced the resolution to refuse a conference with the House and noted his motives in his *Autobiography*. He characterized his actions as "resisting the project of the [Quincy Adams] Administration in respect to the Judiciary Bill."[112] In his estimation, the expansion of the judiciary was a repeat performance of 1801, of a popularly repudiated aristocracy attempting to use the judiciary to achieve its anti-constitutional objectives. Viewing the bill as supported by a minority opposition administration that should never have gained power in the first place, Van Buren amended it to demand judicial representation in a strategic effort to kill it. His action does

---

[110] Frankfurter and Landis, 32.
[111] Geyh, 64.
[112] Van Buren, *Autobiography*, 198.

not suggest that he was anti-court per se; rather, it demonstrates that he took whatever measures were necessary to weaken the minority faction, which by the parameters of his party theory, threatened the Constitution. Once the constitutional party, "the Democracy," was ascendant, judicial expansion would suffice to unify the branches under the control of the perpetual majority. In short, "party appointment" could proceed once the Democracy had re-gained control of the government and could re-set the constitutional ship of state.

II.b. *Failure to Repeal Section 25: Securing Federal Supremacy not the Court*

Amid annual re-introductions of judiciary reform bills, the House took up legislation to repeal Section 25 of the 1789 Judiciary Act.[113] In part, the repeal effort served to warn the Marshall Court not to challenge the Indian Removal Act, which Chief Justice Marshall was known to oppose. While repealing Section 25 would not necessarily remove the Court's jurisdiction to declare the Removal Act unconstitutional – because it would undermine vertical review of state law and state court rulings but not horizontal review of congressional legislation – it nevertheless would put the Court again on notice that open opposition and thus regime disunity would not be permitted.[114] The Court had already adjudicated the 1789 statute's constitutionality, and it found the jurisdiction granted to be appropriate and required by Article III's stipulation that the judicial power "shall be vested in one supreme court" and that that power "shall extend to all Cases ... arising under this Constitution."[115] Repeal of Section 25 would not only eliminate federal review of state law that might conflict with federal statute, but because cases involving federal law often began in state courts, the Court would have limited ability to adjudicate the status of federal law entirely.[116] The repeal effort was an attack on judicial authority in pure Jeffersonian fashion.

The majority of the House Judiciary Committee supported its repeal.[117] Representative James Buchanan authored a minority report, which has been

---

[113] 1 U.S. Stat. 73, 85–6 (1789).

[114] As Magliocca notes, Marshall's opposition to the Removal Act was clear; he wrote to a colleague, "Humanity must bewail the course which is being pursued [by Congress]. Furthermore, Marshall had been a long-time advocate of improving relations with Native Americans, sponsoring a bill, when he served in the Virginia House of Burgesses, to promote marriage between Native Americans and Virginians. See Marshall to Dabney Carr, 21 June 1830, in John Pendleton Kennedy, *Memoirs of the Life of William Wirt, Attorney General of the United States*, 2 vols. (Philadelphia: Lea and Blanchard, 1849), Vol. 2, 253–8, quoted in Magliocca, 35. On the connection between the Cherokee case and the Section 25 repeal effort, see Magliocca, 36–7.

[115] See Justice Joseph Storey's opinion for the Court in *Martin v. Hunter's Lessee*, 14 U.S. 304 (1816).

[116] See generally Marcus and Wexler, 1992.

[117] "Report upon the Judiciary," *Register of Debates*, 21st Congress, Second Session, Appendix, lxxvii.

credited with significant persuasive power.[118] However, it is more likely that because the committee was overwhelmingly Southern in its composition, the majority report was unrepresentative of the broader Jacksonian coalition in the House.[119] Southern Jacksonians tended to be the most anti-judicial wing of that coalition. However, more so than simply anti-judiciary, these men were troubled by the potential for expansive federal power at the expense of individual state sovereignty. They maintained the Anti-Federalist presumption and fear that federal unity, as discussed in Chapter 3, would lead to consolidation of power against the states. For them, Section 25 was an emblem of that drive toward consolidation. As such, the failure of the repeal effort reveals more about the drive to secure federal power than about deference to judicial authority or to the 1789 Judiciary Act per se.

The principle of legislatively conferred jurisdiction was sound doctrine throughout the antebellum era. Judicial authority was considered to rest on congressional assent. As the Court recognized in *Wiscart v. Dauchy* in 1796, "if Congress has provided no rule to regulate our proceedings, we cannot exercise appellate jurisdiction."[120] As late as 1850, Justice Grier articulated the principle that judicial power was soundly grounded in congressionally authorized jurisdiction-granting: "Congress is not bound to enlarge the jurisdiction of the Federal courts to every subject, in every form which the Constitution may warrant."[121] As to stripping jurisdiction, Justice Peter Daniel emphasized in *Cary v. Curtis* (1845) that Congress could do so if it "may seem proper for the public good."[122]

However, repealing Section 25 would undermine the entire logic of federal supremacy. The repeal effort was essentially a restatement of principles underlying Jefferson's Kentucky Resolution. The House committee report "denied that the judicial department of the Federal Government, or all the departments of that Government conjointly, were empowered to decide finally and authoritatively, in questions of sovereignty, controversies between a State and

---

[118] *Register of Debates*, 24–29 January 1831, House of Representatives, 21st Congress, Second Session, 532–42. "Counter-Report Upon the Judiciary," *Register of Debates*, 21st Congress, 2nd Session, Appendix, lxxxi. On Buchanan's persuasive abilities, see Robert J. Pushaw, Jr., "Congressional Power over Federal Court Jurisdiction: A Defense of the Neo-Federalist Interpretation of Article III," *Brigham Young University Law Review* (1997), 882, note 149. For a similar assessment, see Frankfurter and Landis, 44.

[119] To the extent that the House Judiciary Committee was unrepresentative of Jacksonian positions on federal power and states' rights, it was non-informative; it could not provide useful information for the House to credibly position itself. On committees as informative in this regard, see Keith Krehbiel, *Information and Legislative Organization* (Ann Arbor: University of Michigan Press, 1992), 61–150.

[120] *Wiscart v. Dauchy*, 3 U.S. 321 (1796)

[121] *Sheldon v. Sill*, 49 U.S. 441 (1850)

[122] *Cary v. Curtis*, 44 U.S. 236 (1845). On congressional authority to manage jurisdiction, see Robert Clinton, "A Mandatory View of Federal Court Jurisdiction: Early Implementation of and Departures from the Constitutional Plan," *Columbia Law Review* 86 (1986), 1515–621.

Federal Government."[123] In other words, the report took aim at the federal government as a threat to state sovereignty, not at an allegedly countermajoritarian judiciary against the elected branches. Repealing Section 25 struck at the heart of federal judicial power, but the target was *federal* power, not only *judicial* power.

Van Buren held federal supremacy as a bedrock principle of the Constitution. His thoughts on the implications of Jackson's Bank veto made that clear. Repealing Section 25 would severely limit federal authority over the states more generally, with potential implications of weakening congressional authority as much as federal judicial authority. The repeal, therefore, was, for Van Buren, fundamentally anti-constitutional. Furthermore, in general, members of Congress would tend not be inclined to undermine federal power, as they were members of a federal branch. By maintaining Section 25, federal supremacy, not simply judicial power, was preserved. Therefore, that the repeal effort failed can be explained without referencing normative desires either to secure the design of the Founding generation or to defer to judicial authority more generally.[124]

Tellingly, Buchanan's minority report made no mention of the importance of preserving the longer term strength of the judiciary in case Jacksonians should ever find themselves in the minority. In other words, there was no indication in the minority report of a strategic long-term strategy of empowering the judiciary as a means to entrench political aims if Jacksonians lost their congressional majority.[125] But this absence of the very strategy that is so often associated with more contemporary inter-branch relations (see discussion in Chapter 1) is entirely understandable once Jacksonian assumptions about a permanent aristocratic minority opposition, permanent majority standing, and rotation in power or lack thereof are taken into account. Put differently, why would Buchanan make a strategic preservation argument if ideas about the opposition's right to rule and rotation of power remained underdeveloped among this first generation of Democrats? In other words, no clear logic of harnessing judicial power through appointment or through tampering with jurisdiction is voiced. By contrast, the primary rationale for preserving Section 25 was limited to maintaining federal power over the states. Utilizing judicial power as a tool through which to lodge political interest was not discussed.

---

[123] Report upon the Judiciary," *Register of Debates,*" 21st Congress, second session, Appendix, lxxviii.

[124] The repeal effort was voted down 138 to 51.

[125] Mark Graber, "James Buchanan as Savior," *Oregon Law Review* 88 (2009), 131–2. Once the opposition's right to rule and rotation in office was conceded, politicians would be clearer about their longer term interests in maintaining judicial power. As detailed in Chapter 7, Senator John McCain was explicit in maintaining the filibuster against judicial nominees for precisely the reason that his party may be in the minority and need that tool. On party entrenchment in and empowerment of the judiciary preceding electoral loss, see Ran Hirschl, *Towards Juristocracy: The Origins and Consequences of the New Constitutionalism* (Cambridge, MA: Harvard University Press, 2004), 38–49.

II.c. *Jacksonian Bench Expansion: Was It Harnessing Judicial Power?*

President Jackson signed on to an increase of the Supreme Court bench from seven to nine justices in March of 1837 just before Van Buren took office. Jackson pushed for the expansion of the Supreme Court after Marshall's death, and Roger Taney was approved as chief justice.[126] Counterfactually, Jackson could have supported the main alternative to the proposed bench expansion, that is, downsizing the Supreme Court and divorcing justices from circuit-riding responsibilities. This plan would have placed Western states on equal footing while also minimizing any interpretation that the Court should have an expanded role. It also potentially would have allowed for a new layer of circuit courts to be set up and thereby provide Jackson and Van Buren with partisan entrenchment in the federal judiciary. There is little in Jackson's correspondence to indicate why he did not advocate the alternative. However, adding more justices did the least to disturb the existing structure. It is likely that as the first Western president, Jackson wanted to resolve the matter of judicial coverage to those Western states lacking full access before he left office. And the alternative was tainted by its structural resemblance to the Judiciary Act of 1801. Furthermore, expanding the Supreme Court bench no longer harbored the possibility of an entrenched opposition as it had in 1826. By 1837, Van Buren could contend that his constitutional party had fully wrested control over the federal government from the aristocratic minority. Party discipline had provided the means to achieve unified federal government.

Given Jacksonian assumptions – evident in Van Buren's writings – about the opposition's right to rule, the stability of the Constitution, and aspirations toward regime unity, it would be a mistake to consider the Judiciary Act of 1837 a strategic attempt to pack the Court with partisan supporters. The Act did not aim to achieve partisan entrenchment in the judiciary as we might define the concept in the contemporary sense, but "party appointment" within Van Buren's framework that conflated majority, party, and the Constitution.[127] This distinction is important. As long as the "Democracy" remained in control – which it would, according to Van Buren, through his various institutional innovations and which it must because the opposition was by definition a minority faction – bench expansion could not turn constitutional interpretation toward the aspirations of the Hamiltonian minority. By the framework of Van Buren's party theory – which rested on the twin presumptions that the federal branches would remain unified and that the minority would not regain the reins of power if party discipline were sustained – judicial power posed no threat to popular sovereignty or states' rights. Party unity would secure appointment of judges who adhered to those principles. Van Buren contended that he had found the institutional solution to manage opposition, to maintain

---

[126] Magliocca, 66–9.

[127] On partisan entrenchment through judicial appointment, see J. M. Balkin and S. Levinson, "Understanding the Constitutional Revolution," *Virginia Law Review* 87 (2001), 1045–109.

the government in the hands of the constitutional majority, and to achieve the presumption and dream that stemmed from republican ideals, namely, unity among the federal branches.

In short, even as politicians continued to stress neutrality of judges, they maintained that the judiciary should remain in lockstep with the majority. Neutrality was a second-best solution in 1826, but by 1837, under the assumption that the permanent party would henceforth eliminate the possibility of minority aristocratic opposition in governance, federal branch unity could be achieved. The three branches would thereby constitute the dream of unified constitutional leadership rather than division between an entrenched minority aristocratic faction and a majority constitutional party. Indeed, John Calhoun conceded this unitary objective in his struggle against federal consolidation: "judges are, in fact, as truly the judicial representatives of this united majority, as the majority of Congress itself."[128] Judges and elected branches were aligned. For Calhoun, an advocate of the repeal and nullification, this view of the branches was troubling, just as it had been for Anti-Federalist Brutus; for Van Buren, it was the realization of civic and constitutional stability that had eluded the Jeffersonians.

III. Judges as Disloyal Opposition: Van Buren on the *Dred Scott* Case

By Van Buren's logic, so long as judges adhered to the principles of the Democracy, their rulings would pose no threat to the Constitution. Judicial power per se was not the cause for concern. Opposition in the judiciary was. By 1837, properly maintained party discipline, Van Buren contended, had minimized the threat and would continue to do so. Ultimately, to Van Buren's dismay, even getting Jacksonian judges on the Supreme Court did not succeed in eliminating the aristocratic minority faction from a seat within governance. However, Van Buren maintained that this result was not because his ideas were flawed. Rather, he contended that the judges turned out to be clandestine Federalists, members of the aristocratic minority who had long hidden their true proclivities. Nowhere is Van Buren's frustration clearer than in his interpretation of Chief Justice Taney's ruling in the *Dred Scott* case.

Van Buren concurred in Chief Justice Taney's interpretation that the Founders never meant to extend citizenship to individuals of African descent, but Taney went too far.[129] According to Van Buren, the chief justice could have declared Scott not to be a citizen for purposes of the Diversity Clause under which the case had been brought to the federal courts.[130] And he could have ruled against Dred Scott's claim by arguing that while Mr. Scott had traveled

---

[128] John C. Calhoun, "Fort Hill Address," *The Nullification Era: A Documentary Record*, William Freehling, ed. (New York: Harper Torchbooks, 1967), 145. In other words, Calhoun supported states' rights because he saw the three branches as unified against state power.

[129] Van Buren, 1867, 356.

[130] Ibid., 358–62.

to federal free territory, as defined by the Northwest Ordinance, by returning to the slave state of Missouri he essentially re-enslaved himself. However,
Taney's ruling reached beyond this narrow – if still morally reprehensible –
construction to declare that states could not define the bounds and terms
of citizenship.

According to Taney, "It is very clear, therefore, that no State can, by any
act or law of its own, passed since the adoption of the Constitution introduce
a new member into the political community created by the Constitution of the
United States."[131] Taney distinguished between state citizenship and national
citizenship. National citizenship was quite broad for Taney. No citizen of one
state could be denied privileges and immunities if they resided in another as
stipulated in Section 2 of the Constitution's fourth article. However, the status of people of African descent could not fit within this paradigm. It did not
make sense, according to Taney, that representatives of slave states during
the constitutional convention in Philadelphia would have intended to provide
rights to people of African descent at a national level that they would simultaneously deny them within the boundaries of their own states.[132] He relied
on the constitutional ban on the international slave trade in 1808 and on the
clause stipulating the return of property to illustrate that "the negro class"
was considered "a separate class of persons ... not regarded as a portion of
the people or citizens of the Government then formed." Therefore, as regarding the relevant constitutional clause of Article IV, "it is impossible to believe
that these rights and privileges were intended to be extended to them."[133] Put
differently, according to Taney, not only were blacks not historically citizens,
but no state could confer citizenship status on them. Doing so would imply
coverage by the privileges and immunities clause. Intent to provide such coverage was implausible given the existence of slave states. If blacks were not
citizens at the time of the Founding, they could never be citizens because no
state had the authority to alter the boundaries of national political community
established by the Constitution. Granting people of African descent state-level
citizenship would have that effect by virtue of the privileges and immunities
clause in Article IV.

For Van Buren, Taney's denial of the states' right to determine citizenship
and slavery status of its own inhabitants was the real violence committed by
the *Dred Scott* ruling. Taney had rejected the fundamental principle of states'
rights underlying the Democracy, and thus underlying the Constitution. He
denied the states' sovereign right to engage in majoritarian processes to determine whether it would allow slavery within its borders. In theory, Taney's
ruling decimated the logic of states' rights, popular sovereignty, and majority
rule. In practice, the ruling invalidated the Kansas-Nebraska Act of 1854 as

---

[131] *Dred Scott v. Sanford*, 60 U.S. 393 (1857); Taney delivered the opinion of the court.
[132] Belz, 2000, 19–20.
[133] *Dred Scott v. Sanford*, 60 U.S. 393 (1857).

that law allowed states to rely on mechanisms of popular sovereignty to determine their slave or free status.

For Van Buren, the Kansas-Nebraska Act was not just another attempt
by Congress at a policy compromise to avoid the slavery question. It was an
expression of Democratic procedural majoritarianism and thus the embodiment of the Democratic Party's key principle.[134] By denying the constitutional
legitimacy of majoritarian processes agreed to by Congress, Taney abandoned
the fundamental principles of Van Buren's Democracy. In the context of this
betrayal, Van Buren foretold the downfall of his party:

> The Democratic party, always before the able and zealous defender of the
> Constitution ... had entered upon a path which leads directly and inevitably
> to a revolution of the Government in the most important of its functions – a
> revolution which would in time substitute for the present healthful and bene-
> ficial action of public opinion the selfish and contracted rule of a judicial oli-
> garchy, which sympathizing in feeling and acting in concert with the money
> power, would assuredly subvert the best features of a political system that
> needs only to be honestly administered to enable it to realize those anticipa-
> tions of our country's greatness.[135]

For Van Buren, Taney, a Democrat, turned on the Constitution, just has
Hamilton had earlier done. How could Van Buren explain this invalidation
of a congressional measure given that Taney was appointed by Jackson?
Van Buren fell back on the civic republican construction of opposition as
an anti-constitutional threat. The answer was that Taney had always been a
Federalist.[136]

Van Buren went to great lengths to illustrate Taney's Federalist leanings
noting that "he had occupied a distinguished place in the Federal ranks to an
advanced period in his professional life."[137] He characterized the judiciary,
by its very construction, as supportive of sentiments that tend to aristocratic
Hamiltonianism. It would be unreasonable, posited Van Buren, to expect
Taney to be "insensible to the *esprit du corps* which had long prevailed in and
around that high tribunal," and which Van Buren ascribes to Marshall's long
tenure.[138] Taney extended himself in an unnecessary and illegitimate direction by asserting judicial supremacy: "To add a deeper shade to this trespass
upon the time-honored creed of the Democratic party, the anti-Democratic
doctrine was conveyed to the public in a form professing to be a necessary
adjudication in the regular course of the administration of justice, whilst it

[134] Leonard, 2001, 262–5.
[135] Van Buren, 1867, 376.
[136] Like Buchanan, Taney originally identified as a Federalist through the 1820s until his
relationship with Andrew Jackson deepened. See Carl Brent Swisher, *Roger B. Taney*
(New York: Macmillan, 1935).
[137] Van Buren, 1867, 363.
[138] Ibid.

is ... an extrajudicial opinion, voluntarily and not necessarily delivered."[139] Taney, Marshall, and Hamilton were all of a type. They were part of an aristocratic minority hell-bent on undoing the Constitution.

As for President Buchanan's support of *Dred Scott*, Van Buren argued that this Democratic leader was also not a true Democrat: "For the first time since [the party's] ascent to power in the Federal Government, two of the three great departments, the Executive and the Judicial, are presided over by gentlemen who ... had not been bred in its ranks but joined them at comparatively advanced periods in their lives, and with opinions formed and matured in an antagonistic school."[140] Although Buchanan had been a Federalist in the early years of the century, his support for killing the national bank placed him firmly in the Jacksonian majority.[141] However, Van Buren clung to Buchanan's repudiated past association. Assertions or actions by party members contradicting core Democratic principles could only be understood as anti-Constitutional; they must be members of the permanent minority opposition. Van Buren did not recognize Buchanan's strategic deference to Taney as a means of avoiding accountability. His party theory obstructed him from doing so. While Buchanan's move set a precedent of turning to the judiciary to settle controversial matters, for Van Buren it only indicated that he was a member of the minority opposition.[142] So Van Buren embraced multiple sources of constitutional interpretation – president, Court, Congress, and *party* (although not the states) – but the legitimacy of only one.

For Van Buren, the cause of civil unrest in the 1850s was not that the slavery issue was politically untenable, but that Federalist Taney invalidated the political resolutions. Moreover, just as he denigrated members of Monroe's cabinet, Van Buren now disparaged those in Buchanan's cabinet as not true party members only "profess[ing] to belong to the Democratic party until

[139] Ibid., 366.
[140] Ibid., 370–1.
[141] Buchanan was a Federalist and supported the national bank until Jackson's veto message. By Jackson's second term, Buchanan moved in lockstep with the president. See James Buchanan, *The Works of James Buchanan: Comprising His Speeches, State Papers, and Private Correspondence* (1813–1830), John Bassett Moore, ed. (New York: Antiquarian Press, 1960), Vol. 14, and "Buchanan to General Jackson," Vol. 3, 256–7.
[142] The *Dred Scott* case, while maligned in the press and a rallying cry for the Republican Party, did not undermine diffuse popular support for the Court. Stanley Kutler, *Judicial Power and Reconstruction Politics* (Chicago: University of Chicago Press, 1968), 6–29. Madison had once turned to the Court to resolve issues, just as Jackson had. Madison declined to support Pennsylvanian resistance to the Court's ruling in *United States v. Peters*, 9 U.S. 115 (1809). Madison told the Pennsylvania governor that he "is not only unauthorized to prevent the execution of a decree sanctioned by the Supreme Court of the United States, but is expressly enjoined, by statute, to carry into effect any such decree where opposition may be made to it." *Annals of Congress*, 11th Cong. 2260. As Madison tended to support federal authority against the states (see the timidity of his Virginia Resolution relative to Jefferson's Kentucky resolution), this position is not surprising. It maps on to Van Buren and Jackson's antipathy toward nullification and is more supportive of federal authority than judicial power.

after their appointment and election to their present posts."[143] Van Buren was boxed into a corner by the parameters of his distrust of opposition. Buchanan and Taney embraced principles of the minority opposition, and they began to unravel the union. An aristocratic minority, always intent on undermining the Constitution, triggered the civil war.

IV. Conclusion

By focusing on Van Buren's underdeveloped sense of the opposition's right to rule, his advocacy of a new institutional solution – the party – to manage that opposition, and his inherited presumption of federal branch unity, this chapter has explained the position of Jackson and Van Buren toward the judiciary that is neither wholly hostile to judicial power as an undemocratic structural anomaly nor purely opportunistic. By contrast, Van Buren's explanation remained entrenched in the remnants of a fading civic republican idiom that viewed formed, stable, and permanent opposition with grave suspicion.

Van Buren conceptualized his permanent party as an institutional buttress of the Constitution against corruption when the Madisonian architecture proved ineffective. His theory of party shows little recognition of opposition loyalty, of two-party competition, or of expected rotation in office between different policy advocates. It conceded only that an opposition – an aristocratic permanent minority – was an inescapable artifact of history, and that given this reality, a new institutional form was needed to protect the Constitution from that anti-constitutional and conspiratorial threat. By arguing that his Democracy always represented the majority, and that the majority always supported the Constitution, he could tautologically claim – much as Madison had done in his series of essays from 1792 – that his party included the sole supporters of the Constitution and the opposition was anti-constitutional. If that opposition became entrenched in the judiciary, the Constitution would be threatened.

When the Court ruled to the advantage of that permanent minority faction, it engaged in specious interpretation that violated the Constitution's fixed, singular, and discoverable meaning. This is so because, by the parameters of Van Buren's bi-factional view of political history, that minority always defined itself as against the Constitution. As such, the president had the authority to counter the Court's interpretation, but this authority was not without limits, and it was certainly not nearly as expansive as Jeffersonian departmentalism. By recognizing this unique definition of the purpose of party and its implications for political opposition, we can understand how politicians operating with such notions related to judicial authority.

Presidential interpretation was legitimate when it was superior to judicial interpretation. That superiority could be gauged by whether the interpretation aligned with the principles of the Democratic Party, which by Van Buren's

---

[143] Van Buren, 1867, 371.

tautological definition were the Constitution's principles. The president, as leader of the perpetual majority, was more likely aligned with the Constitution than were judges, who could become entrenched when the minority faction attained power either through corruption or misdirection. Unlike Jeffersonian departmentalism, which potentially leads to a chaotic situation of all branches and all states – of "each public officer" – holding equal responsibility to interpret the Constitution and which was grounded in the constitutional logic of separated powers, Van Buren set limits on Jackson's interpretive authority. First, the authority stemmed not only from the president's institutional role as a co-equal branch but also from his connection with the people themselves as the only national officer and as leader of a permanent political party. Second, Jackson's interpretive authority could not be used to undermine federal supremacy. These limits were not grounded in any kind of deference to judicial authority, idea of judicial supremacy, or particular need to maintain judicial power. Rather, they were based on extra-constitutional party leadership, a position never fully countenanced by Jefferson, and on *federal* supremacy, a principle that Jefferson openly questioned despite the Constitution's supremacy clause.[144]

Congressional debates on judicial reform revealed that politicians sought to maintain the post-Chase impeachment notion of the neutral judiciary. Beyond this objective, little agreement existed on how best to achieve it. Judicial neutrality was the Jeffersonian second-best solution when federal branch unity could not be achieved. The ideal itself constructed the judiciary as different, as not clearly as representative of popular sovereignty as the other branches. Similarly, the failure to repeal Section 25 illustrated only that Jacksonians like Van Buren, Buchanan, and the Northern branch of that political coalition supported some balance between federal power and states' rights and maintained no desire to return to circumstances under the Articles of Confederation or to endorse the principles of Jefferson's Kentucky resolution.

In short, by attending to how Jacksonian politicians, particularly Van Buren, reckoned with the inevitability of a permanent organized opposition, we can better identify and understand *variation* in presidential assertions of authority to interpret the Constitution and other tactics toward the judiciary – particularly ignoring the Court – when judges' ruling were perceived as opposing presidential and congressional interest. No longer should all such assertions of interpretive authority or congressional actions of the Jacksonian years be considered simple replays of Jeffersonian departmentalism. Jacksonian positions and actions are distinguishable from those taken by their Jeffersonian fathers. Furthermore, little evidence exists during this period that politicians maintained the idea that judicial authority should be preserved to entrench partisan interests, that is, the more contemporary longer term strategic rationale often used to explain congressional behavior in the late nineteenth century. This absence can be accounted for by understanding that Jacksonian

144 Ibid., 316–7.

political interests were not defined in that manner. Put differently, partisan aim to harness judicial power did not displace the ideal of judicial neutrality because the Democracy was not conceptualized as partisan but as always the majority, as the vehicle of the Constitution itself. For Van Buren, politics was and always had been about supporting or undermining the Constitution. Thus, the eventual "court-packing" provided by the 1837 Judiciary Act can be viewed as achieving the older aim of federal unitary authority, which followed from the traditional republican wariness toward opposition. Bench expansion under Jackson would ensure that the judges would represent the interests of the constitutional party. The anti-constitutional aristocratic minority would be removed from its seat in government. Van Buren understood his single constitutional party as the political solution to the challenge that judicial power posed to the Jeffersonians, namely, regime disunity. Appointing more judges amounted to "party appointment" not "partisan appointment." Unfortunately, for Van Buren, the *Dred Scott* decision seemed to reveal Taney's aristocratic Federalist tendencies.

Van Buren conceptualized his political party as a way to achieve regime unity. When Taney refused to play along, Van Buren could not conceptualize the logic of multiple equally valid interpretations because his view toward opposition was so constrained. Instead, Taney had to be characterized as part of the threatening aristocratic minority hell-bent on undermining the Constitution. Nevertheless, Van Buren's conception of party as not inimical to but supportive of civic health set in motion the foundation for multiple parties to each claim the legitimacy of their own constitutional interpretations. And, as is argued in the next chapter, it was the contingency of a specific circumstance, namely, the threat of national dissolution, that compelled politicians, particularly President Abraham Lincoln, to recognize the opposition's right to rule and, by extension, the validity of multiple interpretations – not just interpreters – of the Constitution. Such recognition would ultimately enable abandoning the idea that constitutional meaning was singular, fixed, and discoverable and open pathways not only for diversity in the modes of interpretation, but also pave a path toward a systematic effort by politicians and judges alike toward further judicial empowerment.

5

"As Party Exigencies Require"

Republicanism, Loyal Opposition, and the Emerging Legitimacy of Multiple Constitutional Visions

In contrast to Martin Van Buren's ideas about a disloyal aristocratic minority opposition and single-party constitutionalism, Abraham Lincoln, as the first Republican president and a consummate party politician, conceded the political opposition's right to rule and endorsed the idea that constitutional interpretations could legitimately vary.[1] Lincoln's ideational innovation was compelled by the secession crisis, and it carried vast consequences for how future politicians would manipulate judicial power. Just as the Framers relocated the source of sovereignty from the legislature to the people in order to stem the crisis of governance created by the Articles of Confederation, and just as Van Buren altered the meaning of party from an institution inimical to civic health to one that promoted civil stability in an effort to end the "corruption" against which the Madisonian design proved ineffectual, Lincoln, seeking to prevent the complete breakup of the republic, would re-define the status of opposition and, with it, the notion of what counted as legitimate constitutional interpretation.

This chapter begins by detailing politicians' ideas about opposition and party during the 1850s and 1860s. The first section examines how early Republican leaders, especially William Seward, characterized Democrats in civic republican terms, that is, as an anti-constitutional conspiracy, and cast Republicans not just as competitors but also in the Van Burenite framework of a singular constitutional party replacement. Many politicians still tended to view stable, permanent, and formed opposition as heralding civil instability, and related, legitimate constitutional interpretation continued to be bound by the strictures of textual originalism such that interpretation only "effectuat[ed] the preexisting sovereign will of those who legitimate the words and structure of the Constitution ... as revealed primarily through textual

---

[1] On Lincoln's support of parties, see David Donald, *Lincoln Reconsidered*, 3rd ed. (New York: Random House, 2001), 164–80, and Michael Pfau, "The House that Abe Built: The 'House Divided' Speech and Republican Party Politics," *Rhetoric and Public Affairs* 2 (Winter 1999), 625–51.

analysis"; therefore, politics continued to operate at the higher stakes of constitutional heights.[2] Little room for compromise existed as politics did not play out as policy debates within an accepted constitutional context; politicians framed their competition as the Framers and Jacksonians had: a battle for the sanctity and preservation of the true Constitution. Party politics was grounded in constitutional interpretation, and parties – Democratic and Republican alike – were characterized in Van Burenite terms of institutionalized representatives and protectors of that interpretation.

The parallels between Seward's and Van Buren's rhetoric bring into clearer relief Lincoln's innovative moves, which are discussed in the chapter's second part. Lincoln was engulfed in constitutional controversies about the balance of state and federal power and the status of slavery, and he pragmatically sought any means available to calm the waters. In a failed attempt to prevent secession, he abandoned the civic republican notion that opposition threatened civil unrest. If his political opposition, as Lincoln would argue, would just try again in the next election rather than exit the Union entirely, then the opposition could not be characterized as anti-constitutional. It was not seeking to destroy the Constitution; how could it, when it obeyed its procedures? Its objectives and viewpoints were simply different, but not anti-constitutional per se.

By Lincoln's logic, whatever manipulations an elected president or congressional majority might make to the judiciary were done to implement the victorious party's particular constitutional vision, which had been ratified by the most recent election. They were not done to protect the true Constitution from a threatening aristocratic conspiratorial minority. If the voting public did not approve, they could easily vote for new leaders and, thus, for a different perspective on constitutional meaning.

The next two sections examine how changing ideas about opposition were evident in congressional action. The third part considers how early Republican characterizations of the Democratic Party as an anti-constitutional conspiracy justified eliminating its influence through judicial re-organization, suppression of congressional representation, and impeachment. Thus, some congressional actions during the Civil War and Reconstruction that were hostile to judicial

---

[2] Johnathan O'Neill, *Originalism in American Law and Politics: A Constitutional History* (Baltimore: Johns Hopkins University Press, 2005), 18, 20. As O'Neill points out, nowhere is the agreement on a single interpretive modality, that is, textual originalism, more apparent and yet such radically different opinions nevertheless yielded than in Chief Justice Taney's ruling and Justice Curtis's dissent in *Dred Scott v. Sanford*. Taney based his decision that people of African descent could never be citizens on the Constitution's "true intent and meaning when it was adopted." *Dred Scott v. Sanford*, 60 U.S. 393, 405. Curtis, coming to the opposite conclusion, agreed on the underlying approach: "When a strict interpretation of the Constitution, according to the fixed rules which govern the interpretation of laws, is abandoned ... we no longer have a Constitution; we are under a government of individual men who, for the time being, have power to declare what the Constitution is according to their own views of what it ought to mean." *Dred Scott v. Sanford*, 60 U.S. 393, 621.

legitimacy can be accounted for by viewing them as broader hostilities toward political opposition, which continued to be characterized in the civic republican language of conspiratorial threat. The fourth part examines congressional Republican manipulations of the judiciary during the late 1860s and early 1870s that seem to more narrowly manipulate the judiciary to support (or at least not block) substantive policy objectives. My distinction between early congressional Republican hostility toward a perceived anti-constitutional conspiracy and later targeted congressional manipulations to exploit the judicial can be contrasted with scholarly framings of Republican behavior as either wholly hostile to or wholly supportive of judicial power. Yet, as detailed in this chapter's fourth section, Republican relations with judicial power were neither wholly one nor the other. Their variation tracks politicians' changing perspectives toward the Court as a potential seat of stable opposition to the governing regime that held Congress and the presidency, marking this period as a transition point from assumptions of civic republicanism and toward those associated with liberal pluralism. And their shift toward harnessing tactics was compelled by undeniable political realities, namely, by the realization that the Van Burenite dream of single-party constitutionalism, to which early Republicans had clung, proved unattainable.

I. Republican Aspirations to Single-Party Constitutionalism

The early Republican Party, which was a diverse coalition of abolitionists, former Whigs, temperance advocates, and evangelical Protestants, came together to "break the back of the Southern-based Democratic Party," which was considered "the executive committee of the Slave Power."[3] Whether the Slave Power included just slave owners, the South, or the whole Democratic Party, Republicans nevertheless consistently characterized it as an internal conspiracy threatening liberty. This fear infused Republican rhetoric prior to and throughout the Civil War as well as during the early years of Reconstruction.[4] The goal of eliminating the Democratic Party, tied as it was to the Slave Power, illustrates the extent to which civic republican assumptions about conspiratorial threat and a political party's primary function as a constitutional protector – ideas put forward by Van Buren in defense of his Democracy – remained potent.

I.a. *The Slave Power Conspiracy and the Constitutional Idea of the Republican Party*
Fear of a Slave Power conspiracy was rooted in the idea that bargains made at the constitutional convention yielded over-representation of Southern interests

---

[3] Garrett Epps, *Democracy Reborn: The Fourteenth Amendment and the Fight for Equal Rights in Post–Civil War America* (New York: Henry Holt, 2006), 51.

[4] On the range of framings of the Slave Power conspiracy, see Michael Pfau, *The Political Style of Conspiracy: Chase, Sumner, and Lincoln* (Lansing: Michigan State University Press, 2005).

in the federal government.[5] This contention "had widespread support in the years before and after the Civil War" and was "deemed a self-evident truth by scores of prominent Northerners."[6] Some Republicans limited the conspiracy to slave owners; others included the entire South or the entire Democratic Party.[7] Journalist and unionist Carl Schurz characterized the Slave Power as an aristocratic cabal lodged in Southern state governments, which not only threatened Northern interests, but which also squashed the rights of Southerners themselves. In his 1859 speech, "True Americanism," delivered at Faneuil Hall in Boston, Shurz explained how the Slave Power harmed Southerners' rights:

> Where is their liberty of the press? Where is their liberty of speech? Where is the man among them who dares to advocate openly principles not in strict accordance with the ruling system? They speak of a republican form of government – they speak of democracy, but the despotic spirit of slavery and mastership combined pervades their political life like a liquid poison.[8]

The Slave Power not only enslaved those of African descent; it also harmed freedoms enshrined by the First Amendment enjoyed by white citizens. The Slave Power's underlying ideology demanded the unconstitutional curbing of liberties of press and speech.

Abraham Lincoln, similarly, focused on the broad conspiratorial threat that the Slave Power posed to fundamental liberties. In an 1858 debate with Stephen Douglas, Lincoln characterized the entire Democratic Party – not just an aristocratic class of Southerners – as engaged in a deliberate strategy to undermine constitutional freedoms, and, in particular, to spread slavery northward:

> there was a tendency, if not a *conspiracy* among those who have engineered this slavery question for the last four or five years, to make slavery perpetual and universal in this nation.... We cannot absolutely know that these exact adaptations are the result of pre-concert, but when we see a lot of framed timbers, different portions of which we know have been gotten out at different times and places and by different workmen ... and when we see these timbers joined together, and see they exactly make the frame of a house or a mill, all the tenons and mortices exactly fitting ... in such a case we feel it impossible not to believe that ... all understood one another from the

---

[5] The fear had some empirical basis. Through 1836 only two presidents were non-Southerners (John Adams and John Quincy Adams); the three-fifths clause gave Southern states, where slavery was far more prevalent, increased House representation, and the construction of circuits courts and the connection of Supreme Court justices to those circuits had yielded a Supreme Court with a distinctly Southern bias. See Akhil Reed Amar, *America's Constitution: A Biography* (New York: Random House, 2005), 351–2.

[6] Leonard Richards, *The Slave Power: The Free North and Southern Domination, 1780–1860* (Baton Rouge: Louisiana State University Press, 2000), 1, 2.

[7] See Pfau, 18–45.

[8] Carl Schurz, *Speeches, Correspondence and Political Papers of Carl Schurz*, Frederic Bancroft, ed. (New York: G. P. Putnam's Sons, 1913), Vol. 1, 57.

beginning, and all worked upon a common plan or draft drawn before the first blow was struck.[9]

Lincoln's rhetoric re-iterated themes offered by his fellow Republican William Seward. Seward, a former Whig and a key figure in launching the Republican Party, characterized Southern slave owners as threatening democracy, but like Schurz he conflated the Slave Power with the entire Democratic Party: "the resources and energies of the Democratic party ... [are] identical with the Slave Power."[10] Also like Schurz, Seward tended to focus less on slavery and more broadly on dangers to freedoms of speech and press.[11] The move was strategic; it was meant to broaden support for the infant party beyond its abolitionist base.

As Seward was considered to be, in many ways, the "architect" of the Republican Party, he represents a Republican analog of Martin Van Buren.[12] It is therefore perhaps unsurprising that Seward held similar aspirations for his Republicans as Van Buren held for his "Democracy," that is, a permanent majority party charged with protecting the Constitution from internal conspiratorial threat. But this is where similarities end. Seward's definition of a party's fundamental purpose was conceptually different from that which Van Buren proposed. First, unlike Democrats, Republicans were defined by a substantive policy commitment: containing slavery. Seward characterized Democratic emphasis on proceduralism – on majoritarian decision-making and states' rights – as its primary deficiency. He maintained that the Democratic Party problematically "has no policy, State or Federal, for finance or trade, manufacture, or commerce, or education, or internal improvements, or for the protection or even the security of civil or religious liberty."[13] Of course, Seward's characterization of the Democrat's lack of clear policy aims begs whether the Republicans could put together a unified program of policy beyond containing slavery.[14]

Notably, in contrast to the anti-party Framers and Whigs, Seward did not contend that Democrats were unworthy by virtue of their elevation of party

[9] Abraham Lincoln, "First Joint Debate at Ottawa," 21 August 1858, in *Political Debates between Abraham Lincoln and Stephen A. Douglas* (Cleveland: Burrows Brothers, 1894), 95.
[10] William H. Seward, "Irrepressible Conflict Speech," Rochester, NY, 25 October 1858, in *History of U.S. Political Parties*, Arthur M. Schlesinger, Jr. (New York: Chelsea House, 1973), Vol. 2, 1238.
[11] See Seward's 1855 speeches, "The Advent of the Republican Party: The Privileged Class" and "The Contest and Crisis," in George E. Baker, ed., *The Works of William H. Seward*, 5 vols. (Boston, 1853–1884), Vol. 4, 225–52.
[12] *New York Herald*, 1 March 1871, quoted in Daniel W. Crofts, "The Union Party of 1861 and the Secession Crisis," *Perspectives in American History* 11 (1977–78), 359.
[13] Seward, "Irrepressible Conflict Speech," 1235.
[14] As Phillip Paludan points out, the first generation of Republicans disagreed on tariff and trade issues, voting extensions to the freed slaves, and federal support for infrastructure. Paludan, "War Is the Health of the Party: Republicans in the American Civil War," in *The Birth of the Grand Old Party: The Republicans' First Generation*, Robert F. Engs and Randall M. Miller, eds. (Philadelphia: University of Pennsylvania Press, 2002), 63–4.

spirit. Party was no longer threatening.[15] Seward eschewed anti-partyism: "I am not actuated by prejudices against that party, or by the prepossessions in favor of its adversary; for I have learned, by some experience, that virtue and patriotism, vice and selfishness, are found in all parties."[16] Yet the underlying theme of Seward's writings, that of an "irrepressible conflict between two opposing and enduring forces," is essentially the same characterization of political history set out by Van Buren. Seward is emphatic that "one or the other system must exclusively prevail," suggesting his belief that a system of ongoing rotation in power among opposing parties was not possible.[17] By linking slaveholders to the Democratic Party, he could posit the anti-constitutional threat that it posed; slave-holders sought to destroy the Constitution. Since "the slaveholders [are] contributing in an overwhelming proportion to the capital strength of the Democratic party, they necessarily dictate and prescribe its policy."[18] Seward, like Van Buren before him, constructed a party charged with maintaining the Constitution against an undemocratic, aristocratic, and conspiratorial threat. The Slave Power now was cast in the role Van Buren once held for the Hamiltonians.

Seward repeated two rhetorical practices evident in Van Buren's justification of Democracy as the constitutional party: first, he conflated majority support with constitutionality and, second, he connected his party's principles to those held by the Framers such that the Constitution's so-called fixed meaning necessarily aligned with Republican positions. In so doing, he, like Van Buren, constructed majority, party, and constitutionalism as mutually reinforcing and ultimately tautological. Seward maintained that Democrats had become a minority faction over time: "It is not a party of the whole union, of all the Free States and of all the Slave States ... it is a sectional and local party, having practically its seat with the Slave States and its constituency chiefly and almost exclusively there."[19] He called his audience to "rush to the rescue of the Constitution."[20] Seward's advocacy of Republicanism as a single constitutional party – as a replacement more than a competitor – is evident in how he diagnosed the fate of Democrats:

> The Democratic party derived its strength, originally, from its adoption of the principles of equal and exact justice to all men. So long as it practiced this principle faithfully, it was invulnerable. It became vulnerable when it renounced the principle, and since that time it has maintained itself, not by virtue of its own strength, or even of its traditional merits, but because

---

[15] The new Republican Party shed much of its Whig predecessors' anti-party bias. See Tyler Anbinder, *Nativism and Slavery: The Northern Know Nothings and the Politics of the 1850s* (New York: Oxford University Press, 1992), 52–94, and Michael Holt, *The Political Crisis of the 1850s* (New York: John Wiley, 1978), 163–9.

[16] Seward, "Irrepressible Conflict Speech," 1229.

[17] Ibid., 1231.

[18] Ibid., 1234.

[19] Ibid., 1233–4.

[20] Ibid., 1237.

there as yet had appeared in the political field no other party that had the conscience and the courage to take up, and avow, and practice the life inspiring principles which the Democratic party had surrendered. At last the Republican party has appeared.[21]

Thus, just as Van Buren maintained, Seward held constitutional principles as stable over time. The Democratic Party was invulnerable – and thus the legitimate perpetual majority – only so long as it maintained these principles. But like any "court" party, it became infected by corruption, which paved the way for a new party to rise and to preserve the Constitution and its fixed and discoverable meaning. If the Democratic Party were once the embodiment of constitutional commitment – and Seward was himself once a Democrat – it no longer was. According to Seward, the "Democratic party must be permanently dislodged from the Government ... [because] the Democratic party is inextricably committed to the designs of the slaveholders."[22] Thus, party and constitutionality were as interconnected for Seward as they were for Van Buren. Electoral competition and political opposition were inevitable, but only one party represented true constitutional meaning; opposition to that meaning was ultimately disloyal.

Further paralleling Van Buren's ideas of a single constitutional party, Seward re-conceptualized the Framers' compromise with the slave system to connect the Republican aims with Founders' intent:

> They preferred the system of free labor, and they determined to organize the Government, and so to direct its activity, that that system should surely and certainly prevail. For this purpose, and no other, they based the whole structure of Government broadly on the principle that all men are created equal and therefore free – little dreaming that, within the short period of one hundred years, their descendants would bear to be told by an orator, however popular, that the utterance of that principle was merely a rhetorical rhapsody; or by any judge however, venerated, that it was attended by mental reservations which rendered it hypocritical and false.[23]

Seward now re-drew the lineage of constitutional principle and meaning, which Van Buren claimed ran from the Founders to the Jeffersonians to his Democracy, from the Founders to the Jeffersonians to the new Republicans. This new lineage was necessary since only one kind of constitutional interpretive modality, namely, textual originalism, was legitimate throughout the mid-nineteenth century. As legal historian Johnathan O'Neill recognizes, "Antebellum constitutional treatises agreed that the Constitution could only mean what it was originally intended to mean."[24] Thus, for Republican principles to be legitimate, they had to be defensible by a textual interpretation of the Constitution, which uncovered the Framers' intent.

[21] Ibid., 1238.
[22] Ibid., 1233.
[23] Ibid., 1231–2.
[24] O'Neill, 21.

By re-drawing this pedigree of party and constitutional principle, Seward could call for an entirely new unified single constitutional-majority Union party that would minimize the sectionalist character of Republicanism.[25] It was not evident that Republicans would emerge as a dominant party in the 1850s or even after Lincoln's victory.[26] Forging a Union Party would eliminate the Democratic Party in the North: "the sine qua non of the Union movement was the assertion that continued opposition by Democrats was disloyalty."[27] When the Union Party, which brought Republicans and War Democrats under the same banner, proved victorious in 1864, Republican aspirations toward a single constitutional party seemed within grasp. The victory was heralded as triggering "a new era of good feeling."[28] As the editors of *Harper's Weekly* put it: "Old party lines do not separate us ... we are at the end of parties."[29]

I.b. The Southern Perspective: The Republican Conspiracy to Undermine the Constitution

While much Republican rhetoric cast Democrats as illegitimate lackeys of the Slave Power's anti-constitutional aims, Southern Democrats cast Republicanism, centered in the North, in similar language. Republicanism was a religious fanaticism seeking to impose policies that would undermine principles of popular sovereignty and federalism. The parallelism of Republican and Democratic criticisms illustrates just how much each was grounded in the civic republican idiom. As one historian notes of the similarities:

> In language curiously reminiscent of Northern attacks on the Southern slave power, disunionists charged that the Republicans intended to enslave the Southern people and establish a tyranny that would shame the worst despots of the ancient and modern world.... By using elements of eighteenth-century republicanism, pro-slavery rhetoric, and antiparty ideology, secessionists built their case on traditional arguments that awakened old anxieties and aroused new fears for the future. The emphasis on irreconcilable differences between North and South transformed the Republicans and large segments of the Northern population into an antislavery monolith.[30]

---

[25] Adam I. P. Smith, *No Party Now: Politics in the Civil War North* (New York: Oxford University Press, 2006), 29–37.

[26] The party's congressional majority was secured by secession. The fluid multi-party context of the 1850s in which Democrats, Whigs, Know-Nothings, and Republicans divided support, suggested that Republican dominance might not be maintained even if the Union war effort succeeded. See Michael Holt, "Making and Mobilizing the Republican Party, 1854–1860," in *The Birth of the Grand Old Party: The Republicans' First Generation*, Robert Engs and Randall Miller, eds. (Philadelphia: University of Pennsylvania Press, 2002), 47–59.

[27] Smith, 42.

[28] Philadelphia *Inquirer*, 17 November 1864, quoted in Mark Neely, *The Union Divided: Party Conflict in the Civil War* (Cambridge, MA: Harvard University Press, 2002), 171.

[29] *Harper's Weekly*, 25 February 1865.

[30] George Rable, *The Confederate Republic: A Revolution against Politics* (Chapel Hill: University of North Carolina Press, 1994), 27–8.

Just as Republicans disparaged Northern Democrats as lackeys of the Slave Power, Democrats saw a Republican conspiracy taking shape in the South. Georgia Governor Joseph Brown warned of this threat: "a portion of our citizens must, if possible, be bribed into treachery to their section, by the allurements of office; or a hungry swarm of abolition emissaries must be imported among us as office holders, to eat out our substance, insult us with their arrogance, corrupt our slaves."[31]

Secessionists framed potential Republican interference in their state's sovereign affairs as part of a New England Puritanical tradition of intolerance, which conflicted with an alleged Southern tradition of liberty such that "the notion of Northern Puritan versus Southern Cavalier became much more than a stock literary device."[32] According to some Southern Democrats, Republican advocacy of government power to impose substantive policy aims without regard for popular and state sovereignty undermined the Constitution's procedural commitments. And these policies dangerously mixed church and state: Republicans threatened constitutional values by "dragging politics into the pulpit."[33] When assessing the Republican gains of 1856 in previously Northern Democratic strongholds, a Democrat wrote President Buchanan:

> We are made up of New England Yankees here with all the superstitions and prejudices of the land of their ancestry. We had all the fanatical Methodist & Baptist preachers against us hurling their anathemas at us from their pulpits on Sundays and from the stump on weekday, and also some of all the other denominations and what is still worse they are all Know nothings and where that is the case you might as well "sing psalms to a dead horse" as to attempt to reach their reason.[34]

The Democratic paper in Cleveland, *Plain Dealer*, in an effort to explain how a formerly Democratic district voted for Republican presidential candidate John Fremont in 1856 by a heavy majority, took note of "those old blue law, blue bellied Presbyterians that hung the witches and banished the Quakers, are determined to convert the people of this region into a race of psalm singers, using the degenerate dregs of the old puritans remaining here to drive the Democrats out."[35] The editor of a Texas paper similarly opined against the dangerous "people and ideas of the New England States [who] have been remarkable in their history, for the violence of their fanaticism and proclivity

---

[31] George Brown, quoted in Rabble, 29.
[32] Rabble, 28. That tradition seems mythic if not false, given slave-state suppression of abolitionist newspapers. See Michael Kent Curtis, "The Curious History of Attempts to Suppress Antislavery Speech, Press, and Petition in 1835–37," *Northwestern University Law Review* 89 (1995), 785–870, and Clement Easton, *The Freedom-of-Thought Struggle in the Old South*, rev. ed. (New York: Harper & Row, 1964).
[33] Clarksville, Tennessee *Jeffersonian*, 30 May 1855.
[34] William Patton to James Buchanan, 7 November 1856, Buchanan Papers, Historical Society of Pennsylvania, quoted in William Gienapp, *The Origins of the Republican Party, 1852–1856* (New York: Oxford University Press, 1987), 432.
[35] Cleveland *Plain Dealer*, 3 December 1856, quoted in Gienapp, 432.

to superstition and intolerance on all subjects connected with religion as they have been for their intelligence, energy and enterprise on all other subjects."[36] A Tennessee editor called stricter naturalization procedures and temperance throwbacks to puritanism: "The Puritans of today, like the Puritans of 1700, conceive themselves to be better and holier than others, and entitled – by divine right as it were – to govern and control the actions and dictate the opinions" of other citizens.[37] An Arkansas paper agreed, characterizing Republican New England as exemplifying "a fanatical zeal for unscriptural reforms, accompanied by a Pharisaical spirit, which says to brethren heretofore cordially acknowledged, 'Stand back, we are holier than you.'"[38]

This anti-Puritan position was, for some, deeper than the rift over slavery. A Virginia newspaper noted that "mutual jealousies of New England and the South do not primarily grow out of slavery. They are deeper, and will always be the chief obstacle in the way of full absolute reunion. They are founded in differences of manner, habits and social life, and different notions about politics, morals and religion."[39] Another paper noted "Abolition is but a small part of their [Republican] programme and probably the least noxious of their measures."[40] The Democratic *New York Herald* declared:

> [The] Republican party majority, usurping the prerogatives of God and conscience, decree that all men must conform to their particular puritanical observance of the Sabbath.... The puritanical and straight laced notions ... are forced down the throats of a population ... and they are compelled to yield obedience to a holy Protestant inquisition.[41]

In short, Southern Democrats saw Republican victory as the end of constitutional proceduralism in favor of a substantive policy program not limited to abolition but including temperance and compelled religious observance. For Democrats, Republican leadership threatened "a scheme for regulating eating or drinking or the industry of the country ... [which was] an effort to govern the World too much" and which was "at war with the real principles of our government as always understood and expounded by the Democratic creed."[42] Disparate elements of Republicanism "were outgrowths of revivalistic religion" that "sprang from similar moral impulses."[43] Republicanism sought nothing less than "to compass its objects by summary seizures, confiscations and extraordinary punishments upon foregone presumptions of guilt, such

[36] Galveston, Texas *Tri-Weekly News*, 17 July 1856, quoted in Joel Silbey, *The Partisan Imperative: The Dynamics of American Politics before the Civil War* (New York: Oxford University Press, 1985), 177.

[37] Memphis *Daily Appeal*, 17 February 1861, quoted in Silbey, 1985, 177.

[38] Arkansas *State Gazette and Democrat*, 11 August 1854, quoted in Silbey, 1985, 177.

[39] Washington *Daily Union*, 24 October 1854, quoted in Silbey, 1985, 178.

[40] Washington *Daily Union*, 20 May 1857, quoted in Silbey, 1985, 179.

[41] *New York Herald*, 23 September 1860, quoted in Silbey, 1985, 181.

[42] Washington *Daily Union*, 26 March 1857, and *Atlas and Argus*, 28 April 1857, quoted in Silbey, 1985, 182.

[43] Gienapp, 47.

as are forbidden by the Bill of Rights."[44] Lincoln's sectional 1860 plurality victory heightened the sense of possible minority tyranny.[45]

By attending to how civic republican assumptions about formed, stable, and permanent opposition underlay both Republican and Democratic rhetoric, in which each cast the other as an anti-constitutional conspiratorial threat, the development of and ideas about political parties are brought back into the discussion of Civil War and Reconstruction politics. The political party, as an institution, has been dropped from recent political-economic analyses of secession and constitutional stability, which has rightly emphasized Southern fears about losing slave property as driving the crisis.[46] However, highlighting only property concerns obscures how Republicans utilized civic republican themes to frame the "Slave Power" as an aristocratic threat to civil stability, ignores Southern claims about the puritanical scope of Republican interventionism, and pays little to no attention to the dominant political institution of the Jacksonian era, that is, the political party.

II. Lincoln: Popular Sovereignty, Constitutional Silence, and Minimal Constraint

In his first inaugural address, Lincoln seems to revive Jeffersonian hostilities toward the Court:

> I do not forget the position assumed by some that constitutional questions are to be decided by the Supreme Court, nor do *I deny that such decisions must be binding in any case upon the parties to a suit* ... while they are also entitled to very high respect and consideration in all parallel cases by all other departments of the Government.... At the same time, the candid citizen must confess that if the policy of the Government upon vital questions affecting the whole people is to be irrevocably fixed by decisions of the Supreme Court ... the people will have ceased to be their own rulers, having to that extent practically resigned their Government into the hands of that eminent tribunal.[47]

Lincoln's assertions that the Court could not be the final arbiter of constitutional meaning, that interpretive authority extended beyond the judiciary, and that constitutionalism is grounded in expressions of popular sovereignty, that is, elections, all carry a Jeffersonian valence. Keith Whittington has argued, "Lincoln rehearsed at length Jefferson's and Jackson's departmentalist

[44] *New York Herald*, 26 October 1860, quoted in Silbey, 1985, 181.

[45] Silbey, 1985, 180.

[46] See Barry Weingast, "Self-Enforcing Constitutions: With an Application to Democratic Stability in America's First Century," http://law.usc.edu/academics/assets/docs/Weingast.pdf (September 2007). "The enormous magnitude of the value of slaves in the Southern economy – in 1860, on the order of GDP for the entire United States – implied that the stakes were very high for slaveholders. Following the rationality of fear, Southerners were episodically deeply concerned about the future of their 'property and their institutions' within the Union."

[47] "First Inaugural Address of Abraham Lincoln," 4 March 1861. Emphasis added.

theories," that Lincoln "offered yet another variation on the departmentalist theme," and that "Lincoln undermined the Court in order to claim constitutional authority for himself."[48] Similarities among Lincoln, Jefferson, and Jackson were noted at the time of the inaugural. The *Louisville Democrat* remarked on Lincoln's inaugural: "Some may censure the general remarks about the decisions of the Supreme Court; but the intelligent reader will see that it is but the old Democratic doctrine of Jefferson and Jackson. If it be a heresy, it is not Lincoln's."[49]

Yet this interpretation skims over distinctions among Jefferson's, Jackson's, and Lincoln's arguments, particularly Lincoln's acceptance of *Dred Scott*: "I do not propose to disturb or resist the decision."[50] His statement appears to accept judicial rulings rather than make any active move against then. It thereby stands in marked contrast to Jefferson's rejection of *Marbury* and Jackson's rejection of *McCulloch* and *Worcester*. Nevertheless, if Lincoln's assertion of presidential interpretive authority was not as forceful as that of his predecessors, neither did it concede judicial supremacy. Lincoln lay between these positions, unwilling to undermine judicial authority and seeking leverage to place limits on some rulings.

This section identifies the coherent rationale underlying this minimalist constraint on judicial authority. Lincoln's characterization of his interpretive authority is based on his re-conceptualization of the meaning of "majority," which maintained a link between constitutionalism and popular sovereignty, as Jefferson and Van Buren had done, but defined that majority as a dynamic rather than static entity, which always defends the Constitution's alleged true meaning. As such, Lincoln promoted the dynamism of constitutional viewpoints, or at least the possibility that multiple legitimate perspectives on meaning followed from the silences of the document. Characterizing majority this way held implications for the opposition's right to rule and expected rotation in power as well as for the legitimacy of elected-branch manipulation of the judiciary to promote a particular constitutional viewpoint.

II.a. *Holding* Dred Scott's *Meaning at Bay by Embracing the Opposition's Right to Rule*

The *Dred Scott* decision was a focal point in Lincoln's 1858 debates with Stephen Douglas. Douglas emphasized process as the means to resolve the crisis over slavery's status. If slavery was an issue to be decided by the people of a given state, then conflict could be avoided by allowing majoritarianism *within* states and non-interference *between* states: "it is none of our

---

[48] Keith Whittington, *Political Foundations of Judicial Supremacy: The Presidency, the Supreme Court, and Constitutional Leadership in U.S. History* (Princeton: Princeton University Press, 2007), 34, 69.

[49] *Louisville Democrat*, quoted in Kutler, 11.

[50] Lincoln at Springfield, 17 July 1858, *The Complete Lincoln-Douglas Debates of 1858*, Paul Angle, ed. (Chicago: University of Chicago Press, 1991), 77.

business in Illinois whether Kansas is a free State or a slave State"; for all that concerned the state of Illinois, which Douglas aspired to represent, was that "when we settled it [i.e., the slavery question] for ourselves, we have done our whole duty."[51] Proceduralism protected liberty – the liberty to own slave property – because it recognized diversity. If democracy were mutual non-interference, Republican aims, for example, ending slavery, tempering alcohol consumption, and compelling particular religious observance, threatened liberty.[52]

Lincoln used Douglas's emphasis on procedural popular sovereignty against him. He framed his Democratic opponent's support of the *Dred Scott* ruling as not holding true to Jacksonian roots:

> The sacredness that Judge Douglas throws around [*Dred Scott*] is a degree of sacredness that has never been thrown around any other decisions.... I ask, if somebody does not remember that a National Bank was declared to be constitutional? ... It was urged upon [Jackson], when he denied the constitutionality of the Bank, that the Supreme Court had decided that it was constitutional; and General Jackson then said that the Supreme Court had no right to lay down a rule to govern a coordinate branch of Government.... I will venture here to say that I have heard Judge Douglas say that he approved of General Jackson for that act. What has now become of all his tirade about "resistance of the Supreme Court"?[53]

If Jackson was justified in asserting an interpretation contrary to the Court's, how could Douglas criticize Lincoln and his supporters as "the enemies of the Constitution"?[54] Lincoln rejected this connection between popular sovereignty and mutual indifference. He, like Seward, contended that more than a commitment to proceduralism must unify a country; a country must hold a substantive understanding of liberty. He viewed slavery as "a moral, a social and a political wrong ... not confining itself merely to the persons or the States where it exists, but that it is a wrong ... that extends itself to the existence of the whole nation."[55] Because protecting slavery necessarily leads to curbs on other rights – such as freedoms of speech, and press – Lincoln characterized it as having a disease-like quality to infect the entire body politic. If liberty were to be ensured, slavery must be contained if not abolished.[56]

Given Lincoln's idea that slavery would undermine the republic, it is hardly surprising that his speeches throughout the late 1850s would cast Democrats

[51] Stephen Douglas, *The Lincoln-Douglas Debates of 1858*, Robert W. Johannsen, ed. (New York: Oxford University Press, 1968), 292, 47.
[52] David Ericson, *The Shaping of American Liberalism: The Debates over Ratification, Nullification and Slavery* (Chicago: University of Chicago, 1993), 117–35.
[53] "Lincoln at Chicago, July 10, 1858," in Angle, 36–37.
[54] "Fifth Joint Debate, at Galesburgh, October 7, 1858," *Political Debates between Abraham Lincoln and Stephen Douglas* (Cleveland, OH: Burrows Brothers, 1894), 219.
[55] Abraham Lincoln, "House Divided," 16 June 1858, http://www.historyplace.com/lincoln/divided.htm. More generally, see Ericson, 136–74.
[56] On the disease metaphor of civic decline in the Slave Power rhetoric, see Pfau, 2005.

as having turned on the Constitution and characterize Republicans as the single constitutional party seeking to replace Democrats entirely. He would, in other words, make claims thematically similar to Van Buren's party theory. In an 1859 letter declining participation in a Jefferson Day celebration in Boston, Lincoln noted the irony of how the professed inheritors of the Jeffersonian ideas, that is, Democrats, had lost their constitutional footing:

> It is both curious and interesting that those supposed to descend politically from the party opposed to Jefferson, should now be celebrating his birth-day in their own original seat of empire, while those claiming political descent from him have nearly ceased to breathe his name everywhere. Remembering too, that the Jefferson party were formed upon their supposed superior devotion to the *personal* rights of men, holding the rights of *property* to be secondary only, and greatly inferior, and then assuming that the so-called democracy of to-day, are the Jefferson, and their opponents, the anti-Jefferson parties, it will be equally interesting to note how completely the two have changed hands as to the principle upon which they were originally supposed to be divided.[57]

In his early speeches, Lincoln utilized a tactic similar to Van Buren's and Seward's bifurcation of political history. He retraced political lineage to link Jeffersonians with Republicans and to cast Democrats in the role of the anti-constitutional party.

What is perhaps more surprising is that if some of Lincoln's rhetoric characterized Democrats as a conspiratorial threat, it also advocated a mild response to the *Dred Scott* ruling:

> We believe ... in *obedience* to, and *respect* for the judicial department of government. We think its decisions on Constitutional questions, *when fully settled*, should control, not only the particular cases decided, but the general policy of the country, subject to be disturbed only by amendments of the Constitution as provided in that instrument itself. More than this would be revolution. But we think the Dred Scott decision erroneous. We know that the court that made it, has often over-ruled its own decisions, and we shall do what we can to have it over-rule this. *We offer no resistance to it.*[58]

This passage from an 1857 speech highlighted a key distinction between Lincoln and his presidential predecessors who had sought to confront, deny, and/or ignore the validity of judicial rulings they opposed. Lincoln would not actively oppose Taney's ruling. He would instead restrict its implications by claiming that while the decision would stand for the parties to the case, the law itself might not be fully settled. Legal meaning, Lincoln maintained, could only be settled over some length of time.

---

[57] Lincoln to Henry Pierce and others, 6 April 1859, in *The Collected Works of Abraham Lincoln*, ed. Roy Basler, http://showcase.netins.net/web/creative/lincoln/speeches/pierce.htm.

[58] Abraham Lincoln, "Speech in Springfield, Illinois," 26 June 1857. *Abraham Lincoln: Speeches and Writings*, 2 vols. (New York: Literary Classics of the United States, 1989), 302–03. Emphasis added.

This characterization was strategic, for time afforded opportunity, an opportunity to persuade the people to elect leaders who could appoint judges who might overturn the ruling. Such instrumental use of judges is evident in Lincoln's characterization of how the *Dred Scott* ruling came to pass in the first place. According to Lincoln, *Dred Scott* was only possible through electoral politics:

> It is my opinion that the Dred Scott decision, as it is, never would have been made in its present form if the party that made it had not been sustained previously by the elections. My own opinion is, that the new Dred Scott decision, deciding against the right of the people of the States to exclude slavery, will never be made if that party is not sustained by the elections. I believe, further, that it is not just as sure to be made as to-morrow is to come, if that party shall be sustained.[59]

For Lincoln, the *Dred Scott* ruling was predicated on Democratic electoral success in 1852 and 1856. This claim implied that elections could be taken as evidence of the status of a given constitutional interpretation. If judicial decisions contradicted the principles of the party most recently victorious at the polls, then politicians could legitimately not enforce the decision beyond the claimants until the ruling became more settled. As such, not only were judicial decisions political as judges may "hold the same passions for party" as Jefferson once claimed and as Lincoln often quoted, but also enforcement of those decisions could be likewise legitimately political. The extent of enforcement could be warranted by a party's electoral success.[60] In short, through this idea that a legal ruling could be affirmed or repudiated by an election, that is, by expressions of popular sovereignty, Lincoln created time to ignore the broader implications of a ruling and avoided undermining judicial authority entirely. If an election registered discontent with a ruling, then the status of law on the question addressed by the case remained unsettled.

Lincoln's focus on time as a factor in presidential interpretive authority distinguished his claim from those put forward by Jefferson and Van Buren. Jefferson held that his authority as president, by virtue of being a co-equal branch, enabled him to reach a different interpretation from that of Congress or the Court. Van Buren maintained that Jackson held that power not merely by virtue of his co-equal position but also because the president was the sole representative of the national majority and leader of the single constitutional party. By contrast, Lincoln held that law could become stable only over time and that the president would become eventually bound by that meaning. Thus, Lincoln's offer of an alternative to judicial authority shares more in common

---

[59] "Fifth Joint Debate, at Galesburgh, October 7, 1858," *Political Debates between Abraham Lincoln and Stephen Douglas* (Cleveland, OH: Burrows Brothers, 1894), 218–9.

[60] "Speech of Hon. Abraham Lincoln, Delivered in Springfield, Saturday Evening, July 17, 1858 (Mr. Douglas was not present)," *Political Debates between Abraham Lincoln and Stephen Douglas* (Cleveland, OH: Burrows Brothers, 1894), 77.

with Daniel Webster's position – reviewed in Chapter 4 – than with Andrew Jackson's. Indeed, Lincoln's construction undermines the logic of the Jackson Bank veto, as the question of the Bank's constitutionally had been settled over a long stretch of time during which presidential action, repeated congressional action, and a Supreme Court ruling had all taken place. Such conservatism, that is, reverence for maintaining tradition and order, was consistent with Lincoln's Whiggish political beliefs.[61] Thus, Lincoln's position on the instability of the law as articulated by Taney in *Dred Scott* is wholly congruent with his earlier defense of judicial decisions on the constitutionality of banks.[62]

The question of slavery's extension to the territories was not comparably settled. Taney's ruling was not "the unanimous concurrence of the judges, without any apparent partisan bias, and in accordance with legal public expectation, and with the steady practice of the departments through our history."[63] If it had been, disobeying it would be "factious, nay, even revolutionary" action; but, given the newness of Taney's interpretation and the vigorous dissent by his brethren, "it is not resistance, it is not factious, it is not even disrespectful, to treat it as not having yet quite established a settled doctrine for the country."[64]

For Lincoln, the more that the people elected leaders who upheld a ruling, the more aligned constitutionalism and popular sovereignty would become and the more law would be settled. For this notion of "congealing" law and an explicit connection between constitutional meaning and election to be non-threatening to Southern interests, Lincoln would also have to claim that the Constitution did not necessarily hold answers to contemporary questions. In essence, he would have to claim that there were multiple plausible renderings of the meaning of the Constitution, not a singular, fixed, and discoverable meaning from the plain written text. He accomplished this in two ways: by focusing on the document's silences and by re-configuring the meaning of majority.

[61] On Lincoln's affiliation with the Whigs and their commitment to tradition, see Joel Silbey, "'Always a Whig in Politics': The Partisan Life of Abraham Lincoln," *Papers of the Abraham Lincoln Association* 8 (1986), 21–2, and Kenneth Stampp, *The Era of Reconstruction* (New York: Vintage, 1965), 24–49.

[62] In a speech to the Illinois Legislature, Lincoln claimed that the judicial ruling that a state bank was constitutional satisfied him. Mark Graber argues that this admission suggests that Lincoln was a judicial supremacist. However, by attending to Lincoln's focus on time and order, we need not cast Lincoln as either a judicial supremacist or a Jeffersonian departmentalist, but instead uncover meaningful variation in the latter category. Defending the Bank fit Lincoln's Whiggish affinity for order and tradition. See Lincoln, Speech in the Illinois Legislature Concerning the State Bank, 11 January 1837, in *The Collected Works of Abraham Lincoln* (1953), Vol. 1, 61–3. For Graber's claim, see his "Popular Constitutionalism, Judicial Supremacy, and the Complete Lincoln-Douglas Debates," *Chicago-Kent Law Review* 81 (2006), 923–52.

[63] Lincoln, 17 July 1858. Taney's ruling was not unanimous, but only two justices dissented. The margin was far from the bare-majority accusations to which 5–4 decisions are often subject.

[64] Ibid.

First, in his First Inaugural, Lincoln made special note of the legitimacy of disagreement on constitutional meaning precisely because the Constitution was silent on so many questions:

> No organic law can ever be framed with a provision specifically applicable to every question.... No foresight can anticipate nor any document of reasonable length contain express provisions for all possible questions. Shall fugitives from labor be surrendered by national or by State authority? The Constitution does not expressly say, May Congress prohibit slavery in the Territories? The Constitution does not expressly say ... From questions of this class spring all our constitutional controversies, and we divide upon them into majorities and minorities.

This framing would not only legitimize the actions a Republican administration might undertake as simply implementing its own interpretation of those silences, but it would also be a means to stem the secession crisis. If constitutionalism were grounded in popular sovereignty, then law would only be settled if reaffirmed continuously by the majority. If Southern slavery interests prevailed in the election of 1864 and Lincoln and the Republicans were rebuked, then the constitutional status of slavery would continue to remain unsettled just as his own 1860 election kept the issue unsettled. If the people continued to vacillate in their convictions toward slavery by electing presidents from parties with different views on its constitutionality, then the constitutionality of slavery would remain unsettled until a consistent electoral pattern emerged. However, if the people re-elected Lincoln or supported an even stauncher advocate of abolition in the future, then the legitimacy of overruling *Dred Scott* would be on even surer footing.

Second, Lincoln's characterization of majoritarian politics is similar to Van Buren's and Jefferson's assertions with one critical caveat, namely, that Lincoln did not view the majority as static. Instead, he stipulated its dynamic nature in his First Inaugural and, more important, that this dynamism was legitimate. To deny it would spell the end of liberty: "A majority held in restraint by constitutional checks and limitations, and *always changing easily with deliberate changes of popular opinions and sentiments*, is the only true sovereign of a free people. Whoever rejects it does of necessity fly to anarchy or to despotism."[65] If constitutional meanings were affirmed via expressions of popular sovereignty, that is, elections, and majorities in those elections were dynamic, then constitutional meaning itself was dynamic. The Constitution's meaning, far from being fixed and singular, was not a settled affair.

In short, through this reconfiguration of the majority, Lincoln held open the possibility that an interpretation of the Constitution explicitly protecting slave-property rights could be implemented *if* that interest acquired the

---

[65] "First Inaugural Address of Abraham Lincoln," 4 March 1861, www.yale.edu/lawweb/avalon/presiden/inaug/lincoln1.htm. Emphasis added.

requisite votes.[66] Instead of seeking those votes through election, six states – South Carolina, Mississippi, Florida, Alabama, Georgia, and Louisiana – seceded from the Union after Lincoln's November 1860 election. By the time of his inaugural in March 1861, five more – North Carolina, Arkansas, Virginia, Missouri, and Tennessee – had held elections for a convention to consider secession. Desperate to hold the Union together, Lincoln utilized his inaugural speech to legitimate his own rule and to calm anxieties about his intentions toward slavery interests. He restricted his aim: "I have no purpose, directly or indirectly, to interfere with the institution of slavery in the States where it exists. I believe I have no lawful right to do so, and I have no inclination to do so."[67] He cited the Republican national platform, which paid homage to state sovereignty: "the right of each state to order and control its own domestic institutions according to its own judgment exclusively, is essential to that balance of powers on which the perfection and endurance of our political fabric depends."[68]

Providing political opposition to the administration with a sense of security was critical to any prospect of maintaining civic stability. Lincoln was compelled to claim that disagreement was not only inevitable and natural given the silences of the Constitution, but that it was also non-threatening to the republic so long as secession did not follow. Lincoln's challenge was to persuade the Southern states that they had a voice in the Union. And to do that, he had to stipulate that Southerners were essentially loyal to the Constitution. Hence, he closed his First Inaugural with "We are not enemies, but friends. We must not be enemies. Though passion may have strained it must not break our bonds of affection."[69]

This statement seemingly holds similar implications as Jefferson's own "we are all Federalists; we are all Republicans." But significant distinctions exist between the two inaugural phrases that hold important implications for how opposition should be treated. First, Lincoln already explicitly endorsed party politics and the notion of two-party competition, including Van Buren's various institutional innovations such as the national convention.[70] Jefferson was

---

[66] Indeed, Lincoln went so far as to mention, in his inaugural, the possibility of a thirteenth amendment that would secure slavery-property interests in the Southern states.

[67] "First Inaugural Address of Abraham Lincoln," 4 March 1861, www.yale.edu/lawweb/avalon/presiden/inaug/lincoln1.htm.

[68] Republican Party Platform of 1860, 17 May 1860, John T. Woolley and Gerhard Peters, *The American Presidency Project* [online]. Santa Barbara: University of California (hosted), Gerhard Peters (database). www.presidency.ucsb.edu/ws/?pid=29620.

[69] Ibid.

[70] Lincoln held few anti-party biases and advocated Whig adoption of Van Burenite innovations, such as the nominating convention, to maintain a united front against the Democrats: "That great fabulist and philosopher, Aesop, illustrated it by his fable of the bundle of sticks; and he whose wisdom surpasses that of all philosophers, has declared that a 'house divided against itself cannot stand.' It is to induce our friends to act upon this important, and universally acknowledged truth, that we urge the adoption of the Convention system." Lincoln, "Circular Letter from Whig Committee," 4 March 1843, in *Collected Works*, Vol. 1, 315.

far more equivocal on such possibilities, often expressing in private letters a desire to eliminate party distinctions rather than maintain them. Second, and more important, Lincoln admitted that the majority could be *wrong*, and thus that the people were eminently persuadable. If the majority could be wrong, and if the majority were only temporary, trying again for electoral victory made more sense than secession. Lincoln admitted this readily: "I do not deny the possibility that the people may err in an election, but if they do, the true cure is in the next election."[71] To another audience, he argued, "though the majority may be wrong ... yet we must adhere to the principle that the majority shall rule. By your Constitution you have another chance in four years ... elect a better man next time. There are plenty of them."[72] These statements, made just before his inauguration, demonstrate Lincoln's contention that the Southern cause could win the next time around, and thus his admission that the Southern claims about slavery and states' rights were not wholly anti-constitutional. Put more generally, he granted that the majority might be wrong and that its legitimacy to rule was based solely on the shifting interests of the electorate, not on the perpetual rightness of its constitutional claims.

In summary, to prevent secession, Lincoln built on the foundation laid by Van Buren when Van Buren emphasized majority rule as the only procedural mechanism that could confer legitimacy to rule. However, he ultimately abandoned Van Buren's and his own earlier civic republican notion of political opposition as an aristocratic minority threat, which each politician relied on to frame his party as a mechanism of civil stability and as a perpetual majority. Instead, Lincoln re-defined majority as only a numerical superiority granting temporary authority to lead.[73] Popular majorities could shift their allegiances. As such, Lincoln conceded ongoing competition of legitimate and loyal interests with expected rotation in office. Nowhere is this idea clearer than in Lincoln's First Inaugural.

Ironically, the secession crisis – when opposition appeared most disloyal to the Constitution – compelled Lincoln to validate his opposition's cause and to suggest that while its constitutional vision was different from his, it was not anti-constitutional per se. If opposition were just another party and not a threat to the Constitution, then multiple parties could exist. And if multiple parties could exist, and parties represented particular takes on constitutional

---

[71] Abraham Lincoln, 12 February 1861, "Fragment of Speech Intended for Kentuckians," in *Collected Works*, Vol. 4, 200.

[72] Abraham Lincoln, 14 February 1861, "Speech at Steubenville, Ohio," in *Collected Works*, Vol. 4, 207.

[73] Mark Graber, *Dred Scott and the Problem of Constitutional Evil* (New York: Cambridge University Press, 2006), 185–99. Lincoln's argument against secession was based on the proposition that it would lead to anarchy as minorities would exit any confederation rather than accept momentary defeat and try again: "If a minority in such case will secede rather than acquiesce, they make a precedent which in turn will divide and ruin them, for a minority of their own will secede from them whenever a majority refuses to be controlled by such minority." Abraham Lincoln, Inaugural Address, 4 March 1861, http://www.yale.edu/lawweb/avalon/presiden/inaug/lincoln1.htm.

meaning, then so too could multiple constitutional viewpoints exist. Lincoln's desperate attempts to stop secession compelled an ideational innovation, namely, a characterization of each political party as making a valid claim on constitutional meaning that it could implement if it won power.

So, for Lincoln, just as for Van Buren, political parties were the source of constitutional vision, but Lincoln granted that multiple parties could legitimately exist. It followed, first, that multiple equally legitimate constitutional visions could exist, and second, that elections were about constitutional meaning, which ultimately set up each election, not just the Founding ratification itself as a moment of popular sovereignty. Therefore, following Lincoln's logic to its conclusion, partisan appointment of judges followed from the choices made by the people themselves, and judicial rulings could and should reflect party principles, which were themselves particular takes on constitutional principles, and those interpretations could legitimately vary. These rulings would be ratified or undermined – and in this sense, law would become stabilized – by the people themselves through election. The more Lincoln and his supporters were elected to office, the more their constitutional visions could be taken to be what the people supported, and the more legitimately they could be implemented through appointment to the judiciary.

In short, judges could be made into or expected to function as not necessarily part of a unified federal regime, but as tools to implement a ruling party's particular constitutional visions. This idea was given full expression by Lincoln's attorney general, Edward Bates: "The Supreme Court is to be a mere party machine, to be manipulated, built up, and torn down, as party exigencies require."[74] Thus, for Lincoln, any party that wins control of the presidency, Congress, or both, as long as it plays by the rules, can implement its constitutional vision. And while Jackson and Van Buren construed judicial outcomes supporting opposition as threats to civic stability, Lincoln held them in stasis, subject to electoral affirmation. Judgeships could now be fully re-conceptualized as the legitimate spoils of victory, allowing for partisan court-packing and yet, given the earlier-established Jeffersonian ideal of judicial independence as political neutrality, politicians would still be vulnerable to criticism if they appeared to be utilizing judges for political objectives. The tension between these two positions is reflected in that clearly partisan manipulations of the judiciary still had to be justified as achieving neutral objectives of efficiency. This pattern is evident in congressional debates on judicial reforms taken up throughout the 1860s, which are discussed in parts three and four of this chapter.

Ultimately, by emphasizing how elections were a mechanism of popular control over constitutional and legal meaning and by developing a new conception of the majority as dynamic, which might shift in its support among the parties seeking power, Lincoln created the flexibility to ignore

---

[74] Howard K. Beale, ed., *The Diary of Edward Bates, 1859–1866* (Washington, DC: American Historical Association, 1933), 553.

the immediate impact of a disagreeable judicial ruling. By linking judicial authority to electoral politics – as the validity of interpretation subject to electoral ratification – Lincoln found a way to maintain judicial authority without deferring to it as supreme. He denied that national governing policy could be "irrevocably fixed by decisions of the Supreme Court."[75] However, if a given issue had "been before the Court more than once" and had "been affirmed and re-affirmed through a course of years," then it would be "even revolutionary, to not acquiesce in its precedent."[76] As such, Lincoln could occupy the quixotic position of placing limits on judicial authority while also ascribing to it legitimate authority, which could be harnessed to serve his political ends. Lincoln could thereby ignore the Court throughout the Civil War and maintain a role for the other branches to interpret the Constitution while not questioning the Court's right to interpret as well.

II.b. *Presidential Constitutional Interpretive Authority during the Civil War*

Presidential confrontations with the Supreme Court continued throughout the Civil War. One clash developed over Lincoln's suspension of habeas corpus, or the right to be brought to trial and respond to charges levied.[77] That conflict began in April of 1861 when Marylanders who held secessionist sympathies attacked Union soldiers traveling through Baltimore to Washington, D.C., to join the Army of the Potomac. If Maryland seceded, the nation's capital would be cut off from the rest of the Union potentially incapacitating the federal government. Lincoln ordered the militia to circumvent Baltimore and suspended habeas corpus rights for those involved in the attacks or who supported secession.[78] If pro-Southern judges released pro-secessionist forces who were tearing up rail lines, supplying the Army of the Potomac would be impossible, and the Union's effort would fail before it had begun.

The suspension issue came to a head when John Merryman, a Baltimore agriculturalist and alleged friend of Chief Justice Taney, was arrested on 25 May 1861 and held at Fort McHenry.[79] No formal charges were announced, but military officials claimed that Merryman was guilty of "acts of treason" including making "open and unreserved declarations" to support activities associated with "the present rebellion" and for "inciting the revolt

---

[75] Lincoln, *Collected Works*, Vol. 4, 268.

[76] Lincoln, *Collected Works*, Vol. 4, 401.

[77] Suspension of the writ is covered in the Constitution's Article I, Section 9: "The Privilege of the Writ of Habeas Corpus shall not be suspended, unless when in Cases of Rebellion or Invasion the public Safety may require it."

[78] Brian McGinty, *Lincoln and the Court* (Cambridge, MA: Harvard University Press, 2008), 66–8.

[79] The *New York Times* (29 May 1861, pages 4–5) reported that Merryman was a "personal friend" of Taney, but the veracity of this claim is unknown. It is likely, however, that Taney, who was a resident of Baltimore for many years, knew of Merryman given the latter's large agricultural holdings and prominence in the Baltimore community.

which resulted in the murder of the Massachusetts soldiers in the streets of Baltimore."[80] Merryman's lawyers requested a writ of habeas corpus from Taney on 26 May. Taney traveled to Baltimore the following day to hold circuit court and issued the writ to General John Cadwalader, who commanded Fort McHenry. However, Cadwalader did not bring Merryman to court on 28 May.[81] In response, Taney declared Merryman's detention unlawful under the logic that the military had no authority to arrest a "person not subject to the rules and articles of war, for an offense against the laws of the United States, except in aid of the judicial authority, and subject to its control."[82] Furthermore, Taney called into question presidential authority to suspend the privilege of the writ. For Taney, only Congress held that authority since the relevant clause was in the Constitution's first article, which dealt with congressional powers, and not in the second article, which dealt with executive powers. But, even if Congress authorized the suspension, Taney still maintained that Merryman could not be detained by military force since civilian courts still operated in Baltimore.[83]

Lincoln turned to his attorney general, Edward Bates, to draft some justification for the presidential suspension. On 5 July, Bates delivered his memo to Lincoln. In it, Bates made two claims. First, Bates relied on the presidential oath of office. That oath included language not only to support the Constitution but also to "preserve, protect, and defend" it. That particular phrasing, according to Bates, bestowed upon the president more emergency authority than on other federal officers. Second, Bates offered an essentially Jacksonian claim that the three branches were co-equal and independent and thus, the president had as much authority to interpret the Constitution as Taney.[84]

Lincoln did not wait for Bates's memo to justify his actions before a special session of Congress on 4 July 1861. He claimed that the powers he invoked were "a fulfillment, not an abandonment, of the rule of law."[85] He characterized the Suspension Clause as "equivalent to a provision – is a provision – that

---

[80] Statement of Cadwalader to Taney, 26 May 1861, in *The War of the Rebellion: A Compilation of the Official Records of the Union and Confederate Armies*, Series II, Vol. I (Washington, DC: Government Printing Office, 1880–1901), 576. The statement regarding Merryman's role in instigating attacks on Northern troops is from the *New York Times*, 30 May 1861, 4.

[81] McGinty, 73–5.

[82] *Ex parte Merryman*, 17 Fed. Cases 144, 147 (C.C.D.Md 1861).

[83] Ibid.

[84] *The War of the Rebellion: A Compilation of the Official Records of the Union and Confederate Armies*, Series II, Vol. II (Washington, DC: Government Printing Office, 1880–1901), 20–30. Robert McGinty, dismisses Bates's second assertion arguing that *Marbury v. Madison* undercut it and that "in the almost half-century since then, the proposition [of judicial supremacy] had not been seriously challenged" (83). McGinty's claim rests on an assumption, disputed in Chapter 3, that Marshall established judicial supremacy in *Marbury*.

[85] Donald, 163. Similarly, Harold Hyman argues that Lincoln never justified his authority by extra-constitutional necessity. See Hyman, *A More Perfect Union: The Impact of the Civil War and Reconstruction on the Constitution* (New York: Knopf, 1973), 127.

such privilege may be suspended when, in cases of rebellion, the public safety *does* require it."[86] Lincoln sidelined Taney's ruling that the power to suspend the privilege of the writ rested with Congress. He maintained only "the Constitution itself, is silent as to which, or who is to exercise the power."[87]

This emphasis on constitutional silences and, by implication, not only on the legitimacy of multiple interpreters (which Jefferson and Jackson obviously granted) but also on the multiplicity of valid interpretations resonated with Lincoln's inaugural claims. Given circumstances surrounding his habeas decision – Congress was not in secession, Baltimore was in tumult, the security of the national capital at stake – action had to be taken. Once again, the contingency of circumstance compelled Lincoln to highlight constitutional silences and ambivalences. He had to show that multiple interpretations were equally valid, and that particular ideational innovation would prove to have lasting effect.

Ultimately, Lincoln did not need to actively assert his authority to interpret the Constitution as the attorney general laid it out. He only needed to stipulate that the Constitution was silent, and given this silence Lincoln's interpretation was just as plausible as Taney's. Lincoln did not even go this far. He removed allusions to Taney's opinion in the official copy of his 4 July address to Congress.[88] Thus, he framed his interpretation as just that, only his and not an assault on Taney or judicial authority more generally.

Lincoln did not engage in the Jeffersonian or Jacksonian sniping with the Court. Lincoln's message to Congress contained no language to the effect of Jefferson's "sappers or miners" or that the Court was powerless to enforce its decisions. Instead, his rationale for the habeas suspension was of a piece with the minimalist constraint on the *Dred Scott* ruling. Both highlighted the unsettled nature of the law on new questions and the plausibility of alternative interpretations, at least until a single interpretation congealed through repetitive announcement and enforcement. Thus, Lincoln's transformation of the meaning of majority, his focus on constitutional silences, and his emphasis on electoral procedures as the source of legitimacy – all of which were stipulated in his First Inaugural – enabled him to hold the precedent of *Dred Scott* at bay and to avoid a direct confrontation with the Court on *Merryman*.

III. Manifestations of Congressional Republican Fears of Disloyal Opposition

Early Republican fear of conspiracy against the Constitution and conflation of the Democratic Party with the Slave Power is evident in congressional Republican rhetoric and action prior to the Civil War, during the conflict,

---

[86] Abraham Lincoln, "Message to Congress," in *The Official Records of the Union and Confederate Armies*, Series IV, I, 311–21.

[87] Ibid.

[88] Douglas Wilson, *Lincoln's Sword: The Presidency and the Power of Words* (New York: Alfred A. Knopf, 2006), 83–5.

and throughout much of Reconstruction. Concerns about an expanding Slave Power underlay Republican criticism of the Kansas-Nebraska Act of 1854 and compelled congressional Republican manipulations of the judiciary during the Civil War. Concerns about a resurgent conspiratorial Slave Power motivated the impeachment of Andrew Johnson, House investigations into impeaching one or multiple Supreme Court justices, and the exclusion of Southern representation in Congress prior to the passage of the Fourteenth Amendment. Again, if we attend to the idea that stable political opposition was viewed as anti-constitutional conspiracy, we can re-evaluate the rationale underlying hostilities toward the judiciary as part of a larger, if waning, set of civic republican assumptions constitutive of political culture, and not simply an attack on judicial review as potentially structurally countermajoritarian.

III.a. *The Slave Power, Kansas, and Broadening Republican Appeal*

The rise of the Republican Party is often connected to the passage of the Kansas-Nebraska Act in 1854, which allowed residents of those territories to determine their slave status when applying for statehood.[89] The new policy splintered the Democratic Party and the declining Whig Party, and it built momentum for a Northern sectional party. Yet Republican ascendance was not a foregone conclusion.[90] The immediate beneficiary of the collapsed Democratic-Whig dynamic was the Know-Nothing Party, a semi-secret society, which Stephen Douglas characterized as "a crucible into which they poured Abolitionism, Maine liquor law-ism [i.e., temperance], and what there was left of Northern Whigism, and then the Protestant feeling against the Catholic, and the native feeling against the foreigner."[91]

---

[89] Eric Foner, *Free Soil, Free Labor, Free Men: The Ideology of the Republican Party before the Civil War* (New York: Oxford University Press, 1995), 93–5; Weingast, "Self-Enforcing Constitutions." Weingast argues that the repeal of the Missouri Compromise led Northern Democrats to desert their party. While this is true, it is not a direct line from the collapse of the Democratic coalition to the rise of Republicans. As Holt, Silbey, and Gienapp argue, nativism provided a strong organizing axis that prevented Republicans from exploiting anti-slavery concerns in the 1854 and 1855 elections. See Holt, 1978; Silbey, 1985; Gienapp, 1987.

[90] To consider the decline of the Jacksonian Democrats with the ascendance of the Republicans conflates the causes of those two events. It obfuscates other issues characterizing national politics of the 1850s such as ethno-cultural politics, for example, anti-Catholicism and nativism, which positioned the American or Know-Nothing Party, not the Republican Party, as replacing the defunct Whigs. See Paul Kleppner, *The Third Electoral System, 1853–1892: Parties, Voters, and Political Cultures* (Chapel Hill: University of North Carolina Press, 1979); Ronald Formisano, *The Birth of Mass Political Parties: Michigan, 1827–1861* (Princeton: Princeton University Press, 1971); Michael Holt, *Forging a Majority: The Formation of the Republican Party in Pittsburgh, 1848–1860* (New Haven: Yale University Press, 1969); Joel Silbey, *The Transformation of American Politics, 1840–1860* (Englewood Cliffs: Prentice-Hall, 1967); Gienapp, 1987. Don Fehrenbacher critiqued this assertion as "reductive" in his "The New Political History and the Coming of the Civil War," *Pacific History Review* 54 (May 1985), 117–42.

[91] *Congressional Globe*, 33rd Congress, 2nd Session, Appendix, 216.

Republican fortunes improved after the "bleeding Kansas" incident. Pro-slavery advocates destroyed the offices of two free-state newspapers and burned the Emigrant Aid Company's Free State Hotel, a center of abolitionist activism. The attack provided an opportunity to broaden Republicanism's appeal beyond its anti-slavery position. "Bleeding Kansans" helped to forge a characterization of a Southern conspiracy against liberties of speech, press, and assembly, which could resonate with a broader electorate.[92] Senator Charles Sumner of Massachusetts exploited this frame in his speech, "The Crime against Kansas."

Sumner used classical civic republican references to illustrate the conspiratorial nature of the Slave Power, framing Mississippi Senator David Atchison as the American Catiline who

> stalked into this [Senate] chamber, reeking of conspiracy, – *immo etuam in Senatum venit*, – and then, like Catiline, he skulked away, – *abiit, excessit, evasit, erupit*, – to join and provoke the conspirators, who, at a distance awaited their congenial chief.... Slavery now stands erect, clanking its chains on the Territory of Kansas, surrounded by a code of death, and trampling upon all cherished liberties, whether of speech, press, the bar, the trial by jury, or the electoral franchise.[93]

Sumner highlighted not only the pervasive intentions of the conspiracy to undermine the constitutional order but also characterized the perpetrators in the civic republican idiom of an aristocratic cabal. He further disparaged the cherished tenet of Democratic proceduralism by noting the perversions to which popular sovereignty could lead when it maintained no underlying substantive principle: "Sir, all this was done in the name of Popular Sovereignty. And this is the close of the tragedy. Popular Sovereignty, which when truly understood, is a fountain of just power, has ended in Popular Slavery; not merely in the subjection of the unhappy African race, but of this proud Caucasian blood, which you boast."[94] By describing a conspiracy against the Constitution, a thematic frame that underlay the partisanship of Federalists, Jeffersonians, Democrats, Whigs, Free-Soilers, and Republicans, Sumner attempted to broaden the threat posed by Southern slavery to attract a wider base of electoral support.

Shortly after Sumner's fiery oratory, Representative Preston Brooks (D-SC) beat the senator on the Senate floor.[95] The assault personified Northern fears about Southern aggression. As one of Sumner's supporters wrote, "The

---

[92] On the processes by which political entrepreneurs broaden the scope of conflict to ensure that their interests remain relevant and attain increased support, see E. E. Schattschneider, *The Semi-Sovereign People* (Chicago: Holt, Rinehart, and Winston, 1983 [1960]), 36–8, 71.

[93] Charles Sumner, *The Crime against Kansas* (Boston: John P. Jewett, 1856), 22–3, 40–1. Catiline refers to Lucius Sergius Catilina, a Roman politician of the first century B.C., who conspired to overthrow the Roman republic.

[94] Ibid., 41.

[95] William Gienapp, "The Crime against Sumner: The Caning of Charles Sumner and the Rise of the Republican Party," *Civil War History* 25 (September 1979), 218–45.

Kansas murders are on the border and border men are always represented and known to be often desperate but to see a senator assaulted in the Senate Chamber no one can find any excuse for it"; another wrote, "It may seem hard to think but still it is true that the north needed in order to *see* the slave aggression, one of its best men Butchered in Congress, or something else as wicked which could be brought home to them. Had it not been for your poor head, the Kansas outrage would not have been felt at the North"; and yet another wrote to Sumner, "The Northern blood is boiling at the outrage upon you. It really sinks Kansas out of sight."[96] The incident's role as a tipping point for Republican electoral viability was not lost on Know-Nothing presidential candidate Millard Fillmore who commented on the strength of John Fremont's 1856 Republican presidential run: "Brooks' attack upon Sumner has done more for Freemont [*sic*] than any 20 of his warmest friends North have been able to accomplish."[97]

Republicans linked "bleeding Kansas" and "bleeding Sumner" to showcase the lengths to which Southerners and, in particular, slave-holders, would go to threaten constitutional principles. In this construction, the aristocratic threat of the Slave Power was not only concerned with maintaining slavery but also with destroying the rights of (and visibly beating) Northern citizens. Days after the Sumner caning, the moderate yet Republican-leaning *New York Times* argued that the Slave Power "will stop at no extremity of violence in order to subdue the people of the Free States and force them into a tame subservience to its own domination."[98] The more extreme New York *Evening Post* asked, "Has it come to this, that we must speak with bated breath in the presence of our Southern masters…. Are we too, slaves, slaves for life, a target for their brutal blows, when we do not comport ourselves to please them?"[99]

III.b. *Fear of a Returning Slave Power: Suppressing Representation and Impeachment after Civil War*

The rhetoric of a Southern Slave Power conspiracy did not die with the defeat of the Confederacy. Instead, it continued to motivate congressional action in the immediate post-war years including the systematic exclusion of Southern members from Congress in 1866 and the passage of the Fourteenth Amendment. Upon the War's end, Democrats called for "The Union as it was and the Constitution as it is," but more radical Republican members of Congress, such as representatives Thaddeus Stevens and John Bingham and Senator Charles Sumner, feared that President Johnson's proposal for re-admission of

---

[96] F. A. Sumner to Charles Sumner, 24 June 1856, Sumner Papers, Harvard University; Henry N. Walker to John S. Bagg, 24 June 1856, John S. Bagg Papers, Detroit Public Library; M. S. Perry to Charles Sumner, 25 October 1856, Sumner Papers, Harvard University, all quoted in Gienapp, 1987, 301–2.

[97] Millard Fillmore to William Graham, 9 August 1856, quoted in Gienapp, 1987, 440. See generally Gienapp, 1987, 165, 235–7, 240–7, 270–5, 297–9.

[98] *New York Times*, 24 May 1856, quoted in Gienapp, 1987, 359.

[99] New York *Evening Post*, 23 May 1856, quoted in Gienapp, 1987, 359.

the Southern states would not just perpetuate antebellum Southern biases of the federal government but exacerbate them.[100] Nowhere was this potential more evident than in the House of Representatives. If former slaves were now to count fully for representational purposes (as one person rather than three-fifths of a person) but still denied the political right of suffrage, former slave states would *increase* their seats in the House of Representatives and continue to not represent African American political interests, interests that congressional Republicans assumed would align with their own.

In response to this possibility, the Republican-controlled Congress refused to administer the oath of office to representatives and senators from former Confederate states when they were to be seated. Although these states had participated in the ratification of the Thirteenth Amendment, which banned slavery, in 1865 – and thus were recognized as states for that purpose – their representatives, nearly all Democrats, were now excluded from Congress. Without their exclusion, it is unlikely that the Fourteenth Amendment would have received the necessary two-thirds approval to go out for state ratification, as it conferred upon the federal government expanded powers to regulate the states for the purpose of ensuring individual rights and thus significantly altered the balance of power between the federal and the state governments.[101]

When defending an early version of the Fourteenth Amendment, which contained a clause stipulating a reduction in congressional representation if states restricted their franchise, Representative Stevens told his fellow members:

> If the amendment prevails, and those States withhold the right of suffrage from persons of color, it will deduct about thirty-seven [representatives], leaving them but forty-six. With the basis unchanged, the eighty-three Southern members, with the Democrats that will in the best time be elected from the North *will always give them a majority in Congress and in the Electoral College. I need not depict the ruin that would follow....* The oppression of the freedmen; the reamendment of their State constitutions, and the reestablishment of slavery would be the inevitable result.... [But] If they should grant the right of suffrage to persons of color, I think there would always be Union white men enough in the South, aided by the blacks, to divide the representation, and thus continue the Republican ascendancy.[102]

Fear of the return of the Slave Power conspiracy underlay the proposal for suffrage guarantees to the new freedmen. Although this version of the amendment did not pass, its language reappeared in what would become the final

---

[100] Eric Foner, *Reconstruction: America's Unfinished Revolution 1863–1877* (New York: Harper and Row, 1988), 176–227.

[101] For a fuller accounting of the procedural anomalies of passage of the Thirteenth and Fourteenth Amendments, see Bruce Ackerman, "Constitutional Politics/Constitutional Law," *Yale Law Journal* 99 (1989), 453–547, and his *We the People: Transformations* (Cambridge: Belknap Press of Harvard University, 1998), 99–252. For a review of this history and a critique of Ackerman's interpretation, see Amar, 2005, 364–80.

[102] Thaddeus Stevens, *Congressional Globe*, 39th Congress, 1st Session, 18 December 1865, 74. Emphasis added.

clause of the second section of the eventual Fourteenth Amendment: "when the right to vote in any election ... is denied to any male inhabitants of such state, being twenty-one years of age, and citizens of the United States ... the basis of representation therein shall be reduced in the proportion which the number of such male citizens shall bear to the whole number of male citizens twenty-one years or age in such state."[103] The clause's wording avoided specifically granting suffrage to freedmen and left determination of voter qualification to the states. However, the penalty would, *if enforced*, induce former Confederate states to enfranchise their former slaves on their own. Either way, the Slave Power would be weakened if not destroyed; it would be rendered a congressional minority due to the penalty or freedmen's votes would limit its representational share since Republican members assumed freedmen would cast ballots for the party of Lincoln, the emancipator. The amendment would, in Stevens's words, do "what the framers intended ... [and] secure perpetual ascendency to the party of the Union; and so as to render our republican Government firm and stable forever."[104] In this statement, once again, a civic republican rhetorical connection between civil stability and constitutional one-party rule is evident as is the association of political opposition with civil strife and constitutional threat.

While Stevens's version of the amendment did not pass, the Joint Committee on Reconstruction did offer two other measures grounded in the more palatable notion that the freedmen were entitled to *civil* rights protections but not necessarily to the *political* right of suffrage. The first bill, the Freedman's Bureau Bill, proposed by moderate Republican senator, Lyman Trumbull, renewed the Freedman's Bureau, established during the last year of the Civil War to ease the transition of the ex-slaves to freedom. The second bill, which became the Civil Rights Act of 1866, secured civil rights, namely, the right to own property, marry, and enter into contracts, against abridgment by state governments; such rights were jeopardized throughout the ex-Confederacy by so-called black codes.[105] To justify federal regulation of the states on behalf of individual rights, Trumbull utilized the Thirteenth Amendment. That amendment did not protect the citizen from government, but by banning slavery, claimed the right of the federal government to protect the citizens from each other.

President Andrew Johnson vetoed both bills claiming that Congress had no authority under the Constitution to pass them.[106] Furthermore, Johnson denied that the Thirteenth Amendment or the Union victory in the Civil War substantially altered relations between the states and the national government or created any significant change in his own power as president. And

[103] United States Constitution, Fourteenth Amendment, Section Two.
[104] Stevens, *Congressional Globe*, 39th Congress, 1st Session, 18 December 1865, 74.
[105] On black codes, see Foner, 1988, 199–201, 208–9. On the nineteenth-century tripartite conception of civil, political, and social rights, see Epps, 31.
[106] Epps, 130–6.

he questioned the legitimate authority of this Congress to pass any legislation while the former Confederate states remained unrepresented. Thus, he alone as president stood as the only fully representational office: "The President of the United States stands toward the country in a somewhat different attitude from that of any member of Congress, chosen from a single district or State. The President is chosen by the people of all the States.... It would seem to be his duty on all proper occasions to present their just claims to Congress."[107] Thus, he maintained the Jacksonian construction of presidential authority: the president was the only officer elected by the people and, as such, functioned as a popular tribune in ways that Congress never could. Furthermore, Johnson claimed a special responsibility toward the excluded Southern states since they had no voice in Congress: "As eleven States are not at this time represented in either branch of Congress, it would seem to be his [the president's] duty on all proper occasions to present their just claims to Congress."[108] For Republican congressmen, such statements likely only confirmed how much Johnson sought to empower the Southern states and restore his own Democratic Party to power. Given perceived links between Democrats and the Slave Power, Republican attribution of Slave Power ambitions to Johnson is hardly surprising.

This fear is evident in congressional debate over the proposed Fourteenth Amendment. Representative Ingersoll of Illinois defended the measure against Johnson's protest by referencing conspiratorial threat: "Carry out the policy of Andrew Johnson, and you will restore the old order of things, if the Government is not entirely destroyed: you will have the same old slave power, the enemy of liberty and justice, ruling this nation again, which ruled it for so many years."[109] This viewpoint underlay the exclusion of Southern representation in the House and the Senate during this debate, and once it became clear that former Confederate and border states were rejecting the proposed Fourteenth Amendment when it went out for ratification, such that it would not have received the necessary support of three-quarters of the states to become part of the Constitution, the Republican-controlled Congress took further action to delegitimize this opposition. It passed the First and Second Reconstruction Acts in March of 1867, both over Johnson's veto. These Acts dissolved the states of the former Confederacy, setting up five military districts in that territory. Re-admission as states into the Union and congressional recognition of House and Senate members were made contingent on ratification of the Fourteenth Amendment.[110] And, Johnson's actions – his vetoes of the

---

[107] Andrew Johnson, Veto Message, presented to the Senate. Reprinted in the *New York Times*, 20 February 1866, 1. While Johnson may have had a legitimate critique that an incomplete Congress could not pass legislation affecting Southern states, particularly when such states were not represented in that body, his own claim to be representative of all the people was unjustifiable as he was not elected by citizens of the ex-Confederacy.

[108] Ibid.

[109] Eben Ingersoll, *Congressional Globe*, 39th Congress, 1st Session, 5 May 1866, 2403.

[110] See Amar, 2005, 364–80.

civil rights bill, the bureau bill, and the reconstruction bills and his campaign against the Fourteenth Amendment – placed him not only in the position of opposing the will of the Republican congressional majority, but cast him as a representative of a conspiratorial opposition threatening to undermine the Union victory and send the nation hurling back toward civil war.

Through impeachment, the Republican congressional majority could assert its authority to save the republic from a president who appeared in words and actions to support the revival of the Slave Power. Johnson's impeachment was preceded by the passage of the Tenure of Office Act, which stipulated that the president could not remove an officer confirmed by the Senate unless the Senate consented to the removal. Johnson vetoed the bill. The veto was overridden, and the new law classified its violation as a "high misdemeanor," foreshadowing the eventual outcome.[111] Johnson retaliated by suspending Secretary of War Edward Stanton and replacing him with General Ulysses S. Grant while the Senate was out of session. When the Senate returned, it disavowed the suspension; Stanton reassumed his position and barricaded himself in his office. Johnson then attempted to establish a new army with General William T. Sherman to lead it. Sherman refused, and shortly thereafter, Johnson fired Stanton, thereby violating the Tenure of Office Act and triggering a House impeachment vote of 126 to 47.[112] Johnson's ill-fated attempt to establish his own army only heightened fears that he intended to reignite civil war. Throughout the North rumors circulated that Johnson would dismiss Congress and install Southern allies. This fear motivated, in part, impeachment proceedings against the president.[113]

III.c. *Judiciary as Slave Power: Removing Southern Opposition during and after the Civil War*

As discussed in Chapter 4, Andrew Jackson's relations with the federal judiciary have been viewed as mostly opportunistic; and the same label has been applied to congressional Republican measures that both contracted and expanded judicial power as circumstances demanded throughout the 1860s. And yet, just as Jackson's actions gained new coherency when attention is paid to opposition legitimacy and the party's role in stipulating constitutional meaning, this same coherency is evident in congressional Republican manipulations in the 1860s of bench size and circuit design. Many of Congress's actions toward the judiciary during the Civil War had the same motivations as that body's refusal to seat Southern delegations to Congress and its impeachment of President Johnson. Put differently, the judiciary was conceptualized as a threatening and conspiratorial opposition supporting the Slave Power.

[111] Richard Neumann, "The Revival of Impeachment as a Partisan Political Weapon" (2006), Hofstra University Legal Studies Research Paper No. 06–22, http://ssrn.com/abstract=923834, 65–6.
[112] Hans Trefousse, *Impeachment of a President: Andrew Johnson, the Blacks, and Reconstruction* (New York: Fordham University Press, 1999), 99–134.
[113] Epps, 241, 253–7.

Stanley Kutler has argued that various Republican measures re-structuring the judiciary taken throughout the 1860s, such as the 1862 Judiciary Act, which re-configured the state composition of the judicial circuits, were not hostile to judicial legitimacy. Rather, they were undertaken to promote judicial efficiency.[114] To a certain extent, Kutler is correct. These actions were not hostile to the power of the judiciary to review legislation. Yet even if they were framed in the language of efficiency, similar to debates preceding the 1837 Judiciary Act, their *effect* re-shaped geographic representation on the bench in ways that revealed hostility not to judicial review and thus not to the judiciary as a structurally undemocratic institution, but rather to Southern Slave Power influence on the bench.

As evidence of congressional concerns with judicial efficiency, Kutler pointed to the mal-apportioned circuits; of the nine, five included Southern states, which only had eleven million inhabitants, while the remaining four had sixteen million inhabitants. Reform was also needed because existing circuits did not cover many of the newly admitted states. Wisconsin, Minnesota, Iowa, Kansas, Florida, Texas, California, and Oregon remained outside the system creating unequal judicial access for citizens. Lincoln proposed a range of options: re-organize the circuits, end Supreme Court Justice circuit-riding, or abolish circuits altogether.[115] Kutler posited that Lincoln "proposed nothing that touched on the basics of judicial power" and that the legislation that followed "was reasonable, just, and obviously quite politic."[116]

Kutler contended that the lack of debate on this reform was "most striking," and that the emphasis on maintaining judicial neutrality during the debate demonstrated sincere interest in promoting judicial efficiency through the least possible changes.[117] Senator Bingham supported judicial reform since it did not make significant change to the system other than shuffling the states in each circuit. And that re-shuffling was justified on the basis of feasible circuit-riding: if the excluded states were to be incorporated into one new circuit, it would be so populous and geographically large that no justice could cover it.[118]

Furthermore, Republicans, like Democrats in the nearly twenty-year debate preceding the Judiciary Act of 1837, attempted judicial reform that would maintain a politically neutral judiciary. What little debate there was on the Judiciary Act of 1862 suggests that politicians sought to maintain independent and neutral judicial authority rather than seek retribution for *Dred Scott*. Indeed, that members of Congress did not take more aggressive anti-judicial

---

[114] Kutler, 7–29.
[115] Abraham Lincoln, First Annual Message, 3 December 1861, John T. Woolley and Gerhard Peters, *The American Presidency Project* [online]. Santa Barbara, CA: University of California (hosted), Gerhard Peters (database): http://www.presidency.ucsb.edu/ws/?pid=29502. In laying out the same three options including the end of circuit-riding, Lincoln shows little deference to the 1789 Act contradicting Geyh's contention of deference to the Founders.
[116] Kutler, 13, 29.
[117] Ibid., 19.
[118] *Congressional Globe*, 37th Congress, 2nd Session, 23 December 1861, 173.

action lends support to the notion that *Dred Scott*, while an unpopular ruling, did not invite reprisal. Senator Kellogg opposed the bill on the grounds that it politicized the Court:

> It is said, however, that this bill does not change the number of judges, and that the President can make his appointments. Sir, if there is any reason in the President's message for desiring a reorganization of the judiciary before he makes his appointments to fill vacancies, is it not a reason against making the change by piecemeal rather than a general measure? ... If we cannot agree upon a general system for the adjustment of this subject, then the Judiciary Committee can report to the House the action desired by the gentleman from Ohio [Mr. Bingham] if it be proper action.[119]

Kellogg framed his objection in terms of pursuing a more uniform reform to maintain the judiciary's independence. He interpreted the bill, which re-drew the districts and diminished the number of circuits including Southern states, as politicizing the Court. Kellogg's objection postponed the bill's consideration but did not prevent its passage in July of 1862.

Yet the bill passed with less debate than its 1837 predecessor, largely because no systemic re-organization was considered – nine circuits were maintained as was circuit-riding – and the expected voices of opposition were obviously not present due to secession. While Northern Democrats remained in Congress, re-scaling the circuit sizes to more adequately reflect Northern population growth would benefit all Northerners regardless of party affiliation. Even if the Act could be framed as political tampering with the Court, Democrats were outnumbered, and by 1863 the Democratic Party was increasingly saddled with accusations of treason.[120]

By re-structuring the circuits, the Judiciary Acts of 1862 and 1866 increased the number of non-Southern justices on the Court so long as the tradition of geographic representation was maintained. As such, redefining the circuit boundaries would rout out opposition. Table 5.1 lists the re-organized circuits before, during, and after the Civil War.

Redesign of circuit boundaries in 1862 and approval of a tenth circuit in 1863 that included California and Oregon enabled Lincoln to appoint five Justices: Samuel Miller, David Davis, Noah Swayne, Stephen Field, and Salmon Chase. By adhering to established tradition of geographic representation, Lincoln avoided appointing Southerners to the bench.[121] By 1866, by maintaining the tradition of geographic representation, only one circuit – the fifth – required judicial appointment from an ex-Confederate state.

[119] Ibid.
[120] Smith, 67–84.
[121] As Kermit Hall has argued, this practice prevented judicial support for nationalist policy: "At least in their institutional structure the federal courts proved resistant to the impact of the Civil War and the first years of Reconstruction. For their part, Republicans emerged as at best reluctant nationalizers." Hall, "The Civil War as a Crucible for Nationalizing the Lower Federal Courts," *Prologue* 7 (Fall 1975), 185.

TABLE 5.1. *Re-drawing Judicial Circuits to Eliminate Southern Supreme Court Justices*

Circuit	1837 Reform Act	1862 Reform Act	1866 Reform Act
First	Maine, Massachusetts, New Hampshire, Rhode Island	Maine, Massachusetts, New Hampshire, Rhode Island	Maine, Massachusetts, New Hampshire, Rhode Island
Second	Connecticut, New York, Vermont	Connecticut, New York, Vermont	Connecticut, New York, Vermont
Third	New Jersey, Pennsylvania	New Jersey, Pennsylvania	New Jersey, Pennsylvania, Delaware
Fourth	**Delaware**, **Maryland**, *Virginia*	**Delaware**, **Maryland**, *Virginia*, *North Carolina*	**Maryland**, *North Carolina*, *South Carolina*, *Virginia*, *West Virginia*
Fifth	*Alabama*, *Louisiana*	*Alabama*, *Georgia*, *Florida*, *Mississippi*, *South Carolina*	*Alabama*, *Georgia*, *Florida*, *Mississippi*, *Louisiana*, *Texas*
Sixth	*Georgia*, *North Carolina*, *South Carolina*	*Arkansas*, **Kentucky**, *Louisiana*, *Tennessee*, *Texas*	**Kentucky**, Michigan, Ohio, *Tennessee*
Seventh	Illinois, Indiana, Michigan, Ohio	Indiana, Ohio	Illinois, Indiana, Wisconsin
Eighth	**Kentucky**, *Missouri*, *Tennessee*	Illinois, Michigan, Wisconsin	*Arkansas*, Iowa, Kansas, Minnesota, *Missouri*
Ninth	*Arkansas*, *Mississippi*	Iowa, Kansas, Minnesota, *Missouri*	California, Oregon, Nevada

Note: Southern states are in **bold**; Confederate states are in **bold *italics***.

Field's appointment, in particular, as the tenth justice has been criticized as an attempt by Lincoln to pack the Court. This appointment has been interpreted as allegedly sought to secure favorable rulings as cases developed questioning executive authority to prosecute the war.[122] Prior to the bench expansion and Field's appointment to the tenth slot, the Court decided the *Prize Cases* 5 to 4, narrowly upholding the president's authorization of a blockade of Southern ports. Given the slim support, Lincoln could plausibly

[122] Silver argued that the closeness of the *Prize Cases* "dictated a packed Court" (84); Kens contends that Republicans "wanted to pack the Court" (95); Rehnquist argued that Lincoln's appointments essentially were "packing the Court," (209–13) but that claim does not suffice to prove that the addition of a tenth justice was a deliberate Court-packing measure in reaction to the *Prize Cases*. See David Silver, *Lincoln's Supreme Court* (Urbana: University of Illinois, 1956), and Paul Kens, *Justice Stephen Field: Shaping Liberty from the Gold Rush to the Gilded Age* (Lawrence: University Press of Kansas, 1997).

be interested in surer judicial footing.[123] However, timing contradicts the idea that bench expansion was a reaction to the ruling; plans for a tenth justice were coordinated before the *Prize Cases* decision was made. And there is ample evidence that the nomination could have been motivated by a variety of reasons aside from expanding Lincoln's emergency powers: (1) Oregon and California remained outside the circuit system even after the 1862 reform; (2) the Court's docket was burdened by California land disputes resulting from the Treaty of Guadalupe-Hidalgo, and Field had experience with such law; and (3) Field's identification as a California Democrat would draw California further into the Union as well as signal Lincoln's interest in crossing party lines in the name of national unity.[124] As such, re-configuring the circuits would eliminate an alleged institutional bolster of the Slave Power. In this way, early congressional Republicans were attempting to achieve what Van Buren thought he might have accomplished through the party appointments in the late 1830s.

Besides altering the composition of the circuits, the 1866 Judiciary Act reduced the Supreme Court bench from ten to seven justices. The 1869 Act then increased the bench from seven justices to nine. These adjustments, occurring in a narrow span of time, have been considered a way to prevent Johnson appointments while giving appointments to President Grant.[125] If this characterization were accurate, why would Johnson sign the 1866 bill? Also, while bench alterations appear to make the Court a Republican plaything, the justices supported these changes.[126] Given that the Supreme Court was almost entirely unable to meet as its full complement in Washington, D.C., when there were ten justices, downsizing the bench would make it a more manageable body. Furthermore, salary increases were more likely if there were fewer justices to be paid. It should be noted, however, that the legislation that passed was not the same as had been supported by Chief Justice Chase. The chief justice sought salary increases, new intermediate appellate courts to relieve the Court's backlog, and a title change from "Chief Justice of the Supreme Court" to "Chief Justice of the United States."[127] The 1866 Act decreased the Supreme bench and gave Chase a new title, but no salary increases were allowed and no intermediate appellate circuit courts were established.[128]

The Act prevented Johnson from nominating men for lower federal judgeships who might be sympathetic to his Reconstruction policy. It also prevented

[123] *The Prize Cases*, 67 U.S. 635 (1867).
[124] McGinty, 179–81. See also Ronald Labbe and Jonathan Lurie, *The Slaughterhouse Cases: Regulation, Reconstruction, and the Fourteenth Amendment* (Lawrence: University Press of Kansas, 2005), 118.
[125] Carson and Kleinerman, 12.
[126] When he was a senator, Chase introduced a bill in 1855 reducing the Court to six justices and ending circuit-riding. The 1869 Act created nine circuit judgeships and required justices to attend at least one term of the circuit court every two years, further lightening their load and attracting their support. See Kutler, 53–6, and Hall, 182–5.
[127] Charles Fairman, *Reconstruction and Reunion, 1864–88, Part One* (New York: Macmillan, 1971), 163–7.
[128] Act of July 23, 1866, chap. 210, 14 Stat. 209.

him from appointing Henry Stanbery to replace the deceased Justice John Catron since the act eliminated Catron's seat. Three days before Johnson signed the Act, the Senate confirmed Stanbery as attorney general. Johnson secured an appointment for Stanbery, Chase got a title, and Congress deprived Johnson of appointments.[129]

Furthermore, prior to the 1866 reform, the Court had done little to foretell its eventual clash with Congress over the constitutionality of Reconstruction policy.[130] Thus, as Kutler argued, reducing the Court's size cannot be understood as congressional retribution against judicial authority, even as he is too hasty in arguing that it did not counter Johnson's authority.[131] And, while the justices' apparent support for the 1866 Act may undercut the claim that Republicans were hostile toward the Court, it does not undermine the idea that some Republicans remained hostile toward Democratic, particularly Southern, opposition. Re-drawing circuit boundaries was a means to eliminate Southern influence. And reducing the membership on the Supreme Court bench would shore up Republican control of the Supreme Court as the seat held by Justice Catron, who was from Tennessee, was eliminated.[132] Furthermore, decreasing the bench size would eliminate Jacksonian influence on the Court as the justices appointed before Lincoln's presidency were each over seventy by 1866 and could be expected to retire soon, solidifying Republican power.

IV. Congressional Republican Harnessing of Judicial Power

The re-structuring of the judicial circuit system fits a pattern of eliminating a threatening opposition from its entrenchment in the federal judiciary. As this section argues, stripping the Supreme Court's jurisdiction in 1868 initially appears similarly motivated. Yet this action was more targeted, and it followed from accepted congressional authority to regulate jurisdiction. So, while jurisdiction-stripping does undeniably impinge on independent judicial authority, it can be a narrow means of doing so. And, as detailed later, that legislators would ultimately deny the precedent effect of this action suggests a desire to maintain judicial authority, not a desire to undercut it.

The Judiciary Act of 1869 can also be understood as a harnessing measure as it increased the Supreme Court bench to nine justices and established new intermediate appellate circuit courts, thereby expanding Republican control over appointments to the lower federal judiciary. If judges are considered arms of their parties – as Lincoln's ideas implied – then Republican constructions of constitutional meaning could spread throughout the federal judiciary

---

[129] McGinty, 267. U.S. Congress, *Senate Executive Journal*, 39th Congress, 1st Session, July 20, 1866, 944, and July 23, 1866, 1043.
[130] On Radical Republican assertions of legislative supremacy against the judiciary, see Walter Murphy, "Who Shall Interpret? The Quest for the Ultimate Constitutional Interpreter," *Review of Politics* 48 (Summer 1986), 410–11.
[131] Kutler, 53.
[132] Ibid., 50–2.

via appointment. If senatorial Republicans and President Grant controlled appointments, they could use them to implement their constitutional vision, seemingly supported by the outcomes of the 1864, 1866, and 1868 elections, which maintained Republican control of Congress and the presidency. How then are the actions taken by Grant and the Republican Senate more akin to partisan harnessing than the bench-packing taken after the Judiciary Act of 1837? They are distinguishable to the extent that the Republicans were *increasingly aware of their own tenuous hold on governing power*. The Republican moves – narrowly limiting the party's authority in certain jurisdictions and then denying that this action had any long-term effect while also expanding the number and reach of judges the Republicans could appoint – follow from their awareness that they could not hold their status as the single constitutional (or even dominant) party and that they could use the judiciary, while they held presidential and congressional power, to promote their constitutional vision and entrench their interests against the Democratic alternative. As such, Republican actions were driven by a desire to secure their partisan objectives if they should lose power whereas Van Buren's earlier actions were motivated by the desire for regime unity; Van Buren never seriously entertained the possibility that his Democracy would fall from power.

IV.a. *The Judiciary as a Policy Tool: Stripping Jurisdiction but Denying the Precedent*

Between 1866 and 1868, the Court did tend to obstruct congressional Reconstruction policy. In *Ex parte Milligan*, the Court ruled against the operation of military tribunals in regions where civil courts functioned, and five justices denied Congress the power to establish a military commission.[133] Congress responded by validating all presidential proclamations made between 4 March 1861 and 1 December 1865 related to ending the rebellion and provided that no court could reverse these proclamations. Essentially, this bill negated *Ex parte Milligan*, but Johnson never signed it.[134] The Court further raised Republican ire by declaring loyalty oaths unconstitutional in *Cummings v. Missouri* and *Ex parte Garland*.[135]

The House passed a bill overruling these loyalty oath rulings. And this action was paired with rhetoric highlighting the extent to which the Supreme Court's members had succumbed to the forces of anti-constitutional and Slave Power conspiracy seeking to overturn the Union victory. According to Representative George Boutwell of Massachusetts:

> If there be five judges upon the bench ... who have not that respect for themselves to enact rules and to enforce proper regulations by which they will

---

[133] *Ex parte Milligan*, 71 U.S. 2 (1866)

[134] Kutler, 69–70.

[135] *Cummings v. Missouri*, 71 U.S. 277 (1867) dealt with loyalty oaths for schoolteachers and *Ex parte Garland*, 1 U.S. 333 (1867) involved a congressional statute requiring federal attorneys to take loyalty oaths.

protect themselves from the foul contamination of conspirators and traitors against the Government of this country, then the time has already arrived when the legislative department ... should exercise its power to declare who shall be officers of the Government in the administration of the law in the courts of the Union.[136]

The Senate was more circumspect and took no parallel actions in response to the loyalty oath cases. In December of 1867, the Senate did pass a bill, put forward by Lyman Trumbull, which provided a five-member quorum of the Supreme Court, which now stood at eight members and to maintain that quorum when membership dropped to seven as provided for by the 1866 Judiciary Act. The House Judiciary Committee then amended this bill to require a two-thirds majority of the bench to invalidate congressional legislation.[137] Another amendment, proposed by Representative Williams of Pennsylvania but not added to the quorum bill, required unanimity on the bench to overturn legislation since the two-thirds requirement "would add one voice only to the number now required to undo the work of Congress ... and ... falls short of the necessities of the case and the high requirements of public duty."[138] However, according to Kutler, the two-thirds amendment, which passed in the House, failed in the Senate because Republicans could not yet determine the extent to which the Court threatened its policy aims: "They could arrive at no consensus on judicial reform so long as they felt no need to react against an obvious transgression on the part of the judiciary."[139] And no judicial action had yet deliberately challenged the core legitimacy of the Senate's Reconstruction plans. Indeed, shortly after announcing its rulings in the loyalty oath cases, the Court indicated its lack of jurisdictional authority to interfere with congressional Reconstruction plans when it refused to grant an injunction against the Reconstruction Acts.[140] The Court skirted the question presented by relying on its political questions distinction enunciated in *Luther v. Borden*.[141] The Court may have been cowed into this position by threatening statements made in the House, but it did not present an immediate oppositional threat to the Republican-controlled Congress. That threat crystallized when the Court accepted jurisdiction in *Ex parte McCardle*.[142]

---

[136] Boutwell, 22 January 1867, *Congressional Globe*, 39th Congress, 2nd Session, 646–47, quoted in Kutler, 71.

[137] Kutler, 72, 74.

[138] Speech of Thomas Williams of Pennsylvania in the House of Representatives, 13 January 1868, *Appendix to the Congressional Globe*, 85.

[139] Kutler, 77.

[140] *Mississippi v. Johnson*, 71 U.S. 475 (1867).

[141] *Luther v. Borden*, 48 U.S. 1 (1849). The Court was asked to decide which of two governments of the state of Rhode Island was legitimate. The Court ruled that it had no proper jurisdiction saying the determination of a state's republican form of government was Congress's responsibility. The case established the idea of political questions, which was elaborated in cases during the mid-twentieth century.

[142] *Ex parte McCardle*, 74 U.S. 506 (1868). Before *Ex parte McCardle*, the Court was not clearly triggering a showdown with Congress. Rulings before *McCardle* indicated that it tried to

William McCardle was a Southern newspaper editor held for trial by a military tribunal for criticizing the military regimes instituted under congressional Reconstruction policy. McCardle sued for a writ of habeas corpus under doctrine established by *Ex parte Milligan*. A lower federal court denied him the writ, and he appealed to the Supreme Court under the auspices of the 1867 Habeas Corpus Act.[143]

Amid a "flood of press reports insisting that McCardle's case was a vehicle for the Court's majority to declare the Reconstruction Acts unconstitutional," congressional Republicans reacted by repealing the Supreme Court's jurisdiction to hear appeals, which had been based on the 1867 Habeas Corpus Act.[144] In *McCardle*, Chief Justice Chase acknowledged congressional authority to manipulate jurisdiction through the Constitution's Exceptions Clause, which states that federal jurisdiction is conferred "with such exceptions and under such regulations as Congress shall make."[145] And the Court acquiesced:

> We are not at liberty to inquire into the motives of the legislature. We can only examine into its power under the Constitution, and the power to make exceptions to the appellate jurisdiction of this court is given by express words. What, then, is the effect of the repealing act upon the case before us? We cannot doubt as to this. Without jurisdiction, the court cannot proceed at all in any cause.[146]

Yet before that judicial retreat took place, the Republican press envisioned the possibility of an oppositional judiciary undermining Reconstruction in favor of a revitalized Slave Power; the *New York Herald* supported pre-emptive congressional action to rein in the Court:

> Shall the opinions of a bare majority of these nine old superannuated pettifoggers of the Supreme Court, *left to the country as the legacy of the old defunct Southern slaveholding oligarchy*, prevail, or shall these old marplots make way for the will of the sovereign people and the national constitution as expounded by Washington and Hamilton, and as established by a million of Union bayonets in a four years' civil war? This is the great question for 1868.[147]

The *Herald's* characterization of the Court is overstated. Again, by 1868, the Court's personnel had substantially changed; it was not the Southern-influenced

---

avoid that possibility. The Republican-oriented press pushed for judicial restraint, and these press reports were used to justify jurisdiction-stripping measures.

[143] Barry Friedman, "The History of the Countermajoritarian Difficulty, Part II: Reconstruction's Political Court," *Georgetown Law Review* 91 (November 2002), 26–39, and Ackerman, 1998, 218–27.

[144] Kutler, 80.

[145] The Exceptions and Regulations Clause is the second clause of the second section of Article Three of the Constitution.

[146] *Ex parte McCardle*, 74 U.S. 506 (1868), 514.

[147] "Congress and the Supreme Court – The Great Issue for the Next Presidency," *New York Herald*, 5 January 1867, 4.

Taney Court. But it is nevertheless telling that the Court could and would still be characterized in the terms of an oppositional conspiracy. The Republican-leaning *Nation* went a step further to call for a range of policies that would limit a potentially anti-Reconstruction Court, even if such policies could not be constitutionally supported by the terms of the Constitution: "there never has existed, and there never is likely to exist, a nation which will allow con-stitutions or any forms of any kind on paper to stand between it and such a change in policy as it deems necessary to its safety."[148] And the *Daily Morning Chronicle* of Washington, D.C., another Republican outlet, called for curbing a Court that upheld claims of state power against the national government, claiming that if it did so, it "would make [the Constitution] a straight waist-coat binding the arms of the nation while its assailants stab it to death."[149] In all of these statements, each newspaper laid the foundations for a more organic or dynamic construction of the Constitution, a construction that must respond to facts on the ground, to newly conceived relationships between the levels of governance.

Representative Wilson, who introduced the jurisdiction-stripping amend-ment, referenced such press reports to defend his proposal:

> When we are told day by day that the majority of the court had practically made up its judgment, not only to pass upon the sufficiency of the return to the writ, which involves the only question properly before them in the McCardle case, but also to do as the court did once before in the Dred Scott case, go outside of the record properly involving the questions really presented for its determination, undertaking to infringe upon the political power of Congress, and declare the laws … unconstitutional, it is our duty to intervene by a repeal of jurisdiction and prevent the threatened calamity falling upon the country.[150]

The histrionic tone distracts from the *limits* of Wilson's claim to restruc-ture the Court's jurisdiction. He made no deeper constitutional claim that Congress could always determine jurisdiction. By referencing the excesses of the *Dred Scott* decision, he argued that the Court ignored its own precedent, which it justly set out in *Luther v. Borden*, by potentially adjudicating ques-tions that were clearly political in nature. As such, he appears to rely on the Lincolnian logic that good law is that which is "affirmed and re-affirmed" and that the Court, ruling as it increasingly had been against Reconstruction policies, was simply not affirming its own precedent on political questions. The jurisdiction-stripping measure, by this logic, ensured only that the Court maintained its own precedent and did not become embroiled in political ques-tions. Wilson's clear message, which echoed Boutwell's rhetoric in the wake of the loyalty oath cases, was that Congress "had to protect the Court from itself" or to protect the Court from its own politicization, which is a familiar

[148] "The Lesson of the Crisis," *Nation*, 17 January 1867, 50.
[149] "The Decision in the Milligan Case," *Daily Morning Chronicle*, 1 January 1867, 2.
[150] *Congressional Globe*, 40th Congress, 2nd Session, 21 March 1868, 2059–60.

theme emanating from the Jeffersonian reconstruction of judicial independence and political neutrality.[151]

Importantly, Boutwell's argument for overturning the loyalty oath rulings, like Wilson's argument supporting jurisdiction-stripping, was not framed as questioning the authority of an unelected judiciary. Boutwell made no mention of doing away with judicial review; the claim was that the Court was backing a treasonous conspiratorial opposition, and as such, its rulings undermined the Constitution. That opposition, those "conspirators and traitors against Government," were the problem to be solved, not the structural abnormality of an unelected judiciary in a democracy or the power of judicial review. This speech also promoted the Court as de-politicized, a quality, Boutwell contended, that was undermined by the Court's rulings in favor of states' rights and Southern objections to Reconstruction in the contest of Union and Republican electoral victory. All rhetorical venom was aimed toward removing opposition to Republican objectives from government, not toward curbing judicial review as an end in itself.[152]

The possibility that the Supreme Court might call into question the constitutionality of the Reconstruction Acts enabled the media to portray it as representing the interests of a conspiratorial opposition, leaving it vulnerable to accusations of treason. *Harper's Weekly* invoked the lexicon of the Southern rebellion to cast aspersions upon the Court: "rebels have already possession of two of the three branches of Government – the Executive and the Judiciary – leaving the Legislative only to the Union men of the country."[153] Opposition to Reconstruction was illegitimate not only because the Union won, but because the ideational paradigm of natural if disloyal opposition continued to color the political beliefs and rhetoric of first-generation Republicans just as it had undergirded Van Burenite Democratic aspirations of the previous generation. Congressional assault on the Court parallels the logic of Johnson's impeachment, that is, routing out an opposition defeated at the polls and on the battlefield to implement a particular constitutional vision.[154]

---

[151] Kutler, 71.

[152] Johnson vetoed the jurisdiction-stripping measure by referencing the Supreme Court's authority. The Court had "been viewed by the people as the true expounder of their Constitution, and in the most violent party conflicts its judgments and decrees have always been sought and deferred to with confidence and impartiality in a greater degree than any other authority." His veto was overridden, and the Court acquiesced by denying jurisdiction in *Ex parte McCardle. Congressional Globe*, 40th Congress, 2nd Session, 25 March 1868, 2094.

[153] "The New Dred Scott," *Harper's Weekly*, 19 January 1867.

[154] Nicole Mellow and Jeffrey K. Tulis, "Andrew Johnson and the Politics of Failure" in *Formative Acts: American Politics in the Making*, Stephen Skowronek and Matthew Glassman, eds. (Philadelphia: University of Pennsylvania Press, 2007). In support of this idea that Republicans endorsed a new constitutional vision, Mellow and Tulis remark, "Johnson covered his narrow and unjust sectionalist motives with plausible, sometimes constitutional argument, whereas his opponents distorted the Constitution, however sound their political motives" (170).

If the jurisdiction-stripping measure in reaction to *ex parte McCardle* was not motivated by claims about the undemocratic structural logic of judicial review, but instead by fears that a Slave Power judiciary would undermine the Reconstruction effort, it was nevertheless narrowly targeted. As Kutler noted, rather than "a drive by the advocates of congressional supremacy," the jurisdiction-stripping "simply marked a Republican reaction toward alleged judicial threats against the Reconstruction program."[155] And, as already detailed in Chapter 4's discussion of the attempt to strip jurisdiction by repealing Section 25 of the 1789 Judiciary Act, Republican action in 1868 followed a clear antebellum doctrine repeatedly articulated by the Taney Court that setting jurisdictional boundaries was within the purview of Congress. In 1845, the Court declared, "the judicial power of the United States ... is ... dependent for its distribution ... entirely upon the action of Congress," and in 1850, "the disposal of judicial power (except in a few specified instances) belongs to Congress."[156] Given this pattern, Mark Graber has argued, "the Chase Court's decision to forego deciding *Ex parte McCardle* while Congress considered stripping jurisdiction was an application of the longstanding principle that federal judicial appellate review existed at legislative whim."[157]

If jurisdiction-stripping was understood not to constitute an assault on judicial authority, Republicans' caginess about their actions appears all the more curious. Debate on jurisdiction-stripping was curt, and rarely was congressional prerogative to modify jurisdiction used to justify the measure. For example, Senator Trumbull downplayed the jurisdiction-stripping measure and denied the bill's relation to possible outcomes of *McCardle*: "It is a bill of very little importance, in my judgment.... [T]he Supreme Court has not decided that any case is pending before it under the [Habeas Corpus] Act of February 5, 1867. No such decision has been made, nor do I believe any such decision ever would be made."[158] In his analysis of congressional actions taken toward the judiciary in the late 1860s, Barry Friedman notes, "Reconstruction-era debates illustrate an odd schizophrenia about subjugation of the Supreme Court to political will. This was apparent with regard to both jurisdiction-stripping and Court-packing."[159] Friedman interprets this behavior to indicate a developing norm of judicial supremacy, but it can also be explained as a strategic decision to achieve a shorter term goal of maintaining Reconstruction policy while not de-legitimizing the very branch – the judiciary – that had been charged with carrying out many Republican policy aims.[160]

---

[155] Kutler, 65.
[156] *Cary v. Curtis*, 44 U.S. 236, 245 (1845); *Sheldon v. Sill*, 49 U.S. 441, 449 (1850).
[157] Mark A. Graber, "James Buchanan as Savior? Judicial Power, Political Fragmentation, and the Failed Repeal of Section 25," *Oregon Law Review* 88 (2009), 113.
[158] *Congressional Globe*, 40th Congress, 2nd Session, 25 March 1868, 2096.
[159] Ibid., 59.
[160] During Reconstruction, the United States lacked administrative capacity to implement the Republicans' constitutional vision and turned to the courts: "Congress placed great reliance on an activist federal judiciary for civil rights enforcement – a mechanism that

In other words, the targeted nature of the attack indicated a strategy of limiting judicial power in a particular policy domain without undermining broad-scale judicial authority that could function as a tool to implement the party's constitutional vision. Limited and targeted jurisdiction-stripping paralleled other congressional moves that shied away from undermining judicial authority. For example, on 30 January 1868, the House ordered a judicial impeachment inquiry of the Supreme Court, even though it is unclear whether any member of the House knew which justice was subject to the inquiry.[161] The only piece of evidence to support a possible impeachment charge was a newspaper story in the *Evening Express* of Washington, D.C., that detailed how "at a private gathering of gentleman of both political parties, one of the justices of the Supreme Court spoke very freely concerning the reconstruction measures of Congress, and declared in the most positive terms that all these laws were unconstitutional, and that the court would be sure to pronounce them so."[162] That the evidence was so minimal and yet that an inquiry was made testifies to ongoing Republican wariness of conspiratorial Slave Power opposition to Reconstruction. The House voted to investigate by a vote of 97 to 57, but shortly after President Johnson was acquitted in his own impeachment trial, the House terminated the inquiry by a voice vote.[163]

Failure to claim the precedence of jurisdiction-stripping and refusal to move ahead on a politicized agenda of judicial impeachment may reflect Republicans' growing fear of losing the Court as a powerful policy tool if these attacks were carried out. Entrenching Republican interests in the judiciary would be especially important if that party lost control of either or both of the elected branches. And the possibility of losing control of the Congress or the presidency was increasingly likely by 1868. As early as 1867, Democrats made strong showings in state elections.[164] Republican-dominated governments in both border and former Confederate states succumbed to electoral defeat in the late 1860s and early 1870s. Although congressional Reconstruction and the Fourteenth Amendment had been, in part, motivated by the Constitution's "republican guarantee" clause, and the Court upheld this rationale in *Texas v. White* and *White v. Hart*, Republicans increasingly shied away from using that clause to overturn state electoral outcomes.[165] Republican Senator William

appeared preferable to maintaining indefinitely a standing army in the South, or establishing a permanent national bureaucracy empowered to oversee Reconstruction." Foner, 1988, 258.

[161] *Congressional Globe*, House of Representatives, 40th Congress, 2nd Session, 862–5.

[162] Ibid., 862. Representative Scofield quoted this passage when he asked that the House authorize an inquiry "into the truth of the declarations therein contained, and report whether the facts as ascertained constitute such a misdemeanor in office as to require this House to present to the Senate articles of impeachment against said justice of the Supreme Court."

[163] Ibid., 865. *Congressional Globe*, House of Representatives, 40th Congress, 2nd Session, 3266.

[164] Friedman, 16.

[165] *Texas v. White*, 74 U.S. 700 (1869); *White v. Hart*, 13 Wall. 646 (1871). The Republican guarantee clause refers to Article IV, Section 4, of the Constitution. On the clause as justification

Stewart of Nevada commented that the clause could not justify federal action to overturn state election outcomes. Congress held "no right to legislate to make them belong to the Republican party."[166] This sentiment, coming from a Republican, was some concession of the inevitability of party competition if not the loyalty of reconstructed Democrats.

IV.b. *Judiciary as a Policy Tool: Judicial Expansion as Partisan Entrenchment*

The Judiciary Act of 1869 increased the size of the Supreme Court bench from seven to nine justices, established nine new circuit judges to alleviate the appellate caseload backlog, and provided pensions at full salary for federal judges who served at least ten years and were over seventy years of age. While Senate debate on judicial re-organization focused on achieving judicial efficiency, Republican Senator Drake of Missouri raised concerns that a new layer of circuit court judges would mimic the problems of the 1801 Judiciary Act: "It [Senate bill S. 44] is no less than a revival after the lapse of more than sixty years of an exploded and defeated and rejected scheme for the reorganization of the judiciary."[167]

Lyman Trumbull met this objection by rehashing the old Federalist claim of the federal judiciary's nationalizing effect. The measure would reunite the nation after the recent civil conflict:

> It was important also, or supposed to be by many, that we should have circuit courts held throughout the reconstructed States of the South and those still unreconstructed by a circuit judge, who should go from State to State and from district to district administering and enforcing the laws of the United States. Perhaps nothing would do more to give quiet and peace to the Southern country than an efficient enforcement of the laws of the United States in the United States courts. That cannot be done and is not done by the district courts as at present organized.[168]

Trumbull was careful to construct the bill's purpose in terms of institutional efficiency rather than partisanship even as the bill might, in effect, support Republican aims.

An alternative, offered by Senator Williams, replaced the proposed intermediate appellate circuit system by appointing ten more Supreme Court justices. This would increase the bench to eighteen judges. The judges would serve in rotation, keeping nine on the bench while the other nine would attend to circuit duties.[169] Senator Stewart, Republican of Nevada, argued against that option. He warned that the proposal would only exacerbate partisan divisions within Congress:

for the Fourteenth Amendment, particularly for its proposal in a Congress in which former Confederate states were excluded, see Ackerman, 1998, 171.

[166] Stewart quoted in Foner, 453.
[167] *Congressional Globe*, Senate, 41st Congress, 1st Session, 23 March 1869, 207.
[168] Ibid., 208.
[169] Ibid., 208–9.

There will be a struggle on the part of the judges as to who shall stay in the Supreme Court and who shall go into the circuits.... The struggle will not be confined to that tribunal, but it will be brought here, and the party in power will be continually devising means whereby the Supreme Court shall be constituted of judges of the same political complexion that the majority in Congress may chance to be. *These conflicts are for all time.* The political complexion of the court will first be ascertained, and then schemes will be introduced to affect it this way or that way. For instance, if the senior judges in commission were sent to the circuits it might leave a very different Supreme Court here from what which would be left if the junior judges in commission were sent out. Such questions would constantly arise if that plan were adopted.[170]

This debate, like that which occurred in the 1820s and 1830s, revealed legislators desperately attempting to maintain and promote judicial independence as political neutrality. The range of plans considered also illustrates little deference to the original design as constructed by the Judiciary Act of 1789. And the statement quoted above showcases an admission that is *new* in comparison with the debates on judicial reform in the 1820s and 1830s. Stewart's words – "these conflicts are for all time" – suggest that party competition was understood as permanent. No single constitutional party would eventually achieve regime unity. Rather, the parties would always squabble over judicial appointment. Given this reality, due diligence to ensure that the judiciary was insulated from this partisanship and to achieve efficiency was even more important.

In the mid-1860s, the Republican press supported manipulating the judiciary to maintain Reconstruction policy. The *New York Herald* wrote: "by increasing or diminishing the number of the judges, the Court may be reconstructed in conformity with the supreme decisions of the war."[171] *Harper's Weekly* likewise asserted that if Reconstruction policies were judicially invalidated, "let the Supreme Court be swamped by a thorough reorganization and increased number of Judges."[172] Yet coverage of these manipulations changed in tone as the decade wore on. By 1870, the *Nation* noted the unstable ground on which politicians would tread if they were to overtly utilize judicial power for partisan ends: "popular reverence for, or confidence in, the Court cannot possibly survive the addition, subtraction, multiplication, and division which it has been undergoing the last five or six years."[173] The magazine's assertion is telling. Republican manipulations had begun to undercut the ideal of judges as de-politicized and neutral arbiters of constitutional meaning. If that image faltered, the Court's value as a tool to pursue policy objectives, particularly if Republicans lost hold on the Congress, presidency, or both, would be lost.

---

[170] Ibid., 210. Emphasis added.
[171] "The Last Decision of the Supreme Court on Military Trials during the War," *New York Herald*, 20 December 1866, 4.
[172] "The New Dread Scott," *Harper's Weekly*, 19 January 1867, 34.
[173] "The Reopening of the Legal-Tender Case," *Nation*, 7 April 1870, 218.

If Republicans wanted to continue to manipulate federal judicial power to serve its objectives, then it could continue to do so only by framing the empowerment in the neutral terms of judicial efficiency. The more Republicans would confer power on the judiciary to achieve its dual policy aims of protecting the rights of a new class of freedmen and to develop a national economy, the more cases would build in the judiciary's backlog.[174] To promote efficiency, the judiciary would need to be expanded and staffed. The two concepts – efficiency and partisan entrenchment – would serve to produce a self-reinforcing cycle. There is no denying that congressional reforms of the judiciary undertaken in 1875 and again in 1891 relieved major inefficiencies in the system.[175] Yet there is also no denying that these reforms were legislated by a Republican-majority Congress and that they would ultimately serve the policy aims of the Republican Party, namely, to facilitate national commercial and economic development. In short, judicial reforms – framed in terms of judicial neutrality and efficiency – would nonetheless advance the Republican Party's constitutional vision.[176] Unable to gain control of the Senate or, for many years, the presidency, Democrats were unable to respond in kind to serve their own particular constitutional vision.[177]

Even within this framework of competitive party politics and the need to maintain judicial neutrality and efficiency, the provisions of the 1869 Judiciary Act increased Republican control over the federal judiciary. For example, the Act allowed President Grant to make several appointments at once, first by elevating district judges to the new circuit position and then by appointing new district judges thereby creating a ladder system.[178] Grant could nominate a raft of new circuit judges, judges who were increasingly authorized to handle disputes regarding Reconstruction policy since Congress had passed a series of acts moving jurisdiction from state to federal courts. Second, the 1869 Act's new pension provision might induce some judges to retire and enable more opportunity for appointment. It was widely known that Chief Justice Taney served on the bench for so long because he relied on his salary; this new pension provision might induce justices to retire at an earlier age.[179]

---

[174] In 1860, the Supreme Court had 310 cases on its docket. By 189, it had 1,816 cases with 623 filed in that year alone. Pending cases in federal trial courts rose from 29,000 in 1873 to 54,000 in 1890. See Felix Frankfurter and James Landis, *The Business of the Supreme Court: A Study in the Federal Judicial System* (New Brunswick: Transaction, 2007), 60, 101–2.

[175] Russell Wheeler and Cynthia Harrison, *Creating the Federal Judicial System*, 3rd ed. (Washington, DC: Federal Judicial Center, 2005), 16–21.

[176] Gillman, 2002.

[177] Republicans held a Senate majority from 1861 until 1913 except for 1879–81 and 1893–5. Republicans held the presidency from 1860 until 1913 with the exception of Andrew Johnson (1865–68) and Grover Cleveland (1885–89 and 1893–97).

[178] Deborah J. Barrow, Gary Zuck, and Gerald S. Gryski, *The Federal Judiciary and Institutional Change* (Ann Arbor: University of Michigan Press, 1996), 37–8.

[179] Edward Bates speculated that Taney, Wayne, Catron, and Grier would have retired if they had had pensions. Beale, ed., 358.

Also, by 1869, Justice Nelson and Justice Grier were in their late seventies, and Grier's brethren had already expressed concerns about his mental fitness.[180] If Grier and Nelson could be induced to retire, Grant could appoint as many as three justices.

While rhetoric of court-packing was avoided during congressional debate, given the ideal of judicial neutrality, the 1869 Act did not preclude partisan utilization of the Court. Such utilization had to be framed in the language of promoting judicial efficiency. But the partisan effect was not lost on Democrats in the House of Representatives, who united to oppose the bill's passage. It passed by a vote of 90 to 53.[181] However, fourteen Republicans joined with these Democrats also signaling that the ideal of judicial independence as political neutrality still held sway.

The effect of Grant's alleged Court-packing is said to be evident in the Court's handling of the constitutionality of paper currency. In 1869, the Court ruled in *Hepburn v. Griswold* that greenbacks or paper money, which was not backed by gold or silver specie but still considered legal tender, as authorized by the Legal Tender Act of 1862, was unconstitutional.[182] The Court reversed its *Hepburn* ruling a year later in the cases of *Knox v. Lee* and *Parker v. Davis*, known collectively as the *Legal Tender Cases*, after new justices were added to the Court.[183] The closeness of the *Legal Tender* ruling (5 to 4), the closeness of the *Hepburn* ruling (4 to 3), and the intervening appointment of Justices Joseph Bradley and William Strong, served as evidence to support accusations of Court-packing. Since the Court's ruling in *Hepburn* was announced on 7 February 1870, and the *Senate Journal* registered the nominations of Bradley and Strong on the following day, the nominations did appear as a direct consequence of the ruling. However, Grant's nominations were sent on 7 February; no Executive Session was held that day so they were not noted until 8 February.[184] In other words, the nominations were sent before any decision on the constitutionality of the Legal Tender Act had been offered.

Defending the administration against criticisms that these nominations converted "an upright and impartial tribunal" into "base compliance with Executive instructions by creatures of the President placed upon the Bench to carry out his instructions," Attorney General Hoar asserted that "there was no more reason to believe those two gentlemen would give a different opinion on the legal-tender question from that which the court first gave than there was that Chief Justice Chase would give a different opinion."[185]

[180] McGinty, 279–80.
[181] Ibid., 38.
[182] *Hepburn v. Griswold*, 75 U.S. 603 (1869).
[183] *Legal Tender Cases*, 79 U.S. 457 (1870).
[184] Sidney Ratner, "Was the Supreme Court Packed by President Grant?" *Political Science Quarterly* 50 (September 1935), 348.
[185] The accusation came from the *New York World*; Hoar's statement is in the *Boston Herald*, 2 November 1876. Both are quoted in Ratner, 348, 349.

Hamilton Fish, Grant's secretary of state, noted to the contrary that the president might have considered Strong and Bradley's position on the legal-tender question:

> Although he [Grant] required no declaration from Judges Strong and Bradley on the constitutionality of the Legal Tender Act, he knew Judge Strong had on the Bench in Pennsylvania given a decision sustaining its Constitutionality, and that he had reason to believe Judge Bradley's opinion tended in the same direction: that at the time he felt it important that the Constitutionality of the Law should be sustained ... [and] he had desired that the constitutionality should be sustained by the Supreme Court.[186]

Thus, although it may not be evident that Grant nominated Bradley or Strong with the *specific* intent of overturning the Court's invalidation of the Legal Tender Act, he nevertheless achieved his preferred policy outcome *by utilizing judicial authority rather than countering the Court directly.*

Opinion, as captured by media outlets, appeared to be on Grant's side. Numerous periodicals criticized Chief Justice Chase for his ruling in *Hepburn*. *Harper's Weekly* criticized the Court for "overstep[ping] the just line of authority and ... [attempting] to restrict Congress in this matter, when the framers of the Constitution decided to leave them free of such restrictions."[187] Similarly, the *Nation* argued that the *Hepburn* ruling incapacitated Congress from raising funds in times of emergency "plunging business into confusion and disheartening the people."[188] The ruling invalidated one of the crucial mechanisms by which Union victory was achieved. It thereby placed the Court on the wrong side of history, a characterization of the Court that was made all the more plausible by Chief Justice Chase's curious position: he ruled the Legal Tender Acts unconstitutional even though he supported them whole-heartedly when he was secretary of the treasury in 1862.[189]

The Court's reversal accorded with the judicial precedent of *McCulloch*. Just as Marshall declared that the national Bank was constitutional on pru-dential grounds, namely, that "an immense amount of property had been advanced" assuming the institution was constitutional, Justice Strong prof-fered a similar argument securing the constitutionality of paper currency: "If it be held by this court that Congress has not constitutional power, under any circumstances, or in any emergency to make treasury notes a legal tender for the payment of all debts ... the government is without those means of self-preservation which, all must admit, may, in certain contingencies, become indispensable."[190] Both rulings relied on the implications of the

---

[186] Hamilton Fish, MS Diary, 28 October 1876, quoted in Ratner, 351. See also Labbe and Lurie, 120, 121.

[187] "Legal Tender," *Harper's Weekly*, 19 March 1870, 179.

[188] "The Legal Tender Decision," *The Nation*, 17 February 1870, 100.

[189] Various machinations undertaken by Chase to secure a majority in *Hepburn*, including the position taken by a confused Justice Grier, also raised skepticism about the validity of the ruling. Ratner, 354–7; McGinty, 278–9.

[190] *McCulloch v. Maryland*, 17 U.S. 316 (1819); *Legal Tender Cases*, 12 Wall. 79 US (1870).

necessary and proper clause rather than a more literal meaning of Congress's enumerated powers.

IV.c. Reprise: Republicans Neither Fully Attack Nor Fully Embrace Judicial Power

Congressional Republican tinkering with federal jurisdiction, circuit composition, and Supreme Court bench size has often been interpreted as reflecting anti-judicial hostilities triggered by the *Dred Scott* decision and as paralleling Jeffersonian sentiment.[191] For example, Charles Evans Hughes referred to *Dred Scott* as "a self-inflicted wound."[192] Others have argued that the ruling led to a "decline in confidence in the Court"[193] such that "judicial power was all but extinct."[194] In this telling, the Supreme Court, weakened by the unpopularity of *Dred Scott*, acquiesced to Republican manipulations.[195]

More recently, legal historians have told a different tale: congressional Republican actions did not undermine judicial power, but vastly expanded it.[196] William Wiecek argues, "In no comparable period in our nation's history have the federal courts, lower and Supreme, enjoyed as great an expansion of their jurisdiction as they did in the years of Reconstruction, 1863 to 1876,"

---

[191] On the traditional thesis of judicial impotence and congressional Republican aggression, see Edward Corwin, "The Dred Scott Decision in the Light of Contemporary Legal Doctrines," *American Historical Review* 17 (October 1911), 52–69; William Dunning, *Essays on the Civil War and Reconstruction and Related Topics* (New York: Macmillan, 1898), and *Reconstruction, Political, and Economic: 1865–1877* (New York: Harper's 1907); John Burgess, *Reconstruction and the Constitution: 1866–1876* (New York: Charles Scribner's Sons, 1903); James Randall, *The Civil War and Reconstruction* (Boston: D. C. Heath, 1937); Charles Evans Hughes, *The Supreme Court of the United States, Its Foundation, Methods and Achievements: An Interpretation* (New York: Columbia University Press, 1928).

[192] Charles Evan Hughes, quoted in Kutler, 3.

[193] Fairman, 21.

[194] Robert Jackson, *The Struggle for Judicial Supremacy: A Study of the Crisis in American Power Politics* (New York: Vintage, 1960), 326.

[195] Another explanation of these manipulations relies less on public esteem than on public apathy. Republicans could weaken judicial authority because the people paid the Court little attention. See Jamie Carson and Benjamin Kleinerman, "Political Institutions and American Political Development: Evolution in the Size of the US Supreme Court," prepared for presentation at the Annual Meeting of the Midwest Political Science Association, Chicago, IL (2001). Yet, as Skowronek has argued, courts were one of the few governing institutions with which people had direct contact in the late eighteenth and early nineteenth centuries. As such, it does not follow that they would have paid little attention to their decisions, especially a decision like *Dred Scott*, which confronted the most contentious issue of the day. See Skowronek, *Building a New American State* (New York: Cambridge University Press, 1982), 27–9. More generally, to assume that ruling would undercut the Court's prestige conflates disagreement with a ruling and hostility toward the institution. The claim confuses specific versus diffuse support (see Chapter 2). As Kutler argues, "A significant body of opinion carefully distinguished its disagreement with the decision from criticism of the institution per se" (10).

[196] See William Wiecek, "The Reconstruction of Federal Judicial Power, 1863–1875," *American Journal of Legal History* 13 (October 1969), 333–59; Kutler, 1968; Eric McKitrick, *Andrew Johnson and Reconstruction* (Chicago: University of Chicago Press, 1960); Foner, 1988, 451–9; and, Friedman, 2002.

and because "to a court, jurisdiction is power," the Court during these years was emboldened by Republican leadership, not cowed into subservience.[197] And by interpreting congressional Republican actions during the late 1860s as harnessing judicial power to serve partisan policy ends rather than undermining judicial legitimacy, legal historian Stanley Kutler usefully distinguished Republican measures from Jeffersonian actions between 1801 and 1805 and Jackson's assertions of presidential constitutional interpretation. Kutler considered these earlier actions to reflect hostility toward the Court as an undemocratic institution.[198] Yet he mischaracterized the Democratic legacy as entirely anti-Court, relying on Jackson's mythologized retort to Marshall on *Worcester v. Georgia* and the Bank veto as evidence of this hostility.[199] And, he drew too sharp distinction between Democratic antipathy toward the judiciary and Republican support for it.

Kutler failed to recognize the parallels that this chapter has sought to draw out. He missed early Republican characterization of stable opposition as a conspiratorial anti-constitutional threat, which was subsequently used to justify re-structuring the Supreme Court bench to eliminate Slave Power influence. Republicans' actions in 1862, 1863, and 1866 are reminiscent of Van Buren's party appointment aims that underlay the Judiciary Act of 1837. As neither Van Buren nor many first-generation Republicans sought to create a stable system of two-party competition and, instead, worked to justify their own party as the single constitutional party, their actions toward judicial authority cannot be explained either as wholly hostile – as Kutler rightly contended – or as simply partisan, which was Kutler's thesis. Lincolnian Republicans and Van Burenite Democrats were more alike than Kutler admitted. Neither was hostile to independent judicial review – neither, for that matter, were the Jeffersonians or many of the Anti-Federalists – but their contention that stable and permanent opposition amounted to an anti-constitutional conspiracy led them to root it out, especially if it were entrenched in the judiciary. When Republican rhetoric is compared with Van Buren's single constitutional partisan rhetoric and both used to contextualize circuit re-shuffling, bench-size alterations, and jurisdiction-stripping, what emerges are not partisan tactics in a stable bi-partisan system, but the attempt to *exclude opposition from the Court altogether and to protect the substantive policy goals that defined Republican constitutional ideology*, at least for the first generation of that party.

These conflicting accounts – of Republicans as wholly hostile to judicial power in the wake of *Dred Scott* and of Republicans as seeking to harness and expand judicial power to secure Reconstruction policy aims – suggest that Republican positions toward judicial power during the Civil War and Reconstruction should not be characterized as all of a piece. Some Republican

[197] Wiecek, 333.
[198] Kutler, 62–3.
[199] Ibid., 30–2.

efforts, especially during the early 1860s, aimed to eliminate their opposition, which they tended to characterize as a conspiratorial threat against the Constitution. Once Republicans recognized their own vulnerability to electoral defeat, that their conceit of single-party constitutionalism could not be realized and needed to be abandoned, and that parties could promote equally legitimate substantive programs – all ideas articulated by Lincoln but made real by a Democratic electoral resurgence in the mid-1870s that brought Reconstruction to its end – they would manipulate the judiciary through narrowly targeted jurisdiction alterations, avoid broadly politically motivated impeachments, and deny the precedent-setting nature of their Court-curbing actions. In short, they would seek to maintain as much judicial power as possible to promote their own partisan interests and constitutional interpretive claims. The limited nature of the later congressional Republican actions suggests that they were attempting to harness judicial power to serve Reconstruction policy goals without necessarily undermining the judiciary's broader legitimacy, which was necessary for that policy to be successfully implemented. As such, there is no need to suggest that members of Congress were seeking to create a burgeoning norm of judicial supremacy. And, by utilizing narrower tactics than their Jeffersonian grandfathers, Republicans set in motion a trend toward realizing partisan aims through judicial authority.

V. Conclusion

The years between 1861 and 1877 are critical in the development of the purpose and meaning of political party, the legitimacy and loyalty of opposition, and the corresponding tactics taken toward opposition entrenched in the judiciary. The transitional character of this period is evident in that the range of congressional and presidential actions taken fit strategies of both undermining judicial legitimacy and harnessing judicial power. The contrast between Seward's and Lincoln's rhetoric illustrates how these years marked the final waning of republic assumptions, which motivated and justified the de-legitimizing tactics. Seward, similar to Van Buren, characterized Republicanism as Van Buren had his Democracy, as holding principles indistinguishable from the Constitution's commitments, which were fixed, singular, and discoverable from the text. Before secession, Lincoln sometimes espoused this viewpoint, but his rhetoric took on a different tone in his 1861 inaugural in which he espoused not only the loyalty of the opposition but the possibility of multiple constitutional meanings in light of that document's so many "silences."

This focus on "silences" was Lincoln's crucial innovation. In its various attempts to deal with the political problem of a judiciary as the seat of stable and formed opposition, each generation of elected political actors constructed a new solution. In their failure to clear the judiciary via impeachment, the Jeffersonians settled on the second-best solution of walling the judiciary off from politics and constructing the new ideal of judicial independence as political neutrality. It was second-best to the extent that constitutionality had to be *severed* from popular sovereignty in seeming denial of the Framers' notion of the judiciary's representative function. In attempting to reconnect popular sovereignty and constitutionalism and to achieve the inter-branch unity that eluded Jeffersonians, Van Buren re-defined the party and maintained party appointment to keep the Hamiltonian minority out of government. Lincoln, facing the Union's collapse, was compelled to approach opposition differently, not to cast it as a threatening minority but to welcome it and characterize his supporters as inherently and rightly unstable.

When Lincoln acknowledged in his 1861 inaugural that "constitutional controversies" divided citizens into "majorities and minorities" and constructed the Constitution as an organic law incapable of being "framed with a provision specifically applicable to every question which may occur in practical administration" such that there will always be a question where "the Constitution does not expressly say," he offered the possibility of multiple equally legitimate interpretations, interpretations that could be rightfully pursued if a party attained the reins of governance through procedurally legitimate means.[200] Put differently, he offered the means to stem the secession crisis by articulating a path to political power for slavery interests that differed from exiting the Union altogether. Parties could disagree on constitutional meaning, and judges could make their rulings. But those rulings were not settled law. They would only become so if they were endorsed by the people, as election outcomes might indicate.

To render this vision non-threatening to Southern interests, Lincoln re-defined the meaning of majority; it was dynamic and granted only temporary authority to lead. He thereby provided a rationale – although it would fail – to keep Southern states from seceding while maintaining his own legitimacy. It enabled him to pursue the particular Republican constitutional vision, freeing his hand to ignore Taney Court objections to his executive prerogatives during the Civil War. Additionally, Lincoln's coupling of judicial authority with democratic affirmation, so that the former rested upon the latter, opened a space to harness judicial power, tailoring that power to suit his partisan aims. His perspective implies a more instrumental use of judicial power; the Court can be used to realize the aims of that partisan majority until such time as that majority loses its hold on power.

If Lincoln maintained, like Jefferson, Jackson, and Van Buren, that there were multiple actors with constitutional interpretive authority, he went a step further to suggest that there were multiple legitimate interpretations. As parties were the vehicles of interpretations, popular support through election would confirm legitimacy to one particular interpretation. And once multiple political parties were expected to compete and each understood as having its own constitutional vision, then each party might legitimately "use the courts to advance their agendas"; otherwise the people would vote those partisans

---

[200] Lincoln, First Inaugural, 4 March 1861.

out of office.[201] But there were definite limits to this strategy, limits made clearer by media response to Republican manipulations by the early 1870s. The earlier normative Jeffersonian construction of judicial independence as political neutrality still held sway. Outright manipulations for partisan gain were to be avoided. Manipulations had to be constructed as serving neutral efficiency objectives.

Lincoln's reframing of party, majority, and electoral competition moved toward contemporary notions of pluralism and away from Van Buren's construction of a single constitutional party and opposition as natural but still anti-constitutional. Historians have praised Lincoln's substantive moral conviction, which was absent from Van Buren's and Stephen Douglas' proceduralism.[202] However, Lincoln's emphasis on the procedures of electoral politics – of the loyalty of all engaged in partisan conflict so long as each respected the rules of competition and the legitimacy of distinct constitutional visions – was just as innovative and perhaps as important. By subjecting a party's constitutional interpretation to repeated electoral ratification, Lincoln laid the foundation to view the document's meaning as not single, fixed, and ultimately discoverable. That ideational shift was a critical step toward a fuller articulation of legal realism and recognition of the strategic value of judicial power.

These ideational moves – granting the loyalty of political opposition and expecting perpetual party competition and legitimate rotation in office – suggest that "the end of the Civil War and Lincoln's tragic death marked the watershed between American republicanism and pluralism."[203] Civic republicanism evolved through the antebellum era to include more pluralist elements; even Lincoln's "understanding of democracy was more pluralist than republican, and more pluralistic than the understandings of most of his predecessors."[204] Lincoln's endorsement of the people as persuadable, of majorities as temporary and as potentially wrong, was a step toward, but not a full realization of, pluralism. It was not a full realization since it was limited to viewing only political parties as institutions capable of representing popular interests and possible constitutional interpretations. Nevertheless, it stood in stark contrast to Van Buren's ideas of a single constitutional party and of political opposition as necessarily seeking to undermine constitutional principles. As such, the ideas initially expressed by Lincoln and evident in some actions of the Republican-dominated Congress mark an idiomatic fault line dividing a premodern party system of Jacksonians and early Lincolnian Republicans. On one side of this fault line, stable opposition is seen as a disloyal and conspiratorial anti-constitutional threat, and aspirations for a single-party constitutionalism are definitive; on the other side is a modern system in which political parties

---

[201] Gillman, 511.
[202] See Allen Guelzo, *Lincoln and Douglas: The Debates that Shaped America* (New York: Simon & Schuster, 2008).
[203] Ericson, 175.
[204] Ibid., 173.

are considered loyal to the Constitution despite differing interpretations and in which rotation in power among these coalitions is expected.

The strategic rationality of antebellum and some Civil War-era animus toward the judiciary is embedded in this civic republican characterization of opposition as illegitimate and dangerous. Through it the judiciary could be framed as the seat of a conspiratorial anti-constitutional threat, and the possibilities for legitimate methods of constitutional interpretation remained limited to textualist originalism. Once these assumptions waned, and Lincoln's pluralistic ideas about loyal opposition and constitutional silences gained favor, multiple legitimate interpretations, a range of interpretive methodologies, and a potential cacophony of interpreters became possible. In this new ideational context, politicians would once again challenge judicial interpretation even as legal scholars and judges engaged in a systematic process to establish judicial renderings of constitutional meaning as authoritative.

PART III

HARNESSING JUDICIAL POWER AND THE POLITICAL IDIOM OF LIBERAL PLURALISM

6

Clashing Progressive Solutions to the Political Problem of Judicial Power

Many accounts of federal judicial politics during the Progressive era – the 1890s through 1930s – note how Republican hold on the Senate and presidency allowed near total control over judicial appointments. Candidates were vetted for "their devotion to party principles and 'soundness' on major economic questions of the day."[1] Judges protected corporate interests against state and federal regulation of workplace conditions, wages, and hours. Judges gave constitutional interpretation a Republican cast, shorthanded by the economic doctrine of laissez-faire and its legal counterpart, liberty of contract.[2]

Federal courts are thereby depicted as countermajoritarian.[3] By resisting popular support for workplace and wage regulation, rulings fomented anti-judge hostility that culminated in Franklin Roosevelt's seemingly Jeffersonian attack in 1937, that is, his proposal to stack the Supreme Court and enlarge the lower federal judiciary to prevent judicial nullification of New Deal policy.[4] The failure to pass various Progressive measures, including FDR's

---

[1] Richard Bensel, *The Political Economy of American Industrialization, 1877–1900* (New York: Cambridge University Press, 2000), 7. Arnold Paul characterizes this jurisprudence as manifestations of class consciousness in his *Conservative Crisis and the Rule of Law* (Ithaca: Cornell University Press, 1960). Jeffrey Segal and Harold Spaeth argue that judges vote their policy preferences in their *The Supreme Court and the Attitudinal Model* (New York: Cambridge University Press, 1993), 304–5. For discussion of conventional and revisionist scholarship, see Barry Friedman, "The History of the Countermajoritarian Difficulty, Part Three: The Lesson of Lochner," *New York University Law Review* 76 (2001), 1383–455.

[2] Michael Les Benedict, "Laissez-Faire and Liberty: A Re-Evaluation of the Meaning and Origins of Laissez-Faire Constitutionalism," *Law and History Review* 3 (1985), 293–331.

[3] This account highlights high rates of judicial invalidation of state legislation. The Supreme Court struck down 275 state laws between 1896 and 1925. Lee Epstein et al., *The Supreme Court Compendium: Data, Decisions, and Developments* (Washington, DC: Congressional Quarterly, 1994), 96–110.

[4] Victoria Hattam, *Labor Visions and State Power* (Princeton: Princeton University Press, 1993); William Forbath, *Law and the Shaping of the American Labor Movement* (Cambridge: Harvard University Press, 1991); Karen Orren, *Belated Feudalism: Labor, the Law, and Liberal Development in the United States* (New York: Cambridge University Press, 1991).

Court-packing proposal, are understood to be evidence of popular and elite acceptance of judicial independence if not outright supremacy.[5]

This chapter challenges this account by focusing attention on assessments of whether, how, and why Progressive proposals failed. Progressives took an inconsistent stance toward federal judicial authority. While some offered the most virulent anti-Court rhetoric since the Jeffersonian years, Progressives proved unable to construct a single solution to the problem of legitimate judicial authority. This failure stemmed from a muddled tradition drawing on incongruent Jeffersonian and Lincolnian strands of Republicanism. As earlier chapters have shown, Jefferson and Lincoln offered distinct solutions to the problem of linking judicial authority to popular sovereignty: Jefferson sought to isolate it from politics and emphasize its neutrality while Lincoln embraced a proto-legal realist perspective, bringing the judiciary into politics and suggesting that interpretation of constitutional silences could be ratified and congealed by election results.

While some Progressives endorsed the Jeffersonian position that law could and should be supplanted by democratic popular will, others advocated a more tempered Lincolnian strategy of holding legal rulings at bay until somehow ratified by the people. Progressive-era politicians took Lincoln's linkage of election and judicial authority in different directions. Some advocated electoral infrastructure to make the connection between legal meaning and popular ratification more explicit. Others, including Franklin Roosevelt (FDR) and some Supreme Court justices, latched onto Lincoln's articulation of constitutional silences to promote the idea of a "living" Constitution that could pragmatically adapt to meet new challenges of industrial expansion. According to one scholar, "Since most of the words and phrases dealing with the powers and the limits of government are vague and must in practice be interpreted by human beings, it follows that the Constitution as practice is a living thing."[6]

---

[5] See Barry Friedman, "The History of the Countermajoritarian Difficulty, Part Four: Law's Politics," *University of Pennsylvania Law Review* 148 (2000), 1060–1, 1059, 1063 ("during the New Deal, it seems apparent that the public was not looking for a rubber-stamp Court," that FDR's plan forced the public "to confront its commitment to an independent judiciary," and that ultimately, the people turned against "political control over the courts, save for the confirmation process"). Kevin Yingling, "Justifying the Judiciary: A Majority Response to the Countermajoritarian Problem," *Journal of Law and Politics* 15 (1999), 121 ("it was Congress and the public who defended the judiciary from Roosevelt's Court-packing plan.... The majority preferred to maintain the Court's structural role as an independent and sometimes countermajoritarian and constitutional arbiter"). Charles Geyh, *When Courts and Congress Collide: The Struggle for Control of America's Judicial System* (Ann Arbor: University of Michigan Press, 2006), 87–8 ("Despite Roosevelt's popularity and the Supreme Court's unpopularity, the court-packing plan lacked majority public approval, had the support of surprisingly few Court critics, and received a tepid welcome in Congress"). William Ross, *A Muted Fury: Populists, Progressives, and Labor Unions Confront the Courts, 1890–1937* (Princeton: Princeton University Press, 1994), 302 (FDR's plan "ultimately failed because it contravened the respect for the judiciary so deeply ingrained in the American character and the Court prudently began to issue decisions that upheld popular reforms").

[6] Charles Beard, "The Living Constitution," *Annals of the American Academy of Political and Social Science* (May 1936), quoted in G. Edward White, *The Constitution and the New Deal*

These "legal realists" endorsed instrumental harnessing of judicial power to serve substantive policy aims, such as protective legislation for female laborers. If judges would interpret the Constitution to promote its contemporary relevance, external electoral mechanisms to control the impact of judicial rulings were unnecessary. Judicial interpretation could be harnessed as a tool to realize social reform. As such, many legal progressives shied away from undercutting judicial authority, as doing so would only close off a viable path that labor unions, women's organizations, and consumer groups might travel to seek change. FDR's judicial reform proposal typified this harnessing strategy. While conventional accounts characterize this plan as pure Jeffersonian redux, as an unabashed attempt to de-legitimize judicial authority, more radical Jeffersonian Progressives recognized how the president was harnessing judicial power for short-term policy gain and declined to support it.

Progressives were so fractured that no single political solution emerged to the problem of connecting judicial authority with popular sovereignty. Amid this incoherence, the Court offered its own solution, which took shape in at least two critical rulings. First, the Court, through Chief Justice Hughes, endorsed the progressive concept of a "living" Constitution, one that yielded not a singular, fixed, and discoverable meaning, but one that could adapt to meet the crisis at hand and which supported different interpretations depending on sociological context and lived experience. In *Home Building & Loan Association v. Blaisdell*, the Court gave full vent to this idea, which laid the foundations for the Court's eventually expansive readings of commerce clause authority to support New Deal legislation.[7] Second, in *United States v. Carolene Products*, the justices abandoned civic republican assumptions including consensualism and state neutrality.[8] The Court, recalibrating to new assumptions that underlay political development and behavior in the other branches and in civil society, endorsed a pluralist notion of politics as competitive, fractious, interest-based, and as not trending toward an identifiable and singular public good. In *Carolene*, the Court reconstituted its own role in this newly recognized order. It replaced civic republican antipathy toward "class

---

(Cambridge: Harvard University Press, 2000), 216. On the move from textual originalism and legal formalism to a pragmatic or "living" constitutionalist approach, see Johnathan O'Neill, *Originalism in American Law and Politics* (Baltimore: Johns Hopkins University Press, 2005) ("in this period thinkers attacked and largely abandoned the established, categorical and deductive ways of thinking about social life, including the nature of law, the Constitution, and adjudication.... The ultimate result ... was the marginalization of the untheorized forms of textual originalism that had become intertwined with economic substantive due process and formalist adjudication. It was replaced by what has aptly been termed a 'pragmatic instrumentalist' approach to the law" [28]). In contrast to legal formalism, which viewed law as a complete and static logical system, such sociological jurisprudence was instrumentalist. In this view law was subject to growth and change, and judges did create law, whether that role was acknowledged or not. See Ernest J. Weinrib, "Legal Formalism: On the Immanent Rationality of Law," *Yale Law Journal* 97 (May 1988), 949–1016, and Roscoe Pound, "The Scope and Purpose of Sociological Jurisprudence, I," *Harvard Law Review* 24 (June 1911), 591–619.

[7] *Home Building & Loan Association v. Blaisdell*, 290 U.S. 398 (1934).
[8] *United States v. Carolene Products Co.*, 304 U.S. 144 (1938).

legislation" with a commitment to ensure participation. Guaranteeing such access – what scholars have called the Court's "pluralism-reinforcing" role – required intervening on behalf of particular groups in a radical departure from republican notions of state neutrality.[9] The Court's move legitimized its own authority, which, once de-coupled from textualist interpretation, had become increasingly strained. And it encouraged politicians to shift strategies from undermining judicial authority to more targeted harnessing of that power for political ends. The Court's justification for intervention in the pluralist process provided the means and motive for individuals, interest groups, and elected officials to harness judicial power rather than de-legitimize it.

This chapter refutes the conventional account of the Progressive era, which focuses on partisan entrenchment and the development of normative judicial supremacy, and offers two revisionist claims: first, Populist, Progressive, and the Court's solutions to the challenge of connecting judicial authority to popular sovereignty were reprisals of and innovations on Lincoln's ideas which were foundational to legal realism, and second, the multiple political solutions offered prevented the development of one around which Progressives could coalesce. Part I of this chapter evaluates Populist approaches while Part II examines Progressive solutions. Part III disputes the claim that the failure of anti-Court actions reflects solely the development of normative judicial supremacy. In line with the expectations laid out in Chapter 2, it details how the congressional Court-curbing legislation of the 1910s and 1930s, often wholly ignored in conventional accounts, was narrow, ambiguous, and symbolic. And it evaluates how the defeat of FDR's proposal can be explained without positing normative judicial supremacy as a causal mechanism. Part IV elaborates on the Court's solution to the challenge of independent judicial authority, highlighting rulings that marked judicial acceptance not only of

---

[9] John Hart Ely, *Democracy and Distrust: A Theory of Judicial Review* (Cambridge: Harvard University Press, 1980), 73–7; William Eskridge, Jr., "Pluralism and Distrust: How Courts Can Support Democracy by Lowering the Stakes of Politics," *Yale Law Journal* 114 (2005), 1279–328; Richard Pildes, "The Supreme Court 2003 Term, Forward: The Constitutionalization of Democratic Politics," *Harvard Law Review* 118 (2003), 28–154. Pildes examines how democracies malfunction when leadership may systematically exclude certain interests unless an enforcement mechanism is introduced. Ely contended that the Court could serve as that mechanism and transformed *Carolene*'s fourth footnote into a defense of unelected judicial power in a democracy. According to Pildes:

> All theories of representative democracy require, at a minimum, that those who exercise power be regularly accountable through elections to those they represent; accountability is a necessary, even if not sufficient, condition of democracy. And ... electoral accountability can exist only when effective political competition generates genuine political choices.... This constantly looming pathology of democratic systems, identified so elegantly by John Hart Ely, means that the vitality of democracy depends upon external institutions that can contain this disease. These institutions need not be courts; viable alternatives, such as independent electoral commissions, exist in many democracies. But the American system generally lacks these intermediate institutions, and constitutional law, almost by default, has come to fill this role. (43–4). (Pildes had various citations in the above quoted passage, which I have purposely not included.)

legal realism, but also of liberal pluralism. Its solution recalibrated judicial purpose from civic republican assumptions and pushed politicians toward the strategy of harnessing judicial power.

I. Populism and the Lawyer Community's Response

Populist antipathy toward judges and courts took on the quality of a gathering storm during the election of 1896, which dissipated shortly thereafter. Criticism focused on the emerging doctrine of "substantive due process."[10] This doctrine positioned property rights against the state's regulatory or "police power." Employment contracts, drawing on the Lincolnian Republican notion of free labor, were understood as property. Given long-standing civic republican assumptions against class-based favoritism, substantive due process held contract negotiations nearly inviolable, such that employees should be free to negotiate the terms of their own employment without state interference; the state should not protect or regulate one class of citizens more than another. However, in practical effect, the doctrine seemed only to empower judges to secure corporate interests against efforts by urban laborers to unionize and farmers to seek price regulations.[11] Although the Court did uphold state regulatory powers in some rulings throughout the late nineteenth century, it maintained its authority to review these regulations in light of due process

[10] On anti-judicial sentiment during the 1896 election, see Alan Westin, "The Supreme Court, the Populist Movement and the Campaign of 1896," *Journal of Politics* 15 (February 1953), 3–41; Michael Kammen, *A Machine that Would Go of Itself: The Constitution in American Culture* (New York: Knopf, 1986), 191–2; Bruce Ackerman, "Taxation and the Constitution," *Columbia Law Review* 99 (1999), 1–58. On 1896 as the culmination of the Populist movement, see Robert Wiebe, *The Search for Order, 1877–1920* (New York: Hill and Wang, 1967) (After the 1896 election, "populism was dead" [105]); and Lawrence Goodwyn, *Democratic Promise: The Populist Movement in America* (New York: Oxford University Press, 1976) (Populism "expired in the autumn of 1896" [514]).

[11] See William Novak, *The People's Welfare* (Chapel Hill: University of North Carolina Press, 1996). According to Novak, the antebellum common law tradition maintained that the government could legitimately regulate and restrict individual freedoms in order to serve public welfare. In the *Slaughterhouse Cases*, 83 U.S. 36 (1873), the Court majority, while maintaining police power, reframed this tradition in a newer constitutional language of "substantive due process" versus "inalienable police powers" (230–48). On state police powers, see Ronald Labbe and Jonathan Lurie, *The Slaughterhouse Cases: Regulation, Reconstruction, and the Fourteenth Amendment* (Lawrence: University Press of Kansas, 2005).

While Novak and other revisionists, like Howard Gillman, ground *Lochner*-era decisions in a common law history of state police powers – and, in Gillman's particular scholarship, in a civic republican notion that would eschew legislation motivated by "class" interests – Friedman (2001) argues that these rulings were viewed as arbitrary: "the law was seen as indeterminate. And ... observers accused judges of applying their own political and class biases, rather than acting consistently with law," 1428. See Gillman, *The Constitution Besieged: The Rise and Demise of Lochner Era Police Powers Jurisprudence* (Durham: Duke University Press, 1993), 19–146. For an overview of revisionist takes on the *Lochner* era, see Paul Kens, "*Lochner v. New York*: Rehabilitated and Revised, but Still Reviled," *Journal of Supreme Court History* (1997), 1–13.

liberties.[12] It thereby moved toward a more robust defense of that liberty once it constructed corporations as also entitled to such liberty.[13] The Court majority endorsed the substantive due process doctrine in 1890 when it invalidated a Minnesota statute regulating rail rates because it did not contain provisions for judicial review of those rates.[14] According to the majority, by denying corporations the right of court review, the state denied corporations their due process rights. By calling the setting of rates "eminently a question for judicial interpretation," the justices characterized the Court as the primary if not the only arbiter of the state's police powers.[15] Such review would increasingly block legislative attempts to regulate industrial expansion.

This characterization of judicial power paralleled moves made in legal academia to re-imagine *Marbury v. Madison* as a foundation for judicial primacy. If judges claimed authority to strike down state and federal legislation, then their legitimacy to do so had to be grounded in something more compelling than the act of ruling. By the 1890s, academics and legal practitioners began to frame *Marbury* as the basis of this authority. What was once primarily considered a case about judicial process and writs of mandamus was thoroughly re-imagined as the foundational cornerstone of judicial review and supremacy.[16]

I.a. *Weaver's and Bryan's Lincolnian Refrains*
In 1892, James Weaver, Populist candidate for president, published *A Call to Action*, which criticized the pattern of judicial review supporting corporate interests under the guise of property rights and due process liberties. Weaver characterized recent instances of judicial review as "dethron[ing] the people who should be Sovereign and enthron[ing] an oligarchy" and held that "freedom has been fired upon" by "our Imperial Supreme Court."[17] Still, contrary to his own hyperbole, he was optimistic about the prospects for rulings favorable to agrarian and labor interests:

[12] On the Court's upholding of state police and regulatory powers, see *The Slaughterhouse Cases, Budd v. New York*, 143 U.S. 517 (1892), and *Reagan v. Farmers' Loan and Trust Co*, 154 U.S. 362 (1894).

[13] On defense of due process rights following the *Slaughterhouse* dissent, see *Munn v. Illinois*, 94 U.S. 113 (1877) and the *Railroad Commission Cases*, 116 U.S. 307 (1886). On the construction of the corporations as persons as entitled to due process protections, see *Santa Clara County v. Southern Pacific Railroad*, 118 U.S. 394, 396 (1886).

[14] *Chicago, Milwaukee, and St. Paul Railway Co. v. Minnesota*, 134 U.S. 418 (1890).

[15] Ibid., 458.

[16] Two constitutional law texts of the early nineteenth century credited *Marbury* with establishing judicial review: Kent's *Commentaries on American Law* (1826) and Story's *Commentaries on the Constitution of the United States* (1833). However, as Davison Douglas notes, "A perusal of nineteenth-century constitutional law treatises published after Kent and Story suggests that *Marbury's* significance lay in its discussion of writs of mandamus and the Court's original jurisdiction, not its treatment of the principle of judicial review." Douglas, "The Rhetorical Uses of *Marbury v. Madison*: The Emergence of a Great Case," *Wake Forest Law Review* 38 (2003), 383.

[17] James Weaver, *A Call to Action* (Des Moines: Des Moines Printing Co., 1892) 134.

We distinctively remember that this same Court and Dred Scott once differed in their conceptions of human rights under our Constitution. But Dred Scott's views are now generally accepted. It is probable that the controversy between the farmers and the Supreme Court will end in the same way ... the great Tribunal must be brought back to a sense of its accountability to the people.[18]

The question was how to bring that tribunal back to a sense of popular accountability. Rather than retaliate with Court-curbing measures, Weaver held the Court up as "the hope and refuge of the people."[19] If constitutional meaning on such new industrial-age questions as regulating monopolistic corporate practices, working conditions, or other issues on the Populist legislative agenda was not yet fully settled, then current rulings were only the ratification of one set of political interests above another.[20] Even if judicial rulings simply reflected political interests, which did not now accord with popular will, Populists like Weaver indicated that they might do so in the future. That sentiment is evident in his commentary on the change in Dred Scott's status. By analogizing *Dred Scott* to contemporary rulings, Weaver held open the possibility that these rulings might similarly fall into disrepute over time. As such, it was not immediately apparent that judicial authority should be actively undermined.

If Weaver had been reticent to undermine judicial legitimacy, three Supreme Court rulings in 1895 left the Court vulnerable to more caustic criticism. First, the Court gutted the Sherman Act by ruling that the E. C. Knight Company, even as it held over 90 percent of the national sugar manufacture capacity, did not violate the anti-trust law. The majority maintained that federal regulatory power extended only to interstate commerce and that commerce was distinct from manufacture.[21] Second, the Court declared the federal income tax unconstitutional. This tax had been widely supported by labor and farm interests to lower the national debt.[22] Third, the Court inverted its logic in *Knight* with its ruling in *In re Debs*.[23] In that case, it upheld injunctions against union strikes because such strikes obstructed commerce. The Court claimed that these strikes were a "conspiracy and

---

[18] Ibid., 133.

[19] Ibid., 86.

[20] Legal scholar James Bradley Thayer, for example, cautioned against viewing interpretation as nothing more than "pedantic and academic treatment of the texts of the constitution and the laws." Thayer, "The Origin and Scope of the American Doctrine of Constitutional Law, Speech before the Congress on Jurisprudence and Law Reform," *Harvard Law Review* (April 1893), 129.

[21] *United States v. E.C. Knight Co.*, 156 U.S. 1 (1895).

[22] *Pollack v. Farmer's Loan and Trust Co.*, 157 U.S. 429 (1895), and *Pollack v. Farmer's Loan and Trust Co.*, 158 U.S. 601 (1895). The first case ruled invalid the tax on income from real estate and municipal bonds. The second held the entire tax unconstitutional. On Populist support for the tax, see Richard Joseph, *The Origins of the American Income Tax: The Revenue Act of 1894 and Its Aftermath* (Syracuse: Syracuse University Press, 2004), 41–6.

[23] *In re Debs*, 158 U.S. 564 (1895).

combination" by railroad workers "to secure unto themselves the entire control of the interstate industrial and commercial business ... of Chicago and
the other communities along the lines of road of said railways."[24] By this
logic, when federal courts issued injunctions to prevent strikes, they were
exercising federal authority to regulate interstate commerce. Hence, manu-
facturing monopolies did not restrain trade, but labor monopolies, that is,
unions, did. The Constitution's commerce clause could suppress labor but
nevertheless be read as impotent against corporate monopoly. The contrast
of *Debs* and *Knight* "underscore[d] the Court's tendency to use the law as a
shield for business and a sword against labor."[25]

Responding to these cases, Sylvester Pennoyer, the populist governor of
Oregon, hyperbolized, "Our government has been supplanted by judicial
oligarchy."[26] He drew parallels to Jefferson's characterization of *Marbury* as
usurping executive and legislative authority. Pennoyer called for the impeachment of any judge who ruled against the federal income tax.[27] Senator Tillman
of South Carolina attacked what he called "the encroachments of the Federal
judiciary," which would lead to "government by injunction in the interests of
monopolies and corporations."[28] Lyman Trumbull criticized *Debs*, which he had
argued before the Court, in Jeffersonian language: "These Federal judges, like
sappers and miners, have for years silently and steadily enlarged their jurisdiction, and unless checked by legislation, they will soon undermine the very pillars
of the constitution and bury the liberties of the people beneath their ruin."[29]

Antipathy toward the judiciary climaxed during William Jennings Bryan's
1896 Democratic campaign for the presidency. While that campaign is mostly
remembered for struggles over currency reform and Bryan's "Cross of Gold"
speech, campaign rhetoric also lashed out against judges.[30] Democratic anti-
judicial sentiment was tonally similar to Republican hostilities triggered by
Dred Scott.[31] Judicial restraint was a central theme of Democrats at their
national convention. In the opening address, Senator John Daniel of Virginia
criticized "the Supreme Court of the United States [for] revers[ing] its settled
doctrine of a hundred years."[32] And the Democratic platform attacked judicial

---

[24] Ibid.
[25] Ross, 28.
[26] Sylvester Pennoyer, "The Income Tax Division and the Power of the Supreme Court to Nullify Acts of Congress," *American Law Review* 29 (1895), 558.
[27] On Pennoyer's use of Marbury, see Davison M. Douglas, "The Rhetorical Uses of Marbury v. Madison: The Emergence of a 'Great Case'," *Wake Forest Law Review* 38 (2003), 397, fn 98.
[28] Tillman, quoted in "The Senate Disgraced," *New York Times*, 29 January 1896, 3.
[29] Trumbull, "Views of Honorable Lyman Trumbull on Existing Political Evils," *American Law Review* 29 (1895), 115.
[30] See Richard Bensel, "A Calculated Enchantment of Passion: Bryan and the 'Cross of Gold' in the 1896 Democratic National Convention," in *Formative Acts: American Politics in the Making*, Stephen Skowronek and Matthew Glassman, eds. (Philadelphia: University of Pennsylvania Press, 2007).
[31] Westin, 38, and Kamman, 191–2.
[32] Daniel, quoted in *Official Proceedings of the Democratic National Convention, Chicago, 1896* (Longansport, IN: Wilson, Humphreys and Company, 1896).

issuance of injunctions as constituting "a new and highly dangerous form of oppression by which Federal judges, in contempt of the laws of the states and rights of citizens, become at once legislators, judges, and juries."[33]

Some press reports framed these Democratic sentiments as undermining notions of judicial independence and foretold an "anarchistic attack," which maintained that party's "old spirit of secession and rebellion against the Constitution."[34] Another suggested that Democrats intended to "pollute the stream of Federal Law at its source by making partisan changes in the Supreme Court."[35] Benjamin Harrison, former Republican president, warned when campaigning for William McKinley that Democrats conspired to see that "our constitutional government is [to be] overthrown" and that he could not "exaggerate the gravity and the importance and the danger of this assault upon our constitutional form of government."[36]

But if in Harrison's Republican hyperbole there existed echoes of Democrat Stephen Douglas, in Bryan's Democratic response there were echoes of Republican Abraham Lincoln's minimalism. Bryan's criticism of the judiciary narrowly focused on the income tax case. He defended judicial authority more generally: "There is nothing in that [Democratic national] platform that assails the integrity or questions the honesty of the Supreme Court of the United States."[37] Speaking at the Democratic convention, Bryan held fast to the idea that the Supreme Court's income tax ruling left the law fundamentally unsettled. He was, in other words, positioning his own possible election as having the same effect that Lincoln constructed for his election's relationship to *Dred Scott*: the election would de-stabilize the ruling. Bryan took care, therefore, to showcase how the ruling was out of line with historical precedents:

> They say we passed an unconstitutional law. I deny it. The income tax was not unconstitutional when it was passed. It was not unconstitutional when it went before the Supreme Court for the first time. It did not become unconstitutional until one judge changed his mind, and we cannot be expected to know when a judge will change his mind.[38]

By focusing on the ruling rather than the legitimacy of the judiciary itself, Bryan, like Lincoln, restricted the scope and scale of his assault.[39] Just as

---

[33] "Democratic Party Platform of 1896," 7 July 1896. John T. Woolley and Gerhard Peters, *The American Presidency Project* [online]. Santa Barbara: University of California (hosted), Gerhard Peters (database). http://www.presidency.ucsb.edu/ws/?pid=29586.

[34] *New York Herald Tribune*, 10 July 1896, 1; *Public Opinion*, 21, 16 July 1896, 76.

[35] *Philadelphia Press*, quoted in *Public Opinion*, 21, 3 September 1896, 298.

[36] Harrison, quoted in Westin, 34.

[37] Bryan, quoted in *Literary Digest*, 21, 31 October 1896, 837.

[38] Bryan, "Cross of Gold" Speech, Democratic National Convention of 1896, http://history-matters.gmu.edu/d/5354.

[39] Notably, Bryan did not directly campaign against the Court; he proposed no changes to structure or decision-making processes. This restraint is a marked contrast with Progressive proposals offered during the election of 1912.

Lincoln indicated that he would observe *Dred Scott*, Bryan would observe the Court's invalidation of the federal income tax: "we expressly recognize the binding force of that decision so long as it stands as a part of the law of the land."[40] Both Lincoln's and Bryan's positions imply a clear understanding that the law in question might not stand for long.[41]

And Bryan's criticism of the tax ruling was not so far beyond the mainstream as suggested by Republican and some press characterizations. While the conservative *New York Sun* supported the ruling, the *St. Louis Post-Dispatch* contended, "To-day's decision shows that the corporations and plutocrats are as securely intrenched [*sic*] in the Supreme Court as in the lower courts which they take such pains to control."[42] The *New York World* offered a more general criticism, not of the Court but of the Constitution:

> The framers of the Constitution could not foresee our conditions. They knew nothing of multi-millionaires or great corporations.... They could not foresee that a time would come when nearly all the burdens of taxation would fall upon the poor and moderately well to do, while the rich paid nothing on their wealth towards the support of the Government. Certainly they did not put any clause into the Constitution with the intent to protect invested wealth against the payment of its fair share. Yet that is precisely the use now to be made of the direct-tax clause under the ruling of the Supreme Court.[43]

Such characterizations of the Constitution as an obstacle to social reform or as incapable of responding to circumstances the Framers could not have imagined would become a continuous refrain among one wing of Progressives. This critique framed the Constitution as a cultural artifact, as an idiosyncratic document of a different era. As such, the Constitution could not be relied upon to respond to the unforeseen problems of industrial expansion. This criticism would underlie some Progressive advocacy of a new institutional architecture, external to the Constitution, to render the Court more in line with expressions of popular will.

---

[40] Arthur Schlesinger, Jr., ed., *History of American Presidential Elections* (New York: Chelsea House, 1971), Vol. 2: 1789–1968, 1853.

[41] Bryan was on stronger ground than Lincoln in claiming the unsettled status of the law. Whereas the Court had repeatedly sided with slavery interests prior to the Civil War, the most recent income tax decision was an outlier. Precedents from the Founding through Reconstruction appeared to maintain the tax's constitutionality. The 1894 statute was modeled on income tax laws passed during the Civil War. That the income tax was now deemed unconstitutional by a one-vote majority highlighted the unsettled nature of the law. See *Hylton v. United States*, 3 U.S. 171 (1796), and *Springer v. United States*, 102 U.S. 586 (1881). See generally, Ackerman (1991), 4–5, 25–8.

[42] Editorial, *New York Sun*, 21 May 1895, 6 ("The wave of the socialistic revolution has gone far, but it breaks at the foot of the ultimate bulwark set up for the protection of our liberties. Five to four, the Court stands as a rock"). Editorial, *St. Louis Dispatch*, quoted in "The Income-Tax Decision," *New York World*, 23 May 1895, 4.

[43] Editorial, *New York World*, 12 April 1895, 4.

I.b. *Responding to the Populist Threat: Lawyers Re-Imagine* Marbury *to Strengthen Judicial Review*

If the principle of judicial review was established and well accepted as even Bryan and Weaver's criticisms indicate, why was there any need to re-imagine *Marbury* and to make that ruling the definitive assertion of judicial authority? As detailed in Chapter 3, in *Marbury*, Marshall re-stated what many of the Founding generation had already granted. While the Constitution nowhere stipulates the power of judicial review explicitly, it is implied and seems to have been assumed by many present at the constitutional convention. And judicial review was continuously justified throughout the course of the nineteenth century without the need to reference *Marbury* as anything particularly groundbreaking. For example, various legal treatises of the mid to late nineteenth century did not cite *Marbury* to justify judicial review.[44] And the Supreme Court tended not to cite the decision. It did not expressly rely on *Marbury* until it ruled in the *Pollock* decisions that the federal income tax was unconstitutional.

These rulings represent a significant turning point in the Court's own justification of its legitimate authority.[45] In an unprecedented fashion, Chief Justice Fuller quoted Marshall's language in *Marbury* extensively. Not only was this explicit reliance on *Marbury* a new tactic for the Court, but so too was the compulsion to justify its authority:

> During the ninety-two years between *Marbury* and *Pollock*, the Court had never once seen it necessary when declaring a congressional statute unconstitutional to defend its power to exercise judicial review by reference to the authority of an earlier decision. In all prior cases, the Court merely asserted its power to declare a congressional statute unconstitutional without specifically citing case authority supporting that course of action.[46]

By singling out *Marbury* as the critical precedent for the authority of review if not for judicial supremacy, Fuller contributed to the contemporaneous academic process of canonizing *Marbury* not only as a "great case," but also as *the* basis of judicial power in a democracy. The case was henceforth more than an example of writs of mandamus and a statement on the extent of the Court's original jurisdiction. That canonization continued throughout the nineteenth and the beginning of the twentieth century, and particularly centered on the centennial of Marshall's appointment as chief justice.[47]

---

[44] Douglas, 382–6.

[45] According to Arnold Paul, a series of incidents including the Haymarket Riots and the Chicago railroad strike of 1894 signaled potential collapse into socialism or anarchy, and many within the conservative legal community viewed the income tax as the institutional embodiment of that trend (160).

[46] Douglas, 395.

[47] Ibid., 398–404. Albert Beveridge, in his *The Life of John Marshall*, articulated what Robert Clinton called the "modern *Marbury*," which is, according to Clinton, a "myth." Beveridge read *Marbury* to stand for judicial supremacy: "In order to assert that the Judiciary rested on the exclusive power to declare any statute unconstitutional, and to announce that the Supreme

It is perhaps unsurprising that this re-conceptualization of *Marbury* would occur concurrently with steps to formalize American legal education and professionalize the practice of law. Standardized legal education did not develop until the 1880s, with Columbia University making initial moves and Harvard University setting the standard.[48] The new appeal to *Marbury* as the succinct and definitive basis for judicial power fit with this process of establishing law as an academic discipline and an elite profession. The decision could be framed as placing the judiciary, judges, and lawyers at the center of good American governance. More importantly, it enabled the builders of this new profession – with its new schools with increasingly standardized curricula and pedagogy (as opposed to the previous system of personal apprenticeship) and extensive network of new bar associations – to cite an already legitimated authority, which is to say, to appeal to constitutional precedent.

This revisionist conception of *Marbury* further legitimized judicial review within this new wave of hostilities because it implied that such power was grounded in one of the earliest acts of governance associated with the Founding period. Thus, the re-imagining of *Marbury* and the professionalization of legal practice worked together to provide lawyers and judges with the intellectual tools necessary to roll back Populist and, later, Progressive legislation, and to frame the authority for such rollback as flowing from one of the earliest decisions in American constitutional law. *Marbury* might only stipulate that the judicial authority to rule on the meaning and constitutionality of law had always existed; nevertheless, specialized, extensive, and formal legal education would ensure that court rulings were superior to those offered by members of the other branches.

II. Constitution as Obstacle or Instrument: Progressive Confusion about Courts

Some Progressive hostilities toward judicial power shared much with their Populist predecessors. Leaders in both movements utilized Lincoln's inaugural claims about constitutional silences to maintain judicial authority while still holding a place for popular ratification of rulings. But while Populist critique, particularly as articulated by Weaver and Bryan, echoed Lincoln's characterization of unsettled law, some Progressives went further to advocate new structural solutions. These Progressives tended to describe the Constitution as an obstacle to social reform, emphasizing instead public opinion as a legitimate source of law in a democracy.

Court was the *ultimate* arbiter as to what is and what is not law under the Constitution, Marshall determined to annul Section 13 of the Ellsworth Judiciary Act of 1789." (Beveridge, *The Life of John Marshall*, Volume 3: *Conflict and Construction, 1800–1815* [Boston: Houghton Mifflin, 1919], 132.) See Clinton, "Precedent as Mythology: A Reinterpretation of Marbury v. Madison," *American Journal of Jurisprudence* 35 (1990), 55–7.

[48] Robert Stevens, *Law School: Legal Education in America from the 1850s to the 1980s* (Chapel Hill: University of North Carolina Press, 1983), 20–72.

Other Progressives contended that the Constitution could function as a conduit of social reform. By this logic, judges construed the Constitution to block reform because of their particular interpretive proclivities toward textual originalism and legal formalism.[49] But a new interpretive methodology, crystallized in Justice Oliver Wendell Holmes's dissents and developed at the new law schools of Yale and Columbia Universities, rejected formalism and the textual originalist claim to a single, fixed, and discoverable meaning and instead sought to bring more flexibility to interpretation so that the Constitution could adapt to changing socioeconomic circumstances. For Holmes and many others who fell into this "legal realist" camp, such as Felix Frankfurter, Louis Brandeis, James Bradley Thayer, and Benjamin Cardozo, a range of legal and often explicitly non-legal factors influenced interpretation.[50] These legal Progressives characterized the Jeffersonian compromise of judicial independence as political neutrality and the subsequent establishment of a wall between law and politics as specious.

For some Progressives, judicial articulation of the law should be granted no special weight in a democracy. They either sought to supplant law with the enlightened rule of public opinion or invented extra-constitutional mechanisms to promote sought-after interpretation, particularly electoral architecture such as judicial recall, that is, the recall of judges, or the more targeted decision recall, which subjected rulings to popular ratification. Others responded to the realist critique by constructing new rules to *legitimize* judicial authority, such as various calls for judicial self-restraint such as Justice Louis Brandeis' *Ashwander* principle; but they also recognized that, through judges who were sympathetic to policy objectives that lay at the base of many legal contests, the courts could become pathways to social reform.[51] As such, the Progressive years are replete with attempts to utilize courts to achieve

---

[49] Legal formalism refers to a late nineteenth-century move in interpretive methodology beyond textual originalism. It maintained originalist focus on intent and textualist focus on the Constitution, but it tended to "get more rigid and scientific"; also, dichotomous categorization was prevalent in legal reasoning, for example, direct versus indirect effects of commerce, the distinction between manufacture and commerce, and so on. O'Neill, 25. See also William Wiecek, *The Lost World of Classical Legal Thought* (New York: Oxford University Press, 1998), 4–7, 89–94.

[50] See Holmes's dissent in *Lochner v. New York*, 198 U.S. 45 (1905), and his rejection of textual formalism's deduction of abstract principles: a constitution "is made for people of fundamentally differing views.... General propositions do not decide concrete cases. The decision will depend on a judgment or intuition more subtle than any articulate major premise.... Every opinion tends to become a law. I think that the word liberty in the Fourteenth Amendment is perverted when it is held to prevent the natural outcome of a dominant opinion." On legal realism, see Wilfred Rumble, Jr., *American Legal Realism* (Ithaca: Cornell University Press, 1968), and Laura Kalman, *Legal Realism at Yale* (Chapel Hill: University of North Carolina Press, 1986).

[51] *Ashwander v. TVA*, 297 U.S. 288 (1936). In a concurring opinion, Justice Brandeis laid out how the Court can and should decide a case without necessarily reaching the constitutional question, thereby suggesting that if a constitutional question can be avoided and the case still be resolved on the merits, then it should be decided that way.

238   *Harnessing Judicial Power and Liberal Pluralism*

Progressive objectives without any new architecture that might tether constitutionalism more directly to expressions of popular sovereignty. If realists claimed that law was merely what "Justices say it is rather than what the framers or you might hope it is," then legal realism provided the intellectual foundations for harnessing judicial power to serve particular policy ends.[52] And this strategy made even more sense within the context of the legal community's explicit attempts to empower judges through its re-imagining of the *Marbury* ruling and establishment of standardized professional schools.

II.a. *Progressive Jeffersonianism: Anti-Partyism, Judicial Legitimacy, and Judicial Recall*

Progressive criticisms of political party and of constitutionalism maintained the same underlying objective, namely, the elevation of national identity above local and state concerns. Progressives derided what they perceived as sectional narrowness and corruption of both the Democratic and Republican parties. They advocated, instead, newer participatory and interest-based organizations that unified identities across partisan and local divisions, a reliance on administrative bureaucracy and government commissions, and a broad new national identity.[53] Two-party competition was diagnosed as "stand[ing] between the people and the government and mak[ing] a fully democratic government impossible"; party government meant nothing more than "stagnation ... commonplace ideas and past issues" or, even worse, a government of "compromise and not principles."[54] While such critique carried moral undertones of Progressive social gospel, secular criticisms were voiced. John Dewey blamed political ills on "'machines' of political parties," which had "hierarchical gradation of bosses from national to ward rulers, bosses who are in close touch with business interests at one extreme, and with those who pander to the vices of the community (gambling, drink and prostitution) at the other."[55] For Dewey, the public participation in conventions and caucuses was simply a means to hold the "masses of men to more or less blind acquiescence."[56]

Some Progressives linked their critique of party with a simultaneous critique of constitutional interpretation. Dewey claimed that Democrats tended to view the Constitution as a static document "maximizing individual and local liberty" and that this construction "necessarily precluded it from serious

---

[52] Franklin D. Roosevelt, Fireside Chat, 9 March 1937. John T. Woolley and Gerhard Peters, *The American Presidency Project* [online]. Santa Barbara, CA, http://www.presidency.ucsb.edu/ws/?pid=15381.

[53] See Eldon Eisenach, *The Lost Promise of Progressivism* (Lawrence: University Press of Kansas, 1994); Wiebe 1966; and Stephen Skowronek, *Building a New American State* (New York: Cambridge University Press, 2008), 165–284.

[54] Samuel Batten, *The Christian State: The State, Democracy, and Christianity* (Philadelphia: Griffith and Rowland Press, 1909), 239–40.

[55] John Dewey and James Tufts, *Ethics* (New York: Henry Holt, 1908), 478.

[56] Ibid.

reflection on objects of national importance."[57] Thus, the Constitution was trapped in the same stultifying localism as the parties of the Jacksonian era; but a new nationalism demanded a new understanding of the Constitution, particularly after the empowerment of federal authority through the thirteenth, fourteenth, and fifteenth amendments. Progressive journalist Herbert Croly made the connection between the localism of political parties and the localist rendering of the Constitution even more explicit:

> American parties had been organized to work with the Constitution, and to supply the deficiencies of that document as an instrument of democratic policy. The organization of a strong official government would not only render the Constitution of less importance, it would also tend to dethrone the party machines. It would imply that the government itself was by way of being democratized, and that the democracy no longer needed to depend upon partisan organizations to represent popular purposes.[58]

The Constitution had certain deficiencies that parties, as an institutional innovation, had rectified. But the perverse outcome was that the government was responsive to the party and not to the people themselves. Parties and the Constitution symbiotically exacerbated the democratic failings of each. As such, Croly recommended the proliferation of non-party organizations, such as civic groups, voter leagues, and women's associations, that might provide more equal and unfettered access to governance while also promoting a shared *national* interest, which the existing parties were diagnosed as inhibiting.[59] Progressive antipathy toward party and claims about the localist construction of the Constitution had a common root.

This branch of the Progressive movement attacked judicial legitimacy in language akin to that of the Jeffersonians. Its anti-partyism and perception of the Constitution as stagnant underlay the idea that law could and should be replaced by popular opinion. Progressive sociologist, Charles Cooley, defined public opinion as "no mere aggregate of separate individual interests."[60] Far from the aggregation of individual wants, public opinion was the realization of individual desire as constrained by recognition of the social good.[61] It was an educated expression of informed criticism. In a democracy, where institutions would form and create public opinion, some Progressives held that "public opinion would (or should) increasingly supplant law and other forms of external coercion in a society."[62]

---

[57] Ibid., 50.
[58] Herbert Croly, *Progressive Democracy* (New York: Macmillan, 1914), 124.
[59] Ibid., 313–17.
[60] Charles Cooley, *Social Organization: A Study of the Larger Mind* (Glencoe, IL: Free Press, 1956 [1909]), 121.
[61] For Progressive views on public opinion, see Franklin Giddings, *Elements of Sociology* (New York: Macmillan, 1898), 155–7, and Arthur Hadley, *The Education of the American Citizen* (New York: Charles Scribner's Sons, 1901), 25.
[62] Eisenach, 77.

Progressives' perception of the Constitution as a fossilized obstacle to reform and their emphasis on public opinion as a source of democratic dynamism gained institutional expression in the movement to subject judges to popular removal, or judicial recall. The reform was instituted at the state level in Oregon in 1908, California in 1911, and Arizona in 1912, as part of a wider movement for direct democracy and public control of politics through initiative, referendum, and recall.[63] Hiram Johnson, the Progressive Republican governor and senator from California, captured the way the rationale for judicial recall rested on conceptions of judges as vulnerable to corruption, the law as static, and public opinion as valorous:

> A judge is but a man, sometimes as good and sometimes fully as bad as we are. He is clothed in authority, it is true, but the minute any man becomes erected into something that does not depend on its own acts for the respect accorded it, that minute it becomes erected into something for worship, something which does not rest on the foundations we built for this country.[64]

The passage suggests that Johnson abandoned or never held the ideal of judicial independence as political neutrality. He embraced an emerging notion of legal contingency or what would become legal realism.

Christopher Tiederman discussed legal realism in his 1890 treatise, *The Unwritten Constitution*. Tiederman contended that judicial opinion would always bend to "the stress of public opinion or private interests."[65] If it were true that, in Tiederman's words, law could be "made to mean one thing at one time, and at another time an altogether different thing," then for Johnson and other Progressives, it was only natural that in a democracy, the law should bend to public interest.[66] In this contention, the Lincolnian foundations of Johnson's ideas are clear. Lincoln also maintained that the Constitution could be read to have different meanings, and that such interpretations would only gain validity the more they were sustained over time by the democratic majority. Likewise, Johnson sought *a mechanism* by which that constitutional interpretation could be more directly compelled to reflect the interest of the majority. Judicial recall elections were the mechanism to ensure that outcome.

Johnson claimed that he would rather have judges pressured by public opinion and the threat of removal than continue to have the Constitution read to support corporate power.[67] Senator Owen of Oklahoma, when proposing a federal judicial recall statute, defended the measure in similar terms. If multiple

[63] Ross, 111–14. For discussion of advantages and disadvantages of judge and decision recall, see *Selected Articles on the Recall: Including the Recall of Judges and Judicial Decisions*, compiled by Edith Phelps (White Plains, NY: H. W. Wilson, 1913).

[64] "Address by Governor Johnson in Los Angeles," *Los Angeles Tribune*, 27 September 1911. Hiram Johnson Papers, Bancroft Library, University of California at Berkeley, part II, Box 43.

[65] Tiedeman, *Unwritten Constitution*, 43, quoted in Howard Gillman, "The Collapse of Constitutional Originalism and the Rise of the 'Living Constitution' in the Course of American State-Building," *Studies in American Political Development* 11 (Fall 1997), 217.

[66] Ibid.

[67] George Mowry, *The California Progressives* (New York: Quadrangle, 1963), 148–9.

interpretations could be sustained, he would rather leave the people in charge of constitutional meaning: "public opinion is a better and safer influence for judges who may be influenced on the bench than the influence of a political boss or his commercial allies."[68]

An indicator of Johnson's priorities to achieve Progressive policy outcomes by whatever means were most expedient was his alternative argument in favor of recall. While with one hand he rejected the ideal of judicial neutrality, with the other he claimed that judicial recall would enhance the normative ideal of judicial independence to the degree that it posed no direct threat to the neutral judge:

> There are two kinds of judges – the judge who decides without inquiry in the past and standing of the litigants before him, except as they come into the open forum, and the judge who decides with an ear listening to every rustle of power behind him, with a thought to which litigant may furthest advance him. The recall will make no weak judge weaker, and no strong judge less strong. It will only remove the corrupt judge. You can't make a coward by putting a pistol to his head. You can only prove him a coward.[69]

Of course, this statement begs the question of how corruption is gauged. In the end, the rationale for judicial recall amounts to little more than the broad construction of judicial impeachment at issue during Samuel Chase's trial, namely, John Randolph's contention that judges could be removed without clear demonstration of criminal wrongdoing. The only difference that Johnson now offered was that judicial recall took impeachment power from the legislature and gave it directly to the people. It turned the extraordinary constitutional process of impeachment into the more quotidian politics of election.

Judicial recall was criticized for undermining the ideal of judicial independence as political neutrality. Progressive Republican Senator William Borah of Idaho – who would, in the 1920s, author a constitutional amendment to constrain judicial decision-making – posited that judicial recall "leaves human rights uncertain and worthless ... destroys values ... and has more than once demoralized and destroyed governments."[70] President William Taft considered judicial recall "so destructive to independence in the judiciary, so likely to subject the rights of the individual to the possible tyranny of a popular majority, and therefore to be so injurious to the cause of a free government."[71] Senator Henry Cabot Lodge summed up the problem of linking judicial authority to democratic politics via recall: "servile judges are a menace to freedom, no

[68] Owen, quoted in Ross, 117.
[69] "Address by Governor Johnson in Los Angeles," *Los Angeles Tribune*, 27 September 1911. Hiram Johnson Papers, Bancroft Library, University of California at Berkeley, part II, Box 43. See also Johnson to A. H. Heflan, 9 September 1911, Hiram Johnson Papers, Bancroft Library, University of California at Berkeley, part II, Box 1.
[70] *Congressional Record*, 62nd Congress, 1st Session, 7 August 1911, 3687.
[71] Taft, quoted in Donald Anderson, *William Howard Taft: A Conservative's Conception of the Presidency* (Ithaca: Cornell University Press, 1973), 231.

matter to whom their servitude is due."[72] The more radical and Jeffersonian Progressive democratic claims triggered concerns of majority tyranny and ignored the long-recognized value of the Court as a potential bulwark against that perversion of democracy that even Jefferson recognized.

II.b. *The Progressives' Lincolnian Refrain: Living Constitutionalism and Decision Recall*

Replacing rule of law with rule by public opinion was not the only Progressive response to the idea that the Constitution could support a range of different substantive policies. Another Progressive solution – whose most prominent advocate was Theodore Roosevelt – was more narrowly targeted to respond to just those decisions that raised Progressive ire. These decisions clustered around the meaning of due process liberty and the balance between individual freedom of contract and state police power to legislate restrictions on that liberty to serve the public welfare. They have come to be known, in shorthand, as *Lochner*-era cases, as that case puts into sharp relief this conflict between legislation for work-hour restrictions and the Court's valorization of freedom of contract.[73]

Many Progressive legal scholars were frustrated by the lack of an identifiably legal principle underlying Court rulings since the *Slaughterhouse* decision. For example, Learned Hand characterized freedom of contract rulings as marking a "great divergence of constitutional decisions and apparent absence of actual principle upon which such cases should be determined."[74] More troubling was the Court's reference to a freedom of contract as a fundamental liberty even though it lacked historical moorings. Hand argued that liberty of contract mangled liberty itself by "disregard[ing] the whole juristic history of the word."[75] Louis Greely contended that it had "no existence in fact."[76] Edward Corwin maintained that it "is not a legal concept at all," but legally sanctions political preferences. It enabled a majority of justices to "sink whatever legislative craft may appear to them to be, from the standpoint of vested interests, of a piratical tendency."[77]

---

[72] Henry Cabot Lodge, "The Compulsory Initiative and Referendum and the Recall of Judges" (address at Princeton University, 8 March 1912), reprinted as Senate Doc. 406, 62nd Congress, 2nd Session, 1912, 17.

[73] The decision struck down a New York statute for maximum work hours for bakers. Other cases include *First Employer's Liability Cases*, 207 U.S. 463, 501, 504 (1908) (invalidating a statute making railroad companies liable for employee injury), *Adair v. United States*, 208 U.S. 274 (1908) (invalidating a statute prohibiting employers from compelling their employees to refrain from participating in labor union activities), and *Loewe v. Lawlor*, 208 U.S. 274 (1908) (ruling that a secondary labor boycott violated anti-trust laws).

[74] Learned Hand, "Due Process Law and the Eight-Hour Day," *Harvard Law Review* 21 (1908), 499.

[75] Ibid., 495.

[76] Louis Greely, "The Changing Attitude of the Courts toward Social Legislation," *Illinois Law Review* 5 (1911), 223.

[77] Edward Corwin, "Review of Goodnow's Social Reform and the Constitution," *American Political Science Review* 6 (November 1912), 271, quoted in *The Green Bag, An Entertaining Magazine of the Law*, Arthur W. Spencer, ed. (Boston: Riverdale Press, 1914), Vol. 26, 436.

Some Progressives, therefore, focused their criticism not on the alleged undemocratic quality of judicial review but more narrowly on the judicial construction of the Fourteenth Amendment. Gilbert Roe, in his influential 1912 text, *Our Judicial Oligarchy*, adopted the Court's construction of the amendment in the *Slaughterhouse Cases*: "Every one knows that the sole intent and purpose of the people in adding this amendment to the Constitution, was to protect the recently emancipated negroes in their rights of citizenship." He complained that the Court perverted the amendment's narrow intent and adopted the *Slaughterhouse* broad dissent to protect "all manner of trusts and corporations, and of contracts and practices, none of which were even in the thought of the people when they adopted the amendment."[78] Similarly, Edward Corwin traced the evolution of the Amendment as a "reinterpretation ... in light of Lockian individualism and of Spencerian *Laissez Faire*."[79] According to this argument, labor interests might be less hindered by the Constitution if the Fourteenth Amendment were repealed entirely.[80]

The Fourteenth Amendment, however, need not be an explicit obstacle. Benjamin Cardozo, who would be appointed to the Supreme Court by President Herbert Hoover, emphasized the ambiguity in the Constitution's phrasing and the changing meaning of key concepts, such as due process liberty, over time. He called due process, which is found in the Fifth and Fourteenth Amendments, "a concept of the greatest generality ... Liberty is not defined." Since "its limits are not mapped and charted," Cardozo wondered, "how shall they be known? Does liberty mean the same thing for successive generations?"[81] Cardozo, like Lincoln, found opportunity within the Constitution's silences, opportunity not only to justify different interpretations but also to advocate the abandonment of nineteenth-century textual originalism and legal formalism that stifled legislative response to industrialization's new challenges. Constitutional meaning was not singular and discoverable but could and should adapt to meet the exigencies of changed circumstance. Cardozo answered his own questions: "May restraints that were arbitrary yesterday be useful and rational and therefore lawful today? May restraints that are arbitrary today become useful and rational and therefore lawful tomorrow? I have no doubt that the answer to these questions must be yes. There were times in our judicial history when the answer might have been no." But for Cardozo, times changed. In the new social order brought by late nineteenth-century industrialization, there needed to be "a new formulation of fundamental rights and duties."[82] Cardozo argued that

---

[78] Gilbert Roe, *Our Judicial Oligarchy* (New York: B. W. Huebsch, 1912), 36–7, 37.
[79] Edward Corwin, *Corwin on the Constitution: The Judiciary* (Ithaca: Cornell University Press, 1981), 126.
[80] Walter Clark, "Some Defects in the Constitution of the United States," *American Law Review* 54 (May 1906), 277–82.
[81] Benjamin Cardozo, *Nature of the Judicial Process* (New Haven: Yale University Press, 1922), 76–7
[82] Ibid., 77, 78.

the old textualism should be abandoned: "Courts know today that statutes are to be viewed, not in isolation or *in vacuo*, as pronouncements of abstract principles for the guidance of an ideal community, but in the setting and the framework of present-day conditions as revealed by the labors of economists and students of the social sciences in our own country and abroad."[83] As such, for legal realists such as Cardozo, the due process clauses need not be obstacles to Progressive objectives as long as they were read with modern industrialization in mind. The question, of course, was how to ensure that the Constitution could be a tool rather than an obstacle.

Theodore Roosevelt offered another pragmatic solution, which exploited these changing ideas about the legitimacy of different interpretive methods. His solution, which held particular rulings up to popular endorsement, was a centerpiece of his unsuccessful bid for re-election in 1912. While his criticism of the judiciary crystallized between 1910 and 1912, the sentiment was evident in his last annual message to Congress in 1908:

> The judges who have shown themselves able and willing effectively to check the dishonest activity of the very rich man who works iniquity by the misman-agement of corporations, who have shown themselves alert to do justice to the wageworker, and sympathetic with the needs of the mass of our people ... these judges are the real bulwark of the courts.... The courts are jeopardized primarily by the action of those Federal and State judges who show inability or unwillingness to put a stop to the wrongdoing of very rich men under modern industrial conditions, and inability or unwillingness to give relief to men of small means or wageworkers who are crushed down by these modern indus-trial conditions; who, in other words, fail to understand and apply the needed remedies for the new wrongs produced by the new and highly complex social and industrial civilization which has grown up in the last half century.[84]

This public statement paralleled Roosevelt's private sentiment that "there is altogether too much power in the bench."[85]

Roosevelt's criticism rested on an assumption that the Constitution was dynamic. And, as Cardozo's writings discussed earlier suggest, Progressive legal thinkers increasingly endorsed this idea. Justice Holmes gave this idea ini-tial prominence in his *Lochner* dissent; the Constitution is "perverted" if it is read to "prevent natural outcome of dominant opinion."[86] He expanded upon

---

[83] Ibid., 81.

[84] Theodore Roosevelt, "Eighth Annual Message," 8 December 1908; John T. Woolley and Gerhard Peters, *The American Presidency Project* [online]. Santa Barbara, CA: University of California (hosted), Gerhard Peters (database), http://www.presidency.ucsb.edu/ws/?pid=29549.

[85] Roosevelt to William White, 30 November 1908, quoted in Henry Pringle, *Theodore Roosevelt: A Biography* (New York: Blue Ribbon Books, 1931), 482.

[86] *Lochner v. New York*, 198 U.S. 45 (1905), 75–76. Cardozo credits Holmes's *Lochner* dissent "as the beginning of an era" in which "a new conception of the significance of constitutional limitations in the domain of individual liberty, emerged to recognition and to dominance" (79, 78).

it in another case, when he argued that "the provisions of the Constitution are not mathematical formulas having their essence in their form; they are organic living institutions."[87] Theodore Roosevelt embraced this idea of the Constitution adapting to socioeconomic circumstance:

> We are now entering on a period when the vast and complex growth of modern industrialism renders it of vital interest to our people that the court should apply the old essential underlying principles of our government to the new and totally different conditions in such fashion that the spirit of the Constitution shall in very fact be preserved and not sacrificed to a narrow construction of the letter.[88]

By defining the Constitution as adaptable, Roosevelt maintained the document's relevance rather than disregard it as a fossil. The Constitution could yield social reform; rule of law need not be *entirely* supplanted by rule by public opinion. A revival of a fading civic republican notion that rights were *constituted* by government and were contingent on public welfare was needed. Reviving this older idea that property liberties are not absolute was the key, for Roosevelt, to maintaining the Constitution's relevance in unforeseen circumstances of industrial growth:

> We are face to face with new conceptions of the relations of property to human welfare.... The man who wrongly holds that every human right is secondary to his profit must now give way to the advocate of human welfare, who rightly maintains that every man holds his property subject to the general right of the community to regulate its use to whatever degree the public welfare may require it.[89]

The Constitution already had within it the terms by which to uphold Progressive policy aims regarding working conditions, maximum-hour limits, and minimum wages. According to Roosevelt, "to give such legislation is not to work a revolution in the Constitution, it is simply to carry out the purpose of the Constitution by facing the fact that new needs exist and that new methods must be devised for reaching these new needs."[90]

In his introduction to William Ransom's influential commentary on judicial authority, *Majority Rule and Democracy*, Roosevelt argued, "the people and not the judges are entitled to say what their Constitution means, for the Constitution is theirs, it belongs to them and not to their servants in office."[91]

---

[87] *Gompers v. U.S.*, 233 U.S. 604 (1914), 610.
[88] Theodore Roosevelt, "The Loss of a Great Public Servant," *The Outlook*, 5 November 1910, reprinted in Theodore Roosevelt IV, *The Roughriders and Men of Action* (New York: Kessinger, 2005), 262.
[89] Theodore Roosevelt, *The New Nationalism* (New York: Outlook, 1910), 23.
[90] Theodore Roosevelt, "Address before the Chamber of Commerce, New Haven CT," 13 December 1910, quoted in Gary Murphy, "'Mr. Roosevelt Is Guilty': Theodore Roosevelt and the Crusade for Constitutionalism, 1910–1912," *Journal of American Studies* 36 (2002), 446.
[91] Theodore Roosevelt, "Introduction," in William Ransom, *Majority Rule and the Judiciary* (New York: Charles Scribner's Sons, 1912), 6.

This sentiment echoed Lincoln's ideas. Roosevelt drew out this connection, using the parallels to frame his own criticisms as hardly reactionary. He contended that his proposals were "in precisely the spirit of Lincoln."[92] And he held to Lincoln's minimalism, placing himself between radicals who called for the elimination of judicial review and rule by public opinion and conservative Republicans who offered no response to the rising tide of popular hostility toward courts and judges:

> I am not prepared to say what, if anything, should be done as regards the Federal judiciary; and I have no sympathy with sweeping general attacks upon it; but I have just as little sympathy with failure to recognize the many and grave shortcomings of the Federal judiciary, including the Supreme Court, during these past three decades or so; and I believe that failure to war against these abuses and unintelligent partisan championship of the court, will in the end do just the reverse of what those who indulge in the championship hope.[93]

If Roosevelt was reluctant to offer a solution to the challenge of *federal* judicial authority, he had already articulated a plan to rein in *state* judiciaries. In January of 1912, in an article in the Progressive periodical *The Outlook*, Roosevelt endorsed subjecting state judicial rulings to popular recall.[94] He elaborated on this plan a month later before the Ohio Constitutional Convention where he kicked off his campaign for the Republican presidential nomination:

> If any considerable number of people feel that the *decision* is in defiance of justice they should be given the right to petition to bring before the people at some subsequent election, special or otherwise, as might be decided and after opportunity for debate has been allowed, the question whether or not the *judge's* interpretation of the constitution is to be sustained.[95]

Whether Roosevelt wanted to see his proposal implemented is a subject of much scholarly debate. It could have been a strategic ploy to distinguish Roosevelt from Taft and to woo Progressives, who had rallied behind Senator Robert LaFollette and who had also made much fodder out of controversial Court rulings.[96]

---

[92] Theodore Roosevelt to Henry Cabot Lodge, 21 September 1910, in *The Letters of Theodore Roosevelt*, Elting E. Morison, ed. (Cambridge, MA: Harvard University Press, 1954), Vol. 7, 134.

[93] Theodore Roosevelt to Henry Stimson, 5 February 1912, in *Letters*, Vol. 7, 495.

[94] Theodore Roosevelt, "Judges and Progress," *The Outlook*, 6 January 1912, 45–6. Roosevelt's timidity in his letter to Stimson highlights the extent to which he sought to maintain strong federal judicial authority. In the *Outlook*, as in a speech delivered in New York in October of 1911, Roosevelt focused his reform on popular recall of *state* court decisions. See *Works of Theodore Roosevelt* (New York: Scribner, 1926), Vol. 16, 206.

[95] Roosevelt, quoted in "Roosevelt's Critics Express Their Views: An Analysis and Criticism of His Utterance on the Recall of Judicial Decisions," *New York Times*, 3 March 1912, 12. Emphasis added.

[96] On judicial decision recall as a ploy to give Roosevelt Progressive credibility, see Stephen Stagner, "The Recall of Judicial Decisions and the Due Process Debate," *American Journal of*

Regardless, many of Roosevelt's letters suggest that he was concerned about "a riot of judicial action looking to the prevention of measures for social and industrial betterment which every other civilized nation takes as a matter of course."[97] His plan, like legal realism itself, had clear Lincolnian roots. Roosevelt himself contended that he was offering no more criticism of the Court than Lincoln had done of *Dred Scott*, which was remarkably less than Jefferson's own sentiment.[98] The proposal for decision recall was essentially a formalization of Lincoln's idea of characterizing elections as signals about whether a legal interpretation was settled. Lincoln, as detailed in Chapter 5, held his own election as a signal that the *Dred Scott* ruling was unsettled. He thereby created flexibility to constrain the precedent effect of the decision.[99] Instead of using presidential elections – with their myriad issues and thus the difficulty to claim a mandate to do anything on a particular issue – Roosevelt wanted to hold specific elections on rulings.[100] Furthermore, as Lincoln would not disturb a decision's impact on the parties to a case, Roosevelt similarly held that whatever the outcome of the decision recall, the law as had been previously decided would still bind the parties involved.[101] As such, Roosevelt's plan maintained judicial authority, while attempting to link expressions of popular sovereignty with judicial power. In essence, Roosevelt disciplined Lincoln's idea that elections could settle law by proposing specific mechanisms to do so.

For Roosevelt, decision recall did not attack judicial legitimacy. It was more targeted than recalling judges. Judicial recall potentially undermined popular

Legal History 24 (July 1980), 258. As a candidate, Roosevelt displaced the standard-bearer, Robert LaFollette, who considered a presidential run in 1912. See Johnson to Unknown, 3 April 1912, Hiram Johnson Papers, Bancroft Library, University of California at Berkeley, part II, Box 42, folder "LaFollette Candidacy Papers." See also Amos Pinchot, William Kent, Gifford Pinchot, and Medill McCormick to Hiram Johnson, 27–8 March 1912, and John D. Fackler, president, Progressive Republican League of Ohio, to Hiram Johnson, 1 April 1912, Hiram Johnson Papers, Bancroft Library, University of California, part II, Box 42, folder "LaFollette Candidacy Papers."

[97] Theodore Roosevelt to Herbert Croly, 29 February 1912, *Theodore Roosevelt Papers*, Series 3A, Reel 374, quoted in Ross, 140.

[98] Theodore Roosevelt, "Criticisms of the Courts," *The Outlook*, 24 September 1910, 149–53. In articles for *The Outlook* in 1911 Roosevelt maintained in Lincolnian fashion that he did not aim to dismantle the courts, and that he only took issue with rulings on particular cases. See Roosevelt, "Nationalism and the New Judiciary," *The Outlook*, 25 February 1911, 383–5. See also 4 March 1911, 488–92, 11 March 1911, 532–36, and 18 March 1911, 574–77. See Pringle, 543–4.

[99] Roosevelt innovated on Lincoln's idea by giving it an institutional structure as opposed to Lincoln's more ethereal claim about law's settlement over time, and this may explain Skowronek's characterization of Roosevelt as an orthodox-innovator of the Lincoln regime. Orthodox-innovators take ideas from a regime's constructive president and expand them, often creating backlash and division in the process. Progressives split on whether to support Roosevelt's judicial scheme. Skowronek, *The Politics Presidents Make: Leadership from John Adams to Bill Clinton* (Cambridge: Belknap Press of Harvard University, 1997), 33–45, 198–259.

[100] Robert Dahl, "Myth of the Presidential Mandate," *Political Science Quarterly* 105 (Autumn 1990), 355–72.

[101] Stagner, 259–60.

support for the courts. Instead, Roosevelt wanted "to show men who wanted to recall judges that what they really meant nine times out of ten was that they wanted to change the decision of the judges on a certain constitutional question."[102] Furthermore, he declared that his proposal would only affect state decisions on constitutional questions. And he did not advocate recall of Supreme Court rulings. Relative to other Progressive ideas, his mechanism for reining in judicial authority was narrow indeed.

Roosevelt's moderation relative to some fellow Progressives is reflected in his endorsement of the doctrine of "rule of reason," which was articulated in the 1911 *Standard Oil* decision. In that ruling, the Court held that certain monopolies that did not harm the public welfare could stand if they were deemed not unreasonable.[103] This flexibility seemed to align with Roosevelt's views of dynamic constitutionalism even if Roosevelt was less sure that the power to determine reasonableness should rest with courts. Roosevelt noted, "I think it is a good thing to have had those decisions."[104]

Despite Roosevelt's clearly articulated restrictions and his praise for the judiciary in general, "the recall of judicial decisions was widely and easily misunderstood."[105] President Taft argued that it would foster a tyranny of the majority.[106] The *New York Times* belittled Roosevelt's January 1912 *Outlook* article, which outlined the rationale for decision recall, as "the craziest article ever published by a man of high standing and responsibility in the Republic" and speculated that it "greatly alarmed the most radical of his followers."[107] Henry Cabot Lodge was not alone among Progressive Republicans when he spoke of his numerous disagreements with his friend, "the Colonel," and that decision recall was one such example.[108] Roosevelt's plan did not receive widespread support even within the Progressive movement. Its platform backed off explicitly endorsing decision recall and settled on vague language. It called only for "restriction of the power of the courts as shall leave to the people the ultimate authority to determine fundamental questions of social welfare and public policy."[109] With Roosevelt's defeat in the November election, the plan lost its most prominent advocate on the national scene.

[102] Roosevelt to William Ransom, 28 April 1912, Roosevelt Papers, Series 3A, Reel 375, quoted in Ross, 143.
[103] The Court articulated the rule of reason in *Standard Oil Co. v. United States*, 221 U.S. 1 (1911) and *United States v. American Tobacco Co.*, 221 U.S. 106 (1911).
[104] Roosevelt, quoted in William Harbaugh, *Power and Responsibility: The Life and Times of Theodore Roosevelt* (New York: Octagon Books, 1975), 379.
[105] Murphy, 452.
[106] William Taft, "The Judiciary and Progress," a speech in Toledo, Ohio, 8 March 1912. Printed by the 62nd Congress, 2nd Session, Document No. 408.
[107] "The Short Way with the Courts," *New York Times*, 6 January 1912, 12.
[108] "Alarms His Own Followers: Recall of Judicial Decision Too Much for the Progressives, Even," *New York Times*, 22 February 1912, 5.
[109] Progressive Party Platform of 1912, 5 November 1912. John T. Woolley and Gerhard Peters, *The American Presidency Project* [online]. Santa Barbara, CA: University of California (hosted), Gerhard Peters (database), http://www.presidency.ucsb.edu/ws/?pid=29617.

II.c. *Working with the System: Women's Legislation and Substantive Due Process*

As Progressive disagreement over judicial recall and decision recall suggests, there was no clear consensus among Progressives about how best to limit or otherwise manipulate judicial power. While there might have been an increasing consensus that the Constitution was interpreted to block social reform, there was little agreement on how to react. Nowhere was this more apparent than in the opposite fortunes of female and male laborers in securing protective legislation before state and federal benches.

Lochner v. New York split the Court 5 to 4 on whether to invalidate a New York state law that mandated a sixty-hour per week limit for bakers. The statute was struck down on due process grounds: "The statute necessarily interferes with the right of contract between the employer and the employees," and that right was understood to be "part of the liberty of the individual protected by the 14th Amendment of the Federal Constitution."[110] According to Justice Peckham, by singling out bakers for protection, New York infringed on the freedom of this particular class of laborers to determine the terms of their own employment contracts. For the Court majority, the legislature construed bakers as incapable of acting on their own behalf suggesting that "bakers as a class are not equal in intelligence and capacity to men in other trades or manual occupations, or that they are not able to assert their rights and care for themselves without the protecting arm of the state."[111] If that were an accurate assessment of bakers, then the Court might have allowed the state to exercise its police powers to provide for this particular class of laborers. From this perspective, *Lochner* did not necessarily contradict the doctrine of police powers. Instead, it constructed a substantive test for the exercise of those powers, a substantive test that judges would arbitrate.[112]

Three years after the *Lochner* ruling, the Supreme Court considered the constitutionality of an Oregon statute, which similarly imposed a per-week ceiling on work hours for women. In *Muller v. Oregon*, the Court ruled unanimously that the state could regulate work-hour limits for *female* laborers in direct contradiction to the *Lochner* precedent.[113] Even though Justice Brewer acknowledged, "women whether married or single, have equal contractual and personal rights with men," the Court nevertheless held that the state could curb their rights.[114] Constitutional scholar Owen Fiss has argued that the important difference between female and male laborers was their access

---

[110] *Lochner v. New York*, 198 U.S. 45 (1905), 54.

[111] Ibid., 58.

[112] See Edward Purcell, Jr., *Brandeis and the Progressive Constitution* (New Haven: Yale University Press, 2000): "The constitutional point was not the assertion of limits on government but the assertion of the judiciary's power to pronounce what those limits were.... Substantive due process meant that the ultimate power to judge the 'reasonableness' of ... legislative actions lay with the federal judiciary" (40).

[113] *Muller v. Oregon*, 208 U.S. 412 (1908).

[114] Ibid., 419.

to political participation. Since women did not hold the vote in national elections and in many state elections, the government could more logically claim women as dependents.[115] Justice Brewer's opinion did note that women could not vote: "It thus appears that, putting to one side the elective franchise, in the matter of personal and contractual rights, they stand on the same plane as the other sex. Their rights in these respects can no more be infringed than the equal rights of their brothers."[116] However, the decision was *not* primarily based on the idea that the state must defend women because they could not defend their own interests through the venues of pluralist democratic politics, a key difference between this ruling and the 1923 *Adkins* decision.[117] Rather, it was grounded in the idea that women were biologically distinct and served a purpose unique to the health of the state in their capacity as wives and mothers. Therefore, the argument that the Oregon law violated *Lochner* "assumes that the difference between the sexes does not justify a different rule respecting a restriction of the hours of labor."[118] This assumption, Brewer maintained, was faulty.[119] By distinguishing between the sexes, the Court accepted the rationale advocated by numerous progressive women's organizations that had lobbied for the protective legislation.

The decision in *Muller* relied on data, compiled by Louis Brandeis and Josephine Goldmark, to "prove" that women were more fragile than men and thus in greater need of protective legislation. Brandeis and Goldmark were recruited to defend the Oregon law by the National Consumers' League (NCL).[120] During the Progressive era new organizational forms like interest groups such as the NCL were a response to a growing sense that existing channels of participation, namely, the political party, were increasingly corrupt and fostered government dysfunction through patronage, which blocked skilled leadership. These new groups were often explicitly anti-party, calling for citizens to abandon their party and instead to advocate their particular interests as farmers, laborers, women, and so on. This proliferation of interest

---

[115] Owen Fiss, *History of the Supreme Court of the United States*, Volume 7: *Troubled Beginnings of the Modern State, 1888–1910* (New York: Cambridge University Press, 2006), 35.

[116] *Muller v. Oregon*, 208 U.S. 412 (1908), 419.

[117] See Part IV of this chapter.

[118] *Muller v. Oregon*, 208 U.S. 412 (1908), 420.

[119] With regard to that gender distinction and the interest of the state, Brewer stated: "That woman's physical structure and the performance of maternal functions place her at a disadvantage in the struggle for subsistence is obvious. This is especially true when the burdens of motherhood are upon her. Even when they are not ... continuance for a long time on her feet at work, repeating this from day to day, tends to have injurious effects upon the body, and, as healthy mothers are essential to vigorous offspring, the physical wellbeing of woman becomes an object of public interest and care in order to preserve the strength and vigor of the race" (422).

[120] The NCL was a national organization that lobbied for protective legislation for women. Theda Skocpol, *Protecting Soldiers and Mothers: The Political Origins of Social Policy in the United States* (Cambridge, MA: Harvard University Press, 1992), 382–94.

groups outside and in rejection of party affiliation provided institutional foundations for what political scientists would identify over the early twentieth century as pluralism, and these new institutions conflicted with the consensual and anti-class assumptions that undergirded civic republicanism. Elisabeth Clemens notes how these new institutions clashed with republican ideals when she identifies their critical quandary: "the puzzle was how 'the people' could employ a model of political organization associated with corrupt corporate lobbying and 'class legislation' that, by definition, were opposed to the common good." Clemens locates the resolution of that puzzle in "a transformation of political norms, motives, and practices" that suggests the slow abandonment of civic republican conceptions and the embrace of liberal pluralism.[121]

Brandeis and Goldmark's legal strategy was to exploit the differences between the sexes, to embrace patriarchal constructions of women's roles as republican wives and mothers, and to argue for protective legislation on these grounds.[122] As Francis Kelly, the NCL's general secretary, argued, "The inescapable facts are, however, that men do not bear the children, are free from the burdens of maternity and are not susceptible to the same measures as women, to the poisons characteristic of certain industries.... Women will always need many laws different from those needed by men."[123] *Muller* was not based on an equality framework but on the idea that state intervention was needed to protect women due to their more fragile state and thereby to ensure healthy republican motherhood.

The argument was not that liberty of contract was per se unconstitutional, but that women were entitled to special state protections given their unique social role.[124] As such, these organizations *relied* on the rationale of substantive due process – the very doctrine that labor groups were often fighting against – to maintain protective legislation passed for female laborers.[125]

[121] Elisabeth Clemens, *The People's Lobby: Organizational Innovation and the Rise of Interest Group Politics in the United States, 1890–1925* (Chicago: University of Chicago Press, 1997), 3. On the new interest groups as an anti-partisan response to the two-party system, see pages 17–40.

[122] While the majority of women's groups assumed sex difference and argued for protective laws, others, like the National Women's Trade Union League, demanded equality legislation. See Holly McCammon, "The Politics of Protection: State Minimum Wage and Maximum Hours Laws for Women in the United States, 1870–1930," *Sociological Quarterly* 36 (Spring 1995), 222–3.

[123] Florence Kelley, quoted in Susan Lehrer, *Origins of Protective Legislation for Women, 1905–1925* (Albany: State University of New York Press, 1987), 6.

[124] The Court did approve work-hour restrictions for male miners. *Cantwell v. Missouri*, 199 U.S. 603 (1905). As Skocpol (1992) argues, the data used in the Brandeis Brief for *Muller* was not gender specific: "women's biological vulnerabilities were highlighted in the 'facts' and expert opinions ... even though most of them were gleaned from European sources that had often advocated protections for workers in general" (394).

[125] Labor organizations, particularly the American Federation of Labor (AFL) under Samuel Gompers, opposed legislative and litigative routes to social reform, particularly as the Court continued to interpret regulations as a constraint on trade union activities in cases like *Loewe v. Lawlor*, 208 U.S. 274 (1908). It also lobbied against legislation to secure minimum wages,

Theda Skocpol has noted that the women's organizations did not challenge the logic of substantive due process but made it "fit" with the legal objectives of maintaining protective legislation for women.[126] Thus, Brandeis's strategy relied on judicial authority and particularly on the legitimacy of courts to review legislation.

That the *Muller* case was brought by a new political institution, an interest group such as the National Consumers' League, whose invention was premised, in part, on the Progressive rejection of parties, exemplifies not only "institutional thickening" that took shape at the turn of the twentieth century but also that more outlets of popular expression other than parties were putting forward claims on constitutional meaning. As parties weakened, these new groups – labor unions, consumer organizations, women's groups – engaged in innovative forms of political participation, advocating new infrastructure such as recall and referenda, but also directly lobbying legislators, seeking access to executive agencies, and supporting litigation when potential rulings placed their policy objectives in jeopardy. Gone were republican claims of common good or at least dueling partisan visions of common good. They were replaced by popular organizational forms of direct engagement seeking particular interests through whatever means necessary, for example, through legislative, executive, and judicial routes: "What changed [during the Progressive era] was not the simple presence of interests, factions, or pressure groups, but the identity of those who organized as factions and the character of their relationship to political outcomes."[127] In other words, lobbying on behalf of particular "class" interests increasingly became the norm, and if the courts were one possible venue to achieve policy objectives, especially given the legal realist assumptions that the law was essentially politics by other means, then utilizing that judicial power could become far more productive than de-legitimizing it. Additionally, as these new groups formed and engaged in litigation, even more claims on constitutional meaning proliferated and were now backed by institutional forms other than parties. The potential chaos of these multiple claims only compelled further the ongoing legal academic project to imagine and assert

---

maximum hours, and workplace safety rules because such legislation, like the Erdman Act of 1898, would hamstring laborers' abilities to bargain privately. In 1914, the AFL passed a resolution to that effect: "the question of the regulation of wages and hours of labor should be undertaken through trade union activity, and not made subjects of laws through legislative enactments" (Skocpol, 211). See George Lovell, *Legislative Deferrals: Statutory Ambiguity, Judicial Power, and American Democracy* (New York: Cambridge University Press, 2003), 51–7, 62, 72, 88–91; Forbath, 1989, 1208, and Paul Kens, *Lochner v. New York: Economic Regulation on Trial* (Lawrence: University Press of Kansas, 1998), 52.

[126] Skocpol, 41, 55–56. See also Karen Orren and Stephen Skowronek, *The Search for American Political Development* (New York: Cambridge University Press, 2004), 98–108. On the separation of gendered legislation from other social reform legislation, see Julie Novkov, *Constituting Workers, Protecting Women: Gender, Law, and Labor in the Progressive Era and New Deal Years* (Ann Arbor: University of Michigan Press, 2001).

[127] Clemens, 29.

judicial interpretive superiority to be grounded in one of the republic's earliest articulations of judicial responsibilities, that is, the *Marbury* ruling.

Furthermore, by ruling that a substantive due process rationale could be summoned or at least not directly challenged to secure protections for female laborers while it could be used to invalidate similar laws for male laborers, the Court positioned itself differently relative to two groups that might otherwise have been natural allies in a broader Progressive anti-Court movement. The disjuncture between *Lochner* and *Muller* showcases how one wing of the Progressive movement could harness judicial support by fitting its aims within the confines of doctrinal analysis while another wing eschewed legislative and judicial routes altogether. Since women's organizations were achieving their objectives through the judiciary, there was no clear reason to advocate measures that might strip it of its powers.

III. Congressional and Presidential Harnessing during the Progressive Era

The conventional account of Progressive anti-judicial sentiment is that judges ruling their partisan preferences triggered a growing wave of popular hostility, and yet, that hostility never materialized as successful statutory curbing of federal judicial power due to the development of normative deference to judicial authority. In this section, I dispute this characterization by discussing examples of congressional and presidential relations with the judiciary. First, I point to successful passage of court-curbing legislation in the 1910s and 1930s. Second, I argue that these actions, as well as FDR's Court-packing proposal, were minimalist and are better thought of as explicit attempts to harness judicial power rather than to undermine judicial legitimacy. They were narrowly targeted measures that often triggered criticism from more radical Progressives. Third, I show that the outcomes of inter-branch conflicts that look like defenses of or deference to independent judicial authority if not judicial supremacy, such as the collapse of a Court-packing initiative, may be explained, at least in part, without referencing sentiment toward the judiciary at all. As such, these outcomes are not sufficient indicators of normative deference to independent judicial authority or judicial supremacy.

III.a. *Congressional Jurisdiction-Stripping and Ambiguous Statutory Language*
In 1914, Congress passed the Clayton Antitrust Act, and in 1932, it passed the Norris-LaGuardia Act. Each piece of legislation stripped federal courts of jurisdiction.[128] Since the American Federation of Labor endorsed both, scholars have suggested that these two Acts reflected the growing power of labor as a political constituency. Regardless, the passage of these measures should call

---

[128] Clayton Antitrust Act of 1914, 38 Stat. 730, codified at 15 U.S.C. § 12–27, 29 U.S.C. § 52–53; Norris-LaGuardia Act of 1932, 47 Stat. 70, codified at (29 U.S.C. § 101 et seq.).

into question, by the terms of the standard definition of attacks on independent judicial authority – reviewed in Chapter 1 – the claim that court-curbing has failed since Reconstruction.[129]

That the Supreme Court ignored the Clayton Act's jurisdiction-stripping provisions and labor protections seems to lend credibility to the judicial supremacy thesis.[130] And yet, the Court upheld similar provisions in the Norris-LaGuardia Act. Explanations for this difference rely on changes in the Court's members: when the Court considered the Clayton Act in 1921, the justices were hostile to labor's demands, but when it considered the Norris-LaGuardia Act twenty years later, the justices – the majority appointed by FDR – had abandoned liberty of contract and substantive due process rationales and were more sympathetic to interpretations supporting labor's objectives.

I offer a different explanation.[131] The Clayton Act and the Norris-LaGuardia Act were attempts to rein in judicial power, the latter more forcefully than the former. But the Court struck down the Clayton Act not simply because the justices held policy preferences opposed to labor interests. Rather, it could do so because the Act's language was *purposively* ambiguous, that is, legislators *recognized* lack of clarity in their own statutory language but were unwilling or unable to alter it.[132] Such purposive ambiguity suggests that members of Congress wanted to use the Act to signal policy responsiveness to their

---

[129] Most studies maintain that attacks – including stripping jurisdiction – have failed since Reconstruction. See Segal and Spaeth, 70–1; Lee Epstein and Thomas Walker, *Constitutional Law for a Changing America: Institutional Powers and Constraints*, 4th ed. (Washington, DC: Congressional Quarterly Press, 2001), 93; Greg Ivers, *American Constitutional Law: Power and Politics*, Volume 1: *Constitutional Structure and Political Power* (Boston: Houghton Mifflin, 2001), 71.

[130] Scholars have pointed to the Supreme Court's invalidation of sections of the Clayton Anti-Trust Act as proof of an anti-labor countermajoritarian Court. In this reading, Congress passed a clear statute supporting unions' right to strike and curbing the Court's ability to enjoin strikes, and the Court ignored legislative intent and the jurisdiction-stripping. See Stanley Kutler, "Labor, the Clayton Act, and the Supreme Courts," *Labor History* 3 (1962); Fortbath, 1991, 154–8; Hattam, 1993, 163–4.

[131] This explanation has been put forth by George Lovell (2003). Lovell makes these arguments about the Clayton Anti-Trust Act and the Norris-LaGuardia Act to illustrate a variety of assumptions in normative and empirical judicial politics scholarship on the Court's countermajoritarian potential. I examine these acts to highlight the jurisdiction-stripping that *did* occur during the Progressive era, thereby contradicting empirical claims about judicial supremacy, and to illustrate that it was narrow or redundant, thereby showing a desire to maintain judicial authority generally.

[132] Purposive ambiguity is distinct from unintentional ambiguity. Judicial interpretation, it has been argued, necessarily reads "between the lines" of an ambiguous statute to determine meaning and leads to judicial policy-making. R. Shep Melnick, *Between the Lines: Interpreting Welfare Rights* (Washington, DC: Brookings Institution, 1994). But ambiguity may be an intentional effort to secure a supportive coalition, that is, support is generated because members believe the proposal means different things. See Robert Katzman, *Courts and Congress* (Washington, DC: Brookings Institution, 1997), 60. This ambiguity may also deflect accountability to the judiciary while reaping the benefits of securing legislation and blaming the Courts if it is subsequently overturned.

constituents, but they did not want to go as far as their constituents might have demanded, and they did not want to take responsibility for acting conservatively. Leading Progressive legal scholars at the time these bills were under consideration clearly recognized how judicial review enabled members of Congress to skirt accountability. The dean of Harvard Law School, Roscoe Pound, pointed out that knowledge that the Court would review a statute would lead legislators to be carelessly vague with their language.[133] Harrison Smalley zeroed in on the *strategic* potential of ambiguity, noting that legislators could depend on the Court during the 1910s to provide a conservative rendering of an ambiguous statute.[134]

I also argue that the jurisdiction-stripping provisions and labor protections in the Norris-LaGuardia Act survived judicial scrutiny not only because new deferential justices were on the Court or because this Act's language was less ambiguous than the wording of the Clayton Act – thereby giving judges less room to interpretively maneuver – but also because its jurisdiction-stripping provisions had *already* been accepted by employers and employees alike, and that these provisions codified as statute the evident jurisprudential trends of recent years.[135] As such, legislators could include them in order to reap electoral benefits without dramatically weakening the judiciary's position. Put differently, the Court could maintain the Norris-LaGuardia Act because its jurisdiction-stripping was redundant to the point that judges had already signaled they were moving in their rulings. In short, the rulings on these Acts were not just effects of new judges or normative deference to judicial authority. They can be explained by identifying indicators of harnessing judicial power, in particular, purposive ambiguity and the symbolic politics of redundant legislation.

III.a.1. *Purposive Ambiguity of the Clayton Act.* In *Duplex Printing v. Deering*, the Court invalidated the Clayton Act and, this ruling is often cast as another instance of the Progressive era's judicial countermajoritarianism.[136] Organized labor had persistently sought relief against injunctions since the mid-1890s, and Samuel Gompers heralded the Clayton Antitrust Act as achieving that aim.[137] Thus, scholars often describe the decision as undoing labor's efforts and countering the stated objective of Democrats and

---

[133] Roscoe Pound, "Courts and Legislation," *American Political Science Review* 7 (August 1913), 378–9.

[134] Harrison Smalley, "Nullifying the Law by Judicial Interpretation," *Atlantic Monthly*, April 1911, 455, 461.

[135] On the claim that Norris-LaGuardia survived judicial scrutiny because its language was clearer than that of the Clayton Act, see Forbath, 1991, 161–2; William B. Gould, IV, *A Primer on American Labor Law*, 3rd ed. (Cambridge: MIT Press, 1993), 23; and, Melvyn Dubofsky, *The State and Labor in Modern America* (Chapel Hill: University of North Carolina Press, 1994), 104, 255–6.

[136] *Duplex Printing v. Deering*, 254 U.S. 443 (1921)

[137] Forbath, 1991, 157.

Progressive Republicans.[138] As George Lovell has shown, however, the ruling was a plausible rendering of an intentionally ambiguous statute. Legislators left the language unclear so that they could appear responsive to constituent demands. If the Court ruled against the Act, then the Court would be a useful electoral foil. It could be presented as a public enemy.

The lawsuit was triggered when the Duplex Printing Press Company refused to recognize the International Association of Machinists as the collective bargaining unit of Duplex employees. In response, the union refused to handle or transport Duplex products. Duplex sought injunctive relief against the boycott. Although district and circuit courts read the Clayton Act to protect the union's action, the Supreme Court granted relief to Duplex.[139]

The Court's decision focused on Sections 20 and 6 of the Clayton Act. Section 20 prohibited judges from issuing injunctions except when it was "necessary to prevent irreparable injury to property, or to a property right, of the party making the application, for which injury there is no adequate remedy in law." It also defined and exempted a specific set of union activities from injunction including quitting or striking, picketing, boycotting, paying benefits to strikers, assembling, and "general," which meant "doing any act or thing which might lawfully be done in the absence of such dispute by any party thereto." Section 6 stipulated "That the labor of a human being is not a commodity or article of commerce" and that

> nothing contained in the antitrust laws shall be construed to forbid the existence and operation of labor, agricultural, or horticultural organizations, instituted for the purposes of mutual help, and not having capital stock or conducted for profit, or to forbid or restrain individual members of such organizations from lawfully carrying out the legitimate objects thereof, nor shall such organizations, or the members thereof, be held or construed to be illegal combinations or conspiracies in restraint of trade under the antitrust laws.

The Section 6 language responded to judicial use of injunctions under federal authority to bar monopolist restraints of trade under the Sherman Act. If labor was defined as not an article of commerce, judicial authority to issue injunctions could not be justified under the Constitution's interstate commerce clause. The legislative language appears to have been intended to limit or reverse the implications of earlier rulings in *In re Debs*, *Loewe v. Lawlor*, and *Adair v. United States*.

To grant the injunction, the Court needed to navigate around Section 20, which seemingly constrained judicial power to enjoin the union from boycotting, and it needed to characterize the union's activity as beyond boundaries defined in Section 6. To do this, Justice Pitney grounded his reasoning in

---

[138] Limiting court-issued injunctions against labor strikes had been a repeated plank of the Democratic Party National Platforms since 1896.

[139] 253 Fed 722, 2nd Circuit, 1918, affirming 247 F. 192; 1917 U.S. District, Southern District New York.

congressional floor speeches. As Lovell has argued, Pitney could use legislative history to this effect because of ambiguities in the language, ambiguities that members of Congress themselves duly recognized and refused to clarify before passing the legislation. Ultimately, *Duplex* rendered the Clayton Act to be "mere legislative codification of the much-criticized judge-made law that was in place before the passage of the Clayton Act," and not as an attempt to refute that tradition and set labor law on a new footing.[140]

The Court's reading of Section 20 focused on whether the union's boycott and the consequential imposition on Duplex's profitability amounted to a violation of property right. Congress had considered an earlier anti-injunction bill, the Pearre bill, which stipulated explicitly that the right to do business was *not* a property right. The AFL lobbied hard for this bill between 1906 and 1912, but this definition of property right, which excluded a right to do business, was dropped from the Clayton bill.[141] As Lovell has argued, this omission did not go unnoticed by members of Congress. In the 1912 and 1914 floor debates on the Clayton bill, legislators pointed to differences between the Pearre language and the Clayton language, and stated that the Court might interpret the lack of a clear definition of property right in the Clayton draft to the detriment of labor aims. Representative MacDonald, a Progressive from Michigan, attempted to amend the legislation by including the Pearre definition of property, but the amendment failed.[142] Representative Martin Madden (R-IL), who opposed the legislation, appreciated that the Clayton language seemed to ensure that labor exemptions from injunctions would be "the rankest nonsense."[143] And Senator Knute Nelson (R-MN) recognized the likelihood that judges would maintain the existing definition of property, that is, they would "hold that the right to carry on business, the right to run a factory, is property."[144] For Nelson, that the Court might read a restriction on property right, without clear congressional articulation of what that restriction might be, constituted "a false promise to labor."[145] He contended that the language served no substantive purpose; it would only lead the Court to reaffirm its prior holdings. Nelson suggested that the entire section without the clear definition of property right was nothing but a symbolic measure to gain labor's support: it was "a sop to encourage and make labor organizations believe

---

[140] Lovell, 101.

[141] Ibid., 125–33. The Peare bill restricted the definition of property right: "no right to continue the relation of employer and employee, or to assume or create such a relation with any particular person or persons, or at all, or to carry on business of any particular kind or at any particular place, or at all, shall be construed, held, considered, or treated as property or as constituting a property right." (HR 18752, 59th Congress. See Hearing before the Committee on the Judiciary of the House of Representatives, 59th Congress, 1st Session, in relation to Anti-Injunction and Restraining Orders [Washington, DC: Government Printing Office, 1906], 6).

[142] Ibid., 9611.

[143] *Congressional Record*, Vol. 51, 9082.

[144] Ibid., 14533.

[145] Ibid., 14534.

they are getting something in this section that is not provided for in the other section."[146] Justice Pitney characterized the statute in ways foreshadowed by Nelson, namely, that it "is merely declaratory of the law as it stood before" and created no substantive change.[147]

As for Section 6, Justice Pitney held that the Clayton Act provided legal recognition of unions but that it did not sanction the boycott.[148] This distinction between organizations and activities seems contrived. What actions could the union undertake as part of its bargaining leverage if not those stipulated in Section 20? Yet the possibility that judges might make a distinction such as this was repeatedly recognized in congressional debate, and clarifications in the language to list specifically protected activities were rejected. Representative Dick Morgan (R-OK) argued that if the language of "activities" was not included, the statute accomplished nothing at all: "It would hardly seem necessary in this day and age of the world to enact a law which merely permits the existence of labor organizations.... If the provisions of our antitrust laws should not apply to labor organizations Congress should in plain and clear language so declare. We should not speak in ... doubtful uncertain, indefinite terms."[149] Gompers wanted language to cover labor *activities* and *organizations*, but President Wilson was unwilling to go along with the change.[150] As such, Section 6 protected labor unions themselves from judicial dissolution, but it did little else. Representative Victor Murdock (R-KA) recognized deflection of accountability in these machinations: "Some friends of labor say that the amendment does exempt organized labor from the provisions of the Sherman antitrust law, but its enemies say that it does not exempt organized labor. Who knows? No man on the floor of this House. Who will determine? The Courts."[151]

Ambiguities in Sections 6 and Section 20 enabled the Supreme Court to read the Clayton Act narrowly, to maintain its jurisdictional authority, and to render the law as nothing more than codification of existing precedent

---

[146] Ibid., 14533.
[147] *Duplex Printing Press Co. v. Deering*, 254 U.S. 443 (1921), 471.
[148] According to Pitney, Section 6 "assumes the normal objects of a labor organization to be legitimate, and declares that nothing in the antitrust laws shall be construed to forbid the existence and operation of such organizations or to forbid their members from *lawfully* carrying out their legitimate objects; and that such an organization shall not be held in itself – merely because of its existence and operation – to be an illegal combination or conspiracy in restraint of trade. But there is nothing in the section to exempt such an organization or its members from accountability where it or they depart from its normal and legitimate objects and engage in an actual combination or conspiracy in restraint of trade. And by no fair or permissible construction can it be taken as authorizing any activity otherwise unlawful, or enabling a normally lawful organization to become a cloak for an illegal combination or conspiracy in restraint of trade as defined by the antitrust laws" (Ibid., 469).
[149] House Report 1168, 63rd Congress, pt. 4.
[150] Wilson was not a clear supporter of the AFL's demands, but he was constrained by the terms of the 1912 Democratic platform to pursue some legislation that could be legitimately construed as providing some relief against injunction (Lovell, 116–7).
[151] *Congressional Record*, Vol. 51, 9542.

rather than a congressional attempt to force the Court onto new ground. Importantly, legislators recognized the possibility of this interpretation. Senators William Borah (R-ID) and Atlee Pomerene (R-OH) both worried that Section 6 did nothing other than confirm what the courts had already stipulated.[152] But the passage of the legislation would nevertheless carry potential electoral benefits, redounding to Progressive Republicans and Democrats. As such, legislative behavior in the passage of the Clayton Act is an example of politically harnessing judicial power. It appears to be an attempt to weaken judicial authority by curbing jurisdiction and thereby reaping potential electoral benefits; however, its ambiguous language leaves room to maintain useful judicial authority while it positions the Court as the unresponsive culprit. Furthermore, given the ambiguous language, judicial invalidation of the act cannot be definitively taken as a countermajoritarian action. Pitney's reading was plausible, and members of Congress had recognized it as possible if not likely. Such recognition suggests that ambiguous language was not wholly unintentional.

III.a.2. *The Jurisdiction-Stripping Redundancy of the Norris-LaGuardia Act.* The Norris-LaGuardia Act, passed in 1932, was less ambiguous than the Clayton Act. According to Lovell, Norris-LaGuardia revealed that Congress was very willing to curb independent judicial authority:

> The statute directly *attacks* the power of federal judges. It seeks to reverse the effects of several Supreme Court decisions by stripping federal courts of jurisdiction to hear many types of cases related to labor disputes. By successfully narrowing the jurisdiction of the federal courts in an effort to reverse a line of Supreme Court decisions, Norris-LaGuardia demonstrates the importance of the congressional power to limit judicial policy making by controlling the jurisdiction of federal courts.... Moreover, by sharply curtailing the use of injunctions in labor disputes, the act dismantled the primary institutional means through which labor organizations were regulated.[153]

By defining jurisdiction-stripping as an attack, Lovell holds to the traditional definition of anti-Court attack summarized in Chapter 1, and as such empirically undermines the validity of the normative supremacy thesis. However, since the legislation removed jurisdiction that judges had already indicated they no longer wanted, the curbing was symbolic, securing electoral capital without wholly undermining courts.[154]

---

[152] Ibid., 13918 and 13912.

[153] Lovell, 162.

[154] The jurisdiction-stripping provision was criticized as infringing on independent judicial authority (see 75 *Congressional Record* 5276). LaGuardia countered that the Court was in danger of losing diffuse support among the public and that such a restriction would help it to recover (75 *Congressional Record*, 5478–9, 5481, 5486). The framers of the court-curbing legislation positioned themselves as friends of judicial authority more generally, recognizing the need to maintain public support for the Court's integrity.

Section 3 of Norris-LaGuardia restricted judges by declaring "yellow-dog" contracts "contrary to the public policy of the United States" and therefore "unenforceable." A yellow-dog contract prohibited employees from joining a union. Section 3's language responded to the Court's ruling in *Adair v. United States*. In that case, the Court ruled that a law, which made it a misdemeanor for employers in the railroad industry to force employees to sign yellow-dog contracts, was invalid because it violated the liberty of both parties to consider and sign whatever kind of contract they wished.[155]

The yellow-dog provision in Norris-LaGuardia together with the *Adair* ruling suggests the onset of a potential inter-branch crisis. However, judicial and employer understandings of the yellow-dog contract had changed since *Adair*. By the late 1920s, the use of yellow-dogs had fallen out of favor with many employers as mechanisms to counter union activities.[156] And judges had grown less willing to support them. When defending the bill against possible judicial nullification, Senator Norris pointed to a pattern of recent rulings more sympathetic to labor. He also noted that the judiciary had provided an unclear pattern in yellow-dog opinions. Given this lack of clear precedent, he averred that the Court might uphold the proposed yellow-dog provision.[157] This sentiment was reiterated by Senator Walsh, who noted Chief Justice Taft's opposition to yellow-dog contracts to indicate a shift in legal thinking: "A wide change has come over the judicial minds of the country as to the question of liberty of contract, the early decisions having been induced, as everybody must now realize, by reason of the judges entertaining antiquated and obsolescent views concerning economic questions."[158] Senator Wagner also emphasized shifts in judicial attitudes that would enable Section 3 to stand.[159]

Besides signaling congressional antipathy toward yellow-dogs, legislators sensed that they were on surer footing to the extent that judges were showing themselves to be less inclined to uphold employers' use of yellow-dogs. In this way, the legislation appears as another example of political harnessing of judicial power. While the Norris-LaGuardia Act *curbs* jurisdiction, thereby responding to popular anti-Court sentiment, it *maintains* broader judicial authority because it strips authority that judges have already signaled they no longer want. The jurisdiction-stripping provisions provided benefits to legislators to the extent that they showcased Congress standing up to a judiciary whose rulings were hostile to labor objectives, but the statute essentially codified the trend of judicial thought at stake. Conflict between courts and

---

[155] That earlier law was Section 10 of the Erdman Act of 1898, which the Court struck down in *Adair*.

[156] Daniel R. Ernst, "Common Laborers? Industrial Pluralists, Legal Realists, and the Law of Industrial Disputes, 1915–1943," *Law and History Review* 11 (1993), 59–100.

[157] *Congressional Record*, Vol. 75, 4683.

[158] Ibid., 5018.

[159] Ibid., 4917.

Congress did not materialize; the Court accepted the jurisdiction-stripping authority of the Congress.[160]

III.b. *FDR's Plan: Fears of Dictatorship and Evidence of Longer Term Time Horizons*

Franklin Roosevelt's 1937 proposal for judicial reform is well-trod territory, and generally, scholars frame the episode as a presidential administration attempting to secure its constitutional and policy priorities against a recalcitrant Court, one of whose members ultimately cracks under a threat to judicial independence.[161] Three explanations are often given for FDR's failure to secure his initial plan for up to six new Supreme Court justices and as many as fifty lower federal court judges. First, the Court's behavior – particularly its rulings in the spring of 1937 and Justice Van Devanter's announcement of retirement in May of 1937 – lowered the sense of urgency.[162] In short, a judicial "switch" staved off the presidential threat while bringing about a constitutional "revolution."[163] Second, FDR was uncharacteristically politically inept.

---

[160] Lower federal cases upheld the jurisdiction-stripping provisions. See *Knapp-Monarch Co v. Anderson, et al.* (7 F. Supp. 332, E.D. Ill. (1934)) and *Cinderella Theater Co., Inc. v. Sign Writers' Local Union No. 591* (D.C. Mich. 1934, 6 F. Supp, 164).

[161] On the Court's liberty-of-contract jurisprudence, FDR's proposal, and the justices' responses, see William Leuchtenburg's *The Supreme Court Reborn: The Constitutional Revolution in the Age of Roosevelt* (New York: Oxford University Press, 1995); Jeff Shesol, *Supreme Power: Franklin Roosevelt v. The Supreme Court* (New York: W.W. Norton, 2010); Conrad Black, *Franklin Delano Roosevelt: Champion of Freedom* (New York: Public Affairs, 2003), 404–52; Marian C. McKenna, *Franklin Roosevelt and the Great Constitutional War: The Court-Packing Crisis of 1937* (New York: Fordham University Press, 2002); Burt Solomon, *FDR v. The Constitution: The Court-Packing Fight and the Triumph of Democracy* (New York: Walker, 2009); Laura Kalman, "The Constitution, the Supreme Court, and the New Deal," William E. Leuchtenburg, "Comment on Laura Kalman's Article," and G. Edward White, "Constitutional Change and the New Deal," all in *American Historical Review* 110 (October 2005), 1046–115.

[162] The Senate Judiciary committee decided against recommending FDR's reform proposal to the full Senate by a vote of 10 to 8 within hours of learning of Van Devanter's decision to resign. It was widely known that FDR had promised the seat to Senator Joe Robinson, who was the lead senatorial advocate of the judicial reform but whom the administration suspected as holding conservative leanings. Leonard Baker points to how Van Devanter's resignation defeated the Court-packing plan in his *Back to Back: The Duel between FDR and the Supreme Court* (New York: Macmillan, 1967), 179. On expectation of Robinson's appointment to the Court and FDR's concerns about his conservative leanings, see Solomon, 199–202, and Shesol, 446–60.

[163] While the Court upheld some state legislation meant to cope with the Great Depression, it struck down the majority of New Deal programs between 1934 and 1935. In 1934, the Court upheld state legislative attempts to mitigate the effects of the Depression: *Home Building & Loan Assn. v. Blaisdell,* 290 U.S. 398 (1934) (upheld a Minnesota law that provided a moratorium on mortgage payments, holding that the law did not violate the Constitution's contracts clause), and *Nebbia v. New York,* 291 U.S. 502 (1934) (upheld New York legislation that set milk prices against the claim that it violated due process rights of shopkeepers to set their own prices). In 1935, the Court struck down various pieces of New Deal legislation, most notoriously *A.L.A. Schecter Poultry Corp. v. U.S.,* 295 U.S. 495 (1935) (invalidating

He allegedly misjudged the implications of his landslide 1936 victory. And he fumbled by being unwilling to compromise on his proposal, making atypical errors when repeatedly offered the opportunity to secure additional justices, but not as many as six.[164] In April, Senate majority leader, Joe Robinson, informed FDR that the Senate would agree to two or three justices. And the Senate continued to consider plans that might give Roosevelt as many as three judges as late as May.[165] That such compromise was possible suggests that

the Recovery Act because through it Congress delegated an unconstitutional amount of authority to the president and because the industry at issue bore an indirect connection to interstate commerce).

The timing of *West Coast Hotel v. Parish*, 300 U.S. 379 (1937) in March of 1937 suggests that FDR's threat to "pack" the Court triggered a judicial "switch-in-time" and brought a "constitutional revolution." Bruce Ackerman characterizes the Court's move – in conjunction with the 1936 election – as part of a larger "constitutional moment." Ackerman, *We the People: Transformations* (Cambridge: Belknap Press of Harvard, 1998), 279–344. Leuchtenberg (1995) claims, "it is not surprising, then, that historians speak of 'the Constitutional Revolution of 1937,' for in the long history of the Supreme Court, no event has had more momentous consequences than Franklin Roosevelt's message of 1937" (162).

Some have argued that FDR's threat compelled Justice Roberts to abandon the four conservative justices – Van Devanter, McReynolds, Sutherland, and Butler. Joseph Alsop and Turner Catledge referred to Justice Roberts's switch as "self-salvation by self reversal" in their *The 168 Days* (New York: Doubleday, Doran, 1938), 143. Numerous scholars commenting on *West Coast Hotel* and subsequent cases that upheld the New Deal suggest that the Court succumbed to political expediency. See Edward Corwin, *Constitutional Revolution* (Claremont, CA: Associated Colleges, 1941), 12, 64, and Benjamin Wright, *The Growth of American Constitutional Law* (Boston: Houghton Mifflin, 1942), 200–208, 256–8.

More recently, scholars contend that Roberts's switch in *West Coast Hotel*, which upheld the state of Washington's minimum-wage law for female labourers, reversing both the ten-month-old *Morehead v. New York ex rel. Tipaldo*, 298 U.S. 587 (1936) ruling and *Adkins v. Children's Hospital*, was consistent with his decision in *Nebbia v. New York*. As such, Roberts's decision to join with conservatives in *Tipaldo* was the outlier, and *West Coast Hotel* is less an indicator of caving to political pressures than of reverting to earlier thinking. More certain is the timing. Roberts's position in *West Coast Hotel* was settled *before* FDR's judicial reform or "Court-packing" plan was announced. The delay in announcing the decision was due, in part, to Justice Stone's illness. See Cushman, *Rethinking the New Deal Court: The Structure of a Constitutional Revolution* (New York: Oxford University Press, 1998), 18–25, and Shesol, 414. While FDR's plan may not have triggered Roberts's shift, that claim does not disprove that Roberts was not aware of or reacting to political pressure: "The years 1935–1937 saw more 'Court-curbing' bills introduced in Congress than in any other three-year (or thirty-five-year) period in history." Michael Nelson, "The President and the Court: Reinterpreting the Court-packing Episode of 1937," *Political Science Quarterly* 103 (1988), 273.

[164] Caldeira (1987) argued that the "Court outmaneuvered the President" (1150). Alsop and Catledge (1938) argued that FDR's victory "caused him to throw caution to the winds ... [and that] he believed that compliance with his wishes had become automatic" (60). Michael Nelson (1988) diagnosed FDR with a "dulled strategic sense in the court-packing episode" (278). James Burns called the Court-packing fight "a stunning defeat for the President," in his *Roosevelt: The Lion and the Fox* (New York: Harcourt Brace, 1956), 315.

[165] Hiram Johnson to Garrett McEnerney, 7 May 1937. ("The compromise propositions are those advanced by Hatch, McCarran, McGill, in substance dealing with an increase in the Supreme Court. In my opinion, they are as bad as the President's proposal, but the timid and

legislators were not wholly concerned with maintaining the Court's institutional integrity or deferring to its independent authority. Harnessing judicial power for partisan policy aims was a politically permissible way to end the constitutional standoff. Yet Roosevelt refused to budge.[166] Furthermore, FDR's uncharacteristic lack of political savvy is evidenced by the clumsy shifting rationale for the plan, which was introduced to Congress as a measure to achieve judicial efficiency and then re-packaged for public consumption a month later as a harsher attack on judicial rulings and an effort to "save the Court from itself."[167] This shift created a sense of disingenuousness that

the weak-kneed are likely to seize upon them, so that they will be able to say that they oppose the President's scheme but were in reality favorable to it by a proposition to give him a part of it.... [O]ur great danger is now increasing the Supreme Court by one, two or three in various ways.") Hiram Johnson Papers, Bancroft Library, University of California at Berkeley, part III, box/reel 17. See also Solomon, 184.

[166] Roosevelt's unwillingness to compromise can be defended on multiple grounds. Administrative records suggest that the president may have believed that his plan had strong popular support. Counts of constituent letters were kept from 17 February 1937 to 14 August 1937. President's Secretary's File, Box 165, folder "Supreme Court, Jan. 1937-July 1937," Franklin D. Roosevelt Presidential Library, Hyde Park, New York.

Additionally, Court decisions upholding New Deal programs were based on slim margins. Roberts's shift offered little assurance. Roosevelt noted the New Deal's precarious footing: "Well, in the last two days the no-man's-land has been eliminated, but see what we have in place of it: we are now in Roberts' Land." See Franklin D. Roosevelt, "Excerpts from the Press Conference," 13 April 1937. John T. Woolley and Gerhard Peters, *The American Presidency Project* [online]. Santa Barbara, CA: University of California (hosted), Gerhard Peters (database), http://www.presidency.ucsb.edu/ws/?pid=15389. FDR's concern was echoed by editors of *The Nation* who noted, "The liberal margin of advantage is the margin of Justice Roberts's very changeable mind." "Is the Supreme Court Going Liberal? *The Nation*, 3 April 1937, 368. Even if FDR secured a Court of eleven justices, if one slot went to stealthy conservative Senate majority leader Joe Robinson or if Roberts again wavered, an eleventh justice would maintain for the New Deal a one-vote majority.

Although Van Devanter's departure meant that the conservative bloc was now broken, FDR promised the opening to Senator Robinson, and he was not a reliable Progressive. If Roberts swung back, FDR's progressive policy agenda would still be precarious. Furthermore, being sixty-four years old, Robinson was hardly the picture of new blood that FDR had premised the reorganization on in the first place. FDR lamented, "If I had three vacancies I might be able to sandwich Joe Robinson in," but as he did not, he refused to announce a replacement until the Senate debate on the Court reform played out. FDR to Henry Morgenthau, quoted in Shesol, 450.

Finally, if FDR was more concerned with altering the course of interpretation than getting judges on the bench, his refusal to compromise might well have been rationally strategic. See James Carson and Benjamin Kleinerman, "A Switch in Time Saves Nine: Institutions, Strategic Actors, and FDR's Court-packing Plan," *Public Choice* 113 (2002), 301–24.

[167] See Franklin D. Roosevelt, "Message to Congress on the Reorganization of the Judicial Branch of the Government," 5 February 1937 ("The personnel of the Federal Judiciary is insufficient to meet the business before them. A growing body of our citizens complain of the complexities, the delays, and the expense of litigation in United States Courts"). John T. Woolley and Gerhard Peters, *The American Presidency Project* [online]. Santa Barbara, CA: University of California (hosted), Gerhard Peters (database) http://www.presidency.ucsb.edu/ws/?pid=15360. Franklin Roosevelt, Fireside Chat, 9 March 1937. ("The Court ... has improperly set itself up as a third House of the Congress – a super-legislature, as one of

undermined legislative and popular support. Third, the plan never had wide or deep public support, which is taken to be evidence of popular approval of the Court. Yet polling data are unclear; it is far from certain that the public preferred to maintain a nine-member court. When the plan was announced, the public was evenly divided, and as late as July 1937, a majority, according to one poll, sought some kind of change to the Supreme Court either through FDR's plan or otherwise.[168] Furthermore, this argument confuses outcome with motive, rendering the plan's failure as evidence of public endorsement of judicial supremacy without exploring possible alternative explanations that have potentially little to do with the judiciary itself.

While FDR's unwillingness to compromise, his hubris stemming from his landslide 1936 victory, and unclear levels of public support play some role in explaining why the judicial reform failed, the judicial reform proposal was not simply executive hostility toward a recalcitrant Court. First, the Roosevelt administration had sought to harness the Court's power and enlist its expertise since its earliest days. The packing plan was the most visible manifestation of an effort spanning two years.[169] Second, congressional opposition to FDR's proposal was *not* motivated by a normative defense of the Court's privileged interpretive role. Indeed, some Progressives opposed FDR's plan because it did not go far enough. They challenged the proposal precisely because it did harness judicial power rather than undermine it. Others opposed it not out of loyalty to the Court, but because they feared a powerful executive.[170]

Members of the Roosevelt administration were well aware of the dubious constitutionality of various pieces of legislation, including National Industrial Recovery Act (NIRA) and the Agricultural Adjustment Act (AAA), which were hurriedly constructed to combat the Great Depression. The NIRA's National Recovery Administration (NRA) was roundly criticized. The nonpartisan

the justices has called it – reading into the Constitution words and implications which are not there, and which were never intended to be there. We have, therefore, reached the point as a Nation where we must take action to save the Constitution from the Court and the Court from itself.") John T. Woolley and Gerhard Peters, *The American Presidency Project* [online]. Santa Barbara, CA: University of California (hosted), Gerhard Peters (database), http://www.presidency.ucsb.edu/ws/?pid=15381.

[168] Gallup and Roper polling from February through April suggest that half of those polled supported the president's plan. That number dropped to less than 40 percent by late May. See George Gallup, "Sharp Drop Recorded since Wagner Decision," *Washington Post*, 23 May 1937, quoted in Solomon, 219. However, Elmo Roper's polling, under the auspices of *Fortune* magazine, still found the public divided and seeking some kind of reform as late as July 1937. See "The Fortune Quarterly Survey: IX," *Fortune*, July 1937, 96–7. In this report, 36.9 percent supported the president's plan while 38.1 percent opposed it, and 18.9 percent sought some kind of alternative reform. On public opinion and the Court-packing plan, see generally, Gregory A. Caldeira, "Public Opinion and the U.S. Supreme Court: FDR's Court-Packing Plan," *American Political Science Review* 40 (1987), 1139–53.

[169] Shesol, 508.

[170] For a similar claim, see Brian Feldman, "Evaluating Public Endorsement of the Weak and Strong Forms of Judicial Supremacy," *University of Virginia Law Review* 89 (2003), 1019–32.

Brookings Institution called the program a failure: "Not only did the program fail to work out as planned, but the plan itself was in our judgment a mistaken one."[171] But beyond the actual effects of the program, others worried about its constitutionality. Felix Frankfurter, for example, advised that judicial review of the NIRA be stalled as long as possible so that the current Act might expire, and Congress might draft a constitutional replacement.[172] Similarly, members of the administration doubted the constitutionality of the first AAA. Secretary of Agriculture Henry Wallace told a fellow cabinet member that he hoped the Court would nullify the program so that Congress would be forced to redesign it.[173] Attorney General Homer Cummings was even more forthcoming with his doubts; in a letter to the president he itemized vulnerable New Deal legislation: "the Wagner Bill, which I regarded as of rather doubtful constitutionality. The Guffey Coal Bill, which I thought was clearly unconstitutional. The A.A.A. amendments [meant to correct previously identified constitutional problems with the legislation], which were not in good condition to meet the constitutional test, and which would have to be strengthened to give them any chance at all."[174] In short, members of the executive branch expressed doubts about the constitutionality of programmatic relief legislation. FDR shrugged these concerns away, instead noting the need to try something: "If it fails, admit it frankly and try another. But above all, try something."[175] When it became clear that the Court was identifying the legislation's constitutional flaws already spotted by the administration, the president advocated a solution that would harness judicial authority in the service of stemming the economic crisis: advisory opinions.

Recognizing the likelihood that the Court would overturn the NIRA and the AAA, FDR considered a constitutional amendment that would require the Court to issue an advisory ruling, at the administration's request, on the constitutionality of any legislation. If the Court held the legislation unconstitutional, but it was passed anyway, the matter would be put to the people in the next election. If the majority party was returned to power, Congress could re-pass the legislation, which would no longer stand for review.[176] In short, FDR's amendment proposal had clear Lincolnian roots. It formalized how law would be congealed over time through popular ratification via the normal election cycle. It also recognized, as Lincoln had, the legitimacy of

[171] "Recovery: Baby Scrubbing," *Time*, 29 April 1935, http://www.time.com/time/magazine/article/0,9171,754595,00.html.

[172] Joseph Lash, *Dealers and Dreamers: A New Look at the New Deal* (New York: Doubleday, 1988), 250–1.

[173] Shesol, 176.

[174] Diary of Homer S. Cummings, 20 June 1935, 82–3, Homer S. Cummings Papers, University of Virginia.

[175] Franklin Roosevelt, *Public Papers and Addresses of Franklin D. Roosevelt, 1928–32,* (New York: Random House, 1938), 646.

[176] Harold Ickes, *The Secret Diary of Harold L. Ickes*: Volume 1, *The First Thousand Days, 1933–1936* (New York: Simon & Schuster, 1953), 13 November 1935, 467–8.

dissenting views of constitutional meaning. And, by adding the advisory role of the Court, FDR was clearly seeking to enlist judicial authority to support their efforts. In short, early judicial hostilities toward New Deal federal programs were not clearly manifestations of a partisan countermajoritarian Court but just as possibly the legitimate recognition of obvious constitutional flaws in hastily constructed legislation, flaws that the Roosevelt administration itself recognized.

The Court unanimously declared the NIRA unconstitutional.[177] The AAA was unconstitutional by a vote of 6 to 3, and shortly after that decision was announced, FDR stepped up discussion of possible ways to bring the Court to heel to ensure his policy aims.[178] On 14 January 1936, he wrote to Cummings to learn more about the "McArdle [*sic*] case" as he was under the impression that "Congress withdrew some act from the jurisdiction of the Supreme Court."[179] The turning point in Roosevelt's thinking from jurisdiction-stripping and constitutional amendments and toward appointing legal realist judges who embraced a "living" Constitution came two weeks later when Cummings criticized those alternatives: "If we had liberal Judges, with a lively sense of the importance of the social problems *which have now spilled over State lines*, there would be no serious difficulty."[180] A year later, FDR announced his proposal to restructure the federal judiciary.[181]

Critical players in the plan's defeat were Senator Burton Wheeler, Democrat of Montana, who was the Progressive Party's vice-presidential nominee in 1924, running on a platform of curbing judicial power, and to a lesser extent, Senator Hiram Johnson, Republican of California, who was the Progressive's vice-presidential nominee in 1912 and who also ran on a platform of curbing courts and made a reputation supporting judicial recall. Neither could be plausibly considered strong supporters of judicial power, much less advocates of judicial supremacy. And yet, in 1937, they stood against FDR's plan, which would likely have secured the substantive progressive legislation they supported and tamed the institution they struggled against for much of their political lives. That Progressives, who had long sought to curb judicial power, refused to support FDR's plan to achieve their policy aims, suggests the need to explain the plan's failure without relying on an underlying normative support of independent judicial authority or judicial supremacy. Wheeler was disappointed that the plan did not get to the underlying root cause of judicial oligarchy and feared executive power; Johnson emphasized FDR's slide toward dictatorship.

[177] *A.L.A. Schechter Poultry Corp. v. U.S.*, 295 U.S. 495 (1935)

[178] *U.S. v. Butler*, 297 U.S. 1 (1936)

[179] Franklin Roosevelt to Homer S. Cummings, 14 January 1936, in President's Secretary's Files, Box 165, Franklin D. Roosevelt Presidential Library, Hyde Park, New York.

[180] Homer S. Cummings to Franklin Roosevelt, 29 January 1936, in President's Personal File Box 1820, Franklin D. Roosevelt Presidential Library, Hyde Park, New York. Emphasis in original.

[181] For a full description of the yearlong process of crafting the Court-packing proposal, see Shesol, 239–306.

Wheeler voted for all New Deal legislation except the National Industrial Recovery Act, and he was no friend of courts and judges.[182] In response to the Court's invalidation of the AAA, he endorsed the idea that the Constitution must adapt to socioeconomic circumstance: "There has been a great deal of talk about the sanctity of the Constitution, but I suggest that constitutions are made for men, not men for constitutions."[183] Wheeler was the first prominent Democrat to endorse FDR in his 1932 bid for the presidency, but early support failed to earn him the vice-presidential nomination, and relations soured. Furthermore, like other Progressives including Johnson and LaFollette, Wheeler questioned FDR's Progressive credentials, and Wheeler's support for the president in his second bid for the office "ranged from the lukewarm to the chilly."[184] Indeed, these senators felt that FDR was "betraying progressive ideals" and found Roosevelt's reputation as the new leader of Progressive causes to be "galling and exasperating."[185] This was no more evident than in Wheeler's concerns about the Court-packing proposal.

Wheeler lamented that it failed to accomplish "one of the things the liberals of America have been fighting for. It merely places upon the Supreme Court six political hacks, the same as the President."[186] The proposal was "a mere stopgap which establishes a dangerous precedent.... There is nothing democratic, progressive, or fundamentally sound in the proposal."[187] Wheeler recognized, to his disappointment, that the plan utilized the judiciary as a tool for policy ends without achieving Progressive objectives of more closely tying the judiciary to popular rule. And the press took note of FDR's minimalism, which was in sharp contrast to a flurry of proposed constitutional amendments – including Wheeler's – that would have altered decision rules, judicial structure, or congressional authority.[188] Thomas Powell, writing in the *New York Times Magazine*, commented that FDR's plan was far less revolutionary: "It involves the least disturbance with existing judicial power of

---

[182] Marian C. McKenna, "Prelude to Tyranny: Wheeler, F.D.R., and the 1937 Court Fight," *Pacific Historical Review* 62 (November 1993), 408–9.

[183] Wheeler quoted in Arthur M. Schlesinger, Jr., *The Age of Roosevelt*, Vol. 3: *The Politics of Upheaval* (Boston: Houghton Mifflin, 2003 [1960]), 488.

[184] Robert Bendiner, "Men Who Would Be President: Burton K. Wheeler," *The Nation*, 27 April 1940, 534.

[185] Shesol, 321.

[186] Wheeler, quoted in Alva Johnston, "President Tamer," *Saturday Evening Post*, 13 November 1937, 51, quoted in McKenna, 416.

[187] Burton Wheeler, with Paul Healy, *Yankee from the West* (New York: Doubleday, 1962), 321.

[188] Wheeler's constitutional amendment stipulated that if the Court invalidated a statute then Congress could veto that ruling by a super-majority of two-thirds of both chambers, that vote taking place only after an election of the House had intervened between the Court's ruling and the vote. This proposal would have concentrated power in Congress and, with its provision for an intervening election – in which the ruling could be an issue for voters to consider – with the people themselves. Wheeler's proposal continued the Lincolnian tradition of linking judicial rulings and the stability of law to electoral consent. 75th Congress, 1st Session, S.J. Res. 80 (15 February [calendar day 17 February], 1937). Note that FDR had aides, Ben Cohen and Thomas Corcoran, work on a very similar proposal while Homer Cummings drafted the Court-packing plan. See Black, 404–5.

any suggestion that has been made. The court may still act as it has acted before.... All that happens is that the present holders of judicial office are given some helpmates to add fresh viewpoints to their counsel."[189] This minimalism raised Progressive ire. Echoing Wheeler's assessment, editors at *The Nation* captured the disappointment that more radical Progressives felt when considering FDR's plan. While the editors ultimately endorsed the plan, they did so reluctantly. For them, the proposal was politically expedient; it "does not go to the roots of our judicial oligarchy, but by reorganizing it seeks rather to perpetuate it."[190]

Hiram Johnson, despite being a life-long Republican and despite considering a run for the presidency in 1932, was pleased with the Democratic Party's nominee that year: "I am very glad the Democrats nominated Roosevelt. I think they have as strong a ticket as they could have."[191] He praised Roosevelt's innovative reaction to his nomination: "The mode in which Roosevelt accepted his nomination and immediately flew to Chicago, and there with a spontaneity we seldom see in politics, spoke his mind to the delegates, fired my imagination."[192] Johnson was happy with the election: "I am extremely anxious to see this administration a success, and short of sacrificing my most cherished principles, I will do anything within my power to aid it."[193] In particular, Johnson thought the new president might make common cause with Progressive Republicans:

> I like Roosevelt immensely. I like his good humor, his geniality, his genuine smile, and what I think was his ready agreement, generally speaking, with progressive principles. He told me that since 1928, the Democratic Party under Raskob and Smith had moved to the right (I quote his language) and he in 1932 was endeavoring to turn it back to the left. He said, in so many words, that he has investigated what had been done in California, and that we thought alike, governmentally, and that he desired to preserve during his administration the cordial relations which the campaign had demonstrated existed between him and the Progressives.[194]

[189] Thomas Reed Powell, "For 'Ills' of the Court: Shall We Operate?" *New York Times Magazine*, 18 April 1937, 26.

[190] "Purging the Supreme Court," *The Nation*, 13 February 1937, 173.

[191] Hiram Johnson to Charles McClatchy, 3 July 1932. Hiram Johnson Papers, Bancroft Library, University of California at Berkeley, part III, box/reel 13. On Johnson's thoughts about running against Hoover for the Republican nomination in 1932, see Johnson to B. B. Meek, 26 December 1931; Johnson to Frank Doherty, 26 December 1931; Johnson to Alex McCabe of Hearst Consolidated Publications, 26 December 1931; Johnson to John Francis Neylen, 26 December 1931 (all inquiring whether anyone might make a successful bid against Hoover in the California primaries). Hiram Johnson Papers, Bancroft Library, University of California at Berkeley, part III, box/reel 13.

[192] Hiram Johnson to Charles K. McClatchy, 8 July 1932. Hiram Johnson Papers, Bancroft Library, University of California at Berkeley, part III, box/reel 13.

[193] Hiram Johnson to Charles K. McClatchy, 11 December 1932. Hiram Johnson Papers, Bancroft Library, University of California at Berkeley, part III, box/reel 13.

[194] Hiram Johnson to Charles K. McClatchy, 29 January 1933. Hiram Johnson Papers, Bancroft Library, University of California at Berkeley, part III, box/reel 13. See also Purcell, 25.

Throughout FDR's first term, Johnson sought the president's support on various initiatives, particularly with regard to the regulation of utilities and curbing the Court's jurisdiction on matters related to utility power companies'
pricing.[195]

The judicial reform proposal soured Johnson's impression. He saw the plan
as part of a larger pattern of executive aggrandizement. When included with
FDR's executive reorganization plan, which FDR proposed three weeks before
the judicial reform plan, and the defunct National Recovery Administration,
which had given the president extensive powers to regulate industry, the pattern proved troubling. Johnson wrote to a friend:

> The President mapped his course immediately after the NRA decision, in
> which the whole court joined. He has been beaten from pillar to post upon
> when he conceived the brilliant idea, and how he conceived it. The other
> day Mrs. O'Day let the "cat out of the bag" (she is the great friend of Mrs.
> Roosevelt, as you know, and a Congresswoman) by saying that of course the
> President wanted control of the Supreme Court.[196]

He clearly contended that FDR's plans concentrated too much power in the
Executive: "the power we [legislators] are giving him, taken in conjunction
with events that are occurring like the 'sit-down' strike, with which he is sympathetic, is mighty ominous, and frankly, I fear for my country."[197] Johnson
held that Congress was relinquishing its check against the president. His primary motivation to defeat the judicial bill was to rein in the president, not
to maintain the integrity of the Court: "Down the road Mr. Roosevelt asks
[us to take] lies Dictatorship. It does not make any difference that that purpose is not in his mind, or that perhaps he, himself, would not be Dictator....
[T]his is the inevitable course he asks us to pursue."[198] In other letters, he
noted, "You can count that we are on the road to dictatorship. I will fight it
until I die. I don't care a damn whether there is anybody with me in it or not"
and that the judicial plan, if accepted, "was the beginning of the end of the
Republic."[199] Further indicating that curbing presidential power was Johnson's
primary goal, Johnson wrote of his disdain for Supreme Court justices. In
other words, he was not motivated primarily to save the Court: "I will go on
fighting this thing as strongly as I know how, although [Chief Justice] Hughes

[195] Hiram Johnson to Charles K. McClatchy (3 letters), 8 February 1934, 20 February 1934,
23 February 1934, and Johnson to Louis Howe, Secretary to the President, 26 March 1934.
Hiram Johnson Papers, Bancroft Library, University of California at Berkeley, part III,
box/reel 16.
[196] Hiram Johnson to John Francis Neylan, 26 February 1937. Hiram Johnson Papers, Bancroft
Library, University of California at Berkeley, part III, box/reel 17.
[197] Ibid.
[198] Hiram Johnson to Raymond Noley, editor of *Today*, 13 March 1937. Hiram Johnson Papers,
Bancroft Library, University of California at Berkeley, part III, box/reel 17.
[199] Hiram Johnson to John Francis Neylan, 26 March 1937, and Johnson to Neylan, 24 July
1937. Hiram Johnson Papers, Bancroft Library, University of California at Berkeley, part III,
box/reel 17.

and [Justice] Roberts have nauseated me. I remember when I was fighting for
the recall of the judiciary in California, I used to say that judges were only
men after all, and damned poor men at that. The Supreme Court Judges are
in the same category."[200] Even in the wake of defeating the president's plan,
Johnson's fears of dictatorship were not laid to rest: "I am suspicious enough
to be on my guard in the future, and to fear for a coup d'etat."[201]

Johnson's opposition to FDR's plan was less influential as his fellow
Republicans stayed publicly silent, letting Democratic senators like Wheeler
and Carter Glass of Virginia trigger an intra-party schism. But Johnson's
characterizations of FDR as a potential dictator were not idiosyncratic.
Robert Taft, son of former president and Chief Justice Taft, editorialized
that FDR's proposal was an attempt "to secure personal control of the entire
government."[202] The president of the American Bar Association opined, "If this
legislation becomes valid ... [w]e shall have said that democracy has failed."[203]
Newspaper magnate Frank Gannet drafted an editorial warning, "This proposal should give every American grave concern for it is a step towards absolutism and complete dictatorial powers" and supported various organized
efforts to defeat the bill.[204] Concerns about FDR's dictatorial potential were
evident in letters from the public as well.[205] As one citizen wrote pleadingly to
Chief Justice Hughes:

> DON'T GIVE UP YOUR JOB! Even if you are old and tired, you can't quit now
> for three years. – we, your fellow-countrymen, need you too much, – for four
> or five years more maybe. You can see that the flood of new Dealism, commu-
> nism or whatnot, will flood our country if you are out of the picture, – YOU
> ARE ONLY AND LAST DIKE AGAINST THAT CATASTROPHE.... YOU HAVE SAVED
> THE COUNTRY ONCE FROM THE FATE THAT HAS FALLEN TO THE RUSSIANS,
> THE ITALIANS, AND THE GERMANS.[206]

Another citizen penned, "It seems to me that the time has come to call a halt
on asking for the executive department of government any further powers....
I ask you what would happen to this country with all the vast powers now
centered in the White House if such a man as Huey Long should attain to the

[200] Hiram Johnson to John Francis Neylan, 13 April 1937. Hiram Johnson Papers, Bancroft Library, University of California at Berkeley, part III, box/reel 17.
[201] Johnson to Neylan, 24 July 1937.
[202] "R. A. Taft Decries Plan," *New York Times*, 7 February 1937, 30.
[203] Frederick Stinchfield, "Address before the Civic and Commerce Association at Minneapolis," 22 February 1937, reprinted in George McJimsey, ed., *Documentary History of the Franklin D. Roosevelt Presidency* (Bethesda, MD: University Publications of America, 2000), Vol. 1, 315.
[204] Frank Gannett, "A Statement by Frank E. Gannett, Publisher, Gannett Newspapers, Released to all American newspapers on February 6," in Roosevelt, Franklin D. Papers as President, Official File, FDR Presidential Library, Hyde Park, NY.
[205] See Leuchtenberg, 1995, 137–8 and 337–45, for additional examples of constituency letters against the plan on the grounds of troubling executive aggrandizement.
[206] Ruth Gustafson to Hughes, 6 February 1937. Papers of Charles Evans Hughes, Library of Congress, box 168, reel 130.

presidency."[207] Others were wary of the concentration of executive power once FDR left office. One first-time voter wrote with flattery and concern:

> You are about to make another ideal change regarding the Supreme Court of the United States, and you can do it with many beneficial results. *Yet, I would like to ask you; what of the future?* After your term in office has expired, what would your ideal government be in the hands of a power-mad individual who had no ideals? With you it has been delicately concentrated ... and under a competent man, but we citizens are aware that not all leaders are Franklin Delano Roosevelts ... there will come a day when we shall be bigger hands in the government than mere first-time voters.... When that day comes, I hope we shall not be forced to lead a civil revolution in order to re-establish an honest government. For these reasons, Mr. President, I beg you to reconsider your plan to revise the judiciary, and visualize our future.[208]

These statements suggest that concerns were not to protect the Court per se, but to limit the powers of the president. They were, of course, offset by numerous letters supporting FDR's proposal.[209] They do not *show* definitive evidence that the public was more supportive or opposed to the plan. They *do* offer the arguments made against it; and one that recurred was to the specter of authoritarianism.

Wheeler was also motivated by fear of executive power. The administration sought Wheeler's support for FDR's judicial reform proposal shortly after it was first announced on 5 February 1937. One of FDR's aides, Ben Cohen, drafted a speech for Wheeler to give on the Senate floor backing the proposal and hoping the Court would alter its decisions. Wheeler never gave it.[210] He broke with the administration and issued a press release on 13 February which, while arguing that the judiciary needed reform, nonetheless sounded the alarm over the executive usurpation inherent in the president's plan:

> The usurpation of the legislative functions by the courts should be stopped. But to give the executive the power to control the judiciary is not giving the law-making power back to the branch of the government to which it rightly belongs, but rather is increasing the dangers inherent in the concentration of power in any one branch of our government.[211]

He followed this press release with a nationally broadcast radio address in which he raised the specter of dictatorship: "Hitler and Stalin talk of their democracies. Every despot has usurped the power of the legislative and judicial

---

[207] Charles Adams to Franklin Roosevelt, 14 July 1937. Roosevelt, Franklin D. Papers as President, Official File, File: OF 41 A-AL Unfavorable, Judiciary Reorganization Act of 1937, FDR Presidential Library, Hyde Park, NY.

[208] Paul Allen to Franklin Roosevelt, 9 March 1937, Roosevelt, Franklin D. Papers as President, Official File, File: OF 41 Unfavorable A-AL, Judiciary Reorganization Act of 1937, FDR Presidential Library, Hyde Park, NY.

[209] See footnote 166.

[210] McKenna, 412–3.

[211] Press Release, 13 February 1937, folder 5, box 8, Wheeler Papers, Montana Historical Society, quoted in McKenna, 414.

branches of the government in the name of the necessity for haste to promote the general welfare of the masses." As immediately as he levied the criticism, Wheeler backtracked, noting that FDR had no conscious intent: "I do not believe that President Roosevelt has any such thing in mind." Regardless of whether the president intended a dictatorship, Wheeler struck the same concern as that first-time voter quoted earlier by saying that "such has been the course of events throughout the world."[212] By laying out a rationale for opposition that did *not* rely on defending judicial independence and acknowledging public disaffection with the Court, Wheeler's defection paved the way for Democrats to break ranks. His move eliminated FDR's ability to paint the opposition as so-called economic royalists represented by the minority Republicans.[213]

In short, FDR's plan succumbed not necessarily to a popular and elite norm that the Court was the privileged constitutional interpreter; opinion polling, while primitive at this time, offers no indication of any great love for the Court. Indeed, a majority appears to have supported some type of reform versus maintaining the status quo, even though no particular reform proposal achieved majority approval. Rather, Progressives, who were not supporters of judicial supremacy and had long histories of actively seeking to bring the Court to heel, led the fight against FDR's plan. Since that plan did not achieve their objective – it merely empowered the president to harness the judiciary's power to endorse a given set of policy aims encapsulated by the New Deal – and enlarged executive power, refusal to endorse the plan could be characterized as seeking to maintain congressional authority against a dictatorial executive. Concern about maintaining judicial integrity per se was plausibly secondary. This characterization fits the expectations of the institutional preservation hypothesis introduced in Chapter 2. Normative judicial supremacy need not be assumed in order to explain the collapse of the Court-packing plan. Neither is it fully empirically evident.

IV. Recasting its Purpose: The Court's Lincolnian Refrain in *Blaisdell* and the Pluralism of *Adkins* and *Carolene*

The Court was not wholly hostile to legislation that aimed to mitigate the worst effects of the economic crisis. Some decisions prior to 1937 indicate sympathy toward such concepts as constitutional adaptability and living constitutionalism. Nowhere are this philosophy and its clash with the strictures of textualist originalism more evident than in Chief Justice Hughes's decision and Justice Sutherland's dissent in *Home Building & Loan Association v. Blaisdell*, delivered in 1934.[214] Hughes was the ideational innovator, exploiting the economic crisis as an opportunity to detail a new approach

---

[212] Wheeler, quoted in Solomon, 123.
[213] Ackerman 1998, 320.
[214] *Home Building & Loan Association v. Blaisdell*, 290 U.S. 398 (1934).

to constitutional interpretation, an approach that had long been articulated in legal academia and in Supreme Court dissents of Justice Holmes, but one that had not yet been cast as a majority ruling. In Hughes's assertions of the Constitution's flexibility to meet and resolve crisis, which grew out of its general phrasing and "broad outline," there are echoes of Lincoln's claims of constitutional silences.

Once FDR's judicial reform proposal collapsed in June of 1937, the range of congressional and presidential solutions to the challenge of linking judicial authority more explicitly with popular sovereignty appeared spent, even though the effort had included more than two hundred constitutional amendments and statutory proposals. Less than a year later, the Court again played ideational innovator and offered its own solution, proffered in the fourth footnote of *United States v. Carolene Products*.[215]

By focusing on *Blaisdell* and *Carolene* as turning points in interpretive methodology and inter-branch relations, respectively, and as critical signals of the re-calibration of the judiciary to the political assumptions of liberal pluralism, my argument departs from many studies of New Deal–era judicial politics. Often scholars emphasize the *West Coast Hotel* decision, which upheld a Washington state minimum-wage law in direct conflict with a decision rendered less than a year earlier, as the switch in judicial philosophy validating government interventionism. *NLRB v. Jones & Laughlin Steel Corporation*, in which the Court upheld New Deal legislation under the commerce clause, maintained this philosophy. *Carolene* is superficially unremarkable in that it continued this pattern of judicial deference to congressional authority to regulate the economy under commerce clause authority.

However, the majority's argument in *West Coast Hotel* was hardly innovative. It was a restatement of civic republican notions of state police powers balanced against rights, and thus constructed rights as contingent on notions of public good. This ruling reclaimed logic evident in *Muller v. Oregon*. Given women's unique role as republican mothers, the state had a special responsibility to ensure that liberty of contract – which the majority now claimed was not stipulated in the Constitution[216] – was *not* absolute:

'The State still retains an interest in his welfare, however reckless he may be. The whole is no greater than the sum of all the parts, and when the individual health, safety and welfare are sacrificed or neglected, the State must suffer.' It is manifest that this established principle is peculiarly applicable in relation to the employment of women, in whose protection the State has

[215] *United States v. Carolene Products Co.*, 304 U.S. 144 (1938).
[216] The majority quoted *Chicago, B. & Q. R. Co. v. McGuire*, 219 U. S. 549 (1897), 567, to this effect: "There is no absolute freedom to do as one wills or to contract as one chooses.... Liberty implies the absence of arbitrary restraint, not immunity from reasonable regulations and prohibitions imposed in the interests of the community." Thus, "this power under the Constitution to restrict freedom of contract has had many illustrations. That it may be exercised in the public interest with respect to contracts between employer and employee is undeniable." *West Coast Hotel Co. v. Parrish*, 300 U.S. 379 (1937), 392–3.

a special interest.... We referred to recognized classifications on the basis of
sex with regard to hours of work and in other matters, and we observed that
the particular points at which that difference shall be enforced by legislation
were largely in the power of the State.[217]

The difference between *Muller* and *West Coast Hotel* was that the former
dealt with work-hours provisions while the latter confronted the constitutionality of a minimum wage. It could be argued that the minimum wage was not
as clearly linked to promoting the physical health of a female labor as work-
hours provisions were. However, minimum wage regulations had been sought
by women's organizations since 1910 and could be articulated within the lexicon of sex difference and republican motherhood utilized in *Muller*.

   Blaisdell and *Carolene* exemplify the Court's ideational innovation. First,
in *Blaisdell*, the Court endorsed the idea of multiple legitimate interpretive
methodologies, giving its imprimatur to living constitutionalism. Second, in
Carolene, the Court not only recognized that civil society and politics were
increasingly organized by a new set of assumptions, but it also found a place
for itself within these assumptions by abandoning ideals of consensualism
and the corresponding fear of opposition that defined civic republicanism and
embracing, if not serving as the guardian of, the interest-based competition
characterizing pluralist politics.

IV.a. Blaisdell: *Living Constitutionalism and the Eclipse of Nineteenth-Century Textual Originalism*

The concept of "living constitutionalism," as should now be clear, stands for
the principle that "judges are men ... made of human stuff like the rest and
sharing with us the common limitations and frailties of human nature."[218] As
such, law is always in the process of being interpreted. The philosophy thereby
abandons the notion that the Constitution holds a singular, fixed, and discoverable meaning and obliterates the dichotomous distinction between law
and politics: "The distinction between a government of laws and a government of men is absurd."[219] According to Justice Holmes, judicial rulings were
not textualist discoveries based on abstract principles deduced in a scientific
manner as formalists might hold; rather, case outcomes were manifestations
of "the felt necessities of the time, the prevalent moral and political theories,
intuitions of public policy, avowed or unconscious, even the prejudices which
judges share with their fellow men."[220] For legal realists such as Holmes, interpretation was contingent on lived circumstance and, indeed, necessarily political. And, more fundamentally, the Constitution allowed it to be so precisely
because it was only the broadest outline of principles, whose meaning was
necessarily subject to dispute and provided the flexibility to meet the needs of
current circumstance.

[217] Ibid., 394–5.
[218] Howard Lee McBain, *The Living Constitution* (New York: Macmillan, 1928), 2.
[219] Ibid., 3.
[220] Oliver Wendell Holmes, Jr., *The Common Law* (Boston: Little, Brown, 1881), 1.

This interpretive philosophy, which resonates with the themes of Lincoln's first inaugural address, is evident in Chief Justice Hughes's ruling in *Home Building & Loan Association v. Blaisdell*. At stake was a 1933 Minnesota statute, the Mortgage Moratorium Law, which granted temporary relief from foreclosure and altered the terms of contractual mortgage payments so that people might not lose their homes. The law was challenged on the basis that it violated the Constitution's contracts clause.[221] Speaking for a majority of five justices, Hughes upheld the law by rationalizing that the Constitution's broad guidelines must make allowances for changing circumstances: "When the provisions of the Constitution, in grant or restriction are specific, so particularized as not to admit of construction, no question is presented.... But where constitutional grants and limitations of power are set forth in general clauses, which afford a broad outline, the process of construction is essential to fill in the details."[222] Precisely because the Constitution is not specific – precisely because there exist ambiguities or silences – steps must be taken to deduce the meaning of the abstract phrasing. But no longer must that deductive process be grounded solely in the text. For Chief Justice Hughes a range of external considerations must, by necessity, come into play: "we must consider the relation of emergency to constitutional power, the historical setting of the contract clause, the development of the jurisprudence of this Court in the construction of that clause, and the principles of construction which we may consider to be established."[223] Circumstances might induce judges to "fill in the details" in one particular way, but different circumstances might induce them to do so in another way. Interpretation was therefore legitimately contingent, and if it were not so, the Constitution would be nothing but an obstacle to meeting the unforeseen challenges of modern society. Hughes calls these new circumstances "the complexity of our economic interests," which has "inevitably led to an increased use of the organization of society in order to protect the very bases of individual opportunities."[224] In other words, the Minnesota law is simply recognition that if no action had been taken, not only would individual contracts have gone into default, but the housing market would have collapsed. Action was necessary to preserve public welfare, and so the Minnesota law fell within the recognized police power.[225]

Justice George Sutherland vigorously dissented, focusing on how Hughes's ruling violated the interpretive principles underlying textualist originalism. For Sutherland, "the whole aim of construction, as applied to a provision of

---

[221] "No State shall ... pass any ... Law impairing the Obligation of Contracts," Article I, Section 10, Clause 1.
[222] *Home Building & Loan Association v. Blaisdell*, 290 U.S. 398 (1934), 427.
[223] Ibid., 426.
[224] Ibid., 443.
[225] By grounding the justification in police power, Hughes revealed how even a non-textualist approach clung to assumptions of identifiable public good, which flowed from a civic republican idiom. In this way, the case shares much with the underlying due process logic articulated in *Slaughterhouse*; the state could restrict the rights of some to ensure the public welfare of the whole. See G. Edward White, 2002, 211–14.

the Constitution, is to discover the meaning, to ascertain and give effect to the intent, of its framers and the people who adopted it.... As nearly as possible we should place ourselves in the condition of those who framed and adopted it."[226] Sutherland emphasized how the contracts clause was adopted in circumstances of economic crisis, when "the American people found themselves in a greatly impoverished condition," not unlike, he contended, current circumstances.[227] The clause was to prevent a legislature from favoring debtors at the expense of creditors, which was exactly what the Minnesota legislature did. Current circumstance did not justify alternative construction. No alternative was possible. By the strictures of textualist originalism, the Constitution could have one meaning: "It does not mean one thing at one time and an entirely different thing at another time."[228]

Of course, that claim of temporal contingency was at the center of efforts to maintain the Constitution through times of crisis. Lincoln had relied on it in his attempts to stave off secession and to tie interpretation to popular sovereignty. Now, Chief Justice Hughes relied on it to stave off the worst economic collapse in American history. In *Blaisdell*, Hughes was "squarely confronted ... between an interpretive theory of the Constitution that saw its provisions as having fixed meaning ... and an interpretive theory – the 'living Constitution' theory that treated the meaning of the Constitution as capable of radically changing with time."[229] Unwilling to endorse either extreme, Hughes attempted compromise, siding with the underlying logic of the latter theory, but also noting that the upheld statute was temporary, an emergency response to meet the crisis and would expire. Furthermore, Hughes framed his endorsement of living constitutionalism as fully conforming to jurisprudential tradition that was opposed to the radical departure in interpretive methodology which the Sutherland dissent proclaimed it to be. To do so, Hughes relied on Chief Justice Marshall's claim in *Marbury* that the Constitution can be "adapted to the various *crises* of human affairs."[230] In other words, now that *Marbury* had been deliberately re-imagined by legal scholars and judges since the late nineteenth century to function now as the definitive bedrock of judicial authority, Hughes relied on it to validate the contention that the purpose of judicial interpretation was not to discover a singular meaning, but to ensure that the Constitution could adapt to meet the exigencies of contemporary life. In short, by relying on *Marbury*, Hughes attempted to ground legal realism, ironically, within originalist recourse to the Founders' intent.

The underlying pattern of ideational innovation is the same in each instance thus far discussed: for each innovator, crisis provided opportunity to take a

---

[226] *Home Building & Loan Association v. Blaisdell*, 290 U.S. 398 (1934), Justice Sutherland dissenting, 454.

[227] Ibid., 455.

[228] Ibid., 450.

[229] White, 212.

[230] *Home Building & Loan Association v. Blaisdell*, 290 U.S. 398 (1934), 344.

formerly unpopular or even illegitimate notion – as living constitutionalism, which had thus far lived only through dissents – and frame it as the solution to contemporary problems. Yet there were limits on what each innovator could do. For Hughes, the limits were the entrenched Jeffersonian notion of judicial independence as political neutrality and continuing civic republican assumptions – at least within judicial thinking – against class legislation; his ruling could not appear to be siding with debtors and law to be mere politics despite the academic claims of legal realists. He, therefore, grounded the decision in existing precedent of state police power, even as *Blaisdell* dealt with the contracts clause and not the due process clause implicated in other police power cases such as *Slaughterhouse* and *Muller*. Nevertheless, by endorsing the underlying logic of "living constitutionalism," the chief justice was calibrating the Court to ideas about constitutional meaning that had already taken root in the elected branches of the state and federal governments and that were evident in state and federal legislation at issue during the Progressive era. With textualist originalism so clearly articulated by Sutherland and so markedly positioned as the dissent in *Blaisdell*, the Court, while still relying on some republican assumptions, had forcefully acknowledged the legitimacy of alternative methodologies to construct (as opposed to derive) constitutional meaning.

IV.b. Carolene: *The Court's Adjustment to the Political Assumptions of Liberal Pluralism*

If in *Blaisdell* Chief Justice Hughes relied on republican assumptions to legitimize the Court's ideationally innovative endorsement of living constitutionalism, then the *Carolene* ruling marked the Court's abandonment of those assumptions and its re-orientation to pluralist ideas, which increasingly underlay the organizational forms of American politics. *Carolene* may be otherwise unremarkable in that it continued the post-1937 pattern of judicial deference to congressional authority in economic matters, but the ruling's importance as a signal of the Court's recognition of the pluralist idiom stems from its fourth footnote. Here, the Court staked out new territory on which to exert its authority. It held that it would *not* defer to Congress when it viewed the legislative process to malfunction by consistently blocking certain interests from participating. The Court noted that dysfunction might be systemic when it involved recognizably "insular and discrete minorities." Through this footnote, the Court recognized the political process as pluralist, that is, as a competitive forum of represented interests. In so doing, it adopted a construction of politics that Lincoln had begun to articulate.

The Court went *further* than Lincoln. By recognizing that certain groups might not have equal access, the Court identified power differentials within interest-based pluralism that Lincoln had not. In effect, the Court granted some legitimacy to the justification offered by slave-property owning interests for seceding. In the late 1850s, as a consequence of demographic developments, this interest had become a discrete and insular minority, unable to secure majorities in the House and potentially the Senate.[231] Now, in 1938, the Court used that phrase to antithetical effect: to recognize the interests of the descendants of former slaves who had systematically been excluded from the post-Reconstruction political order.

Carolene was not the Court's first recognition of American democracy as interest-based pluralism. Its decision in *Adkins v. Children's Hospital* had proven a false start in this regard.[232] It did so because it assumed, as Lincoln did in his articulation of representational dynamics, that participants were equal. In *Adkins*, the Court failed to recognize power differentials that it ultimately acknowledged in *Carolene*.

In *Adkins*, the Court declared a minimum-wage law for female laborers in the District of Columbia to be unconstitutional. The rationale for the law was similar to that for other protective legislation, which the Court validated in *Muller v. Oregon. Muller* maintained maximum-hour limits because it linked women's health to the public good and national interest. It thereby separated women as a group outside the otherwise allegedly plausible assumptions of employee-employer equality underlying liberty of contract rationale. *Muller's* ruling could potentially be used to justify minimum-wage legislation, which would emphasize "women's dependence, their inequality in bargaining, and the impact of low wages paid women on public health and morals."[233] Without a minimum wage, women could not thrive as republican mothers, leading to an array of social and moral ills.[234] Since minimum-wage and maximum-hours legislation rested on a lexicon of sex difference, advocates of this position, including Felix Frankfurter and the National Consumer League's Florence Kelley, were suspicious of the movement for sexual equality, represented by Alice Paul's National Women's Party (NWP), and the battle for an Equal Rights Amendment (ERA).

Giving voice to the fear that an ERA would undermine maximum-hour and minimum-wage laws by subjecting women as men's equals to the harsh rationale of liberty of contract Kelley wrote to Frankfurter:

> There is at this moment an insanity prevalent among women.... This insanity expresses itself in eager demands for identical treatment.... It is idle to explain to them that, if these ideals prevail ... the statutory working day and legal wage, the provision of seats when at work, for rest rooms, and all other special items which are more necessary for women more than for men, (however much men may need them), will all be swept away.[235]

[231] On these demographic shifts through the antebellum era, see Mark Graber, *Dred Scott and the Problem of Constitutional Evil* (New York: Cambridge University Press, 2006), 5, 92, 126–8.

[232] *Adkins v. Children's Hospital*, 261 U.S. 525 (1923).

[233] Joan Zimmerman, "The Jurisprudence of Equality: The Women's Minimum Wage, the First Equal Rights Amendment, and *Adkins v. Children's Hospital*, 1905–1923," *Journal of American History* 78 (June 1991), 201.

[234] Kelley lays out this essentially republican construction of women and rights in her book, *Some Ethical Gains through Legislation* (New York: Macmillan, 1905).

[235] Kelley to Roscoe Pound, 3 June 1921, folder 4, box 29, Pound Papers, quoted in Zimmerman, 207.

Frankfurter warned Paul: "What you are attempting is fraught with the greatest dangers."[236] He advised: "The seeds of litigation against the power to enact social legislation for women should not be sown in a new amendment."[237]

Kelley and Frankfurter's fears were prescient. In *Adkins*, the Court distinguished *Muller* and maximum-hours legislation as having a direct connection to women's health compared with minimum wages and argued that the sex difference rationale was precluded by the Nineteenth Amendment's passage:

> The ancient inequality of the sexes, otherwise than physical, as suggested in the *Muller* case has continued "with diminishing intensity." In view of the great – not to say revolutionary – changes which have taken place since that utterance, in the contractual, *political* and civil status of women, culminating in the Nineteenth Amendment, it is not unreasonable to say that these differences have now come almost, if not quite, to the vanishing point.... [W]oman is accorded emancipation from the old doctrine that she must be given special protection or be subjected to special restraint in her contractual and civil relationships.[238]

According to the Court, by granting women the right to vote, the Nineteenth Amendment placed men and women on equal footing within the pluralist setting of American democracy. By having the vote, women's interests could sufficiently compete. Explicit protections were no longer needed. In this setting of formal equality, minimum-wage law was considered by the republican terms of class legislation.[239] For Frankfurter, *Adkins* spelled the end of a sex difference rationale.[240]

The Court revisited the relationship between political equality and interest representation in *Carolene*. At issue was the constitutionality of a federal statute banning interstate shipment of "filled milk" – milk reconstituted with vegetable oil – because it was deemed injurious to public health. The Court not only claimed that Congress could pass this legislation under its commerce clause authority, but also that the Court was compelled to presume that such legislation was not class-biased because all interests affected by the legislation's passage were represented during its consideration. In other words, the Court assumed the pluralist construction of democratic politics

---

[236] Frankfurter to Paul, 30 June 1921. Felix Frankfurter Papers, box 153, reel 96–97, Library of Congress, Washington, DC.

[237] "Memorandum on the Proposed Amendment to the United States Constitution presented by the National Woman's Party," drafted by Frankfurter, 21 July 1921. Felix Frankfurter Papers, box 153, reel 96–97, Library of Congress, Washington, DC.

[238] *Adkins v. Children's Hospital*, 261 U.S. 525 (1923), 553. Emphasis added.

[239] Sutherland used the Nineteenth Amendment as Kelley and Frankfurter feared judges might interpret the ERA. In dissent, Chief Justice Taft maintained that the amendment referenced political participation and did not bear on contract negotiation nor alter women's physical attributes on which protective legislation was justified.

[240] Frankfurter to Jesse Adkins, 16 April 1923 (expressing agreement with *Adkins'* disapproval of the Court's ruling and his push for re-argument). Felix Frankfurter Papers, box 153, reel 96–97, Library of Congress, Washington, DC.

as interest-based and conflict-ridden. It found no basis to justify the appellee's assertion that Congress's concerns about the injurious potential of filled milk were mere cover for discrimination and thereby class-based legislation. Instead, the ban was a legislative judgment based on proceedings and evidence in which affected interests were represented.[241]

The Court did not stop there. In its fourth footnote, it laid out the limits by which a statute would be presumed constitutional. Justice Stone maintained that the pluralist system of interest representation functioned when Congress passed the particular statute at issue. But that process could malfunction, and when that occurred, the presumption of constitutionality would not hold. The Court would henceforth be particularly attentive when it reviewed cases and controversies involving the Bill of Rights, the Fourteenth Amendment, and "whether prejudice against discrete and insular minorities may be a special condition, which tends seriously to curtail the operation of those political processes ordinarily to be relied upon to protect minorities, and which may call for a correspondingly more searching judicial inquiry."[242] Stone accepted a presumption of equality in representation that constituted an underlying assumption of liberal pluralism. He accepted that in a well-functioning pluralist democracy in which all persons with affected interests were represented, the Court had much less justification to intervene. He also recognized that liberal pluralist assumptions did not always describe real politics. By pointing to discrete and insular minorities, Stone recognized power differentials that Lincolnian pluralism did not. This acknowledgment carved a new rationale for the judiciary's purpose in a democracy. Judges would serve as overseers of pluralist representation. When such representation did not function, that is, if it operated to the perpetual exclusion of certain interests, judges would step in to act on behalf of those minority interests.

Furthermore, in contrast to Lincoln's pluralism – which was essentially party-based since he inherited from Van Buren the idea that parties were vehicles of constitutional interpretations – the Court's take on pluralism carried no such institutional limitations. It was interest-based. It thereby recognized the changing nature of the participatory landscape at the end of the Progressive Era, that is, that a range of organizations and other forms had developed, which had not supplanted political parties but could nevertheless represent group interests. Interests could now be carried into the legislative arena by a far more diverse array of increasingly entrenched institutions – interest groups, social movement organizations, non-profit legal organizations, the people themselves – than just partisan politicians.

---

[241] According to the Court: "Regulatory legislation affecting ordinary commercial transactions is not to be pronounced unconstitutional unless, in the light of the facts made known or generally assumed, it is of such a character as to preclude the assumption that it rests upon some rational basis within the knowledge and experience of the legislators (*United States v. Carolene Products Co.*, 304 U.S. 144 [1938], 152).

[242] Fourth Footnote, *United States v. Carolene Products Co.*, 304 U.S. 144 (1938).

In short, through *Carolene's* fourth footnote the Court recognized pluralist assumptions as ordering contemporary politics and reformulated its
own role accordingly. In doing so, it moved beyond Lincoln's articulation of
pluralism in two ways: by noting power differentials and by noting the range
of institutional forms through which participation occurred. By stipulating
that it would closely scrutinize legislation beyond its rational basis when it
affected interests of discrete and insular minorities, the Court abandoned its
position of neutrality that accorded with early civic republican assumptions
about the role of the state and the problems of class-based legislation. It also
set itself as a "pluralism-reinforcing" overseer, which paradoxically meant
that it would intervene in some circumstances but be aloof in others. And by
broadening its range of possible actions, the Court described the characteristics that groups had to demonstrate to activate judicial intervention on their
behalf. It thereby provided a road map on how to construct circumstances
under which judicial power could be effectively harnessed. If a group could
formulate its grievance in a particular way, it might trigger heightened levels
of judicial scrutiny. As such, it might better be able to utilize judicial authority to achieve its aims.

V. Conclusion

This chapter examined how and why a range of Populist and Progressive measures that might more closely link popular sovereignty to judicial authority
were not implemented. Explanations for the failure to alter the judiciary or
undermine judicial legitimacy need not rely on the development of a norm of
deference to judicial authority. A normative claim leaves the passage of Court-
curbing legislation in the 1910s and 1930s unexplained, and it downplays
the range of Progressive approaches to the problem of judicial authority.
That range – which included supplanting the rule of law with public opinion to establishing new electoral infrastructure to increasing the number of
judges – illustrates how much Progressives were encumbered by the weight of
Jeffersonianism and Lincolnian Republicanism as two distinct approaches to
that problem.

The Lincolnian and Jeffersonian foundations of Populist and Progressive
criticism of judicial authority are evident in Populist rhetoric and Progressives'
efforts to institutionalize popular control over a law's status via judicial recall
or decision recall and in some Progressives' views of political parties. Anti-
party views were evident in Progressive endorsement of new interest groups
and in their resurgent hope that a Progressive party might replace corrupt
party competition. Even as Progressivism created new forms of interest
representation that accorded with the competitive political logic of pluralism, it maintained affinities with the republican idiom, for example, single
party constitutionalism, consensualism, and singular public good, that faded
throughout the nineteenth century. Progressives defined "reform as revival,

and what they wished to revive clearly evoked republican themes."[243] Since Progressivism embraced republican assumptions, and republicanism is associated with aggressive restrictions on judicial authority given fear of opposition, the spike in proposals during the 1910s and 1920s that undermine judicial legitimacy – seen in Chapter 1 – can be accounted for by attending to the role played by these political ideas.

While Progressive solutions that aimed to link judicial power with the people did not come to pass, the Court's solution to the political problem of judicial power, offered in *Carolene's* fourth footnote, placed it in the conflicted position as both detached guardian of the democratic process and periodic active intervener in that process. If legal realism – with its supposition that law was not a formal system of discoverable principles with singular and fixed meaning and thus that no wall existed between law and politics – undercut the rationale of an unelected judiciary, the Court tried to re-establish the logic of "guardian review" through *Carolene*. Whereas the original logic of review rested on the representational rationale flowing from textualist originalism and the act of ratification, judicial legitimacy was now recalibrated and rationalized on pluralistic terms in which multiple interpretations were granted legitimacy. Once again the political problem of judicial power was resolved. The Jeffersonian solution was to cordon off the unrepresentative judiciary from politics altogether. Van Buren's resolution relied on the single constitutional party from which judges would be selected and whose principles they would represent. Lincoln's resolution was granting that the Court rightly represented particular viewpoints, which could be popularly ratified through the normal cycle of elections. In *Carolene*, the Court resolved the problem by fully calibrating its legitimacy to the new pluralist assumptions increasingly defining American politics.

By the terms of living constitutionalism, there was no fixed and singular meaning consecrated by the popular sovereign and embedded in the constitutional text for judges to discover. As such, the Court seemed to lose any special claim on interpretive authority. One solution to the potential legitimacy crisis was to ground the realist jurisprudence of constitutional adaptation, perhaps ironically, within the language of originalist intent. This strategy is evident in Hughes's reliance on *Marbury* in *Blaisdell*. Another was to cast *Lochner*-era jurisprudence as problematic by its own textualist methodology and to cast rulings like *West Coast Hotel* as textually adherent: "The Constitution does not speak of freedom of contract" and as such "The *Adkins* decision [which had voided minimum wages for female laborers] was a departure of the true application of the principles governing the regulation by the State of the relation of employer and employed." As in *Blaisdell*, Sutherland issued a textualist retort in *West Coast Hotel*: "To say ... that the words of the Constitution mean today what they did not mean when written ... is to rob that instrument of the essential element which continues it in force as the people have

---

[243] David Ericson, *The Shaping of American Liberalism* (Chicago: University of Chicago Press, 1993), 175–6.

made it."[244] Not until it could endorse its non-textualist non-originalist methodology on its own terms and ground its legitimate authority in a non-textualist rationale would its legitimacy crisis be possibly overcome.

Legal realist principles, which dominated the post-1937 Court at least through much of Chief Justice Burger's tenure, and which compelled a new pluralist justification for guardian review, left the Court vulnerable to perpetual accusations that it was not neutral among different social groups or classes. The justification violated the entrenched ideal – taken root since the Chase impeachment – of judicial independence as political neutrality even as it recognized the power imbalances and dysfunctions in American pluralism. Furthermore, it highlighted the conditions under which the Court would intervene. As such, it stipulated circumstances under which judicial power could be harnessed to achieve political objectives. If a group could plausibly contend that it met the descriptors triggering heightened scrutiny, then judicial power could be mobilized to achieve that group's objectives. It is no wonder that groups ranging from women to gays and lesbians to evangelical Christians have sought to qualify as "suspect classes" deserving higher scrutiny under the logic of *Carolene's* fourth footnote.[245]

The Court's new justification in *Carolene* emphasized that institution's exteriority from the political process and its deliberate interference with it. If such intervention were to go unchallenged, the Court would need to claim that when it ruled, its pronouncements carried unique finality. Put differently, once judicial authority was no longer premised on discovering and defending the fixed, singular, and discoverable meaning consecrated by the popular sovereign, but rather took on a role as intervening to promote functioning democratic politics, the only way to compel observance of its particular interpretation would be to assert its superiority. Judges now had to claim explicitly their own supremacy. Such claims would be made in *Cooper v. Aaron* and repeated in *Baker v. Carr* when the Court stepped in to desegregate public schools and to regulate legislative apportionment. Both cases relied on the Court's purpose as ensuring access to effective representation, that is, on the rationale put forward in *Carolene*.[246] Assertions of such finality

---

[244] *West Coast Hotel v. Parish*, 300 U.S. 379 (1937), Justice Sutherland dissenting, 404.

[245] Strict scrutiny refers to a threshold of judicial review. Other levels include intermediate scrutiny and rational basis review. Each attaches to a particular "suspect class." Legal development has centered on which group triggers which level. See Erwin Chemerinsky, *Constitutional Law: Principle and Policies*, 3rd ed. (New York: Aspen, 2006), 694–6, 752–8, 782–9.

[246] *Cooper v. Aaron*, 358 U.S. 1 (1958) (ruling that Arkansas must desegregate its schools). The ruling rested on an assertion of judicial supremacy, which the Court said was articulated in *Marbury*: "In 1803, Chief Justice Marshall, speaking for a unanimous Court … declared … 'It is emphatically the province and duty of the judicial department to say what the law is.' This decision declared the basic principle that the federal judiciary is supreme in the exposition of the law of the Constitution, and that principle has ever since been respected by this Court and the Country as a permanent and indispensable feature of our constitutional system." 358 U.S. 18. *Baker v. Carr*, 369 U.S. 186 (1962) (ruling that legislative apportionment was justiciable). In doing so, the Court intervened in how legislatures should be organized to ensure that they were maximally representative and that particular interests were not excluded.

did not clearly follow from John Marshall's rulings – even as the attempts to re-imagine *Marbury* beginning in the late nineteenth century might suggest – but the Court would seize upon these statements to clothe this new position in a seemingly long tradition. It is little wonder that the Warren Court would trigger scholarly preoccupation with the countermajoritarian difficulty since – as detailed in the next chapter – it based its authority on the *Carolene* overseer and interventionist rationale rather than on the Framers' representational rationale, which made sense only if it were assumed that the popular sovereign had declared a fixed, singular, and discoverable constitutional meaning.

7

A Polity Fully Developed for Harnessing (I)

Living Constitutionalism and the Politicization of Judicial Appointment

As reviewed in the previous chapter, in the vacuum created by Progressive failures to connect more directly judicial rulings on constitutional meaning to the shifting passions of quotidian politics, the Court put forth its own solution, one that, in part, abandoned the Jeffersonian construction of judicial independence as political neutrality in favor of the precepts of legal realism. In doing so, the Court cast its role in pluralist democracy as ensuring functional democratic processes, which might require periodically intervening in them. Judicial authority was no longer premised on the Framers' idea of representing the popular sovereign but on an overseer capacity that identified and corrected the potential failings of democracy. Lacking an operational rationale grounded in representative purpose equal to the elected branches, the Court's legitimate authority was without clear mooring. In such circumstance, judges – with the aid of legal scholarship from newly established law schools such as Columbia, Harvard, and Yale – asserted the supremacy of their own interpretation.

This resulting "Great Supreme Court" that could "stand up to both Congress and the states in defense of newly created rights" was epitomized by Earl Warren's stewardship from 1954 through 1968. Liberal Democrats "abandoned their prior fears of conservative or reactionary Courts" and supported the Warren Court, in part, because its rulings progressed in lockstep with a president and a congressional majority that embraced "a comprehensive ideology of Great Society liberalism."[1] Since this characterization of judicial authority – offered by the Justices themselves in *Cooper v. Aaron* and *Baker v.*

---

[1] The first quotation is from H.W. Perry, Jr., and L. A. Powe, Jr., "The Political Battle for the Constitution," *Constitutional Commentary* 21 (Winter 2004), 651. At this time, liberal Democrats viewed the Court as marching in complementary fashion toward a unified goal of the New Deal-Great Society vision. On a Great Court working with the elected branches to secure "Great Society" aims, see Mark Tushnet, *The New Constitutional Order* (Princeton: Princeton University Press, 2003). The second quotation is from Tushnet, "The Politics of Constitutional Law," *Texas Law Review* 79 (2000). The quoted passage is taken from an earlier draft available at SSRN: http://ssrn.com/abstract=237551, p. 8.

Carr[2] – aligned with the policy interests of many within the New Deal-Great Society coalition, the Court *appeared* to serve the constitutional vision of the dominant political party that defined the parameters of policy development.

The Court's repeated articulation of its own interpretive supremacy within the factious politics of democratic pluralism only further incentivized politicians to harness this power to their own ends. In the wake of the *Carolene* ruling, hostility toward the judiciary worked itself out in a political context where liberal pluralism was the dominant organizing rationale of all three federal branches of government, where multiple interpretive methodologies reigned, and where an array of participatory institutions – political parties, interest groups, and social movements – could claim the legitimacy of their own conceptions of constitutional meaning. In this context, rhetorical hostility toward the Court continued almost unabated. But the jurisdiction-stripping that was advocated rarely prevailed, and when it did, it achieved little beyond the observable trajectory of the Court's own moves. Tactics undermining judicial legitimacy more directly, such as politically motivated impeachment, were never acted upon. As detailed in this chapter and the next, measures ranging from increasing the size of the lower federal judiciary, to expanding the use of presidential signing statements, to transferring jurisdiction between federal and state courts in the War on Terror, to filibustering judicial appointees were more clearly employed to harness judicial power for partisan ends. These actions are not indicators of politicians' deference to courts, and they are not clearly indicators of outright hostilities toward courts either. Instead, they are actions meant to harness a judiciary that has, since *Brown v. Board of Education*, set itself up as increasingly powerful.[3]

As laid out in Chapter 2, when assumptions associated with competitive interest-based pluralism structure the range of rational preferences and legitimate actions political actors may have and pursue, they are more likely to engage in tactics that harness judicial power to achieve policy aims than to undermine judicial legitimacy. These tactics include stripping jurisdiction on a particular policy matter or transferring jurisdiction between state and federal courts in hopes of securing a desired judicial outcome. Hostile rhetoric may remain, but it will likely be paired with legislation that does little beyond what the Court has already done through its own decision-making. Politicians may draft ambiguous statutes that invite judicial review as this not only passes accountability from legislators to judges, but also enables legislators to claim credit for passing laws even if they are overturned by judges, a situation that can usefully position judges as undemocratic foils. Or as passage of legislation undermining judicial authority becomes increasingly popular and likely, politicians might seek ways to avoid acting upon it. Such avoidance may not stem from any deference to the Court per se but because that legislation could

---

[2] *Cooper v. Aaron*, 358 U.S. 1; *Baker v. Carr*, 369 U.S. 186.
[3] *Brown v. Board of Education* (I), 347 U.S. 483 (1954).

undermine a longer term strategic interest in maintaining judicial power. Or, Congress might avoid this legislation because passing it might weaken another power base. In other words, concerns about the Court's integrity and independence might be secondary to other political challenges that passage of the legislation might present.

This chapter and the following one detail how hostilities toward the judiciary took shape in a polity fully developed for judicial harnessing, by which I mean a civil society in which all branches of government and all institutions of political participation tend to operate under the assumptions associated with liberal pluralism. This chapter examines attempts to manipulate the judiciary from the 1950s through the 1970s, when legal realism was the ascendant interpretive philosophy and when the three federal branches appeared to work in unison to develop and protect a range of identified constitutional rights. This chapter also examines the emphasis on judicial appointment and subsequent politicization of the lower federal judiciary. Chapter 8 focuses on the conservative insurgency from the 1980s onward and its innovative attempts to solicit judicial power through a range of new mechanisms – including the development of contemporary originalism as well as the innovative use of presidential signing statements – precisely because appointment opportunities were not immediately available. Both chapters aim to validate the four expectations laid out above, which were initially introduced in Chapter 2.

Part I of this chapter details how isolated segregationist criticism of Supreme Court rulings blossomed by the mid to late 1950s into a cross-sectional and bi-partisan anti-Court coalition. Between 1955 and 1958, at least one Court-curbing measure became law, and others attained overwhelming support in the House and nearly passed in the Senate. This fact is troubling for any claim that a norm of deference to judicial authority characterized politicians' position since the end of the nineteenth century. It is less troubling for my theory, which predicts not that attacks against independent judicial authority will subside once political assumptions about competitive loyal opposition take hold, but that they change in mode. They narrow in scope and accomplish little more than where the Court has already trended in its own rulings. Part II examines politicians' reactions as the Court's racial jurisprudence focused on school integration through busing. It discusses congressional consideration of judicial impeachment and the Nixon administration's attempts to utilize judicial appointment as a voter-mobilization issue. Passage of Court-curbing legislation in the 1970s demonstrates that the Congress did little more than the Court already indicated it would do, which allowed members of Congress to claim credit for battling an "activist Court" while *not* substantially limiting its powers. Part III examines President Carter's appointment strategy after the largest expansion of the federal judiciary took effect in 1978; how, despite his own claims to be guided by neutral objectives, his efforts politicized the lower federal courts; and how that expansion set the stage for the conservative insurgency's innovative moves once Reagan was elected in 1980.

I. The Near Misses of Jurisdiction-Stripping in the 1950s

In his recent study of congressional Court-curbing, Charles Geyh character-ized hostilities toward the Warren Court, which included impeachment threats against the chief justice and Justice William Douglas and jurisdiction-stripping legislation drafted between 1955 and 1958, as having "failed miserably." In Geyh's assessment, the impeachment outcry "amounted to little more than expletives intended to display the depths of the speakers' dissatisfaction." And Geyh linked congressional authority to strip jurisdiction not to the more recent examples of the Clayton Act or the Norris-LaGuardia Act but to the Reconstruction-era *McCardle* case. In Geyh's estimation, the failures of anti-Court activists in the 1950s showcased a fully developed norm of popular and elite-level deference to independent judicial authority, which only highlighted how the *McCardle* precedent "stood alone like the proverbial cheese, increas-ingly aged and malodorous."[4]

And yet assessments by scholars such as Robert McClosky, offered when these aggressive statements and proposed actions against judicial power were occurring, portrayed them as "a firebell in the night" which came "shockingly close to succeeding."[5] Chief Justice Warren believed the jurisdiction-stripping legislation "came dangerously close to passing."[6] And more recently, legal scholar, Lucas Poe, claimed that the "anti-Court measures, though not as all-encompassing as the [FDR] Court-packing plan, had come far *closer* to passage than Roosevelt's initiative."[7]

Hostilities toward independent judicial authority were triggered by the Court's unanimous ruling in *Brown v. Board of Education*, which held that segregation of public education violated the equal protection clause of the Fourteenth Amendment.[8] For all its moral correctness, the Court did not offer much by way of legal arguments against desegregation. The justification, instead, accorded with judicial attempts to stake out a role in a pluralist democracy as articulated in *Carolene*. Because segregation, according to the Court, "generates a feeling of inferiority ... that may affect their [African Americans'] hearts and minds in a way unlikely to ever be undone," it undermined education's purpose of preparing a student to "adjust normally to his environment."[9] Once Warren framed education

---

[4] Charles Geyh, *When Courts and Congress Collide* (Ann Arbor: University of Michigan Press, 2006), 109–10.

[5] Robert McCloskey, "Reflections on the Warren Court," *Virginia Law Review* 51 (November 1965), 1258.

[6] Earl Warren, *The Memoirs of Earl Warren* (Garden City, NY: Doubleday, 1977), 313.

[7] Lucas Powe, Jr., *The Warren Court and American Politics* (Cambridge, MA: Belknap Press of Harvard University, 2000), 133.

[8] To reach a similar outcome for the District of Columbia, the justices used the due process clause of the Fifth Amendment since the Fourteenth Amendment applied only to the states and since the Fifth Amendment lacked an equal protection clause. The Court linked equal protection and due process as "both stemming from our American ideal of fairness." *Bolling v. Sharpe*, 347 U.S. 497 (1954).

[9] *Brown v. Board of Education* (I), 347 U.S. 483 (1954).

as the bedrock of a healthy democracy – "education is perhaps the most important function of state and local governments ... [as] it is the very foundation of good citizenship" – school segregation could be framed as undermining functioning pluralism, and thus the Court needed to step in.[10] To make this argument, the Court relied on psychological data.[11] Going beyond legal justifications to strike down a law left the justices vulnerable to claims that they had moved beyond the parameters of their role. Despite approving the result, many scholars wondered whether *Brown*'s style of reasoning, which appeared unrestrained by constitutional text and legislative history, might constitute the Court as a "naked power organ" in which judicial preferences would substitute for interpretation and thereby destroy any kind of political neutrality which still grounded the legitimacy of the Court's pluralist overseer capacity.[12]

That fear formed the basis of much of the anti-judicial criticism that came in *Brown*'s wake. Nevertheless, the history of this consequent Court-curbing legislation aligns with expectations that follow from my theory. As the remaining sections of Part I illustrate, this legislation cannot be dismissed as the angry voice of an unrepresentative congressional minority. Indeed, much of this Court-curbing legislation was a common carrier of cross-sectional and bi-partisan interest that overcame many of the collective action problems that often plague Congress. Second, the attacks were narrowly focused on jurisdiction, suggesting attempts to limit judicial power in a targeted way without wholly undermining judicial authority. Third, bills that would have more broadly undermined federal legitimacy – through impeachment or by validating nullification doctrine – were not considered for a vote. Fourth, bills that did nearly pass in the Senate were narrow or ambiguous; the one bill that did pass was so vague that supporters of the Court as well as its detractors claimed victory. In other words, circumstances surrounding attacks on judicial authority in the 1950s do not easily bear out claims of normative deference to judicial authority, but do fit the expectations laid out in Chapter 2 of how attacks on judicial authority take shape in a polity calibrated to the competitive politics and assumptions of loyal opposition that define pluralism.

I.a. *Isolated Southern Reactions to* Brown v. Board of Education

Following *Brown*, numerous Southern legislators called for judicial restraint, judicial impeachment, or other measures that might discipline the Supreme Court. Five state legislatures resurrected the theory of nullification to stop the

---

[10] Ibid.

[11] Footnote 11 of *Brown* (I) cites six psychological studies as evidence that the *Plessy* claim that separation does not connote any state sanction of inferiority is invalid. It also cites Gunnar Myrdal's *An American Dilemma: The Negro Problem and Modern Democracy* (1944). The Court was well aware that *Brown* would be published in newspapers and widely read throughout the country and structured its language accordingly.

[12] Herbert Wechsler, "Toward Neutral Principles of Constitutional Law," *Harvard Law Review* 73 (1959), 12.

decision from being enforced.[13] These states appeared to act against the tide of history. According to legal scholar Walter Murphy, "After 1950, every careful student of constitutional law knew that, given the climate of judicial – as well as national – opinion, the 'separate but equal' formula was doomed."[14]

Yet although the Court had been chipping away at the legal basis for segregation since the 1930s, *Brown* should not be considered inevitable; the machinations taken – including numerous delays and repeated oral arguments – as well as the justices' own notes indicate that *Brown* was a difficult decision.[15] The justices were well aware that a ruling to desegregate public schools could be met with evasion or outright resistance. Such a ruling called for re-structuring the primary cultural institution of seventeen states and the District of Columbia, an action of unprecedented scale and one demanded by an institution without enforcement mechanisms. Chief Justice Vinson, before he died between *Brown*'s first and second argument, leaned toward waiting for Congress to move first.[16] Justice Reed maintained that the time was not ripe to declare school segregation unconstitutional. Justice Frankfurter, who supported desegregation in the nation's capital on due process grounds, was less sure of the equal protection argument that compelled desegregation in the states. And ruling against segregation smacked of the very activism he had often publicly accused judges of prior to 1937.[17]

Political party support for the *Brown* ruling was vague or weak. The 1956 national party platforms suggested that robust endorsements were not forthcoming:

> The Republican Party accepts the decision of the U.S. Supreme Court that racial discrimination in publicly supported schools must be progressively eliminated. We concur in the conclusion of the Supreme Court.... This

---

[13] See acts of Alabama 1956, No. 42; Georgia Laws 1956, House Resolution 185; Mississippi General Laws 1956, Senate Concurrent Resolution 125; South Carolina Act of 14 February 1956; Virginia Acts of Assembly 1956, Senate Joint Resolution 3. For arguments politicians made to deny the validity of *Brown*, see Charles Fairman, "The Supreme Court, 1955 Term," *Harvard Law Review* 70 (November 1956), 83–188. Gallup polling in 1956 showed over 70 percent of whites outside of the South agreed with *Brown*. In states where desegregation would occur, 16 percent of whites agreed with *Brown*. George Gallup, *The Gallup Poll: Public Opinion 1935–1971*, 3 vols. (New York: Random House, 1972), Vol. 2,1401.

[14] Walter Murphy, *Congress and the Court: A Case Study in the American Political Process* (Chicago: University of Chicago Press, 1962), 80.

[15] In 1938, the Court ordered that Lloyd Gaines be admitted to the University of Missouri Law School (*State of Missouri ex rel Gaines v. Canada et. al*, 305 U.S. 337 (1938)). In 1950, the Court held that a black man should be admitted to the University of Texas Law School as separate facilities could not be considered equal and that denial of admission violated equal protection under the Fourteenth Amendment (*Sweatt v. Painter*, 339 U.S. 629 (1950)).

[16] *Brown* was ordered for re-argument with the instruction that litigators investigate the intent of the Fourteenth Amendment. Michael Klarman suggests that one reason for re-argument was to buy time to attain a unanimous ruling. Klarman, *From Jim Crow to Civil Rights: The Supreme Court and the Struggle for Racial Equality* (New York: Oxford University Press, 2004), 301.

[17] Ibid., 292–312.

progress must be encouraged and the work of the courts supported in every legal manner by all branches of the Federal Government to the end that the constitutional ideal of the law, regardless of race, creed or color, be steadily achieved.[18]

Republicans accepted the ruling rather than heartily supporting it. Democrats were more equivocal possibly to avoid alienating their Southern wing and provoking another "Dixiecrat" defection:

> Recent decisions of the Supreme Court of the United States relating to segregation in publicly supported schools and elsewhere have brought consequences of vast importance to our Nation as a whole and especially to communities directly affected. We reject all proposals for the use of force to interfere with the orderly determination of these matters by the courts.[19]

Noting only "consequences of vast importance," the statement could hardly be more ambiguous. And its rejection of force held two possible meanings: first, opposition to violence by Southern citizens and officials to obstruct implementation of the ruling, and second, advocacy of restraint from the executive and Congress when considering enforcement lest violence ensue. To this degree, the platform mimicked that language of the Southern Manifesto delivered on 12 March 1956.[20]

The Manifesto, known formally as a Declaration of Constitutional Principles, was drafted by Senator Strom Thurmond of South Carolina and revised by Senator Richard Russell of Georgia; nineteen senators and eighty-two representatives from eleven Southern states signed it.[21] It charged the Court with substituting "naked power for established law" and as engaging in "a clear abuse of judicial power" that "climaxes a trend in the Federal Judiciary undertaking to legislate, in derogation of the authority of Congress, and to encroach upon the reserved rights of the States and the people."[22] Like the Democratic platform, the Manifesto utilized a double meaning of force. The signatories pledged themselves "to use all lawful means to bring about a reversal of this decision which is contrary to the Constitution and to prevent the use of force in its implementation" and beseeched their constituents to "scrupulously refrain from disorder and lawless acts."[23] By emphasizing law over force and suggesting that enforcement would trigger violence, these politicians not only framed the Court as usurping congressional power

---

[18] Republican Party Platform of 1956.

[19] Democratic Party Platform of 1956. On the Dixiecrat revolt, see Joseph Lowndes, *From the New Deal to the New Right: Race and the Southern Origins of Modern Conservatism* (New Haven: Yale University Press, 2008), 26–34.

[20] *Congressional Record*, 84th Congress, Second Session, Vol. 102, part 4 (12 March 1956) (Washington, DC: U.S. Government Printing Office, 1956), 4459–60.

[21] The majority of the Texas delegation did not sign. See Tony Badger, "Southerners Who Refused to Sign the Southern Manifesto," *Historical Journal* 42 (1999), 517–34.

[22] *Congressional Record*, 84th Congress, Second Session, Vol. 102, part 4 (March 12, 1956), 4459–60.

[23] Ibid.

and upsetting the state-federal balance but also as fostering civic instability. While the signatories acknowledged that in opposing desegregation, they "constitute[d] a minority in Congress," they were hopeful that "a majority of the American people ... will in time demand that the reserved rights of the States and of the people be made secure against judicial usurpation."[24] They did not have to wait long.

I.b. *Forging an Anti-Court Coalition beyond the Segregated South*
In 1955, Representative Mendel Rivers (D-SC) proposed a jurisdiction-stripping bill, which transferred the Supreme Court's appellate jurisdiction on school desegregation to federal district courts.[25] Southern district courts, given traditions of patronage and senatorial courtesy, were staffed by judges sympathetic to local segregationist interests. However, the bill did not receive widespread support outside of the Southern delegation. The chair of the House Judiciary Committee, Emmanuel Cellers, a Northern Democrat who supported *Brown*, buried the bill. No action was taken in the Senate.

Later that year, the Court delivered a series of rulings protecting civil liberties, which were increasingly unpopular given national security concerns associated with early Cold War anti-communism. In *Slochower v. Board of Education of New York City*, the Court ruled that a professor could not be fired for invoking Fifth Amendment protections not to testify before a congressional committee investigating his possible connections to the Communist Party.[26] In *Cole v. Young*, the Court held that the Summary Suspension Act of 1950 did not permit summary dismissal of government employees in non-sensitive areas.[27] In *Pennsylvania v. Nelson*, the Court overturned a conviction under a state sedition act on the reasoning that federal legislation in the same policy area, the Smith Act of 1940, superseded state law.[28] This doctrine of pre-emptive federalism stipulated that if federal and state legislation operated in the same field, federal law took precedence. It developed through commerce clause litigation and was used to overturn state anti-union right-to-work legislation, which operated on the same field as the Wagner and Taft-Hartley Acts. In *Nelson*, this doctrine was used to invalidate state sedition laws. In so

[24] Ibid.
[25] House Resolution 3701, 84th Congress, 1st Session (1955).
[26] *Slochower v. Board of Education*, 350 U.S. 551 (1956).
[27] *Cole v. Young*, 351 U.S. 536 (1956). Employees could be dismissed if questions of loyalty surfaced only after normal civil service procedures had been taken.
[28] *Pennsylvania v. Nelson*, 350 U.S. 497 (1956). The Smith Act or Alien Registration Act (18 U.S.C. § 2385) made it a federal crime to "knowingly or willfully advocate, abet, advise, or teach the duty, necessity, desirability or propriety of overthrowing the Government of the United States or of any State by force or violence, or for anyone to organize any association which teaches, advises or encourages such an overthrow, or for anyone to become a member of or to affiliate with any such association." In *Nelson*, the Court relied, in part, on the Smith Act to demonstrate the redundancy of the Pennsylvania sedition law to bolster its claim that sedition against the states was punishable under federal law, and thus state law could be invalidated unless the state provided a compelling local interest.

ruling, the Court now linked economic and national security conservatives by providing a common doctrinal enemy.[29]

Through *Nelson*, the Court invalidated forty-two state sedition laws, and suddenly, the segregationist claim that federal judicial power had upset the state-federal balance no longer looked like a racist ploy. Northerners spear-headed congressional response to the pre-emption decisions. Representative Mason of Illinois asked, "where is the usurpation of States' rights by the United States Supreme Court going to end?"[30] Senator Mundt of North Dakota drafted legislation to overturn *Cole v. Young* aiming to "plug another hole in the defense bastions of America which has been created by another unrealistic and unhappy decision by six isolated members of our Supreme Court."[31] In short, the Court's application of the pre-emptive federalism doctrine to invalidate state sedition laws and state labor laws fostered a community of common interest. A coalition of Southern segregationists, anti–New Deal Republicans, and security-conscious anti-communist politicians coalesced around reactionary Court-curbing measures, and a policy remedy was already at hand.[32]

Representative Smith of Virginia, an economic conservative who had sponsored the Smith Act of 1940, introduced H.R. 3 on 5 January 1955 before the civil liberties decisions were announced. The bill eviscerated pre-emptive federalism by stipulating that no act of Congress could be construed to operate to the exclusion of state laws on the same or similar subject matter unless the congressional act explicitly stated its intent to do so.[33] In the wake of the pre-emption decisions, the bill garnered support from business interests including the National Association of Manufacturers, the U.S. Chamber of Commerce, and the American Farm Bureau Federation. It was opposed initially by the American Federation of Labor and Congress of Industrial Organizations (AFL-CIO), who saw the bill as a threat to federal labor protections and, following the Court's civil liberties rulings, by Americans for Democratic Action and the NAACP.[34] The American Bar Association (ABA) did *not* adopt a resolution formally supporting the Court, foreshadowing more clashes between the Court and the ABA.[35]

---

[29] On pre-emptive federalism, see Murphy, 90–3.

[30] *Congressional Record*, 84th Congress, 1st Session, Vol. 101-a, 6384.

[31] Ibid., 10173.

[32] See S. 3606, S. 3617, H.R. 10335, and H.R. 10344 from the 84th Congress, 2nd Session (1956). The legislation was a "common carrier," meaning that several groups supported it because each saw it as serving their particular aim.

[33] The language of H.R. 3 is "No act of Congress shall be construed as indicating an intent on the part of Congress to occupy the field in which such act operates, to the exclusion of all state laws on the same subject matter, unless such act contains an express provision to that effect." H.R. 3, 84th Congress, 1st Session (1955).

[34] Murphy, 92–4.

[35] "Recent Attacks upon the Supreme Court: A Statement by Members of the Bar," *American Bar Association Journal* 42 (1956), 1128–9. The organizational strength of the legal profession did not immunize the Court from attack. Thus, during the 1950s, it would be naïve to think the ABA would support a strong judiciary, just as Arnold Paul (1960) pointed out that during the 1890s, it would be wrong to assume that lawyers were uniformly against restricting federal judicial power to issue injunctions against labor strikes.

Also, the Governor's Conference, while not officially endorsing H.R. 3, did support the legislation's purpose citing that its members were "gravely concerned by decisions of the Supreme Court of the United States which have held that Congressional enactments supersede state laws on the matters involved and thereby pre-empt those fields for the federal government alone."[36] H.R. 3 was reported out of committee in the summer of 1956 only after its scope was narrowed to affect only state sedition laws. The bill maintained the broader pre-emption doctrine to protect pro-labor and pro-civil rights decisions. Smith shelved it and waited for a more opportune moment.

Amid impeachment and jurisdiction-stripping threats, the Court did not pull back. In May of 1956, in *Schware v. Board of Bar Examiners* the Court ruled that the state bar could not block admission of a former Communist Party member on grounds that such membership constituted a lack of good moral character.[37] In a companion case, *Konigsberg v. State Bar*, the Court ruled that although Konigsberg published criticism of American participation in the Korean War and testimony had been given of his attendance at Communist Party meetings, he could not be denied admission to the state bar.[38]

Denying state bars the ability to block communists paled in comparison to the potential impact of the Court's overturning of a perjury conviction of a New Mexico labor leader in *Jencks v. United States*.[39] Jencks's attorneys sought access to FBI files containing testimony of two witnesses against Jencks, but lower courts denied access to the FBI files. Speaking for the majority, Justice William Brennan ruled that not only could the trial judge have access to the files but that the defense should have access as well. The ruling was widely regarded as a setback to FBI anti-communist efforts and as threatening national security. FBI Director J. Edgar Hoover lobbied Congress to reverse the ruling, and a day after the Court's ruling, at least ten bills were introduced in the House that would minimize the decision's effect.[40]

Shortly thereafter, on Monday, 17 June – a day memorialized by Hoover as "Red Monday" – the Court issued four rulings that further stymied anti-communist efforts. In *Service v. Dulles et. al.*, the Court reversed John Service's discharge from the foreign service. While granting that Secretary of State Dean Acheson had "absolute discretion" to dismiss officers on concerns of disloyalty and security, the Court noted that Service had been subjected to a series of departmental loyalty investigations and cleared each time. Therefore, the Court ordered that Service be reinstated on the grounds that the department's regulatory procedures had not been followed. In *Watkins v. United States*, the Court

[36] *1956 Proceedings of the Governor's Conference* (Chicago: Conference of State Governors, 1956), 188, quoted in Murphy, 96.
[37] *Schware v. Board of Bar Examiners*, 353 U.S. 232 (1957).
[38] *Konigsberg v. State Bar*, 353 U.S. 252 (1957).
[39] *Jencks v. United States*, 353 U.S. 657 (1957).
[40] Arthur Sabin, *In Calmer Times: The Supreme Court and Red Monday* (Philadelphia: University of Pennsylvania Press, 1999), 145–51.

constricted congressional inquisitorial power suggesting that anti-communist investigations constituted "broad-scale intrusion into the lives and affairs of private citizens." In *Sweezy v. New Hampshire*, a professor at the University of New Hampshire claimed that questions about his lectures violated his First Amendment rights; by using the Fourteenth Amendment to incorporate First Amendment freedoms against state action, the Court restricted state inquisitorial power. In *Yates v. United States*, the Court reversed the convictions of fourteen communist leaders under the Smith Act, in part, on the grounds that the term "organize" in the Smith Act was vague. Essentially, the ruling prevented prosecutions under the Smith Act from continuing.[41]

Finally, a week after Red Monday, in *Mallory v. United States*, the Court overturned a rape conviction on the grounds that District of Columbia police did not arraign the African American defendant, Andrew Mallory, in a prompt manner, delaying his arraignment for nearly eight hours during which time he was subjected to polygraph tests and confessed. The majority argued that the delay violated Rule 5(a) of the Federal Rules of Criminal Procedure, which commanded arraignment "without unnecessary delay." Since Mallory's confession was obtained during this delay, it was considered inadmissible.[42]

Taken together, all of these rulings – touching on national security concerns, bar admissions, and police procedures – galvanized a broadening congressional coalition that sought to challenge judicial authority in some manner. In this environment of multiple unrelated interests offended by judicial rulings, Court-curbing legislation could be a common carrier, appealing to politicians for diverse reasons. Even presidential support for the Court was limited. Days after Red Monday, Eisenhower was posed a question at a press conference:

> As is well known, the judiciary cannot defend itself as the legislative and executive branches can and do. Right now the Supreme Court, prominently including some Justices appointed by you, are under heavy attack for a series of decisions they have made defending the rights of individual citizens under the Constitution. In view of the fact that the Court is unable to answer back ... do you think there is a danger of these attacks being intemperate?[43]

Eisenhower continued his earlier pattern of equivocating on desegregation cases by now characterizing the civil liberties decisions as "some that each of us have very great trouble understanding."[44] And again, the American Bar Association (ABA) was not a pillar of support. During its summer conferences, it refused to back the Supreme Court against growing public outcry. Instead,

---

[41] *Service v. Dulles et al.*, 354 U.S. 363 (1957); *Watkins v. United States*, 354 U.S. 178 (1957); *Sweezy v. New Hampshire*, 354 U.S. 234 (1957); *Yates v. United States*, 355 U.S. 66 (1957); see Sabin, 151–72.

[42] *Mallory v. United States*, 354 U.S. 449 (1957).

[43] 26 June 1957, "The President's News Conference," John T. Woolley and Gerhard Peters, *The American Presidency Project* [online]. Santa Barbara, CA: University of California (hosted), Gerhard Peters (database), http://www.presidency.ucsb.edu/ws/?pid=10822.

[44] Ibid.

the organization's Committee on Communist Strategy criticized the Court for "hav[ing] rendered the United States incapable of carrying out the first law of mankind – the right of self-preservation."[45] The full ABA accepted the committee's report at a conference in London to which Chief Justice Warren had been invited, convincing him that he was "sandbagged into coming to London to garner publicity for a simultaneous attack on the Court."[46] The Court was increasingly left without allies in government and in the legal profession.

I.c. *Court-Curbing Legislation in the 85th Congress*

With this broadening constituency of grievance holders, the 85th Congress secured passage of the Court-curbing Jencks Act, and the House passed five additional Court-curbing measures, including a re-packaged H.R. 3.[47] The legislative histories of the Jencks Act and the collapse of the other House measures in the Senate suggest that a viable anti-Court coalition had developed and that these bills were not doomed from the start by a powerful norm of deference to judicial authority. The legislative histories also give some evidence of how attacks would take shape in a polity when politicians are more inclined to harness judicial power than to wholly undermine its legitimacy. As this section details, as these six bills traveled toward passage in the Senate, they were de-fanged to allow legislators the maximum credit-claiming benefit of battling against judicial authority without undermining politically useful judicial power. And politicians retreated from legislation that would undermine judicial legitimacy just when passage was within reach.

On 24 June 1957, a bill drafted by Assistant Attorneys General Warren Olney III and Wilson White was introduced in the House as H.R. 7915 and the Senate as S. 2377. In response to the *Jencks* decision, it provided that no statements or reports of any person other than the defendant would be given to defense counsel except after a witness testified. Defense could petition for the statement but could have access only to those parts that bore on events discussed in testimony. The trial judge would inspect the reports, and then give whatever portions he deemed appropriate to defense counsel.[48] To secure passage of the bill, the subcommittee chair, former Progressive and New Dealer Senator O'Mahoney (D-WY) framed it as a clarifying statute rather than a Court-curbing reaction.[49] Of course, the bill included severe restrictions on defendant access that Brennan's opinion for the Court had considered invalid. Brennan, for example, declared that statements and reports must be handed over to the defendant; the Jencks bill in its original form, allowed for no such possibility.

Responding to pressure from civil liberties advocates and counter pressure from the FBI and the Justice Department, the Senate legislation went through

---

[45] Warren, *Memoirs*, 322.
[46] Powe, 100.
[47] 18 U.S.C §3500.
[48] Murphy, 131–4.
[49] Ibid., 134.

multiple drafts. The final version fell in line with liberals' demands to the point that it was not clearly a repudiation or affirmation of the *Jencks* decision. By sponsoring a jury trial amendment to the bill, which Southerners had attempted but failed to attach to the recently passed civil rights bill, O'Mahoney ensured that Southern anti-Court vitriol would not mar the *Jencks* debate. Indeed, during that debate, Senator Dirksen proposed two amendments to strengthen the bill in line with Justice Department and FBI demands and rebuke the Court, but no Southerner supported the amendments despite segregation-ists' desire to curb the Court. The Senate passed the conference report by 74 to 2 on 30 August 1957. The House passed it unanimously on 31 August.[50] Ultimately, the Act was hailed by friends and foes of the Court. It ratified part of *Jencks*, but it codified Justice Burton's more limited concurrence rather than Brennan's majority opinion. Even as the *New Republic* editorialized that the legislation "is not in our judgment the catastrophe for civil liberties that some liberals have claimed," some national coverage indicated that its pas-sage was a victory against "Earl Warren's Supreme Court's pro-communist victory."[51] Yet, according to one historian, the Jencks Act "only whetted the anti-Court coalition's appetite for more legislation."[52]

Six other bills – the Jenner-Butler Bill initiated in the Senate and five others initiated in the House – were more hostile to independent judicial authority than the Jencks Act. Senator William Jenner (R-IN), on 26 July 1957, introduced S. 2646, which eliminated the Supreme Court's appellate jurisdiction on an unprecedented scale. It stripped the Court's ability to hear cases involving con-tempt of Congress, the Federal Loyal-Security Program, state anti-subversive statutes, regulation of employment and subversive activities in schools, and admission to the bar. The bill essentially curbed jurisdiction that permitted rul-ings in *Slochower, Young, Nelson, Service v. Dulles et al., Watkins, Sweezy, Yates, Schware*, and *Konigsberg*. Given the Jenner bill's application to a range of controversial cases, it received support not only from Southern segregationists, but also from security conservatives who feared internal communist subver-sion. Opposition to the bill was voiced by Northern liberals such as O'Mahoney and Celler, who chaired relevant committees. By the conclusion of hearings, on 30 April 1958, the Jenner bill was replaced by the more moderate but still aggressive Jenner-Butler Bill, which curbed jurisdiction on bar admission cases, reversed *Nelson* by re-instating state sedition laws thereby striking a blow at pre-emption doctrine, and clarified the meaning of "organize" in the Smith Act to reverse *Yates* and continue anti-communism prosecutions.[53]

Meanwhile, the House was busy passing Court-curbing legislation by wide margins. On 18 March 1958, the House passed H.R. 8361, which curbed federal jurisdiction to issue writs of habeas corpus to persons convicted in state courts. On 17 June 1958, it passed a revised H.R. 3, which eliminated the judicial doctrine of pre-emptive federalism discussed above by a vote of 241 to 155. On 2 July it passed H.R. 11477, which overturned *Mallory* and allowed for evidence to be entered even if it had been acquired during a delay of arraignment, by a vote of 294 to 79. On 10 July it passed an amended version of the Senate's moderate S. 1411. The House bill reversed *Cole v. Young* and extended summary suspension power of federal department heads to all positions regardless of whether they were considered sensitive or not. This bill passed by 298 votes to 46. Finally, on a voice vote on 12 August 1958, the House passed H.R. 13272, which reversed *Yates*. Many of these bills were statutory revisions, but H.R. 3 was a more direct attack on judicial authority as it redefined state and federal power, upsetting twenty years of judicial doctrine supporting New Deal economic policy and underlying, in part, the rationale for desegregation.

On 5 August the Senate Judiciary Committee reported S. 654 favorably out of committee. That bill, more limited than Jenner-Butler, would reverse *Nelson* and reinstate state sedition laws. On 6 August the Senate version of H.R. 8361, which curbed habeas corpus jurisdiction, and S. 337, which was the Senate version of H.R. 3, were reported favorably out of committee. Senate majority leader, Lyndon Johnson, sensing that this legislation threatened to divide his Democratic Party into Northern and Southern factions, tried to diffuse anti-Court momentum by bringing to the floor the most innocuous bill first, namely, the bill clarifying the section of the Federal Code at issue in *Mallory*. The Senate Judiciary Committee amended the legislation by adding the vague term "reasonable" in front of "delay" such that evidence could not be determined inadmissible "solely because of reasonable delay." The term's ambiguity would invite judicial interpretation, thereby potentially saving rather than overruling the implications of the *Mallory* decision. Adding the adjective, "reasonable," appealed to civil libertarians and Democratic liberals; it also served to pass accountability on the statute's meaning from the Congress to the Court. The amended bill passed and conference with the House was set to unify the chambers' versions.[54]

Rather than satisfy the anti-Court coalition, progress on the *Mallory* bill spurred it to press for more legislation. Senator Thurmond forced Johnson's hand to bring the Jenner-Butler Bill, up for debate and vote by threatening to attach the more controversial H.R. 3 to every bill remaining on the Senate's calendar.[55] Johnson called up a bill dealing with federal appellate procedure and yielded to Senator Jenner who attached Jenner-Butler as an amendment. While seemingly provoking a rancorous debate, Johnson did so because he had already garnered enough votes to kill the legislation called up. In other words, Johnson allowed it to be attached it to what he presumed to be a dead bill in order to kill

---

[54] *Congressional Record*, 85th Congress, 2nd Session, Vol. 104a, 18511.
[55] Murphy, 207.

the Jenner-Butler Bill, which threatened to divide and weaken his Democratic Party. On the following day, the amendment was tabled by 49 to 41 votes.

Johnson then moved for debate on S. 654. Senator John McClellan (D-AK) substituted H.R. 3 for S. 654. Johnson assured liberals that he had the votes to kill H.R. 3, and by substituting S. 654 with the more extreme legislation, killing H.R. 3 would clear the docket of both Court-curbing bills simultaneously. Johnson had convinced Senator Thomas Hennings (D-MO) to move to table Jenner-Butler, and now Hennings moved to table discussion of H.R. 3. However, the motion unexpectedly *failed* by a vote of 46 to 39.[56] Johnson had not secured the votes as he thought he had. The seven-vote margin opened the possibility that the more extreme H.R. 3 (relative to S. 654) could pass. Amid some senators calling for an immediate vote on H.R. 3 to capture momentum, Johnson called a motion to adjourn that was carried strikingly by a vote of 70 to 18.

H.R. 3 came up for a vote the following day, and Johnson warned Senator Dirksen (R-IL) that a tied vote was in the offing. Such a tie would compel Vice President Richard Nixon to vote. Nixon was known to oppose the bill, but voting against it would only alienate him from the security and economic conservatives within his own party, thereby jeopardizing his presidential aspirations. As the votes came in, it became apparent that the anti-Court coalition might eke out a one-vote victory. When Senator Kerr (D-OK), whom Johnson failed to convince to stay off the floor, entered the chamber, Johnson hustled him to the cloakroom for one last persuasive effort. When the Senate clerk called for Kerr's vote, Johnson held him in the cloakroom and Democratic whip, Mike Mansfield, called out that Kerr was not in the building. At that point, the vote was tied at 40 to 40. Johnson may have wanted to force a Nixon vote as he harbored his own presidential ambitions. By preventing Kerr from voting, Johnson stopped a member of his own party from casting a deciding vote, which could have widened the rift between Northern and Southern Democrats, while forcing Nixon to do so. However, Senator Bennett (R-UT), who had met earlier with minority leader Dirksen, cast the deciding vote to defeat HR. 3 by 41 to 40. Bennett thereby saved both Nixon from alienating Republican conservatives by having to vote against the bill and Johnson from alienating Northern Democrats by preventing Kerr from voting for the bill.[57]

---

[56] Between the tabling of S. 2646 and debate on H.R. 3 / S. 654, Senator Douglas, a liberal Democrat of Illinois, moved to attach an amendment to the appellate procedural bill to which S. 2646 had been attached. Douglas's amendment stated Congress's full endorsement of the Supreme Court's desegregation rulings. This move may have been an effort by the liberal senator to expose the partly racist motivations underlying the anti-Court movement, but it may also have galvanized supporters of H.R. 3. Either way, it did break whatever momentum was earned by tabling S. 2646 that could have fed into a tabling of H.R. 3. Murphy, 208–10.

[57] Murphy, 214–7. Bennett's vote is somewhat confusing since he had earlier indicated to the National Association of Manufacturers, of which he was president in 1949, that he would support H.R. 3. Yet Bennett's vote aligned with many in his party including Nixon and the Justice Department. And if Bennett had voted for H.R. 3, he might have provoked a filibuster,

The Jenner-Butler Bill, H.R. 3, and S. 654 failed. S. 1411 came out of conference, but the Senate conferees were unhappy because the bill maintained extensive summary suspension power for department heads; they convinced Johnson not to call it for a vote. Left on the docket were the habeas corpus bill, which threatened a divisive debate within the Democratic Party, and H.R. 11477, the *Mallory* bill, which had been sent to conference. At conference, conservatives sought an amendment defining "reasonable," but liberals balked. By doing so, they could keep the statutory language ambiguous and open to judicial interpretation. However, they were outvoted, and an amendment defining "reasonable" passed. Liberals now threatened a filibuster, which Johnson was eager to avoid since he wanted to prepare for the coming election and because a filibuster would only highlight the Democrats' sectional rift. Liberals offered a way out: Rule 27 did not allow new material to be added to a bill when it was in conference, and the amendment defining "reasonable" constituted new material. Once Johnson ruled on that point of order, the bill would be killed and the session could end; he ruled accordingly.[58]

What do these parliamentary machinations suggest for anti-Court legislation's likelihood of passage and why it collapsed at the moment of political opportunity? Since the bills were common carriers serving the aims of a diverse range of politicians, basic difficulties of collective action cannot fully explain their failure. First, the Jencks Act had been widely demanded by the press, members of Congress, and the executive branch. Therefore, securing some version of the legislation would garner valuable electoral capital. And while congressional action had been demanded in the immediate wake of the *Jencks* ruling, low levels of press coverage of the outcome demonstrate that judicial decisions do not hold high public salience. This lack of salience gave politicians the flexibility to pass legislation that was not as aggressive as first demanded. Second, the Jenner-Butler Bill was similarly de-fanged. The five jurisdiction-stripping clauses were reduced to one involving admission to the bar. Third, and most telling, was the senators' reversal when confronted with the near passage of H.R. 3. The motion to table the measure was defeated by a seven-vote margin, indicating that there were enough votes to secure passage. But, at the moment of opportunity to rebuke the Court, senators pulled back, voting to adjourn by an overwhelming majority.

Accounting for this reversal requires acknowledging that politicians have both short- and longer term interests. In Chapter 2, I noted that politicians are interested in achieving policy, gaining elections, *and* maintaining powers of their home institution. Such institutional interest is evident in Johnson's

which would have prevented adjournment. Adjournment was crucial as elections were only two months away, and Bennett's fellow Republican senator from Utah, Arthur Watkins, was facing a tough re-election battle since he chaired the committee that censured Senator McCarthy, and McCarthy's anti-communism was popular among Utah's electorate. Thus, Bennett might have wanted to prevent a filibuster so that Watkins could campaign.

[58] Murphy, 217–23.

attempts to push the Court-curbing bills through quickly to avoid party division as much as in Senator Butler's vote to save both the Senate from a debilitating filibuster and his vice president from placing a vote on the record. In Chapter 2, I also suggested that politicians may learn how to avoid damaging constitutional crises while exploiting them for political gain, that is, capitalizing on battling the Court while also accepting loss, because that loss may actually maintain the strategic value of judicial power in the longer term. This lesson is only possible if entrenched judicial opposition is not considered wholly threatening to civic stability more generally. By 1958, the rhetoric of civic instability and internal subversion characteristic of the early Cold War had died down. As Powe notes:

> While cloaked in "Cold War hysteria," the summer of 1958 was four years after domestic anticommunism peaked in Congress and McCarthy's public disgrace. More than domestic security was at work. Southerners had found the rhetoric of anticommunism brought allies, but the southern concern was blacks, not reds. What had been drawing together in the 84th and 85th Congresses was a coalition that wanted the Court brought to heel for decidedly different reasons.[59]

So, were anti-Court forces simply outmaneuvered? If that were the only reason, why were senators like Kerr pinned down in cloakrooms so they could not vote and others like Bennett voting against their previously stated policy interests? One answer is that politicians balance short-term gain against longer term interests. In accounting for reversal on H.R.3, Walter Murphy offers a similar assessment:

> Backing the Majority on procedural points [like adjournment] is customary, yet there was more to the matter: a fear, felt by a number of *institutionally oriented* senators, that in approving a bill as drastic as HR. 3 the Senate might be upsetting not only the federal-state political balance, but also what might be described as a balance of power among the three branches of the federal government.[60]

The bills rebuking *Mallory* and *Cole* operated at the statutory level, but H.R. 3, to the contrary, struck at the heart of the constitutional relationship between state and federal power, which resurfaced after *Brown* as Southern politicians revived nullification. By tabling H.R. 3, Senators might lower the stakes of politics.[61] While it is likely that they had various reasons to vote to adjourn, ranging from simply being tired after a long day of debate to supporting their majority leader, it is also plausible that having registered their positions in the *Congressional Record*, they had staked out their positions well enough to mollify constituents. Undermining the Court's authority further might do

---

[59] Powe, 134.
[60] Murphy, 259. Emphasis mine.
[61] A similar dynamic is apparent in actions of the so-called Gang of Fourteen in 2005, discussed later.

more harm than good. In Murphy's words, "they did not want to strike down a current foe who might someday be a needed ally."[62]

To summarize, liberals in the House and the Senate sought to limit threats to civil liberties posed by the Jencks Bill, to gut much of the jurisdiction-stripping of the original Jenner Bill, and to limit the impact of any bill repudiating *Mallory* by inserting vague language into the statute. In this way, their behavior appears initially to map on to a claim about normative deference to judicial authority; however, the larger context of the passage of anti-Court legislation in the House by wide margins and the near passage of H.R. 3 in the Senate calls out for a different explanation. I have offered one by highlighting that the attacks were narrow and targeted and showing that some of their failures can be accounted for by attending to concerns about the institutional power of party that places concerns about judicial integrity in a decidedly secondary position. First, by minimizing the scope of the Jencks Bill, politicians could claim that they battled against the Court and maintained the FBI's ability to operate while also not undermining the Court's authority to rule on civil liberties. The bill could satisfy constituents clamoring for congressional action to battle communism while meeting constituent demand for civil liberties protections against anti-communist fervor. Second, anti-Court sentiment and legislation were not limited to a minority within Congress. A coalition of segregationists, national security conservatives, and economic conservatives formed to endorse H.R. 3. As such, collective action problems cannot sufficiently address the legislation's failure in the Senate. Third, this episode illustrates institutional preservation. H.R. 3, for example, redefined the relationship between state and federal power by rebuking a pivotal judicial principle underlying New Deal policy. The bill's breadth undercut judicial legitimacy, and senators backed away from it when its passage seemed likely. Jurisdiction-stripping, by contrast, while not coming to fruition in the 1950s, resurged and *passed* in the 1970s as desegregation traveled North.

II. Nixon: Judicial Impeachment, Stripping Jurisdiction, and Appointment Power

Presidential and congressional relations with judicial authority became increasingly tense in the late 1960s and early 1970s, particularly as Court decisions moved from calling for school desegregation toward advocating active integration through busing schemes in states outside the old Confederacy. Richard Nixon capitalized on rising public discontent by supporting measures to limit judicial authority in school segregation cases as well as by making judicial appointment a campaign issue. In addition to detailing Nixon-era inter-branch tensions, which included threats and passage of jurisdiction-stripping, threats of judicial impeachment, and politicized appointment, my aims in this section are, first, to show how congressional jurisdiction-stripping on matters related

---

[62] Murphy, 261.

to busing was redundant to the Burger Court's rulings and thus operated to symbolic effect, and second, to illustrate how broader assaults on judicial legitimacy, such as politically motivated impeachments, did not succeed. Therefore, I contend that it is empirically incorrect to claim that jurisdiction-stripping did not occur during the 1970s as a normative theory of judicial supremacy implies. It is more appropriate to examine how the jurisdiction-stripping that did occur is evidence of the narrow and symbolic attack expected in a polity developed for harnessing judicial power for partisan aims.

II.a. *Nixonian Harnessing: Judicial Appointment, Impeachments, and the Southern Strategy*

Nixon narrowly edged out Hubert Humphrey in the three-way 1968 presidential race. The popularity of George Wallace's third party confirmed how racial politics might be exploited for Republican gain. Wallace's strong showing demonstrated that hostility to integration was not regionally isolated.[63] Taking such lessons to heart, Nixon built on earlier Republican attempts to gain a foothold in the once solid Democratic South.[64] Part of that strategy, as this section will discuss, involved assuring his growing Southern constituency that he would bring the Court to heel through appointments or otherwise.[65] And 1968 appears to many scholars to be a turning point in the politicization of appointment power. As one historian has noted, "earlier rejections [by the Senate of judicial nominees] and controversies had been episodic, many of them having dynamics unique to themselves" and the "events of 1968 started an era of confirmation battles in a long-running war for control of the Supreme Court."[66]

[63] Nixon received 43.42 percent of the popular vote to Humphrey's 42.72 percent; Wallace received 13.53 percent. Jeremy Mayer, *Running on Race: Racial Politics in Presidential Campaigns, 1960–2000* (New York: Random House, 2002), 68. Dan Carter, *From George Wallace to Newt Gingrich: Race and the Conservative Counterrevolution, 1963–1994* (Baton Rouge: Louisiana State University Press, 1996), 9.

[64] Earl Black and Merle Black, *The Rise of Southern Republicans* (Cambridge: Belknap Press of Harvard University, 2002). Characterizing the open knowledge of the Southern strategy, Nixon biographer, Garry Wills wrote, "The Right just will not learn to keep its mouth shut to work on a strategy without confessing it." Garry Wills, *Nixon Agonistes: The Crisis of the Self-Made Man* (New York: Houghton Mifflin, 1979), 251.

[65] Since *Brown*, the Court sparked a widening coalition of hostile members of Congress as it ruled on the legitimacy of electoral reapportionment schemes, civil liberties, obscenity laws, criminals' rights, school prayer, and sexual privacy. On reapportionment: *Baker v. Carr*, 369 U.S. 186 (1962), and *Reynolds v. Sims*, 277 U.S. 533 (1964). On civil liberties, see discussion in Part I. On obscenity law: *Stanley v. Georgia*, 294 U.S. 557 (1969). On criminal procedure: *Gideon v. Wainwright*, 372 U.S. 335 (1963) and *Miranda v. Arizona*, 384 U.S. 436 (1966). On school prayer: *Engel v. Vitale*, 370 U.S. 421 (1962). On privacy, see *Griswold v. Connecticut*, 381 U.S. 479 (1965).

[66] Richard Neumann, "The Revival of Impeachment as a Partisan Political Weapon," Hofstra University Legal Studies Research Paper No. 06–22 (2006), 107, http://ssrn.com/abstract=923834. The pattern of interest group mobilization, congressional partisan rancor, and heightened public awareness that is now associated with Supreme Court appointments is relatively new. This claim does not negate that Supreme Court appointments were

During the campaign, Nixon and Wallace capitalized on antipathy toward judicial rulings to mobilize voters. Wallace's American Independent platform hearkened back to Progressive-era proposals that explicitly undermined independent judicial authority. It called for two reforms:

> It shall be our policy and our purpose, at the earliest possible time, to propose and advocate and urge the adoption of an amendment to the United States Constitution whereby members of the Federal judiciary at District level be required to face the electorate and his record at periodical intervals; and, in the event he receives a negative vote upon such election, his office shall thereupon become vacant, and a successor shall be appointed to succeed him.[67]

The second proposal was to modify appointment and tenure on the Supreme Court: "With respect to the Supreme Court and the Courts of Appeals ... this amendment require[s] reconfirmations of the office holder by the United States Senate at reasonable intervals."[68]

By contrast, the Republican Party emphasized gaining control over judicial appointment: "Public confidence in an independent judiciary is absolutely essential to the maintenance of law and order. We advocate application of the highest standards in making appointments to the courts, and we pledge a determined effort to rebuild and enhance public respect for the Supreme Court and all other courts in the United States."[69] The difference in Republican weight

controversial or that nominees were defeated in the nineteenth and early twentieth centuries. Judicial nomination fights have, to some extent, always exhibited some partisan rancor. See the failed nomination of Roger Taney as associate justice following his support of Jackson against the National Bank or the anti-Semitic attacks on Woodrow Wilson's nominee, Louis Brandeis. See J. Myron Jacobstein and Roy M. Merskey, *The Rejected: Sketches of the 26 Men Nominated for the Supreme Court but Not Confirmed by the Senate* (Milpitas: Toucan, 1993), 35–41, and Henry Abraham, *Justices and Presidents: A Political History of Appointments to the Supreme Court*, 3rd ed. (New York: Oxford University Press, 1992), 181–4. However, Neuman argues that the modern practice of interest group mobilization and the ongoing partisan battle over control of the Court in which justices are repeatedly asked how they would rule on certain issues began in 1968. Lee Epstein and Jeffrey Segal, who maintain "political clashes over candidates for the Supreme Court are not a new phenomenon," concede that "since the Haynsworth nomination, interest groups have become an even more regularized part of the process." Epstein and Segal, *Advice and Consent: The Politics of Judicial Appointment* (New York: Oxford University Press, 2005), 2, 95.

[67] American Independent Party Platform of 1968, 13 October 1968, John T. Woolley and Gerhard Peters, *The American Presidency Project* [online]. Santa Barbara, CA: University of California (hosted), Gerhard Peters (database), http://www.presidency.ucsb.edu/ws/?pid=29570.
[68] Ibid.
[69] Republican Party Platform of 1968, 5 August 1968, John T. Woolley and Gerhard Peters, *The American Presidency Project* [online]. Santa Barbara, CA: University of California (hosted), Gerhard Peters (database), http://www.presidency.ucsb.edu/ws/?pid=25841. That a third party would advocate more extreme measures to undermine judicial legitimacy and emphasize its countermajoritarian potential by illustrating the need for election or re-appointment is not surprising. These third-party attacks may be less constrained in their advocacy precisely because they are third parties; freed from a realistic prospect of governing, they offer more creative reforms. They are not as concerned with maintaining their institutional standing or capacities in the elected branches precisely because they are not well represented (if at all) in those branches.

on appointment versus the Independent/Wallace emphasis on altering judicial structure not only draws attention to the freedom of third-party bids to make more extremist claims, but also highlights the Republican aim to *harness* judicial power to promote Republicans' constitutional vision, particularly as it related to criminal justice reform and school desegregation.

Republicans were careful to distinguish between attacking the Court's authority to make a decision versus attacking the decision itself. Nixon's director of communications, Herbert Klein, emphasized this distinction to James Sheply, editor of *Time* magazine. Klein was annoyed by the periodical's framing of Nixon's stance toward the judiciary. The magazine recounted Nixon's attendance at the swearing-in of Chief Justice Burger as significant since it demonstrated the president's "offer [of] symbolic support to an institution that he himself had attacked so harshly during last year's election campaign."[70] Klein pointed out that Nixon never attacked the Court as an institution; he characterized the story as "bad reporting" because "it turns criticism of decisions into criticism of the institution."[71] Klein emphasized how Nixon "has at all times defended the institution of the Supreme Court, its independence, and the traditional value of an independent executive, judicial and legislative branch of government."[72] By focusing on the ruling rather than the institution, Nixon allies, like Klein, pointed to the need to change the decision-maker, not change the institution. During the 1968 campaign, Nixon promised to appoint judges who adhered to "a strict interpretation of the Supreme Court's role" and who were "thoroughly experienced and versed in criminal laws and its problems," because "recent Court decisions have tended to weaken the peace forces, as against the criminal forces, in this country."[73] Nixon's appointment strategy was part of the broader Southern strategy, which included increasing Southern representation throughout the executive branch.[74]

The contentious nature of Supreme Court appointments came to the fore shortly after Robert Kennedy's assassination in June 1968. That event threw the Democratic presidential nomination process into chaos. In the wake of the assassination, Chief Justice Warren told President Johnson of his intent to resign. Timed appropriately, Warren's departure would offer Johnson another Court appointment and keep the judiciary on track as legally entrenching the Great Society programs. Furthermore, since Warren and Nixon held a long-standing animosity toward one another, and if Warren considered Nixon the likely victor in November given the chaos of the Democratic nomination, it is not beyond the pale to suggest that he would seek to deny him a

[70] "The Legacy of the Warren Court," *Time*, 4 July 1969, http://www.time.com/time/magazine/article/0,9171,840195,00.html?iid=chix-sphere.

[71] Hebert Klein to James Shepley, 11 July 1969. Nixon Presidential Archives, National Archives and Records Administration, White House Special Files: Staff Member and Office Files, John Ehrlichman, Box 34, Folder "Supreme Court 510."

[72] Ibid.

[73] Excerpts from *Nixon on the Issues* attached to letter from Klein to Shepley, ibid.

[74] Dean Kotlowski, *Nixon's Civil Rights: Politics, Principle, and Policy* (Cambridge: Harvard University Press, 2001), 19–20.

Court nomination.[75] Warren had not considered the Senate response. Hoping to maintain a vacancy for a possible Republican presidential appointment, Senate Republicans filibustered Johnson's nomination of Abe Fortas to the chief justice seat.[76] This was the first time the filibuster had been successfully used to deny a judicial appointment.[77] When Nixon won the presidency, he nominated Warren Burger for the chief justice slot and, later that year, Justice Fortas was accused of shady financial dealings with convicted financier Louis Wolfson.[78] Fortas resigned so "that the Court may not continue to be subjected to extraneous stress which may adversely affect the performance of its important functions."[79] Although the Justice Department's investigation could not verify whether Fortas's relationship with Wolfson violated any law, it did convene a grand jury against Fortas's wife, Carol Agger, to consider charges of obstruction of justice in an unrelated issue.[80] The Nixon administration appeared to apply pressure to earn another bench slot.

With that second vacancy, Nixon could make good on his promise to appoint a Southern justice. He nominated Clement Haynsworth. When the Senate rejected Haynsworth, Nixon nominated G. Harold Carswell, who was considered more conservative and less qualified than Haynsworth, even by Nixon's aides.[81] Unsurprisingly, Carswell was defeated. Frustrated, Nixon attempted to earn political capital by suggesting that these defeats represented congressional anti-Southern bias. The president lamented, "After the Senate's action yesterday in rejecting Judge Carswell, I have reluctantly concluded that it is not possible to get confirmation for a judge on the Supreme Court of any man who believes in the strict construction of the Constitution, as I do, if

---

[75] Powe, 2000, 467–9.

[76] Fred Graham, "Critics of Fortas Begin Filibuster, Citing Propriety," *New York Times*, 26 September 1968, A1; Robert Albright, "Fortas Debate Opens with a Filibuster," *Washington Post*, 26 September 1968, A1.

[77] Neumann, 109; Jacobstein and Merskey, 135.

[78] William Lambert, "Fortas of the Supreme Court: A Question of Ethics: The Justice ... and the Stock Manipulator," *Life*, 9 May 1969, 32.

[79] Abe Fortas to Earl Warren, 14 May 1969. Nixon Presidential Archives, National Archives and Records Administration, White House Special Files: Staff Member and Office Files, Presidents' Personal Files, Box 8. On Fortas's resignation, see Laura Kalman, *Abe Fortas: A Biography* (New Haven: Yale University Press, 1990), 370–3, and generally Bruce Allen Murphy, *Fortas: The Rise and Ruin of a Supreme Court Justice* (New York: William Morrow, 1998).

[80] Robert Shogan, *A Question of Judgment: The Fortas Case and the Struggle for the Supreme Court* (Indianapolis: Bobbs-Merrill, 1972), 263; John Dean, *The Rehnquist Choice: The Untold Story of the Nixon Appointment that Redefined the Supreme Court* (New York: Free Press, 2001), 10.

[81] The *New York Times* editorialized that with Carswell's nomination, Nixon aimed to "lower the significance of the Court by the appointment of an incompetent." Quoted in Jacobstein and Merskey, 148. Nixon aide Jeb Stuart Magruder admitted that "few of us thought he was qualified." And Clark Mollenhoff said of Carswell that he "wouldn't have defended him under any circumstances." Both are quoted in Bruce Kalk, "The Carswell Affair: The Politics of a Supreme Court Nomination in the Nixon Administration," *American Journal of Legal History* 42 (July 1998), 282.

he happens to come from the South."[82] Nixon then invoked the idea of geographic representation; the South deserved a seat because "over 25 percent of the people live in the South. The South is entitled to proper representation on the Court."[83] Despite such protestations, Nixon nominated and the Senate confirmed Harry Blackmun, a Northerner.

The Nixon administration then promoted a congressional investigation of Justice William O. Douglas in hopes of forcing a resignation or triggering impeachment proceedings.[84] As early as 4 June 1969, only weeks after Fortas stepped down, the administration began to keep track of the investigation. One internal memo indicated that "it has been reliably determined from a confidential source that at least two newspapers with nationwide circulation are attempting to develop a story revealing further impropriety on the part of Justice Douglas" and that "the newspaper feels it is on to a Fortas type exposure."[85] The impeachment attempt smacked of "reprisal for Richard Nixon's two Senate defeats in the Haynsworth and Carswell cases" especially since House minority leader Gerald Ford announced his intent to launch an investigation of Douglas four days after Carswell's nomination was defeated.[86]

Ford focused attention on Douglas's alleged improprieties by suggesting that if nominees had to be held to a standard of lack of sensitivity on values such as civil rights – which had been invoked against Haynsworth and Carswell – then justices should endure similar scrutiny on other social values such as pornography about which Douglas had been notoriously liberal. Yet this standard was flouted as absurd by mainstream media: "different standards apply to a sitting judge [than to a nominee]. After all, no one seriously considered impeaching

[82] Richard Nixon, "Remarks to Reporters about Nominations to the Supreme Court," 9 April 1970, John T. Woolley and Gerhard Peters, *The American Presidency Project* [online]. Santa Barbara, CA: University of California (hosted), Gerhard Peters (database), http://www.presidency.ucsb.edu/ws/?pid=2455.

[83] Ibid. A day later, twenty-eight senators objected in writing to Nixon's claim about an anti-Southern bias, explaining that the majority felt neither Haynsworth nor Carswell, given their demonstrated ambivalence toward civil rights legislation, was qualified to serve. Letter to Richard M. Nixon, 10 April 1970. Signed by Senators McGovern, Bayh, Burdick, Gravel, Hart, Inouye, Ribicoff, McGee, Metcalf, Mondale, Moss, Muskie, Tydings, Young, Brooke, Eagleton, Goodell, Hartke, Cannon, Proxmire, Javits, McIntyre, Gore, Symington, Cranston, Harris, Fulbright, and Williams. Nixon Presidential Archives, National Archives and Records Administration, White House Special Files: Staff Member and Office Files, H.R. Haldeman, Box 139.

[84] John Ehrlichman characterized Nixon as "from the beginning ... [being] interested in getting rid of William O. Douglas." Ehrlichman, *Witness to Power: The Nixon Years* (New York: Simon & Schuster, 1982), 116.

[85] Jack Caufield to John Ehrlichman, 4 June 1969, Subject: Newspapers investigate possible Justice Douglas impropriety. Nixon Presidential Archives, National Archives and Records Administration, White House Special Files: Staff Member and Office Files, John Ehrlichman, Box 34, Folder, "510 Supreme Court."

[86] "Impeach Douglas?" 27 April 1970, *Time*, http://www.time.com/time/magazine/article/0,9171,909119,00.html.

Judges Haynsworth and Carswell, despite the criticism that barred them from the Supreme Court."[87] Ford rejected that argument. He advocated a broad definition of impeachment, one that Senator Giles and Representative Randolph invoked against Justice Chase. According to Ford, who admitted that "there are too few cases to make very good law" on what constitutes the underlying principle of an impeachable offense, such an offense amounted to "whatever a majority of the House of Representatives considers to be at a given moment in history; conviction results from whatever offense or offenses two-thirds of the other body considers to be sufficiently serious to require removal of the accused from office."[88] With a burgeoning coalition of Republicans who sought to shape the Court through appointments and conservative Southern Democrats angered by judicial rulings on issues including obscenity, civil rights, civil liberties, and criminal justice, many authored by Douglas, it was an open question whether impeachment charges might have been filed in the more extremist House: "Douglas' impeachment is by no means impossible" opined *Time* magazine.[89]

Ford was outmaneuvered by Democrats. While he gave charges against Douglas on the House floor, Representative Andrew Jacobs, Jr., filed a resolution to impeach Douglas.[90] Although Jacobs was a Douglas supporter, he worried that an impeachment would inflame the sectional divisions in the Democratic Party. His resolution specified that the investigation be conducted by the House Judiciary Committee, which was chaired by the liberal Celler rather than by the Rules Committee, which was chaired by a Mississippi segregationist, who likely would have supported the impeachment if only to secure a seat for a Southern justice.[91] Cellers's committee produced a report of over 900 pages clearing Douglas of all allegations.[92]

By 1972, Nixon secured four appointments to the Supreme Court. At a July 1972 White House meeting to discuss campaign strategy, Nixon's chief of staff, H. R. Haldeman, emphasized the value of these appointments as a vote-mobilization issue: "One of the more important issues of the campaign – in terms of basic differences [with McGovern] – there probably isn't a greater difference than in attitudes toward the courts and law enforcement. The way you demonstrate that is to point out the kind of people we have appointed to the Court – make an asset of it."[93] Haldeman stressed that the promised aim

[87] Ibid.
[88] House Floor Speech: Impeach Justice Douglas, Box D29, Gerald Ford Congressional Papers, Gerald Ford Library, http://www.ford.utexas.edu/library/speeches/700415a.htm.
[89] "Impeach Douglas?" 27 April 1970, *Time*.
[90] James Simon, *In His Own Image: The Supreme Court in Richard Nixon's America* (New York : D. McKay, 1973), 405.
[91] Ibid.
[92] Associate Justice William Douglas: Final Report of the Special Subcommittee on H. Res 920 of the Committee on the Judiciary, 91st Congress. [microform] (Washington, DC: U.S. Government Printing Office, 1970).
[93] "Memorandum for the President's File" from Ray Price, Subject: Meeting with Price Staff – July 24, 1972. Nixon Presidential Archives, National Archives and Records Administration,

of 1968 to reshape the judiciary had not yet been completed; acknowledging this unfinished business would motivate voters to keep Nixon in office: "On the Court, we have made a beginning – an important one. There are still a lot of 5 to 4 decisions. For a real imprint on the courts – *not just the Supreme Court* – it takes longer than four years. If we were to be voted out of office, the gains would be wiped out."[94] Nixon's advisors demonstrated an intention not only to make Supreme Court appointments an election issue but also to politicize lower court appointments.[95] This memo captures the administration's continued emphasis on appointment as a tool to shape the judiciary and utilize it to realize the policy and constitutional vision that Nixon ascribed to the Republican Party. Judicial appointment held out the potential for the most effective judicial harnessing *as long as judicial constitutional visions remained aligned with those of the president's party.* Given the pattern of Warren Court support of the Great Society, the Nixon administration had little reason to view partisan entrenchment through judicial appointment as improbable.[96]

II.b. *Fungible Legislation and Attacking Integrative School Busing Schemes*

Nixon exploited unpopular Court-ordered busing schemes to mobilize his "silent majority" and to continue Republican inroads among Southern racial conservatives.[97] Importantly, however, the fungible nature of his and

White House Special Files: Staff Member and Office Files, President's Meeting Series, Box 86. Epstein and Segal characterize the connection between judicial appointment and Nixon's attempt to broaden the Republican connections to the South: "Nixon was nearly obsessed with making appointments that would help his 1972 reelection bid, and in particular ... with enhancing the Republican party's appeal to southerners by appointing a justice from that region" (57). In particular, Nixon reached across party lines to nominate the conservative Democratic, yet importantly, Virginian, Lewis Powell to the Supreme Court bench.

[94] Ibid. Emphasis added.
[95] See discussion of this point in Section III of this chapter.
[96] The problems with this assumption are discussed in this book's Conclusion.
[97] See Reg Murphy and Hall Gulliver, *The Southern Strategy* (New York: Scribner's, 1971), and Joseph Aistrup, *The Southern Strategy Revisited* (Lexington: University Press of Kentucky, 1996), 18–64. While busing has been characterized as a racial codeword, it is not clear that Nixon advocated the policy because of any deeply seated racism. See Joan Hoff, *Nixon Reconsidered* (New York: Basic Books, 1995), 79. On racial code words, see Tali Mendelberg, *The Race Card* (Princeton: Princeton University Press, 2001). Nixon advisor, Harry Dent, offered the administration's official line following a 1969 Conference of Southern state Republican parties in New Orleans: "this Administration has no Southern strategy but rather a national strategy which, for the first time in modern times, includes the South, rather than excludes the South from full and equal participation in national affairs ... the Democrats seem to have written the South out of the Union, but the Republican Party is writing the South into the Union on an equal basis." Dent, "Memorandum for the President, Subject: Report on Southern GOP Conference at New Orleans," 8 December 1969, Richard Nixon Presidential Archives, National Archives and Records Administration, White House Special Files: Staff Member and Office Files, Harry Dent, Box 8, 1969 Southern GOP (Folder 1 of 3).
    Nixon was a racial moderate. See Kotlowski, 2001, and Lawrence McAndrews, "The Politics of Principle: Richard Nixon and School Desegregation," *Journal of Negro History* 83

congressional approaches to the challenge of stopping busing indicates that jurisdiction-stripping was not necessarily an attack on judicial authority per se. As this section argues, stripping jurisdiction was one of numerous tactics to secure a policy outcome suggesting that the policy was the main object, not the undermining of judicial authority. Haldeman indicated in his notes from daily staff meetings that Nixon did not want to undermine judicial authority directly. In this way, Nixon's relationship with the Court on busing matters reflected Klein's note to the editor of *Time* cited in the previous section. Nixon sought to *utilize* judicial power to support his administration's objectives. Thus, Haldeman noted the administration's strategy with reference to busing: "This is a very historic crisis. Country must not move in wrong direction. Must hit it effectively – In a way that will affect the court.... *Have to say in way that doesn't throw down gauntlet to Court too directly.* Must mobilize decent opinion."[98]

The battle over busing began with successful passage of the Civil Rights Act (CRA) in 1964. Antagonism toward busing markedly increased after the Supreme Court's unanimous 1971 decision in *Swann v. Charlotte-Mecklenburg Board of Education*, which ruled that busing was an appropriate remedial measure to advance a unitary and integrated school system, and especially after *Keyes v. School District No. 1* (1973), which opened Northern school systems to desegregation measures even absent a history of de jure segregation; however, congressional antipathy toward busing was evident as early as debate on the CRA.[99] The CRA's Title IV, Section 2000c-6, imposed explicit limits on utilizing busing: "Nothing herein shall empower any official or court of the United States to issue any order seeking to achieve a racial balance in any school by requiring the transportation of students or pupils from one school or another."

While some anti-busing legislation of the early 1970s did seek to curb the federal courts' jurisdiction or to limit the remedies the courts could access to

---

(Summer 1998), 187–200. As Jeremy Mayer, 2002, notes, the Republicans in 1960 "had put their strongest civil rights ticket forward, along with a platform that was at least as competitive with the Democrats, and lost significant ground among blacks. The Nixon campaign of 1960 was the high tide for racial liberalism in the Republican Party, which they have never approached since" (39).

98 Haldeman Notes, 20 February 1970, Richard Nixon Presidential Archives, National Archives and Records Administration, White House Special Files: Staff Member and Office Files, Box 41. Emphasis added.

99 *Swann v. Charlotte-Mecklenburg Board of Education*, 402 U.S. 1 (1971); *Keyes v. School District No. 1* 413 U.S. 189 (1973). In 1964, the Supreme Court refused review of a case of alleged school segregation in Gary, Indiana. The lower court ruling indicated that in the absence of de jure segregation, the school board had no obligation to act. *Bell v. School City of Gary, Indiana*, 324 F. 2nd 209 (7th Cir. 1963), cert denied, 377 U.S. 924 (1964). This case was mentioned in debate on the 1964 CRA. During debate, Hubert Humphrey, the Senate's floor manager, assured Senator Robert Byrd (D-WV) that the fund-withholding provisions of the bill could not be applied to cases of de facto segregation to secure racial balancing. *Congressional Record*, 4 June 1964, 12715–17.

secure the right of access to equal education, politicians advocated a range of ways to halt busing. This variety stems, in part, from the fact that once Congress passed the CRA, the Court no longer stood alone against segregationist forces. Thus, the old argument that desegregation was advanced by the unelected and undemocratic branch no longer functioned. Limits were now sought on a range of relevant enforcement bureaucracies.

Secretary John Gardner, head of the Department of Health, Education, and Welfare (HEW), zealously enforced desegregation under the CRA, even threatening to cut federal funds to Chicago given evidence of city-enforced school segregation.[100] The HEW threat was a gift to Southern anti-busing activists because it showed that the North was not exempt from busing. The possibility for a cross-sectional and cross-party coalition against busing, at least in the House, was in the offing.[101] In 1966, the House secured passage of an amendment that would forbid HEW to require busing to achieve racial balance. Another amendment, later known as the Whitten amendment, which would prohibit any desegregation plans beyond freedom-of-choice schemes, failed by only nine votes.[102] This budding bi-partisan coalition secured an amendment to the Model Cities Act, a cornerstone of Johnson's Great Society Program, stipulating that desegregation was not required to participate in the program.[103]

Congressional and presidential maneuvering shifted in 1968 when, in *Green v. New Kent County School Board*, the Court recognized "an affirmative duty to take whatever steps might be necessary to convert to a unitary system in which racial discrimination would be eliminated root and branch."[104] By putting the Court on the side of active integration as opposed to desegregation, the ruling opened the door to busing as a remedy, seemingly ignoring the legislative history of the Civil Rights Act. Presidential candidates capitalized on the ruling by coming out forcefully against busing. George Wallace advocated wholesale repeal of the Civil Rights Act.[105] Nixon utilized the CRA's language opposing "racial balancing" to support a moderate claim: he supported desegregation but opposed busing as a particular means to that end because the CRA itself forbade it.[106] Nixon could thereby distinguish himself

[100] The Department of Health, Education, and Welfare was later divided into the Departments of Health and Human Services and the Department of Education.
[101] Orfield, 1975, 85–7.
[102] Gary Orfield, *Must We Bus? Segregated Schools and National Policy* (Washington, DC: Brookings Institution, 1978), 239. See discussion of Nixon administration attempt to soften the Whitten amendments and place responsibility with the courts.
[103] 80 Stat. 1257. See *Congressional Record*, 14 October 1966, 26922 and 26927.
[104] *Green v. County Sch. Bd. of New Kent County*, 391 U.S. 430 (1968).
[105] George Wallace, *Hear Me Out* (New York: Droke House, dist. by Grosset & Dunlap, 1968), 18; Mayer, 85–6.
[106] See *Nixon on the Issues* (New York: Nixon-Agnew Campaign Committee, 1968), 98. Whether or not Nixon's anti-busing position was simply a code word for more deep-seated racism is unclear. Joan Hoff (1994) offers a sympathetic view suggesting that Nixon pushed hard on civil rights in line with Johnson's earlier achievements. Stephen Ambrose,

from Wallace's racist rhetoric while also wooing Southern and urban Northern voters wary of busing schemes.[107] He focused on education rather than integration: "My view, generally speaking, is that there has been too much of a tendency for both our courts and our Federal agencies to use the whole program of what we would call school integration for purposes which have very little to do with education," and "education should come first. Let it be our long-range objective to have it the integrated kind of education, but only when it works out in ways in which education does not suffer." Nixon also attempted to widen the scope of the conflict by acknowledging that "when you are talking about desegregation, let's understand it, it just isn't a Southern problem. You have de facto segregation in the North."[108] Thus, Nixon implied that busing could travel northward. In Nixon, opponents of busing in the North and South would have an ally.

Once in office, Nixon continued to oppose busing. Initially, he focused attention on the bureaucracy rather than the courts. Repositioning the Department of Health, Education, and Welfare (HEW) on desegregation would woo Southern voters.[109] Shortly after the 1969 inauguration, Harry Dent advised HEW Secretary Finch on how to handle busing:

by contrast, characterized Nixon as "being dragged kicking and screaming into desegregation on a meaningful scale." Stephen Ambrose, *Nixon: The Triumph of a Politician, 1962–1972* (New York: Simon & Schuster, 1989), 471. McAndrews, 1998, suggests that Nixon's position in favor of the principle of desegregation but opposed to the practice of busing mapped onto dominant popular sentiment at the time. Some have called anti-busing stances an instance of "symbolic racism." See John McConahay and Joseph C. Hough, Jr., "Symbolic Racism," *Journal of Social Issues* 32 (1972), 23–45, and Donald Kinder and David Sears, "Prejudice and Politics: Symbolic Racism versus Racial Threats to the Good Life," *Journal of Personality and Social Psychology* 40 (1980), 414–31. Others suggest the position is not racist per se, but grounded in assessment of costs and benefits to families with children. See McKee J. McClendon, "Racism, Rational Choice, and White Opposition to Racial Change: A Case Study of Busing," *Public Opinion Quarterly* 49 (Summer 1985), 214–33.

[107] On Nixon's strategic centrism in 1968, see Kotlowski, 19. See also Jonathan Rieder, "The Rise of the 'Silent Majority,'" in *The Rise and Fall of the New Deal Order, 1930–1980*, Steve Fraser and Gary Gerstle, eds. (Princeton: Princeton University Press, 1989), 243–68.

[108] These statements by Nixon are taken from a telecast of an interview in Charlotte, North Carolina, which had been reported by the *New York Times*, 13 September 1968. They were compiled as part of a packet that Harry Dent sent to Southern Republican chairpersons to clarify Nixon's stance on school desegregation. In a memo to other administration officials, Dent was careful to note that while "these reports are sent on plain letterhead ... they [the Southern leaders] know from where they come," suggesting the hushed nature of the "Southern strategy." Harry Dent to John Ehrlichman, Bob Haldeman, Bryce Harlow, Herb Klein, Ron Zeigler, and John Sears, 7 February 1969, Richard Nixon Presidential Archives, National Archives and Records Administration, White House Special Files: Staff Member and Office Files, Harry Dent, Box 8, 1969 Southern GOP (Folder 1 of 3).

[109] Southern House Representatives had already attempted to raise broad antagonism toward HEW by inserting a directive into that department's annual appropriations bill that half of all federal funds must be used to investigate school segregation *outside* of the South. Pub. L. 90–577 (1968), section 410. Doing so would widen the scope of conflict, under the idea that once integration traveled north, Northerners would join the anti-busing coalition.

> I tried to stress to him [Finch] the importance of emphasizing to the pub-
> lic that education will come first. He might want to also add that the
> Administration does not support the concept of bussing for the purpose of
> trying to achieve racial balance. Putting both points together in one state-
> ment would serve to reassure people in the North and South that this will not
> be a wild Administration on the subject of guideline implementation.[110]

A July 1969 statement of HEW policy on desegregation accordingly emphasized procedures to "improve, rather than disrupt, the education of the children concerned."[111] It stressed that "it is not our purpose here to lay down a
single, arbitrary date by which the desegregation process should be completed
in all districts, or lay down a single, arbitrary system by which it should be
achieved."[112] HEW and the Department of Justice were clearing a way to retreat
from the Johnson administration's enforcement standards. In another characteristic indicator of harnessing, the statement looked to the Court, quoting
the *Green* decision to supportive effect: "there is no universal answer to the
complex problems of desegregation."[113] The statement used judicial authority
to prop its own proposal. There was no direct attack on that authority.

The Nixon administration attempted to harness judicial power beyond
using it to legitimize its position on busing. It also sought to pass accountability to the Court and thus to maintain the Court as a potential scapegoat. The
administration's approach to the Whitten amendments is representative. These
amendments would have prevented HEW's use of federal funds to compel a
school district to bus students, close schools, or eliminate freedom-of-choice
plans. They were attached to H.R. 13111, which passed in the House in 1969
and traveled to conference reconciliation. In September of 1969, Secretary
Finch advised John Ehrlichman, White House Counsel to President Nixon,
that the administration needed a backup plan if the Senate or the conference
committee maintained the Whitten amendment. Finch recommended substitute language: "No part of the funds contained in this Act may be used
to force any school district to take any actions not constitutionally required
involving the busing of students, the abolishment of any school or the assignment of any student attending elementary or secondary school to a particular
school against the choice of his or her parents or parent."[114] The language was

---

110 Harry Dent to Herb Klein, 25 February 1969, Richard Nixon Presidential Archives, National
Archives and Records Administration, White House Special Files: Staff Member and Office
Files, Harry Dent, Box 8, 1969 Southern GOP (Folder 1 of 3).

111 "School Desegregation Statement by the Department of Justice and the Department of
Health, Education, and Welfare," 5 July 1969, Richard Nixon Presidential Archives,
National Archives and Records Administration, White House Special Files: Staff Member
and Office Files, Harry Dent, Box 8, 1969 Southern GOP (Folder 1 of 3).

112 Ibid.

113 Ibid.

114 Robert Finch to John Ehrlichman, 16 September 1969, Richard Nixon Presidential Archives,
National Archives and Records Administration, White House Special Files: Staff Member
and Office Files, John Ehrlichman, Box 34, Folder "School Busing (Whitten Amendments).
Emphasis in original.

essentially identical to that in the Whitten provision except for the insertion of the phrase "not constitutionally required." That phrase was *an invitation for judicial interpretation*. If the amendment passed, it allowed Congress to look strong against busing. It created the potential to maintain HEW funding by passing accountability to a pro-busing Court. HEW would get its money and the administration and Congress could both blame the Court to their respective electoral benefit.

While Finch maintained that his proposed language was "simple and straightforward, leaving unmistakably clear the limitations on the Department's authority to enforce Title VI of the Civil Rights Act," he also noted that it would force opposition into a narrow frame: "the language has some political appeal in that it could be opposed only by directly attacking the Constitution or court decisions."[115] And such direct attacks on judicial legitimacy were to be avoided at all cost. The language achieved two objectives. First, it took heat off HEW and the administration for enforcing busing, placing the administration firmly on record as opposing busing. Second, it freed the administration to move forward with desegregation plans by passing responsibility to judges to read exceptions into the statute. It left open the possibility that in some cases busing schemes may be constitutionally required. But that determination was removed from the executive branch and lodged with the Court.

Nixon's response to the Court's ruling in *Alexander v. Holmes* was another example of harnessing judicial power.[116] The Justice Department sought to delay desegregation of a Mississippi school district, but in *Alexander*, the Supreme Court issued a per curiam opinion that rebuked the call for delay.[117] In March of 1970, Nixon responded by issuing, a "Statement about Desegregation of Elementary and Secondary Schools," in which he re-affirmed his support for *Brown* and his objection to busing. He urged that plans for compliance with desegregation should come from local school boards, "provided they act in good faith and within Constitutional limits," that racial imbalance, if de facto to the extent that it results "genuinely from housing patterns," cannot "by itself be cause for Federal enforcement actions," and that "transportation of

---

[115] Ibid.
[116] *Alexander v. Holmes County Bd. of Ed.*, 396 U.S. 1218 (1969). Leon Panetta, *Bring Us Together* (Philadelphia: Lippincott, 1971), 350–55; Orfield,1978, 243, 285–91; Kotlowski, 34.
[117] The administration's advocacy of delay in Mississippi was, in part, triggered by a letter from Senator John Stennis (D-MS), who called for the delay in HEW desegregation plans. Stennis issued the veiled threat: "AS CHAIRMAN OF THE SENATE ARMED SERVICES COMMITTEE I HAVE MAJOR RESPONSIBILITIES HERE IN CONNECTION WITH LEGISLATION DEALING WITH OUR NATIONAL SECURITY, BUT I WILL NOT HESITATE ONE MOMENT TO LEAVE MY DUTIES HERE AT ANY TIME TO GO TO MISSISSIPPI OR DO WHATEVER ELSE MAY BE REQUIRED TO HELP PROTECT THE PEOPLE OF MISSISSIPPI AND TO PRESERVE OUR PUBLIC SCHOOL SYSTEM. Stennis to Richard Nixon, 11 August 1969. Included in a memo from Ken Belieu to Bryce Harlow, undated but marked "urgent." Richard Nixon Presidential Archives, National Archives and Records Administration, White House Special Files: Staff Member and Office Files, Ehrlichman, Box 34, Folder "School Busing."

pupils beyond normal geographical school zones for the purpose of achieving racial balance will not be required."[118] He also emphasized busing's alleged potential to undermine social institutions: "several recent decisions by lower courts have raised widespread fears that the Nation might face a massive disruption of public education: that wholesale compulsory busing may be ordered and the neighborhood school virtually doomed."[119] He backpedaled in his next sentence: "A comprehensive review of school desegregation cases indicates that these latter are untypical decisions, and that the prevailing trend of judicial opinion is by no means so extreme."[120] This statement seems to follow from advice offered at Nixon's staff meeting on 21 February 1970 – quoted earlier – to avoid throwing down a gauntlet directly against the Court.

In short, Nixon attempted to align himself with widespread support for desegregation, but not busing, while avoiding a direct attack on judicial legitimacy.[121] He stressed his agreement with Chief Justice Burger, who indicated earlier that year in *Northcross v. Board of Education* that the extent to which "transportation may or must be provided" to promote desegregation remained unclear.[122] In doing so, Nixon signaled that, through Burger, he was turning the Court against integrationist policy, a promise made to Southerners at the 1968 Republican national convention.[123] And by keeping busing in the public discourse during an election year, Nixon "used the busing issue in a strident campaign to put a new conservative majority on Capitol Hill."[124] Haldeman's notes of Nixon's staff meetings indicate that the president "Wants Dems – especially Muskie and Kennedy – put on spot – for or against busing."[125] Keeping conversation on this topic active might force Democrats to make a move.

Burger answered the question he posed in *Northcross* a year later in *Swann*, but not in the definitive way Nixon might have hoped. A unanimous Court endorsed racially conscious remedial measures such as "gerrymandering of

[118] "Statement about Desegregation of Elementary and Secondary Schools," 24 March 1970, John T. Woolley and Gerhard Peters, *The American Presidency Project* [online]. Santa Barbara, CA: University of California (hosted), Gerhard Peters (database), http://www. presidency.ucsb.edu/ws/?pid=2923.

[119] Ibid.

[120] Ibid.

[121] See Orfield's, 1978, survey of polling data, 108–8.

[122] Ibid. *Northcross v. Board of Education*, 397 U.S. 232 (1970).

[123] Jeffrey Rosen, "Can Bush Deliver a Conservative Supreme Court?" *New York Times*, 14 November 2004, Week in Review, 1. "By promising to appoint strict constructionists, Mr. Bush has embraced the mantra of every Republican president since Richard Nixon, who first made that promise in his 1968 campaign."

[124] Orfield, 1978, 245.

[125] Haldeman Notes, 23 February 1970, Richard Nixon Presidential Archives, National Archives and Records Administration, White House Special Files: Staff Member and Office Files, Box 41. See also a similar statement from the notes on 26 February 1970: "Get a response from Kennedy and Muskie.... Do they support busing?"

school districts and attendance zones ... pairing, 'clustering,' or 'grouping' of schools" and recognized that while busing was inconvenient, it was a constitutionally required remedy to realize the aims laid out in *Brown*:

> Absent a constitutional violation there would be no basis for judicially ordering assignment of students on a racial basis. All things being equal, with no history of discrimination, it might well be desirable to assign pupils nearest their homes. But all things are not equal in a system that has been deliberately constructed and maintained to enforce racial segregation. The remedy for such segregation may be administratively awkward, inconvenient, and even bizarre in some situations and may impose burdens on some; but all awkwardness and inconvenience cannot be avoided in the interim period when remedial adjustments are being made to eliminate the dual school systems.[126]

The ruling maintained the de facto/de jure distinction that Nixon brought to light. The Court stated that it was concerned with dismantling dual school systems and not with the ways in which the state might conceivably maintain segregated schools without an *explicit* statute to that effect: "We do not reach in this case the question whether a showing that school segregation is a consequence of other types of state action, without any discriminatory action by the school authorities, is a constitutional violation requiring remedial action by a school desegregation decree. This case does not present that question and we therefore do not decide it."[127] While the decision endorsed busing, as did three other rulings handed down on the same day, it rejected racial balancing: "The constitutional command to desegregate schools does not mean that every school in every community must always reflect the racial composition of the school system as a whole."[128] Furthermore, Burger imposed limits on the remedy; it must be "reasonable, feasible, and workable."[129] It could not "significantly impinge on the educational process," suggesting that if busing entailed long rides, it would be deemed inadequate.[130] By stipulating that busing was an "interim corrective measure," he assured that it would eventually end and that the federal court's role was limited: "in the absence of showing that either the school authorities or some other agency of the State has deliberately attempted to fix or alter demographic patterns to affect racial composition of the schools, further intervention by a district court should be unnecessary."[131] While *Swann* supported busing, Burger was careful to structure the opinion to avoid inter-branch backlash as much as possible.

[126] *Swann v. Charlotte-Mecklenburg Bd. of Education*, 402 U.S. 1 (1971).
[127] Ibid.
[128] Ibid. The three other cases were *Davis v. Board of Commissioners*, 402 U.S. 33 (1971); *McDaniel v. Barresi*, 402 U.S. 39 (1971); and *North Carolina Board of Education v. Swann*, 402 U.S. 42 (1971).
[129] Ibid.
[130] Ibid.
[131] Ibid.

Far from a watershed decision supporting busing against Nixon's aims, Burger's ruling in *Swann* was a circumscribed acknowledgment that busing was a necessary counter to statutory or de jure segregation.[132] While the decision approved of busing as an appropriate tool to achieve integration, it set limits on the extent to which that tool could be used and the narrow responsibilities of the federal courts to ensure that integration continued over time. It consciously avoided the question of whether busing was the required remedy for de facto school segregation. Thus, the ruling attempted to balance the acknowledged logistical difficulties and unpopularity of busing with the constitutional demands to reach the goal set out by *Brown*. Viewing *Swann* in this light allows us to better understand the minor purpose and ultimate effect that the Court-curbing legislation to come, detailed in the next section, in fact had.

Swann shifted Nixon's focus from the bureaucracies toward the judiciary in order to stop busing schemes. Prior to the ruling, the administration centered its efforts on limiting HEW's enforcement. It harnessed judicial power either by passing accountability for interpretation of statute – as in the case of the Whitten Amendments – or citing Court rulings as legitimizing administration positions. Prior to *Swann*, the Nixon administration demonstrated the ways it strove to harness judicial power to positive political effect.

II.c. *Passing Redundant, Ambiguous, and Symbolic Court-Curbing Legislation*

Court jurisdiction in matters related to busing was ultimately curbed in two statutes. The Educational Amendments of 1972 and the 1974 reauthorization of the Elementary and Secondary Education Act (ESEA) imposed restrictions on remedies, that is, limited when courts could authorize busing. As this section details, the legislation was redundant to the Court's earlier rulings, suggesting that "the limitations were more symbolic than real."[133] So, although the attack on judicial authority did pass, that is, jurisdiction was stripped, it took shape as expected in a polity developed for judicial harnessing, namely, it was symbolic and served electoral credit-claiming goals. Politicians could go on record against busing and the Court without diminishing judicial power any further than judges already had by imposing limits upon themselves.

The first specifically anti-judiciary proposal, as opposed to limits on HEW enforcement, was an amendment to the 1972 higher education bill, sponsored by Representative William Broomfield (D-MI); it restricted implementation of court orders requiring busing until all appeals were tried. If it had passed, the Court's ruling in *Alexander v. Holmes* would have been negated. The amendment is also interesting to the extent that it came from a Northerner as busing

---

[132] Bernard Schwartz, *Swann's Way: The School Busing Case and the Supreme Court* (New York: Oxford University Press, 1986), 100–184.

[133] Gary Orfield, "Congress, the President, and Anti-Busing Legislation, 1966–1974," *Journal of Law and Education* 4 (January 1975), 132.

schemes proceeded in Detroit following *Bradley v. Milliken*.[134] The House bill
passed, forcing the Senate to take it up in 1972, an election year.

In the Senate, legislation delaying court-ordered busing until all appeals
were exhausted failed by one vote. In a context where jurisdiction-stripping
or remedial constraints would likely pass, given their broad support and low
electoral cost, Senate majority leader, Mike Mansfield, and Senate minority
leader, Hugh Scott, sponsored an amendment to their chamber's version of
the bill that would delay enforcement, but it would do so only until mid-
1973.[135] The proposal "was a very significant change of principle"; the Senate
acknowledged that it was "necessary to endorse a 'compromise' action restraining the authority of the judicial branch."[136] In short, no norm of deference
to judicial authority appears to have bound even the more moderate upper
legislative chamber.

The Mansfield-Scott amendment inserted the phrase "except as the
Constitution requires" into the House language thereby creating a plausible
opening for the judiciary to overrule Congress and continue to enforce busing. In other words, the proposed language, similar to dynamics discussed in
Chapter 6, allowed legislators to claim they had taken action against busing
and the Court, but kept open the possibility that busing might continue.[137]
The amendment also stood against "racial balancing" by banning the use
of federal monies for that purpose; but this provision was *redundant* as the
Court in *Swann* explicitly indicated it was not racial balancing and had no
intention of doing so. As such, that part of the compromise was symbolism.
However, the amendment failed at conference suggesting that members of the
House believed that a large enough coalition backed curbing judicial author-
ity. The Senate passed the bill by 63 to 16; the House did so by 218 to 180.[138]

---

[134] *Bradley v. Milliken*, 338 F. Supp. 583 (1971). The Michigan congressional delegation's turn
against busing may therefore have been more related to local rulings than to the Supreme
Court's ruling in *Swann*, which was limited to Southern desegregation. Two other amendments came from Northerners, but like earlier moves, these attempted to stop busing by cutting off funding rather than curbing jurisdiction. Representative Ashbrook (R-OH) wanted to
prohibit use of federal funds for transporting students or teaching in any school adhering to
a court-ordered busing scheme. Representative Green (D-OR) wanted to prohibit federal
officials from urging integration. This proposal would prevent HEW from cutting funding
to school districts segregating their students because, in so doing, they would be encouraging
integration. Orfield, 1978, 250–1. See also Orfield, 1975, 104–7, and *Congressional Record*,
4 November 1971, 10407–58, 10416–7.

[135] Orfield, 1978, 253.

[136] Orfield, 1975, 108.

[137] The language had little to no effect. In *Keyes v. School District No. 1* (1973) the Court
(7 to 1) blurred the lines between de jure and de facto segregation. Justice Brennan ruled
that if plaintiffs demonstrated that one part of the Denver school system is segregated,
even without statute authorizing a dual system, the system must prove that that segregation
was not intended on a system-wide basis. In so ruling, the Court brought the possibility of
busing north.

[138] Orfield, 1975, 109.

When Nixon signed this bill, he issued a signing statement calling its anti-busing language "inadequate, misleading and entirely unsatisfactory."[139] Prior to signing it and only days after George Wallace won the Florida primary, Nixon offered two statutory proposals, considered under the titles "Equal Educational Opportunities Act" and "Student Transportation Moratorium Act," which represented the president's strongest position against the federal courts. The measures were undoubtedly an attempt to shore up Nixon's credentials against busing and to stake a centrist position between Wallace and the Democrats.[140] They imposed a moratorium on busing until 1 July 1973 and prioritized the remedies that the courts might offer to end desegregation, with busing as a last resort.[141]

It is not entirely clear how Nixon's moratorium language was substantively different from the Mansfield-Scott compromise, which was less harsh than the House amendment that had already passed. Put differently, Nixon's contribution was redundant. To the extent that the Nixon proposal sought to define busing as a measure of last resort, it went beyond Burger's own caveats in *Swann*. It made that principle more concrete by prohibiting busing for children in grades one through six and allowed limited busing for students in grades seven through twelve. However, the Court had *already* recognized in *Swann* and *Green* that remedial measures, particularly busing, could not be used if they were detrimental to students' educational success. While more specific in its judicial limits, the proposal's objectives did not appear all that distinct from the limits that Chief Justice Burger had already sought to impose on lower federal courts in *Swann*. Even so, Nixon's proposals were criticized by the legal academic community, and the administration could point to only conservative professor Robert Bork as supportive.[142]

---

[139]   Richard Nixon, "Statement on Signing the Education Amendments of 1972," 23 June 1972, John T. Woolley and Gerhard Peters, *The American Presidency Project* [online]. Santa Barbara, CA: University of California (hosted), Gerhard Peters (database), http://www.presidency.ucsb.edu/ws/?pid=3473.

[140]   The Democratic National Platform of 1972 clearly supported busing: "There are many ways to desegregate schools: School attendance lines may be redrawn; schools may be paired; larger physical facilities may be built to serve larger, more diverse enrollments; magnet schools or educational parks may be used. Transportation of students is another tool to accomplish desegregation," John T. Woolley and Gerhard Peters, *The American Presidency Project* [online]. Santa Barbara, CA: University of California (hosted), Gerhard Peters (database), http://www.presidency.ucsb.edu/ws/?pid=29605.

[141]   "Address to the Nation on Equal Educational Opportunities and School Busing," 16 March 1972, John T. Woolley and Gerhard Peters, *The American Presidency Project* [online]. Santa Barbara, CA: University of California (hosted), Gerhard Peters (database), http://www.presidency.ucsb.edu/ws/?pid=3775, and "Special Message to the Congress on Equal Educational Opportunities and School Busing,"17 March 1972, John T. Woolley and Gerhard Peters, *The American Presidency Project* [online]. Santa Barbara, CA: University of California (hosted), Gerhard Peters (database), http://www.presidency.ucsb.edu/ws/?pid=3776.

[142]   Orfield, 254. See Robert Bork, *Constitutionality of the President's Busing Proposals* (Washington, DC: American Enterprise Institute, 1972).

In the hands of House Representatives, Nixon's proposal became rabidly anti-integrationist. The House strengthened the restrictions by limiting busing to the "closest" or "next-closest" school to the student's home, and it allowed for federal courts to re-open previous cases so that the law could apply retro-actively thereby dismantling existing court-ordered busing schemes.[143] Since the bill came to the Senate floor in October of 1972 and Congress would soon recess for the election, a filibuster was possible.[144] Cloture failed three times, and Congress recessed without taking action on Nixon's proposal.[145] Nixon vowed to continue the fight against busing and the federal judiciary in Congress's next session, but his agenda was precluded by the deepening Watergate investigations and possible impeachment.[146]

The opportunity to continue the battle against busing and to curb federal court jurisdiction to enforce busing came in 1974 when the Elementary and Secondary Education Act was set to expire. During debate on the proposed education bill, Representative Esch (R-MI) offered a series of anti-busing amendments, which passed by a vote of 293 to 117 and which were similar to the House amendments of 1972.[147] The Senate began debate on the bill in May 1974, which was too far from the end of session to contemplate a fili-buster. Senators sought a compromise that would register objection to busing. To that end, Senator Bayh (D-IN) offered an amendment that forbade busing unless courts deemed "all alternative remedies are inadequate."[148] Once again, the proposed language left it to the courts to determine the standard of ade-quacy and deflected accountability while preserving the ability to attack the judiciary if it continued to maintain busing as a remedy. The Bayh proposal has been considered "more rhetoric than substance," and anti-busing sena-tors criticized it for doing "absolutely nothing to change the situation as it exists" and as "simply a ploy in order to prevent the Senate ... from voting on this all-burning, all compelling, all-pervasive issue of school busing."[149] The amendment did little more than reaffirm what the Court had already said in *Swann*. It continued the tradition of passing accountability to judges with one hand while passing legislation that chastised judges with the other.[150] The House amendments were tabled in the Senate, but only by a single vote, which again suggests that numerous senators exploited the opportunity to make the symbolic gesture of striking out against judicial authority, indicating that it

[143] *Congressional Record*, 17 August 1972, 2888–2907.
[144] Senator Griffin (D-MI) had in 1967 helped block a Whitten amendment to the Elementary and Secondary Education Act that would have prohibited federal funding for busing pur-poses; now he switched sides on the issues in the wake of *Bradley*. He now shepherded the bill to passage and secured enough votes to invoke cloture.
[145] *New York Times*, 7 October 1972, 1. The Senate's last attempt to invoke cloture to end the filibuster failed on 12 October 1972. *Congressional Record*, 35330.
[146] Orfield, 1975, 111.
[147] Congressional Record, 26 March 1974, 8281–2.
[148] *Congressional Record*, 15 May 1974, 14862.
[149] Orfield, 1978, 363; Congressional Record, 15 May 1972, 14864–5, 14866–7.
[150] Orfield, 1975, 126; Congressional Record, 15 May 1974, 8192–3.

would earn them electoral capital.[151] Senators at least felt that demonstrating deference to the judiciary would *not* earn them political capital with their constituents, which undermines the idea that deference to judicial supremacy is a pervasive popular norm. The Bayh amendment passed 56–36.[152]

Ironically, the bill produced at conference, rather than curbing federal jurisdiction, authorized a *new* area of judicial discretion. Since 1954, desegregation cases remained open and litigants could file new motions with federal judges to revisit whether desegregation orders were proceeding apace. The new bill authorized federal judges to close these cases, limiting desegregation cases to one ruling that would remedy de jure segregation. Once that ruling was ordered, the court could relinquish jurisdiction, which would essentially close it to re-examination if the school district were to resegregate. The bill harnessed judicial power, in this case by widening judicial discretion, to achieve an anti-integrationist outcome.[153] But again, the bill did not achieve anything that the Court had not already acceded to, namely, the idea that busing must be a limited remedy and that children could not be bused beyond the "school closest or next closest to his place of residence which provides the appropriate grade level and type of education for such student."[154]

The Senate passed the legislation on 24 July 1974; the House did so on 31 July.[155] The Court decided *Milliken v. Bradley* six days prior to the House vote. In *Milliken* the Court held that busing could only occur within the boundaries of a school district, essentially ending integrationist busing because it ensured the success of "white flight" to suburban areas beyond city limits. The legislation was not only redundant, but the Court went even further than the legislation. The legislation had allowed for integration to include the next-closest school, which could have been across the city line, but now *Milliken* prevented such a school from being part of any desegregation remedy. Congress removed judicial powers in areas from which the Court had already shied away. Once again, legislators may have manipulated judicial power through some degree of jurisdiction-stripping, but it only did so after the Court self-regulated.

In summary, congressional attacks on court-ordered busing in the 1970s reveal three patterns. First, legislation did not only target the judiciary, indicating that altering busing policy as opposed to undermining judicial authority, was the real aim.[156] Much of the anti-busing legislation was targeted at

---

[151] The anti-busing constitutional amendment, which had a House majority and was endorsed by Nixon, never gained widespread popular support; an Opinion Research Corporation poll from 13 March 1973 indicated that 30 percent of respondents favored the amendment banning busing, while 57 percent favored a statutory ban. Appendix of U.S. Commission on Civil Rights, "Public Knowledge and Busing Opposition: An Interpretation of a New National Survey" (Washington, DC: U.S. Government Printing Office, 1973), 2.

[152] Ibid., 14924, 14926.

[153] Orfield, 1978, 266.

[154] *Congressional Record*, 23 July 1974, 24543–44, text of bill sec 215(a).

[155] Ibid., 24 July 1974, 26111–12 and 31 July 1974, 16128.

[156] On anti-busing legislation as fungible, see Edward Keynes, *The Court vs. Congress: Prayer, Busing, and Abortion* (Durham: Duke University Press, 1989), 206–44. That the anti-busing

HEW enforcement. Second, a cross-party coalition in the House managed to pass numerous bills curbing judicial power. Nixon advocated these measures, and even the allegedly mild-mannered Senate supported court-curbing legislation. This circumstance raises doubts as to whether any claim of normative deference among politicians to judicial authority or an elite norm of judicial supremacy is empirically valid. Parallel to congressional dynamics of jurisdiction-stripping in the 1950s, anti-busing policies, including but not limited to jurisdiction-stripping, could not gain traction until a coalition of supporters broadened beyond Southern Democrats. That coalition building, as in the 1950s, was spurred by Court rulings, most prominently *Swann*, which began to directly affect Northern states. Tellingly, the Michigan delegation was at the forefront of anti-busing legislation as much as, if not more than, any Southern state delegation.

Third, while a deluge of court-curbing proposals came in *Swann*'s wake, the legislation that passed – the 1972 Educational Amendments and the 1974 ESEA – did *not* limit the Court's authority beyond what the Court had already imposed on itself. Some of this legislation actually widened judicial discretion, although it did so with the intent to secure anti-busing policy aims. While impinging on judicial power to rule in particular ways, either by curbing jurisdiction or proscribing the remedies, the legislation did not seek to undermine the Court's wider legitimacy to rule. In 1972, when referencing his H.R. 13534, which would stop federal courts from ordering busing if a local school board was already following an HEW-approved desegregation plan, Representative Dingell (D-MI) admitted his intention to harness judicial power. The legislation was "an attempt to *guide the hands and ways of the courts* into perhaps the most expeditious and satisfactory conclusion to the cases before them."[157] Similarly, on a different bill that would prohibit student assignment to schools based on race, Senator Gorton (R-WA) was explicit in endorsing harnessing: "we are not attempting to directly reverse Supreme Court decisions but, to put it more delicately, simply to *guide* the Supreme

---

movement was motivated to achieve a specific policy result rather than to engage a constitutional question about the balance of powers is reflected in the shape of popular outcry. Anti-busing campaigns were local; no national anti-busing campaign was mounted with any degree of success, and the protest and violence that characterized Boston, Canarsie, and Detroit in the early and mid-1970s was triggered when busing infiltrated those neighborhoods. Popular remedies by individuals were not to coordinate a large-scale movement against judicial authority but to leave jurisdictions where busing was ordered, by moving altogether or relocating children out of the public school system. See Ronald Formisano, *Boston against Busing* (Chapel Hill: University of North Carolina Press, 1991), 3–7, 80–2, 146–8, 172–202, 210. On localism of the anti-busing movement, see also Steven Taylor, *Desegregation in Boston and Buffalo* (Albany: State University Press of New York, 1998). As one legal scholar has recently characterized the anti-busing activism, "their fight was about *their* schools and children, and very little else." Eric Citron, "Constitutional Change and the End of Integration: From *Swann* to *Milliken* in the Constitutional Politics of the 1970s." Unpublished manuscript on file with the author.

[157] House Judiciary Committee, *Busing Hearings*, part I (1972), 502. Emphasis added.

Court into a slightly different channel."[158] These legislative proposals relied on the accepted authority of courts to rule. Gorton's dismissal of a direct reversal is particularly telling as to do so would be a step toward undermining judicial legitimacy. By the time the 1974 ESEA became law, the Court had already obliged with its majority ruling in *Milliken v. Bradley*, which allowed members of Congress to credit-claim on passing the ESEA without actually restricting judicial authority.

There is no denying that following Nixon's appointments the Court retreated from busing; as such, appointments can trigger policy change through judicial review.[159] With *Milliken*, the Court backed off busing. Yet the Nixon administration – especially given *Swann* and *Keyes* – demonstrated that appointments alone could not ensure a judicial realignment toward the political leanings of the administration. The Court's hand had to be further controlled if its *own* constitutional vision was to give way or be shaped to conform to the president's. A few years later, under the guidance of former Nixon appointees, young lawyers in the Reagan administration's Justice Department hit upon a new tool that might utilize judicial power without undermining judicial authority or the ideal veneer of judicial neutrality: presidential signing statements. That innovation is taken up in Chapter 8.

III. Appointment and Obstruction: Maintaining Vacancies to Harness Judicial Power

If judicial interpretation can promote policy objectives, then controlling who is on the bench is yet another way that presidents – through their nomination power – and senators – through their advise and consent authority and through procedural maneuvers to delay a nominee's consideration – can manipulate judicial power.[160] Through appointment the president and the majority party in the Senate, particularly in an instance of unified government, can potentially harness judicial power par excellence. This section examines evidence of how and why the confirmation process has become increasingly politicized since the 1970s. While appointments to the Supreme Court have perhaps always been contentious to a degree, the newer development is the politicization of lower court appointments. Discussion of the kinds of judges

---

[158] Senate Judiciary Committee, Subcommittee on Separation of Powers, *Busing Hearings* (1981), 9. Emphasis added.

[159] This "attitudinal model" suggests that judges can be arrayed on a left-right one-dimensional policy space. See Jeffrey Segal and Harold Spaeth, *The Supreme Court and the Attitudinal Model Revisited* (New York: Cambridge University Press, 2002).

[160] For discussion of how presidents and senators utilize appointments to transform the political makeup of the federal judiciary and alter judicial rulings (if, of course, one assumes that judicial rulings, if not necessarily motivated by judges' partisan leanings, have partisan effects supportive of one party's policies versus another's), see Sheldon Goldman, "Reagan's Judicial Legacy: Completing the Puzzle and Summing Up," *Judicature* 72 (April–May 1989), 318–30, and Carl Tobias, "Rethinking Federal Judicial Selection," *B.Y.U. Law Review* (1993), 1257–86.

that a presidential candidate favors is consistent election fodder, and interest groups have come to participate in and publicize not only Supreme Court appointments but also appointments to federal district courts and courts of appeals.[161] This trickle down the hierarchy began under Nixon, was exacerbated by Carter-era reforms, and reached a crisis in recent years that threatened congressional shutdown and the elimination of a critical tool of democracy: the filibuster.[162]

III.a. *Jimmy Carter Politicizes the Lower Federal Judiciary*

The ability to control policy through judicial appointment, and thus the consequent politicization of appointment, is not new. In the weeks preceding FDR's announcement of his judicial reform plan, Judge William Denman of the Ninth Circuit, wrote to FDR, "The New Deal needs more federal judges."[163] Similarly, after the *Adkins* decision, Florence Kelley lamented that her dispute with the National Women's Party was a distraction from the real agenda of harnessing the Court's power to stand behind the social reform her group advocated: "My debates with the Woman's Party are one per cent against an Amendment which will never be adopted, and 99% for women judges and a responsible Court."[164] Even as evidence exists that judicial appointments shifted from patronage motivations in the nineteenth century to policy motivations in the early twentieth century, that recognition was intermittent – especially with regard to the lower federal judiciary – until at least the Carter presidency.[165] The development of senatorial courtesy – whereby the president defers to a senator's preferences when appointing a judge to a district or circuit

---

[161] See Patrick Healy, "Seeking to Shift Attention to Judicial Nominees," *New York Times*, 6 October 2008.

[162] On the crisis of judgeship vacancies throughout the federal judiciary, see Chief Justice John Robert's "2010 Year-End Report on the Federal Judiciary." He writes, "Each political party has found it easy to turn on a dime from decrying to defending the blocking of judicial nominations, depending on their changing political fortunes. This has created acute difficulties for some judicial districts" (7–8), http://www.supremecourt.gov/publicinfo/year-end/2010year-endreport.pdf.

[163] Denman, quoted in Sheldon Goldman, *Picking Federal Judges: Lower Court Selection from Roosevelt through Reagan* (New Haven: Yale University Press, 1997), 32.

[164] Kelley to William Bigelow, 12 December 1923, "Correspondence: Press and Periodicals, Good Housekeeping," folder, Box B 20, National Consumers' League Papers, quoted in Joan G. Zimmerman, "The Jurisprudence of Equality: The Women's Minimum Wage, the First Equal Rights Amendment, and *Adkins v. Children's Hospital*, 1905–1923," *Journal of American History* 78 (June 1991), 225.

[165] Rayman Solomon, "The Politics of Appointment and the Federal Court's Role in Regulating America: U.S. Courts of Appeals Judgeships from T.R. to F.D.R.," *American Bar Foundation Research Journal* 9:2 (1984), 285–343. Solomon argues that through FDR's administration, presidents utilized lower judicial appointments for patronage purposes or, in the case of Taft and Hoover, to boost the professionalism of the federal judiciary. By contrast, FDR, beginning in his second term, utilized his appointments to achieve policy ends; however, even FDR's assessment of the judicial-policy nexus was limited according to Solomon: "the importance to policy of lower court judgeships was not perceived until after the courts had blocked several of the administration's regulatory experiments" (342).

court of which that senator's state is part – testifies to how lower federal judicial appointments were considered a source of patronage to secure broader inter-branch comity.[166] As one legal scholar notes, "prior to the Nixon administration, policy considerations and/or ideological ones didn't often take primacy in lower court selection processes."[167]

As detailed earlier, Nixon exploited judicial appointment as a part of a strategy to secure the Republican Party's viability in the South. While his struggles with securing Supreme Court appointees garnered much media coverage, the administration was keenly aware of how shaping the *lower* federal judiciary could have electoral and policy benefits. Nixon aide, Tom Huston, bluntly detailed the strategy:

> Perhaps the least considered aspect of presidential power is the authority to make appointments to the federal branch, not merely the Supreme Court, but to the district and circuit court benches as well. Through his judicial appointments a president has the opportunity to influence the course of national affairs for a quarter of a century after he leaves office.[168]

While Nixon aides articulated the idea of utilizing lower court appointment to serve ideological and policy purposes, and not only for patronage, President Carter put the idea into full effect.

When Carter signed the Omnibus Judgeship Act of 1978, he authorized the largest expansion of federal judgeships in American history; the statute created 152 federal judgeships.[169] It is not clear that Carter's immediate objective was to secure Democratic policy aims on the bench. It is unnecessary to show that Carter's motive was such anyway. More important for the argument made in this book is that Republican reaction framed it as having that effect.

Rather than defer to senatorial courtesy to fill these new judgeships, Carter, ever the administrative bureaucrat, established the United States Circuit Judge

[166] Such inter-branch comity is shown by the high rates of approval senators give to presidential judicial appointments. The direction of the comity, however, is contested. Early studies suggested that senators were deferential to the president. See Harold Chase, *Federal Judges: The Appointing Process* (Minneapolis: University of Minnesota Press, 1972). More recent game-theoretic models suggest the deference runs in the opposite direction: presidents anticipate whom senators might support or oppose and nominate accordingly. Randall Calvert, Matthew McCubbins, and Barry Weingast, "A Theory of Political Control and Agency Discretion," *American Journal of Political Science* 33 (1989), 588–611, and Byron Moraski and Charles Shipan, "The Politics of Supreme Court Nominations: A Theory of Institutional Constraints and Choices," *American Journal of Political Science* 43 (1999), 1069–95. On senatorial courtesy, see Sarah Binder and Forrest Matzman, "The Limits of Senatorial Courtesy," *Legislative Studies Quarterly* 29 (February 2004), 5–22.

[167] Elliot Slotnick, "A Historical Perspective on Federal Judicial Selection," *Judicature* 86 (July–August 2002), 14, and Kermit Hall, *The Politics of Justice: Lower Federal Judicial Selection and the Second Party System, 1829–61* (Lincoln: University of Nebraska Press, 1979), 173.

[168] Tom Charles Huston to Richard Nixon, Memorandum for the President, 1–2, 25 March 1969, White House Central Files, FG 50, the Judicial Branch (1969–1970), Nixon Presidential Library, National Archives and Records Administration, College Park, MD.

[169] Pub. L. No. 95–486, 92 Stat. 1629. See generally, Tobias, 1993, 1259–64.

Nominating Commission.[170] The commission was a set of thirteen panels –
one for each circuit – composed of presidential appointees charged with recommending nominations for a judgeship.[171] The commission aimed to divorce
the judiciary from partisan politics and patronage. However, while this innovation accorded with the myth of judicial neutrality, Carter directly linked
judicial appointment to Democratic preferences for increased diversity.[172] In
his executive order establishing the commission, he indicated that the panel
would make "special efforts" to seek out women and minority candidates to
diversify the federal bench and that it seek candidates who demonstrated a
"commitment to equal justice under the law," which was taken, by opponents,
as a euphemism for alleged liberal judicial activism that the Nixon administration sought to suppress.[173] The importance of the Omnibus Judges Act and
Carter's perspective on filling the positions was not simply that by working
with a Democratically controlled Congress he could stack the lower federal
judiciary. Rather, Carter stipulated guidelines for appointment that could be
understood by the Republican opposition to fulfill Democratic policy aims
rather than adhere to the ideals of the judicial neutrality myth.[174]

Carter's oxymoronic bureaucratic politicization through his executive
order highlighted the importance of appointment. The terms of that order
left Carter vulnerable to the accusation that he sought judges who would
rule in particular ways on substantive values. The 1980 Republican platform
stated so. It then identified Republican policy aims and how Reagan's judicial
appointments would achieve them:

> Under Mr. Carter, many appointments to federal judgeships have been par-
> ticularly disappointing. By his partisan nominations, he has violated his

[170] Executive Order 12059, "United States Circuit Judge Nominating Commission," 11 May
1978, John T. Woolley and Gerhard Peters, *The American Presidency Project* [online]. Santa
Barbara, CA: University of California (hosted), Gerhard Peters (database), http://www.
presidency.ucsb.edu/ws/?pid=30796. On Carter's technocratic obsession with bureaucracy,
see Stephen Skowronek, *Presidential Leadership in Political Time: Reprise and Reappraisal*
(Lawrence: University Press of Kansas, 2008), 86–92.
[171] The commission was not charged with making recommendations for district courts.
Senatorial courtesy was more easily avoided with circuit court appointments as multiple
states made up one circuit; with multiple states came multiple senators, and it would have
been difficult for the president to defer to the approval of only one of these senators.
[172] Policy preferences for increased diversity follow from similar objectives of the McGovern-
Fraser reforms implemented by the Democratic Party in 1972 to increase representation of
women, racial minorities, and youth.
[173] On "equal justice" as a euphemism for liberal judicial activism, see Slotnick, 15. None of
Carter's actions were particularly surprising. He announced during the 1976 election campaign his intent to establish these commissions and to focus on diversifying the bench. See
Jimmy Carter, *The Presidential Campaign, 1976*, Vol. 1, part 1. Prepared for the Committee
on House Administration. 95th Congress, 2nd Session, 1978, 494. In doing so, Carter was
following a national trend in judicial reform taking root in the states that made appointment
procedures more transparent. Alan Neff, "Breaking with Tradition: A Study of the U.S.
District Nominating Commissions," *Judicature* 64 (December–January 1981), 257–78.
[174] Of course, it is ironic that the president who oversaw the collapse of the New Deal coalition
attained a judicial outcome that had eluded the regime's creator.

explicit campaign promise of 1976 and has blatantly disregarded the public interest. We pledge to reverse that deplorable trend, through the appointment of women and men who respect and reflect the values of the American people.... We will work for the appointment of judges at all levels of the judiciary who respect *traditional family values* and the *sanctity of innocent human life.*[175]

Reagan administration actions on appointment illustrate partisan control over lower court appointments. To realize the promise of this platform, Reagan eliminated Carter's commission. He placed responsibility for advising judicial selection with the Justice Department's Office of Legal Policy.[176] The new process was criticized as "engage[ing] in the most systematic philosophical screening of judicial candidates seen in the nation's history."[177] Democrats placed concerns about Reagan judicial appointments at the top of their 1984 national platform. Democrats alleged, "the President who appointed James Watt will appoint the Supreme Court majority for the rest of the century."[178] While Democrats continued to focus on the Supreme Court, Republicans maintained a broader focus on the entire judiciary. The Reagan campaign continued the ideas set out by Nixon aides:

We commend the President for appointing federal judges committed to the rights of law-abiding citizens and traditional family values. We share the public's dissatisfaction with an elitist and unresponsive federal judiciary. If our legal institutions are to regain respect, they must respect the people's legitimate interests in a stable, orderly society. In his second term, President Reagan will continue to appoint Supreme Court and other federal judges who share our commitment to judicial restraint.[179]

While the platform endorsed "congressional efforts to restrict the jurisdiction of federal courts," most emphasis was on getting particular judges on the bench under the assumption that doing so would produce particular judicial outcomes supportive of partisan policies.[180] Thus, the approaches of Nixon, Carter, and Reagan to lower court appointments were strikingly similar; these

---

[175] Republican Party Platform of 1980, 15 July 1980, John T. Woolley and Gerhard Peters, *The American Presidency Project* [online]. Santa Barbara, CA: University of California (hosted), Gerhard Peters (database), http://www.presidency.ucsb.edu/ws/?pid=25844. Emphasis added.

[176] David O'Brien, "Judicial Roulette." Report of the Twentieth Century Fund Task Force on Judicial Selection (Background Paper) (New York: Priority Press, 1988); Tobias 1267–8. President G.W. Bush eliminated his administration's connections with the ABA's review process for judicial appointments. See Joan Biskupic, "Bush's Conservatism to Live Long in the U.S. Courts," *USA Today*, 14 March 2008, A4.

[177] Goldman, 1989, 319–20.

[178] Democratic Party Platform of 1984, 16 July 1984, John T. Woolley and Gerhard Peters, *The American Presidency Project* [online]. Santa Barbara, CA: University of California (hosted), Gerhard Peters (database), http://www.presidency.ucsb.edu/ws/?pid=29608.

[179] Republican Party Platform of 1984, 20 August 1984, John T. Woolley and Gerhard Peters, *The American Presidency Project* [online]. Santa Barbara, CA: University of California (hosted), Gerhard Peters (database), http://www.presidency.ucsb.edu/ws/?pid=25845.

[180] Ibid.

presidents "treated their lower court judicial selection responsibilities as primary domestic policy making opportunities, and [all] presidents generated public controversy over the clear ideological bent in their appointments."[181]

By 1988, the Democratic national platform recognized the policy implications of a lower federal judiciary dominated by Reagan and potentially G.H.W. Bush appointees. However, Democrats framed their concerns with language of multiculturalism and a need for gender and racial diversity on the bench – indicating Carter's impact on Democratic approaches to appointment – as opposed to seeking direct policy objectives:

> **WE BELIEVE** that we honor our multicultural heritage by assuring equal access to government services, employment, housing, business enterprise and education to every citizen regardless of race, sex, national origin, religion, age, handicapping condition or sexual orientation; that these rights are without exception too precious to be jeopardized by Federal Judges and Justice Department officials chosen during the past years – by a political party increasingly monolithic both racially and culturally – more for their unenlightened ideological views than for their respect for the rule of law.[182]

While this platform continued the affirmative action policy impetus reminiscent of Carter's executive order, four years later, Bill Clinton attempted to break free of the dominant paradigm of identity politics defining Democratic politics to that point.[183] He adopted the more direct Nixonian approach and "promised to reshape the character of the federal courts, reversing the trend ... under the Reagan and Bush Administrations."[184] By 1992, Reagan and Bush had appointed 550 of 837 federal judges.[185] Yet Democrats who thought that a Clinton presidency would provide appointees who eschewed a resurgent conservative originalism were disappointed by Clinton.[186] Following Carter's legacy, Clinton achieved an unprecedented level of diversity on the federal bench, but his administration was criticized for caving at the first sign of opposition to judicial nominees.[187] As one legal scholar argued, "After 1992, judicial nominations went from low priority to no priority, a practice

[181] Eliot Slotnick, "Federal Judicial Recruitment and Selection Research: A Review Essay," *Judicature* 71 (1988), 317.

[182] Democratic Party Platform of 1988, 18 July 1988, John T. Woolley and Gerhard Peters, *The American Presidency Project* [online]. Santa Barbara, CA: University of California (hosted), Gerhard Peters (database), http://www.presidency.ucsb.edu/ws/?pid=29609.

[183] Perhaps the most telling indicator of this shift was Clinton's criticism of the rap artist, Sista Soulja, who allegedly advocated black-on-white violence in the wake of the 1992 Los Angeles riots. See Paul Frymer, *Uneasy Alliances: Race and Party Competition in America* (Princeton: Princeton University Press, 1999), 5.

[184] Stephen Labaton, "President's Judicial Appointments: Diverse, but Well in the Mainstream," *New York Times*, 17 October 1994, A15.

[185] Robert Marquand, "As Goes the White House, So Go Federal Judges," *Christian Science Monitor*, 31 October 1996, 1.

[186] On the resurgence of originalism in the 1970s through the 1990s, see Chapter 8.

[187] Labaton, 1994. Rorie L. Spill and Kathleen A. Bratton, "Clinton and the Diversification of the Federal Judiciary," *Judicature* 84 (March–April 2001), 256–61.

he [Clinton] began while serving as Arkansas's governor … and after 1994 [when Republicans gained control of both chambers of Congress], he refused to exhaust political capital on judicial fights."[188]

III.b. *Obstruction: Majority Party Committee Action and Minority Party Filibusters*

The flipside of controlling who can serve on the bench is manipulating who is kept off the bench through various means of obstructing the appointment process. There are essentially two tools for this purpose. During divided government, the majority party in Congress may bottle up the president's appointments in committee. During unified government, the minority party in Congress can use the filibuster. Both tactics are evident during the Clinton and G.W. Bush years.

Clinton diversified the bench by appointing women, African Americans, and Latinos, and he tended to select moderate jurists who did not inspire confidence among liberals that the conservative tide of the Reagan and Bush years might be halted.[189] The appointment of Ruth Bader Ginsburg to the Supreme Court was a case in point, leading one commentator at the time to suggest that Clinton "isn't seeking to politicize the court the way Reagan and Bush did."[190] By 1994, when Republicans took control of Congress, some commentary contended that rather than offer nominations that might counterbalance Reagan and Bush nominees, Clinton sought candidates amenable to the Republican-controlled Senate.[191]

However, the strategy of nominating moderates did not succeed in a polarized Congress. With Republicans in control of the Senate, action on appointees was held up in committee. Ultimately, Clinton condemned the Senate Judiciary Committee's refusal to hold the necessary hearings. Such unprecedented inaction created a "vacancy crisis in our courts" constituting a "real threat to our judicial system."[192]

President G.W. Bush's victory in 2000 did not necessarily foreshadow conservative judicial appointments or the politicization evident under Nixon, Carter, or Reagan. Bush's record as governor in Texas allegedly demonstrated a moderate approach to appointment similar to Clinton's. Thus, as the *New York Times* reported in 2000, "Even those who do not support Mr. Bush say that while his appointees are regarded as conservative and business-oriented,

[188] Martin Garbus, *Courting Disaster* (New York: Henry Holt, 2002), 34.

[189] Warren Richley, "Clinton Remaking Reagan Bench," *Christian Science Monitor*, 17 February 1999, 1.

[190] James Simon, dean of New York Law School, quoted in Chris Reidy, "Clinton Gets His Turn," *Boston Globe*, 8 August 1993, 69.

[191] Ana Puga, "Clinton Judicial Picks May Court the Right," *Boston Globe*, 29 December 1994, 1.

[192] William Clinton, The President's Radio Address, 27 September 1997, John T. Woolley and Gerhard Peters, *The American Presidency Project* [online]. Santa Barbara, CA: University of California (hosted), Gerhard Peters (database), http://www.presidency.ucsb.edu/ws/?pid=54684.

they are not fiercely ideological."[193] Events would unfold differently. In the wake of the terrorist attacks of 11 September 2001 and the president's extraordinarily high approval ratings, Bush put the Senate on notice of his intention to get "good conservative judges appointed to the bench and approved by the Unites States Senate."[194] Not only would judicial appointments to the lower federal bench remain politicized and garner much interest among the Republicans' evangelical base but it would also trigger a crisis that threatened to alter radically how the Senate would operate.

Aside from a brief period in late 2001 and 2002 when Democrats held a Senate majority, Democrats were the Senate minority party for all but the last two years of Bush's presidency.[195] As such, they could not use the tactic that Republicans had employed in the 1990s. Rather than bottling up nominees in committee, Democrats relied on the unique senatorial tool of the minority: the filibuster.

A filibuster on judicial nomination had been used only once before to successful effect. In 1968, Republicans filibustered Abe Fortas's nomination to the chief justice position to maintain a vacancy for Nixon to fill if he won the presidency. During the G.W. Bush presidency, Democrats filibustered to prevent appointment of *lower* court judges. While senators had been able to privately obstruct judicial nominees via senatorial courtesy and the "blue slip" since the late nineteenth century, the *public* use of the filibuster was a clear innovation.[196] With Senate Republicans holding as many as fifty-four seats after the 2004 election, majority leader Bill Frist threatened that if Democrats' filibusters prevented hearings on Bush's nominees, he would invoke a "nuclear option" of eliminating the filibuster on judicial appointments.[197] Democrats threatened to shut down the Senate altogether. Minority leader Harry Reid (D-NV) fired back "If they [Republicans] ... decide to do this, it's not only wrong, they will rue the day they did it, because we will do whatever we can do to strike back.... I will, for lack of a better word, screw things up."[198]

[193] Jim Yardley, "Bush's Choices for Court Seen as Moderates," *New York Times*, 9 July 2000, 1.
[194] Reuters, "President Says "Good, Conservative" Judges Needed," *San Diego Union-Tribune*, 29 March 2002, A6; Neil Lewis, "Divisive Words: Judicial Appointments," *New York Times*, 18 December 2002, http://query.nytimes.com/gst/fullpage.html?res=9F0CE7DC123 DF93BA25751C1A9649C8B63.
[195] The Democrats' brief time as the Senate majority party was a consequence of Senator Jim Jefford's (VT) defection from the Republican Party to a status of Independent.
[196] Some scholars suggest that the filibuster – as just one more obstruction tool – is nothing new. See David Law, "Appointing Federal Judges: The President, the Senate, and the Prisoner's Dilemma," *Cardozo Law Review* 26 (2005), 491–500. Others highlight the filibuster as unprecedented. See John Cornyn, "Our Broken Judicial Confirmation Process and the Need for Filibuster Reform," *Harvard Journal of Law & Public Policy* 27 (2003), 188.
[197] In a speech to the Federalist Society, Frist was explicit: "One way or another, the filibuster of judicial nominees must end." William Frist quoted in Helen Dewar and Mike Allen, "GOP May Target Use of Filibuster," *Washington Post*, 13 December 2004, A01. Whether Lott had the authority to kill the filibuster is contested. See Robert Klotz, "The Nuclear Option for Stopping Filibuster," *PS: Political Science & Politics* 37 (2004), 843–6.
[198] Reid, quoted in Dewar and Allen.

The stakes of the debate were heightened not only by extensive media coverage of what could have been an esoteric argument about procedural rules, but also because interest groups publicized the conflict on lower federal judges in ways not seen previously, a circumstance attesting to the increasing number and kinds of institutions that claimed a stake in constitutional interpretation. While presidents and their aides have recognized the policy and legacy impact of making appointments to the lower federal courts at least since the Nixon administration, the public salience of these lower appointments has historically been rather low. While interest groups had been prominently involved in Supreme Court nomination battles, at least since Robert Bork's hearings in the mid-1980s, the attention brought on lower federal court appointments in 2005 by interest groups was unprecedented.[199] The high level of media coverage and interest group exposure potentially prevented the leadership of either party from compromising.[200]

In May of 2005, fourteen senators drafted the "Memorandum of Understanding on Judicial Nominees," which offered a way to break through the standoff.[201] This "Gang of Fourteen" negotiated that Democratic signatories would vote for cloture, that is, an end to the filibuster, on three of the Bush lower court nominees, Priscilla Owen, Janice Rogers Brown, and William Pryor. In exchange, Republican signatories agreed "to oppose the rules changes in the 109th Congress, which we understand to be any amendment to or interpretation of the Rules of the Senate that would force a vote on a judicial nomination by means other than unanimous consent or Rule XXII." By effectively taking these fourteen senators out of the voting pool either to maintain a filibuster or to invoke the rules-changing nuclear option, the crisis was averted.[202]

Why would these senators defy their parties' leadership? One possibility is that the compromise was popular, but evidence suggests that this explanation

---

[199] On interest group participation in the Bork nomination battle, see Lauren Bell, *Warring Factions: Interest Groups, Money and the New Politics of Senate Confirmation* (Columbus: Ohio State University Press, 2002).

[200] Gregory Wawro and Eric Schickler note that the media coverage and interest group participation intensified costs: "audience costs for backing down seemed to be central to the dynamics of the conflict.... Democratic and Republican leaders preferred confrontation to compromise because they knew they would be penalized by their allied groups should they be seen as caving in." Wawro and Schickler, *Filibuster: Obstruction and Lawmaking in the U.S. Senate* (Princeton: Princeton University Press, 2006), 270. A conservative leader highlighted how much Frist had at stake: "he has to see to it that the Bush judicial nominees are confirmed.... If he fails, then he is dead as a presidential wannabe." Richard Lessner, executive director of the American Conservative Union, quoted in Charles Babington, "Frist Likely to Push for Ban on Filibusters," *Washington Post*, 15 April 2005, A4.

[201] The Gang of Fourteen included John McCain (R-AZ), Lindsay Graham (R-SC), John Warner (R-VA), Olympia Snowe (R-ME), Susan Collins (R-ME), Mike DeWine (R-OH), Lincoln Chafee (R-RI), Joe Lieberman (D-CT), Robert Byrd (D-WV), Ben Nelson (D-NE), Mary Landrieu (D-LA), Daniel Inouye (D-HI), Mark Pryor (D-AK), and Ken Salazar (D-CO).

[202] The Memorandum can be viewed at http://www.nationalreview.com/pdf/compromise.pdf.

is flawed. Gallup polling does indicate that a majority of Americans wanted to maintain the filibuster. However, despite media coverage and interest group action to publicize the conflict, polling also indicated that most Americans did not pay much attention to the conflict.[203] Given low public salience, it is unlikely that politicians would have received much capital for bucking their parties. It is more likely that the Gang of Fourteen might suffer some electoral *cost* since each party's bases were paying more attention to this battle than the general public. Indeed, John McCain was viewed with suspicion by much of the Republican evangelical Christian base for his participation in the compromise well after it had been brokered.[204]

A more plausible explanation might highlight how senators understood the nuclear option as diminishing their own institutional position. The compromise avoided the procedural question as to whether the Senate could, through a simple majority vote, alter the institutional rules. It did not contain procedures for avoiding the nuclear option in the future. Because its language remained vague – "nominees should only be filibustered under extraordinary circumstances" – Democrats retained filibuster and Republicans retained the right to threaten that tactic.[205] Put differently, the compromise managed to postpone a conflict rather than resolve it. Moreover, a 200-year-old cherished tool of the Senate was at stake. While Frist's plan would maintain the filibuster for issues other than judicial appointment, a precedent of working around one of the few minority tools would have been set. And the process of judicial appointment has historically deferred to minority interests as the norm of senatorial courtesy had long held. Invoking simple majority rule on judicial appointments may have killed not only the tradition per se, but more importantly it would have eliminated this significant reservoir of senatorial power against the executive.[206] And ending the filibuster would have eliminated Republicans' ability, if they found themselves in the minority in the future, to have a weapon against Democratic judicial nominees. While political scientists often cast longer term interests like institutional preservation as secondary, Senator John McCain's justification for his participation in the Gang of Fourteen constitutes a direct rebuttal to this assumption: "If we don't protect the rights of the minority … [i]f you had a liberal president and a Democrat-controlled Senate, I think that it could do great damage."[207]

The compromise illustrated not only senators' interest in maintaining their institution's rules, but it also indicated that senators wanted to maintain

203 Shickler and Wawro, 273.
204 Michael Luo, "McCain Extends His Outreach, but Evangelicals Are Still Wary," *New York Times*, 9 June 2008 and Richard Baehr, "The Base Is Wrong about the Gang of 14," *Realpolitics.com*, 30 January 2008, http://www.realclearpolitics.com/articles/2008/01/the_base_is_wrong_about_the_ga.html.
205 http://www.nationalreview.com/pdf/compromise.pdf.
206 Wawro and Schickler, 272.
207 McCain, quoted in Ronald Brownstein, "McCain Sees 'Slippery Slope' in Filibuster Ban," *Los Angeles Times*, 11 April 2005, A9.

their ability to manipulate judicial power by obstructing future appointments. Such action and longer term interest is only strategically rational under assumptions that parties might operate, with some frequency, as a loyal opposition.

The Gang of Fourteen's actions to achieve a bi-partisan breakthrough speak not only to the potential for centrist moderation even in an atmosphere of heightened party polarization, but also that politicians maintain longer term interests beyond electoral incentives. Furthermore, the compromise freed Senate leadership from both parties to continue their rhetorical antagonism and play to their respective party bases. Ultimately, the compromise was not motivated to maintain unity among a divided party – as were Lyndon Johnson's actions in the late 1950s or Michael Mansfield's compromise on busing in the early 1970s – but to preserve the institutional capacity of Congress to manipulate judicial power in the future.

In summary, while Nixon transformed judicial appointment into a campaign issue, Carter's 1978 executive order on how judicial vacancies should be filled transformed Nixon's idea into political reality. Reagan continued this tradition. Clinton refused to expend political capital on appointments, tending not to defend them against Republican attack and to select moderate jurists.[208] Yet, although he attempted to avoid conflict, a Republican-dominated Senate bottled his appointments in committee.[209] When Democrats attempted to limit Bush's influence on the federal courts, their minority status meant they were limited to the much more visible filibuster. Because Republicans could thwart Clinton in committee, their actions were less publicly salient. It was easier then for Republicans to frame senatorial Democrats as obstructionist, even though at the time of the conflict, Bush had already secured more of his judicial appointments than Clinton ever did.[210]

Obstruction appears to be a preferred mechanism in a polity fully developed for harnessing judicial power. If controlling judicial authority hinges on securing appointment, then obstruction prevents the president from creating a judiciary that could align with his policy objectives. It also maintains vacancies for future presidents that may align with the congressional party impeding the appointment process. Furthermore, the focus on appointment belies an underlying concession to legal realists about how we think about the Constitution, namely, that multiple interpretive methods are plausible, and that politicians want to ensure that a particular interpretive method is

[208] Katharine Seelye, "Dole, Citing 'Crisis' in the Courts, Attacks Appointments by Clinton," *New York Times*, 20 April 1996, Section 1, 1. On advocacy of judicial impeachment as a tactic during the Clinton administration akin to Gerald Ford's advocacy against Justice William Douglas, see Tom Delay, "Impeachment as a Valid Answer to a Judiciary Run Amok," *New York Times*, 6 April 1997, Section 4, 1.

[209] Richard Fleisher and Jon Bond, "Congress and the President in a Partisan Era," in *Polarized Politics: Congress and the President in a Partisan Era*, Jon Bond and Richard Fleisher, eds. (Washington DC: CQ Press, 2000), 1–8.

[210] Dewar and Allen, A1.

adhered to by a majority of judges. Conservatives' efforts to achieve that goal through a revival of originalism are detailed in the next chapter.

While politicized judicial appointment is hardly new to the extent that Supreme Court nominees have often been contentious, obstruction has changed over time. It has not only increased in quantity in the 1990s and early 2000s, but in quality. It has focused more on lower federal courts. Given the number of court appointments a president has opportunity to fill over one or two terms, the politics of obstruction may become a permanent campaign over judgeships. Appointment is likely to remain a campaign issue to mobilize the base as well as a contentious issue regardless of divided or unified government given procedural rules that allow for appointees to be held up in both circumstances.[211]

IV. Conclusion

Theories of normative and strategic deference to judicial authority suggest that court-curbing legislation succumbs, for different reasons, to perils of collective action. This chapter has shown that congressional measures to curb judicial power in the 1950s and the 1970s were often common carriers of multiple interests, essentially overcoming collective action problems. Why would they fail? The short answer is that they often did *not* fail. The Jencks Act, the 1974 Elementary and Secondary Education Act, and – as discussed in the next chapter – the 2005 Detainees Treatment Act, and the 2006 Military Commissions Act all passed. This outcome is not fully accounted for by current reliance on normative judicial supremacy. So, I have focused on a different question: how did the legislation that passed serve elected leaders' dual aims: first, *seeming* to rein in the courts to respond to constituency demand, and second, not undermining judicial power, which is useful in achieving policy ends as well as in scapegoating the Court as an undemocratic foil. I provided evidence of politicians' actions toward the judiciary in a context where each branch accepts and operates under the assumptions of liberal pluralism. As such, the polity is fully developed for harnessing the judiciary for political ends. To be clear, my theory does not predict that attacks on judicial authority will subside. Instead, I point to how they have changed in form. For example, they tend to strip jurisdiction rather than attempt any kind of broadly undermining attack as defined in Chapter 1. And this jurisdiction-stripping would often be ambiguous, narrow, or even redundant to the Court's already identifiable jurisprudential trends. We might also expect politicians to back off legislation, not necessarily out of a desire to maintain the institutional integrity of the

---

[211] See John McCain's assurances when he ran for president in 2008: "I have my own standards of judicial ability, experience, philosophy, and temperament. And Chief Justice Roberts and Justice Samuel Alito meet those standards in every respect. They would serve as the model for my own nominees if that responsibility falls to me." McCain, "Remarks by John McCain on Judicial Philosophy," 6 May 2008, http://i.usatoday.net/news/mmemmottpdf/mccain-on-judges-may-6–2008.pdf?loc=interstitialskip.

Court, but because such legislation may undermine a politician's power base, for example, the party or the branch.

That jurisdiction-stripping legislation did pass in the 1950s and 1970s undercuts the empirical validity of a norm of deference to judicial authority. That it only nibbled at the edges of jurisdiction validates expectations about its narrow scope. That other legislation, such as the 1974 Elementary and Secondary Education Act, was redundant to Court rulings verifies expectations of their symbolic purpose.[212] Expectations that such legislation would be purposively ambiguous are confirmed by attempts to insert the term "reasonable" at conference on the *Mallory* legislation in the late 1950s. They are further evident in HEW Secretary Finch's support of adding the phrase "not constitutionally required" at conference to diffuse the potential impact of the Whitten Amendments. Finally, backing off legislation that undermines judicial legitimacy cannot be taken to indicate deference to independent judicial authority. Rather, the legislation may expose rifts in the party and thus damage its unity and the power of its leaders. This is particularly true when parties have deep-seated sectional rifts as the Democrats did throughout the New Deal/Great Society regime, which collapsed by the late 1970s. Such possibility would account for Lyndon Johnson's actions as Senate majority leader on the court-curbing legislation in the 1950s.

Yet, as parties realigned, unified, and polarized from the 1980s onward, why would senators choose to secure their longer term interests instead of immediate short-term gains, especially if such action could be electorally costly? Why did the Gang of Fourteen act? Retaining the filibuster maintained the ability of either party, regardless of its position in Congress, to manipulate judicial appointments. Maintaining the filibuster made sense when politicians assumed that they would lose control of Congress, that is, that their party would ultimately end up in the position of the loyal opposition. Obstructionist politics were thereby secured for both parties and irrespective of circumstances of unified or divided government.

Maintaining the filibuster when considering judicial appointment is essentially the flipside of securing judicial appointments. The battle over judgeships, especially as it has seeped downward to encompass the entire federal judiciary, suggests that hostilities toward judges have transformed into a permanent campaign, irrespective of a particular ruling. These battles are unlikely to subside unless they become electorally costly. As the 2005 conflagration demonstrated, given their low salience among the broader public but their high salience among particular constituents, such as the conservative, particularly evangelical, right, high costs may be unlikely. But in the early 1980s, during Reagan's first term as president and even with a Senate

---

[212] That it is symbolic should not be taken to mean that it has no effect, especially when judges must reconcile it with existing law and existing jurisprudence. *Its redundancy may have unanticipated consequences and muddy the logic of precedent.* For the purposes of this argument, such legislation is tailored for credit-claiming and electoral purposes.

Republican majority, opportunity for lower federal judicial appointment did not substantially materialize. The administration secured only twenty-four additional appeals court judgeships in 1983. But without any expansion similar to the scale of the 1978 Omnibus Act, it developed new ways to harness judicial power, which included the deliberate development and/or revival of a once defunct interpretive method, namely, originalism, and the creation of a device meant to solicit judicial authority, namely, the presidential signing statement.[213] These two innovations are taken up in the next chapter.

[213] John De Figueiredo and Emerson Tiller, "Congressional Control of the Courts: A Theoretical and Empirical Expansion of the Federal Judiciary," *Journal of Law and Economics* 39 (October 1996), 443.

A Polity Fully Developed for Harnessing (II)

A Conservative Insurgency Innovates and a Self-Styled Majoritarian Court Responds

New Deal policy aims and the Court's post-1937 interpretive emphasis on living constitutionalism promoted specification of un-enumerated rights. Foremost among these contentious judicially constructed rights was a right to privacy, detailed in *Griswold v. Connecticut*.[1] To avoid criticism plaguing the *Lochner* Court's discovery of un-enumerated rights within the Fourteenth Amendment's due process clause, such as liberty of contract, the majority in *Griswold* grounded its holding in constitutional text. Justice Douglas's ruling specified "penumbras" and "emanations" of the Bill of Rights suggesting a right to privacy.[2] Justice Goldberg's concurrence, true to the precepts of living constitutionalism, anchored the right outside the text and in "'the traditions and [collective] conscience of our people to determine whether a principle is 'so rooted [there] ... as to be ranked fundamental.'"[3] Yet, to avoid falling prey to the claim that he was entrenching his own values, Goldberg argued that the right to privacy drew on the *original* meaning of the Ninth Amendment, which held that the rights enumerated in the first eight amendments did not constitute an exhaustive list, but that "others" are "retained by the people." Of course, as Justices Black and Stewart's dissents made clear, simply referencing constitutional text in and of itself did not constitute valid interpretation. The living constitutionalist approaches of the majority "turn[ed] somersaults with history."[4]

For many legal scholars and judges, privacy doctrine represented the same challenges posed by unrestrained judicial power that liberals charged had been evident in *Lochner*-era rulings.[5] The self-imposed restraints – ranging from

---

[1] *Griswold v. Connecticut*, 381 U.S. 479 (1965)

[2] Ibid., 482, 484.

[3] Ibid., 493. Goldberg concurring and quoting *Snyder v. Massachusetts*, 291 U.S. 97, 105.

[4] Ibid., Stewart dissenting, 530.

[5] *Eisenstadt v. Baird*, 405 U.S. 438 (1971) (ruling that the denial of contraception to single people violated the Fourteenth Amendment's equal protection clause); *Roe v. Wade*, 410 U.S. 113 (1973) (ruling that absolute prohibitions on abortion violated the right to privacy). On equation of privacy doctrine with substantive due process, see Christopher Wolfe, *The Rise*

judicial deference to the legislature to reasoned judicial judgment – offered little security against potentially expansive judicial interpretation.[6] This crisis provided an opportunity for political entrepreneurs to re-imagine a modern textualist originalism as the solution.

Originalism is said to legitimize judicial constitutional interpretation because it provides a strict underlying interpretive principle: interpretation must be grounded in the text of the Constitution, which represents the singular and precise act of popular sovereignty. That act fixed the meaning of the text, and that original meaning always trumps meanings that might have been given to it by subsequent generations: "The central tenet of originalism as it is often understood is the existence of a clear demarcation between the original meaning of a constitutional provision and its subsequent interpretation. The originalist ... is the interpreter who knows the difference and acknowledges it by according authority to the founders rather than their successors."[7] Of course, what counts as evidence of this original meaning is hotly debated among contemporary originalists.

While scholars revived originalism as a means to restrain judicial interpretation from devolving into the imposition of particular values by unelected overseers of pluralist democracy, it was ultimately taken up as the constitutional vision of a conservative insurgency that came to power with Ronald Reagan. In other words, while scholars concerned with the increasing criticism of the judiciary since *Brown* revived the interpretive methodology as a way to secure institutional legitimacy, the Reagan administration latched onto it as the constitutional vision of the contemporary Republican Party. This insurgency transformed originalism into a tool to align the judiciary with Republican objectives and, more importantly, to present those objectives not as partisan policy aims but as constitutional imperatives flowing from an uncontestable reading of the original meaning of the Constitution. As Reva Siegel and Robert Post note of the partisan capture of originalism: "the power of originalism in fact lies ... in the way it aligns constitutional vision and constitutional law. If one examines how the theory of originalism has been

---

of *Modern Judicial Review: From Constitutional Interpretation to Judge-Made Law*, revised ed. (Lanham, MD: Rowman & Littlefield, 1994) ("But in *Griswold v. Connecticut* (1965), the Court resurrected *Lochner's* doctrine for quite different purposes while trying to deny it was doing so" [289]); Robert George, "Judicial Usurpation and Sexual Liberation: Courts and the Abolition of Marriage," 17 *Regent University Law Review* (2004–2005); and, Richard A. Epstein, "Substantive Due Process by Any Other Name: The Abortion Cases," *Supreme Court Review* (1973). ("Thus in the end we must criticize both Mr. Justice Blackmun in *Roe v. Wade* and the entire method of constitutional interpretation that allows the Supreme Court in the name of Due Process both to 'define' and to 'balance' interests on the major social and political issues of our time" [185].)

[6] On self-restraints to confer legitimacy to judicial ruling once textualism was abandoned during the mid-twentieth century, see Neil Duxbury, *Patterns in American Jurisprudence* (New York: Oxford University Press, 1995), 205–300, and Melvin Urofsky, *Felix Frankfurter: Judicial Restraint and Individual Liberties* (Boston: Twayne, 1991), 148–57.

[7] H. Jefferson Powell, "Rules for Originalists," *Virginia Law Review* 73 (1987), 676.

deployed outside the academy to mobilize support among the political constit-
uencies responsible for electing conservative presidents like Reagan, George
H. W. Bush, and George W. Bush, it becomes clear that originalism's appeal
grows out of the conservative constitutional ideals it expresses."[8]

This chapter details how the conservative insurgency attempted to harness judicial power to secure its partisan aims and how it has not yet fully
succeeded. Part I focuses on the revival of originalism. When the lawyers
in the Reagan administration recognized that Nixon's appointments to the
Supreme Court did not produce reversals of Warren Court decisions, were
denied an early opportunity to appoint additional federal judges to balance
Carter appointments in the late 1970s, and were unable to secure statutory
or constitutional language to overturn reviled rulings on abortion, school
prayer, busing, and criminal rights, they turned to originalism as a political strategy. That strategy began with a public campaign, spearheaded by
Reagan's attorney general, Edwin Meese III, to bring originalism's tenets into
the public discourse as *the* legitimate form of interpretation. Additionally,
Republicans sought to ensure that originalism not only produced outcomes in
line with Republican objectives but that it also did not upset rulings that the
broader public had come to accept, namely *Brown*, especially as early proponents of originalism, including Thomas Grey and Raoul Berger, suggested that
originalism could not sanction desegregation. Ultimately, Meese contended
that originalism endorsed departmentalism, but the Reagan administration
refrained from directly challenging the Court on its rulings, suggesting that
Reagan-era inter-branch relations are not a simple replay of Jeffersonian hostilities. Instead, Reagan's Office of Legal Counsel (OLC) developed a new
way to solicit the Court's authority and to make originalist interpretation
known via innovative use of presidential signing statements. Part II examines this innovation as well as the revival of jurisdiction-stripping legislation
to provide further evidence against normative judicial supremacy, highlight
evidence validating expectations of symbolic politics, and suggest that even
when the Court behaves in ways that appear supremacist, its rationale is limited. Part III examines how despite inroads made by originalism in academia
and think tanks, that interpretive method has not attained a consistent hold
on the Supreme Court. According to one historian, "Although it is clear that
originalism substantially reoriented constitutional theory, its influence on the
Court was not as deep.... [T]he Rehnquist Court still cannot be regarded
as originalist in orientation."[9] The same assessment may hold for the current Roberts Court. Instead, having reconciled itself to pluralist assumptions

[8] Robert Post and Reva Siegel, "Democratic Constitutionalism," in *The Constitution in 2020*, Jack Balkin and Reva Siegel, eds. (New York: Oxford University Press, 2009), 30. See also Robert Post and Reva Siegel, "Originalism as a Political Practice: The Right's Living Constitutionalism," *Fordham Law Review* 75 (2006), 545–74.
[9] Johnathan O'Neill, *Originalism in American Law and Politics* (Baltimore: Johns Hopkins University Press, 2005), 205.

and recognizing increased polarization of American politics, the Court has positioned its rulings as representing the majoritarian interests of the people themselves. Recent cases are discussed as exemplars of this pattern, and what this pattern means for attempts to harness judicial power is assessed.

I. Originalism: Reviving an Interpretive Method in order to Harness Judicial Power

After 1937, the textual originalism defining nineteenth-century jurisprudence fell from prominence as the single legitimate methodology. This is nowhere more apparent than in the circumstances surrounding the re-argument of *Brown*. The Supreme Court asked litigants in *Brown* to brief specifically on whether the framers of the Fourteenth Amendment contemplated desegregated schools; Chief Justice Warren's subsequent statement that petitioners' briefs were, at best, "inconclusive" not only endorsed the realist notion, voiced once by Justice Frankfurter that "no one knows what was intended," but also, more generally, committed to the waste bin originalist emphasis on discoverable intent or fixed meaning.[10] However, if originalism was eclipsed by the promotion of a "living Constitution," it was by no means dead, and "consideration of historical evidence of original intent remained an important component of arguments about proper constitutional interpretation and the role of the Court" after *Brown*.[11] Indeed, criticism of *Brown*, which emphasized the ruling's dismissal of text and its reliance on social scientific data rather than legal reasoning, spurred concern over the legitimacy of judicial authority and laid seeds for developing a more systematic and deeply theorized originalism, which bloomed in the 1970s and 1980s.

A comprehensive discussion of the resuscitation, evolution, and balkanization of originalism into a range of theories about what counts as original meaning is beyond this book's scope and purpose.[12] Nevertheless, a brief

---

[10] *Brown v. Board of Education of Topeka*, 347 U.S. 483 (1954), 489; Frankfurter is quoted in Mark Tushnet and Katya Lezin, "What Really Happened in *Brown v. Board of Education*," *Columbia Law Review* 91 (1991), 1906.

[11] O'Neill, 71.

[12] For discussions of the development of originalism, see O'Neill, 2005, and Dennis Goldfarb, *The American Constitution and the Debate over Originalism* (New York: Cambridge University Press, 2005). On the splintering of originalism, see James Fleming, "The Balkanization of Originalism," *Maryland Law Review* 67 (2007) (noting "there are numerous varieties of originalism.... It all began with the conventional 'intention of the Framers' originalism. Then it became the 'intention of the ratifiers' originalism. Of course we also have the 'original expectations and applications' originalism.... Then came 'original meaning' originalism.... Then came 'broad originalism.' ... Now comes 'the new originalism (so characterized by Keith Whittington) as distinguished from 'the old originalism'" (11). On originalism as framers' intentions, see Raoul Berger, *Government by Judiciary* (Cambridge: Harvard University Press, 1977). On originalism as the ratifiers' intentions, see Robert Bork, *The Tempting of America: The Political Seduction of the Law* (New York: Touchstone, 1990), 144. On originalism as expectations and application, see Sotirios Barber and James Fleming, *Constitutional Interpretation: The Basic Questions* (New York: Oxford University Press, 2007), 84–91.

review of originalism's resurgence makes clear that an emerging legal conservative movement, which gained adherents in the 1970s and 1980s particularly after the Federalist Society was established in 1982, sought to harness the judiciary through advocacy of originalism. The interpretive approach, if adopted, could position the judiciary to serve conservative policy aims, including overturning *Roe v. Wade* and breaking through the wall of separation between church and state constructed by the Warren and Burger Courts.[13]

The Warren Court's rulings – which demanded separations of church and state, protected rights of the criminally accused, involved the Court in what had previously been considered political matters of reapportionment, and established rights to privacy – were criticized as based in little else than "a curious mixture of law-office history and vaulting legal logic," which "mangled constitutional history."[14] As was evident in Nixon's presidential campaigns discussed in the previous chapter, by the late 1960s and early 1970s, there was a growing sense among legal academics and the public that the Court was straining the limits of its legitimacy. Attention to the history, text, and structure of the Constitution, rather than to external considerations such as moral philosophy, natural law, contemporary values, or political circumstances was increasingly advocated as the means for the Court to regain its moorings, especially after *Roe*.[15] Even scholars who supported the substantive outcome

On originalism as original meaning, see Antonin Scalia, *A Matter of Interpretation: Federal Courts and the Law* (Princeton: Princeton University Press, 1997), 38, and Randy Barnett, *Restoring the Lost Constitution: The Presumption of Liberty* (Princeton: Princeton University Press, 2004), 89–94. On originalism as broad "translation," see Lawrence Lessig, "Fidelity in Translation," *Texas Law Review* 71 (1993), 1171–3. On the new originalism as fidelity to original public meaning but not necessarily judicial restraint or deference to legislative enactment, see Keith Whittington, "The New Originalism," *Georgetown Journal of Law and Public Policy* 2 (2004), 599–614.

[13] On the development of the conservative legal movement, see Steven Teles, *The Rise of the Conservative Legal Movement: The Battle for Control of the Law* (Princeton: Princeton University Press, 2008).

[14] On separation of church and state: *School District of Abington Township v. Schemp*, 374 U.S. 203 (1963) (holding that laws requiring the reading of the Lord's prayer and Bible verses in public school violated the establishment clause because the law must have a primary secular purpose that neither promotes nor inhibits religion). On rights of the criminally accused: *Escobedo v. Illinois*, 378 U.S. 478 (1964) (holding that if someone under arrest requests an attorney present, the request must be honored), and *Miranda v. Arizona*, 384 U.S. 436 (1966) (holding that persons under arrest must be informed of their rights). On reapportionment: *Baker v. Carr* 369 U.S. 186 (1962) (holding that the Court could order reapportionment of state legislative districts based on the Fourteenth Amendment's equal protection clause). On privacy: *Griswold v. Connecticut* 381 U.S. 479 (1965) (holding that a state ban on contraception for married couples violated a fundamental right to privacy grounded in the Bill of Rights). The assessment of privacy doctrine as defined in *Griswold v. Connecticut* (1965) is Alfred Kelley's. See Kelley, "Clio and the Court: An Illicit Love Affair," *Supreme Court Review* (1965), 150, 135.

[15] See John Hart Ely, "The Wages of Crying Wolf: A Comment on *Roe v. Wade*," *Yale Law Journal* 82 (April 1973), 920–49; Epstein, 1973; and Robert Bork, "Neutral Principles and Some First Amendment Problems," *Indiana Law Journal* 47 (1971), 1–36.

in that case criticized the ruling because it did not contain even the pretext of interpretation as anything more than values imposition by the justices.[16]

Nowhere is this concern more evident than in Raoul Berger's writings. Berger contended that living constitutionalism would lead judicial authority to run amok. While he endorsed the judicial deference to the legislature characterizing the New Deal Court after 1937, he worried that the underlying jurisprudential philosophy that gave rise to the conflict between Roosevelt and the Court, namely, the notion that the Constitution could be adapted by judges to meet contemporary needs, conferred too much power on the judiciary, upsetting the separation of powers and majoritarian thrust of American democracy. Self-imposed limits were false hope since they were subject to judicial discretion. Instead, judicial ruling needed clear grounding in text to legitimize interpretive authority. Berger's turn to textualist originalism was therefore compelled by the same concerns evident in Alexander Bickel's promotion of "passive virtues," or Justice Brandeis's *Ashwander* principle. Each sought to restrain the judiciary. In Berger's view, lack of restraint had resulted in *Brown*. Berger, unlike his contemporary Bickel, argued that *Brown* could not be justified by the text or history of the Fourteenth Amendment.[17]

For Berger, the 39th Congress's debate on the Fourteenth Amendment clearly illustrated that none of its framers contemplated school segregation to fall within its equal protection clause, and thus that the text's original meaning could not be read to support *Brown*. By contrast, Alexander Bickel claimed that the amendment's language was intentionally broad, such that even though the 39th Congress might not have endorsed school desegregation, the text itself could be abstracted to support contemporary mores. While Bickel saw grave dangers in limiting interpretation to the bounds of original meaning, being sure to criticize the originalist outcomes put forth by Chief Justice Taney in *Dred Scott* and Justice Sutherland in *Blaisdell*, he nevertheless observed, "it is a long way from rejection of the Taney-Sutherland doctrine to the proposition that the original understanding is simply not relevant."[18] While acknowledging the importance of uncovering original meaning, he argued that doing so was not a "mechanical exercise," and, more important, that original meaning is not the only relevant factor in interpreting constitutional provisions; so is "the line of their growth."[19] Bickel conceded that "the obvious conclusion to which the evidence ... easily leads is that section I of the fourteenth amendment ... was meant to apply neither to jury service, nor suffrage, nor antimiscegenation statutes, nor segregation."[20] But Bickel differentiated between a statute and a constitutional amendment; if the Court were

[16] O'Neill, 99.
[17] Berger, 1977, 37–51, 166–220.
[18] Alexander Bickel, "The Original Understanding and the Segregation Decision," *Harvard Law Review* 69 (November 1955), 3.
[19] Ibid., 5, 6.
[20] Ibid., 58.

interpreting the former in *Brown*, then desegregation would not follow. Yet the Court was interpreting a constitutional amendment, and for Bickel, that made all the difference:

> We are dealing with a constitutional amendment, not a statute. The tradition of a broadly worded organic law not frequently or lightly amended was well-established by 1866, and, despite the somewhat revolutionary fervor with which the Radicals were pressing their changes, it cannot be assumed that they or anyone else expected or wished the future role of the Constitution in the scheme of American government to differ from the past. Should not the search for congressional purpose, therefore, properly be twofold? One inquiry should be directed at the congressional understanding of the immediate effect of the enactment on conditions then present. Another should aim to discover what if any thought was given to the long-range effect, under future circumstances, of provisions necessarily intended for permanence.[21]

For Bickel, the living constitutional approach, which emphasized long-range effects of constitutional text, was an originalist principle. To justify this claim that the text had long been held to be judicially adaptable to meet lived circumstance, Bickel relied on Chief Justice Marshall's dictum in *McCulloch v. Maryland*, "that it was a *constitution* they were writing, which led to a choice of language capable of growth."[22] Berger responded that Marshall's dicta were taken out of context by the living constitutionalists to support their own political ends. That dicta, understood in the context of when and why it was written, could not support the expansive interpretive objectives of the living constitutionalists.

Thomas Grey, another critical figure in contemporary originalism's development, was more circumspect than Berger, perhaps because he recognized the moral correctness of *Brown* and therefore sought an interpretive means to maintain *Brown* while still offering a way to legitimize judicial interpretation. Rather than claim that judicial adaptation was an originalist principle as Bickel had, Grey dichotomized interpretive methods. In one of the first influential articles to take note of originalism's resurgence, Grey construed two approaches: interpretivism and non-interpretivism. The former referred to originalist interpretation, while the latter referred to methods that looked past the Framers' intent to other guidelines for decision-making. Indeed, Grey favored interpretive pluralism because many cherished rights could not be maintained through originalist technique: "very little of our constitutional law of individual rights has any firm foundation in the model of judicial review which traces from *Marbury v. Madison* to the jurisprudence of Mr. Justice Black."[23] While he recognized that interpretivism, or what came to be known as contemporary originalism, was historically deeply rooted, Grey

---

[21] Ibid., 59.
[22] Ibid., 63.
[23] Thomas Grey, "Do We Have an Unwritten Constitution," *Stanford Law Review* 27 (1975), 718.

argued against discarding non-interpretivism altogether: "I do not think that the view of constitutional adjudication outlined by [interpretivist] commentators is sufficiently broad to capture the full scope of legitimate judicial review. It seems to be that the courts do appropriately apply values not articulated in the constitutional text and appropriately apply them in determining the constitutionality of legislation."[24] Grey advocated an interpretive methodological pluralism that paralleled the institutionalized liberal pluralism of the political realm. Not only were multiple readings plausible, but also multiple interpretive methodologies were plausible and necessary to maintain rights. What was needed was not adherence to one methodology, originalism or otherwise, but embrace of multiple interpretive techniques and a concerted effort to articulate how each was a legitimate path to constructing the meaning of the Constitution's provisions.

As detailed by Raoul Berger, originalism faced its own set of legitimacy problems; the interpretive approach could not clearly reach the unanimous ruling in *Brown*. And, as Grey noted, such rulings were defensible but only on non-originalist terms, which themselves were coming under scrutiny. Berger's exclusion of *Brown* spurred attempts to bring *Brown* within originalist purview.[25] Attorney General Meese laid out how an originalist understanding of *Brown* was possible in a 1985 speech to the Federalist Society in which he critiqued an earlier speech given by Justice Brennan, which laid out principles of living constitutionalism.[26] For Meese, the danger of Brennan's constitutional philosophy was that any attempt to read the Constitution in light of evolving standards of human dignity led not only to the outcomes Brennan sought to praise, but also to outcomes reviled. Evolving standards, which eschewed the original meaning of the constitutional text, according to Meese were exactly what grounded *Dred Scott v. Sanford* and which had also curbed the Fourteenth Amendment to fit the development of Jim Crow laws and thereby permit the incorrect rulings in the *1883 Civil Rights Cases* and *Plessy v. Ferguson*. *Brown*, by contrast, flowed from the original meaning of the Fourteenth Amendment's text:

> When the Supreme Court sounded the death knell for official segregation in the country ... [it] was not giving new life to old words, or adapting a "living," "flexible" Constitution to new reality. It was restoring the original principle of the Constitution to constitutional law. The Brown Court was correcting the damage done fifty years earlier, when in *Plessy v. Ferguson*, an earlier Supreme Court had disregarded the clear intent of the framers of

[24] Ibid., 705.
[25] See Michael McConnell, "Originalism and the Desegregation Decisions," *Virginia Law Review* 81 (1995), 947–1140.
[26] William Brennan, Jr., "Speech to the Text and Teaching Symposium," delivered at Georgetown University, Washington, DC, 12 October 1985; Edwin Meese, III, "Speech before the D.C. Chapter of the Federalist Society Lawyers Division, delivered on 15 November 1985; both reprinted in *Originalism: A Quarter-Century of Debate*, Steven G. Calabresi, ed. (Washington, DC: Regnery, 2007), 102.

the Civil War Amendments to eliminate the legal desegregation of blacks, and had contrived a theory of the Constitution to support the charade of "separate but equal" discrimination.[27]

In a striking reversal from Berger's discussion of the Fourteenth Amendment, Meese argued that the doctrine of separate-but-equal was nothing more than the unseemly importation of late nineteenth-century racism into the amendment, not a true reading of its meaning. Meese constructed originalism to achieve outcomes approved by the wider public, but also to question those rulings garnering less support, namely *Roe*, and thereby bring originalism in to line with modern Republicanism and make it more publicly acceptable.

Indeed, the Reagan administration found originalism appealing because it offered a constitutional interpretive philosophy that secured its policy aims when alternative attempts to do so had already proven ineffectual. For example, congressional conservatives advocated a range of jurisdiction-stripping measures and constitutional amendments to restore school prayer, prevent busing, and curb access to abortion. These proposals failed. Nixon's strategy of explicitly transforming judicial appointment into an electoral issue and then appointing "strict constructionists" only proved that "electoral success was not enough" to roll back the un-enumerated rights articulated by the Warren Court.[28] Even though Nixon had placed four justices on the Supreme Court, Chief Justice Burger's rulings on privacy, school integration, religious expression, which tended to adhere to Warren-era precedent, demonstrated that Republican capture of the presidency produced a judicial "counter-revolution that wasn't."[29] With appointment opportunities initially lacking and jurisdiction-stripping strategies failing to manipulate judicial power to support partisan aims, lawyers in the Reagan administration turned to promoting originalism as its guiding judicial philosophy, since this philosophy could be shaped to render the administration's policy aims. The Reagan Justice Department, which now oversaw the judicial nomination process, sought out judges who endorsed originalism.[30] As appointment opportunities lagged, the administration focused on promoting the philosophy through a public campaign.

With *Brown* nestled within originalist purview, originalism no longer ran counter to contemporary popular support for racial equality, and a concerted effort to foster public understanding of originalism was made. Originalism most clearly entered the popular imagination in the mid-1980s after Ronald Reagan's attorney general, Edwin Meese III, gave a series of well-publicized speeches on the concept. Since these speeches introduced modern originalism to the public, critics of this jurisprudential philosophy tend to view it simply as

---

[27] Meese, 15 November 1985, 77–8.
[28] Teles, 1.
[29] Vincent Blasi, ed., *The Burger Court: The Counter-Revolution That Wasn't* (New Haven: Yale University Press, 1983).
[30] See Dawn Johnsen, "Ronald Reagan and the Rehnquist Court on Congressional Power: Presidential Influences on Constitutional Change," *Indiana Law Journal* 78 (2003), 363–412.

the conservative version of legal realism, that is, as a jurisprudential approach meant to do little more than sustain conservative policy objectives by cloaking them in the legitimizing terms of Framers' intentions. Yet, as one legal historian has countered, "Originalism was not, however, merely a call for conservative results in constitutional adjudication.... [I]n one form or another its appeals to the principles and rhetoric of limited government and consent-based politics, as well as its traditional understanding of the nature of constitutional interpretation, had long been characteristic features of American constitutionalism."[31] And yet, as this book has emphasized, to suggest that ideas have long histories does not negate the possibility that they can be put intentionally into the service of new political ends, even ends that might be antithetical to the purposes under which such ideas were originally conceived.

Originalist emphasis is evident in Reagan's comments during the investiture of Chief Justice William Rehnquist and Justice Scalia, which were, like Meese's speeches, part of a larger project to "transform the values that underlie judicial interpretation of the Constitution ... [and] to challenge and discredit the basic values that had generated the Warren Court precedents."[32] Recounting the constitutional convention in his remarks, Reagan reminded his listeners that the Founders "settled on a judiciary that would be independent and strong, but one whose power would also, they believed, be confined within the boundaries of a *written* Constitution and laws."[33] And he advocated judicial restraint, but not restraint flowing from deference to Congress; restraint followed from interpretive method, and the Constitution's text restrained judicial interpretation. Thus, the Court could be restrained and still overturn a legislative act. In other words, originalism itself was the basis of judicial restraint. Other interpretive methods, by contrast, were illegitimate judicial activism. As such, originalism supported Reagan's flirtation with Jeffersonian departmentalism: "It would always be the totality of our constitutional system, with no one part getting the upper hand. And that's why the judiciary must be independent. And that is why it must exercise restraint."[34] If the judiciary did not proceed by terms of originalism, it necessarily upset the balance of powers.

Meese took Reagan's flirtation and its justification by originalist terms further a month later.[35] In a speech given at Tulane University, Meese distinguished between the Constitution as the founding document and constitutional law as what the Supreme Court interprets the document to mean: "constitutional law

---

[31] O'Neill, 134.

[32] Post and Siegel, 2009, 29.

[33] Ronald Reagan, "Remarks at the Swearing-In Ceremony for William H. Rehnquist as Chief Justice and Antonin Scalia as Associate Justice of the Supreme Court of the United States," 26 September 1986, John T. Woolley and Gerhard Peters, *The American Presidency Project* [online]. Santa Barbara, CA, http://www.presidency.ucsb.edu/ws/?pid=36494.

[34] Ibid.

[35] Edwin Meese, III, "The Law of the Constitution," delivered at Tulane University, 21 October 1986, reprinted in *Originalism: A Quarter-Century Debate*, Steven Calabresi, ed. (Washington, DC: Regnery, 2007).

is what the Supreme Court says about the Constitution in its decisions resolving the cases and controversies that come before it."[36] This distinction re-opened the argument that each branch had the responsibility to engage in constitutional interpretation. By separating the Constitution from the Supreme Court's constitutional law, Meese created the possibility that constitutional law could be misinterpretation, that is, that it does not follow from original meaning, as *Plessy*, *Dred Scott*, or *Lochner* had not, and thus needed to be overturned.

Even as Meese named presidents who, similar to Reagan, experienced conflict with the judiciary, his distinction between Constitution and constitutional law did not simply reconstruct the Jeffersonian or Jacksonian assertions of equal right to interpretation: "For the same reason that the Constitution cannot be reduced to constitutional law [expounded by the Supreme Court], the Constitution cannot simply be reduced to what the Congress or the President say it is, either. Quite the contrary. The Constitution, the original document of 1787 plus its amendments, is and must be understood to be the standard against which all laws, policies, and interpretations must be measured."[37] In contrast to earlier departmentalism, Meese attempted to recapture the logic of interpretation that Marshall laid out in *Marbury*, namely, that each branch held the responsibility to represent and protect the original act of popular sovereignty. Now Meese claimed that the legitimacy of the interpretation was based in whether it reflected the meaning understood at the time of that original act. Therefore, Meese rested the legitimacy of presidential interpretive authority not solely on the notion of coordinate powers (as Jefferson and Jackson had), nor on the authority conferred by party leadership (as Jackson, Lincoln, and FDR had), but on the rightness of a particular interpretive method. Presidential constitutional interpretive authority flowed from the original meaning of the Constitution itself. Alternative interpretative methodology undermined the basis of presidential interpretive authority, and confused constitutional law with the Constitution.

While laying the groundwork to defy judicial interpretation, rather than openly challenge the Court as Jefferson had or take a more limited challenge that Lincoln had, Meese participated in the process of contestation and persuasion, through his public rhetoric and through advocacy of a new institutionalized mechanism – the presidential signing statement – to convince Supreme Court Justices of the rightness of originalist methodology. It is to that new technique that this chapter turns.

II. Reagan's Legacy: the G.W. Bush Administration's Harnessing of Judicial Power

The G. W. Bush administration pursued at least two strategies to manipulate judicial power to enhance its own power. The first built on an innovation of

---

[36] Ibid., 102.
[37] Ibid., 106.

the Reagan justice department, namely, drafting of signing statements, which, in part, offer judges a statutory interpretation distinct from legislative history. The signing statement would make intent more ambiguous and invite judicial interpretation. The second is jurisdiction-stripping, in particular, removing the Supreme Court's appellate jurisdiction on habeas rights for "enemy combatants" in the War on Terror. Neither strategy has worked effectively. Supreme Court majorities have so far ignored signing statements although they have been cited in dissent. The Court has – by slim margins – ignored recent congressional efforts to strip and transfer habeas jurisdiction in both the Detainee Treatment Act of 2005 and the Military Commissions Act of 2006. In this way, the recent decision in *Boumediene v. Bush* perhaps constitutes the strongest evidence of assertions and acceptance of judicial supremacy.[38] However, the Court's claims turn out to be rather narrow and restrained.

II.a. *Signing Statements as Tools to Harness Judicial Power*
Signing statements are presidential commentary on legislation signed into law.[39] While they have long been an executive practice, until the Reagan administration they tended to be little more than "public announcements containing comments from the President" akin to "a press release."[40] Lawyers in the Reagan Office of Legal Counsel explored ways to enhance executive power, curtailed in the wake of Watergate.[41] They struck upon the signing statement as a means to that end. These lawyers sought to use the statement to guide judicial interpretation of statute.[42] The statement could signal that

---

[38] *Boumediene v. Bush*, 553 U.S. 723 (2008).

[39] James Monroe issued the first signing statement, and Jackson, Tyler, Lincoln, Andrew Johnson, Grant, Theodore Roosevelt, Wilson, Franklin Roosevelt, Truman, Eisenhower, Lyndon Johnson, Nixon, Ford, and Carter each issued a small number of statements. Louis Fisher, *Constitutional Conflicts between Congress and the President*, 5th ed. (Lawrence: University Press of Kansas, 1997), 123–5. For the history of signing statements, see T. J. Halstead, "Presidential Signing Statements: Constitutional and Institutional Implications," Congressional Research Service Report for Congress. Updated 17 September 2007, http://www.fas.org/sgp/crs/natsec/RL33667.pdf.

[40] Statement by Senator Patrick Leahy (D-VT), Ranking Member, at a Senate Judiciary Committee Hearing on "Presidential Signing Statements," 27 June 2006, http://judiciary. senate.gove/hearing.cfm?id=1969.

[41] Charlie Savage, *Takeover: The Return of the Imperial Presidency and the Subversion of American Democracy* (New York: Little, Brown, 2007), 70–84, 229–49.

[42] Signing statements serve purposes beyond this guidance function. First, by declaring parts of a law unenforceable, they may act as an informal line-item veto since the line-item veto was declared unconstitutional in *Clinton v. New York*, 524 U.S. 417 (1998). Second, they may function as directives to agencies regarding how a statute should be implemented. However, as detailed in this section, Reagan administration lawyers struck upon the guidance function first. Christopher Kelley disagrees with this assessment, arguing instead that the purpose of the signing statement was not "to affect judicial decision making" but to "influence the administrative agencies as much if not more than to influence judges" (1). Yet, I contend that while the signing statement had as one of its purposes to consolidate executive power, memos from the Reagan Justice Department clearly stipulate that using signing statements to augment the legislative record and provide an alternative route for interpretation was a high

the president preferred a particular interpretation. By opening another path of interpretation, the statement attempts to bring the judiciary to the president's side, to utilize judicial authority for executive policy aims rather than counter or undermine it.

On 2 April 1985, Acting Deputy Attorney General D. Lowell Jensen wrote to Fred Fielding, counsel to the president, citing displeasure at Reagan's failure to attach a statement to the Pacific Salmon Treaty Act. Although the Justice Department outlined how the bill might violate executive authority, no statement was issued. Jensen contended that Reagan missed an opportunity since signing statements "perform important functions by placing an interpretation on a statute" and give "instructions to the agency charged with the administration of a statute."[43] Jensen's first claim, that the statement could offer an alternative to legislative history and imprint executive interpretation on statutory meaning, was the focus of another memo addressed to Attorney General Meese drafted in August of that year.

That memo was authored by Federalist Society founders Steven Calabresi and John Harrison. It begins, "The abuse of legislative history is a major way in which legislative power is usurped by activist courts, ideologically motivated congressional staffers and lobbying groups." It outlines how judges have no written alternative to legislative history to serve as "a guide to the interpretation of statutory language."[44] The remedy, Calabresi and Harrison suggested, was "a potentially powerful, if so far unused tool: Presidential signing statements."[45] The immediate challenge was that signing statements were not part of legislative history even if, in the young lawyers' words, they were better than congressional committee reports as guides to statutory meaning since the former "represent an entire branch's view of the matter."[46] By contrast, committee reports represent only the majority of a committee not the entire Congress. Given that statements were not published and thus not immediately accessible to lawyers and judges, Calabresi and Harrison recommended that Meese take the following actions: (1) publish the signing statements; (2) give speeches to spread awareness about them; (3) ask the Litigation Strategy Working Group, which has been called "a brain trust of about fifteen political appointees drawn from throughout the Justice Department," to consider how

priority. See Christopher Kelly, "A Matter of Direction: The Reagan Administration, the Signing Statement, and the 1986 Westlaw Decision," *William & Mary Bill of Rights Journal* 16 (2007), 283–306.

43 D. Lowell Jensen to Fred F. Fielding, 2 April 1985, http://www.archives.gov/news/samuel-alito/accession-060–89–269/Acco60–89–269-box3-SG-ChronologicalFile.pdf.

44 Steve Calabresi and John Harrison, Memo for the Attorney General on Presidential Signing Statements, 23 August 1985, http://www.archives.gov/news/samuel-alito/accessuib-060–89–269/Acco60–89–269-box3-SGChronologicalFile.pdf.

45 Ibid.

46 Ibid. For a discussion of an enacting congressional coalition and whether statutory outputs capture legislative intent, see McNollgast, "Legislative Intent: The Use of Positive Political Theory in Statutory Interpretation," *Law & Contemporary Problems* 57 (1994), 3–37.

to disseminate statements to staff attorneys to familiarize thems with the document; and (4) have the OLC draft law review articles on behalf of Meese encouraging judicial use of signing statements to interpret statute.[47]

On 3 September 1985, Kenneth Cribb, counselor to the attorney general, sent memos to Charles Fried, acting solicitor general; James Spears, acting assistant attorney general in the Office of Legal Policy; and Ralph Tarr, acting assistant attorney general in the Office of Legal Counsel, seeking assessment of Calabresi and Harrison's idea.[48] In a memo dated 25 October 1985 from Spears to Cribb, Spears concentrates *exclusively* on whether and how the signing statement can be used as an interpretive device to guide judicial interpretation of statute. According to Spears, this tactic relies on how judges understand intent, that is, whether it is derived from what legislators meant when debating a bill or whether it is derived from what a "reasonable person" may take the statute to mean. If intent were the former, then signing statements would have no use, since they are drafted after congressional debate. However, if intent were the latter, then "the relevance of a Presidential signing statement as an aid to legislative interpretation increases dramatically" because "unlike the subjective 'congressional intent' standard, the 'meaning of the statute' test focuses upon an objective analysis of what other [*sic*] perceive it to mean – and that public perception would be influenced by the President's interpretation of the statute." Ultimately, Spears recommended that to use signing statements toward this end, they needed to be included alongside publication of the law itself in the United States Code Congressional and Administrative News (USCCAN) in hopes that "the mere proximity of the statement of the legislation and its procedural history will encourage attorneys to make greater use of documents."[49]

Three days later, Ralph Tarr responded to Cribb's request with a memo outlining purposes signing statements have historically served: (1) executive agencies use them as guides to interpret statute and direct their actions; (2) Congress uses them as signals of presidential interpretation, particularly when the president believes a provision to be unconstitutional, and (3) courts cite them "in describing the underlying intent of a statute."[50] Tarr spent most of

---

[47] Ibid. The characterization of the Litigation Strategy Working Group is from Savage, *Takeover*, 233.

[48] T. Kenneth Cribb, counselor to the attorney general to Charles Fried, acting solicitor general, 3 September 1985. T. Kenneth Cribb, counselor to the attorney general to James M. Spears, acting assistant attorney general, Office of Legal Policy, 3 September 1985. T. Kenneth Cribb, counselor to the attorney general to Ralph Tarr, acting assistant attorney general, Office of Legal Counsel, 3 September 1985, http://www.archives.gov/news/samuel-alito/accession-060–89–269/Acco60–89–269-box3-SG-ChronologicalFile.pdf.

[49] James M. Spears, acting assistant attorney general, Office of Legal Policy to T. Kenneth Cribb, Jr., counselor to the attorney general, 25 October 1985, http://www.archives.gov/news/samuel-alito/accession-060–89–269/Acco60–89–269-box3-SG-ChronologicalFile.pdf.

[50] Ralph W. Tarr, acting assistant attorney general, Office of Legal Counsel to T. Kenneth Cribb, 18 October 1985, http://www.archives.gov/news/samuel-alito/accession-060–89–269/Acco60–89–269-box3-SG-ChronologicalFile.pdf.

the memo elaborating this third use, listing cases in which the federal courts and the Supreme Court raised executive interpretation as an important guide, particularly *INS v. Chadha*, *EEOC v. Home Ins. Co.*, and *Clinton D. Mayhew Inc. v. Wirtz*.[51] Tarr wrote "that it should be possible to have signing statements join the material other than congressional debates and reports that courts use to determine the meaning of a statute."[52] The memo analogized such deference to that already displayed to bureaucratic agencies as evident in *Chevron* and to the attorney general's views in *State of Vermont v. Brinegar*.[53] Given this precedent, Tarr concluded, "there is no reason that the same rules of statutory construction that make these materials legitimate tools for courts confronted by ambiguous statutes should not also apply to Presidential signing statements."[54]

In February 1986, about a year after these memos began to circulate, Samuel Alito, Jr., deputy assistant attorney general in the Office of Legal Counsel, summarized for the Litigation Strategy Working Group the primary purpose of the administration's use of signing statements: "Our primary objective is to ensure that Presidential signing statements assume their rightful place in the interpretation of legislation." For Alito, the problem was that "in interpreting statutes, both courts and litigants (including lawyers in the Executive branch) invariably speak of 'legislative' or 'congressional' intent. Rarely if ever do courts or litigants inquire into the President's intent." Alito repeated ideas outlined by Calabresi and Harrison, namely, that although the statement had been "often little more than a press release," an "interpretive signing statement" would "increase the power of the Executive to shape the law" and "by forcing some rethinking by courts, scholars, and litigants, it may help to curb some of the prevalent abuses of legislative history."[55] In short, all of these memos highlighted offering judges an alternate route to interpret a statute in line with presidential interests. They sought to harness judicial authority rather than to directly counter it.

[51] *INS v. Chadha*, 462 U.S. 919 (1983); *EEOC v. Home Ins. Co.*, 672 F. 2nd 252, 265 (2nd Cir. 1982); *Clinton D. Mayhew Inc. v. Wirtz*, 413 F. 2nd 658, 661 (4th Cir. 1969).

[52] Tarr memo, 18 October 1985.

[53] *Chevron v. Natural Resources Defense Council*, 467 U.S. 837 [1984]; *Vermont v. Brinegar*, 379 F. Supp. 606 (D. Vt. 1974). This memo did not specifically cite *Chevron*; however, the Court found in that case that it would defer to agency implementation of statute if congressional intent was unclear. See Christopher Kelley, "The Law: Contextualizing the Signing Statement," *Presidential Studies Quarterly* 37 (December 2007): 741.

[54] Tarr, memo, 18 October 1985. Meese followed up on these memos by writing to the West Publishing Company requesting that signing statements be published in the USCCAN. The company agreed to do so on 26 December 1985, and the CEO of West noted that the statements would be "of interest and of help to the legal profession. I am surprised nobody thought of it before." Dwight Opperman to Edwin Meese III, 26 December 1985, http:// www.archives.gov/news/samuel-alito/accession-060–89–269/Acc060–89–269-box3-SG-ChronologicalFile.pdf.

[55] Samuel Alito, Jr., deputy assistant attorney general, Office of Legal Counsel to the Litigation Strategy Working Group, 5 February 1986, http://www.archives.gov/news/samuel-alito/accession-060–89–269/Acc060–89–269-box6-SG-LSWG-AlitotoLSWG-Feb1986.pdf.

This interpretive signing statement was widely utilized by President George
W. Bush.⁵⁶ And it is perhaps more innovative than the presidential veto to the
degree that it manipulates the construction of law without directly confronting congressional or judicial authority. In the veto process, a bill is presented
to the president and must be signed or vetoed within ten days. If vetoed, the
bill returns to Congress, which may then override the veto with a two-thirds
majority in both chambers. In other words, crafting law requires a dialogue
between the legislative and executive branch, and the veto is a component
of that dialogue, whether it comes as a threat or is actually used.⁵⁷ By exe-
cuting a law, but nevertheless holding out the possibility that it may not be
enforced at the president's discretion, as many of the Bush signing statements
did, the president forecloses a congressional response. Recognizing this problem, members of Congress have called for legislation to stifle the influence
of these statements by refusing to allocate funds for their publication, limiting their accessibility for judicial citation, or by directly preventing citation
altogether.⁵⁸

⁵⁶ Bush has included multiple constitutional objections within a single statement (see Kinopf
and Shane, 2007). According to one count, Bush's objections center on vague assertions
of the power of the unitary executive, or the idea that presidential power drawn from the
Constitution is inherent, that is, that such powers need not be explicitly stated but are
implied, and exclusive, that is, no other branch can legitimately encroach on presidential power. By one count, 82 of 505 signing statements based objections on the "power to
supervise the unitary executive." Phillip Cooper, "George W. Bush, Edgar Allan Poe, and
the Use and Abuse of Presidential Signing Statements," *Presidential Studies Quarterly* 35
(September 2005), 522. On unitary executive theory, see Steven Calabresi and Kevin Rhodes,
"The Structural Constitution: Unitary Executive, Plural Judiciary," *Harvard Law Review*
105 (April 1992), 1153–216 and Christopher S. Yoo, Steven G. Calabresi, and Anthony J.
Colangelo, "The Unitary Executive in the Modern Era, 1945–2004," *Iowa Law Review* 90
(2005), 601–731. Furthermore, Bush statements have been ambiguous, citing general claims
about executive constitutional authority rather than specifying clear objections to a particular section of the statute. In one assessment, the statements of Reagan, G. H. W. Bush, and
Clinton are "respectful and specific," "explicitly acknowledged the role of the Congress in
reaching accommodation while claiming the president's role in resolving problems in first
person," and their "proposed course of action is specific and well documented." By contrast,
G. W. Bush's statements "follow none of these precedents," and they "do not necessarily specify sections of bills that infringe executive authority, much less precisely how those infringements will be countered." David Birdsell, "George W. Bush's Signing Statements: The Assault
on Deliberation," *Rhetoric & Public Affairs* 10 (2007): 340, 342.
⁵⁷ Charles Cameron and Nolan McCarty, "Models of Vetoes and Veto Bargaining," *Annual
Review of Political Science* 7 (May 2004): 409–35. On the veto and signing statement as rhetoric, see Karlyn Campbell and Kathleen Jamieson, *Presidents Creating the Presidency: Deeds
Done in Words* (Chicago: University of Chicago Press, 2008).
⁵⁸ On withholding of funds, see H.R. 264, 110th Congress, 1st Session (2007), in particular
§ 3(a) and 3(b). On banning their use by judges, see S. 1747, 110th Congress, 1st Session
(2007), § 4 and H.R. 3045, 110th Congress, 1st Session (2007), § 4. The Bush signing statement is considered quantitatively and qualitatively distinct from its predecessors. Senators
Arlen Specter (R-PA) and Patrick Leahy (D-VT) have argued that through his signing
statements, Bush has upset the balance of powers among the three federal branches. Andy
Sullivan, "Specter to grill officials on Bush ignoring laws," REUTERS, June 21, 2006,http://

In short, by drafting signing statements the president comments on the law's constitutionality. Executive power seemingly encroaches on a traditionally judicial responsibility, namely, to say what the law is. Yet, because the president signs the bill into law, this extra-judicial interpretation is less blunt than Jackson's departmentalist veto or Lincoln's containment of *Dred Scott*. Through the interpretive signing statement, presidents can articulate an alternate constitutional interpretation and ensure that, if the law is challenged, courts have multiple options to gauge statutory intent. Since the statements posit *possible* rather than *definitive* presidential action, it is more difficult to contain this executive prerogative.[59]

The signing statement, as has been utilized by the Bush administration, offers an interpretation of statute that is potentially distinct from that gleaned from legislative history. As such, the statements point judges to an alternative foundation for ruling if the law becomes subject to litigation. If the judiciary is ideologically aligned with the executive, then that strategy is more plausible. And by asserting only possible action, rather than making a definitive veto, the president hamstrings congressional response.

The Reagan-era intention behind the interpretive signing statement and the Bush-era attempts to utilize the statement to guide judges have not worked out.[60] The Supreme Court has refused thus far to utilize these statements. But

---

www.washingtonpost.com/wp-dyn/content/article/2006/06/21/AR2006062101594.html; see Statement of Senator Patrick Leahy, Ranking Member, Judiciary Committee Hearing on Presidential Signing Statements, 27 June 2006, at http://judiciary.senate.gov/member_statement.cfm?id=1969&wit_id=2629.

[59] Since Bush signing statements "do not apply particularized constitutional rationales to specific scenarios, nor do they contain explicit measurable refusals to enforce a law," it is not clear how review would proceed. On withholding of funds, see H.R. 264, 110th Congress, 1st Session (2007), in particular § 3(a) and 3(b). On banning their use by judges, see S. 1747, 110th Congress, 1st Session (2007), § 4 and H.R. 3045, 110th Congress, 1st Session (2007), § 4. Recognizing this dilemma, the ABA called for legislation that may more easily enable judicial review of signing statements, which may ultimately backfire to the extent that, in doing so, the Court would be compelled to recognize the statement as part of the legitimate record of a statute's meaning. In its 2006 report, the ABA cites this problem: "For individual plaintiffs, a signing statement might well elude the case or controversy requirement because the immediate injury is to the lawmaking powers of Congress. The President thus becomes the final judge of his own constitutional power, and he invariably rules in favor himself." Therefore, the Association calls for legislation that would provide Congress or any agent of Congress legal standing "in any instance in which the President uses a signing statement to claim the authority, or state the intention, to disregard or decline to enforce all or part of a law, or interpret such a law in a manner inconsistent with the clear intent of Congress." *Report of the Task Force on Presidential Signing Statements and the Separation of Powers Doctrine*, 25.

[60] Steven Calabresi, one of the original architects, has become ambivalent on whether the signing statement should become a tool of judicial interpretation. In 2006, Calabresi wrote that "the use of presidential signing statements as legislative history is more subject to doubt that I thought when I first argued for the idea in the Reagan Justice Department twenty years ago." Calabresi and Daniel Lev, "The Legal Significance of Presidential Signing Statements," *The Forum* 4 (2006), 6. And he recounted that while he "initially thought of signing statements

recent judicial moves point toward that possibility. Justice Scalia scolded his brethren for not treating the statement as an indication of a statute's intent. His position is ironic since Scalia tends not to rely on so-called external instruments to interpret law such as legislative history and instead relies on the text itself and how the words' meanings might be understood by comparing their use intra-textually, that is, how they are used throughout the Constitution in various clauses, and by gathering their meaning through use of dictionaries and other sources at the time of the drafting.[61] Yet in his dissent in *Hamdan v. Rumsfeld*, Scalia noted, "in its discussion of legislative history the court wholly ignores the president's signing statement, which explicitly set forth his understanding that the [Detainee Treatment Act] ousted jurisdiction over pending cases."[62] Justices Thomas and Alito joined in this dissent. Alito, as noted above, drafted one of the memos highlighting how statements could be used for the very purpose Scalia argued. Therefore, even if the original aim of signing statements represents only a minority view on the Court, as previous chapters discussed, minority views can become majority views over time. As one scholar characterized the aim of using signing statements as statutory history, this "may be of more importance in the long term than any other impact of the signing statements."[63]

II.b. *Jurisdiction-Stripping to Win the War on Terror: A Case of Judicial Supremacy?*

The strongest case for the existence of a general norm of judicial supremacy is seemingly demonstrated by the Supreme Court's refusal to acknowledge that Congress has repeatedly stripped its jurisdiction on habeas rights for "enemy

as presidential legislative history," his view has narrowed; he sees them now as "important vehicles by which presidents can control subordinates in the executive branch" (Calabresi, quoted in Savage, *Takeover*, 234).

[61] On Scalia's textualism and his consistent refusal to look at legislative history as a reference of legislative intent, see his *A Matter of Interpretation: Federal Courts and the Law* (Princeton: Princeton University Press, 1998), and Steven Calabresi and Gary Lawson, "The Unitary Executive, Jurisdiction Stripping, and the Hamdan Opinions," *Columbia Law Review* 107 (2007), 1002–48.

[62] *Hamdan v. Rumsfeld*, 548 U.S. 557 (2006), Scalia, J., dissenting. The DTA had a presidential signing statement in which Bush further limited jurisdiction, and which formed part of the foundation of Justice Scalia's dissent in *Hamdan*, which assessed the constitutionality of the DTA. Scalia would have dismissed the case since Congress exercised its Exceptions Clause power to tailor federal jurisdiction. However, before the Senate voted on the jurisdiction-stripping provision that would become § 1005(e) of the law, Senator Carl Levin (D-MI), who authored that amendment with Senator Lindsay Graham (R-SC), argued that the provision "will not strip the courts of jurisdiction over those [pending] cases. For instance, the Supreme Court jurisdiction in *Hamdan* is not affected." *Congressional Record* S12,755 (Daily Edition, 14 November 2005). Of course, after the DTA was passed, Senator Kyl (R-AZ) suggested the precise opposite characterization. See *Congressional Record*, S14,264 (Daily Edition, 21 December 2005).

[63] Phillip Cooper, *By Order of the President: The Use and Abuse of Executive Direct Action* (Lawrence: University Press of Kansas, 2005), 520.

combatants." Yet even as the Court claimed jurisdiction by the slenderest of margins in the 2008 ruling in *Boumediene v. Bush*, it did so on narrow grounds and in a somewhat incoherent way. My aim in this section, then, is to acknowledge the Court's claim of supremacy when the status of habeas rights are involved, but also to argue that the Court acknowledged this to be a fundamentally special case. The supremacy claim as articulated by the Court rests on narrow grounds. In other words, I take the most difficult case for the validity of my theory and show that the Court's articulation of its supremacy, precisely because it is narrow, convoluted, and distinguished as special, fits with expectations that judicial supremacy tends not be a widespread norm.

Relevant jurisdiction-stripping began in 2005 when Congress passed the Detainee Treatment Act (DTA). The DTA declared "no court, justice, or judge shall have jurisdiction to hear or consider" any habeas corpus or other action filed by a non-citizen detained at Guantanamo Bay.[64] Detainees could not appeal their "enemy combatant status" as determined by military tribunals or Combatant Status Review Trials (CSRTs) except through a path ending at the D.C. Court of Appeals rather than the Supreme Court.[65]

In the 2006 case, *Hamdan v. Rumsfeld*, the government contended that the DTA's jurisdiction-stripping applied retroactively. Therefore, the Supreme Court did not have authority to hear the case.[66] Justice Steven's opinion for the majority held that it was unnecessary to reach the constitutional question of Article III jurisdiction-stripping. Rather, it held "through ordinary principles of statutory construction" that the legislative intent of jurisdiction-stripping

[64] Detainee Treatment Act of 2005, Pub. L. No. 109–148, 119 Stat. 2739. § 1005(e). The act received coverage mostly because it was spearheaded by former prisoner-of-war Senator John McCain (R-AZ) as a response to the Abu Ghraib torture scandal. The stripping of habeas corpus jurisdiction tended to be overshadowed by coverage of the battle between President Bush and Senator John McCain over the statutory ban on torture included in the DTA.

[65] Ibid., § 1005(e)(2)(C)(ii); § 1005(e)(3)(B)(i); § 1005(e)(3)(D)(ii). Military commissions had not been used in the United States since World War II prior to 9/11. See Louis Fisher, *Military Tribunals and Presidential Power: American Revolution to the War on Terrorism* (Lawrence: University Press of Kansas, 2005), and Johan Steyn, "Guantanamo Bay: The Legal Black Hole," *International and Comparative Law Quarterly* 53 (2004), 1–15. Bush's use of these commissions has been critiqued as "ignoring all the changes to military law over the past sixty years and instead reinstituting a rough-justice trial system." See Savage, *Takeover*, 137–8. The Bush administration rests much of its legal authority for its 2001 Military Order on FDR's proclamation and cites the Supreme Court's decision in *Ex parte Quirin*, in which the Court unanimously ruled against the defendants' habeas claims that the military commissions by which they were tried were legally constituted. *Ex parte Quirin*, 317 U.S. 1 (1942) Yet, as Fisher notes, Roosevelt's order was targeted toward particular men already identified as Nazi saboteurs, while the Bush order includes a much larger class of individuals, which has been extensively critiqued. See Neal Katyal and Laurence Tribe, "Waging War, Deciding Guilt: Trying the Military Tribunals," *Yale Law Journal* 111 (2002), 1259–311 and Harold Hongju Koh, "The Case against Military Commissions," *American Journal of International Law* 96 (2002), 337–44.

[66] *Hamdan v. Rumsfeld*, 548 U. S. 557 (2006). As discussed in the previous section, Scalia accepted this argument.

was not clear and that the omission of clear language was *deliberate*. According to Stevens, the DTA's legislative history detailed that Congress rejected retroactive application and, in doing so, Congress rejected "the very language that would have achieved the result the Government urges." Such rejection, according to Stevens, "weigh[ed] heavily against the Government's interpretation."[67] The omission of language specifying retroactive jurisdiction-stripping, was for Stevens "an integral part of the statutory scheme that muddies whatever 'plain meaning' may be discerned."[68]

Therefore, upon determining that it still had jurisdiction, the Court ruled the administration-established military tribunals unconstitutional.[69] The Court left open the possibility that an alternatively constructed tribunal might pass constitutional muster. In his concurrence, Justice Breyer laid out possible presidential and congressional reaction to *Hamdan*:

> The Court's conclusion ultimately rests upon a single ground: Congress has not issued the Executive a "blank check." Cf. *Hamdi v. Rumsfeld*, 542 U. S. 507, 536 (2004) (plurality opinion). Indeed, Congress has denied the President the legislative authority to create military commissions of the kind at issue here. Nothing prevents the President from returning to Congress to seek the authority he believes necessary.[70]

Weeks before the closely contested 2006 midterm election, in which Republicans lost their majority in the Senate and the House, Congress passed the Military Commissions Act (MCA) on a near party-line vote.[71] The bill re-established military tribunals for trying enemy combatants, and it stripped the Supreme Court of habeas jurisdiction. It lodged that jurisdiction, in most cases, with the United States Court of Appeals for the District of Columbia.[72] This court was granted "exclusive jurisdiction to determine the validity of a final judgment rendered by a military commission."[73]

---

[67] Ibid., 11, 14.

[68] Ibid., 19.

[69] First, they were not established by either the Authorization to Use Military Force of 2001 or the Detainee Treatment Act of 2005. Second, the offense of which Hamdan was accused did not conform to the historical use of military commissions; it took place prior to the conflict as well as occurred outside the region of conflict, and the charge against Hamdan of "conspiracy" was not considered a war crime. Ibid., 30, 36, 38–40.

[70] Ibid., J. Breyer, concurring, 1.

[71] In the House, the MCA received 219 Republican votes for passage and 39 Democratic votes for passage; 160 Democrats voted against the bill as did 7 Republicans and 1 Independent. Seven Democrats and 5 Republicans did not vote. In the Senate, 53 Republicans voted for the bill as did 11 Democrats; 32 Democrats voted against the bill as did 1 Republican. One Independent voted for the bill in the Senate; 1 voted against it, and 1 Republican did not vote, http://www.govtrack.us/congress/vote.xpd?vote=s2006–259 and http://www.govtrack.us/congress/vote.xpd?vote=h2006–491.

[72] PL 109–366 – adopted 17 October 2006. See Section 3, "Military Commissions," Subchapter VI – Post-Trial Procedures and Review of Military Commissions, Section 950g, "Review by the United States Court of Appeals for the District of Columbia and the Supreme Court."

[73] Ibid.

The MCA offered a two-stage process to determine enemy combatant status: first, the status would be determined by a CSRT, and second, that determination could be appealed to the D.C. Circuit Court. The MCA undercut the logic of *Hamdan's* reliance on the Geneva Convention to guarantee defendants' due process rights by stipulating that the Court could no longer cite the Geneva Convention as relevant law.[74] And, in response to Scalia's *Hamdan* dissent, the jurisdiction-stripping cited in the DTA signing statement now had congressional sanction in the MCA.[75] The Supreme Court was seemingly cut out of the process and, as such, the MCA is perhaps the strongest example of jurisdiction-stripping as an assault on judicial legitimacy since *McCardle*.

On 20 February 2007, the United States Court of Appeals for the District of Columbia ruled 2 to 1 in *Boumediene v. Bush* to uphold the Military Commissions Act to the extent that it eliminated federal jurisdiction on habeas corpus challenges brought by "enemy combatants."[76] On 5 December 2007, the Supreme Court heard appeal, which challenged the MCA's curbing of habeas jurisdiction.[77]

On 13 June 2008, the Supreme Court ruled 5 to 4 that terrorist suspects were entitled to the writ of habeas corpus and could challenge their detention in federal courts. In so ruling, the Court decided two questions. First, were the jurisdiction-stripping measures in the DTA and MCA constitutionally valid?[78]

---

[74] Ibid. See Section 5, "Treaty Obligations Not Establishing Grounds for Certain Claims," Subsection (a): "No person may invoke the Geneva Conventions or any protocols thereto in any habeas corpus or other civil action or proceeding to which the United States, or a current or former officer, employee, member of the Armed Forces, or other agent of the United States is a party as a source of rights in any court of the United States or its States or territories."

[75] Ibid. See Section 7, "Habeas Corpus Matters," Subsection (a).

Section 2241 of title 28, United States Code, is amended by striking both the subsection (e) added by section 1005(e)(1) of Public Law 109–148 (119 Stat. 2742) and the subsection (e) added by section 1405(e)(1) of Public Law 109–163 (119 Stat. 3477) and inserting the following new subsection:

(e)(1) No court, justice, or judge shall have jurisdiction to hear or consider an application for a writ of habeas corpus filed by or on behalf of an alien detained by the United States who has been determined by the United States to have been properly detained as an enemy combatant or is awaiting such determination.

(2) Except as provided in paragraphs (2) and (3) of section 1005(e) of the Detainee Treatment Act of 2005 (10 U.S.C. 801 note), no court, justice, or judge shall have jurisdiction to hear or consider any other action against the United States or its agents relating to any aspect of the detention, transfer, treatment, trial, or conditions of confinement of an alien who is or was detained by the United States and has been determined by the United States to have been properly detained as an enemy combatant or is awaiting such determination.

[76] Stephen Labaton, "Court Endorses Law's Curbs on Detainees," *New York Times*, 21 February 2007, http://www.nytimes.com/2007/02/21/washington/21gitmo.html.

[77] Relevant case law suggests that no suspension follows if a substitute is provided. See *Swain v. Pressley*, 430 U.S. 372, 381 (1977). ("The substitution of a collateral remedy which is neither inadequate nor ineffective to test the legality of a person's detention does not constitute a suspension of the writ of habeas corpus.")

[78] The Court did not reach the question of whether the jurisdiction-stripping in the DTA was constitutionally valid because the timing of the *Hamdan* case and the passage of the DTA

Second, if yes, how could the Court rule to secure habeas rights for suspects deemed "enemy combatants" by the CSRTs?[79]

The Court acknowledged that the jurisdiction-stripping was valid, but it then ignored the statute on the basis that it was overridden by the *fundamental right* of habeas protection. The slim majority held that Section 7 of the Military Commissions Act "denies the federal courts jurisdiction to hear habeas corpus actions pending at the time of its enactment ... so that, if the statute is valid, petitioners' cases must be dismissed."[80] The majority then discussed the ongoing colloquy between Congress and courts characterizing the development of statute, noting that the MCA was drafted as a direct response to the Court's ruling in *Hamdan*, where it invoked a "clear statement rule" and invited Congress to draft a law that clearly stipulated its intent. The Court found the MCA to have done just that:

> If the Court invokes a clear statement rule to advise that certain statutory interpretations are favored in order to avoid constitutional difficulties, Congress can make an informed legislative choice either to amend the statute or to retain its existing text. If Congress amends, its intent must be respected

meant that the jurisdiction-stripping would have had to have been retroactive. The Court decided that it was not retroactive, not that it could not hold henceforth.

[79] On the second question, the majority held that while Congress could replace habeas review with an alternative review, the alternatives provided by the DTA and MCA were inadequate. The DTA limited judicial review of the status designation to the facts established by a CSRT. This procedure was criticized because the detainee was not entitled to see evidence used to determine enemy combatant status. See Combatant Status Review Tribunals Order of the Deputy Secretary of Defense of July 7, 2004, 12 paragraph a, http://www.defenselink.mil/news/Jul2004/d20040707review.pdf. See Melissa Patterson, "Surely You Didn't Mean 'No' Jurisdiction: Why the Supreme Court's Selective Hearing in *Hamdan* Is Good for Democracy," *Harvard Law & Policy Review* 1 (2007), 282.

The Constitution's privilege of the writ of habeas corpus allows the opportunity for a prisoner to demonstrate his or her detention to be unlawful or erroneous. The procedures of CSRT did not, in the majority's view, provide this opportunity: "At the CSRT stage the detainee has limited means to find or present evidence to challenge the Government's case, does not have the assistance of counsel, and may not be aware of the most critical allegations that the Government relied upon to order his detention. His opportunity to confront witnesses is likely to be more theoretical than real, given that there are no limits on the admission of hearsay" (*Boumediene v. Bush*, 553 U. S. 723 [2008], 7).

If the CSRT model was inadequate, the question arose as to whether the DTA allowed the Court of Appeals to conduct review of the CSRT proceedings. The Court found the DTA to be silent on this question, an omission it called "troubling," and assumed that "congressional silence permits a constitutionally required remedy" (Ibid., 59). In other words, the Court read the remedy as implied. Such silences in the MCA raise the question as to whether they were deliberate by Congress so that politicians might secure political capital for passing a measure that is harsh on terrorists while leaving the Court to secure constitutional rights and, thus, taking the "fall" for appearing soft on terrorism.

The majority stipulated that within this silence the DTA might be interpreted to allow "petitioners to assert most, if not all, of the legal claims they seek to advance, including their most basic claim: that the President has no authority under the AUMF [Authority to Use Military Force] to detain them indefinitely" (Ibid., 59).

[80] *Boumediene v. Bush*, 553 U. S. 723 (2008), 5.

even if a difficult constitutional question is presented. The usual presumption is that Members of Congress, in accord with their oath of office, considered the constitutional issue and determined Opinion of the Court the amended statute to be a lawful one; and the Judiciary, in light of that determination, proceeds to its own independent judgment on the constitutional question when required to do so in a proper case.[81]

The Court sought to avoid direct confrontation with the Congress on the question of whether the latter could strip the Court of jurisdiction; it followed deferential logic of avoiding the constitutional question. It went further than *Hamdan* in that the *Boumediene* majority *conceded* that Congress could jurisdiction-strip, that the MCA had legitimately done so, and that the Court of Appeals ruled appropriately.

The problem was that the MCA's denial of habeas protections was *fundamentally* unconstitutional. The jurisdiction-stripping and the constitutional question were not separable, and, as such, the jurisdiction-stripping was voided. The Court invalidated the jurisdiction-stripping while affirming Congress's general authority to take such action. The majority denied its supremacy by acknowledging that the general principle and practice of jurisdiction-stripping was in and of itself valid. But, then it denied the particular validity of the DTA and MCA's jurisdiction-stripping by defining habeas as a *fundamental* right.

Having ruled the DTA unconstitutional, the majority proceeded to question whether it could be amended to make it constitutional. The answer appears to be no: "We do not imply DTA review would be a constitutionally sufficient replacement for habeas corpus but for these limitations on the detainee's ability to present exculpatory evidence.... Petitioners have met their burden of establishing that the DTA review process is, on its face, an inadequate substitute for habeas corpus."[82] The Court appears to have ended the very interbranch colloquy it praised in the first part of its decision. By now repeatedly ruling presidential and congressional construction of military tribunals to be inadequate, the Court has not only negated the possibility of jurisdiction-stripping by statute, but it has also asserted its own supremacy to rule on the extent of presidential and congressional authority. Justice Scalia stated as much in his dissent:

> If the understood scope of the writ of habeas corpus was "designed to restrain" (as the Court says) the actions of the Executive, the understood *limits* upon that scope were (as the Court seems not to grasp) just as much "designed to restrain" the incursions of the Third Branch. "Manipulation" of the territorial reach of the writ by the Judiciary poses just as much a threat to the proper separation of powers as "manipulation" by the Executive.[83]

---

[81] Ibid., 7–8.
[82] Ibid., 63.
[83] Ibid., J. Scalia dissenting, 8–9.

Yet even as the Court asserted its supremacy on habeas protections, such assertions are *not* new. For example, the Nixon administration, responding to concerns that the Warren Court expanded criminals' rights to use federal habeas protections to challenge convictions in state courts, wrote legislation to rein in these protections.[84] That legislation did not pass. The Burger and Rehnquist Courts demonstrated less concern for the rights of convicted criminals, with majorities ruling *against* their habeas rights in *Wainwright v. Sykes* and *Teague v. Lane*.[85] Congress exerted some claim on the extent of habeas rights when it passed and President Clinton signed the Antiterrorism and Effective Death Penalty Act (AEDPA) of 1996.[86] However, importantly, this Act did not clearly do much beyond what the Rehnquist Court had already accomplished through judicial interpretation to foreclose access to habeas remedies. Of course, legislation that was redundant to jurisprudential trends is, as has been argued already, useful for purposes of political capital: "The fact that the courts had already done most of what the Republican legislation sought to accomplish was largely irrelevant from a politician's point of view" because passing the AEDPA would allow for electorally valuable position-staking and credit-claiming.[87] The pattern of passage of the AEDPA mimicked that of the jurisdiction-stripping that passed in the 1970s, that is, Congress passed a statute that required what the Court had already trended toward through its interpretation. Congress could thereby claim credit, but the Court's power was not substantially curbed. The AEDPA case is different from the busing legislation to the extent that rather than embracing the statute, the Court moderated its impact.[88] As one scholar has judged, through its

---

[84] Powe, 2000, 379–44. Larry W. Yackle, "The Habeas Hagioscope," *Southern California Law Review* 66 (1993), 2353–5.

[85] *Wainwright v. Sykes*, 433 U.S. 72 (1977); *Teague v. Lane*, 489 U.S. 288 (1989). In *Wainwright*, the Burger Court established a series of rules that would foreclose access to federal habeas courts on procedural claims. If the state had a procedural rule regarding the filing of federal claim and a prisoner had not met the parameters of that rule such that the Supreme Court would not grant review, then review by a federal habeas court could similarly be refused. In *Teague*, the Rehnquist Court ruled that so-called new rules that could be discovered between a state court's conviction and a federal habeas decision were no longer enforceable in habeas matters except if the state court had made an egregious error. Essentially the Court curbed habeas rights in line with what had been sought by the Nixon and the Reagan administrations. Mark Tushnet and Larry Yackle, "Symbolic Statutes and Real Laws: The Pathologies of the Antiterrorism and Effective Death Penalty Act and the Prison Litigation Reform Act," *Duke Law Journal* 47 (October 1997), 7–9.

[86] Pub. L. No. 104–134, 110 Stat. 1214 (1996).

[87] Tushnet and Yackle, 21.

[88] See rulings in *Edwards v. Carpenter*, 529 U.S. 446 (2000), and *Williams v. Taylor*, 529 U.S. 420 (2000). In *Edwards*, the Court ruled that the while Robert Carpenter, who was convicted on charges of aggravated murder and aggravated robbery, could not seek relief on a habeas claim, it affirmed that procedural errors brought about by bad lawyering, if they rose to a constitutional level, could qualify a convicted individual for habeas relief. In *Williams*, the Court upheld a prisoner's right to seek an evidentiary hearing on a series of constitutional questions that implicated the fairness of the original trial.

decisions reviewing the AEDPA, "the Court communicated to Congress that the Court had already gutted habeas and would assume responsibility for any further tinkering."[89] In matters of habeas, the Court reigns supreme.

The majority in *Boumediene* appeared to follow the logic of judicial supremacy, but that logic is premised on narrow grounds. While it might appear unclear as to how an inter-branch colloquy of statutory construction would continue after this ruling, the decision cut off the dialogue because of the special or fundamental nature of habeas protections. Of course, if jurisdiction-stripping cannot stand when fundamental rights are involved, the question of what counts as a fundamental right and who gets to make such classification arises.

To invoke one example on a contentious matter, consider that members of the House have proposed numerous laws to limit federal jurisdiction to review the Defense of Marriage Act so as to prevent rulings supporting same-sex marriage.[90] However, in a context where marriage is a fundamental right, as the Court ruled in *Loving v. Virginia*, and if jurisdiction-stripping is trumped in matters of fundamental rights, jurisdiction-stripping may be a hardly effective tool.[91] Indeed, the California Supreme Court has recognized marriage as a fundamental right and ruled that same-sex marriage must be constitutionally recognized on that basis.[92] And, more recently, a lower federal court has ruled similarly.[93]

On the other hand, habeas protections could be distinguished from other fundamental rights, such as marriage, to the extent that habeas is "super

[89] Lucas A. Powe, Jr., "The Not-So-Brave New Constitutional Order," *Harvard Law Review* 117 (2003), 670.

[90] See, for example, in the 108th Congress, (2003–4), H.R. 3313 (to amend title 28, United States Code, to limit federal court jurisdiction over questions under the Defense of Marriage Act [DOMA]), H.R. 38393 (to limit the jurisdiction of the federal courts). In the 109th Congress (2005–6), see H.R. 1100 (to amend title 28, United States Code, to limit federal court jurisdiction over questions under the Defense of Marriage Act). In the 110th Congress (2007–8), see H.R. 724 (to amend title 28, United States Code, to limit federal court jurisdiction over the Defense of Marriage Act). One such ruling on DOMA was issued on Thursday, 8 July 2010. Judge Joseph Tauro (appointed by President Nixon) for the federal district court in Massachusetts declared the Defense of Marriage Act unconstitutional because it violated the Tenth Amendment and because it violated the equal protection clause of the Fourteenth Amendment. *Gill et al. v. Office of Personnel Management et al.*

[91] *Loving v. Virginia*, 388 U.S. 1 (1967). "Marriage is one of the 'basic civil rights of man,' fundamental to our very existence and survival."

[92] *In re Marriage Cases*, Ct. App 1/3 Nos. A110449, A110450, A10451, A110463, A110651, A110652, San Francisco County, JCCP No. 4365. Six consolidated cases: *City and County of San Francisco v. State of California* (A110449 [Super. Ct. S.F. City & County, No. CGC-04–429539]); *Tyler v. State of California* (A110450 [Super. Ct. L.A. County, No. BS-088506]); *Woo v. Lockyer* (A110451 [Super. Ct. S.F. City & County, No. CPF-04–504038]); *Clinton v. State of California* (A110463 [Super. Ct. S.F. City & County, No. CGC-04–429548]); *Proposition 22 Legal Defense and Education Fund v. City and County of San Francisco* (A110651 [Super. Ct. S.F. City & County, No. CPF-04–503943]); *Campaign for California Families v. Newsom* (A110652 [Super. Ct. S.F. City & County, No. CGC-04–428794]).

[93] *Gill et al. v. Office of Personnel Management*, 699 F.Supp.2d. 374 (D.Mass., 2010)

fundamental" or definitional to democratic governance whereas other fundamental rights as included in the Bill of Rights do not rise to this level.[94] In other words, habeas may be in a class by itself. Habeas has a much longer history and existed prior to the Constitution; it is within the original constitutional text and not the first ten amendments that make up the Bill of Rights, which might suggest a deeper or special status. Therefore, refusal to support jurisdiction-stripping in this area may be distinguishable. Jurisdiction-stripping on other matters may remain a useful tactic to control the judiciary.

In this section, I have identified two tactics that the Bush administration has employed to harness judicial power rather than wholly undermine the judiciary's legitimacy. The first was an innovative use of signing statements to present alternative statutory meaning, a move with roots in the Reagan administration. The second was the transfer of jurisdiction from the Supreme Court to military tribunals and the D.C. Court of Appeals. While the Court has refused to treat signing statements as signals of statutory meaning, dissents stipulate that they might be so treated and keep that possibility open. And, while the Court has seemingly run roughshod over Congress's recent attempts to control jurisdiction, this case of judicial supremacy has been narrowly confined and articulated as a special case given the right at stake. The Court repeatedly recognized congressional authority to control federal jurisdiction, which suggests that deference runs the other way: from judges to legislators rather than legislators to judges.

III. The Majoritarian Court

A rift between judicial interpretation and the constructive assumption of judges as partisans of the respective parties and presidents who appointed them became evident once New Deal-Great Society liberalism collapsed by 1980. Even within the Reagan regime of the last thirty years, which was, in part, premised on harnessing judicial power through the appointment process and through a public campaign meant to promote originalism, an *independent* Great Court-centered constitutional vision persisted.[95] Although Republicans have dominated judicial appointment since 1968, rulings by the Burger and Rehnquist Courts indicating clear "partisan entrenchment" are difficult to identify. As Steven Teles has argued, electoral victory no longer ensures constitutional visions as the institutions of popular participation, each with its own constitutional vision, have flourished. The non-electoral mobilization that Teles examines is the formation in the 1980s and 1990s of the conservative

[94] Jeremy Waldron makes a similar argument about a ban on torture as "operates in our law as an archetype – that is as a rule which has significance not just in and of itself, but also as the embodiment of a pervasive principle." I would suggest that habeas protections might similarly qualify as a "legal archetype." Jeremy Waldron, "Torture and Positive Law: Jurisprudence for the White House," *Columbia Law Review* 105 (October 2005), 1687.

[95] See Tushnet, 2003, and Stephen Skowronek, *The Politics Presidents Make: Leadership from John Adams to Bill Clinton* (Cambridge: Belknap Press of Harvard University, 1997), 287–446.

legal movement, which promoted originalist interpretive methods in the legal academy and in the public imagination.[96] Only recently have implications of this movement manifested themselves through the appointments of John Roberts and Samuel Alito.

But before these appointments, reversals of Warren and Burger Court rulings were not forthcoming. The Rehnquist Court charted a new federalism jurisprudence, but on other questions that motivated the conservative evangelical base of the contemporary Republican Party – for example, abortion, gender equality, gay rights, and school prayer – rulings have been far from counterrevolutionary.[97] Even the new federalism, which hammered the nail in the coffin of the New Deal and Great Society's constitutional rationales, has been viewed as a *majoritarian* move in that the rulings often align with public opinion.[98]

III.a. *Three Examples of the Majoritarian Court*
In this chapter's last section, I use the phrase "majoritarian Court" in a more active sense to connote how justices themselves have used evidence of national consensus as an extra-legal justification for their decision-making.[99] By briefly

---

[96] Teles, 3.

[97] Three cases stand out as reversals in federalism jurisprudence: *United States v. Lopez*, 514 U.S. 549 (1995) (striking down a federal act banning possession of a gun in a local school zone as beyond congressional commerce authority); *Printz v. United States*, 521 U.S. 898 (1997) (striking down federal authority to regulate hand gun purchase under the necessary and proper clause); and *Morrison v. United States*, 529 U.S. 598 (2000) (striking down the Violence against Women Act of 1994 as exceeding congressional authority under either the commerce clause or the Fourteenth Amendment). For examination of the Rehnquist Court's federalism jurisprudence as something less than a judicial revolution, see Keith Whittington, "Taking What They Give Us: Explaining the Court's Federalism Offensive," *Duke Law Journal* 51 (2001) ("Although not quite amounting to a revolution in American constitutional law, the recent federalism cases are nonetheless striking" [477]), and Powe (2003) ("Despite all the Republican appointees, the Court did not become revolutionary" [680]). The Rehnquist Court upheld *Roe v. Wade*. It extended gender equality in *United States v. Virginia*, 518 U.S. 515 (1996). It provided constitutional sanction to some gay rights in *Romer v. Evans*, 517 U.S. 620 (1996) and *Lawrence and Garner v. Texas*, 539 U.S. 558 (2003). It maintained a ban on school prayer: *Lee v. Weisman* 505 U.S. 577 (1992) and *Santa Fe Independent School District v. Doe*, 530 U.S. 290 (2003). Since Roberts's and Alito's appointments, some retrenchment has occurred; a congressional ban on late-term abortion procedures was upheld (5 to 4) in *Gonzalez v. Carhart*, 550 U.S. 124 (2007) as was plausible gender discrimination in *Ledbetter v. Goodyear Tire and Rubber Co.*, 550 U. S. 618 (2007). On the federalism shift as revolutionary, see Martin Garbus, *Courting Disaster* (New York: Henry Holt, 2002), 121–60.

[98] Neal Devins, "The Majoritarian Rehnquist Court?" *Law and Contemporary Problems* 67 (2004), 63–81, and Barry Cushman, "Mr. Dooley and Mr. Gallup: Public Opinion and Constitutional Change in the 1930s," *Buffalo Law Review* 50 (2002), 7–102.

[99] Doing so highlights an awareness of and reaction to the countermajoritarian critique and may be meant to deflect such criticism. Chief Justice Roberts explicitly discussed his concern that the Court not be polarized: "In Roberts's view, the most successful chief justices help their colleagues speak with one voice. Unanimous, or nearly unanimous, decisions are hard to overturn and contribute to the stability of the law and the continuity of the Court; by contrast, closely divided, 5–4 decisions make it harder for the public to respect the Court as an impartial institution that transcends partisan politics." Jeffery Rosen, "Roberts's Rules," *The Atlantic*, January/February 2007, http://www.theatlantic.com/doc/200701/john-roberts.

reviewing recent rulings in three contentious arenas of social politics – gay rights, death penalty, and abortion – I show how the Court has grasped at national consensus, however it defines the concept, as a marker of its majoritarian footing. Seemingly aware that the judicial solution to the Court's role in a democracy – as overseer of and periodic intervener in the political process – has failed to quell and even fomented public outcry against judicial authority, justices have repeatedly emphasized how their rulings capture a national consensus.[100]

For a majoritarian Court, judicial action is restrained *reaction*. Rulings maintain or consolidate the status quo; they give legal voice to an already apparent pattern of national political consensus. The Court identifies that consensus in a variety of ways: by reviewing the trend of passed state and/or federal legislation, by citing the balance of opinion among legal scholars, by noting the decline of prosecution even as a relevant statute remains in effect, by discussing legal patterns abroad, or by ruminating on popular reliance on expectations that follow from a particular legal interpretation when setting personal goals and aspirations. Justices have cited one or more of these markers of consensus in cases involving gay rights, the death penalty, and abortion regulation.[101] In doing so, the Court has positioned itself as a last mover, as putting a legal imprimatur on choices already made. When it has not cited these markers – as it did not in a recent abortion case, *Gonzales v. Carhart* – it has held its ruling subject to future consideration via "as-applied" challenges.

In *Lawrence v. Texas*, the Court ruled six to three that criminalization of consensual homosexual sex between two adults violated the Fourteenth Amendment's due process clause. The ruling, which overturned the decision in *Bowers v. Hardwick*, was grounded in the Court's privacy jurisprudence.[102] The majority not only cited the trend of state legislation but also noted that the *Bowers* majority failed to recognize the emergent pattern of national consensus in 1986. In *Lawrence*, the Court rejected the claim made in *Bowers* that "Proscriptions against homosexuality have ancient roots"; it emphasized, "there is no long-standing history in this country of laws directed at homosexual conduct as a distinct matter."[103]

---

[100] Gillman argues that the shift from a jurisprudence anchored in popular sovereignty to one anchored in "living constitutionalism" exacerbated hostilities toward courts: "While there is no evidence that this theoretical shift has led to a diminution of the Court's role in the political system, it is likely that it has made judicial authority more vulnerable to the modern preoccupation with the 'countermajoritarian difficulty.'" Gillman, "The Collapse of Constitutional Originalism and the Rise of the Notion of the 'Living Constitution' in the Course of American State-Building," *Studies in American Political Development* 11 (Fall 1997), 194.

[101] *Lawrence and Garner v. Texas*, 539 U.S. 558 (2003); *Kennedy v. Louisiana*, 554 U.S. 407 (2008); *Planned Parenthood of Southeastern Pennsylvania et. al. v. Casey, Governor of Pennsylvania*, et. al. 505 U.S. 833 (1992).

[102] *Bowers v. Hardwick*, 478 U.S. 186 (1986).

[103] Ibid., 192; *Lawrence v. Texas*, 539 U.S. 558 (2003), 568.

The Court further identified "an emerging awareness that liberty gives substantial protection to adult persons in deciding how to conduct their private lives in matters pertaining to sex."[104] A range of evidence suggested increasing acceptance of homosexual relations. The Court cited the trend of state legislation: "The 25 States with laws prohibiting the relevant conduct referenced in the *Bowers* decision are reduced now to 13, of which 4 enforce their laws only against homosexual conduct."[105] It also took note of global trends rejecting criminalized homosexuality.[106] Finally, the Court recognized the low regard in which *Bowers* was held among legal scholars at the time of that ruling.[107] An explicit rejection of *Bowers* was necessary not only on the contention that anti-sodomy laws violated a liberty claim but to bring the Court's jurisprudence in line with state legislative trends. The Court was the *last* mover, and was only giving legal codification to demonstrated national trends.

A slimmer majority of five justices articulated a similar argument in the Court's recent analysis of the death penalty as violating the Eighth Amendment's ban on cruel and unusual punishment. In *Kennedy v. Louisiana*, the Court invalidated a Louisiana statute providing the death penalty in cases of child rape. In death penalty cases, the Court is guided by "objective indicia of society's standards, as expressed in legislative enactments and state practice with respect to executions." While the Court noted, "consensus is not dispositive," much of the ruling identified patterns of legislation in order to characterize the Louisiana statute as an outlier of societal standards.[108] The Court pointed out that "44 States have not made child rape a capital offense," as well as that an option to do so at the federal level had been rejected.[109] Based on this pattern, the majority declared:

> The evidence of a national consensus with respect to the death penalty for child rapists, as with respect to juveniles, mentally retarded offenders, and vicarious felony murderers, shows divided opinion but, on balance, an opinion against it. Thirty-seven jurisdictions – 36 States plus the Federal Government – have the death penalty ... [but] only six of those jurisdictions authorize the death penalty for the rape of a child. Though our review of national consensus is not confined to tallying the number of States with applicable death penalty legislation, it is of significance that in 45 jurisdictions, petitioner could not be executed for child rape of any kind.[110]

---

[104] *Lawrence v. Texas*, 539 U.S. 558 (2003), 572.

[105] Ibid., 573.

[106] Citing European Court of Human Rights rulings, the Supreme Court majority characterized *Bowers* as out of step with "values we share with a wider civilization." Ibid., 576.

[107] "Criticism of *Bowers* has been substantial and continuing, disapproving of its reasoning in all respects, not just as to its historical assumptions." Ibid.

[108] *Roper v. Simmons*, 543 U.S. 551 (2005), 563; *Kennedy v. Louisiana*, 554 U.S. 407 (2008), 10. Louisiana introduced the death penalty for the rape of a minor under the age of thirteen in 1995. Georgia, Montana, Oklahoma, South Carolina, and Texas followed suit; yet these states placed additional qualifications on when the death penalty could be invoked.

[109] Ibid.

[110] Ibid., 15.

Beyond this tally of laws as indicator of sociopolitical norms, the Court noted a tendency not to invoke the death penalty despite its availability. The majority emphasized that no execution for child rape or other non-homicide offense had been performed in over forty years.[111] On statistical and legislative patterns, the majority concluded, "there is a social consensus against the death penalty for the crime of child rape."[112]

The Court's ruling may have stalled an emergent trend from taking shape. Louisiana was the first state to pass such a statute, and five states followed suit, some only a year before the Court rendered its judgment. The ruling might have recognized the wrong pattern and prevented a more recent legislative pattern on death penalty use for child rape from emerging. The Court acknowledged this criticism that it "becomes enmeshed in the process, part judge and part the maker of that which it judges." Such criticism brings to the fore the very basis of the Court's accommodation and recalibration to pluralist politics. Yet it rejected the argument; it claimed it did not have the power to stall "evolving standards of decency" that have marked a "maturing society" in general, and its Eighth Amendment jurisprudence in particular.[113]

That the Court would downplay the power of its intervention is striking in light of its abortion jurisprudence. The Court *relied* on the effect of its intervention to justify maintaining a woman's right to choose to abort a fetus. When *Roe v. Wade* was reconsidered in 1992 in *Planned Parenthood v. Casey*, the majority, in part, upheld *Roe* because the ruling had shaped popular expectations:

> The inquiry into reliance counts the cost of a rule's repudiation as it would fall on those who have relied reasonably on the rule's continued application.... [F]or two decades of economic and social developments, people have organized intimate relationships and made choices that define their views of themselves and their places in society, in reliance on the availability of abortion in the event that contraception should fail. The ability of women to participate equally in the economic and social life of the Nation has been facilitated by their ability to control their reproductive lives. The Constitution serves human values, and while the effect of reliance on *Roe* cannot be exactly measured, neither can the certain cost of overturning *Roe* for people who have ordered their thinking and living around that case be dismissed.[114]

The Court recognized its intervention as influencing ideas about women's socioeconomic equality. Its rulings upholding *Roe* have set women's expectations of access to abortion as part of a way to maintain their socioeconomic development and status. Thus, the Court made a prudential claim; it avoided

---

[111] Ibid., 23.
[112] Ibid.
[113] Ibid., 36.
[114] *Planned Parenthood of Southeastern Pennsylvania et al. v. Casey, Governor of Pennsylvania, et al.*, 505 U.S. 833 (1992), 855–7.

overturning *Roe* because too many women rely on access to abortion when making their life choices. That the Court would highlight its intervention as reason for maintaining its ruling in one case but deny the effect of intervention in another serves to point out that the judicial solution to the problem of judicial authority – that of overseer and intervener – subjects the Court to accusations of arbitrariness.

The most recent abortion ruling stakes out a rationale different from national consensus, one that acknowledges the contingency of legal interpretation and, as such, seemingly sets limits on rulings and opportunities for their reconsideration. In *Gonzales v. Carhart*, the Court upheld the federal Partial-Birth Abortion Ban Act of 2003, claiming that it did not impose an undue burden on a woman seeking an abortion, the standard articulated in *Casey*.[115] The Court ruled that the statute was narrowly constructed to prevent the use of the "dilation and extraction" procedure in the second trimester while permitting alternative abortion methods. Nor was the law void for vagueness as it responded to criticisms of a Nebraska statute that the Court invalidated eight years earlier.[116] Justice Ginsburg criticized:

> Today's decision is alarming. It refuses to take *Casey* and *Stenberg* seriously. It tolerates, indeed applauds, federal intervention to ban nationwide a procedure found necessary and proper in certain cases by the American College of Obstetricians and Gynecologists (ACOG). It blurs the line, firmly drawn in *Casey*, between previability and postviability abortions. And, for the first time since *Roe*, the Court blesses a prohibition with no exception safeguarding a woman's health.[117]

By this view, the ruling reversed the trend of abortion jurisprudence in a stealth manner. And yet, Justice Kennedy's opinion for the majority set limits on the ruling's effect by leaving possibility for further consideration of the statute. He noted that another "situation ... might develop" in which the 2003 Act might be considered unconstitutional, that the Court's decision might change in the face of an "as-applied" challenge, and that through such challenges constitutional meaning is rendered less opaque.[118] Such challenges would keep the meaning of the Act and the ruling in potential flux.

III.b. *The Majortiarian Court and the Permanent Campaign against Judges*

The majoritarian rationale for judicial authority positions the Court as a reactive institution in contrast with recent accusations by politicians and interest group leaders who have made much of judicial activism. Explicit judicial

---

[115] Partial-Birth Abortion Ban Act of 2003 (Act). 18 U.S.C. § 1531.
[116] *Stenberg v. Carhart*, 530 U.S. 914 (2000).
[117] *Gonzales v. Carhart*, 550 U.S. 124 (2007), Ginsburg, J., dissenting, 3.
[118] Ibid., 38. Kennedy cited Richard Fallon's statement: "As-applied challenges are the basic building blocks of constitutional adjudication." Fallon, "As Applied and Facial Challenges and Third-Party Standing," *Harvard Law Review* 113 (2000), 1328.

reliance on national consensus seems to suggest that on issues involving contentious matters such as abortion, gay rights, and the death penalty, the Court has attempted to stake out a centrist and majoritarian position, a position that aligns with trends in public opinion and patterns of state legislation. This idea of national consensus bears some superficial resemblance to a popular sovereignty claim. However, the newer *majoritiarian* rationale for independent judicial authority that flows from the national consensus framework differs from the original *representational* rationale that underlay judicial legitimacy.

This newer rationale is not simply a return to the original rationale of the Court as equally serving representative purpose. That original purpose was grounded in the assumption that the Constitution had a singular, fixed, and discoverable meaning, a meaning ratified by the people in a public act of unprecedented large scale, and a meaning that judges, like elected politicians, were committed to protect against threatening alternatives. As alternatives are now not always considered threatening but, in fact, plausible renderings, and since the Court rejected the textualist basis of its authority in *Blaisdell* and *Carolene*, the Court's search for national consensus is now not grounded in constitutional authority but in the trappings of quotidian politics: in legislation, in public opinion, and in popular expectation. These more explicit expressions of contemporary democratic politics are needed to justify the ruling as the judges themselves lack the democratic legitimacy that followed from their original and now lost characterization as representatives of popular sovereignty. Constitutional meaning is now up for grabs; different visions are held by numerous interests, contested in diverse forums, and ratified by numerous mechanisms. The Court turns to these forums and mechanisms to justify its particular interpretive rendering.

As speechifying during the 2008 presidential campaign illustrated, the Court's majoritarian approach has failed to prevent characterizations of "activist judges" and politicians' exploitation of this epithet as a voter mobilization tactic, particularly among conservatives. Republican presidential nominee, John McCain, reprised the rhetoric of countermajoritarianism: "Assured of lifetime tenures, these judges show little regard for the authority of the president, the Congress and the states. They display even less interest in the will of the people."[119] The judicial majoritarian strategy fails to quell these hostilities

---

[119] McCain, quoted in Elisabeth Bumiller, "McCain Assures Conservatives of His Stance on Judges," *New York Times*, 7 May 2008, A22. Some of candidate John McCain's speeches in the spring of 2008 are a case in point. He criticized Barack Obama's vote against John Roberts's nomination as embodying support for liberal activism: "And just where did John Roberts fall short, by the senator's measure? Well, a justice of the court, as Senator Obama explained it – and I quote – should share 'one's deepest values, one's core concerns, one's broader perspectives on how the world works, and the depth and breadth of one's empathy.'" According to McCain, this perspective amounts to an "attempt to justify judicial activism"; and he scolded Obama for allegedly not supporting anyone but "an elite group of activist judges, lawyers and law professors who think they know wisdom when they see it – and they see it only in each other." McCain, quoted in Elisabeth Bumiller, "McCain Criticizes Democratic Rivals on 'Activist' Judges," in nytimes.com's "The Caucus" blog, 6 May

because in order to stake out these rulings, justices cut narrowly at precedents social conservatives claim to want wholly overturned; the pattern of rulings suggest that no definitive reversal is forthcoming. On the other hand, liberals are upset as these decisions lay the groundwork for a gradual or stealth reversal. Judicial majoritarianism only manages to set the stage for continuous attacks on judges, additional attempts to harness the Court's power, particularly through appointment, and outcry when these strategies fail. The results have been an odd combination of the Court claiming legitimacy on similar majoritarian terms as elected politicians and a populist interest group-driven permanent campaign against judges.

IV. Conclusion

Bearing witness to the disconcerting reality that Nixon's appointments to the Supreme Court did not bring the desired counter-revolution against the Warren Court's living constitutionalism, the Reagan administration sought new ways and revived old ones to harness judicial power to promote its policy ends. One innovation was the transformation of the signing statement into a tool to solicit or guide judicial opinion by purposively creating ambiguity in the statute's meaning. To the extent that these statements provide alternatives to legislative intent, they increase the possible meanings of the statute. As such, the purposive ambiguity hypothesis is validated by the innovative use of the interpretive signing statements even as the strategy has, as yet, been unsuccessful, in swaying a majority of the Court.

Additionally, that jurisdiction-stripping did pass in the 1990s and in the early 2000s again undercuts the empirical validity of a norm of deference to judicial authority at the level of elites or the voting public. That the 1996 Antiterrorism and Effective Death Penalty Act was, in various ways, redundant to already made Court rulings verifies expectations of symbolic politics. And even where judicial supremacy seems most evident – when the Court rejects the Congress's attempts at jurisdiction-stripping in *Boumediene* in marked distinction from the judicial deference shown in *ex parte McCardle* – the Court's move remained cautious and limited. It acknowledged congressional prerogative, but carved out a narrow exception for the fundamental habeas right.

But perhaps the most important innovation of the conservative insurgency was its partisan seizure of originalism. Textual originalism did not begin as a politicized reaction by opponents of the Warren Court's controversial decisions. It is deeply grounded in American legal thought. And, as it was developed in its modern form, primarily in the work of Raoul Burger and Thomas Grey, it did not carry a partisan valence; instead, it was motivated by the same

2008, 12:12 P.M. See http://thecaucus.blogs.nytimes.com/2008/05/06/mccain-criticizes-democratic-rivals-on-activist-judges/?scp=1&sq=judges%20activism%20mccain%20elections&st=cse.

concerns held by liberal legal scholars as Alexander Bickel and John Hart Ely to prevent judges from abusing their authority by imposing their own values. Yet, when the Reagan administration was denied an early opportunity to appoint federal judges to counterbalance the recent stocking of the judiciary under Carter, administration lawyers grasped any way to foster legal change to serve the conservative insurgency. And it attempted to shift the norms of interpretation by promoting originalism through speeches and establishing conservative legal networks that had not heretofore existed. In short, by creating professional and educational networks, legal advocates of the Reagan administration built a pool of like-minded jurists who could promote originalism from the bench once opportunities for appointment presented themselves.

But attempting to ensure that originalism was perceived as not "just another tool for pragmatic manipulation by the Court and modern theorists who typically equate judging with legislating," contemporary originalism's proponents have pushed the method's tenets to the breaking point, defining originalism by various formulas – intent, application, public meaning, and so on – in a desperate attempt to include rulings supported by the citizenry at large, namely *Brown*, but to exclude decisions publicly reviled such as *Dred Scott v. Sanford*, *Plessy v. Ferguson*, *Lochner v. New York*, and *Korematsu v. United States*.[120] Through this ideational elaboration, undertaken most directly by Edwin Meese, originalism could become a closed system, presenting itself not as an alternative methodology to living constitutionalism but claiming that living constitutionalism yielded necessarily incorrect if not illegitimate and dangerous outcomes.

And yet, the Rehnquist Court, despite numerous appointments by Ronald Reagan and George H. W. Bush, did not fully adopt originalism. Rather than presenting itself as the guardians of the original act of public sovereignty, the Court in a range of rulings has utilized quotidian pluralist democracy to cast itself as the majoritarian branch in contrast to the increasingly polarized and partisan representatives occupying Congress and the White House. Thus, even the newest rationale for judicial legitimacy, while departing, to some extent, from the interventionist logic of *Carolene*, remains structured by the underlying assumptions of democratic pluralism rather than the textualist originalism that was wedded to a "civic" republican perspective on politics. As such, critical precedents that conservative originalists say they would like to see overturned – like *Roe* – have remained in place and the underlying privacy doctrine has not been curbed but relied upon not only to ensure constitutional recognition of gay rights, but potentially to open the door to a new problem for many political conservatives: same-sex marriage.

Recent appointments by former President George W. Bush raise the possibility that originalism may make further inroads.[121] But beyond the head-counting politics of judicial appointment, Meese's elaboration of originalism may lay

---

[120] O'Neill, 11.
[121] See further discussion in the Conclusion.

foundations within constitutional development for a return to the illegitimacy of opposition that marked much of the nineteenth century. Progressive
legal scholars hold that possibility at bay by noting how originalism is nothing more than a tool to achieve particular partisan objectives or a "'living
constitutionalism' for the right."[122] For these scholars, contemporary originalism does not rebuild a wall that separates law from politics and thereby
re-secures the legitimacy of judicial interpretation; rather, it articulates conservative politics as law. Progressive response has focused on developing a
methodological approach and liberal constitutional vision that might secure
liberal policies.[123] But this advocacy sidesteps the potential for instability
inherent in contemporary originalism's basic premise, namely, that it presents
itself as a closed logic of absolutes. Whereas progressive constitutionalism,
grounded in legal realism, concedes that law is politics and that multiple interpreters and interpretations must challenge one another within the constructs
of democratic pluralism, originalism remains wedded to the primacy of its
own rightness, holding not only that law is not politics but that it can only
remain "not politics" if interpretation is originalist in orientation. According
to one scholar, "originalism, rightly conceived, *has to be* the best – or indeed
the only – conception of constitutional interpretation. Why so? Because
originalism, rightly conceived, just *has to be*. By definition. In the nature of
things – in the nature of the constitution, in the nature of law, in the nature of
interpretation, in the nature of fidelity in constitutional interpretation!"[124] It
is therefore worth considering whether contemporary originalism – which had
been, at first, elaborated and extolled by Thomas Grey and John Hart Ely as
a legitimate interpretive method when *paired* with non-originalist technique
yielding a methodological pluralism in constitutionalism parallel to the pluralism of the political realm – has since evolved (or, indeed, regressed) into the
ideational foundation to promote the *illegitimacy* of dissenting views about
constitutional meaning and thus to revive the very political instabilities characterizing the first century of inter-branch relations.

---

[122] Post and Siegel, 2009, 30.
[123] Post and Siegel, 2009, write, "Just as the New Right advanced a constitutional nomos rooted
in images of family, religion, and social control, so progressives need to articulate a convincing vision that will express their own distinctive commitments" (31).
[124] Fleming, 12. Emphasis in original.

Conclusion

On the Return of Opposition Illegitimacy and the Prospects for New Development

This book has traced the changing politics of hostilities toward the federal judiciary. Episodic conflicts between courts and the elected branches have been with us from the beginning of our constitutional history. They suggest a persistent and still unresolved problem over the place of an independent judiciary in a democracy. But these attacks have not been all of a piece, suggesting that this phenomenon is not merely the result of a constitutional design flaw of an unelected judiciary in an otherwise democratic republic. Their variation reflects systemic changes ongoing within the polity at large, changes that mark the development of American democracy and reveal processes of ideational and institutional change that structure the assumptions underlying rationally strategic political behavior. In particular, shifts in how elected actors understood the legitimacy and loyalty of opposition – evident in changing positions they took on threats posed by and purposes of political parties – have had a pronounced effect on politicians' solutions to the challenge of independent judicial authority. New responses to judicial power emerged in each period as politicians eyed different possibilities for democratic politics and reconsidered the utility of courts accordingly.

This account stands in stark contrast to received understandings of anti-court sentiment, hostility toward judges, and the tactics used to manipulate judicial power. Scholars have long been aware of the episodic manifestations of the problem of judicial authority in American politics. And most analysis has fallen under the rubric of the countermajoritarian difficulty, which positions the separate federal branches in checking formation and then relates the judiciary's particular legitimacy crisis to its unelected status. More recently, political scientists and legal scholars have moved past Madisonian notions of separated and checked powers in an effort to assess how judicial power and authority have been politically constructed to ensure partisan policy aims, and thus how the branches often cooperate rather than challenge one another. While pointing to the unwarranted assumptions within the previous paradigm, this more recent model swung too far, since it failed to address those instances when genuine elected branch and popular hostility toward the judiciary was evident, except to treat them as more the exception than the rule. Those scholars who focus on these inter-branch tensions tend to characterize them as epiphenomenal to electoral realignment, ignoring the inconsistencies within realignment theory; more important for the argument advanced here, they do not consider how institutional and ideational change affected the way in which hostilities toward judicial authority manifested themselves and changed over time. Elected branch conflicts with judicial authority were symptomatic of larger electoral shifts and were resolved – even if that resolution took a longer time due to the greater length of time judges have spent on the bench in recent years – either through appointment or a political game of pressure, challenge, and brinksmanship.

These models have not attended to the *changing* nature of politicians' responses and to the effect that each new response had in altering the platform for the next. As such, many have missed the profound transformation that has gradually taken place in institutional politics and constitutional government overall as well as the variation in the solutions proposed to resolve the political problem of judicial power. They have not taken seriously the possibility of ideational change over time, which structures the limits of legitimate political behavior. And they have often not considered institutional development – particularly the institutional thickening, which created new and increasingly entrenched interests in both protecting judicial power and challenging received constitutional meanings – and how this development may have altered the ways in which manipulations of and hostilities toward judicial authority come to pass. Indeed, by examining the processes and patterns of institutional and ideational development, we can recognize a history that has left us to confront issues very different from those with which we began.

Scholars who contend that normative development of judicial supremacy is the causal mechanism underlying changing behavior over time toward the judiciary are sensitive to the new institutional relationships and underlying ideational changes and assumptions that have emerged from these episodes. But they appear to have overstated the amelioration of the problem. On inspection, there is little definitive evidence that a publicly accepted norm of deference to the judiciary or elected-branch deference to judicial supremacy has emerged. In the final analysis, the developmental effect is subtler and less settled.

By contrast, the movement I have traced is evident less at the level of the public, where episodic hostility toward the judiciary remains intense, than at the elite level, where politicians have gradually figured out how to deflect public anger from direct assaults on judicial power itself into more intense efforts to harness that power for political ends. This is where the development of legitimate opposition and the focus on courts' and parties' changing relationship to each other has had its most profound effect. Before opposition was deemed legitimate, before multiple understandings of constitutional government were considered credible, before politicians expected their opponents to gain power and to pursue their own constitutional visions as a matter of course – in short, when civic republican ideas structured the assumptions underlying political rationality and strategy – the judiciary was considered as a potential repository for alternatives that, by definition, threatened constitutional government itself. After opposition was deemed legitimate and loyal, after multiple understandings of the Constitution were considered credible, after politicians came to expect that their opponents would periodically gain power and would naturally seek to implement their own vision – in short, when notions of conspiracy and threat were gradually supplanted by the pluralist values of competition, trust, and persuasion – politicians came to understand the potential for using independent judicial power instrumentally to achieve particular partisan goals.

Thus, the political problem of judicial power has not only been about the structural anomaly of an unelected branch in an otherwise democratic polity. Rather, it is deeply embedded in underlying and changing assumptions about the legitimacy and loyalty of opposition and the interpretive disagreements held by those opposing forces. It has fostered distinct resolutions since the Founding, including the judiciary as part of a unified representative regime, the judiciary as set apart from politics and upheld as a paragon of neutrality discovering the plain meaning of text, the judiciary as protector of democratic procedure, the judiciary as authoritative arbitrator among multiple constitutional possibilities, and the judiciary as reactive and fundamentally majoritarian.

The Court has not been a mere pawn in these developments. Engaged from the start in their own struggle for legitimacy, judges have been keenly sensitive to the changing political environment in which they have acted and positioned themselves differently over time. The settlement on judicial independence as political neutrality following Chase's impeachment anchors one side of this development; the judicial move to stake out a role for courts in the pluralist politics rumbling out of the New Deal anchors the other. From the start, Federalists grounded the legitimacy of judicial independence in what I have referred to as a *representational* rationale. Each of the federal branches, whether elected or not, were constructed to represent equally the Constitution as an act of popular sovereignty. The Framers made accommodations for when the people might once again speak in a similar fashion; the Constitution laid out the parameters of that formal process in its fifth article. But until that time, the power of governance – whether held by the elected politician or the judge – drew from these leaders' capacities to represent the popular sovereignty as it was expressed in the act of ratification. As such, judicial legitimacy rested on textual originalist analysis. Yet that logic began to break down almost as soon as it was constructed. The Framers had not counted on and made little accommodation for the Jeffersonian claim that popular sovereignty could be expressed through more quotidian electoral politics, that is, in ways other than the Constitution's fifth article. Jefferson's more democratic assertion created the feared possibility of regime disunity or the realization of opposition entrenched in governance. With little understanding of legitimate much less loyal opposition, the Constitution's meaning became intolerably contested. For the Framers, such was a prelude to civil instability.

Failing to find a way to re-secure unity in governance, Jeffersonians settled on a second-best solution. They cast judges out of politics altogether and re-imagined the idea of judicial independence to mean not just separation from political corruption but as total political neutrality. While this solution did not weaken the drive to align the judiciary with the president and or the congressional majority's constitutional vision, this notion of judicial neutrality constricted the means to achieve that end, compelling rhetoric of judicial reform framed as efficiency. Subsequent generations have struggled to solve the challenge that the Jeffersonians confronted. Each has offered a diverse range of solutions identified and evaluated in this book. Their parameters have been explained as reflecting ideas about opposition and party politics that gradually changed over time and came to embody assumptions that we recognize today as modern interest-based liberal pluralism. So while Thomas Jefferson, Andrew Jackson, Abraham Lincoln, Franklin Roosevelt, and even Ronald Reagan did make similar claims – each thereby earning the appellation of departmentalist president – their claims were grounded in different assumptions, and their corresponding actions toward judicial power reflected these changing ideas.

I. The Themes of this Book and the Prospects for Change

By attending to shifts in politicians' perceptions of and ideas about the threat posed by opposition, we reorient our understanding of elite and popular hostilities toward expressions of judicial power. These hostilities do not simply reflect an eventual tipping point of antagonism toward judicial review's countermajoritarian potential within each instance, but a more gradual shift in perspective among political leaders toward opposition as no longer threatening civic stability. As such, political ideational development and constitutional development are linked. Numerous scholars have pointed to the Civil War as a tipping point in constitutional development such that disagreements on constitutional meaning would no longer descend into threats of violence or secession but rely on persuasion and, ultimately, trust; I have tried to isolate the ideational foundations for that shift in perspective in the oft-recognized shift from civic republicanism to liberal pluralism as the underlying idiom of political assumption and behavior, which has also been assessed as pivoting on the Civil War and Reconstruction. In other words, I have highlighted how a common set of assumptions and a gradual shift in those assumptions underlie constitutional culture and strategic political rationality. My aim has been to link constitutional and political development through the exploration of changing ideas over time, in ways overlooked by legal academics, historians, and political scientists; these scholars, partly because of the isolation of each discipline from the other in the contemporary university, too often operate independently of one another's insights.

By reorienting the focus of inter-branch relations toward commonly held ideas about opposition – which structure constitutional culture and limit legitimate political strategy and interests – and thus away from the cyclic and static models of design flaw and electoral realignment to explain anti-judicial tension, we can reach new conclusions and find possible extensions for further research. First, by focusing on the politics of legitimate and loyal opposition rather than on the structural form of the judiciary and its potential for countermajoritarian judicial review, we can better specify the nature of the political concern surrounding judicial power at different historical moments. Thus, during the early republic, federal judges were often depicted as threatening regime unity; however, that notion of regime unity seems remarkably out of place or at least unsustainable in our contemporary era of recurring "divided government." Given contemporary politicians' recognition that divided government is likely, we might therefore expect their calculations to shift, particularly taking into consideration longer range objectives that might not have been at the forefront when their predecessors considered divided government not only unlikely but inherently dangerous to the stability of the republic.

Second, while the case studies focused on elaborating how elected officials responded to the perceived threats and opportunities created when judges acted at odds with an administration's constitutional vision, the underlying theoretical aim has been to understand how agent rationality and strategy interact with structural context. That structure can be institutional and ideational, and it can constrain the range of legitimate options an actor may choose to pursue when attempting to achieve substantive change. This orientation helps us grapple with how strategic rationality is historically situated.

At the same time, this book has outlined a general pattern of ideational change observed in each episode of inter-branch conflict, namely, how entrepreneurial agents may frame particular circumstances as a crisis, which ultimately serves as an opportunity to push the limits of the pre-existing ideational context. Each new innovation – whether it be the notion of judicial independence as political neutrality, the legitimacy of a political party, the loyalty of a political opposition, an interventionist Court charging itself with protecting the integrity of pluralist democracy, or the revival and re-imagining of textual originalism – is layered on the next, creating an expanding repertoire for politicians to pull from when criticizing a particular ruling and fundamentally reshaping how the political problem of judicial power is recognized and how solutions are offered. This book has striven to highlight the institutional thickening, particularly over the course of the twentieth century, which has expanded the number of invested actors and the range of power bases from which these actors might challenge and/or promote constitutional meaning, thereby ultimately displacing the political party as the primary purveyor of such meaning; it has also examined the phenomenon of ideational thickening, namely, how new ideas are generated from crisis but do not necessarily wipe the slate clean of older assumptions. Instead, the innovations interact with older notions, creating conflict and opportunity for change. Thus, the seemingly separable ideas of judicial neutrality and political manipulation of the judiciary find dual expression in contemporary originalism. Similarly, the Court re-conceptualizes the Framers' representational rationale for judicial legitimacy, which was grounded in the precepts of early textualist original-ism, and refits it to a new representational logic as overseer of democratic pluralism; it thereby legitimizes legal realism and living constitutionalism as well as positions the Court as a majoritarian institution.

Third, when conceptualizing the actions elected-branch actors take to con-trol judicial power, this book has pointed toward an expanded list of possi-bilities and has differentiated between the strategies of undermining judicial legitimacy and harnessing judicial power. In particular, given that election provides no guarantee of interpretive change – even when judicial appoint-ments are made – it is necessary both to think beyond appointment to other previously recognized strategies that might harness judicial power and legit-imacy to serve partisan aims, such as jurisdiction-stripping, and to consider wholly new strategies, such as the "interpretive" signing statement. Drafting presidential signing statements to be used by judges for interpretive guidance is not about undermining judicial authority as much as about relying on it and seeking to channel it toward particular political ends. The "interpretive" signing statement was invented by contemporary conservatives and paired with rhetorical emphasis on originalism as the only interpretive methodol-ogy that maintains judicial neutrality. The interpretive signing statement itself highlights just how much the Jeffersonian construction of legitimate judicial authority as neutral and the Lincolnian construction of such authority as rightly political gain simultaneous expression in the most recent instance of conservative manipulations of judicial power.

Finally, my argument suggests that the shift toward viewing opposition as legitimate and loyal (and possessing a consequent right to rule) developed over time, gaining ground during Lincoln's presidency, and becoming entrenched after Reconstruction, such that the Civil War's conclusion heralded a new spirit of trust and persuasion over the old republican assumptions of conspir-acy, threat, and instability; however, there is no immediate reason to believe this result is fixed. Circumstances may develop in which political opposition could be once again considered illegitimate or disloyal. We witnessed rhetoric to this effect during the height of McCarthyism in the early 1950s, and it has characterized some aspects of the 2008 presidential campaign. The notion of illegitimate opposition has existed since the Founding, and there are differing views as to whether and why it resurfaces in political rhetoric. Nevertheless, it certainly remains a potentially potent rhetorical trope.[1]

As we note the recurrence of this rhetoric suggestive of illegitimate opposi-tion in our contemporary political culture, we should attend to who is articu-lating these ideas and to whom are they speaking. In other words, normative

[1] Richard Hofstadter, *The Paranoid Style of American Politics and Other Essays* (Cambridge: Harvard University Press, 1964).

acceptance of the opposition's right to rule may be more apparent among political elites than the voting public. For example, during the 2008 presidential campaign, John McCain stated that his opponent, Barack Obama, was a good man from whom Republicans had nothing to fear, and Obama similarly stated that McCain was honorable; these statements indicate that a norm of loyal opposition holds among political elites even if it may not be as diffuse among the wider citizenry.[2] Representative Joe Wilson's September 2009 outburst during a presidential address in Congress on health care reform, during which he accused President Obama of lying, may appear, at first glance, to be an exception to this assessment; however, take note of the Republican leadership's reaction. Senate Minority leader, Mitch McConnell (R-KY), said, "I think we ought to treat the president with respect, and anything other than that is not appropriate." House Republican Whip, Eric Cantor (R-VA), similarly stated, "Obviously, the president of the United States is always welcome on Capitol Hill. He deserves respect and decorum." He also called Wilson's apology "the appropriate thing to do."[3] In short, responsible and loyal opposition is supported, but accusations of lying, which imply that Obama's policy aims are destructive to the essence of constitutional government, are simply over the line.

Some examples of the rhetoric of disloyal opposition are evident as well in the contemporary popular discourse about judicial power. A recent *New York Times* best seller characterized some judges – judges who offered an interpretation of the Constitution clearly disagreeable to the author – in terms that are strikingly reminiscent of Jeffersonian-era fears of opposition undermining the Constitution's stability and longevity: "Judicial activists are nothing short of radicals in robes – contemptuous of the rule of law, subverting the Constitution at will, and using their public trust to impose their policy preferences on society. In fact, no radical political movement has been more effective in undermining our system of government than the judiciary."[4]

The statement's consequent danger lies in its hyperbole. Its author subtitles his book, "How the Supreme Court is destroying America." But such extremist claims only obfuscate legitimate concerns about the nature and extent of judicial authority in the United States. And, as former Justice O'Connor noted – as cited in this book's Introduction – most Americans remain relatively uninformed about the courts and a judge's role in American democracy. As such, they remain vulnerable to misinformation and potentially swayed by such dangerous overstatement and mischaracterization.

It should be unsurprising that the author of this best seller is a staunch advocate of contemporary originalism. As discussed in the conclusion of

---

[2] Elisabeth Bumiller, "McCain Draws Line on Attacks as Crowds Cry 'Fight Back,'" *New York Times*, 11 October 2008, A12

[3] McConnell and Cantor are quoted in Carl Hulse, "In Lawmaker's Outburst, a Rare Break of Protocol," *New York Times*, 10 September 2009, A26.

[4] Mark Levin, *Men In Black: How the Supreme Court Is Destroying America* (Washington, DC: Regnery, 2005), 22.

Chapter 8, contemporary originalism, with its focus on absolute meaning, may undermine the very possibility of legitimate disagreement about constitutional meaning; it could thus construct a constitutional culture that may reinforce and encourage a political culture in which opposition is treated as threatening if not ultimately disloyal. Thus, the development of contemporary originalism over the course of the 1980s, 1990s, and early 2000s and its focus on the absolute rightness of a particular constitutional interpretation – even if scholars claim it has had limited impact on the Court itself (and this claim may be contestable once recent rulings by the Roberts Court are considered) – corresponds with partisan polarization in Congress and in the electorate over the same years. And it may have found popular expression in the frenzied atmosphere characterizing rowdy town hall meetings on healthcare reform during the summer of 2009, the rise of Tea Party conservatism, and the neo-populist outcry to take back government.[5]

Recent rulings by the Roberts Court suggest that contemporary originalism has gained a stronger foothold than it had in its predecessor.[6] By holding that a fundamental right to bear arms cannot be infringed upon in *District of Columbia v. Heller*, at least five Supreme Court justices endorsed originalism.[7] At the same time, originalism may be losing its ideational integrity in legal academe. Some scholars have suggested that "we are all originalists now," such that legal realists and living constitutionalists have been vanquished; however, originalism itself has changed greatly over time and has come to include within its ranks the scholarship of numerous realists, to the point that its coherence has been strained to the breaking point.[8] Indeed, once a legal scholar can thoughtfully claim that originalist premises support

---

[5] On the rise of congressional party polarization, see Kenneth Poole and Howard Rosenthal, *Congress: A Political-Economic History of Roll Call Voting* (New York: Oxford University Press, 1997), and David Rhode, *Parties and Leaders in the Postreform House* (Chicago: University of Chicago Press, 1991). On recent rising levels of partisanship among the mass electorate, see Marc Hetherington, "Resurgent Mass Partisanship: The Role of Elite Polarization," *American Political Science Review* 95 (September 2001), 619–31. On hostilities during 2009 town hall meetings with members of Congress, see Ian Urbina, "Beyond Beltway, Heath Debate Turns Hostile," *New York Times*, 7 August 2009, A1. On the neo-populism of the current moment, see Scott Rasmussen, *In Search of Self-Governance* (Asbury Park, NJ: Rasmussen Reports, LLC, 2009).

[6] On Heller as the triumph of originalism on the Court, see Reva Siegel, "Dead or Alive: Originalism as Popular Constitutionalism in *Heller*," *Harvard Law Review* 122 (2008), 191–245.

[7] *District of Columbia v. Heller*, 554 U.S. 570 (2008) (ruling 5 to 4 that a District of Columbia ban on handguns in the home violates the Second Amendment). More recent rulings such as *McDonald v. Chicago*, 561 U.S. ___ (2010), which extends Heller's logic to apply to states and localities by incorporating the Second Amendment further suggest originalism's hold on the Roberts Court. Note, however, that a majority could not agree on which Fourteenth Amendment clause – due process or privileges and immunities – enabled incorporation, and this lack of a majority rationale may limit the ruling's effect as precedent.

[8] See James Fleming, "The Balkanization of Originalism," *Maryland Law Review* 67 (2007–08), 11–13.

a constitutional right to choose to terminate a pregnancy, that is, to support the very decision whose overturning motivated originalism's revival, then the dividing line between originalism and living constitutionalism blurs into incoherence.[9] And we might rightly begin to wonder whether we are approaching the "end of originalism."[10] Ironically, just when originalism seems to have reached its pinnacle on the Court, there may be early signs of paradigmatic collapse in the academy.

Indeed, only a year ago, some journalists lamented that originalism's limited conception of judicial power – its non-realist conception of judicial power – had won out. Evidence of such victory was found in the confirmation hearings of now-Justice Sonia Sotomayor. President Obama's aspiration to appoint a justice with empathy was taken by his political opponents to mean utilizing the Court for particular political purposes.[11] Conservatives clung to the judge-as-umpire analogy initially articulated by now Chief Justice John Roberts during his own confirmation hearings as proof that they, and originalism itself, held to the norm of judicial neutrality thereby casting alternative methods as politically motivated and contrary to judicial independence.[12] But, as this book has demonstrated, such superficial dichotomies leave the rich and nuanced history of constitutional development profoundly misunderstood, mischaracterizing the objectives of presidents like Jefferson, Van Buren, Lincoln, FDR, and Reagan. And they only perpetuate the widespread lack of popular understanding of courts, judges, and the Constitution.

Nevertheless, a year later, during her own hearings for appointment as associate justice, Elena Kagan seemed to back off the judge-as-umpire analogy just a bit. In response to a question from Senator Kyl (R-AZ), Kagan stated, "There are cases where it is difficult to determine what the law

[9] Jack Balkan offers a loose or moderate originalism in which he argues that judges can be bound by the written text of the Constitution but that they do not have to apply those words in the "original expected" way. As such, constitutional law is always in the process of developing, and therefore, originalist premises can ironically be inverted to support living constitutionalist ends, for example, the identification of a fundamental right to an abortion under the privacy doctrine that follows from the Fourteenth Amendment's due process clause. See Balkin, "Abortion and Original Meaning," *Constitutional Commentary* 24 (2007), 295–303.

[10] Jeffrey Shaman, "The End of Originalism," *San Diego Law Review* 47 (2010), 83–108.

[11] Sheryl Gay Stolberg, "In Court Pick, Obama Seeks Experience of Real World," *New York Times*, 23 May 2009, A16.

[12] J. Scott Orr and Robert Cohen, "Enter the New Chief Justice," *The Star-Ledger*, 30 September 2005, 1. Senator John Cornyn's reaction to the empathy standard was emblematic of Republican response and for its reliance on the concept of a judge as a neutral umpire: "The problem is you've got to call balls and strikes as a judge and the ethnicity focus – the focus on sex and on race and saying that there may be different outcomes depending who the judge is – is antithetical to the whole idea of the rule of law objective and neutral justice. And that's the reason why this deserves some questions." Cornyn quoted in Janie Lorber, "The Sunday Word: Confirmations and Torture Investigations," The Caucus: The Politics and Government Blog of the Times, 12 July 2009, http://thecaucus.blogs.nytimes.com/2009/07/12/the-sunday-word-confirmations-and-torture-investigations/?scp=37&sq=republican%20reaction%20to%20empathy%20standard%20for%20judges&st=cse.

requires. Judging is not a robotic or automatic enterprise, especially on cases that come before the Supreme Court." At the same time, she, perhaps prudently, rejected President Obama's call for judicial empathy, noting abstractly "I think it's law all the way down."[13] Thus, even as she adhered to the norm of judicial neutrality, she distanced herself from strict adherence to textualist originalism, at least to the extent of suggesting that a singular fixed meaning of the Constitution can be discovered and applied as if by an apolitical robot. And, in her defense of Justice Thurgood Marshall – for whom she clerked – Kagan rejected the notion of judicial activism as remotely meaningful and embraced the *Carolene* rationale of the Court as the guarantor of functioning pluralist democracy: "Marshall's whole life was about seeing courts take seriously the claims that were generally ignored anywhere else."[14] Kagan's statement does not amount (yet) to an articulate elaboration of a coherent alternative to contemporary originalism that reaches much past the living constitutionalist theory of the twentieth century, but it nevertheless suggests that originalist inroads on the Court may have been held at bay. And given originalism's tendency toward absolutism and the corresponding strife that may cause, even such limited assurances are comfort to those who consider dissent over constitutional meaning not only unavoidable but the marker of a healthy democratic republic.

II. Taking Responsibility for a Politicized Court

Anti-court and anti-judge rhetoric is hardly new. Yet traditional framings of federal judges as unelected, undemocratic, and therefore fundamentally anomalous, lead to characterizations of anti-court hostility as proceeding along a reactionary continuum. By this viewpoint, repeated disagreement with rulings reaches a point whereby the Court's institutional legitimacy loses its footing.[15] This account compels recommendations that judges should not reach too far ahead of public opinion lest they highlight their precarious position. So, when "Impeach Earl Warren" billboards were plastered across the South, scholars such as Charles Black, Robert McClosky, and Alexander Bickel advised judicial restraint and outlined the "passive virtues."[16] Put differently, this construction of anti-judicial hostilities leaves the onus on the judge to alter her behavior. It focuses on only half of the dynamic at play.

---

[13] "Kagan Disregards Obama View on Empathy," *The BLT: The Blog of the Legal Times*, 29 June 2010, http://legaltimes.typepad.com/blt/2010/06/kagan-disregards-obama-view-on-empathy.html.

[14] Kagan, quoted in Dahlia Lithwick, "The Kagan Hearings: A Woman in Full," Slate.com, 29 June 2010, http://www.slate.com/id/2258135/entry/2258630/.

[15] Michael Klarman, *From Jim Crow to Civil Rights: The Supreme Court and the Struggle for Racial Equality* (New York: Oxford University Press, 2004), 465.

[16] Charles Black, *The People and the Court* (New York: Macmillan, 1960); Robert McCloskey, *The American Supreme Court* (Chicago: University of Chicago Press, 1960), 230; Alexander Bickel, *The Least Dangerous Branch: The Supreme Court at the Bar of Politics* (New Haven: Yale University Press, 1986).

My characterization of more recent anti-judicial hostilities as not necessarily seeking to broadly undermine judicial legitimacy but as harnessing judicial power for political purposes draws attention to the other half of that dynamic. No matter how judges rule, their decisions will often trigger hostile criticism because that criticism is politically useful. Politicians' accusations of and promises to rein in "judicial activism" potentially mobilize voters and serve short-term aims of winning office. And yet, the generally low public salience of the judiciary and the obtuseness of many of the cases with which it deals enables politicians to avoid turning their rhetoric into realizable action, action that may damage longer term interests realized through strong judicial power. Even when judges highlight within their rulings how those rulings align with national consensus, the politician's strategy of harping on activist judges is not kept at bay. Rather, the Court's majoritarian strategy leaves it exposed to attack from all sides of the political spectrum. Regardless of judicial behavior, the political circumstance is ripe for a campaign of simmering hostility against judges and a perpetual politicization of judicial appointment.

Judicial interpretation is political, not because judges simply clothe their political preferences in legal language, but because their rulings are used by politicians to great and potentially damaging political effect. They may damage public support for courts and judges. They may inflame differences of opinion among the citizenry and thereby raise the stakes of politics to dangerous heights. Ultimately, they transform the judicial appointment process itself from a great debate about judicial philosophy and constitutional interpretation into a forum for shallow position-staking marked by reliance on increasingly meaningless but politically charged and electorally symbolic catch phrases, such as judicial activism. This catastrophic collapse of the potential of these hearings is perpetuated by the mistaken conceit that judges have the final say on what the Constitution means or that the Constitution must mean what the majority of the Court says it means. By promoting either judicial supremacy and/or the absolutist premise that follows from textualist originalism, the people not only cede control over their Constitution, but they lose the ability and the imperative to understand it themselves.

It is all too easy to cast blame on judges as the perpetrators of this development, for they are unelected, removed, elitist, and deeply mysterious characters. The judiciary's empowerment has been a century-long project consisting of building ever more professionalized schools and interest groups, gaining authority over its own affairs, and elaborating its own powers through academia and through judicial rulings so that it becomes not merely constructed but increasingly self-evident and natural. But the blame for the politicization of an ever more powerful judiciary lies with the politicians as much as with the judges. Perhaps the concept of blame implies an unwarranted and unhelpful normative bias. In this book, I have sought to demonstrate that the current state of our judicial politics is the consequence of a long developmental process, a process in which our leaders have articulated and attempted numerous solutions – both political and judicial – to the challenge posed by independent judicial authority in a democratic republic. These solutions have been offered in good faith to realize more fully the democratic aspirations defining our common heritage. If we recognize this faith, we might be less inclined to view our politicians and judges with such derision. Instead, we might come to see that governance is as much like those who lead as it is like those who are led: inherently flawed, eminently renewed, and more often than not, a process of trial and error.

Index

Acheson, Dean, 294
Adair v. United States (1908), 242n73, 256,
    260
Adams, Abigail, 99, 135
Adams, John, 6, 152
    and election of 1800, 100
Adams, John Quincy, 90, 102, 146, 152, 158
    and election of 1824, 142
    on impeachment, 117, 119
Adkins v. Children's Hospital (1923), 250,
    277–9, 282, 324
Agger, Carol, 306
Agricultural Adjustment Act, 264–5, 267
*A.L.A. Schechter Poultry Corp, v. United
    States* (1935), 261n163, 266
*Alexander v. Holmes County Board of
    Education* (1969), 314, 317
Alito, Samuel, 4, 351, 354, 363
American Bar Association (ABA), 293, 295–6
American Farm Bureau Federation, 293
American Federation of Labor (AFL), later
    AFL-CIO, 253, 293
American Independent Party (Wallace
    candidacy), 304
American Revolution of 1776, 56
Americans for Democratic Action, 293
Ames, Fisher, 97
Annals of Congress, 36
Anti-Federalism (Anti-Federalists), 74,
    77–78, 86, 89, 104, 147
    and acceptance of the Constitution of
        1787, 90
    and Martin Van Buren's characterization
        of, 141
Antiterrorism and Effective Death Penalty
    Act (AEDPA) of 1996, 360–1, 369
Arendt, Hanna, 57

Articles of Confederation, 73, 104, 138, 168,
    170
Ashwander principle, 237, 342
Ashwander v. Tennessee Valley Authority
    (1936), 237n51
Atchison, David, 194

Baker v. Carr (1962), 283, 285–6, 341n14
Baltimore American, 119, 122
Bates, Edward, 189, 191–2
Bayard, James, 116, 126, 127
Bayh, Birch, 320–1
Bennett, Robert, 299, 301
Benson, Lee, 50
Berger, Raoul, 339, 344
    on judicial restraint, 342–3
    on textualist originalism, 342–3, 369–71
Bickel, Alexander, 20, 381
    on *Brown v. Board of Education*, 342–3
    and the countermajoritarian difficulty,
        20–22
    on judicial restraint, 342–3, 370
Bill of Rights, 84, 89, 129, 280, 362
Bingham, John, 195, 200
Black, Charles, 381
Black, Hugo, 337, 343
Blackmun, Harold, 307
Blair, John, 81–82
"Bleeding Kansas," 194
Blount, William, 115
    Impeachment of, 116, 127
Bolingbroke, Lord Henry, 92, 93
Borah, William, 241, 259
Bork, Robert, 319, 331
Boudinot, Elias, 81
Boumediene v. Bush (2008), 57–60, 348, 355,
    361, 369

Boutwell, George, 205–6, 208, 209
Bowers v. Hardwick (1986), 364, 365
Bradley, Joseph, 215, 216
Bradley v. Milliken (1971), 318
Brandeis, Louis, 237, 342
 and *Muller v. Oregon* (1908) and "Brief,"
  250–1
Breckenridge, John, 108
Brennan, William, 294, 296, 297, 344
Brewer, David, 250
Breyer, Stephen, 256–7
Brookings Institution, 265
Brooks, Preston 194
Broomfield, William, 317
Brown, Janice Rogers, 331
Brown, Joseph, 178
Brown v. Board of Education (1954), 286,
  288–92, 316, 317, 338, 339, 370
 and difficulty of decision, 290
 as "living constitutionalism," 340
 as originalist, 344–5, 370
 as pluralism reinforcing, 188–9
 Political party support of, 290–1
 as a rejection of originalism, 340
 Southern reaction to, 289–92
Brutus, 77–78, 84, 97
Bryan, William Jennings, 232–5
 "Cross of Gold" speech, 232
 Democratic candidacy of, 232–5
Buchanan, James, 132, 178
 and Repeal of Section 25 of the 1789
  Judiciary Act, 159–61
 and support for *Dred Scott* ruling, 166–7
Budd v. New York (1892), 230n12
Burger, Warren, 283, 303, 305, 341, 360, 363
 on school busing to achieve integration,
  315–19
 Swann ruling of, 315–16
Burges, Tristam, 155
Burgess, Susan, 27
Burt, Robert, 137
Burton, Harold, 297
Bush, George H. W., 328, 339
Bush, George W., 329, 333, 339, 347, 362,
  370
 Characterization as moderate, 329–30
 and presidential signing statements, 352–4
Busing (school integration), 309–17
Butler, Pierce, 100, 262n163

Cadwalader, John, 191
Calabresi, Steven, 349–50
Caldeira, Gregory 48, 49
Calder v. Bull (1798), 83

Calhoun, John, 137
Callender, James, 121
Cantor, Eric, 378
Cantwell v. Missouri (1905), 251n124
Cardozo, Benjamin, 237, 243
Carriage Tax Act, 82
Carswell, G. Harold, 306–7, 308
Carter, Jimmy, 287
 and judicial appointments, 324–9, 333, 370
Cary v. Curtis (1845), 160
Catron, John, 204
Ceaser, James, 139
Cellers, Emmanuel, 292, 308
Chase, Salmon, 201, 203
 Ruling in *Ex parte McCardle*, 207
 Ruling in *Hepburn*, 216
Chase, Samuel, 13, 29, 73, 83, 104, 112, 308
 on constitutionality of the Repeal Act of
  1802, 109
 and criticism of appointment to the
  Supreme Court, 120
 and eight articles of impeachment, 126
 Impeachment of, 85, 103, 104, 113–29, 374
 on the Judiciary Act of 1802, 110
 on a strike in response to the Repeal Act,
  110–11
Cherokee removal, *see Worcester v. Georgia*
  (1832)
*Chevron v. Natural Resources Defense
  Council* (1984), 351
*Chicago, Milwaukee, and St. Paul Railway
  Co. v. Minnesota* (1890), 230n14
Civic republicanism, 45, 54–64, 67–68, 370
 as collapsing after the Civil War and
  Reconstruction, 221–2, 375
 and conspiracy theory, 57, 172–7
 and Jeffersonian hostilities toward judicial
  authority, 71–131
 and Martin Van Buren's characterization
  of political opposition, 141–5
 and party competition, 177–80
Civil Rights Act of 1866, 196
Civil Rights Act of 1964, 310–12
Civil Rights Cases of 1883, 344
Civil War, 43, 56, 171, 172, 190–2, 221–2,
  375, 377
Clay, Henry, 142, 143, 156
Clayton Antitrust Act, 253, 254, 255–9, 288
Clear statement rule, 258–9
Clemens, Elisabeth, 251
Cleveland Plain Dealer, 178
Clinton, William J., 328, 329, 360
 Judicial appointment strategy of, 328–9,
  333

Clinton D. Mayhew Inc. v. Wirtz (1969), 351
Cole v. Young (1956), 292, 293, 297, 301
Columbia University, 236, 237, 285
Columbian Centinnel, 106
Combatant Status Review Trials (CSRTs),
    355, 357–60
Communist Party, 294
Congressional Globe, 36
Congressional Record, 36, 301
Connecticut Courant, 124
Constitutional amendments, 32
    Eighth Amendment, 365–6
    Fourteenth Amendment, 196
    on judicial structure and authority, 32, 34,
        36–39
    Thirteenth Amendment, 196
Cooley, Charles, 239
Cooper, Thomas, 120
Cooper v. Aaron (1958), 47, 283, 285
Cooper v. Telfair (1800), 81, 83
Corwin, Edward, 242, 243
Countermajoritarian difficulty, 7, 19–31
    and the Supreme Court's response, 15
Court-curbing tactics, 31–42
Courts
    and civic republicanism, 54–64
    and liberal pluralism, 54–64, 272–84
    and party development, 4–10, 64–67,
        374–5
Crawford, William, 142
Cribb, Kenneth, 350
Croly, Herbert, 239
Cummings, Homer, 265
Cummings v. Missouri (1867), 205

Dahl, Robert, 22–24, 47
Dallas, Alexander, 100
Daniel, John, 232
Davis, David, 201
Declaration of Constitutional Principles,
    291–2
Declaration of Independence, 129
Defense of Marriage Act of 1994, 361
DeLay, Tom, 2
Deman, William, 324
Democratic Party, 132–4
    and 1896 national platform, 232–3
    and 1956 national platform, 290–1
    and 1988 national platform, 328
    Associated with "Slave Power," 172–7,
        192–204
    Development of, 138–45
    Perceptions of early Republican Party,
        177–80

Sectional rift of, 298–302
    as a single constitutional party, 138–45
Democratic-Republican Clubs, 91
Dent, Harry, 312
Departmentalism, 32–33, 168–9, 181, 220–1,
    346–7, 375
Detainee Treatment Act (2005), 30, 334, 348,
    354, 355–62
Devins, Neal, 24
Dewey, John, 238–9
Dingell, John, 322
Dirksen, Everett, 299
District of Columbia v. Heller (2008), 379
Douglas, Stephen, 132, 173, 181–2, 221, 233
Douglas, William, 288
    Impeachment attempt against, 307–8
    Ruling in *Griswold*, 337
Drake, Charles, 212
Dred Scott v. Sanford (1857), 14, 134, 139,
    163–7, 181, 185, 192, 200, 208, 217,
    218, 231, 232, 233, 247, 342, 344,
    347, 370
    in the Lincoln-Douglas Debates, 181–3
    Lincoln's interpretation of, 183–5
Duplex Printing v. Deering (1921), 255–6

Educational Amendments of 1972, 317–23
Edwards v. Carpenter (2000), 360n88
EEOC v. Home Ins. Co. (1982), 351
Ehrlichman, John, 313
Eisenhower, Dwight, 23
    and alleged frustrations with Earl
        Warren, 23
    on support for *Brown* and desegregation,
        295
    on support for civil liberties rulings of
        1957, 295
Eisenstadt v. Baird (1971), 337n5
Election of 1800, 100–103
Election of 1824, 142–3
Elementary and Secondary Education Act
    (ESEA) of 1974, 317–23, 334, 335
Ely, John Hart, 57, 370
"Enemy combatants," 354–62
Epstein, Lee, 49
Equal Rights Amendment, 278
Esch, Marvin, 320
Escobedo v. Illinois (1964), 341n14
Evarts Act, 30, 214
Ex parte Garland (1867), 205
Ex parte McCardle (1868), 206–12, 266,
    288, 357, 369
Ex parte Merryman (1861), 191–2
Ex parte Milligan (1866), 205, 207

Exceptions Clause of the U.S.
    Constitution, 33

Family Research Council, 2, 53n45
    Sponsoring of Justice Sunday Telecast, 2, 3
Federal Bureau of Investigation (FBI), 294,
    296, 302
Federal Rules of Criminal Procedure, 295
Federalism (Federalists), 71, 74, 84, 86, 91,
    92, 104, 113, 118
    and James Madison's depiction of, 95
    and Martin Van Buren's characterization
        of, 141
    and position on legitimacy and loyalty of
        political opposition, 87–103, 133
Federalist 9, 92, 93
Federalist 10, 5, 61, 92, 94, 96, 142, 143
Federalist 37, 88
Federalist 49, 88
Federalist 51, 142, 143
Federalist 65, 115
Federalist 78, 76–77
Federalist 80, 78
Federalist Society, 341, 344, 349
Ferejohn, John, 25–26, 29
Field, Stephen, 201, 202–3
Fielding, Fred, 349
Filibuster (in the U.S. Senate), 33, 286, 320,
    324, 335
    of Fortas as Earl Warren's replacement,
        306, 330
    as harnessing judicial power, 34, 329–34
    of lower federal judges, 329–34
Fillmore, Millard, 195
Finch, Robert, 312, 313, 314, 335
First Employer's Liability Cases (1908),
    242n73
Fish, Hamilton, 216
Fiss, Owen, 249
Ford, Gerald, 307–8
Fortas, Abe, 306, 307, 330
Fourteenth Amendment, 196, 280
    Due process clause, 243
    Progressive Era consideration of repeal of,
        243
Frankfurter, Felix, 158, 237, 265
    on difficulty of *Brown* decision, 290, 340
    on sex difference and protective legislation,
        278–9
Freedman's Bureau, 196
Fremont, John, 178, 195
French Revolution of 1789, 57
Fried, Charles, 350
Friedman, Barry, 210–11

Frist, William (Bill), 330, 332
Fuller, Melville, 235
Fundamental rights, 361–2

Gallatin, Albert, 100, 117
Gang of Fourteen, 331–4, 335
Gannet, Frank, 270
Gardner, John, 311
Gazette of the United States, 107
Gerry, Elbridge, 84
Geyh, Charles, 28–30, 158, 288
Gibson, James, 48, 49
Giffords, Gabrielle, 63
Giles, William Branch, 100, 107, 308
    on impeachment of Samuel
        Chase, 123–4
Gillman, Howard, 25
Gingrich, Newt, 10
Ginsburg, Ruth Bader, 329
    Dissent in *Gonzales v. Carhart*, 367
Glass, Carter, 270
Goldberg, Arthur, 337
Goldmark, Josephine, 250–1
Gompers, Samuel, 255, 258
Gompers v. United States (1914), 245
Gonzales v. Carhart (2007), 364, 367
Gordon, James, 90
Gore, Al, 6
Gorton, Slade, 322–3
Graber, Mark, 25, 210
Grant, Ulysses S., 199, 203, 205, 214
    and Court-packing, 212–17
Great Depression, 264
Great Society programs, 285, 309, 311, 362,
    363
Greely, Louis, 242
Green v. New Kent County School Board
    (1968), 311, 313, 319
Grey, Thomas, 339, 344
    and originalism or interpretivism, 343–4,
        369–71
Grier, Robert, 160, 215
Griswold, Roger, 108
Griswold v. Connecticut (1965), 337–8,
    341n14
Grutter v. Bollinger (2003), 24n22

Habeas corpus, 207, 210, 359–62
Habeas Corpus Act of 1867, 207, 210
Haldeman, H. R., 308–9, 310, 315
Hamdan v. Rumsfeld (2004), 3n10, 354,
    355–7, 358
Hamdi v. Rumsfeld (2004), 356
Hamilton, Alexander, 76, 78, 84, 92, 93

as characterized by Martin Van Buren,
140–45, 165
and the need to expand the lower federal
judiciary, 106
on the scope of impeachment, 115
Hand, Learned, 242
Hanna, James, 90
Harper, Robert Goodloe, 97, 101, 102
on representing Samuel Chase at his
impeachment trial, 125–6
Harper's Weekly, 177, 209, 213, 216
Harrison, Benjamin, 233
Harrison, John, 349–50
Harvard University, 236, 285
Hayburn, William, 81
Hayburn Case (1795), 81–82, 111
Haynsworth, Clement, 306, 307, 308
Health, Education, and Welfare (HEW),
Department of, 311
and enforcement of school busing policy,
311–17
Hennings, Thomas, 296
Henry, Patrick, 90
Hepburn v. Griswold (1869), 215
Hirschl, Ran, 25
Hoar, Ebenezer R., 215
Hofstadter, Richard, 57
Holmes, Oliver Wendell, 237, 273, 274
*Home Building & Loan Association v.
Blaisdell* (1934), 227, 272, 274–7, 282,
342, 368
Hoover, Herbert, 243
Hoover, J. Edgar, 294
Hughes, Charles Evans, 270, 272
on *Dred Scott*, 217
on *Home Building & Loan v. Blaisdell*,
275
Hume, David, 92, 93–94
Humphrey, Hubert, 303
Huston, Tom, 325
Hylton v. United States (1796), 81, 82, 141

Impeachment, *see* judicial impeachment
Impeachment, non-judicial, 36, 114–16
In re Debs (1895), 231, 232, 256
Indian Removal Act, 159
Ingersoll, Ebon, 198
INS v. Chadha (1983), 351
International Association of Machinists, 256
Invalid Pensions Act of 1792, 81–82
Iredell, James, 76, 83, 84, 120

Jackson, Andrew, 14, 32, 56, 152, 199, 347, 375
as compared to Jefferson, 135

as compared to Lincoln, 180–1
and the election of 1824, 142–3
and relations with the Supreme Court, 132,
134–5, 218–19
and veto of the national bank, 145–9, 218
Jacobs, Jr., Andrew, 308
Jefferson, Thomas, 6, 32, 97, 282, 347, 374,
375, 377, 380
as compared to Jackson and Lincoln,
180–1, 187–8
and the election of 1800, 100–103, 104
on impeaching John Marshall, 124
on impeachment of John Pickering, 118
on impeachment of Samuel Chase, 122
and the Kentucky Resolution, 98–99
and position toward judicial authority,
84–86
and position toward party, 96
Jencks Act, 296–302, 334
Jencks v. United States (1957), 294
Jenner, William, 297
Jenner-Butler Bill, 297–302
Jensen, D. Lowell, 349
Johnson, Andrew, 195–9, 203
as compared to Andrew Jackson, 199
Impeachment of, 199, 209, 211
as part of the "Slave Power," 198–9
and veto of the Civil Rights Act of 1866,
197
and veto of the Freedman's Bureau Act, 197
Johnson, Hiram, 240, 266
Opposition to FDR's Court-packing plan,
268–70
Support for judicial recall, 240–1
Johnson, Lyndon B., 298, 353
on replacing Earl Warren, 305
as senate majority leader, 298–302, 335
Joint Committee on Reconstruction, 196
Judicial activism, 1, 67, 368–9, 382
definition of, 1n1
and rhetoric of, 1–2, 51–52
Judicial impeachment, 29, 31, 34–35, 287
of Judge John Pickering, 116–19
of Justice Samuel Chase, 113–30
as undermining judicial authority, 34–35
Judicial neutrality, 13
and the 1826 congressional debate, 151–9
and the 1860s congressional debate, 200
and Chief Justice John Roberts, 16n38
and civic republicanism, 228–9
Public assumption of, 48–49
as resolution of the impeachment of Justice
Samuel Chase, 128–9, 131, 163
and Senator John Cornyn, 16n38

Judicial recall, 29, 31
  Progressive movement for, 238–49
  as undermining judicial legitimacy, 34–35
Judicial review, definition of, 20, 48
  as criticized by Brutus, 77–78
  as discussed by Andrew Jackson, 136
  and early judicial articulation of, 80–84
  as examined in *Federalist* 78, 76–77
  and Framers' ideas about, 74–80
  as "pluralism-reinforcing," 228n9
Judicial supremacy, 27–31, 32, 285–6, 373
Judiciary Act of 1789, 30, 37n71, 79–80,
    105, 106, 111, 112, 151, 152
  and possible repeal of Section 25, 135, 136,
    138, 159–61, 210
Judiciary Act of 1801, 103, 104, 105, 106,
    113, 155
Judiciary Act of 1802, 105, 109–10
Judiciary Act of 1807, 151
Judiciary Act of 1837, 141, 151, 162–3,
    200–202, 205, 218
Judiciary Act of 1862, 200, 201–2
Judiciary Act of 1866, 201–2, 203, 206
Judiciary Act of 1869, 203, 204–5, 212–17
  Comparisons with the 1801 Judiciary
    Act, 212
Judiciary Reorganization Bill of 1937 (FDR
    Court-Packing Plan), 7, 19, 26, 28, 30,
    105, 261–72, 288
  as harnessing judicial power, 35, 267–8
  Public opinion of, 270–2
Jurisdiction stripping, 33
  as harnessing judicial power, 34–35
  and the Reconstruction Congress,
    205–12
Justice at Stake, 31, 53n45
"Justice Sunday" telecasts, 3–4

Kagan, Elena, 380–1
Kansas-Nebraska Act of 1854, 164–5, 193
Kellogg, William, 201
Kelly, Francis, 251, 278–9, 324
Kennedy, Anthony, 2
  Decision in *Gonzales v. Carhart*, 367
  Decision in *Lawrence*, 365
Kennedy, Robert, 305, 315
Kennedy v. Louisiana (2008), 365–6
Kentucky Resolution of 1798, 98–99, 108,
    135, 136, 168
Kerr, Robert, 299, 301
Keyes v. School District No. 1 (1973), 310,
    323
King, Jr., Martin Luther, 55
King, Rufus, 91

Klein, Herbert, 305, 310
"Know-Nothing" Party, 193, 195
Knox v. Lee (1870), 215
Konigsberg v. State Bar (1957), 294
Korean War, 294
Korematsu v. United States (1944), 370
Kramer, Larry, 82, 102–3
Kutler, Stanley, 200, 204, 218–19
Kyl, John, 380–1

LaFollette, Robert, 246
Laissez-faire, 225, 243
Landis, James, 158
Lawrence v. Texas (2003), 24n22, 49, 364–5
Legal realism, 227, 237–8, 240–1, 252, 274,
    283
Legal Tender Act of 1862, 215, 216
Legal Tender Cases (1870), 215–16
Legitimate opposition, 5, 11, 372–383
  and constitutional interpretation, 6, 12,
    14, 45
  and Federalist position toward it, 87–103
  and Jackson's position toward it, 134–8
  and political idiom, 54–64, 67–68
  and political party development, 6–9, 12,
    88–96, 373–4
  and secession, 118
Leonard, Gerald, 133, 134, 143
Liberal pluralism, 45, 54–64, 67–68, 221–2,
    286, 375
  and *Adkins v. Children's Hospital*, 278–9
  and *Carolene Products*, 277–81
  and Court development, 64–67, 375
Liberty of contract, 225
Lincoln, Abraham, 6, 14, 32, 61, 62, 170,
    218–19, 233, 277, 282, 347, 375, 377,
    380
  Connections to Progressive ideas about
    judicial recall, 240, 246, 247
  on *Dred Scott*, 181–90
  on *Ex parte Merryman*, 191–2
  and first inaugural address, 180, 220
  and ideas about political parties, 171,
    183–90, 220–1
  and interpreting constitutional silences,
    180–92, 219
  on Jackson's national bank veto, 184–6
  on the "Slave Power" conspiracy, 173–4
Litigation Strategy Working Group, 349, 351
"Living" Constitution, 226–8, 274–7, 340,
    369
Livingston, Edward, 156, 157
Lochner v. New York (1905), 237n50, 337,
    347, 370

Holmes's dissent, 244–5
Peckham's ruling, 249
Locke, John, 74, 243
Lodge, Henry Cabot, 241–2, 248
Loewe v. Lawler (1908), 242n73, 251n125, 256
Louisville Democrat, 181
Lovell, George, 25, 256, 257, 259
Loving v. Virginia (1967), 361
Loyal opposition, 5, 11, 372–83
   and constitutional interpretation, 6, 12, 14, 45
   and originalism, 16
   and political idiom, 54–64, 67–68
   and political party development, 6–9, 12, 88–96, 373–4
   and Republican characterizations of, 172–7, 192–204
   on return of illegitimate opposition, 5n17, 10
   and secession, 118
   and the Tea Party, 10
Luther v. Borden (1849), 206, 208

Madden, Martin, 257
Madison, James, 5, 61, 83–84, 88, 90, 92, 100, 132, 142, 152, 372
   as characterized by Martin Van Buren, 140–45
   and essays on political parties, 95–96, 107, 144, 167
   and *Federalist 10*, 92, 94–95
   and veto of the national bank, 146
   and Virginia Resolution, 84, 98–99
Majority Rule and Democracy, 245
Mallory v. United States (1957), 295, 298, 300, 301, 302
Mansfield, Mike, 299, 318, 333
Marbury, William, 111
Marbury v. Madison (1803), 10, 28, 47, 74, 80, 83, 86, 105, 108, 111, 147, 230, 232, 276, 282, 284, 343
   as "rediscovered" in the 1890s, 230, 235–6
Marshall, John, 74, 80, 84, 108, 109, 162, 216, 218, 276, 343
   and Andrew Jackson's baiting of, 134–5
   and *Marbury v. Madison*, 111–12
   and *McCulloch v. Maryland*, 136–7, 216–17
   on opposition to Indian Removal Act, 159
   on possibility of striking in reaction to the Repeal Act, 110
   and possible impeachment charges against, 124

Marshall, Thurgood, 381
Mason, George, 115
McCain, John, 63, 377–8
   and rhetoric of "activist judges," 368–9
   as member of Gang of Fourteen, 332–3
McCardle, William, 207
McCarthyism, 377
McClellan, John, 296
McClosky, Robert, 288, 381
McConnell, Mitch, 378
McCulloch v. Maryland (1819), 132, 135, 136, 149, 150, 181, 216, 343
McDonald v. Chicago (2010), 379
McGovern, George, 308
McKinley, William, 233
McReynolds, James, 262n163
Meese III, Edwin, 339, 348, 350
   on *Brown*, 344
   on originalism, 344–7, 370–1
"Memorandum of Understanding on Judicial Nominees" (2005), 331
Mercer, John, 154, 155
Merryman, John, 190–1
Military Commissions Act of 2006, 3n10, 30, 334, 348, 356–62
Miller, Samuel, 201
Milliken v. Bradley (1974), 321, 323
Miranda v. Arizona (1966), 341n14
Mississippi v. Johnson (1867), 206
Model Cities Act of 1966, 311
Monroe, James, 88, 139–40, 152
Morehead v. New York ex. rel. Tipaldo (1936), 262n163
Morgan, Dick, 258
Morris, Aldon, 55
Mugler v. Kansas (1887), 28n41
Muller v. Oregon (1908), 249–53, 273, 274, 277, 278
Munn v. Illinois (1877), 230n13
Murdock, Victor, 258
Murphy, Walter, 290, 301
Muskie, Ed, 315

Nation, 208, 213, 216, 268
National Association of Manufacturers, 293
National Consumers' League, 250–3, 278
National Gazette, 95
National Industrial Recovery Act, 264–5, 268
National Intelligencer, 122
National Recovery Administration, 30, 264–5
National Republicans, 143, 144
National Women's Party, 324

Nebbia v. New York (1934), 261n163
Nelson, Knute, 257–8
Nelson, Samuel, 215
New Deal, 66, 264–6, 362, 363, 374
New Republic, 297
New York Herald, 179, 207, 213
New York Sun, 234
New York Times, 248, 378
New York Times Magazine, 267
New York World, 234
Nicholson, James, 122
Nixon, Richard, 24, 302–23, 360, 368
    Competition with George Wallace, 311–12
    Judicial appointment strategy of, 303–9,
        325, 369
    and jurisdiction-stripping, 26, 28, 287, 302
    Opposition to busing to achieve school
        integration, 311–12, 314–15
    and pursuing judicial impeachment, 287
    Support of *Brown,* 314
    as vice president, 296
*NLRB v. Jones & Laughlin Steel
    Corporation* (1937), 273
Norris, George, 260
Norris-LaGuardia Act, 253, 254, 255,
    259–61, 288
Northcross v. Board of Education (1970),
    315–16
Nullification doctrine, 135, 136, 137–8

Obama, Barack, 10, 63, 378, 380, 381
O'Connor, Sandra Day, 1, 54, 378
Office of Legal Counsel, Reagan
    Administration, 339, 348–52
Office of Legal Policy, Reagan
    Administration, 327
Olney III, Warren, 296
O'Mahoney, Joseph, 296, 297
Omnibus Judges Act of 1978, 325–7, 336
O'Neill, Johnathan, 176
Opposition, *see* legitimate opposition and
    loyal opposition
Originalism, 16, 52–53, 338, 370–1, 376–7,
    378–9
    Benjamin Cardozo's argument against,
        243–4
    and the conservative legal movement, 53
    and early textualism, 86, 222, 376
    in the Reagan administration, 338–40
    Rejection of, 237, 243–4, 274–7
    Revival of, in mid-twentieth century, 338,
        340–47, 369–71
    and the speeches of Edwin Meese, III,
        344–7

Strains on contemporary originalism,
        379–81
    and the writings of Raoul Berger, 342–3
    and the writings of Thomas Grey, 343–4
Our Judicial Oligarchy, 243
Outlook, 246, 248
Owen, Priscilla, 331
Owen, Robert, 240

Pacific Salmon Treaty Act of 1985, 349
*Parents Involved in Community Schools v.
    Seattle District No. 1* (2007), 49
Parker v. Davis (1870), 215
Partial-Birth Abortion Ban Act of 2003, 367
Patterson, William, 80, 110
    and *Stuart v. Laird* ruling, 112
Paul, Alice, 278–9
Pearce, Duttee, 157
Peckham, Rufus, 249
Pennoyer, Sylvester, 232
Pennsylvania v. Nelson (1956), 292, 293,
    297, 298
Philadelphia Aurora, 107–8, 122
Pickering, John, 113
    Impeachment of, 116–19
Pickering, Timothy, 117, 123, 124
Pitney, Mahlon, 256–7, 258, 259
Planned Parenthood v. Casey (1992), 24n22,
    364, 366–7
Plessy v. Ferguson (1896), 344, 347, 370
Plumer, William, 118, 120, 123
Police power, 229–30
Political parties, definition of
    and Abraham Lincoln's ideas about,
        180–90
    and founding generation antipathy toward,
        88–96
    and James Madison's essays on, 95–96
    and judicial development, 4–10, 64–67,
        374–5
    and Martin Van Buren's ideas about,
        138–51
    as party systems, 87–88
    Progressive antipathy toward, 238–42
    and William Seward's ideas about, 174–7
Pollack v. Farmers' Loan and Trust Co.
    (1895), 231n22, 235
Pollack v. Farmers' Loan and Trust Co.
    (1896), 231n22, 235
Pomerene, Atlee, 259
Populism, 228–36, 281–2
    and James Weaver's position toward the
        Supreme Court, 230–1
Posner, Richard, 48

Post, Robert, 338
Pound, Roscoe, 255
Powe, Lucas, 288
Powell, Alfred, 157
Preemptive federalism doctrine, 292–3
Presidential signing statements, *see* signing
    statements
Prize Cases (1867), 202–3
Progressive Era, 14–15, 30, 225–84
Progressives, 225–84
    Criticism of the Constitution, 238–49
    Criticism of political parties, 238–42
    Judicial decision recall, 242–8
    Judicial recall, 238–42
    Public opinion, 238–42
Pryor, William, 331

Railroad Commission Cases (1886), 230n13
Randolph, Edmund, 81–82
Randolph, James, 100, 308
    and impeachment of Samuel Chase, 119,
        123–7
Ransom, William, 245
Reagan, Ronald, 1, 32, 287, 362, 369, 375,
    380
    Judicial appointment strategy of, 327–8,
        333, 370
    Office of Legal Counsel, 339, 348–52
    Office of Legal Policy, 327
    and originalism, 338–47
    and presidential signing statements,
        348–52
Reagan v. Farmers' Loan & Trust Co.
    (1894), 230n12
Reconstruction, 43, 56, 64, 171, 195–9,
    205–12, 213, 217, 375
Reconstruction Acts, 198–9, 206, 209
"Red Monday," 294–5
Reed, Stanley, 290
Register of Debates, 36
Rehnquist, William, 331, 346, 360, 363
Reid, Harry, 330
Repeal Act of 1802, 104, 106, 107–10, 111,
    121, 129
Republican Party, 1, 51, 170, 363
    and 1860 national platform, 187
    and 1956 national platform, 290–1
    and 1968 national platform, 304–5
    and 1980 national platform, 326–7
    and 2000 national platform, 53
    Conflicting Jeffersonian and Lincolnian
        traditions, 226–8
    Development of, 172–80
    as a single constitutional party, 172–7, 218

Rivers, Mendel, 292
Roane, Spencer, 130
Roberts, John, 4, 339, 363, 379, 380
Roberts, Owen, 262n163, 270
Robinson, Joseph, 262
Roe, Gilbert, 243
Roe v. Wade (1973), 24n22, 36, 49, 337n5,
    341, 367
Roosevelt, Franklin D., 7, 32, 375, 380
    and 1937 Judiciary Reorganization Bill
        (Court-Packing Plan), 7, 19, 26, 28,
        30, 152, 225–6, 253, 261–72, 324
Roosevelt, Theodore
    Advocacy of judicial decision recall, 242–9
    Progressive Party presidential candidacy,
        246–9
    Publications in the periodical, *The
        Outlook*, 246
Roper v. Simmons (2005), 365n108
Ross, John, 108
Russell, Richard, 291

*Santa Clara County v. Southern Pacific
    Railroad* (1886), 230n13
Scalia, Antonin, 346, 354
    Dissent in *Boumediene*, 359
    Dissent in *Hamdan*, 354
Schiavo, Terri, 2
*School District of Abington Township v.
    Schemp* (1963), 341n14
Schurz, Carl, 173, 174
Schware v. Board of Bar Examiners (1957),
    294
Scott, Hugh, 318
Secession, 102, 186–9
Second National Bank of the United States,
    138
    and Jackson's Veto of it, 145–9
Sedgwick, Theodore, 106
Sedition Act of 1798, 86, 96–99, 104, 116,
    120
Segal, Jeffrey, 49
Senatorial courtesy, 324–5
Service, John, 294
Service v. Dulles et. al. (1957), 294, 297
Seward, William, 170, 183, 219
    and comparisons to Martin Van Buren,
        171, 174, 219
    and establishment of Republican Party,
        174–7
Sex equality and protective legislation,
    249–53, 278–9
Sheldon v. Sill (1850), 160
Sheply, James, 305

Sherburne, John Samuel, 117
Sherman, William T., 199
Sherman Anti-Trust Act, 231
Siegel, Reva, 338
Siemers, David, 94, 96
Signing statements, 33, 348–54, 377
"Silent majority," 309
Skocpol, Theda, 252
Skowronek, Stephen, 32
Slaughterhouse Cases (1873), 229n11,
    230n12, 242, 243, 277
"Slave Power," 172–7, 192–204, 207, 211
Slochower v. Board of Education (1956),
    292, 297
Smith, Howard, 293, 294
Smith, William, 83
Smith Act (Alien Registration Act) of 1940,
    292–3, 295
Sotomayer, Sonia, 380
Southern Christian Leadership Conference,
    55
Southern Manifesto, *see* Declaration of
    Constitutional Principles
Spears, James, 350
St. Louis Post-Dispatch, 234
Stanbery, Henry, 204
Standard Oil Co. v. United States (1911), 248
Stenberg v. Carhart (2000), 367
Stevens, John Paul, 355–6
Stevens, Thaddeus, 195, 196–7
Stewart, Jon, 1
Stewart, Potter, 337
Stewart, William, 211–12
Stone, Harlan, 280
Strong, William, 215, 216
Stuart v. Laird (1803), 105, 109, 111, 112
Substantive due process, 253
Summary Suspension Act of 1950, 292
Sumner, Charles, 194–5
Supreme Court, *see* Courts
Sutherland, George, 262n163, 272, 342
    Dissenting in *Home Building & Loan v.
    Blaisdell*, 275–7
*Swann v. Charlotte-Mecklenberg Board of
    Education* (1971), 310, 315–20, 322, 323
Swayne, Noah, 201
Sweezy v. New Hampshire (1957), 295, 297

Taft, Robert, 270
Taft, William Howard, 28, 260
    against judicial recall, 241, 246
Taft-Hartley Act (The Labor-Management
    Relations Act) of 1947, 292–3
Taney, Roger, 14, 133, 161, 214, 342

and ruling in *Dred Scott*, 163–7
and ruling in *Ex parte Merryman*, 190–2
Tarr, Ralph, 350–1
Tea Party, 379
Teague v. Lane (1989), 360
Teles, Steven, 362–3
Tenure of Office Act, 199
Texas v. White (1869), 211
Thayer, James Bradley, 237
Thomas, Clarence, 354
Thurmond, Strom, 291, 298
Tiederman, Christopher, 230
Tillman, Benjamin, 232
Time Magazine, 305
Treaty of Guadalupe-Hidalgo, 203
Trumbull, Lyman, 197, 206, 210, 212, 232
Tulane University, 346

Union Party, 177
United States Chamber of Commerce, 293
United States Circuit Judge Nominating
    Commission, 325–6
United States v. American Tobacco Co.
    (1911), 248n103
United States v. Butler (1936), 266
United States v. Callender (1801), 120–1
United States v. Carolene Products (1938),
    65, 66, 227–8, 273, 274, 277–81, 286,
    288, 368, 370, 381
    Footnote Four, 280–1, 282, 383–4
United States v. E. C. Knight Co. (1895),
    231, 232
United States v. John Fries (1800), 120
United States v. Yale Todd (1794), 81, 82

Van Buren, Martin, 5, 14, 61, 88, 131–60,
    170, 203, 205, 219–21, 282, 380
    on Andrew Jackson's relationship with the
        Supreme Court, 135, 138–51, 167–9
    as builder of the Democratic party,
        138–45, 167–9
    and characterization of Jefferson's position
        on judicial impeachment, 114
    as compared to Abraham Lincoln, 187–8
    and correspondence with James Madison,
        140n38
    Defense of Andrew Jackson's veto of the
        national bank, 147–51
    on *Dred Scott*, 163–7
    on judicial reform, 158–9
    and Judiciary Act of 1837, 162–3
    and position on judicial power, 132, 184
Van Devanter, Willis, 261, 262n163
Vanhorne's Les see v. Dorrance (1795), 80n46

Vinson, Fred, 290
Virginia Resolution of 1798, 84, 98

Wagner Act (National Labor Relations Act)
    of 1935, 292
Wainwright v. Sykes (1977), 360
Wallace, George, 303–4, 311–12, 319
Wallace, Henry, 265
Walsh, Thomas, 260
War on Terror, 286, 348, 354–62
Warren, Earl, 19, 285, 297, 309, 340, 346,
    363, 369
  Calls for impeachment of, 381
  and countermajoritarian judicial rulings,
    20, 23, 284, 381
  on jurisdiction-stripping legislation of the
    1950s, 288
  Retirement of, 205
Washington, George, 81, 90, 119
Washington Daily Morning Chronicle, 208
Washington Evening Express, 211
Watergate scandal, 320, 348
Watkins v. United States (1957), 294–5, 297
Weaver, James, 230–1
Webster, Daniel, 147–8
  on reform of the federal judiciary, 153–4
West Coast Hotel v. Parish (1937), 66,
    262n163, 273, 274, 282

Wheeler, Burton, 266
  Opposition to FDR's Court-packing plan,
    267–8, 271–2
Whig Party, 133, 140, 143, 172, 174, 193,
    194
White, Wilson, 296
White v. Hart (1871), 211n165
Whitten amendment, 311, 313–14
Whittington, Keith, 25, 27, 32, 180
Wicklffe, Charles, 155–6
Wiecek, William, 217
Williams, Thomas, 206
Williams v. Taylor (2000), 360
Wilson, Henry, 208, 209, 212
Wilson, James, 81–82, 121
Wilson, Joe, 378
Wilson, Woodrow, 258
Wiscart v. Dauchy (1796), 160
Wolcott, Oliver, 120
Wolfson, Louis, 306
Worcester v. Georgia (1832), 132, 134, 138,
    147, 150, 181, 218
Wright, John, 157

Yale University, 237, 285
Yates v. United States (1957), 295, 297,
    298
Yellow-dog contracts, 260–1